The Great Seljuk Empire

THE EDINBURGH HISTORY OF THE ISLAMIC EMPIRES
Series Editor: Ian Richard Netton

Available or forthcoming titles

The Umayyad Empire
Andrew Marsham

The Early Abbasid Empire
Matthew Gordon

The Almoravod and Almohad Empires
Amira Bennison

The Seljuk Empire of Anatolia
Sara Nur Yildiz

The Great Seljuk Empire
A. C. S. Peacock

The Fatimid Empire
Michael Brett

The Mamluk Empire
Jo van Steenbergen and Patrick Wing

The Ayyubid Empire
Gerald Hawting

The Mongol Empire
Timothy May

The Safavid Empire
Andrew J. Newman

The Ottoman Empire
Gökhan Çetinsaya

www.euppublishing.com/series/ehie

The Great Seljuk Empire

A. C. S. Peacock

EDINBURGH
University Press

Edinburgh University Press Ltd
The Tun – Holyrood Road
12 (2f) Jackson's Entry
Edinburgh EH8 8PJ
www.euppublishing.com

Typeset in 11/13pt Adobe Garamond Pro by
Servis Filmsetting Ltd, Stockport, Cheshire
and printed and bound in Great Britain by
CPI Group (UK) Ltd, Croydon CR0 4YY

A CIP record for this book is available from the British Library

ISBN 978 0 7486 3825 3 (hardback)
ISBN 978 0 7486 3826 0 (paperback)
ISBN 978 0 7486 3827 7 (webready PDF)
ISBN 978 0 7486 9807 3 (epub)

Published with the support of the Edinburgh University
Scholarly Publishing Initiatives Fund.

Contents

Box Text

Illustrations

Figures

Maps

Abbreviations

Journals and Encyclopaedias

BSOAS	*Bulletin of the School of Oriental and African Studies*
EI^2	*Encyclopaedia of Islam* (Leiden, 1960–2007)
EIr	*Encyclopaedia Iranica* (London, Costa Mesa, etc., 1982–, and www.iranicaonline.org)
JAOS	*Journal of the American Oriental Society*
JRAS	*Journal of the Royal Asiatic Society*
IJMES	*International Journal of Middle East Studies*
ZDMG	*Zeitschrift der Deutschen Morgenländischen Gesellschaft*

Editions of Commonly Cited Texts

Bayhaqi, *Tarikh*	Abū'l-Faḍl Bayhaqī, *Tārīkh-i Bayhaqī*, ed. Khalīl Khaṭīb Rahbar (Tehran, 1376)
Bundari, *Zubda*	Bundārī, *Zubdat al-Nuṣra*, ed. M. Th. Houtsma as *Histoire des Seljoucides de l'Irâq par Bondârî d'après Imâd al-dîn al-Kâtib al-Isfahânî* (Leiden 1889) (Recueil de textes relatifs à l'histoire des Seljoucides, II)
Husayni, *Akhbar*	Ṣadr al-Dīn ʿAlī al-Ḥusaynī, *Akhbār al-Dawla al-Saljuqiyya*, ed. Muḥammad Iqbāl (Beirut, 1984)

Ibn al-'Adim, *Bughya*	Ibn al-'Adīm, *Bughyat al-Ṭalab fī Ta'rīkh Ḥalab: al-tarājim al khāṣṣa bi-ta'rīkh al-Salājiqa*, ed. Ali Sevim as *Buğyat at-Ṭalab fî Târîḫ Ḥalab Selçuklularla İlgili Haltercümeleri* (Ankara, 1976)
Ibn al-Athir, *al-Kamil*	Ibn al-Athīr, *al-Kāmil fī 'l-Ta'rīkh*, ed. C. Tornberg (Beirut, 1965–7)
Ibn al-Jawzi, *al-Muntazam*	Ibn al-Jawzī, *al-Muntaẓam fī Ta'rīkh al-Mulūk wa'l-Umam*, ed. Muḥammad 'Abd al-Qādir 'Aṭā and Muṣṭafā 'Abd al-Qādir 'Aṭā (Beirut, 1995)
Nishapuri, *Saljuqnama*	Nīshāpūrī, Ẓahīr al-Dīn, *Saljūqnāma*, ed. A. H. Morton (Cambridge, 2004)
Sibt, *Mir'at*	Sibṭ b. al-Jawzī, *Mir'āt al-Zamān fī Ta'rīkh al-A'yan: al-Ḥawādith al-khāṣṣa bi-ta'rīkh al-Salājiqa bayna al-sanawāt 1056–1086*, ed. Ali Sevim as *Mir'âtü'z-Zeman fî Tarihi'l-Âyan* (Ankara, 1968)
Sibt, *Mir'at*, ed. Ghamidi	Sibṭ b. al-Jawzī, *Mir'āt al-Zamān fī Ta'rīkh al-A'yān (481–517/1088–1123)*, ed. Musfir b. Sālim al-Ghāmidī (Mecca, 1987)

Note on Transliteration, Conventions and Geographical Terminology

The term Seljuk might also be reasonably transliterated several different ways: Seljūq, Saljūq or Seljük. Trying to give an impression of mediaeval Turkish pronunciation while remaining faithful to the standard transliteration of Arabic and Persian is well nigh impossible. In the text I have favoured a simplified system of transliteration of Arabic, Persian and Turkish personal and geographical names, and names of texts. Full diacritics will be found in the bibliography and the index. Technical terms and quotations from Arabic or Persian are given full diacritics in line with the usual British conventions.

References to *Encyclopaedia of Islam* (*EI*^{2}) and the *Encyclopaedia Iranica* (*EIr*) are given simply to the article heading without page or volume numbers as the online versions are widely used today, and in the case of *EIr* many are only available online.

Many geographical terms have changed their meaning since the Middle Ages. Here, the Sultanate of Iraq refers not to modern Iraq, but to roughly western Iran and central modern Iraq. To avoid confusion I prefer to use the term Jibal for western Iran, and Arab Iraq for territories west of the Zagros in modern Iraq. Iran rarely appears in mediaeval texts, and when it is used here it has a purely geographical sense to describe the Iranian plateau; it does not carry any political connotations. Azerbaijan is used in its mediaeval sense of northwestern Iran. Syria refers to the historical Bilad al-Sham, that is, the modern republic of Syria and its immediate neighbours, Lebanon, northern Jordan, Palestine, the Hatay. Khurasan, too, is used with its historical meaning, an area that extends far to the east beyond the confines of the modern Iranian province of Khurasan (see pp. 1–2 below), up to the River Oxus.

Translations are my own, except where otherwise indicated. Published translations, where available, are listed in the bibliography.

Acknowledgements

I am grateful to numerous individuals and organisations who have facilitated the preparation of this book. Oya Pancaroğlu, Jürgen Paul and Scott Redford shared their thoughts on aspects of the Seljuks with me at various times, and provided me access to their work in advance of publication. Lorenz Korn also generously sent me copies of his articles on Seljuk architecture, and David Wasserstein gave me useful insights into David Alroy's rebellion. David Durand-Guédy kindly agreed to read the entire text at short notice, and offered many valuable comments and corrections. I am very grateful to Deborah Tor for her meticulous reading of the manuscript and her incisive remarks. I have benefited greatly from the contribution of both these colleagues, but, naturally, all errors of fact or interpretation are my own.

Tim Williams of the Merv Archaeological Project, Bernard O'Kane and Raya Shani very kindly made photographs available to me which are reproduced in this book as acknowledged. Images were also supplied by the British Museum, the Metropolitan Museum New York, the Biblioteca Nacional, Madrid, the Bibliothèque nationale de France, the Burrell Collection, Glasgow, the Walters Art Museum Baltimore, and the Freer Gallery of Art. I thank them all for their assistance and granting permission for the reproduction of materials in their collections. The accompanying maps were prepared by Chris Green.

I am also extremely grateful to the Gerda Henkel Stiftung, Düsseldorf, for providing me with funding to pay a visit to Seljuk monuments in Turkmenistan and Iran in 2012, which was invaluable in gathering material for this book. The School of History at the University of St Andrews also provided funding for research trips and materials for which I am thankful.

Above all, I am grateful to my family, and especially my wife Liz for supporting my work, and tolerating my sometimes protracted absences in the Seljuk world.

St Andrews – Istanbul
October 2013

For Liz and Alexander

Introduction

In Sha'ban 429/May 1038, the eastern Iranian city of Nishapur, one of the great cultural and economic centres of the Islamic world, opened its gates to new Turkish rulers. The Ghuzz, as the Nishapuris called them, consisted of 'two or three hundred horsemen, a banner, two beasts of burden, and with the whole group having a generally ragged and battered aspect'.[1] When, later, their leader, Tughrıl, made an appearance in the city, he was no more prepossessing than his followers, who

> looted the inhabitants. It said that when [Tughrıl] saw an almond pastry [*lawzinj*] he ate it, saying, 'These are good noodles [*ṭutmāj*], but lack garlic.'[2] The Ghuzz saw camphor, and, thinking it was salt, said, 'This salt is bitter.' Many other such things are related of them.[3]

These Ghuzz were also known as the Türkmen, or sometimes, the Seljuks (Arabic *al-saljuqiyya*), after Tughrıl's ancestor, Seljuk, who had converted to Islam and died at the beginning of the eleventh century in Jand, a remote outpost of the Islamic world situated in the northwest of modern Kazakhstan, in the great Eurasian steppe that was the Turks' homeland. Recent converts to Islam, in large part nomadic tent-dwellers, the Seljuks seemed like barbarians to the settled population of the Iranian world. However, by 431/1040, they had seized not just Nishapur, but also all of the vast surrounding province of Khurasan – historically comprising most of modern eastern Iran,

1 Bayhaqi, *Tarikh-i Bayhaqi*, ed. Khalil Khatib Rahbar (Tehran, 1376), 883; translation from C. E. Bosworth, *The Ghaznavids: Their Empire in Afghanistan and Eastern Iran, 994–1040* (Edinburgh, 1963), 255. For Nishapur and Khurasan on the eve of the Seljuk invasions, see Bosworth, *The Ghaznavids*, esp. 145–61.

2 Read *ṭutmāj* not *qutmāj* as in the text (but as per the ms variants listed in the critical apparatus). On *ṭutmāj*, a classic Turkish noodle dish in which garlic is an essential ingredient, see Paul D. Buell, 'The Mongol Empire and Turkicization: the Evidence of Food and Foodways', in Reuven Amitai-Preiss and David Morgan (eds), *The Mongol Empire and its Legacy* (Leiden, 1999), 211, 216.

3 Ibn al-Athir, *al-Kamil fi 'l-Ta'rikh*, ed. C. Tornberg (Beirut, 1965–7), IX, 483.

Turkmenistan and northern Afghanistan[4] – one of the foremost commercial, cultural and intellectual centres of the Islamic world, the birthplace of the New Persian literary language,[5] and home to rich traditions of Arabic literature and Islamic scholarship. The Seljuk takeover of Khurasan laid the foundations for an empire that would sweep away the established political order in the central lands of the Islamic world, and would endure for more than a century.

There had been Turks in the Middle East before the Seljuks. Where the Islamic world adjoined the Eurasian steppe, on the borders of Iran and the Muslim-ruled lands of Central Asia (Khurasan and Transoxiana, the latter comprising roughly modern Uzbekistan), nomadic Turks were familiar. Stereotypes of their uncouthness were deeply entrenched in Arabic literature even before the first Seljuk incursions.[6] The Turks were most famous, however, as military slaves, in which capacity they had been employed since the ninth century by the ʿAbbasid caliphs who ruled most of the Middle East. Occasionally, these slave soldiers, such as the Tulunids in Egypt (245/858–292/905), had even established their own polities. Indeed, the Ghaznavid state that controlled Khurasan at the time of the Seljuk conquests was itself of Turkish slave origin.

The Seljuks were different. As propaganda produced for their court boasted, they were free, not slaves.[7] Unlike the earlier military slaves, they came accompanied by their families and their livestock, and their advance consisted of great nomadic migrations which permanently transformed the demography of the parts of the Middle East where they settled. With the coming of the Seljuks, Iran, Anatolia, northern Syria and parts of southern Caucasia all started to acquire the Turkish populations that exist there to this day, although they were reinforced by subsequent waves of migration, especially in the thirteenth century.

4 There is also a modern Iranian province of Khurasan, which represents only a fraction of the area meant historically by the term.

5 This was the version of Persian, written in the Arabic script, that first came into regular use as a literary and administrative language in tenth-century Khurasan, and is essentially the same language that is in use in modern Iran, Tajikstan and Afghanistan today.

6 Richard N. Frye and Aydın M. Sayılı, 'The Turks in the Middle East before the Saljuqs', *JAOS*, 63/iii (1953), 194–207; Yehoshua Frenkel, 'The Turks of the Eurasian Steppes in Medieval Arabic Writing', in Reuven Amitai and Michal Biran (eds), *Mongols, Turks and Others: Eurasian Nomads and the Sedentary World* (Leiden, 2005), 201–41. In general on the medieval Turkish peoples, see Peter B. Golden, *An Introduction to the History of the Turkic Peoples: Ethnogenesis and State Formation in Medieval and Early Modern Eurasia and the Middle East* (Wiesbaden, 1992).

7 Ibn Hassul, *Kitab Tafdil al-atrak ʿala saʾir al-ajnad*, ed. Abbas Azzavi as 'Ibni Hassulün Türkler hakkında bir eser', *Belleten*, 4 (1940) (Arabic text as separately paginated *ilave*).

The Seljuk conquests marked the beginning of a millennium of domination of the Middle East by peoples of steppe or Turkish origin, among them the Mongols in the thirteenth to fourteenth centuries, their contemporaries the Mamluks of Syria and Egypt, and later the Timurids and the Ottomans. Even dynasties which were not themselves ethnically Turkish, such as the Ayyubids and the Safavids, often relied on a Turkish soldiery, and were profoundly influenced by Turkish culture – so much so that they were sometimes perceived by outsiders to be Turkish themselves. The Kurdish Ayyubids, for example, were sometimes known as the 'Ghuzz'.[8]

Despite their regular depiction as barbarians, something all too often reflected in the secondary literature as much as the primary sources,[9] the Turks in fact possessed their own sophisticated political traditions derived from the heritage of the steppe. Turkish empires had existed in Central Asia since the sixth century, and the Seljuks themselves seem to have originated from the ruins of the last great non-Muslim Turkish empire, the Khazar state which dominated southern Russia and the north Caucasus between the eighth and tenth centuries.[10] The Ghaznavids (366/977–582/1186), the most important Turkish Muslim dynasty to date, embarrassed by their servile origins, had sought to legitimise themselves by emulating the practices of established Islamic states like the 'Abbasids, and to participate in the prestigious Perso-Islamic culture of Khurasan by claiming illustrious Iranian descent.[11] In contrast, the Seljuks vaunted their origins through their alien Turkish names, and introduced new political symbols and practices which originated on the steppe, such as the *ṭughrā*, the stylised bow and arrow that symbolised possession of authority, or the *atabeg*, the military guardian of a prince. Such customs were also adopted by later dynasties: the *ṭughrā* remained in use until the end of Ottoman period (see pp. 126–8, 320 below), and the Seljuks were succeeded

[8] Cf. Ibn Hatim, *Kitab al-Simt al-Ghali al-Thaman fi Akhbar al-Muluk min al-Ghuzz bi'l-Yaman*, ed. G. R. Smith as *The Ayyūbids and Early Rasūlids in the Yemen (567-694/1173–1295)* (Cambridge, 1974), I, 15: *awwal man malaka al-Yaman min al-ghuzz Banū Ayyūb* – 'the first of the Ghuzz to rule Yemen were the Ayyubids'.

[9] See, for example, the influential comments of Barthold, whose study of pre-Mongol Central Asia remains an essential work of scholarship: 'The Saljuqids could not assimilate themselves completely to the Sāmānids and the Ghaznavids, because up to the end they remained strangers to all culture . . . An illiterate sovereign certainly could not follow the intricate bureaucratic administration of his extensive possessions, and this duty lay exclusively with the wazīr' (W. Barthold, *Turkestan Down to the Mongol Invasion* (London, 1928), 308).

[10] For an introduction to the Khazars, see D. M. Dunlop, *The History of the Jewish Khazars* (Princeton, 1954), and see further the discussion and references in Chapter 1, p. 24.

[11] See C. E. Bosworth, 'The Heritage of Rulership in Early Islamic Iran and the Search for Dynastic Connections with the Past', *Iran*, (1973), 61–2.

Map I.1 The Middle East in the eleventh to twelfth centuries: settlements and geography

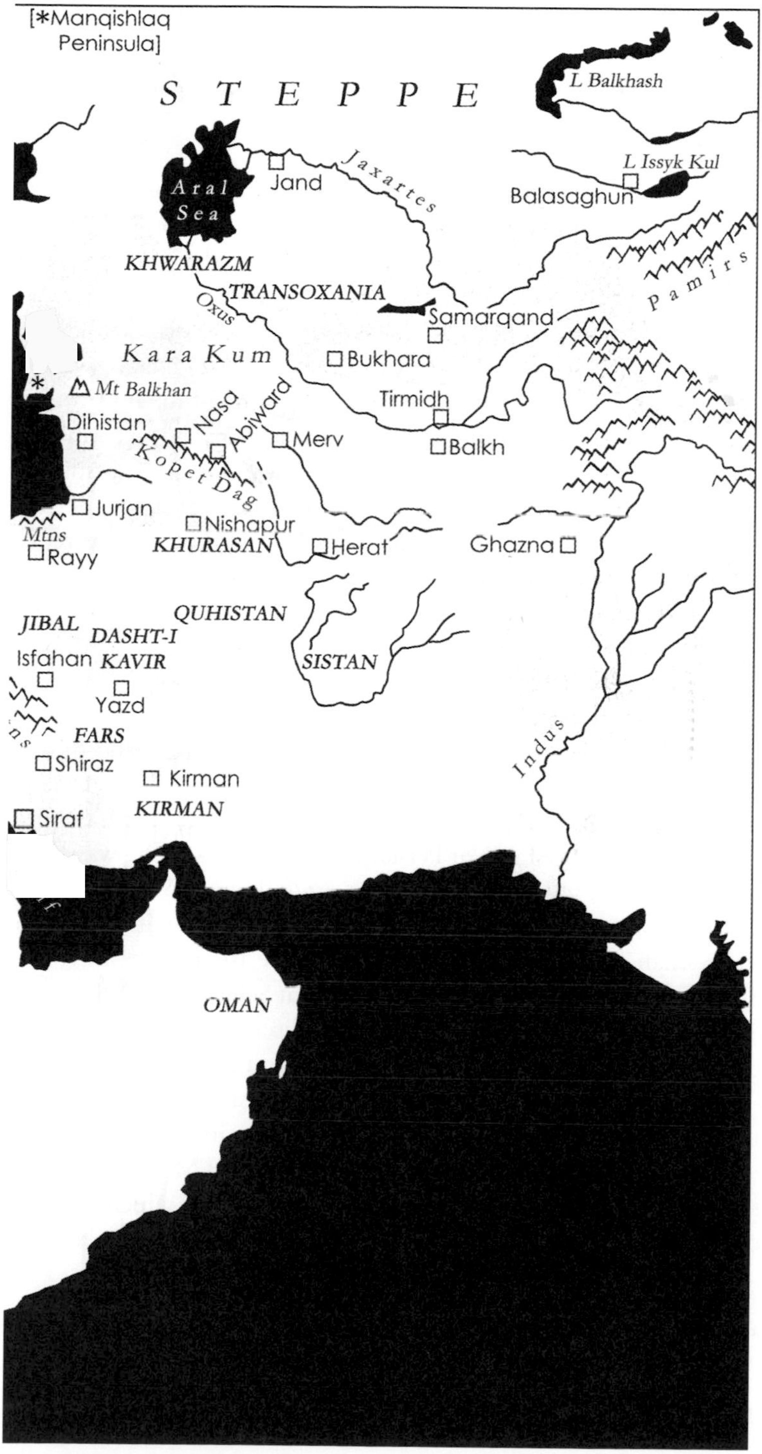
[*Manqishlaq Peninsula]
STEPPE
L Balkhash
Jaxartes
Aral Sea
Jand
L Issyk Kul
Balasaghun
KHWARAZM
TRANSOXANIA
Pamirs
Oxus
Samarqand
Kara Kum
Bukhara
Mt Balkhan
Tirmidh
Dihistan
Nasa
Abiward
Merv
Balkh
Kopet Dag
Jurjan
Mtns
Nishapur
Rayy
KHURASAN
Herat
Ghazna
JIBAL
QUHISTAN
DASHT-I KAVIR
Isfahan
SISTAN
Yazd
FARS
Shiraz
Kirman
Indus
Siraf
KIRMAN
OMAN

in the west by a plethora of dynasties that called themselves *atabegs*. The steppe political heritage first introduced into the Islamic world by the Seljuks would exert an important influence on the ideology and institutions of later empires.[12]

The Great Seljuk Empire

The scale of the state the Seljuks founded dwarfed any earlier Muslim Turkish polity – indeed, in terms of area, it was second only to the 'Abbasid caliphate at its height and was considerably larger than any of the other contemporary Muslim empires such as the Fatimids in Egypt or the Almoravids in Morocco and Spain. By the late eleventh century, the lands that recognised Seljuk suzerainty stretched from Palestine in the west to as far as Kashghar in what is now China in the east. Even the somewhat reduced empire of the mid-twelfth century still reached from Iraq to Samarqand in Central Asia, and, according to the calculation of one contemporary traveller, took four months to cross.[13]

These lands, comprising most of the heartland of mediaeval Islamic civilisation, were bound together by the dominance of Islam and its culture, by the common political heritage of the 'Abbasid caliphate (128/750–637/1258) to which all were nominally subject, and by historic road networks that were traversed by scholars, pilgrims and merchants. They were populated by a massively diverse range of religious, linguistic and ethnic groups: there were nomads and sedentaries, Arabs, a plethora of different ethnically Iranian groups, not to speak of the various Georgian, Armenian, Greek and Syriac-speaking Christians, as well as Jews, Zoroastrians and other smaller remnants of pre-Islamic religions. Although an exact equivalent for the word 'empire' does not exist in pre-modern Arabic or Persian, and the Seljuk polity was called simply a *dawla* (dynasty), *salṭana* (sultanate) or *mulk* (kingdom), the modern term seems entirely appropriate for a state that encompassed without doubt greater diversity than any of its contemporaries in the Islamic world. It also serves to distinguish the subject of this book, the Great Seljuk Empire, from the smaller Seljuk polities that arose on its peripheries (discussed further below).

The Great Seljuks dominated the Middle East and Islamic Central Asia between *c.* 431/1040 and 552/1157. For most of its history, the empire was divided into a western and eastern half, and it lacked a single capital city or political centre. In the east, the main seat of Seljuk rule was Merv, in modern Turkmenistan. In the west, several different cities between which the sultans moved seasonally served as capitals: Rayy near modern Tehran, Isfahan,

12 See, for example, Joseph Fletcher, 'The Turco-Mongolian Monarchic Tradition in the Ottoman Empire', *Harvard Ukrainian Studies*, 3–4 (1979–80), 236–51; and pp. 318–20 below.

13 Benjamin of Tudela, *The Itinerary of Benjamin of Tudela: Travels in the Middle Ages*, trans. A. Asher (New York, 2010), 109.

Baghdad and, later, Hamadhan. These western territories were known as the Sultanate of Iraq. Iraq here is meant in its mediaeval sense, and thus comprises western Iran (historic 'Iraq al-'Ajam, Persian Iraq, also known as the Jibal) as well as 'Iraq al-Arab (Arab Iraq), corresponding to the central and southern parts of the modern state of Iraq (the north of which, along with parts of southeastern Turkey and northeastern Syria, was known as the Jazira – the 'island' between the Tigris and Euphrates rivers).

From 511/1118, the Seljuk sultans of Iraq recognised the suzerainty of the Great Seljuk ruler Sanjar, based in Khurasan, who was known by the title of *al-sulṭān al- a'ẓam*, 'the Greatest Sultan'. The sultans of Iraq are sometimes referred to as the 'Lesser Seljuks'. The Sultanate of Iraq survived the Great Seljuk collapse in 1152–7, only finally disappearing in 1194. These later Seljuks of Iraq claimed to be inheritors of the Great Seljuk Empire, but their state was, in reality, very different. The largely powerless sultans remained in office to give legitimacy to the actual rulers, the Ildegüzid dynasty, who had originated as slave soldiers in the Seljuks' service. The complex history of the Iraq sultanate between 552/1157 and 590/1194 is treated only briefly here, as it is properly a separate subject.

The term Seljuk without further qualification is thus here used to describe the Great Seljuk Empire, just as it is in the primary sources. Other branches of the Seljuk family also controlled territories on the peripheries of the empire, which are only treated tangentially here. Kirman in southern Iran (and Oman too) was between *c.* 440/1048 and 582/1186 ruled by its own Seljuk dynasty, the descendants of Tughrıl's nephew Qavurt b. Chaghrı. Their relationship with their cousins, the Great Seljuk rulers, was often tense, especially in the eleventh century. There were also the Seljuks of Syria (471/1076–511/1117), descended from Chaghrı's grandson Tutush, who were themselves divided into two rival branches, one based at Aleppo in the north and one at Damascus. The most important of these offshoots of the family were the descendants of Seljuk's great-grandson Sulayman, who ruled Anatolia from *c.* 483/1081 to 707/1308. In the late twelfth and early thirteenth centuries the Anatolian Seljuks became one of the leading powers of the eastern Mediterranean. Any one of these dynasties deserves a monograph in its own right; the Seljuks of Anatolia, in particular, ruled a previously Christian land and their history relies on entirely different sources and presents quite distinct problems from the Great Seljuks.[14]

[14] A useful introduction covering all the various Seljuk dynasties with bibliography is C. E. Bosworth, 'Saldjuḳids', *EI*[2]. See also on the Anatolian dynasty A. C. S. Peacock, 'Saljuqs. III. Anatolia', *EIr*, and A. C. S. Peacock and Sara Nur Yıldız (eds), *The Seljuks of Anatolia: Court and Society in the Medieval Middle East* (London, 2013).

The Great Seljuk Empire also encompassed many other vassal rulers, ranging from Bedouin Arab chiefs in Iraq like the Mazyadids and ʿUqaylids, to dynasties like the Bawandids on the Caspian coast of Iran who could trace their roots back to pre-Islamic times. Rabbi Benjamin of Tudela, who visited the Seljuk lands in the mid-twelfth century, stated that no fewer than forty-five kings were subject to the sultan's authority.[15] One might quibble with the exact number, but the general picture is fair. Surrounded on all sides by Seljuk territories was, from the late eleventh century, the state of the Ismailis in the Alburz mountains of northern Iran, in Quhistan in eastern Iran, and in parts of Syria, which did not recognise Seljuk suzerainty. No effort is made to deal with these numerous states except insofar as they are relevant for understanding Seljuk history.

The Seljuks were not interested in enforcing conformity to the practices or ideals of an imperial centre. The empire did not even have a uniform currency: although sultans certainly did strike coins in their own names, individual areas used whatever type of coinage precedent, convenience and local circumstances dictated: Byzantine coins in Syria, Fatimid ones in Baghdad, the old Nishapuri dinar in Khurasan, and so on.[16] Vassals could often rule their territories in their traditional ways provided they recognised the Seljuk sultans' suzerainty, remitted tribute and performed obligations of military service. To people in the Seljuk world, above all the Seljuk sultans themselves, political authority, indeed the political viability of the empire itself, was expressed not through institutions, but through personal ties of loyalty and obligation between patrons and their vassals.[17] The impact of Seljuk rule thus varied greatly from place to place. Some areas perhaps rarely saw a Turk, while others were fought over repeatedly by rival contenders for the sultanate and their Türkmen, Bedouin and Kurdish allies. It is only through detailed, regional studies that we can understand the fluctuating impact of Seljuk rule in different locations, and these should be a priority for future scholarship.[18]

[15] *The Itinerary of Benjamin of Tudela*, 109. On the date of Benjamin's visit, see further p. 275, n. 126 below.

[16] Stefan Heidemann, *Die Renaissance der Städte in Nordsyrien und Nordmesopotamien: Städtische Entwinklung und wirtschaftliche Bedingungen in ar-Raqqa und Harran von der Zeit der beduinischer Vorherrschaft bis zu den Seldschuken* (Leiden, 2002), 387.

[17] For a study of these concepts in a slightly earlier Buyid period, which in general holds true for the Seljuks, see Roy Mottahedeh, *Loyalty and Leadership in an Early Islamic Society* (London, [1981] 2001).

[18] The recent studies of David Durand-Guédy on Isfahan, Vanessa van Renterghem on Baghdad, Stefan Heidemann on the Jazira and Jean-Michel Mouton on Damascus represent a welcome start in this direction. Khurasan has received rather less attention, although the works of Richard Bulliet and Jürgen Paul should be noted.

Such a vast realm could not be run without the contribution of subject peoples, and Persian-speakers from Khurasan played an especially important role in the administration of the empire in the eleventh century. They were deployed in western Iran, Iraq and Syria as well as Khurasan, making the Seljuk Empire in some respects as much a Khurasani empire as a Turkish one. In culture and art, as much as political traditions, the Seljuk period saw the spread of Khurasani traditions to the west of their realms. As a result, the period is characterised by a fusion of Turkish, Persian and Islamic influences, and later dynasties, the twelfth- and thirteenth-century successor states to the Seljuks such as the Syrian Zangids and Ayyubids, sought to appropriate this Seljuk legacy for themselves. Thus, while recognising the diversity of the Seljuk lands, there is also a need for an empire-wide perspective. It is that perspective that the present study seeks to present.

Modern Scholarship on the Seljuks and the Scope of this Book

The eleventh and twelfth centuries witnessed profound social and religious change throughout the Middle East, beyond the Seljuk lands as well as within them. More and more Christians and Jews were converting to Islam, giving the region a much more markedly Muslim character. The quintessential Muslim institution of learning, the madrasa, first became widespread in this period, while Sufism also gained a much wider popularity and acceptability. By the end of the twelfth century, the Islamic world looked not just more Muslim, but more Muslim in a way that is familiar today. Indeed, one scholar has written that, 'Many Saljuq institutions lasted in their outward forms (though the terminology was in some cases changed) until the twentieth century; and without a knowledge of these, and an attempt to trace them back to earlier times, we cannot fully comprehend the questions that began to agitate Iran in the nineteenth century and the solutions sought to them.'[19] While many of these developments are undoubtedly the culmination of longer processes, some seem to have been spread or facilitated by Seljuk rule and its import of Khurasani practices to the central Islamic lands of Iraq and Syria.

Despite the indubitable significance of the period, our understanding of it remains very limited owing to the comparative absence of research on the Seljuks. Although there are a number of monographs treating individual aspects of Seljuk history, no book-length scholarly study of the dynasty has previously appeared in any western language.[20] The most comprehensive works

[19] A. K. S. Lambton, 'The Internal Structure of the Saljuq Empire', in J. A. Boyle (ed.), *The Cambridge History of Iran, vol. V: The Saljuq and Mongol Periods* (Cambridge, 1968), 203.

[20] The contribution by Aziz Basan, *The Great Seljuqs: A History* (London, 2010), despite its

on Seljuk political and dynastic history to date are those by twentieth-century Turkish scholars, particularly Kafesoğlu, Köymen, Sevim and Merçil, whose principal relevant publications are listed in the bibliography and are referred to selectively in the notes. These contributions have not yet been superseded in detail (nor is that the aim of the current book), but they are dated by their nationalistic assumptions of the Turks' unique genius for state foundation.[21] Moreover, they tend to favour a narrative of rulers and battles over analysis. The Soviet scholar S. G. Agadzhanov's study of the Seljuk state in Central Asia is also valuable for a more general understanding of the dynasty.[22] In the west, we are indebted to Anne Lambton's pioneering studies of Seljuk administration, George Makdisi's work on religion, and Claude Cahen's research on political history and historiography. Their work has been continued by the major contributions of Edmund Bosworth and Carole Hillenbrand. Despite the seminal importance of these works, it must be said that Seljuk studies (especially of political history – art history fared rather better) have been relatively neglected outside Turkey, perhaps because comparatively few scholars command all the necessary research languages – Arabic and Persian for the primary sources, Turkish for the secondary literature. Although recent years have seen an upsurge of interest in the Seljuks,[23] many basic questions remain unresolved.

Given this absence of research on many areas, this book does not purport to offer a synthetic overview of the consensus of scholarship, as there is both too little scholarship and, in what there is, too little consensus. Rather, it is an attempt to offer a personal interpretation of the empire's

promising title, largely consists of a summary of older Turkish scholarship on the dynasty. See the review by Jürgen Paul in *Eurasian Studies*, 9 (2011), 268–71.

21 See Martin Strohmeier, *Seldschukische Geschichte und türkische Geschichtswissenschaft: die Seldschuken im Urteil moderner türkischer Historiker* (Berlin, 1984). An impression of Turkish scholarship and its highly politicised nature can also be gained from Gary Leiser (ed. and trans.), *A History of the Seljuks: İbrahim Kafesoğlu's Interpretation and the Resulting Controversy* (Carbondale, 1988). A useful recent addition to this scholarship is Osman G. Özgüdenli, *Selçuklular, vol. I: Büyük Selçuklu Devleti Tarihi (1040–1157)* (Istanbul, 2013), the first of a projected three-volume series which appeared while the current work was in the final stages of preparation. While adopting the same narrative, chronological approach as earlier Turkish scholars, Özgüdenli's work is particularly useful for being based on a very wide range of modern Iranian and Turkish scholarship, as well as western works.

22 S. G. Agadshanow, *Der Staat der Seldschukiden und Mittelasien im 11.–12. Jahrhundert* (Berlin, 1994). See further the review by Carole Hillenbrand, *Journal of the Royal Asiatic Society*, 3rd Series, 2 (1996), 255–7.

23 A sampling of this recent scholarship may be found in the valuable collection edited by Christian Lange and Songül Mecit, *The Seljuqs: Politics, Society and Culture* (Edinburgh, 2011).

history, which it is hoped will go some way to filling this lacuna in scholarship as well as acting as a stimulus to future research. We commence with two chapters that offer a narrative political history of the Seljuk state from its origins to its collapse in 1194. Although much of this ground has already been covered by Edmund Bosworth in a magisterial survey which will doubtless remain the standard work on the political history of the Iranian world for the foreseeable future, the approach here differs in two respects.[24] First, Seljuk history frequently forces us to look beyond even the greater Iranian world of Iran, Iraq and Central Asia, into Syria, the Jazira and Anatolia. Secondly, Bosworth was unable to use Sibt b. al-Jawzi's chronicle, which was published in the same year as his survey. This text (discussed further below) is especially important for the detailed information it gives on the activities of the nomadic Turks, especially in Syria and Iraq, between 1055 and 1092, which it is vital to consider in any account of this formative period of the Seljuk Empire. For the subject of the second chapter, the period between 1092 and 1194, our picture has changed less dramatically, but our sources are now supplemented by the relatively recently published chronicles of Nishapuri and Qummi, and a small but important body of secondary literature. I have not sought to detail every revolt, or every contortion of the phenomenally complex political history of the twelfth century. For these readers should still refer to Bosworth, or the Turkish literature mentioned above. Rather, my aim has been to give the reader an impression of the overarching trends in Seljuk political history, their causes and their consequences.

The subsequent six chapters deal with topics that are key to understanding the Seljuk Empire and its development. A particular theme we will seek to investigate is the role of Turks, nomads and steppe culture and their interaction with the empire's Perso-Islamic traditions, which have often been privileged by previous scholarship. As Lambton put it, '[the Seljuks'] Muslim upbringing prepared them for a rapid acceptance of the Muslim world and the [latter's] imperial ['Abbasid] tradition in its broad outlines. But the usages of the steppe and the nature of the armed forces of the Seljuks necessarily modified the imperial structure somewhat.'[25] The nature and extent of this modification has rarely been investigated, however, owing to the problematic nature of our sources (on which more below).

24 C. E. Bosworth, 'The Political and Dynastic History of the Iranian World (A.D. 1000–1217)' in J. A. Boyle (ed.), *The Cambridge History of Iran, vol. V: The Saljuq and Mongol Periods* (Cambridge, 1968), 1–202.

25 Ann K. S. Lambton, *Continuity and Change in Medieval Persia: Aspects of Administrative, Economic and Social History* (Albany, NY, 1988), 11.

Chapter 3 examines Seljuk political concepts, such as sovereignty, succession and legitimacy, considering the dual legacy of the steppe and the Perso-Islamic tradition. In this context we also look at the thorny question of the Seljuk relationship with the 'Abbasid Caliphs who played a crucial role both in providing legitimacy for the Seljuks in the broader Islamic world, but who also were constantly striving to assert their own authority at the Seljuks' expense. Central to any understanding of Seljuk political and cultural life is the royal court, the *dargāh*, which forms the subject of Chapter 4. In Chapters 5 and 6 we consider the other two main groups who ran the empire: the predominantly Persian bureaucrats and the largely Turkish military; Chapter 7 considers the role of religion in the empire; whereas most surveys concentrate exclusively on Islam, here we attempt to give due weight to the important role of Jewish and Christian communities as well. The final chapter seeks to offer an overview of the economic and social organisation of the empire.

The Seljuk Empire and the way it functioned changed considerably over its one and a half centuries of existence, but it is only very occasionally that the evidence allows us to understand how and why it did. Scholars have sometimes taken the reign of Malikshah (r. 464/1072–485/92) as more broadly representative of a classical age of the Seljuk Empire.[26] However, Malikshah's reign was in many ways quite anomalous, and in any event one should be wary of extrapolating broader trends from limited evidence. We really cannot say at the moment, for instance, to what extent the military forces at the disposal of Sultan Sanjar in the middle of the twelfth century differed in organisation or financing from those of Malikshah. We therefore cannot begin to discuss whether there might have been any relationship between any putative differences and Sanjar's poor battlefield performance (at least in his later reign) as opposed to Malikshah's success. In practice, it is not possible to avoid some generalisations about 'Seljuk' practices in a work of this size; but these should be read with a health warning that they must be nuanced by future research that we must hope will tease out the similarities and differences of Seljuk rule across the empire.

The Sources for the History of the Great Seljuks

Any attempt to study the Seljuk Empire as a whole soon comes up against a major obstacle in the extreme unevenness of our evidence. As for most of the mediaeval Islamic world, few archival documents have come down to us.

[26] The essay of Lambton, 'The Internal Structure of the Saljuq Empire', is a good example of this tendency.

Our main sources are therefore the Arabic and Persian chronicles without which it would be impossible to piece together the barest narrative of Seljuk history.[27] They confront us with the problems which will be familiar to students of mediaeval Islamic history. The chronicles are primarily literary artefacts, intended to promote a certain version of the past for a variety of purposes, such as the author's (or his patron's) political or moralistic agenda, or his factional loyalties. The chronicles are generally written much later than the events they describe; and they concentrate almost exclusively on the elites of the court – sultans, amirs and bureaucrats. A problem peculiar to the Seljuk case is that the chronicles tend to concentrate on the west of the Seljuk realm; despite its undoubted importance, events in Khurasan are covered much more scantily. Furthermore, the chronological coverage is patchy: the period between 485/1092 and 511/1118 (from the death of Sultan Malikshah to the accession of Mahmud) is particularly poorly documented, even in the west.

Perhaps most seriously of all, Seljuk history was written not by the conquerors, but by the conquered. We have only fleeting glimpses of the Seljuks' own view of themselves and their past: most of our sources were composed by authors writing in Persian and Arabic who lived in the great urban centres of the eastern Islamic world. As the quotation that opens this chapter suggests, many regarded the Seljuks with undisguised contempt as an alien and barbaric force. Even mediaeval historians and poets who are sympathetic to the dynasty tended to propagandise on its behalf by using terms of reference that might have been persuasive to an audience in the settled lands of Islam, but do not necessarily reflect what the Seljuks themselves found important. As a result, such sources tend to underestimate the role of nomads and Turkish culture in the empire, or even at times to whitewash it out entirely.

The principal exception is a lost work called the *Maliknama* (*Book of the King*), which seems to have, at least in part, relied on oral Turkish sources and to have presented something of the Seljuks' own view of their origins. Although Arabic and Persian versions of the *Maliknama* were widely used by historians of the thirteenth century, it has been preserved most extensively in the fifteenth-century version by Timurid historian Mirkhwand's great general history, the

[27] For surveys of Seljuk historical writing, see Claude Cahen, 'The Historiography of the Seljuqid Period', in Bernard Lewis and P. M. Holt (eds), *Historians of the Middle East* (London, 1962), 59–78; Julie Scott Mesiami, *Persian Historiography to the End of the Twelfth Century* (Edinburgh, 1999), 141–280; Carole Hillenbrand, 'Some Reflections on Seljuq Historiography', in Antony Eastmond (ed.), *Eastern Approaches to Byzantium* (Aldershot, 2000), 73–88; A. C. S. Peacock, 'Court Historiography of the Seljuq Empire in Iran and Iraq: Reflections on Content, Authorship and Language', *Iranian Studies*, 47 (2014), 327–45.

Rawdat al-Safa, rewritten to suit the literary tastes of the day. In any event, the *Maliknama* is of use only for the earliest period of Seljuk history; from the mid-eleventh century onwards, all our sources are written by outsiders.[28]

None of our extant chronicles was composed within the Great Seljuk Empire. Except for the very early period, up to *c.* 431/1040, when we have the valuable evidence of the contemporary Ghaznavid bureaucrats Bayhaqi and Gardizi, plus the *Maliknama*, the earliest surviving chronicles date to the late twelfth century. Earlier chronicles were certainly written, as we know from later references and citations. An attempt has been made, for instance, to reconstruct an early twelfth-century history, the *'Unwan al-Siyar* by al-Hamadhani, on the basis of quotations in the Mamluk author al-'Ayni.[29] Fragments of this work are also preserved along with quotations from other early sources in the thirteenth-century history of Aleppo, the *Bughyat al-Talab* by Ibn al-'Adim.[30]

Two of the surviving works were composed in the Jibal, under the nominal rule of the Seljuk sultans of Iraq. The brief Persian *Saljuqnama* of Zahir al-Din Nishapuri was written around 1177 for the Seljuk prince (and future sultan) Tughrıl III (d. 590/1194), to inspire him with examples of ideal rulership taken from the behaviour of his ancestors. Although the original text has only recently been published,[31] Nishapuri's *Saljuqnama* served as the source of many later Persian works dealing with the Seljuks, of which the most famous is the *Rahat al-Sudur* written by another member of Tughrıl III's circle, Rawandi, but completed and dedicated after his death to the Anatolian

28 Claude Cahen, 'Le Maliknameh et l'histoire des origines seljukides', *Oriens* 2/i (1949), 31–65 (English translation, 'The Malik-nama and the History of Seljuqid Origins', in C. Edmund Bosworth (ed.), *The Formation of the Classical Islamic World, vol. 9: The Turks in the Early Islamic World* (London: Ashgate, 2007)); also on this source, A. C. S. Peacock, *Early Seljūq History: A New Interpretation* (London, 2010), 8–9, 27–32, 38–41, 43–6.

29 Abu l-Hasan Muhammad b. Abi 'l-Fadl 'Abd al-Malik al-Hamadhani, *Qit'a Ta'rikhiyya min kitab 'Unwan al-Siyar fi Mahasin Ahl al-Badw wa l-Hadar, aw al-Ma'arif al-Muta'akhkhira, wa bi-Dhaylihi Shadharat min kitab Umara' al-Hajj*, ed. Shayi' 'Abd al-Hadi al-Hajiri (Tunis, 2008).

30 See C. Edmund Bosworth, 'Towards a Biography of Niẓām al-Mulk: Three Sources from Ibn al-'Adīm', in Geoffrey Khan (ed.), *Semitic Studies in Honour of Edward Ullendorf* (Leiden, 2005), 299–308.

31 Zahir al-Din Nishapuri, *Saljuqnama*, ed. A. H. Morton (Cambridge, 2004). Other later chronicles which draw on Nishapuri are Rashid al-Din's *Jami' al-Tawarikh* and Yazdi's *al-'Urada fi 'l-Hikaya al-Saljuqiyya* (both fourteenth century). On the embellishments of these later authors, see Alexander H. Morton, 'Qashani and Rashid al-Din on the Seljuqs of Iran', in Yasir Suleiman (ed.), *Living Islamic History: Studies in Honour of Professor Carole Hillenbrand* (Edinburgh, 2010), 166–177. In this work, Nishapuri and Rawandi have generally been used in preference to later, embellished derivatives.

Seljuk sultan Ghiyath al-Din Kaykhusraw I (d. 608/1211). The second Jibali work, also in Persian, is *Dhayl-i Nafthat al-Masdur* by the bureaucrat Najm al-Din Qummi, also during the lifetime of Tughrıl III. It focuses on the bureaucrats of the Sultanate of Iraq from the 1130s onwards; although it has been known to scholarship since the 1970s, it has been generally neglected, perhaps because of the general lack of scholarly interest in the period it covers.[32]

Roughly contemporary is perhaps the single most important Seljuk chronicle, the Arabic *Nusrat al-Fatra* by the famous bureaucrat 'Imad al-Din al-Isfahani, Saladin's secretary. Composed in Syria, it covers the whole sweep of Seljuk history, but again with special reference to the activities of the bureaucratic class of which Isfahani was a member (see p. 205). Despite its importance, the *Nusrat al-Fatra* has not yet been published in its entirety and is wrongly thought by many scholars to have been lost.[33] Instead, it has been generally known through a thirteenth-century abridgement by Bundari, the *Zubdat al-Nusra*, which is cited here according to the 1889 edition by Houtsma, as the complete text remains inaccessible to most, and largely unanalysed.[34]

Two further important sources originate in Baghdad. The first, *al-Muntazam fi 'l-Ta'rikh* by the Hanbali scholar Ibn al-Jawzi (d. 597/1200), contains much valuable information, some of it first-hand, about politics and sometimes daily life in a city which every Seljuk ruler sought to possess. Events beyond Baghdad rarely feature except where they affect the city, but Ibn al-Jawzi's grandson, Sibt b. al-Jawzi (d. 654/1256), produced a history known as the *Mir'at al-Zaman* which is much broader in scope. For our purposes, Sibt b. al-Jawzi's work – which remains inadequately published[35] – is

32 On this work, see K. A. Luther, 'A New Source for the History of the Iraq Seljuqs: The *Tarikh al-Vuzara*'', *Der Islam*, 45 (1969), 117–28; Stephen Fairbanks, 'The *Tarikh al-Vuzara*': A History of the Saljuq Bureaucracy', PhD dissertation, University of Michigan, 1977.

33 The unique manuscript is preserved in the Bibliothèque nationale in Paris, MS arabe 2145. For the differences between the mansuscript and the published abridged text, see David Durand-Guédy, 'Un fragment inédit de la chronique des Salğūqides de 'Imād al-Dīn al-Iṣfahānī: le chapitre sur Tāğ al-Mulk', *Annales Islamologiques*, 39 (2005), 205–22.

34 Bundari, *Zubdat al-Nusra*, ed. M. Th. Houtsma as *Histoire des Seljoucides de l'Irâq par Bondârî d'après Imâd al-dîn al-Kâtib al-Isfahânî* (Leiden, 1889) (*Recueil de textes relatifs à l'histoire des Seljoucides*, II).

35 The parts dealing with the reigns of Tughrıl, Alp Arslan and Malikshah were published by Ali Sevim as *Mir'âtü'z-Zeman fi Tarihi'l-Âyan* (Ankara, 1968); Sevim subsequently produced a new edition of the same sections in *Belgeler: Türk Tarih Kurumu Dergisi*, 14/xviii (1989–1992), 1–260, but the lack of an index makes this rather hard to use. For this reason, the 1968 edition has been preferred here. Later parts of the chronicle were published by 'Ali Ghamidi.

exceptionally valuable because he drew on a now lost eleventh-century history by a Baghdadi resident, Ghars al-Niʿma, which offers an eyewitness view of the Seljuk conquests, and contains particularly valuable information about the Türkmen in Iraq and Syria not preserved in other sources.

Otherwise, we are reliant on thirteenth-century sources, without which it would be impossible to construct any meaningful history of the Seljuks. The most important are a mid-thirteenth-century monograph on the Seljuks, Husayni's *Akhbar al-Dawla al-Saljuqiyya*, which shares a common source with Isfahani, but does contain some independent information, especially for the later twelfth century; and Ibn al-Athir's (d. 630/1233) *al-Kamil fi 'l-Ta'rikh*, a universal history which draws extensively on now lost sources for the Seljuks. Although Ibn al-Athir's work seems a model of dispassionate annalistic historiography, it needs to be treated with care, as the author was sympathetic to the Zangid dynasty of Mosul which his father had served. The dynastic founder, ʿImad al-Din Zangi (d. 546/1146), had been a senior Seljuk amir (commander). This personal connection doubtless influenced Ibn al-Athir's positive portrayal of Zangi and his role in the Seljuk state in the early twelfth century.

Some thirteenth-century Persian works should also be mentioned: Juzjani (writing in Delhi in *c.* 658/1260) is helpful mainly for the collapse of the Seljuk Empire in the east and Seljuk relations with the Ghurid and Qarakhitay states, while his contemporary Juwayni (writing in Mongol-occupied Baghdad) is good on the Seljuks' relations with their vassals the Khwarazmshahs and the Ismailis of northeastern Iran. We also have, from the late eleventh century and especially the twelfth century, a developing tradition of local historiography in Persian – works devoted to an individual city or province, reflections of a local patriotism. Local histories of Fars, Isfahan, Herat, Sistan and the town of Bayhaq (Sabzawar) in Khurasan shed light on aspects of Seljuk rule.[36] In the west, Arabic histories of Aleppo by Ibn al-ʿAdim, of Mayyafariqin (modern Silvan in southeastern Turkey) by

All editions fail to represent the substantial differences between the extant manuscripts. A new edition of the work by Kamil al-Juburi et al. (Beirut, 2013) came to my attention too late to be used here.

36 Ibn al-Balkhi, *Farsnama*, ed. G. Le Strange and R. A. Nicolson as *The* Fársnáma *of Ibnu'l-Balkhí* (Cambridge, [1921] 1962); ʿAbd al-Rahman Fami Harawi, *Tarikh-i Harat*, facsimile edition prepared by Muḥammad Husayn Mir Husayni and Muhammad Rida Abuni Mihrizi (Tehran, 1387); *Tarikh-i Sistan*, ed. Muhammad Taqi Bahar (Tehran 1381); Ibn Funduq, *Tarikh-i Bayhaq*, ed. Ahmad Bahmanyar (Tehran, n.d.). Mafarrukhi's *Kitab Mahasin Isfahan*, ed. ʿArif Muhammad ʿAbd al-Ghani (Damascus, 2010) contains limited but valuable information on Isfahan. For a discussion with further references. see David Durand-Guédy, *Iranian Elites and Turkish Rulers: A History of Iṣfahān in the Saljūq Period* (London, 2010).

Ibn Azraq al-Fariqi, and of Damascus by Ibn al-Qalanisi are valuable for understanding the Seljuk impact on Syria and the Jazira.

Apart from chronicles, a number of collections of Seljuk archival documents have survived, of which by far the most important for our purposes is the *'Atabat al-Kataba*, originating from the chancery of the Great Seljuk sultan Sanjar (r. 511/1118–552/1157), which offers an insight into the functioning of Seljuk government in twelfth-century Khurasan.[37] Diplomas of appointment to various positions such as governor, tax collector or qadi comprise the bulk of this collection. Such documents, written in the elaborate prose known as *inshā'*, were preserved largely as practical manuals of style for bureaucrats to emulate. As a result, they often lack information of crucial importance to the historian, such as the date and even the name of their addressee. Closely related to the *'Atabat al-Kataba*, but including additional documents from Sanjar's chancery, is the largely unpublished St Petersburg *inshā'* collection.[38] A third collection, *al-Muhktarat min al-Rasa'il*, comes from Isfahan, but most of the documents are from the second half of the twelfth century and thus falls slightly outside the focus of this book, although it is of interest for the later Seljuks and the Ildegüzids.[39]

[37] 'Ali b. Ahmad Muntakhab al-Din Badi' Atabak al-Juwayni, *'Atabat al-Kataba: majmu'a-yi murasalat-i diwan-i sultan Sanjar*, ed. Muhammad Qazwini and 'Abbas Iqbal Ashtiyani (Tehran, [1329] 1389).

[38] A number of the St Petersburg documents were published by V. V. Bartol'd, *Turkestan v Epokhu Mongolskogo Nashestviya. Chast' 1: Teksty* (St Petersburg, 1898); some also appeared in German translation by Heribert Horst, *Die Staatsverwaltung der Grosselǧūqen und Ḫōrazmšāhs (1038–1231)* (Wiesbaden, 1964). The most detailed examination of the St Petersburg documents and their relationship to the *'Atabat al-Kataba* is Mehmed Altay Köymen, 'Selçuklu devri kaynaklarına dâir araştırmalar. I. Büyük Selçuklu İmparatorluğu devrine ait münşeat mecmuaları'. This was slated to be published in the *Ankara Üniversitesi Dil ve Tarih-Coğrafya Fakültesi Dergisi*, 8 (1951), 539–648, but never actually appeared. An offprint is held in the Türk Tarih Kurumu in Ankara.

[39] *Al-Mukhtarat min al-Rasa'il*, ed. Ghulamrida Tahir and Iraj Afshar (Tehran, 1378). Some of these documents have been studied by Durand-Guédy in *Iranian Elites and Turkish Rulers*, 8-10, 230–255. See also David Durand-Guédy, 'Diplomatic Practice in Saljuq Iran: A Preliminary Study based on Nine Letters about Saladin's Campaign in Mesopotamia', *Oriento Moderno*, 89/ii (2008), 271–96 and David Durand-Guédy, 'The Türkmen–Saljuq Relationship in Twelfth-century Iran: New Elements based on a Contrastive Analysis of Three inšā' Documents', *Eurasian Studies* (special issue, *Nomads in the Political Field*, eds Johann Büssow, David Durand-Guédy and Jürgen Paul), 9 (2011), 11–66. For information on other collections of Seljuq documents, see Horst, *Staatsverwaltung*, 7–12. Note, too, the *inshā'* collection of the Seljuk *mustawfi* of Baylaqan in the Caucasus around 1100, although many documents are literary rather than archival: Mas'ud b. Namdar, *Sbornik Rasskazov, Pisem i Stikhov*, ed. V. M. Beylis (Moscow 1970), and the discussion in Vladimir Minorsky and Claude Cahen, 'Le recueil transcaucasien de Mas'ûd b. Nâmdâr (debut du

The coverage offered by these collections is quite limited, and none survive from the eleventh century.

Despite the lack of surviving chronicles and documents from the Seljuk realm, there was a rich tradition of literary production in both Arabic and Persian. Indeed, poems written in praise of rulers, viziers and other senior figures in the Seljuk state comprise in some periods the main extant contemporary evidence. However, their use by historians has to date been quite limited, as their references to historical events are usually very vague.[40] Poetry rarely supplements our factual knowledge from the chronicles. It is more valuable for the impression it provides of court life, the great festivals and ceremonies that were celebrated there, and for giving a certain 'atmosphere' to the period. There are also normative sources, like the two 'mirrors for princes' of the late eleventh century, Nizam al-Mulk's *Siyasatnama* (on which see further below pp. 66–7) and the *Qabusnama* of a Seljuk vassal prince, the Ziyarid ruler Kayka'us b. Iskandar. In both instances they are more useful for understanding the ideal than the reality.

There are many other literary sources which contain tangential information about aspects of politics, religion and culture under the Seljuks, including those written by Jewish and Christian authors. My aim here has been simply to give an impression of the principal sources on which our knowledge of the period is based. Inevitably, these concentrate heavily on rulers, wars and battles, and have little to say about everyday life. It is very difficult for the historian to escape this bias, particularly when the main alternative source for social and economic history, archaeology, is extremely undeveloped in most of the lands of the Seljuk Empire (the sophisticated work ongoing at Merv is an exception). The problem is compounded by the fact that comparatively little material evidence in the form of artefacts has survived from most of the Seljuk lands, especially from the period up to the middle of the twelfth century which is our focus here. Only architectural monuments provide us with any significant corpus of reasonably securely dated material.

Where possible, I make use of this material evidence. However, despite the limitations of the written sources, they contain a vast trove of information the potential of which has not yet begun to be realised. So far, the chronicles

VIe/XIIe siècle)', *Journal Asiatique*, 237 (1949), 93–142. Further on Seljuk documents, see the bibliography in Özgüdenli, *Selçuklular*, 309–10.

40 See G. E. Tetley, *The Ghaznavid and Seljuk Turks: Poetry as a Source of History* (London, 2009); poetry has also been used extensively by Abbas Iqbal for the study of Seljuk bureaucrats: *Wizarat dar 'ahd-i salatin-i buzurg-i Saljuqi az tarikh-i tashkil-i silsila ta marg-i Sultan Sanjar 432–552* (Tehran, 1338).

have largely been used as mines of dates and data, but they deserve to be read much more critically and carefully. Indeed, the fact that our principal source, Isfahani's *Nusrat al-Fatra*, has been published only in a bowdlerised abridgement rather than the critical edition that a major work by one of the masters of classical Arabic prose deserves, and has in fact wrongly long been regarded as lost by many scholars in the field, suggests the extent of the work remaining to be done.

1

The Rise of the Seljuks: From the Eurasian Steppe to the Gates of Cairo, *c.* 965–1092

Contemporaries struggled to understand the Seljuk conquests. The Armenian historian Aristakes Lastiverttsi, writing in the 1070s of events some thirty years earlier, could comprehend their speed and savagery only as a sign of divine anger with his native land:

> [T]he gate of Heaven's wrath opened upon our land. Numerous troops moved forth from T'urk'astan [Turkestan], their horses were as fleet as eagles, with hooves as solid as rock. Well girded, their bows were taut, their arrows sharp, and the laces of their shoes were never untied . . . They sped like lions, and like lion cubs, they mercilessly threw the corpses of many people to the carnivorous beasts and birds . . . [God] poured His wrath down upon us by means of a foreign people, for we had sinned against Him.[1]

For the settled Muslim population, the Turks were scarcely less alien or alarming. Contemporary intelligence reports from Khurasan quoted by the Ghaznavid historian Bayhaqi complain that the Seljuks and their nomadic followers, the Türkmen, 'damage every place and people; they steal everything they find, and much evil comes from them'.[2]

However, another Armenian chronicler, Matthew of Edessa (d. *c.* 1136) gives a very different impression of Seljuk campaigns under the third Seljuk sultan Malikshah in the 1070s:

> Malikshah . . . marched forth at the head of a formidable army composed of innumerable warriors. He came and entered the Roman empire in the West [i.e., Byzantium] in order to take over that region. This sultan's heart was filled with benevolence, gentleness, and compassion for the Christians; he

[1] Aristakes Lastiverttsi, *History*, trans. Robert Bedrosian (New York, 1985) 64–5, 66 (= Armenian text edited by Yuzbashian, 63–4) (available at www.rbedrosian.com). By 'the laces of their shoes were never untied' Aristakes means they were constantly on the move.

[2] Bayhaqi, *Tarikh*, 720.

> showed fatherly affection for all the inhabitants of the lands [he traversed] and so gained control of many towns and regions without resistance.[3]

This perceived transformation of the Seljuks from a barbarous force of warriors into architects of a civilised empire is often associated with Malikshah's great vizier, Nizam al-Mulk (d. 485/1092). As one contemporary put it, 'he was the one who built the Seljuk state',[4] by introducing the norms of Perso-Islamic governance. A different source, however, remarks of Tughrıl (d. 455/1063), that he was 'the first of the Seljuk kings and the one who built their state'.[5] Both characterisations have a measure of truth. It is perhaps not surprising that contemporaries were confused. The sudden collapse of the existing empires in western Asia in the mid- to late eleventh century – the Ghaznavids, Buyids and Byzantines – before the Seljuks is not easily explained today, and the apparent suddenness of the transformation from war band to empire is as bewildering as the scale and rapidity of the conquests.

By the middle of the eleventh century, something resembling a Seljuk state had emerged – a polity that struck coins, had some sort of a bureaucracy, and raised taxes, to use a fairly minimal definition. However, *pace* Matthew of Edessa, even under Malikshah it was still often the Türkmen rather than the sultans who spearheaded expansion, launching campaigns that reached far into Anatolia, Egypt, Arabia and the Caucasus. Yet alongside this process of empire-building, tension was growing between some groups of nomads and the Seljuk sultans. The latter's leadership was by no means accepted, even (or especially) by other members of the Seljuk family, who were often able to mobilise Türkmen support for their own claims. For the Seljuk sultans, these Türkmen-backed rebels represented a much more serious threat to their authority than any external threat. Understanding the empire's formation is thus not merely a question of tracing the emergence of state institutions, but also of examining the fate of the force which had created the empire, the nomadic Turks themselves, whose political concepts remained rooted in the world of the steppe where not merely descent, but also personal charisma was required to establish a claim to leadership.[6] We therefore must start with the steppe background from which these Turks emerged.

3 Matthew of Edessa, *Armenia and the Crusades, Tenth to Twelfth Centuries: The Chronicle of Matthew of Edessa*, trans. Ara Dostourian (Lanham, MD, 1993), 154.

4 Ibn al-'Adim, *Bughyat al-Talab fi Ta'rikh Halab: al-tarajim al-khassa bi-ta'rikh al-Salajiqa*, ed. Ali Sevim as *Buğyat at-Ṭalab fī Tārīḫ Ḥalab: Selçuklularla İlgili Haltercümeleri* (Ankara, 1976), 90; Bosworth, 'Towards a Biography of Nizam al-Mulk', 303.

5 Sibt, *Mir'at*, 107.

6 See Peacock, *Early Seljūq History*, 60–3.

The Oghuz and the Emergence of the Seljuks

In the sacred heart of the pre-Islamic Turkish world in Mongolia, an eighth-century inscription in Turkish runes provides our earliest references to the Oghuz (the Turkish form of Arabic and Persian 'Ghuzz').[7] Bilge Qaghan, ruler of the Gök Türk Empire (552–774), which stretched from Manchuria to the Black Sea steppes, erected this monument to the memory of his younger brother Kül Tigin in 732. The inscription surveys the history of the Gök Türk Empire, which Bilge Qaghan and Kül Tigin had rescued from destruction at the hands of various enemies, both the Chinese and various Turkish groups, of whom the Oghuz are one.[8] Yet Bilge Qaghan also refers to the Oghuz as 'my own people', and they are one of the main groups to whom the inscription is addressed. These Oghuz played a prominent role in the fighting between various nomadic groups that accompanied the demise of the Gök Türks in the mid-eighth century. After this we know very little about the Oghuz until they appear in Islamic sources of the ninth and tenth centuries in the west of the Eurasian steppe, around the Volga River.

Writing at the court of Malikshah in the late eleventh century, the physician Sharaf al-Zaman Marwazi attempted to explain the origins of the dynasty's ancestors. He traced the Oghuz migrations westwards back to the struggles for pasture among nomadic groups in Central Asia displaced by the new power of Liao, a nomadic dynasty from Manchuria, better known in Islamic history as the Qarakhitay,[9] who were to play a crucial role in the destruction of the Great Seljuk Empire in the mid-twelfth century (pp. 103–6 below). The rise of the Liao/Qarakhitay did, indeed, have profound consequences for the steppe, but it is unlikely that they were behind the Oghuz

[7] For the early Oghuz and the background of the steppe world from the sixth century more generally, see: Peter B. Golden, 'The Migrations of the Oğuz', *Archivum Ottomanicum*, 4 (1972), 45–84 (reprinted in Peter B. Golden, *Nomads and their Neighbours in the Russian Steppe: Turks Khazars and Qipchaqs* (Aldershot, 2003) (study V); Peter B. Golden, 'The Turks: Origins and Expansion', in Peter B. Golden, *Turks and Khazars: Origins Institutions and Interactions in Pre-Mongol Eurasia* (Farnham 2010), (study I); C. Edmund Bosworth, 'The Origins of the Seljuqs', in C. Lange and S. Mecit (eds), *The Seljuqs: Politics, Society and Culture* (Edinburgh, 2011). On the Gök Türk empire, see Denis Sinor, 'The Establishment and Dissolution of the Türk Empire', in Denis Sinor (ed.), *The Cambridge History of Early Inner Asia* (Cambridge, 1990), 285–316; Ahmet Taşagıl, *Gök Türkler I –II–III* (Ankara, 2012). For the Orkhon inscriptions, see Talat Tekin, *Orhon Yazıtları* (Ankara, 1988).

[8] There are also references to the 'Toquz Oghuz' (Nine Oghuz [tribes]). It is not clear whether these are a distinct group from the Oghuz. See Golden, 'The Migrations of the Oghuz', 48.

[9] *Sharaf al-Zaman Tahir Marvazi on China, the Turks and India*, ed. and trans. Vladimir Minorsky (London, 1942), 29–30.

migrations westwards. Oghuz had been noted in Islamic Central Asia even before the ninth-century rise of the Liao. Ibn al-Athir records that: 'These Ghuzz are a people who moved from the furthest frontier regions of the Turks to Transoxiana in the days of al-Mahdi, and converted to Islam.'[10] This would put the Oghuz migration between *c.* 158/775 and 169/785, the dates of the Caliph al-Mahdi's reign. The credibility of the report is strengthened by the fact we know of other Turkish people who were on the move westwards in the same period,[11] following the collapse of the Gök Türk empire.

Originally, the term Oghuz seems to have meant something like a nomadic 'confederation',[12] but from the mid-eighth century a distinct Oghuz cultural and linguistic identity started to emerge within the broader family of groups who identified themselves as Turks.[13] At roughly the same time, these Oghuz started to form what scholars have regarded as a 'state' in the southern parts of what is now Kazakhstan and Russia – the Volga–Syr Darya region.[14] This enormous, largely flat steppe region would provide ample pasture space for the sheep, camels and horses on which a nomadic existence depended. Nomads migrated vast distances within it to secure the essential necessities of their lifestyle – pasturage for their flocks: cool dry high land in summer (*yaylāq*, modern Turkish *yayla*) and lower lying warm winter grounds, often by rivers (*qïshlāq, kışlak*). A Mamluk source records that one group of Oghuz regularly migrated between winter pastures at Balasaghun by Lake Issyk Kul (in modern Kyrgyzstan) and summer ones by the Volga, a distance of roughly 1,500 miles, and there is some evidence to suggest a similar pattern may have been true of the Seljuk clan.[15] However, not all Oghuz were nomads. Along the Syr Darya River, on the northern and eastern frontiers of the Islamic world, there were quite a number of Oghuz-populated towns.[16] Yengi-Kent ('New town', also known by its Persian name, Dih-i naw, 'New village'), for instance, served as the winter quarters of an Oghuz *yabghu*, a chief's title inherited from the Gök Türk empire.[17]

State is probably too grand a term for these political structures. The

[10] Ibn al-Athir, *al-Kamil*, XI, 176

[11] Golden, 'The Turks: Origins and Expansion', 20–1.

[12] Golden, 'The Migrations of the Oghuz', 47.

[13] *Ibid.*, 57.

[14] See Peacock, *Early Seljūq History*, 21–6.

[15] *Ibid.*, 24.

[16] *Ibid.*, 54–5. In addition, see now Peter Golden, 'Courts and Court Culture in the Proto-urban and Urban Developments among the pre-Chinggisid Turkic Peoples', in David Durand-Guédy (ed.), *Turko-Mongol Rulers, Cities and City Life* (Leiden, 2013), esp. 22–31, 50–1.

[17] Golden, 'Türk Imperial Tradition', 50–5.

imperial legacy of the Gök Türk empire and the sacral title of *qaghan* were inherited not by the Oghuz, but by the Khazar empire based on the Volga (eighth–tenth centuries) to which many Oghuz chiefs were in some sense – at least in theory – subject.[18] It is in the Khazar state that we find our earliest reference to Seljuk and his father Duqaq. According to accounts composed for the courts of the first two Seljuk sultans, Tughrıl and Alp Arslan, the ancestors of the dynasty served the Khazar ruler as military commanders.[19] This suggests that by the mid-tenth century Duqaq and Seljuk were active in the area to the west of the Aral Sea, near the Khazar capital of Itil on the Volga. In common with much of the Khazar elite, they may have adhered to the Jewish faith.[20]

The Migration of Seljuk

Sometime in the late tenth century the Seljuk family broke decisively with the Khazars.[21] The details are hazy. Ibn Hassul, a bureaucrat at Tughrıl's court, claimed that the rebel was Seljuk himself,[22] but the *Maliknama* attributes the revolt to Seljuk's father Duqaq.[23] Meanwhile, Arabic chronicles suggest that the Oghuz collaborated with an attack by the Rus' on Itil in 965, which struck a fatal blow to the Khazar empire and may indicate the broader context for the revolt.[24] Mirkhwand's version of the *Maliknama*, on the other hand, attributes the break with the Khazars to court intrigues, and goes on to recount how Seljuk

> thought much about how to save himself. He decided to flee into exile. When he had decided on flight, with a hundred horsemen, 1500 camels and 50,000 sheep he headed for the lands of Samarqand.[25]

18 *Ibid.*

19 See the discussion of these accounts in Peacock, *Early Seljūq History*, 27–35.

20 On Judaism in the Khazar empire, see Peter B. Golden, 'The Conversion of the Khazars to Judaism', in P. B. Golden, H. Ben-Shammai and A. Rona-Tas (eds), *The World of the Khazars* (Leiden 2007), esp. 144 (reprinted in Golden, *Turks and Khazars*, study XI). See further Chapter 7 below.

21 The principal secondary literature on this period is: Cahen, 'Le Maliknameh', *passim*; Mehmet Altay Köymen, *Büyük Selçuklu İmparatorluğu Tarihi, vol. I: Kuruluş Devri* (Ankara, 1979), 18–36; Peacock, *Early Seljūq History*, 16–47.

22 Ibn Hassul, *Tafdil al-Atrak*, 49.

23 Mirkhwand, *Rawdat al-Safa* (Tehran, 1338), IV, 235; cf. Bar Hebraeus, *Chronography*, I, 235.

24 Golden, 'Migrations', 77–9; Peacock, *Early Seljūq History*, 34–5; Bosworth, *The Ghaznavids*, 220; Ibn al-Athir, *al-Kamil*, VIII, 565.

25 Mirkhwand, *Rawdat al-Safa*, IV, 236.

The migration (dated only by a fourteenth-century source to 375/985–6)[26] brought Seljuk and his followers to the town of Jand, near modern Kyzylorda in western Kazakhstan. Jand was the heart of an Oghuz principality which was a vassal of Khwarazm, the northernmost Muslim province in Central Asia. Khwarazm, ruled by the Ma'munid dynasty, was itself theoretically subject to the Samanid state (204/819–390/999) that dominated Transoxiana and Khurasan. Disputes over pasture and taxes soon broke out between Seljuk and the local Oghuz ruler, the *yabghu* 'Ali and his son Shahmalik.[27] Although Islam existed within the Khazar domains,[28] Jand, through its subjugation to Khwarazm, would have been the first Muslim-ruled area that Seljuk and his followers encountered. It was there that Seljuk is said to have embraced the faith of Islam, and to have recruited support from 'the Turks of that frontier who incline towards holy war',[29] with whose aid he was able to establish himself in a position of authority.

The motives for Seljuk's conversion are opaque (see pp. 246–7 below), but the impetus behind his migration in the first place is scarcely any clearer. In addition to the reason the *Maliknama* gives us – the break with the Khazars – modern scholars have suggested that climate change may have forced the nomadic Seljuks to migrate to escape a shortage of pasture on the steppe.[30] It is true that some scientific evidence does point to increased aridity in the Aral Sea region around this period,[31] but this is hardly conclusive, as it usually takes more than one single factor to spark a migration. Moreover, the *Maliknama* suggests this was not a mass movement of people: rather, it was a small-scale exodus led by one specific aristocratic nomadic chief, Seljuk, and his personal followers, accompanied by their most valuable possessions – their livestock. Far from being a sudden deluge of people onto an unsuspecting sedentary world, the migration was initially too slight an occurrence to be noted by Muslim chroniclers.

The Descendants of Seljuk in Islamic Central Asia

When Seljuk died in Jand around the beginning of the eleventh century, according to tradition at the age of 107 around 399/1009,[32] the Muslim

26 Hamdallah Mustawfi, *Tarikh-i Guzida*, ed. 'Abd al-Husayn Nawa'i (Tehran, 1339), 426; cf. Peacock, *Early Seljūq History*, 37, and Cahen, 'Le Maliknameh', 37–8.

27 Bosworth, 'Origins', 17–18; Peacock, *Early Seljūq History*, 38, 40.

28 Cf. Golden, 'The Conversion of the Khazars', 144–5, 148.

29 Mirkhwand, *Rawdat al-Safa*, IV, 237; cf. Ibn al-Athir, *al-Kamil*, IX, 474.

30 The main proponents of this view are Richard Bulliet and Ronnie Ellenblum. See further the discussion in Chapter 8.

31 See the climatological evidence discussed in Peacock, *Early Seljūq History*, 45.

32 Ibn al-Athir, *al-Kamil*, IX, 474; Özgüdenli, *Selçuklular*, 33; Köymen, *Büyük Selçuklu İmparatorluğu Tarihi*, I, 26–7.

lands to the south were wracked by political tumult. Out of the wreckage of the Persianate Samanid empire of Khurasan and Transoxiana, two Turkish states were emerging.[33] Transoxiana fell to Qarakhanid dynasty (382/992–607/1222), also nomads recently converted to Islam, whose main base was Balasaghun. Khurasan and the lands to the south of the Oxus fell to the nascent Ghaznavid empire, whose rulers were descendants of Sebüktegin (d. 387/997), a Turkish slave soldier. Although nomads were employed in their military, the Ghaznavids modelled themselves on the Samanid state from which they had originated. Arabic and Persian were the court languages, and Sebüktegin's descendants had Arabic names like Mahmud and Mas'ud, not Turkish ones. Their power was based on the domination of urban centres, and they fought the Qarakhanids over the remnants of the Samanid state. Khwarazm was itself annexed by the Ghaznavids in 408/1017, putting an end to the Ma'munid dynasty of Khwarazmshahs. The Ghaznavid governors, however, proved as anxious as their Ma'munid predecessors to take advantage of Khwarazm's location near major nomadic migration routes and its remoteness from the rest of Islamic Central Asia to assert a privileged position of autonomy.[34]

These political changes had a number of causes, such as the weakening of the Samanid economy with the exhaustion of its silver mines.[35] In addition, the borders of Islamic Central Asia were becoming home to an ever increasing number of desperate Turks, pushed out of their traditional pasturelands and politically leaderless, owing to the collapse of nomadic confederations and the emergence of new ones, convulsions which were perhaps exacerbated by the rise of the Liao.[36] In 408/1017–8, for instance, the Qarakhanids themselves

[33] See Peter B. Golden, 'The Karakhanids and Early Islam', in Denis Sinor (ed.), *The Cambridge History of Early Inner Asia* (Cambridge, 1990), 358–61; Bosworth, *The Ghaznavids*, 27–47; Bosworth, 'Political and Dynastic history', 5–11; Köymen, *Büyük Selçuklu İmparatorluğu Tarihi*, I, 30–70. In general on the Qarakhanids, see also C. E. Bosworth, 'Īlek-Khāns or Ḳarakhānids', *EI*²; and in more detail, Boris Kochnev, *Numizmaticheskaya Istoriya Karakhanidskogo Kaganata (991–1209)* (Moscow, 2006).

[34] See the discussion in Jürgen Paul, 'The Role of Ḫʷārazm in Seljuq Central Asian Politics, Victories and Defeats: Two Case Studies', *Eurasian Studies*, 6 (2007–8), 1–17.

[35] For discussion, see Thomas Noonan, 'The Onset of the Silver Crisis in Central Asia', *Archivum Eurasiae Medii Aevii*, 7 (1987–91), 228–48; Roman K. Kovalev, 'Mint Output in Tenth-century Bukhara: A Case Study in Dirham Production and Monetary Circulation in Northern Europe', *Russian History/Histoire Russe*, 28/i–iv (2001), 245–71; Roman K. Kovalev, 'The Production of Dirhams in the Coastal Caspian Sea Provinces of Northern Iran in the Tenth–Eleventh Centuries and their Circulation in the Northern Lands', *Archivum Eurasiae Medii Aevii*, 19 (2012), 133–83, with further references.

[36] Golden, 'The Karakhanids and Early Islam', 363–4; also Peter B. Golden, 'The Qipchaqs of Medieval Eurasia: An Example of Stateless Adaptation in the Steppes', in G. Seaman and D. Marks (eds), *Rulers from the Steppe: State Formation on the Eurasian Periphery* (Los

were attacked by a huge number of unidentified pagan 'Turks', allegedly more than 300,000 households strong.[37] It seems likely that the increase in the Seljuks' strength in this period from the small band that had migrated to Jand may be attributed to their ability to appeal to this reservoir of disaffected, leaderless nomads.

Seljuk had himself apparently been drawn into these convulsions, supporting the last Samanid ruler against the Qarakhanids.[38] It was probably as a result of this that the Seljuks were granted summer pastures near Samarqand and winter ones near the Samanid capital of Bukhara.[39] They also maintained a connection with Khwarazm, the northeastern portions of which – roughly modern Karakalpakstan – continued to serve as a major winter pasture for the Seljuks into the 1030s.[40]

The Oghuz, the Türkmen and their Social Organisation

Oghuz who converted to Islam became known as Türkmen as early as the tenth century.[41] Muslim writers, however, frequently continued to apply the term Oghuz (or Ghuzz) to describe even Muslim Türkmen, usually with distinctly pejorative connotations. On the other hand, some groups described as Türkmen by the sources were evidently still pagan.[42] Although historically there were town-dwelling Oghuz/Türkmen, both terms usually denote that an individual or group is a nomad. In this book, we generally use 'Türkmen' to refer to the Seljuks' nomadic subjects, except when quoting from primary sources that use Ghuzz, or when that term is so well-entrenched that to use Türkmen would be anachronistic (for example, the great Ghuzz revolt against Sanjar in 1152–7).

The term Turk is used by the Muslim sources both to refer to the Ghuzz/Türkmen, and to other Turkic-speaking groups who were not

Angeles, 1991), 142–7 (reprinted in Golden, *Nomads and their Neighbours*, study IX); *Sharaf al-Din Marvazi, loc cit.*

37 Ibn al-Athir, *al-Kamil*, IX, 297.

38 Mirkhwand, *Rawdat al-Safa*, IV, 237; Ibn al-Athir, *al-Kamil*, IX, 474.

39 Nishapuri, *Saljuqnama*, 5; cf. Mirkhwand, *Rawdat al-Safa*, IV, 237.

40 Bayhaqi, *Tarikh*, 693, 1113–15; Paul, 'The Role of Ḫʷārazm', 6, n. 6. Peacock, *Early Seljūq History*, 43.

41 On the terms Oghuz and Türkmen, see Peacock, *Early Seljūq History*, 48–53; also David Durand-Guédy, 'Goodbye to the Türkmen? The Military Role of Nomads in Iran after the Saljuq Conquest', in K. Franz and W. Holzwarth (eds), *Nomadic Military Power, Iran and Adjacent Areas in the Islamic Period* (Wiesbaden, in press).

42 See Peacock, *Early Seljūq History*, 124–5; cf. Juwayni, *'Atabat al-Kataba*, 19.

Oghuz, such as the Qarluqs (perhaps the single most important component in the Qarakhanid state), Pechenegs and Qipchaqs. A detailed contemporary description of the Turks' language, poetry and customs has come down to us in the form of the *Diwan Lughat al-Turk*, a Turkish–Arabic dictionary composed by the émigré Qarakhanid prince Mahmud al-Kashghari in Seljuk Baghdad, completed around 1077. Despite Kashghari's detailed ethnographic information, much remains mysterious about the social organisation of these Turks. He divides the Oghuz into twenty-four (or, according to another version, twenty-two) tribes – but their names virtually never feature in early accounts of eleventh-century Seljuk history.

Instead, contemporary authors like Bayhaqi depict the nomads as coalescing around aristocratic Turkish leaders, after whom they were known – the *Yınaliyan* are the followers of Ibrahim Yınal, the *Saljuqiyya* or *Saljuqiyan* the adherents of the descendants of Seljuk and so on. Thus, *Saljuqiyya* has no implication of shared blood, and some nomadic groups were also known after geographical regions, not people (the 'Iraqiyya, the Balkhan-Kuhiyan). Certainly, the tribe was a much less significant social organism among the Turks than it was among the Arabs, and Kashghari's Oghuz tribes seem to represent an attempt to legitimise the Turks' role in the Islamic world by giving them the same status as Arabs.[43] It is not until the second quarter of the twelfth century that any of Kashghari's tribes start to appear in our sources; the reasons for their growing significance in this period are not yet clear, and require further research. After the Mongol invasions in the thirteenth century, interest in tribal origins seems to have intensified among the Turkic peoples of the Middle East, and was projected by onto earlier periods by writers of the fourteenth and fifteenth centuries.

After Seljuk's death, his elder son Arslan Isra'il became the most prominent member of the family. We find him intervening in Transoxianan politics in support of a Qarakhanid prince, 'Ali Tegin, who attempted around 411/1020–1 to establish himself as ruler in Bukhara.[44] 'Ali Tegin faced opposition from both his brother Ilek Khan and the latter's supporter Mahmud, the

[43] See A. C. S. Peacock, 'From the Balkhān-Kūhīyān to the Nāwakīya: Nomadic Politics and the Foundations of Seljuq Rule in Anatolia', in Jürgen Paul (ed.), *Nomad Aristocrats in a World of Empires* (Wiesbaden, 2013), 55–80, esp. 57–62, for a detailed consideration of these issues.

[44] On the political situation in Transoxiana and Khurasan, see Bosworth, *The Ghaznavids*, esp. 234–40; Golden, 'The Karakhanids and Early Islam', 362–5; Köymen, *Büyük Selçuklu İmparatorluğu Tarihi*, I, 68–78.

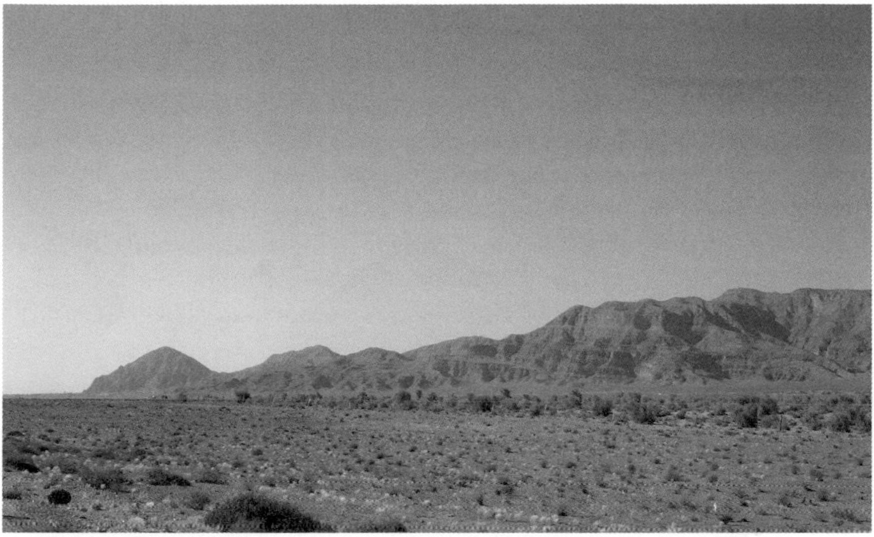

Figure 1.1 Mount Balkhan, western Turkmenistan, was a major base for the Türkmen

Ghaznavid sultan (r. 388/998–421/1030), who crossed the Oxus to remove the pretender. On the steppe outside Bukhara, Mahmud first encountered Arslan's nomadic followers encamped; he 'saw the strength of the Seljuks, and the force and large numbers they possessed'.[45] This is one of the earliest references to the Seljuks [*al-saljuqiyya*] in a sense which clearly refers to rather more than just the immediate family of Seljuk and his descendants.

Mahmud's response was to arrest and imprison Arslan Isra'il, doubtless hoping that without their leader, the supporters of the Seljuks would disperse – a reasonable assumption, given the fissiparous nature of political formations on the steppe. Indeed, Mahmud allowed them to cross the Oxus and tried to disperse them in Khurasan, effectively making them Ghaznavid subjects. Some were exiled to remote Mount Balkhan in the west of modern Turkmenistan. Mahmud's actions had profound consequences both for the Seljuk family and for his own territories. First, some nomads still maintained a loyalty to their imprisoned leader, especially the groups that had been exiled to Mount Balkhan (the 'Balkhan-Kuhiyan' – see Figure 1.1). Resentful of the Ghaznavid mistreatment of Arslan Isra'il and seeking to escape from Mahmud's control, some nomads, principally the Balkhan-Kuhiyan, started to migrate westwards, through the Ghaznavid territories and beyond, to

[45] Ibn al-Athir, *al-Kamil*, IX, 475; for a different version of Mahmud's relations with Arslan Isra'il, see Nishapuri, *Saljuqnama*, 6–8.

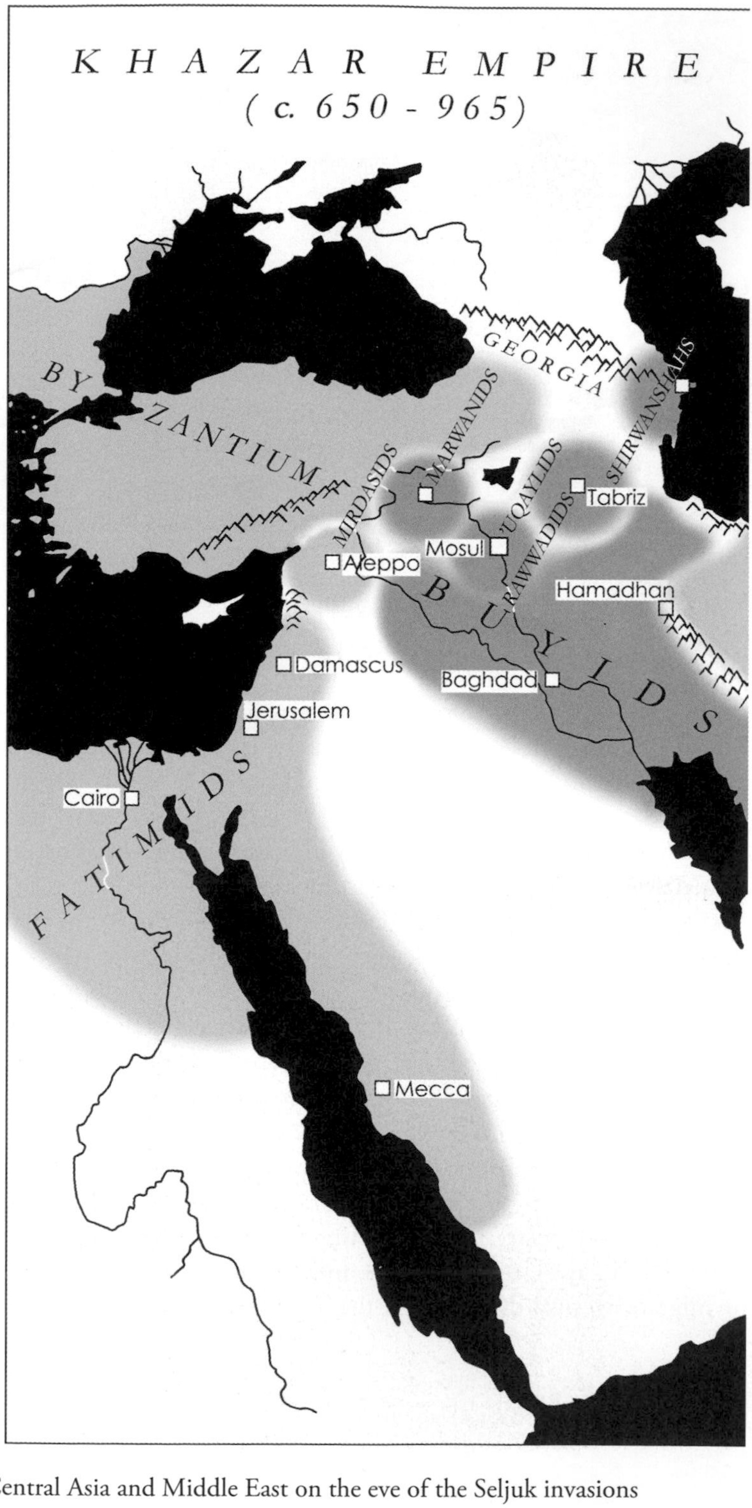

Map 1.1 Central Asia and Middle East on the eve of the Seljuk invasions

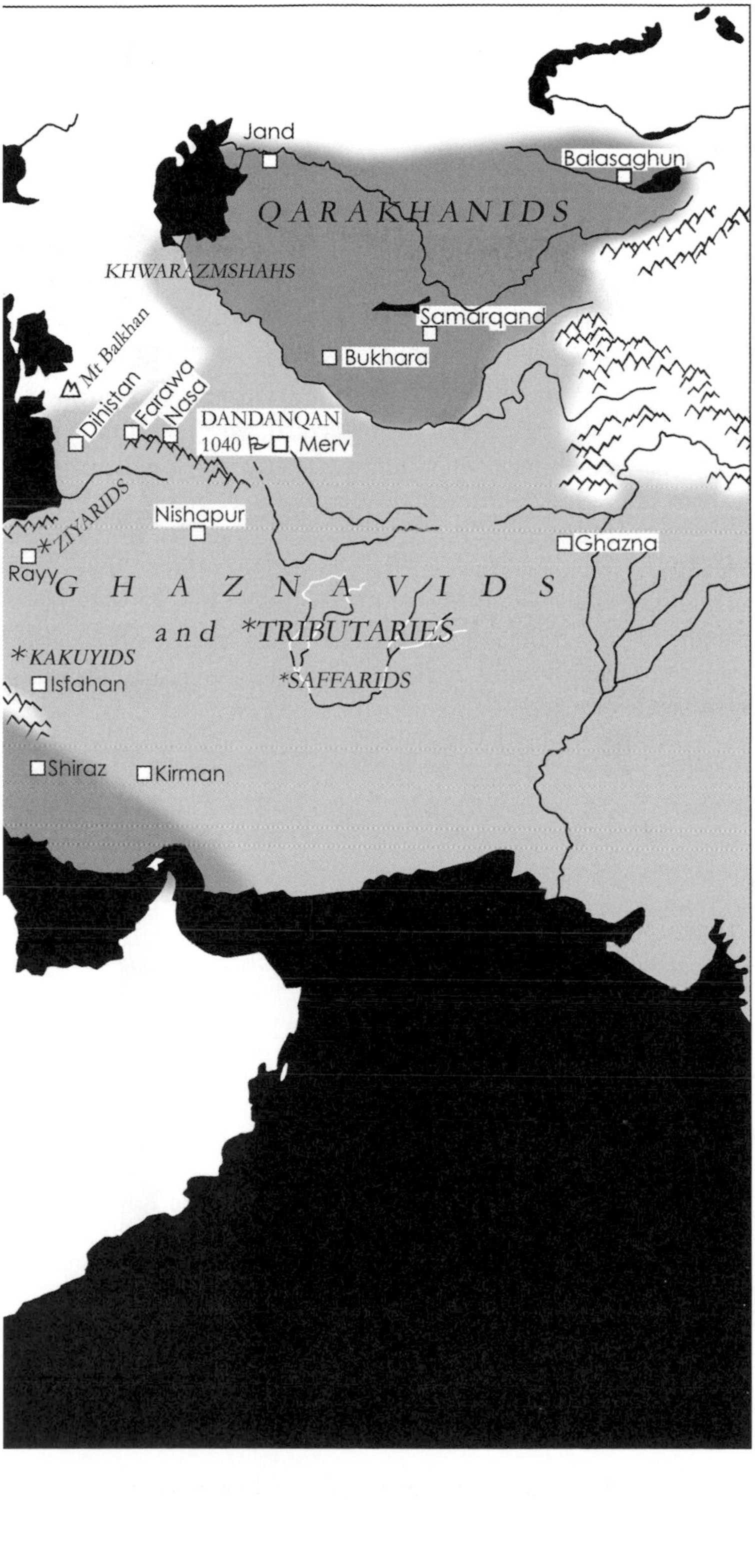
Jand
Balasaghun
QARAKHANIDS
KHWARAZMSHAHS
Samarqand
Bukhara
Mt Balkhan
Dihistan
Farawa
Nasa
DANDANQAN
1040
Merv
*ZIYARIDS
Nishapur
Ghazna
Rayy
GHAZNAVIDS
and *TRIBUTARIES
*KAKUYIDS
Isfahan
*SAFFARIDS
Shiraz
Kirman

the west of Iran, ʿIraq-i ʿAjam. Owing to their association with this region, the migrants were now dubbed ʿIraqiyya, although they penetrated as far as Azerbaijan and eastern Anatolia, which, with their vast pasturelands, represented an ideal location for their flocks.[46] The numbers of the ʿIraqiyya were small: the first group of migrants to the west consisted of 2,000 men.[47] Many more, however, remained in Khurasan, where some were recruited into the Ghaznavid army.[48]

The second consequence of the imprisonment of Arslan Isra'il was the outbreak of a struggle between the other descendants of Seljuk for leadership. The details of this are obscure, but it seems the Qarakhanid ʿAli Tegin still envisaged himself as the Seljuks' ultimate suzerain. By around 421/1030 the sons of Arslan's younger brother Mika'il, Tughrıl and Chaghrı, had emerged as leaders of resistance to ʿAli Tegin,[49] but their ascendancy was far from universally accepted. Arslan Isra'il's own son Qutlumush and his descendants would challenge the heirs of the Mika'ilids, and the discrepancies in the treatment of these events in different versions of the *Maliknama* suggests that its compilers struggled to find a convincing narrative of the rise of Tughrıl and Chaghrı that would dispel doubts about their entitlement to the leadership.[50] Later sources also play down the role of a third Seljuk, Musa Yabghu, who certainly occupied an equal position to Tughrıl and Chaghrı, and possibly even a senior one.[51] Bayhaqi, for instance, our main contemporary source, talks of three leaders, not just two – Tughrıl, Chaghrı and Yabghu.[52]

46 On these, see Peacock, 'From the Balkhān-Kūhīyān to the Nāwakīya', 59–64.

47 Ibn al-Athir, *al-Kamil*, IX, 377–9, 476.

48 *Ibid.*, IX, 478, [Masʿud] *istakhdama baʿḍahum wa-muqaddamuhum Yaghmur*.

49 *Ibid.*, IX, 476–7; Mirkhwand, *Rawdat al-Safa*, IV, 242–3; Peacock, *Early Seljūq History*, 65–6. Another account is given by Bayhaqi, *Tarikh*, 669, 693–4, who cites a letter purportedly written by the Seljuk leadership, where they claim they had had a good relationship with ʿAli Tegin, which broke down when he was succeeded by his two inexperienced sons.

50 Peacock, *Early Seljūq History*, 41; Peacock, 'From the Balkhān-Kuhīyān to the Nāwakīya', 63–4.

51 See, for example, ʿAbu Saʿid b. ʿAbd al-Hayy Gardizi, *Zayn al-Akhbar*, ed. Rahim Ridazada Malik (Tehran, 1384), 292, where Yabghu appears as the Seljuk with whom Masʿud negotiates. Yabghu is also a senior Turkish title. For more details on him, see Osman G. Özgüdenli, 'Musa Yabghu', *EIr*.

52 Bayhaqi, *Tarikh*, 693, 714–15; Bosworth, *The Ghaznavids*, 221–2, 226, 244. Three leaders are also mentioned in Mirkhwand, *Rawdat al-Safa*, IV, 246, but the third one is called ʿInanj Beg b. Seljuk'; Inanj was a title used by Musa as is confirmed by numismatic evidence. See Peacock, *Early Seljūq History*, 64, esp. n. 127.

The Seljuks in Khurasan and the Ghaznavid Collapse, 1034–40

Around 425/1034, Tughrıl and Chaghrı suffered a major defeat at the hands of ʿAli Tegin and his allies, forcing them to flee Transoxiana: 'Their possessions and their children were taken, many of their women and offspring were imprisoned, and necessity made them cross to Khurasan'.[53] First, they took refuge in Khwarazm, which in any event was one of their traditional pastures, but they were also encouraged by the ambitious Ghaznavid governor, Harun, who hoped to use them to support his efforts to conquer Khurasan from his suzerain.[54] When Harun was murdered by Ghaznavid agents in April 426/1035,[55] the Seljuks were again forced to flee, heading south across the barren wastes of the Kara Kum desert. Initially, they made for the great oasis city of Merv, but perhaps it was too well defended, for they then diverted westwards to take refuge in the town of Nasa, lying in the northern foothills of the Kopet Dagh mountains.[56] They had arrived on the edges of Khurasan, the province which was one of the 'jewels in the crown' of the Ghaznavid sultan Masʿud (421/1030–432/1041).[57]

'Khurasan is lost!' (*Khurāsān shud*), the Ghaznavid governor of Khurasan, Abu 'l-Fadl Suri, is said to have declared as soon as he heard of the Seljuks' arrival.[58] This was an exaggeration: having been chased out of both Transoxiana and Khwarazm the Seljuks scarcely seem to have been invincible and, in fact, they preferred negotiation to force. A letter preserved by Bayhaqi allegedly signed by Tughrıl, Chaghrı and Musa Yabghu explains their travails, and asks Suri to intercede with the sultan on their behalf:

> If [the sultan] sees fit, he will accept us as his servants, so that one of us will pay homage to him at his exalted court and the others will undertake whatever service the sultan commands, and we will rest in his great shadow. He should grant us the province of Nasa and Farawa which is on the edge of the desert so that we can put down our possessions and rest. We will not allow any evil doer from Mount Balkhan, Dihistan, the borders of Khwarazm and the banks of the Oxus to appear, and we will fight the ʿIraqi and Khwarazmian Türkmen. If – God forbid – the sultan does not agree, we do not know what will happen, for we have nowhere else to go.'[59]

[53] Ibn al-Athir, *al-Kamil*, IX, 477.
[54] Bayhaqi, *Tarikh*, 1117.
[55] See Paul, 'The Role of H̱ʷārazm', 6–8.
[56] Bayhaqi, *Tarikh*, 693; Ibn al-Athir, *al-Kamil*, IX, 477.
[57] Bosworth, *The Ghaznavids*, 250.
[58] Bayhaqi, *Tarikh*, 693.
[59] *Ibid.*, 694.

On receipt of this letter, the Ghaznavid vizier commented 'up to this point this has been an affair [of dealing with] shepherds . . . now they have become amirs who seize provinces',[60] but Gardizi confirms that the Türkmen's main aim was to secure pasture. Indeed, as late as 429/1038, when several of the leading cities of Khurasan had accepted Seljuk suzerainty, their leaders were still claiming that their ambitions were limited to pastureland.[61]

This may not have been wholly disingenuous. Securing pasture for his followers is one of the main tasks of a nomadic chief, for without pastures the Türkmen's livestock would die, imperilling their own survival. Türkmen in such a position would naturally gravitate towards a new leader: ultimately, then, the question of securing pasture was also one of ensuring the continuing leadership of the Seljuk family.[62] Even the promise to fight other Türkmen may have been sincere: after all, such Türkmen would present a threat to the Seljuks' control of these new pastures, and some – such as those who remained loyal to the line of Arslan Isra'il – represented a challenge to the Mika'ilids' leadership. There is little evidence that at this date either Tughrıl or Chaghrı, or any of their other relatives had any designs to establish their own polity.[63]

Mas'ud proved unable to settle on a coherent policy. Initially, mindful of the trouble caused by the 'Iraqiyya whom his father Mahmud had let through, the sultan rejected the Seljuks' demands and prepared to campaign in person against them.[64] Given that Khurasan was suffering from a series of bad harvests and famine,[65] the arrival of the Seljuks may have seemed like an intolerable additional burden, and a threat to the tax base of the province. However, the expedition was a disaster, and Mas'ud's army met a humiliating defeat in a Türkmen ambush at Nasa in Sha'ban 426/June 1035.[66]

Following this debacle, Mas'ud gave in to the Seljuk demands, granting

60 *Ibid.*, 694.

61 Gardizi, *Zayn al-Akhbar*, 287, 292.

62 See Peacock, *Early Seljūq History*, 60–1.

63 Nishapuri, however, claims that the imprisoned Arslan Israil urged Tughrıl and Chaghrı to seek kingship (*dar ṭalab-i mulk sakht bikūshīd*), but this is clearly a later fiction designed to legitimise the Mika'ilid takeover. Nishapuri, *Saljuqnama*, 8.

64 Bayhaqi, *Tarikh*, 695–6.

65 Cf. Bosworth, *The Ghaznavids*, 259–60. For famine, see Bayhaqi, *Tarikh*, 942–3, 949–50 (in Khurasan in 431); Nasir-i Khusraw, *Safarnama*, ed. Muhammad Ghanizada (Berlin, 1341), 5 (at Qazwin in 438); Ibn Funduq, *Tarikh-i Bayhaq*, ed. Ahmad Bahmanyar (Tehran, n.d.), 268, 273 (famine in Bayhaq in the seven years up to 429/1038); Bosworth, *The Ghaznavids*, 250–1, 260–1.

66 Bayhaqi, *Tarikh*, 708, 711–13; Gardizi, *Zayn al-Akhbar*, 288–9; Mirkhwand, *Rawdat al-Safa*, IV, 255; Peacock, *Early Seljūq History*, 74–5.

Figure 1.2 Chaghrı's first fief, the desert city of Dihistan, Turkmenistan. In the foreground are the remains of the city's walls

them diplomas of recognition for rule over the three main towns lying in the northwest foothills of the Kopet Dagh, with the ancient Iranian title of *dihqān*. Chaghrı received the steppe city of Dihistan (see Figure 1.2), Tughrıl was granted Nasa, while Farawa went to Musa Yabghu (another indication that, in fact, the Seljuk leadership was a triumvirate at this date – and Bayhaqi was in a position to know as he actually drew up the diplomas).[67] There was nothing especially startling about such a move. Governments throughout the Islamic world tended to be decentralised, and regions distant from the main administrative centres were easy prey to local strongmen, whom rulers often preferred to recognise rather than fight. This step emboldened the Seljuks, and in Muharram 428/November 1036, they sent an embassy demanding greater prizes: the grant of the towns of Sarakhs, Abiward (Figure 1.3) and Merv itself. The arrangement envisaged was basically a tax farm: the Seljuks wanted to keep Ghaznavid administrators in place, but have the taxes paid to themselves rather than to the sultan in return for military service – the offer of keeping out other, less desirable groups of Türkmen was repeated.[68]

The Seljuks had evidently resolved not to wait for Masʿud's answer, for Chaghrı was already conducting manoeuvres in Balkh hundreds of miles away from Dihistan, provoking fears that he was about to march on Ghazna itself.[69] The threatened Ghaznavid response caused this Seljuk party to retreat

[67] Bayhaqi, *Tarikh*, 714–15; cf. Ibn al-Athir, *al-Kamil*, IX, 481 who also mentions Musa Yabghu.

[68] Bayhaqi, *Tarikh*, 727.

[69] *Ibid.*, 727–8; Ibn al-Athir, *al-Kamil*, IX, 481.

Figure 1.3 The ruins of the Seljuk city of Abiward, Turkmenistan, in the shadow of the Kopet Dagh mountains that form the frontier of Khurasan with the steppe (and today of Iran and Turkmenistan)

to Farawa and Nasa,[70] but it was too dilatory to deter the Türkmen, whose raids continued.[71] With almost no warning, all of Khurasan except Balkh fell to the Seljuks in 428–9/1037–8.[72] The sudden Ghaznavid collapse is bewildering, not least because it is so ill-attested. The conquest of the great city of Merv, for instance, is not even distinctly recorded; the last Ghaznavid garrison is mentioned in 428/1037, but later the same year sources allude to Chaghrı's presence there.[73] Nishapur, too, may have fallen as early as 428/1037, judging by the earliest extant Seljuk coin struck there bearing that date, although literary sources put the conquest firmly in the following year.[74]

Nonetheless, we can identify some of the main factors that contributed to the Ghaznavid collapse. Formidable though the Ghaznavid military was, it faced insuperable logistical and tactical difficulties. Their heavy armour and their use of elephants – a tactic learned from India intended to terrify their foes – slowed them down and it made it impossible to operate in the desert

70 Bayhaqi, *Tarikh*, 740, 745.

71 *Ibid.*, 757.

72 Ibn al-Athir, *al-Kamil*, IX, 459.

73 See Peacock, *Early Seljūq History*, 90–2; Ibn al-Athir, *al-Kamil*, 479–80; Husayni, *Akhbar*, 8–9; Bayhaqi, *Tarikh*, 753. The most detailed account of these years is Köymen, *Büyük Selçuklu İmparatorluğu Tarihi*, I, 197–335.

74 Richard Bulliet, *The Patricians of Nishapur: A Study in Medieval Islamic Social History* (Cambridge, MA, 1972), 204, n. 10; Sadi S. Kucur, 'A Study on the Coins of Tughrıl Beg, the Sultan of the Great Seljuqs', in Carmen Alfaro, Carmen Marcos and Paloma Otero (eds), *XII Congreso Internacional de Numismática, Madrid, 2003. Actas I* (Madrid, 2005), 1602.

or steppe where resources were scarce. In individual battles, the Ghaznavids tended to get the upper hand, but the Seljuks usually evaporated into the steppe before a direct confrontation could take place.[75] When in 431/1040 Mas'ud finally managed to capture Tughrıl's base at Nasa, it did him precious little good for the Türkmen had merely melted away to the traditional stronghold of Mount Balkhan, far into the steppe where the Ghaznavids were incapable of following them.[76] Even tracking down the lightly armed and highly mobile enemy was an enormous struggle, for the Seljuks did not aim to garrison towns. The prevailing famine in Khurasan meant that the Ghaznavid army struggled to find supplies, 'but the Seljuks did not care about that for they are content with little'.[77] The Seljuks' manoeuvrability also meant that Ghaznavid forces were massively overstretched by having to defend the whole vast region stretching from Jurjan by the Caspian to the Oxus. As a result, even important cities were left with wholly inadequate garrisons, or with no garrison at all. Some major centres lacked walls.[78] Such cities were thus easy prey for the Seljuks.

In the absence of Ghaznavid authority, it was left to urban notables to decide how to react. Some towns, such as Abiward, seem to have defected to the Seljuks on the initiative of these local elites,[79] and Nishapuri may well record something of the truth when he cites a letter sent by Tughrıl and Chaghrı to the caliph al-Qa'im in which they claimed that 'the notables and famous people of Khurasan requested us to protect them'.[80] Years of over-taxation, religious oppression, and Mas'ud's own personal venality and incompetence meant that Ghaznavid governance was regarded with suspicion and sometimes outright hostility by many groups in Khurasan.[81] At the same time, urban society in Khurasan was fragmented by factionalism.[82] A decision made by the elite – or one group of it – to accept Seljuk authority

75 Peacock, *Early Seljūq History*, 79–80.

76 Bayhaqi, *Tarikh*, 936, 937; cf. Gardizi, *Zayn al-Akhbar*, 285; Mirkhwand, *Rawdat al-Safa*, IV, 254. Further on the inability of Ghaznavid armies to operate in the steppe, see Bosworth, *The Ghaznavids*, 241–52; Peacock, *Early Seljūq History*, 80; Bayhaqi, *Tarikh*, 908.

77 Ibn al-Athir, *al-Kamil*, IX, 480; cf. Bosworth, *The Ghaznavids*, 251–2.

78 Bosworth, *The Ghaznavids*, 252, 261; Paul, 'The Seljuq Conquest(s) of Nishapur'.

79 Gardizi, *Zayn al-Akhbar*, 293; cf. Muhammad b. Munawwar, *Asrar al-tawhid fi maqamat al-Shaykh Abi Sa'id*, ed. Muhammad Rida Shafi'i Kadkani (Tehran 1366), I, 156, according to which the people of Abiward and Mayhana supported the Seljuks. See also Mirkwand, *Rawdat al-Safa*, IV, 250, on pro-Seljuk feeling among the urban elite of Merv.

80 Nishapuri, *Saljuqnama*, 13.

81 Bosworth, *The Ghaznavids*, 79–80, 84–90, 227–30, 258–61, 266.

82 See Chapter 8, esp. pp. 312–14.

might be opposed by other social groups. In Merv, Herat and Nishapur, the Seljuks faced popular rebellions which seem to have been instigated by the lower social classes, and it was these, rather than Ghaznavid forces, which on occasion temporarily evicted the Seljuks.[83]

Ghaznavid armies continued to operate in Khurasan for two years after the Seljuk takeover of most of the region in 428–9/1037–8. For the reasons outlined above, although sometimes successful in restoring Ghaznavid authority in areas, they were unable to secure the province. The final Ghaznavid collapse was precipitated by one of the few pitched battles in the contest for Khurasan, at the small town of Dandanqan near Merv on 8 Ramadan 431/23 May 1040.[84] An army led by Masʿud was heading from Nishapur to Merv to seek out the Seljuks, but the Ghaznavid force was exhausted from the long desert road and the shortage of supplies, and fighting broke out between the sultan's personal guard and the ordinary soldiers over water. Chaghrı, meanwhile, who had been shadowing the army's march across the desert, pounced just as these Ghaznavid forces were setting about each other. The defeat was total, and Masʿud fled southwards to save what he could of his empire. He was killed soon afterwards, toppled in a court coup on his way to India to try to recruit forces with which to fight the Seljuks.[85]

In an oft quoted passage, Mirkhwand claimed that the Seljuks had made Khurasan 'ruinous, like the dishevelled tresses of the fair ones or the eyes of the loved ones, and it became devastated by the pasturing of [the Türkmen's] flocks'.[86] Gardizi tells us how Ghaznavid officials in Khurasan 'were continually sending letters [to Masʿud] with the information that the violence and evildoing of the Türkmen had gone beyond all measure'.[87] Without denying the damage cause by the Türkmen and their livestock, they cannot have been solely to blame. The deployment of large Ghaznavid armies across the province for several years must have placed a massive burden on Khurasan's already stretched resources.[88] As Ghaznavid authority ebbed away, urban militias (*ʿayyārs*) proliferated, terrorising the population,[89] while rivalries between cities also led to strife, with the people of Tus and Abiward ganging

[83] See Paul, 'Histories of Herat', 106–7; Paul, 'The Seljuq Conquest(s) of Nishapur', 578–9; Peacock, *Early Seljūq History*, 89–94.

[84] Bayhaqi, *Tarikh*, 961–5; Gardizi, *Zayn al-Akhbar*, 293–4; Husayni, *Akhbar*, 12; Ibn al-Athir, *al-Kamil*, IX, 482–3; Mirkhwand, *Rawdat al-Safa*, 258.

[85] Ibn al-Athir, *al-Kamil*, IX, 487; cf. Gardizi, *Zayn al-Akhbar*, 294.

[86] Mirkhwand, *Rawdat al-Safa*, IV, 102; trans. from Bosworth 'Political and Dynastic History', 20.

[87] Gardizi, *Zayn al-Akhbar*, 291.

[88] Cf. Bosworth, *The Ghaznavids*, 249–52, 260.

[89] Ibn al-Athir, *al-Kamil*, IX, 483; Gardizi, *Zayn al-Akhbar*, 292.

up to try to sack Nishapur.[90] Pro-Seljuk narratives emphasise Tughrıl's role in restoring order and cracking down on the *'ayyārs*,[91] but even hostile sources suggest Seljuk rule was welcomed by some. The Ismaili poet Nasir-i Khusraw, a vigorous opponent of the new rulers, was moved to berate the population of Khurasan for their predilection for Seljuk rule:

> Why are you deceived by the rule of the Turk (i.e. the Seljuks)? Remember the glory and strength of Mahmud of Zavulistan (i.e. Mahmud of Ghazna).[92]

The Formation of the Seljuk Empire

Tughrıl, Chaghrı and the Internal Struggle for Supremacy

After Dandanqan, the Seljuks could hardly believe their luck. Ibn al-Athir recalls how Chaghrı's men 'did not dismount for three days, and would not be parted from their horses except when they needed to eat and drink and so on, out of fear of the return of Mas'ud's army'.[93] When the scale of their victory became clear, the Seljuks sought to secure control of Khurasan. While Chaghrı set off to seize Balkh,[94] Tughrıl entered Nishapur. This time the Seljuks were to stay. For most of the populace, though, there was no sudden transformation. The Seljuks had already learned to rely heavily on existing Khurasani officials. Bayhaqi tells us of 'an aged and eloquent man from Bukhara' who had served as their ambassador to the Ghaznavids, while we also read of a Seljuk governor (*wālī*) of Juzjan who was crucified by Sultan Mas'ud when he retook the town.[95] Bayhaqi, relying on Ghaznavid intelligence reports, records how Tughrıl seated himself on Mas'ud's throne in Nishapur and asked for guidance from the qadi installed by the previous regime stating that, 'We are new men and strangers, and we do not know the Persians' customs.'[96]

The first conquest of Nishapur in 428 or 429/1037 or 1038 (depending on whether we accept the date given by the coins or the chronicles) features in several sources as the turning point when Tughrıl started to act as an Islamic ruler rather than merely a nomad chief. Tughrıl, we are told, prevented the Türkmen from sacking the town until the conclusion of the month of

[90] Paul, 'The Seljuq Conquest(s) of Nishapur', 579–80; Peacock, *Early Seljūq History*, 89; Ibn al-Athir, *al-Kamil*, IX, 434–5.
[91] Paul, 'The Seljuq Conquest(s) of Nishapur', 580–1.
[92] Nasir-i Khusraw, *Diwan*, ed. Mujtaba Minuwi (Tehran, 1353), 117, l.9.
[93] Ibn al-Athir, *al-Kamil*, IX, 483.
[94] *Ibid.*, IX, 483–4; cf. Nishapuri, *Saljuqnama*, 11; Mirkhwand, *Rawdat al-Safa*, IV, 259.
[95] Bayhaqi, *Tarikh*, 712; Ibn al-Athir, *al-Kamil*, IX, 481.
[96] Bayhaqi, *Tarikh*, 885.

Ramadan. However, when the holy month was over, inspired by a recent congratulatory message from the caliph that urged him to respect the lives and property of Muslims, he continued to withhold the promised looting. Chaghrı was restrained from leading the Türkmen to plunder only by his brother's threat to kill himself.[97]

It may be doubted whether these principles of Islamic governance were really taken to heart, even by Tughrıl. The story does not appear in our main contemporary source, Bayhaqi, and the later chronicles aim to legitimise the Seljuks by portraying them as rulers in the Sunni Perso-Islamic tradition, worthy successors to the Samanids and Ghaznavids. Nomads remained the basis of Tughrıl's and Chaghrı's power. Thus, on his second occupation of Nishapur, Tughrıl gave the Türkmen free reign to sack the city.[98] As one less favourably disposed chronicler commented, 'Tughrıl made [other] people's property the stipends for his followers, who would come and go as they pleased.'[99]

Nonetheless, an ideological change over the five years since the victory at Nasa is apparent, with dreams of conquest and empire supplanting the traditional aim of securing pasture. The striking of our first Seljuk coins at Nishapur in 428 and 429/1037–8, inscribed with the names of Tughrıl and the caliph, confirms that Tughrıl was beginning to view himself as a ruler in the Islamic tradition, and suggests the emergence of one of the basic elements of a state: the ability to mint coins.[100] This shift is also suggested by an agreement between the leading members of the Seljuk family after the second conquest of Nishapur, which partitioned the lands conquered and to be conquered.[101] Musa Yabghu was assigned Herat, and Chaghrı the eastern territories, from Nishapur to Merv. Tughrıl, meanwhile, took the west, and

97 Bar Hebraeus, *Chronography*, I, 198; Bundari, *Zubda*, 8; Husayni, *Akhbar*, 7–11, 17; Ibn al-Athir, *al-Kamil*, IX, 457–9.

98 Ibn al-Athir, *al-Kamil*, IX, 483.

99 Hamadhani, *'Unwan*, 166.

100 Kucur, 'A Study on the Coins of Tughrıl', 1602–3.

101 The accounts of this differ, evidently as a result of an attempt by the chroniclers to cover up the profound differences between Tughrıl and Chaghrı. Bundari, *Zubda*, 8–9, states that Chaghrı held the territories from the Oxus to Nishapur, while Ibrahim Yınal received Quhistan and Jurjan, and Musa Yabghu's son Abu 'Ali al-Hasan got Herat, Bushanj, Sistan and Bilad al-Ghur. Husayni's account agrees with this, except that he states that the territories from Nishapur to the Oxus were allotted to Chaghrı by Tughrıl: Husayni also emphasizes Chaghrı's subject status by referring to him with the title *malik* as opposed to Tughrıl whom he calls sultan. Nishapuri (*Saljuqnama*, 14) states that Chaghrı took Merv and most of Khurasan, Musa Yabghu Bust, Herat, Isfizar and Sistan, while Chaghrı's son Qavurt was granted Tabas and Kirman, while Tughrıl was allotted the as yet unconquered west. Arslan Isra'il's son Qutlumush was granted Jurjan and Damaghan, while Yaquti b. Chaghrı was allotted Abhar, Zanjan and Azerbaijan. Cf. Shimizu, 'The Bow and Arrow', 94–5.

Nishapur seems to have remained in the peculiar situation of being claimed by both Tughrıl and Chaghrı.[102]

After Dandanqan, Tughrıl emerges in the sources as the leading member of the family – to such an extent that one historian has accused Chaghrı of being 'colourless'.[103] Chaghrı does virtually disappear from our sources, yet he remained in Merv until his death in 451/1059, successfully repelling Ghaznavid attempts to re-occupy Khurasan, and initiating the Seljuk conquest of the remote province of Sistan.[104] Musa Yabghu, meanwhile, seems to have held on to Herat until about 446/1054–5 – the date of his last known coin – after which he was ousted by Chaghrı's son Alp Arslan, but his fate is obscure.[105] The fact that we are only adequately informed about Tughrıl reflects the problems of our sources rather than the relative importance of the two brothers. After *c.* 431/1040 – not just the date of Dandanqan, but also the point at which our major source for the early Seljuks, Bayhaqi's chronicle concludes, as well as the work of his contemporary Gardizi – we are almost entirely reliant on lost Arabic chronicles preserved by Ibn al-Athir and Sibt b. al-Jawzi. With their western focus, they naturally concentrate on Tughrıl, who was operating in the region, rather than Chaghrı, who remained in Khurasan, which was of little interest to them. Moreover, the prestige that accrued to Tughrıl through his conquest of Baghdad, the seat of the caliphate, further encouraged chroniclers to concentrate on him at the expense of Chaghrı.

Several fragments of evidence suggest, however, that Tughrıl's supremacy was far from assured. When the *partitio imperii* was agreed, Chaghrı's portion would have represented the bulk of the territories actually held by the Seljuks, while Tughrıl won the uncertain reward of as yet unconquered territories. In addition, the east – Chaghrı's portion – has connotations of seniority in Turkic culture: with both the Gök Türks and the Qarakhanids, the rulers of the eastern divisions of the empire, considering it to be superior.[106] The numismatic evidence shows that Chaghrı, as

102 Shimizu, 'The Bow and Arrow', 94–6.

103 Cl. Cahen, '<u>Ch</u>ag<u>h</u>rï', *EI*².

104 Bosworth, 'Čağri Beg Dāwud', *EIr*. For his death date, see now Osman G. Özgüdenli, 'Selçuklu paraların ışığında Çağrı Bey'in ölüm tarihi meselesi', *Ankara Üniversitesi Dil ve Tarih-Coğrafya Fakültesi Tarih Bölümü Tarih Araştırmaları Dergisi*, 22(35) (2004), 155–70.

105 See Özgüdenli, 'Musa Yabghu'; Ibn al-Athir, *al-Kamil*, X, 34. Note, too, the verses celebrating the fall of Yabghu by the contemporary poet Bakharzi, suggesting, contrary to Ibn al-Athir, that Musa Yabghu was humiliated on his fall: 'Ali b. al-Hasan al-Bakharzi, *Hayatuhu wa-Shi'ruhu wa-Diwanuhu*, ed. Muhammad al-Tunji (Beirut, 1994), 84: 'A state has fallen with Yabghu; I gave thanks when it fell / It had grown up with him, but now has turned against him.'

106 Peter B. Golden, 'Imperial Ideology and the Sources of Unity amongst the pre-Cinggisid

well as Tughrıl, used the Turkic symbol of sovereignty, the bow and arrow motif (see further pp. 126–7 below).[107] Ibn al-Athir states that since Rajab 428/1037 Chaghrı had appropriated the honour of having himself named as the 'king of kings' (*malik al-mulūk*) in the *khuṭba*, the Friday sermon, delivered in the mosques of Merv.[108] Chaghrı's son Qavurt, the ruler of Kirman, mentioned only his father and not Tughrıl on his coins, and called Chaghrı the same title, *malik al-mulūk*.[109] By this the ancient Persian title *shāhanshāh* is probably meant,[110] which was also used by Tughrıl (see p. 137 below). Thus, the titulature and symbols of rule suggest that Chaghrı saw himself at very least as equal to Tughrıl, if not as his superior.

It is unlikely that Chaghrı – after all, the victor of Dandanqan –would simply have ceded his claim to suzerainty to his brother. Indeed, a local chronicle of the province of Sistan, apparently put together in the eleventh century, suggests enduring tension between Tughrıl and Chaghrı. Each claimed the right to appoint Sistan's governor (through the issuance of a decree, or *manshūr*), have coins struck in his own name (*sikka*), and his name mentioned as ruler in the *khuṭba*, the sermon at Friday prayers – and each appointed rival governors who fought one another for control of the province between Rajab 446/October 1054 and Jumada II 448/August 1056.[111] This dispute was thus conducted not just by force of arms, but also through the

Nomads of Western Eurasia', *Archivum Eurasiae Medii Aevi*, 2 (1982), 52–3; Peter B. Golden, 'Türk Imperial Tradition', 50.

107 Shimizu, 'The Bow and Arrow', *passim*; Bulliet, 'Numismatic Evidence', *passim*; Osman G. Özgüdenli, 'Yeni paraların ışığında kuruluş devri Selçuklularında hakimiyet münasebetleri hakkında bazı düşünceler', *Belleten*, 45(242/4) (2002), 547–70. See further the discussion in Chapter 3.

108 Ibn al-Athir, *al-Kamil*, IX, 479–80; Husayni, *Akhbar*, 8; cf. Mirkhwand, *Rawdat al-Safa*, IV, 250. Further evidence of Chaghrı's seniority to Tughrıl may be suggested by the parallels drawn between the two brothers and the Parthian rulers drawn by Tughrıl's court poet Gurgani. See M. Molé, '"Vis u Ramin" et l'histoire seldjoukide', *Annali: Istituto Orientale di Napoli*, 9 (1960), 14–17.

109 Özgüdenli, 'Yeni paraların ışığında', 550; Özgüdenli, 'Selçuklu paraların ışığında Çağrı Bey'in ölüm tarihi', 165–6.

110 The usage of *malik al-mulūk* as an equivalent to *shāhanshāh* is attested in Buyid times. See Heribert Busse, 'The Revival of Persian Kingship under the Buyids', in D.S. Richards (ed.), *Islamic Civilisation, 950–1150* (Oxford, 1973), 64–5.

111 See C. E. Bosworth, *The History of the Saffarids of Sistan and the Maliks of Nimruz (247/861 to 949/1542–3)* (Costa Mesa, 1994), 383–5; *Tarikh-i Sistan*, ed. Muhammad Taqi Bahar (Tehran, 1381), 349–55. Musa Yabghu was also caught up in fighting in this region – he apparently regarded himself as having a claim to Sistan as a result of the *partitio imperii*. Tughrıl supported Musa Yabghu in Sistan, and also came in person to assist him in recapturing Herat which he had lost to a local rebellion. Tughrıl may have seen Musa Yabghu as a convenient means of keeping Chaghrı's ambitions in check. See Özgüdenli, 'Musa Yabghu'.

use of symbolism, which was both traditionally Turkic – such as the bow and arrow motifs on the coins – and Islamic: the *manshūr, sikka* and *khuṭba.* It is impossible to know how often the sort of proxy war between the two brothers that Sistan saw was repeated elsewhere, given the lack of comparable local sources for this date. Certainly, other members of the Seljuk family very rarely even mentioned Tughrıl's name on their coins,[112] suggesting that they shared a reluctance to accept his claims to suzerainty. These disputes over leadership and the system of territorial division would persist for most of the empire's existence.

Tughrıl's Conquest of Iran, 1038–55

Tughrıl's great achievement was the conquest of the Iranian plateau and Iraq, which was crowned by his entrance into Baghdad in 447/1055 and subsequent coronation as sultan (pp. 48–50, 164–5 below). These territories were ruled by various princes of the ethnically Iranian Buyid dynasty, although in peripheral areas like the Caspian (where the Buyids themselves had originated, in the province of Daylam), Azerbaijan and the Caucasus other ruling houses – Iranian, Kurdish and Arab – preserved their independence.[113] The Buyid state was divided into several large appanages, of which Shiraz and Baghdad were the most important, each held by a different member of the family. Competition between rival Buyid princes for these appanages rendered the political system inherently unstable. Much of western Iran was dominated by another Iranian family of Caspian Daylamite origin, the Kakuyids, based in Isfahan, who alternately recognised Buyid and Ghaznavid suzerainty.[114]

For the first decade after Dandanqan, the northern Jibal – basically the Hamadhan to Rayy axis – formed the core of the Seljuk territories to the west of Khurasan. Although Tughrıl's troops intervened in Fars at the request of the warring local Buyids, that province was not occupied.[115] The only other part of the Iranian plateau to experience direct Seljuk rule at this point was Kirman, where Chaghrı's son Qavurt had established himself as ruler during the period

[112] Özgüdenli, 'Yeni paraların ışığında', 558–62.

[113] See Bosworth, 'Political and Dynastic History', 23–41, for an overview. On the Buyids, see Heribert Busse, *Chalif und Grosskönigen: die Buyiden in Iraq (945–1055)* (Beirut, 1969); Tilman Nagel, 'Buyids', *EIr*. The most detailed study of Tughrıl's reign remains Mehmet Altay Köymen, *Tuğrul Bey ve Zamanı* (Istanbul, 1976). See also George Makdisi, *Ibn 'Aqil et la résurgence de l'Islam traditionaliste au XIe siècle* (Damascus, 1963), 89–119; C. E. Bosworth, 'Ṭoghril (I) Beg', *EI*².

[114] C. E. Bosworth, 'Dailamīs in Central Iran: The Kākūyids of Jibāl and Yazd', *Iran*, 8 (1970), 73–95.

[115] Ibn al-Athir, *al-Kamil*, IX, 585–6.

around 1048–51.[116] The 1050s saw a rapid expansion of Tughrıl's territories, with wide-ranging campaigns designed to bring local rulers much more closely to heel. The questionable loyalty of Abu Mansur b. 'Ala' al-Dawla, the Kakuyid ruler of Isfahan, encouraged Tughrıl to depose him. Tughrıl finally entered Isfahan in Muharram 443/May–June 1051 after a year-long siege.[117] A major expedition in 446/1054–5 brought the submission of Vahsudan of Tabriz, Abu 'l-Aswar of Ganja, Nasr al-Dawla of Diyar Bakr and the Arab Quraysh b. Badran from the 'Uqaylid Bedouin dynasty of Mosul.[118]

The Iranian plateau fell to Tughrıl less by violent conquest than by negotiation, with local Iranian and Kurdish princes usually left in place provided that they acknowledged Tughrıl's sovereignty and, most importantly, paid him off. 'Tughrıl sent to the king of the Daylamites inviting him to obedience [i.e., to acknowledge Tughrıl's sovereignty] and demanding money from him' as Ibn al-Athir succinctly expresses one example of this behaviour.[119] Even Tughrıl's siege of a major prize such as Isfahan (438/1046–7), subsequently to become the Seljuk capital, was bought off.[120] Intervention often seems to have been purely opportunistic: when Tughrıl invaded the Caspian provinces of Jurjan and Tabaristan in 433/1041–2, this was simply an attempt to take advantage of the squabbling among the local Ziyarid dynasty, who, characteristically, were left in place subject to a cash payment.[121]

This is not to say that the Turkish takeover was entirely peaceful. The 'Iraqiyya, notorious for the destruction they left behind, and rejecting Tughrıl's authority,[122] had been operating on the Iranian plateau since at least *c.* 420/1029.[123] Rayy, Tughrıl's main base, was in fact first occupied by a group of 'Iraqiyya led by one Qızıl.[124] Similarly, Hamadhan in the Jibal, a region noted for its rich pastureland and so ideal for sustaining a nomadic host, had been occupied by the 'Iraqiyya in 430/1038–9, several years before Tughrıl's cousin Ibrahim Yınal seized the area in 433/1041–2.[125] Tughrıl is reported to have responded to the Buyid ruler Jalal al-Dawla's complaints:

116 See Erdoğan Merçil, *Kirman Selçukluları* (Ankara, 1989), 10–16.

117 Ibn al-Athir, *al-Kamil*, IX, 562–3; see Durand-Guédy, *Iranian Elites*, 71–3.

118 Ibn al-Athir, *al-Kamil*, IX, 598–9, 600.

119 *Ibid.*, IX, 508.

120 *Ibid.*, IX, 534; cf. the submission of the Marwanid ruler of Diyar Bakr: Bar Hebraeus, *Chronography*, I, 206; but note also the variant account in al-Fariqi, *Ta'rikh*, 160.

121 Ibn al-Athir, *al-Kamil*, IX, 496–7.

122 *Ibid.*, IX, 508.

123 *Ibid.*, IX, 381, 382, 384–5, 495. See also Bosworth, 'Dailamīs in Central Iran', 77–8; Peacock, *Early Seljūq History*, 69, 85, 139, 141.

124 See Bar Hebraeus, *Chronography*, I, 198–9; Ibn al-Athir, *al-Kamil*, IX, 381.

125 Ibn al-Athir, *al-Kamil*, IX, 384, 496, 506–7; Bosworth, 'Dailamīs in Central Iran', 80.

> These Türkmen (*al-Turkmān*) were our slaves, servants, subjects and followers. They were obedient and served our court, and when we arose to arrange the affairs of the Ghaznavid house and we were charged with dealing with Khwarazm, they headed off to Rayy where they created havoc and destruction. We mustered our armies from Khurasan against them, determined that they should seek mercy and take refuge in forgiveness. Pride took possession of them and decency deserted them, and we must return them humble to our banners and give them a taste of our harshness as a reward for rebels.[126]

In addition to the challenge from the 'Iraqiyya, the loyalties of Tughrıl's cousin Ibrahim Yınal were often in doubt. Tughrıl was afraid that Ibrahim 'would make himself master of Persia, and cause the armies of the Turcoman Ghuzzaye [i.e., the Ghuzz] to rebel with him',[127] and Ibrahim's three major revolts indicate this was no vain worry.[128] However, the relationship was much more complex than simply a challenge from an ambitious relative. Sometimes Ibrahim Yınal appears in the sources as Tughrıl's chief aid and assistant; likewise, not all 'Iraqiyya were hostile to Tughrıl. Some of their leaders were linked by marriage ties to Tughrıl, and continued to reside in Rayy after Tughrıl's entry to the city.[129] Indeed, the 'Iraqiyya were also employed as mercenaries by local Iranian rulers such as the Kakuyids of Isfahan and Vahsudan, the lord of Tabriz.[130]

Tughrıl's own armies remained overwhelmingly Türkmen-based, and this too had consequences for the nature of early Seljuk rule. Not just his men, but also their dependants and their livestock needed to be fed. A single Türkmen family may have owned around 100 sheep for subsidence, meaning that a 3,000-strong army – the size of the force with which Tughrıl entered Nishapur in 429/1038[131] – would have been accompanied by 300,000 sheep, to say nothing of other, larger livestock.[132] These numbers put immense

[126] Ibn al-Athir, *al-Kamil*, IX, 389.

[127] Bar Hebraeus, *Chronography*, I, 213.

[128] Ibn al-Athir, *al-Kamil*, IX, 556, 639–40, 645.

[129] Peacock, *Early Seljūq History*, 69–71, 142–3; Peacock, 'From the Balkhān-Kūhīyān to the Nāwakīya', 62–4.

[130] Ibn al-Athir, *al-Kamil*, IX, 381, 382, 384–5, 495. See also Bosworth, 'Dailamīs in Central Iran', 77–8; Peacock, *Early Seljūq History*, 69, 85, 139, 141.

[131] Bayhaqi, *Tarikh*, 884; Bosworth, *The Ghaznavids*, 256.

[132] See the discussion in Peacock, *Early Seljūq History*, 83–9. The sole statement of numbers of livestock for this early period is that provided by Mirkhwand's version of the *Maliknama* (see p. 24 above) for Seljuk's migration, which gives a figure of 500 sheep, although it is not clear whether this is meant to represent Seljuk's personal wealth or that of his followers, and to what extent these can be distinguished. Malikshah is said to have possessed some

pressure on the countryside, exacerbating the famines from which Khurasan was suffering in this period. As the Syriac Christian chronicler Bar Hebraeus (d. 1286), who drew on the *Maliknama* tradition, puts it:

> In every place where his troops meet together they plunder, and destroy and kill. And no one district (or, quarter) is able to support them for more than one week because of their vast number. And from sheer necessity they are compelled to depart to another quarter in order to find food for themselves and their beasts.[133]

To keep his men loyal, Tughrıl needed to provide them with plunder and pasture – the traditional duties of a nomadic chief. From approximately 1045 onwards, the attention of Ibrahim Yınal and Tughrıl was directed towards the south Caucasus, eastern Anatolia and northwestern Iran, rich in the pasturelands that were lacking in much of the arid Iranian plateau, and which had already been subject to 'Iraqiyya penetration since 420/1029.[134] Ibn al-Athir specifically connects these campaigns with the limitations of the existing Seljuk territories:

> A large number of Türkmen from Transoxiana came to [Ibrahim Yınal], and he said, 'My territories are too small for you and to support your needs. The best thing is to go to attack Anatolia, fight in God's path, plunder, and I will come in your wake and assist you.'[135]

As before, the Seljuk leadership was following where the 'Iraqiyya had led. These campaigns were not intended to annex territory, and no attempt was made to garrison strongholds or tax the inhabitants. They were determined by the Türkmen's ecological needs, focusing on areas of summer and winter pastures (Figure 1.4), and attacking towns and fortifications in their immediate vicinity which might threaten their control of the pastures, but largely ignoring other potential targets.[136]

In some respects, then, the first years of Seljuk hegemony on the Iranian plateau thus had a curiously indistinct character. Beyond a few cities which served as Seljuk bases, such as Rayy and Hamadhan, Tughrıl made little effort

12,000 animals by a fourteenth-century chronicler (Ahmad b. 'Ali Katib, *Tarikh-i Jadid-i Yazd*, ed. Iraj Afshar (Tehran, 1386), 54).

133 Bar Hebraeus, *Chronography*, I, 202; cf. *ibid.*, I, 204.

134 See A. C. S. Peacock, 'Nomadic Society and the Seljuq Campaigns in Caucasia', *Iran and the Caucasus*, 9 (2005), 205–30, with a chronology at 227–9; Peacock, *Early Seljūq History*, 139–40.

135 Ibn al-Athir, *al-Kamil*, IX, 546.

136 See Peacock, 'Nomadic Society', *passim*; Peacock, *Early Seljūq History*, 144–51.

Figure 1.4 Summer pastures (*yayla*) in eastern Anatolia, offering ample grazing for Türkmen flocks (Çayıryolu, Bayburt Province, Turkey)

to assert direct rule. For many city dwellers, little changed immediately, and not just the descendants of Seljuk but also local princes continued fighting among each other, sometimes recruiting aid from various Turks, ranging from Tughrıl himself to Ibrahim Yınal to the 'Iraqiyya.[137] The Iranian plateau was thus not so much the object of a deliberate campaign of conquest than the backdrop against which these rivalries were fought out. These characteristics may explain why so few of our sources except Ibn al-Athir dwell on the Seljuk takeover: for pro-Seljuk chroniclers like Nishapuri and Husayni there was little to report in the way of heroic victories.

From the same period we have clear evidence of some kind of Seljuk administration. In the cities that were directly subject to Tughrıl's control he installed 'agents' (*nuwwāb*), if at least the example of Hamadhan is anything to go by, where they are attested in 436/1044–5. Their main function, most probably, was to extract revenue from the city. In the same year, Ibn al-Athir tells us, Tughrıl appointed his first vizier, Abu 'l-Qasim 'Ali b. 'Abdallah al-Juwayni, suggesting a further move towards the norms of Perso-Islamic governance,[138] while around the same time a man named Khwaja Muwaffaq, a member of an ancient and prominent local family, is mentioned as Tughrıl's

[137] See, for instance, Ibn al-Athir, *al-Kamil*, IX, 496–7, 512, 519–20, 532–4, 536–7, 573–4.

[138] For both the *nuwwāb* at Hamadhan and Juwayni's appointment, see Ibn al-Athir, *al-Kamil*, IX, 526. The early Seljuk viziers are discussed by Harold Bowen, 'Notes on some Early Seljuqid Viziers', *BSOAS*, 20/i (1957), 97–110 and by Iqbal, *Wizarat*, 36–43. See also Qummi, *Dhayl-i Nafthat al-Masdur*, 139–40. It is possible that Juwayni in fact had predecessors, but the chronology of these early viziers is hopelessly confused.

agent (*khwāja*) in Nishapur.[139] In 435/1044, Caliph al-Qa'im despatched an embassy to Tughrıl offering him titles and formal recognition as ruler in the hope that he might be dissuaded from further advances.[140] We have very little information indeed about conditions in Chaghrı's territories, but similar administrative arrangements probably prevailed there: Chaghrı had an official (*mutawallī*) who looked after affairs in Balkh, and it was in the latter's service that the famous Nizam al-Mulk started his career in the Seljuk bureaucracy.[141] Around the same time, Nasir-i Khusraw was serving Chaghrı as an official in the 'sultanic' revenue and finance department in Merv.[142] His conversion to Ismailism occurred as a result of a vision he had when sent on an official business trip to Marw al-Rud in Rabi' II 437/October–November 1045.[143]

Thus, by the mid-1040s, a mere decade after their arrival in Khurasan, the Seljuks had acquired many of the institutions of Islamic statehood, the first signs of which we noted as early as *c.* 1038: a bureaucracy, viziers, government departments, recognition by the caliph, and the regular striking of coinage.[144] Moreover, Seljuk governance gradually became something more than merely an exercise in revenue collection. In the Isfahan region, after the Seljuk conquest of 443/1051, a generous system of tax relief was instituted to tempt peasants back to the lands they had abandoned, forts were constructed to ensure the security of roads, and Nasir-i Khusraw admired Isfahan's prosperity under Tughrıl's rule.[145] It was, however, a state that was still dominated by the requirements of the Türkmen, whose relationship to the Seljuk family remained both intimate and fraught with tension.

Tughrıl and Iraq, 1055–63

Seljuk aid had been seen by several Iranian rulers as a winning formula for securing their own positions locally, and it seems that it was with the same purpose that Tughrıl was invited to intervene in Arab Iraq. The 'Abbasid Caliph al-Qa'im (r. 422/1031–467/1067) had long had tense relations with the Buyids, who, as Shi'ites, scarcely acknowledged his authority. A Sunni reaction had set in, and al-Qa'im's vizier, Ibn Muslima, was noted for his fanatical hatred of the Shi'a. While al-Qa'im initially seems to have regarded

139 Nasir-i Khusraw, *Safarnama*, 4; Bulliet, *Patricians of Nishapur*, 118–19.

140 Bar Hebraeus, *Chronography*, I, 203–4; Ibn al-Athir, *al-Kamil*, IX, 522; Ibn al-Jawzi, *al-Muntazam*, XV, 289.

141 Ibn al-Athir, *al-Kamil*, X, 207; Ibn al-'Adim, *Bughya*, 65–6.

142 Nasir-i Khusraw, *Safarnama*, 2: *az jumla-i mutaṣṣarifān dar amwāl wa a'māl-i sulṭānī*.

143 *Loc. cit.*

144 For the coinage, see Kucur, 'A Study on the Coins of Tughrıl'; Coşkun Alptekin, 'Selçuklu paraları', *Selçuklu Arastırmaları Dergisi*, 3 (1971), 435–591.

145 Durand-Guédy, *Iranian Elites*, 106–8; Nasir-i Khusraw, *Safarnama*, 138.

the Turks with a good measure of suspicion, Ibn Muslima established friendly relations with Tughrıl.[146] As Buyid authority in Iraq collapsed over the reign of al-Malik al-Rahim (440/1048–447/1055), an array of contenders for power emerged. Prime among them was Ibn Muslima's arch rival, the Shi'ite-leaning general al-Basasiri, commander of the Turkish slave troops in Baghdad, who had recently expanded his power by occupying Basra and Anbar. To survive, Ibn Muslima needed to thwart his rival's ambitions, and did not hesitate to stir up sectarian tensions between Baghdad's restive Sunni and Shi'ite populations to discredit al-Basasiri.[147]

Ibn Muslima and Tughrıl seem to have prepared the ground for intervention carefully. Tughrıl's image as a Sunni ruler was burnished by his proclamation of a persecution (*miḥna*) of various heretical religious groups, launched simultaneously in Baghdad and Nishapur in 445/1053, shortly after Tughrıl's receipt of titles from the caliph. The symbolic intent of the *miḥna* is underlined by the fact it does not seem to have been implemented anywhere else.[148] In 447/1054, the Türkmen raided Ahwaz and, on Tughrıl's instructions, occupied Khuzistan,[149] on the eastern borders of Arab Iraq. Tughrıl then himself advanced to Khuzistan, claiming that he intended to perform the pilgrimage to Mecca and to lead an expedition against the Fatimids of Egypt[150] – another piece of propaganda designed to emphasise his credentials as a legitimate Muslim ruler, for the Sunni world regarded the Ismaili Fatimids as heretics. It seems few were convinced, for rumours of an impending Seljuk invasion racked Baghdad. In the event, al-Basasiri fled, and Tughrıl entered the city peacefully in Ramadan 447/December 1055, welcomed by a splendid procession of local notables. Even before his arrival, the caliph had proclaimed the *khuṭba* in Tughrıl's name, a traditional sign of recognition of a new ruler.[151]

146 Ibn al-Athir, *al-Kamil*, IX, 580, 602, 609. See Peacock, *Early Seljūq History*, 117. Ibn Muslima's first cousin once removed was Ibn Mika'il, who served as vizier to Tughrıl (see Bowen, 'Notes', 108; Carla L. Klausner, *The Seljuk Vizierate: A Study of Civil Administration 1055–1194* (Cambridge, MA, 1973), 57). The caliph's wariness is demonstrated by (a) his letter sent to Tughrıl before the first conquest of Nishapur, urging him to abstain from plunder; and (b) the embassy sent in 1044 which seems to have been intended to discourage any further advances by Tughrıl, and to make peace between him and the Buyid Jalal al-Dawla.

147 Ibn al-Athir, *al-Kamil*, IX, 607–8; on these two, see M. Canard, 'al-Basāsirī', *EI*²; Cl. Cahen, 'Ibn al-Muslima', *EI*².

148 See Peacock, *Early Seljūq History*, 109–18 for this episode, and Chapter 7 below, p. 268.

149 Ibn al-Athir, *al-Kamil*, IX, 602–3.

150 *Ibid.*, IX, 609; Ibn al-Jawzi, *al-Muntazam*, XV, 238; Bar Hebraeus, *Chronography*, I, 207–8.

151 Ibn al-Athir, *al-Kamil*, IX, 610.

Tughrıl's stay in the city was short-lived. The Iraqi countryside could not support his Türkmen troops, and prices doubled as the latter devastated the agricultural land around Baghdad and systematically plundered its villages.[152] Although the Türkmen stationed in the immediate vicinity of Baghdad initially seem to have been better behaved, misunderstandings with the local populace resulted in riots, and the billeting of soldiers on the Baghdadis was so unpopular that the caliph was forced to intervene.[153] In Dhu 'l-Qi'da 448/ January 1057, thirteen months after their arrival, Tughrıl and his troops withdrew to campaign in northern Mesopotamia.[154] The way to Baghdad lay open before al-Basasiri. Generously financed by the Fatimids, al-Basasiri had little difficulty in winning over the Bedouin chiefs of northern Mesopotamia such as the 'Uqaylids who had seen their lands repeatedly ravished by the Türkmen.[155] For a year, from Dhu 'l-Qi'da 450/December 1058 to Dhu 'l-Qi'da 451/December 1059, the *khuṭba* in Baghdad was said in the name of the Fatimid caliph, while Shi'ite control was asserted with the crucifixion of Ibn Muslima – the arch enemy of the Shi'ites of Baghdad – and the exile of the 'Abbasid caliph.[156]

A much greater challenge to Tughrıl remained internal threats to his leadership. In the last days before al-Basasiri's seizure of the city, a convoluted – if short-lived – plot had been hatched in Baghdad by Tughrıl's wife Altunjan and his vizier Kunduri to install Altunjan's son by a previous marriage to the Khwarazmshah as ruler. The pretender, Anushirwan, attracted no support, and Tughrıl's wife soon dissociated herself from the plot, all of whose conspirators appear to have been eventually restored to favour without further punishment.[157] More serious was the third great revolt of Ibrahim Yınal, which was Tughrıl's real reason for neglecting Baghdad. The rebellion was funded and supported by the Fatimids and al-Basasiri, but Tughrıl's cousin had also been able to capitalise on the Türkmen unrest. The nomads, dependent on pastureland for their flocks, seem to have found Iraq's mix of arid desert and marsh intolerable (p. 224 below), and

152 *Ibid.*, IX, 613.

153 Sibt, *Mir'at*, 7–8; Ibn al-Athir, *al-Kamil*, IX, 626; Ibn al-Jawzi, *al-Muntazam*, XVI, 3–4.

154 Bundari, *Zubda*, 13; Ibn al-Athir, *al-Kamil*, IX, 627; Sibt, *Mir'at*, 13–14; Bar Hebraeus, *Chronography*, I, 209.

155 For example, Sibt, *Mir'at*, 11, *wa-khawwafahum mā ya'ūlu ilayhi amr al-'arab min al-ghuzz.*

156 On these events, see Ibn al-Athir, *al-Kamil*, IX, 639–50; Ibn al-Jawzi, *al-Muntazam*, XVI, 30–8, 44–6; Sibt, *Mir'at*, 26–62; Bar Hebraeus, *Chronography*, I, 213–14; *The Fatimids and Their Successors in Yaman: The History of an Islamic Community. Arab edition and English summary of volume 7 of Idris 'Imad al-Din's* 'Uyun Al-Akhbar, ed. Ayman Fu'ad Sayyid (London, 2002), 69–75.

157 Sibt, *Mir'at*, 32–4.

increasingly resented Tughrıl for bringing them there. A further reason for resentment may have been Tughrıl's attempts in the wake of the occupation of Baghdad to recruit a corps of slave soldiers (*mamlūks*), a sign of the growing conformity of Seljuk practice with that of most Islamic states of the time – but also a development which threatened to dilute the role and influence of the Türkmen,[158] even if Tughrıl was never able to dispense with them entirely.[159]

As the price for their support, the Türkmen extracted from Ibrahim two telling concessions: that, in the event of his victory, he would not make them return to Iraq; and that he would not make peace with his cousin under any circumstances.[160] Tughrıl was obliged to call on Chaghrı's sons Alp Arslan, Qavurt and Yaquti to help him, and thousands of Türkmen were killed in the uprising which ended with Ibrahim Yınal's execution.[161] The lesson of the Türkmen's loathing for Iraq and the possible trouble this might provoke as a rallying point for dissent could not be forgotten. On defeating al-Basasiri, Tughrıl delegated the administration of Baghdad to the amir Bursuq and sold off its taxation rights,[162] spending a mere two weeks in the city before heading off to the Jibal.[163] Judging by a letter Tughrıl sent to his erstwhile ally Quraysh b. Badran from the Banu 'Uqayl, he had no intention of returning.[164] Indeed, when Tughrıl demanded the hand of the caliph's daughter – an approach that was regarded by al-Qa'im as an impertinent outrage[165] – the caliph attempted to impose the condition that Baghdad should become Tughrıl's permanent place of residence as a means of making the prospect of the sultan marrying his daughter less attractive.[166] Nonetheless, opposition to Tughrıl from within his family and from some groups of Türkmen was as virulent as ever. In 453/1061, Arslan Isra'il's son Qutlumush launched a rebellion which attracted huge Türkmen support,[167] while shortly before Tughrıl's death his step-son Anushirwan attempted for a second time to seize the throne for himself.[168]

[158] Peacock, *Early Seljūq History*, 94–8.
[159] *Ibid.*, 98; and see further pp. 221–5 below.
[160] Ibn al-Athir, *al-Kamil*, IX, 639–40; Sibt, *Mir'at*, 31–2.
[161] Ibn al-Athir, *al-Kamil*, IX, 645.
[162] *Ibid.*, X, 8; also Idris 'Imad al-Din, *The Fatimids and Their Successors in Yaman*, 69ff.
[163] Sibt, *Mir'at*, 71–2; he entered the city on 17 Safar 452/23 March 1060, and left on 2 Rabi' I/6 April.
[164] *Ibid.*, 56–7.
[165] *Ibid.*, 76. See the discussion below, Chapter 3, p. 141.
[166] *Ibid.*, 76.
[167] *Ibid.*, 77, 82, 84, 101.
[168] *Ibid.*, 100.

Tughrıl died on Friday, 8 Ramadan 455/4 October 1063, aged seventy, in Rayy, the city which served as his principal base throughout his reign and where he was buried.[169] His character was, it seems, a mystery even to the mediaeval chroniclers, for he is described as both 'intelligent, mild-tempered and extremely tolerant' and 'cruel and tyrannous' by the same source.[170] His achievement is indubitable: the lands subject to the Seljuks by his death spread from Transoxiana to the borders of Syria, from the Gulf far into the Caucasus. His role had been transformed from that of nomad chief to the greatest ruler in the eastern Islamic world. However, for all Tughrıl posed as defender of the caliphate, had grandiose Islamic and Iranian titles showered upon him, including the new coinage of sultan, and held a court at which poets praised him lavishly in the Arabic he did not understand (pp. 181–2, 195 below), his room for manoeuvre remained limited by the ecological requirements of the Türkmen on whom he continued to rely, and by the constant threat to his claims to suzerainty from other members of his family.

The Seljuk Empire under Alp Arslan, 1063–72

Despite several marriages, Tughrıl died childless, having appointed as his successor his infant nephew Sulayman, who was backed by the vizier Kunduri,[171] doubtless in the hope of obtaining vast power during a regency for the child. However, Sulayman's elder brother, Alp Arslan, ruler of Khurasan since his father Chaghrı's death in 451/1059, had already started to advance westwards on hearing rumours of Tughrıl's malady.[172] After seeing off the challenge of Qutlumush, who died in battle outside Rayy,[173] Alp Arslan turned to deal with Kunduri, whom he swiftly had imprisoned, executed and replaced with his own vizier, Nizam al-Mulk, who had served him in Khurasan.[174] Tughrıl's and Chaghrı's lands, stretching from Iraq to Transoxiana, were now united for the first time under one ruler. However, this was no time for consolidation. Alp Arslan's reign witnessed a relentless series of campaigns, usually headed by the sultan himself, which took him the length and breadth of the empire. Although these campaigns would culminate in the sultan's famous

[169] Although some sources claim Tughrıl had made Isfahan his capital, he seems to have had relatively little to do with the city. See Durand-Guédy, *Iranian Elites*, 76–7.

[170] Ibn al-Athir, *al-Kamil*, X, 28: *kāna ʿāqilan ḥalīman min ashadd al-nās iḥtilāman . . . wa-kāna ẓalūman, ghashūman, qāsiyyan*. On Tughrıl's age at his death, see also Sibt, *Mirʾat*, 108.

[171] Sibt, *Mirʾat*, 97, 100, 108.

[172] *Ibid.*, 101–2, 108–10; cf. Ibn al-Athir, *al-Kamil*, X, 29.

[173] Husayni, *Akhbar*, 30; Ibn al-Athir, *al-Kamil*, X, 36; Sibt, *Mirʾat*, 107, 110.

[174] On Kunduri's end, see Sibt, *Mirʾat*, 124–9. The most detailed study of Alp Arslan's reign remains Mehmet Altay Köymen, *Alp Arslan ve Zamanı* (Ankara, 1983); on Alp Arslan's defeat of his opponents, see Makdisi, *Ibn ʿAqil*, 121–7.

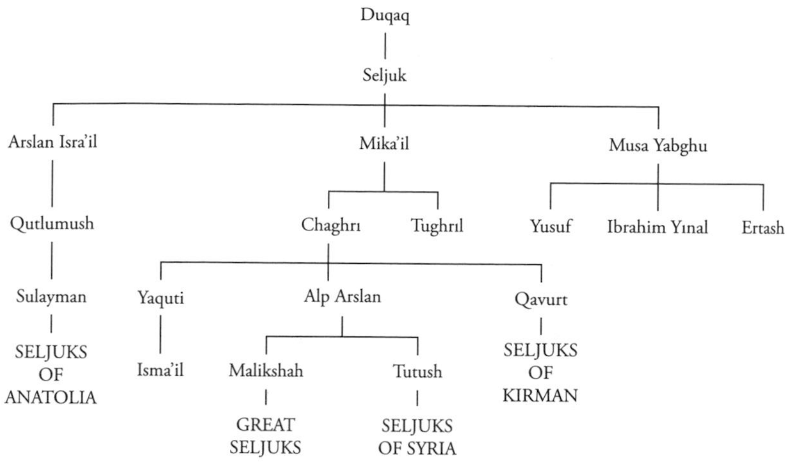

Figure 1.5 Genealogical tree of the first generations of the Seljuk family, showing the emergence of the various ruling branches of the family

victory over Byzantium at Manzikert in eastern Anatolia in 463/1071, they were driven at least as much by the exigencies of internal politics as by the desire for expansion.

Some campaigns aimed to bring the sultan's errant relatives to heel, such as Alp Arslan's brother Qavurt, the ruler of Kirman (see Figure 1.5). Although Qavurt had recognised Alp Arslan's accession by having his name mentioned in the *khuṭba*, he also demanded his 'share in his inheritance', which he sought to assert by capturing Shiraz and threatening Isfahan.[175] Alp Arslan was obliged to head in person no fewer than three expeditions against him, and it was not until the beginning of Malikshah's reign that Qavurt was finally captured and killed, although even then his descendants were left in control of Kirman and its outremer territory of Oman.[176]

Campaigns were also directed at imposing sultanic authority on the Türkmen, such as those in Central Asia in 457–8/1064–5 which explicitly targeted 'wrong-doing' (i.e., rebellious) Türkmen.[177] Given that much Türkmen settlement was concentrated on the borders of the empire, where pasture was much more freely available than in arid central Iran or Iraq, these campaigns could also be legitimised to a wider audience as jihad,

175 Sibt, *Mir'at*, 118; Bundari, *Zubda*, 30–31; Durand-Guédy, *Iranian Elites*, 77.

176 See Merçil, *Kirman Selçukluları, passim*. Also Afdal al-Din Kirmani, *Saljuqiyan wa Ghuzz dar Kirman*, ed. Bastani Parizi (Tehran, 1373).

177 Sibt, *Mir'at*, 131; Ibn al-Athir, *al-Kamil*, X, 49.

holy war, against the Seljuks' non-Muslim neighbours. For instance, one of Alp Arslan's first acts as sultan, three months after his entry to Rayy, was to launch a major expedition into the Caucasus. Accompanied by his vizier Nizam al-Mulk and son Malikshah, he advanced northwest from Marand up the River Kur through Nakhchivan, burning and plundering his way through southern Georgia before seizing the great Armenian trading city of Ani, then in Byzantine hands.[178] His victories, relayed in letters to Baghdad, clearly had great propaganda value in representing the sultan as a doughty fighter for Islam; but in reality they were not intended to annex territory. Just as with earlier campaigns in the region, no Seljuk garrisons were installed, and existing fortifications were razed. As much as jihad, the aim was to allow the sultan to carry out the traditional nomad chief's role of securing pasture and plunder, to cement bonds of loyalty with his nomadic subjects, and to appeal to disaffected Türkmen after the death of Qutlumush.[179] That such a campaign should take priority over dealing with Qavurt or any of the sultan's other relatives suggests both that there was more at stake than merely the territorial expansion of the empire, and underlines the extent to which Alp Arslan still felt himself to be beholden to a nomadic constituency.

Alp Arslan seems to have been especially concerned by the activities of a Türkmen grouping called the Nawakiyya, who started to settle in Syria and the borders of Anatolia around the beginning of his reign. Exactly who the Nawakiyya were is unclear, but they may well have been connected with the earlier Balkhan-Kuhiyan and 'Iraqiyya, who now disappear from the record. Their leaders were often of aristocratic, even Seljuk birth. A certain Ibn Khan, who operated around Aleppo, is described as a Türkmen prince; Qutlumush's son Sulayman was a Nawakiyya leader, as was the sultan's brother-in-law Arisighi/Eresghen/Erbasghan (the reconstruction of the name is unclear).[180]

The Nawakiyya were widely used by various parties in Syria – including the Fatimids – as mercenaries or auxiliaries.[181] Owing to his poor relations with Alp Arslan, Erbasghan and his followers sought to enter Byzantine service, threatening to destabilise Byzantine–Seljuk relations. Initially, despite the loss of Ani, the Byzantines had sought amicable rela-

178 Husayni, *Akhbar*, 35–40; Ibn al-Athir, *al-Kamil*, X, 37–41; Sibt, *Mir'at*, 117. On the campaign, see Marius Canard, 'La campagne arménienne du sultan salǧuqide Alp Arslan et la prise d'Ani en 1064', *Revue des études arméniennes*, 2 (1965), 239–59.

179 See Peacock, 'Nomadic Society', for a discussion.

180 Peacock, 'From the Balkhān-Kūhīyān to the Nāwakīya', 64–8.

181 Sibt, *Mir'at*, 133, 143, 153; Ibn al-Athir, *al-Kamil*, X, 60; Ibn al-'Adim, *Bughya*, 21.

tions with the Seljuks, and these seem to have been sealed by a formal treaty.[182] For reasons which are unclear, the Byzantines offered Erbasghan and his men shelter; perhaps they believed they could use them against other Türkmen, or as a bargaining chip, or simply sought to take advantage of their military prowess. The emperor Romanus was anxious to assert Byzantine power in eastern Anatolia and northern Syria, against which he had launched expeditions that captured the town of Manbij and threatened Aleppo,[183] although at the time these territories were not subject to the Seljuk Empire.

Romanus' Syrian campaigns seem to have worried Alp Arslan much less than his aid to these Nawakiyya, and the sultan threatened to break the truce if Erbasghan and his Nawakiyya were not handed over.[184] The sultan had marched to Syria to impose his authority over local Arab rulers such as the Mirdasids of Aleppo (who were also employing Nawakiyya troops), and then advanced on the Diyar Bakr (itself a major Türkmen winter pasture).[185] When he heard that Romanus was leading a great army eastwards, aiming to cement the emperor's authority by putting an end to the Turkish raids which had plagued the plateau for the last forty years, Alp Arslan seized the opportunity to divert his army to confront the emperor who had given shelter to his Nawakiyya enemies. The two forces met at Manzikert, north of Lake Van, in 463/1071; the Byzantines were routed, and Romanus taken prisoner.[186]

Manzikert is conventionally considered one of the great turning points in world history, opening the way to the collapse of the Byzantine empire in Anatolia and the establishment of Turkish rule there. However, both Byzantine and Muslim sources agree that Alp Arslan offered Romanus generous peace terms, involving merely the concession of a few frontier fortresses such as Edessa and the payment of an indemnity. Rather than his defeat

182 Sibt, *Mir'at*, 122, 147: Alp Arslan's ambassador to Romanus sent to seek the return of the Nawakiyya refers the *hudna* (peace treaty) between them.

183 For these operations, see Ibn al-ʿAdim, *Bughya*, 40; Ibn al-Athir, *al-Kamil*, X, 60; Sibt, *Mir'at*, 136–7, 139.

184 Sibt, *Mir'at*, 146–7; for a more detailed analysis and translation of the passage, see Peacock, 'From the Balkhan-Kūhīyān to the Nāwakīya', 68–70.

185 Peacock, *Early Seljūq History*, 137, 146–8, 150; Sibt, *Mir'at*, 136, 142; Ibn al-Athir, *al-Kamil*, X, 60; Ibn al-ʿAdim, *Bughya*, 17–18.

186 See the detailed analysis and translation of sources in Carole Hillenbrand, *Turkish Myth and Muslim Symbol: The Battle of Manzikert* (Edinburgh, 2007), which also includes a useful bibliography of the extensive literature on the battle; also Peacock, 'From the Balkhān-Kuhīyān to the Nāwakīya'. A collection of primary sources on the battle giving the original Arabic and Persian texts and Turkish translations has also been published: Faruk Sümer and Ali Sevim (eds), *İslam Kaynaklarına Göre Malazgirt Savaşı (Metinler ve Çevirleri)* (Ankara, 1971).

Figure 1.6 Seljuk Turks (middle, described as 'Persians') fighting Byzantines (right), as depicted in the twelfth-century manuscript of the Byzantine *Chronicle of John Skylitzes* (Biblioteca Nacional, Madrid. MS Graecus Vitr 26-2, fol. 234v)

in battle, it was the ensuing civil war with his Byzantine rivals that cost Romanus his throne and led to the collapse of Constantinople's authority across much of the Anatolian plateau. The vacuum left by this collapse did open the way to the formation of Turkish principalities in Asia Minor. Moreover, the defeat at Manzikert highlighted Byzantium's weakness to the wider world, and it inspired broader Christian fears of the empire's imminent demise before Islam.[187]

With his dual victories over Christendom at Ani and Manzikert, it is not surprising that both Muslim and Christian sources portray Alp Arslan as a religiously motivated warrior for Islam. Matthew of Edessa, for instance, describes him as 'the venomous serpent of the Persians', and in phrases reminiscent of Aristakes calls him 'the instrument of divine wrath' who 'spread the flaming fire of death to all the Christian faithful and filled all Armenia with blood, the sword and enslavement'.[188] Matthew records how, on the conquest of Ani, the great silver cross on the cathedral was taken and placed on the entrance to the mosque of Nakhchivan for believers to step on in contempt.[189] Sibt b. al-Jawzi mentions similar stories of the desecration of crosses,[190] suggesting a policy of deliberately stressing the jihad element of these campaigns. For Ibn al-Athir, meanwhile, these military victories were not the sole cause for celebration. The sultan was a man who acted piously in

187 See Chapter 2 below.
188 Matthew of Edessa, *Armenia and the Crusades*, 102.
189 *Ibid.*, 104.
190 Sibt, *Mirat*, 148.

accordance with the precepts of Islam, giving alms to the poor, was fond of having histories of past kings and their behaviour read out to him, and was solicitous in preventing his soldiers from plundering his subjects' property.[191]

In reality, like Tughrıl, Alp Arslan had his price: Matthew of Edessa also relates how the Armenian king of Kars managed to buy off Alp Arslan's threatened attack by offering vassalage, cash and a lavish banquet.[192] Even for his Muslim subjects, the experience of Alp Arslan's rule was nothing like as appealing as Ibn al-Athir portrays, judging by the account of the contemporary Baghdadi diarist Ibn al-Banna'. In a letter to the caliph, Ibn al-Banna' lamented the injustice of his age:

> As for the learned men, no word of theirs is heard, nor is any order of theirs obeyed. As for the virtuous men, they silently keep to their homes. As for those who are trustworthy officials, to whom the virtuous men complain of the trouble which they experience for the sake of religion, they lighten its burden upon them, and exert their efforts in good causes, either by that which they remove, or by that which they do. Some of them have died and passed on to God – to Whom might and majesty belong! – may God be pleased with them, and others wait. They have already become the targets of the oppressors, who pursue them in their dependents, in their possessions, and in their affairs. Thus they have become preoccupied with themselves away from all occurrences and affliction.[193]

This passage does not ascribe blame for the oppression and injustice, but other passages in Ibn al-Banna's diary suggest that he held the Seljuks responsible. The terror that might be inspired merely by rumours of the sultan's approach to Baghdad with his army is described:

> An announcement was made on the west bank [of Baghdad] to the effect that whoever owns a shop, and other property which may be plundered, should move it and keep himself in a state of preparation, on account of what has been rumoured concerning the arrival of the King [Alp Arslan]; for he has armies with him whose quartering in residences cannot be trusted. On hearing the announcement, the people became greatly disturbed.[194]

191 Ibn al-Athir, *al-Kamil*, X, 75. Further on the image of Alp Arslan as a pious Muslim as presented by the Muslim primary sources, see D. G. Tor, '"Sovereign and Pious": The Religious Life of the Great Seljuq Sultans', in C. Lange and S. Mecit (eds), *The Seljuqs: Politics, Society and Culture* (Edinburgh, 2011), esp. pp. 42–5, but see also the comments below (pp. 250–2).

192 Matthew of Edessa, *Armenia and the Crusades*, 104.

193 George Makdisi, 'Autograph Diary of an Eleventh-century Historian of Baghdad, IV', *BSOAS*, 19/ii (1957), 299, § 130.

194 George Makdisi, 'Autograph Diary of an Eleventh-century Historian of Baghdad, II', *BSOAS*, 18/ii (1956), 249, § 6.

Such rapacity was practiced not only by ordinary soldiers, but by high-ranking Seljuk officials. Ibn al-Banna' records one attempt by Alp Arslan to admonish his governor of Baghdad:

> A good written decision, regarding the Muslims, was issued by the Sultan – May God make mighty His assistance to him! The 'Amid [Seljuk governor of Baghdad] was ordered to desist from molesting the Muslims, and to refrain from what he was demanding of them by way of house-rents for past years, and other such schemes. He would say to them: 'You are foreign residents in the houses of the Turks, and I want the rent from you!', and similar demands, such as mattresses and other things.[195]

Especially striking is the '*amīd's* pride in his status as a Turk, and his contempt for the settled population of Baghdad, the 'foreign residents' in the Turks' rightful property. Such attitudes were not easily overcome. On the one hand, Ibn al-Banna' does confirm Ibn al-Athir's stories of Alp Arslan trying to rein in his soldiery, through a 'written decision', itself suggesting the growing bureaucratisation of aspects of the Seljuk state. On the other hand, it seems that the '*amīd's* arbitrary imposition of taxes and seizure of property was common practice, for Sibt b. al-Jawzi also refers to Alp Arslan's vain efforts to control the rapacity of his Turkish officials.[196] This picture is confirmed by sources dealing with Isfahan, which also reveal discontent with arbitrary and exorbitant levels of taxation.[197] In many ways, then, Alp Arslan's reign represents continuity with Tughrıl's. Alongside lip-service to the precepts of Islamic rulership, the sultan continued to act much as a nomadic chief, seeking to defeat not just the infidel enemies of Islam but also rivals within his own family, and to consolidate his authority not just over the Seljuks' newly conquered lands but also over his Türkmen subjects.

Malikshah and Nizam al-Mulk, 1072–92

Alp Arslan's murder at the age of forty in Rabi' I 465/October 1072 by the banks of the Oxus River, on campaign to subjugate the Qarakhanids of Transoxiana, was followed by the customary struggle for the succession (detailed on p. 132). However, the army that had accompanied the sultan to the Oxus remained loyal to his young son Malikshah at the urging of the vizier Nizam al-Mulk.[198] Hindsight has seen Malikshah's reign as the apogee

195 George Makdisi, 'Autograph Diary of an Eleventh-century Historian of Baghdad, V', *BSOAS*, 19/iii (1957), 442, § 182.

196 Sibt, *Mir'at*, 121–2.

197 Durand-Guédy, *Iranian Elites*, 110–12, 118–19.

198 On Alp Arslan's murder and the succession, see Bundari, *Zubda*, 45–6; Husayni, *Akhbar*,

of Seljuk rule (see Map 1.2), with the sultan 'acknowledged in the *khuṭba* from the borders of China to the extremities of Syria and from the northernmost lands of Islam to Yemen'.[199] Malikshah sent an expedition to assert Seljuk authority in Mecca in the Hijaz (which under Alp Arslan had briefly recognised Seljuk suzerainty)[200] and Yemen, capturing Aden by the Indian Ocean.[201] The Byzantine empire – at least according to Islamic sources – was reduced to paying tribute to the Seljuks.[202] Campaigns in Central Asia allowed Malikshah to repel the Qarakhanids from the key frontier city of Tirmidh on the Oxus which they had captured at the beginning of his reign,[203] and in 482/1089 he was able to seize the Qarakhanid bases of Samarqand and Bukhara, even advancing as far as Kashghar.[204] Subject princes would 'kiss [Malikshah's] letters out of awe and honour for him', or so Isfahani, for whom this sultan's reign was a model compared to which all others fell short, would have us believe.[205] Contemporary Seljuk propaganda commemorated the sultan's campaigns in stone: inscriptions and reliefs on the walls at Amid (modern Diyarbakır in southeastern Turkey) dated to 481–2/1088–90 have been interpreted as serving as a 'victory monument' (*mashhad al-naṣr*) that immortalised to the city's surrender to Malikshah after a two-year siege (Figures 1.7(a) and (b)).[206]

In fact, the most spectacular advances were made by Türkmen groups, whose relationship with the sultan remained ambiguous. On the one hand, some Türkmen attacks seem to have been encouraged by Malikshah; on the other, some Türkmen leaders constituted a major threat to Malikshah's personal authority. We will assess first the Türkmen expansion on the frontiers of the Seljuk Empire; we will then turn to deal with the internal situation, specifically the vizier Nizam al-Mulk and his relations with Malikshah on the one hand, and the Türkmen on the other.

53–5; Ibn al-Athir, *al-Kamil*, X, 73–4; Sibt, *Mir'at*, 160, 164–6; Matthew of Edessa, *Armenia and the Crusades*, 136–7.

199 Ibn al-Athir, *al-Kamil*, X, 211. For studies of the reign, which generally echo this adulatory tone, see İbrahim Kafesoğlu, *Sultan Melikşah Devrinde Büyük Selçuklu İmparatorluğu* (Istanbul, 1953); Bosworth, 'Political and Dynastic History', 66–102; Makdisi, *Ibn 'Aqil*, 128–40; David Durand-Guédy, 'Malekšāh', *EIr*.

200 Ibn al-Athir, *al-Kamil*, X, 61; Sibt, *Mir'at*, 184, 193, 198–9, 205.

201 Bundari, *Zubda*, 70; Ibn al-Athir, *al-Kamil*, X, 203–4.

202 Husayni, *Akhbar*, 72.

203 Ibn al-Athir, *al-Kamil*, X, 77, 92.

204 *Ibid.*, X, 171–4.

205 Bundari, *Zubda*, 56.

206 Joachim Gierlichs, 'A Victory Monument in the Name of Sultan Malikshah in Diyarbakır: Medieval Figural Reliefs used for Political Propaganda?', *Islamic Art*, 6 (2009), 51–79.

Figure 1.7(a) Malikshah's 'victory monument' at Amid (Diyarbakır): Tower 40, showing the ensemble of inscriptions and reliefs

Figure 1.7(b) Malikshah's 'victory monument' at Amid (Diyarbakır): Tower 40, detail. Above the panel are the damaged remains of an eagle, symbolising the sultan's power; the galloping horses on each side have been interpreted as symbolising the Seljuk campaign against Amid (see Gierlichs, 'Victory Monument', 51–3)

Türkmen Expansion in the Age of Malikshah

The activities of two Türkmen chiefs, Artuq and Atsız, suggest the complexities of the Türkmen's role in Malikshah's empire. Artuq had plundered Basra and the date-filled oases of al-Ahsa' on the east coast of Arabia in 469/1086. Despite the wanton attack on Basra, Artuq seems to have continued to be regarded with favour by Malikshah, and he was later allotted territories in the Jibal[207] – rather more suitable, ecologically, for a Türkmen. Indeed, as during his campaign into al-Ahsa', Artuq had attacked the local Qarmatians, an Ismaili Shi'ite group, he was personally thanked by the caliph. Later we find Artuq assisting sultanic forces in operations in Syria,[208] although later he rebelled, using Türkmen support to carve out a base for himself there.[209] Under Artuq's descendants, his territories in the Jazira became an independent polity, the Artuqid state, that drew on Great Seljuk practice and precedent.[210]

The career of the Khwarazmian Türkmen Atsız b. Awaq was likewise characterised by both tension and cooperation with the Seljuk sultan. Atsız ruled what Turkish scholars have described as a Nawakiyya principality (*beylik*) in Syria.[211] Initially, Atsız seems to have operated with the consent of the sultan, gradually pushing Fatimid forces out of most of the coast and Jerusalem in 463/1070 onwards, and finally capturing Damascus in 468/1075. Indeed, Atsız's Türkmen forces were supplemented by 3,000 slave soldiers sent by Malikshah.[212] However, Atsız overreached himself with a disastrous campaign against Egypt in 469/1076–7. Initially, he met with some success, plundering the Nile Delta for two months while the main Fatimid army was campaigning in Upper Egypt. A Jewish witness resident in Cairo, Solomon Ben Joseph Ha-Cohen, recorded with horror Atsız's pillaging and desecration, both in Egypt and previously in Jerusalem:

> They entered Fustat [Cairo], robbed and murdered
> And ravished and pillaged the storehouses

207 Sibt, *Mir'at*, 235.

208 On his campaigns, see Sibt, *Mir'at*, 181, 193, 193, 206, 213, 216. See further Ali Sevim, 'Sultan Melikşah devrinde Ahsa ve Bahreyn Karmatilerine karşı Selçuklu seferi', *Belleten*, 24(94) (1961), 209–32.

209 Sibt, *Mir'at*, 235–6.

210 On them, see Carole Hillenbrand, *A Muslim Principality in Crusader Times: The Early Artuqid State* (Istanbul, 1990).

211 Ali Sevim, *Suriye ve Filistin Selçukluları Tarihi* (Ankara, 1983), 49, 63–84; and in English on these events, see Taef El-Azhari, *The Saljuqs of Syria during the Crusades, 463–549 AH/1070–1154 AD* (Berlin, 1997), 34–46.

212 Sibt, *Mir'at*, 175.

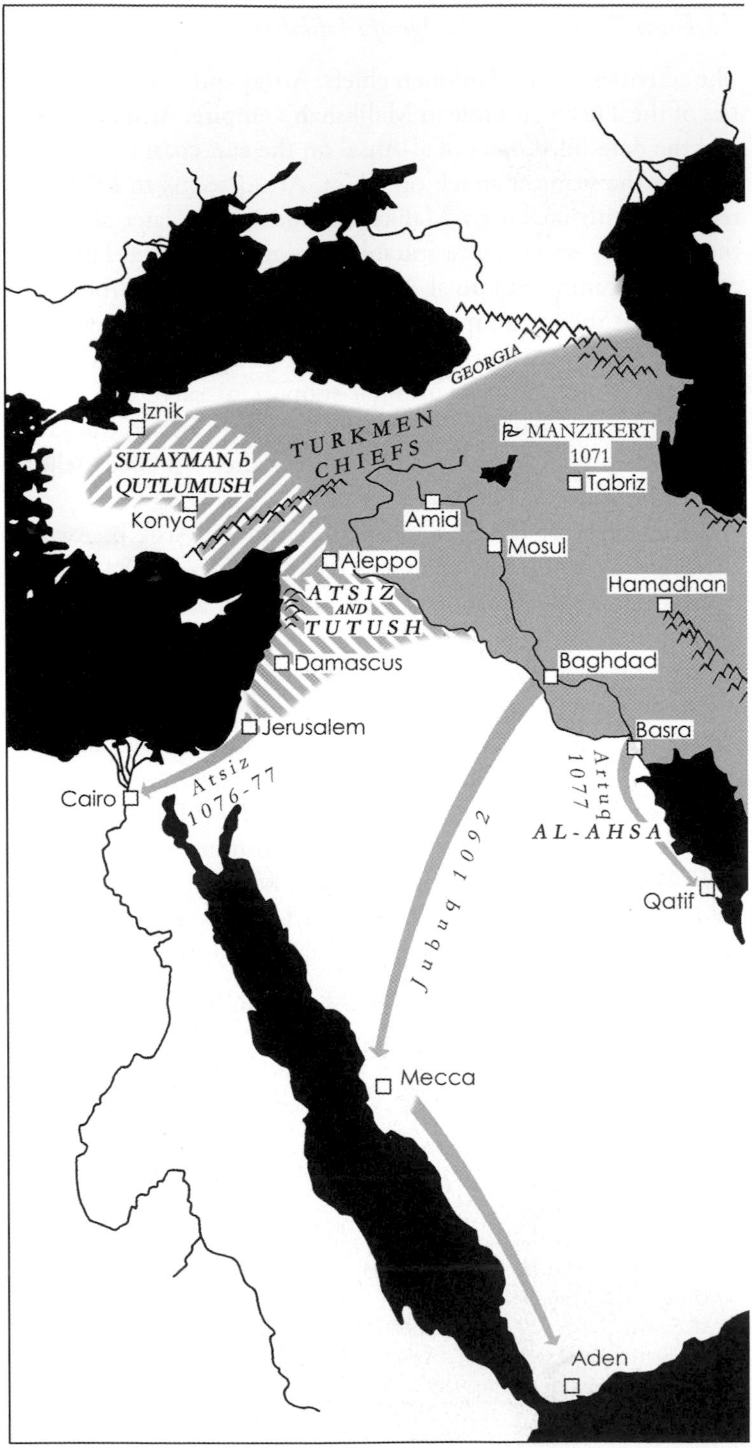

Map 1.2 The expansion of the Seljuk Empire under Malikshah

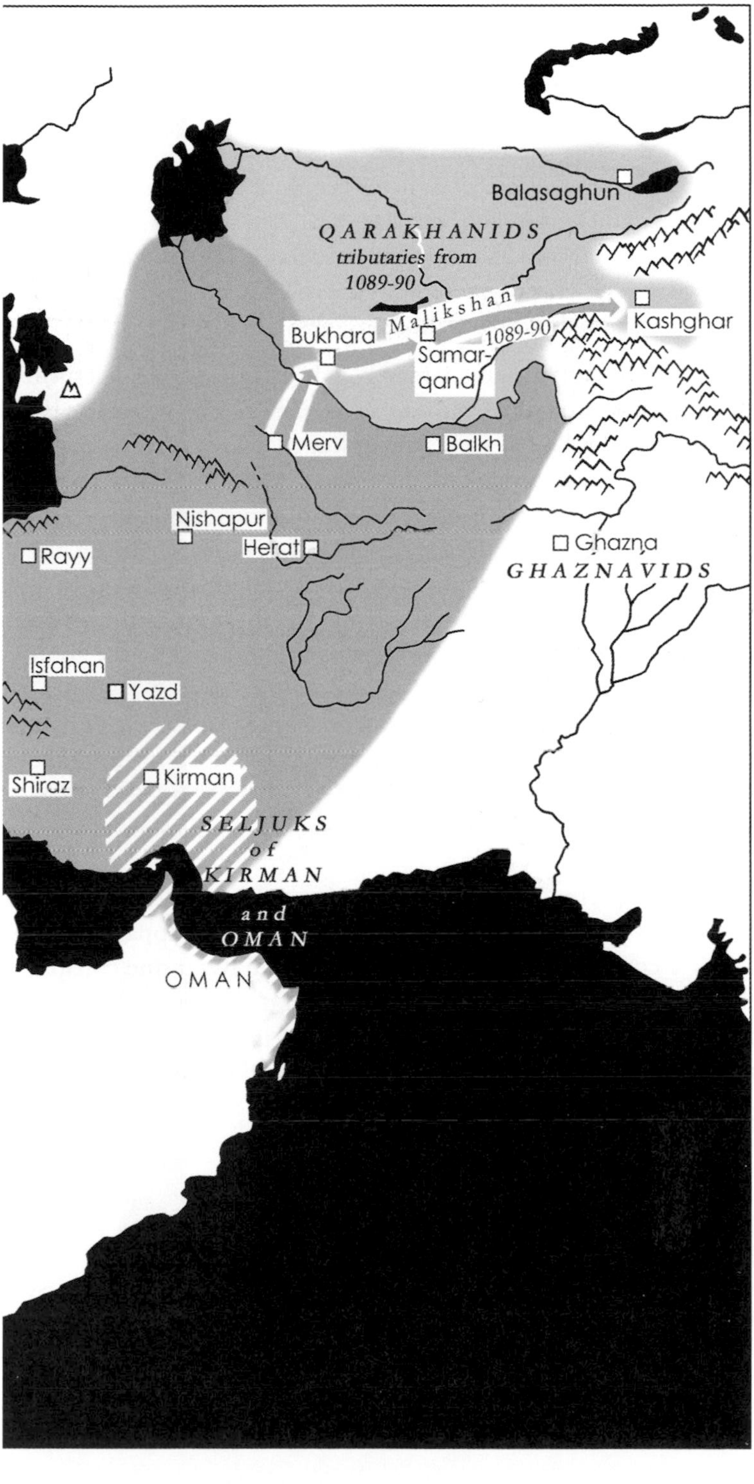
Balasaghun
QARAKHANIDS
tributaries from
1089-90
Malikshah
1089-90
Kashghar
Bukhara
Samar-
qand
Merv
Balkh
Nishapur
Herat
Rayy
Ghazna
GHAZNAVIDS
Isfahan
Yazd
Shiraz
Kirman
SELJUKS
of
KIRMAN
and
OMAN
OMAN

They were a strange and cruel people
Girt with garments of many colours, armed and officered
And capped with helmets, black and red
They trumpet like elephants, and roar as the roaring ocean . . .
They laid waste the cities and they were made desolate.
God remembered what they had done to the people of Jerusalem,
That they besieged them twice in two years,
And burned the heaped corn and destroyed the palaces,
And cut down the trees and trampled upon the vineyards,
Despoiled the graves and threw out the bones.[213]

The Fatimid general Badr al-Jamali marched north, inflicting a crushing defeat on the Türkmen army at Cairo on 22 Rajab 469/19 February 1077, from which only Atsız and a few of his men escaped alive.

The defeat at Cairo also marked the end of the Nawakiyya polity in Syria. Malikshah had evidently been minded to annex Syria anyway, for as early as 468/1075–6 he had tried to appoint his brother Tutush there. Atsız had successfully appealed against the decision on the grounds that: 'I am the obedient slave and the sultan's deputy in these lands; I take from them nothing but what I spend on my sustenance and that of the soldiers with me, and I send to the treasury 30,000 dinars every year.'[214] In other words, Atsız expected to be left alone if he sent a suitable amount of tribute to the sultanic treasury. Despite the appointment of Tutush in the wake of the Cairo debacle, it was not until 482/1089–90 that Syria and the Jazira came firmly under the control of either Malikshah's relatives, or governors appointed by him.[215]

The greatest long-term consequence of Atsız's achievement in capturing Syria from its weak Fatimid rulers would not become apparent in the Middle East for a couple more decades. Alongside the Byzantine collapse at Manzikert, Atsız's capture of Jerusalem – which had now been under Muslim rule for some four hundred years – was represented in Europe as a threat to Christendom, and in 1074 Pope Gregory II announced his intention 'to take

[213] Solomon ben Joseph Ha-Kohen, *The Turkoman Defeat at Cairo*, ed. and trans. Julius. H. Greenstone (Chicago, 1906), 163. For Muslim sources, see Sibt, *Mir'at*, 182–6; Ibn al-Athir, *al-Kamil*, X, 103–4; El-Azhari, *The Saljuqs of Syria*, 40–50.

[214] Sibt, *Mir'at*, 197, see also *ibid.*, 178, where Atsız proclaims that he has captured Syria without imposing a burden on the treasury.

[215] On the establishment of Tutush and other Seljuk governors in Syria, see Heidemann, *Die Renaissance der Städte*, 148–52; also Sevim, *Suriye ve Filistin Selçukluları*, 96–126; El-Azhari, *Saljuqs of Syria*, 60–70.

up arms against the enemies of God and push forward even to the sepulchre of the Lord under his supreme leadership'.[216]

It would, however, be up to Malikshah's successors to deal with the Crusaders. As far as Malikshah was concerned, a more intractable problem was Anatolia, where the Nawakiyya Türkmen were led by a member of the Seljuk family, Arslan Isra'il's descendant Sulayman b. Qutlumush.[217] With the collapse of Byzantium into civil war following Manzikert, the Türkmen had been able to spread to the far west of Anatolia, into the region of Bithynia that would later foster the Ottoman state, whose ample pasturelands appealed to nomads. Sometime in, or more likely, before 1081, Sulayman gained control of the ancient city of Nicaea (modern İznik). Anna Comnena described the situation:

> [T]he godless Turks were in sight, living in the Propontis area, and Sulayman, who commanded all the east, was actually encamped in the vicinity of Nicaea. His sultanate was in his city . . . The whole countryside of Bithynia and Thynia was unceasingly exposed to Sulayman's foragers; marauding parties on horseback and on foot were raiding as far as the town now called Damalis [Üsküdar] on the Bosphorus itself; they carried off much booty and all but tried to leap over the very sea. The Byzantines saw them living unafraid and unmolested in the little villages on the coast and in sacred buildings.[218]

The Türkmen were not simply a nuisance. They were also potentially valuable allies to the various contenders for the Byzantine crown. Like all mercenaries, the Turks' loyalties were flexible, so Sulayman found himself supporting first Michael Doukas and then Nikephoros Botaneiates in their short-lived efforts to assert themselves as emperor. Desperate to secure support, another pretender to the crown, Nikephoros Melissenos, handed over control of the cities of 'Asia, Phrygia and Galatia' to his Turkish allies.[219]

By 1081, the year conventionally given as the beginning of the Seljuk Sultanate of Anatolia (or Rum), Sulayman b. Qutlumush was thus in control

216 Cited in Christopher Tyerman, *God's War: A New History of the Crusades* (London, 2006), 49; cf. Malcolm Barber, *The Crusader States* (New Haven, 2012), 10–11.

217 For these events, see Claude Cahen, 'La première pénétration turque en Asie Mineure', *Byzantion*, 18 (1946–8), 5–67 (reprinted in Claude Cahen, *Turcobyzantina et Oriens Christianus* (London, 1974); the interpretation is derived from Peacock, 'From the Balkhān-Kūhīyān to the Nāwakīya', 70–4.

218 Anna Comnena, *The Alexiad*, trans. E. R. A. Sewter (Harmondsworth, 1969), III.vi, p. 129. Anna Comnena's work is our main source for Turkish activity in western Anatolia in the late eleventh century, but presents major problems of chronology. See Peter Frankopan, *The First Crusade: The Call of the East* (London 2012), 43–6.

219 See Peacock, 'From the Balkhān-Kūhīyān to the Nāwakīya', 71.

of a large part of western and central Anatolia. His ambitions, however, remained further east, to unite the Nawakiyya under his leadership. He had earlier fought Atsız for leadership of the Syrian Nawakiyya,[220] and having secured a base in Anatolia, he again set out for Syria, capturing Cilicia and Antioch in 475/1083–5 and attacking Aleppo in 479/1086. Although outwardly professing loyalty to Malikshah, these attacks within the lands of the Great Seljuk sultanate itself suggest that like his father Qutlumush, Sulayman had his sights set on leadership of all the Seljuk Türkmen, in other words to displace Malikshah himself. The gravity of the crisis forced Malikshah to march in person to Syria, although in the event Tutush killed Sulayman in battle before the sultan arrived.[221] Sulayman's sons were captured and exiled to Khurasan, while Malikshah despatched his amirs Bozan and Bursuq to impose his authority over the Anatolian Türkmen, although with little success. Anna Comnena recounts that the sultan even offered the Byzantine emperor Alexios an alliance to clear Bithynia of Türkmen, whom he evidently continued to regard as his errant subjects.[222] The Nawakiyya polity in Anatolia, however, survived in the form of the Seljuk Sultanate of Rum. Sulayman's son Qılıj Arslan eventually escaped from captivity to return to Anatolia in triumph, confirming its independence from the Great Seljuks. After Malikshah, the Seljuk sultans in Khurasan and Iraq were too preoccupied with their internal affairs to intervene in Anatolia.

Nizam al-Mulk and his *Siyasatnama*

By far the most famous Seljuk vizier is Nizam al-Mulk (408/1018–485/1092),[223] and by far the most famous work of Seljuk literature is his *Siyasatnama* (*Book of Policy*), sometimes known as the *Siyar al-Mulūk* (*The Conduct of Kings*). Although the attribution of this book to Nizam al-Mulk has sometimes been questioned, it is accepted as authentic by most scholars

220 Sibt, *Mir'at*, 174–5.

221 *Ibid.*, 237–40, 243–4; Ibn al-Athir, *al-Kamil*, X, 138, 140, 147–8.

222 Anna Comnena, *The Alexiad*, VI, ix. See further Frankopan, *The First Crusade*, 52–5, 62–3.

223 For overviews of Nizam al-Mulk's career, see H. Bowen and C. E. Bosworth, 'Niẓām al-Mulk', *EI*²; Omid Safi, *The Politics of Knowledge in Premodern Islam: Negotiating Ideology and Religious Inquiry* (Chapel Hill, NC, 2006), 47–79; Durand-Guédy, *Iranian Elites*, 112–29; also, Neguin Yavari, 'Nizam al-Mulk Remembered: A Study in Historical Representation', PhD dissertation, Columbia University, 1992. Important primary sources include Ibn al-'Adim, *Bughya*, 59–94; Subki, *Tabaqat al-Shafi'iyya al-Kubra*, ed. Mahmud Muhammad Tanahi and 'Abd al Fattah Muhammad Hulw (Cairo, 1964), IV, 309–23; Ibn Khallikan, *Wafayat al-A'yan wa-Anba' Abna' al-Zaman*, ed. Yusuf 'Ali Tawil and Mariyam Qasim Tawil (Beirut, 1998), II, 109–11; see also Bosworth, 'Towards a Biography of Niẓām al-Mulk'.

today. Written in Persian, it purports to advise the ruler on how to run the Seljuk state, and Lambton described it as 'an administrative handbook'.[224] While it is sometimes called a 'mirror for princes', it contains little of the advice about the sultan's private conduct in hunting, drinking and feasting typical of contemporary examples of the genre. Nizam al-Mulk constantly holds up as an ideal the practice of the Samanid, and especially the Ghaznavid realm where he had started his bureaucratic career.

A first version of the text was prepared for presentation to Malikshah between 479/1086 and 484/1091, and a second part was added in 484/1091. In other words, it was composed right at the end of Nizam al-Mulk's career, just as evidence suggests he was beginning to lose the sultan's confidence (see p. 71 below). The book contains several barely disguised *ad hominem* attacks on Nizam al-Mulk's rivals, above all his arch-enemy in the bureaucracy Taj al-Mulk, and the latter's patron Terken Khatun, Malikshah's wife. These enemies are accused of secret adherence to Ismailism, repeated examples of the dangers of which are given in the text.[225] At one point Nizam al-Mulk writes: 'The Master of the World [Malikshah] has become weary of his humble servant . . . One day The Master will realize [the] iniquity and criminal deeds [of these enemies] – when I have disappeared. Then he will know the measure of my devotion and loyalty to this victorious empire.'[226]

The *Siyasatnama* thus represents an attempt by Nizam al-Mulk to save his position at court by discrediting his enemies and showing how only he can solve what seem to have been growing administrative and fiscal problems within the empire (pp. 70–1 below). Far from being a simple administrative handbook, its prescriptions are often better evidence for what Seljuk practice was not rather than what it was; and frequently Nizam al-Mulk sorrowfully notes that such-and-such a practice used to be done but has fallen into abeyance. Rather than an advertisement for the success of the Persian bureaucrats at acculturating the Seljuks to their norms, it is testimony to their limitations.

224 A. K. S. Lambton, 'The Dilemma of Government in Islamic Persia: The *Siyāsat-nāmah* of Niẓām al-Mulk', *Iran*, 22 (1984), 55.

225 See Safi, *Politics of Knowledge*, 67–74; Durand-Guédy, *Iranian Elites*, 114–15; also Neguin Yavari, 'Mirror for Princes or a Hall of Mirrors? Nizam al-Mulk's *Siyar al-Mulūk* reconsidered', *al-Masāq*, 20/i (2008), 47–79.

226 Nizam al-Mulk, *Siyar al-Muluk (Siyasatnama)*, ed. Hubert Darke (Tehran, 1340), 255–6; trans. Hubert Darke, *The Book of Government or Rules for Kings: The Siyar al-Muluk or Siyasat-nama of Nizam al-Mulk* (Richmond, [1978] 2002), 188–9.

Nizam al-Mulk and the Transformation of the Seljuk Empire

Internally, the most striking development of Malikshah's reign was the exponential increase in the power of the vizier, Nizam al-Mulk. Not for nothing do some chroniclers refer to the period as '*al-dawla al-Nizamiyya*', the Nizam's state,[227] whilst modern scholars have described him as 'the real ruler of the Seljuk empire'.[228] The fourteenth-century biographer Subki agreed, saying that his vizierate was 'not just a vizierate, it was above the sultanate'.[229] Although Nizam al-Mulk had served as vizier through Alp Arslan's reign, his own account indicates he had a somewhat chilly relationship with the sultan.[230] According to Ibn al-Athir, Malikshah voluntarily entrusted his vizier with complete powers shortly after his accession, seeing him as the only man who could prevent the military's incessant plundering of the civilian population. Malikshah not only rewarded him with lands, but even the title of *atabeg*, meaning 'father of a prince', signifying his role as guardian to the youthful sultan.[231]

A different, and rather more convincing, explanation of Nizam al-Mulk's ascendancy is given by Sibt b. al-Jawzi. To cement his own position, and that of his nominal master, Nizam al-Mulk implemented a policy of cutting the old Turkish aristocracy down to size. The vizier was behind the killing of Malikshah's aunt Gawhar Khatun, who retained the support of a substantial band of Türkmen,[232] and the execution of Chaghrı's son Qavurt – who had sought the sultanate for himself on Alp Arslan's death – and the blinding of his sons. Qavurt's plea to Malikshah for his life suggests the bitter resentment with which some regarded Nizam al-Mulk's policies:

> Do not destroy this house by killing me and listening to the bureaucrats – meaning Nizam al-Mulk – as to what to do with me. Do with me what is fitting for Turks and I will give you the like of what you lost when your father died. I will go to Syria and Egypt and I shall surrender my whole land to you.[233]

It was to no avail, and the executions were carried out. When the army learned of this, they were in uproar and 'cursed Nizam al-Mulk to his face,

227 Ibn al-Athir, *al-Kamil*, X, 33; cf. Ibn Khallikan, *Wafayat*, IV, 375.

228 Bowen and Bosworth, 'Niẓām al-Mulk'; cf. Safi, *Politics of Knowledge*, 43–4.

229 Subki, *Tabaqat*, IV, 316–17.

230 Nizam al-Mulk, *Siyar al-Muluk*, 129, trans. 96; see, however, the comments in Yavari, 'Mirror for Princes or a Hall of Mirrors?', 55–6.

231 Ibn al-Athir, *al-Kamil*, X, 79–80. On the meaning of the term *atabeg*, see Ibn Khallikan, *Wafayat*, I, 339. See further Chapter 2 below.

232 Sibt, *Mir'at*, 173, 176.

233 *Ibid.*, 163–4.

and cursed Malikshah, and disassociated themselves from him, saying "This is not what Alp Arslan bequeathed. According to his will, Qavurt Beg was to receive Kirman and Fars . . .".' Nizam al-Mulk asked the terrified Malikshah 'Do you want to manage this affair or shall I?' Malikshah abjured responsibility, and Nizam al-Mulk resolved the crisis by buying off the troops with money and land grants.[234] The crisis demonstrated Nizam al-Mulk's growing power, the sense of sultanic impotence and the increasing break with the nomadic past, and the bitterness these changes engendered in some.

A break can also be seen in Malikshah's own behaviour. Malikshah spent much less time on campaign compared with Tughrıl and Alp Arslan. Isfahan became firmly established as the sultan's main place of residence, although in the last years of his reign Malikshah tended to winter in Baghdad. While Alp Arslan had spent little more than a year out of his decade-long sultanate in Isfahan, Malikshah resided there for well over half his reign. The city also served as the burial place of Malikshah, his sons and grandsons, and prominent servants of the state like Nizam al-Mulk.[235] Malikshah's choice of a capital far away from the centres of Türkmen settlement around Hamadhan, Rayy, Merv and Azerbaijan may be connected with the growing distance between the sultan and his nomadic subjects.[236]

Posterity remembered Nizam al-Mulk's three decades as vizier kindly. The idea of a strong bureaucracy was attractive to the *kuttāb* class who later lost power to amirs, and it is largely they who wrote our sources. 'Imad al-Din al-Isfahani (drawing at least partly on the account of a contemporary, Ibn al-Simnani, d. 493/1100) illustrates the esteem in which Nizam al-Mulk was held by later generations:

> He became vizier at a time when the order of the realm was weakened, and the decrees of religion had been altered at the end of the Daylamite state [i.e., the Buyids] and the beginning of the Turks' state [i.e., the Seljuks]. The lands had been destroyed by their toing and froing, and were impoverished and depopulated. Hostile hands took control of them and became strong, while mourners bewailed the territories and the calamities [that had befallen them]. [Nizam al-Mulk] restored the realm to order [*a'āda al-mulk ilā 'l-niẓām*],[237] and religion to its proper state. He made the provinces flourish and he built constantly. The custom was that taxes were collected from the land and spent on the army; previously no one had held a land-grant [*iqṭā'*].

234 *Ibid.*, 164.

235 Durand-Guédy, *Iranian Elites*, 76–83, 320–1.

236 *Ibid.*, 88–90; cf. Peacock, *Early Seljūq History*, 144–51.

237 A play on Nizam al-Mulk's name, also indicating his seizure of control. One might alternatively translate 'he restored the realm to Nizam al-Mulk'.

> Nizam al-Mulk realised that taxes were not being collected from the land owing to its poor condition, nor was revenue being realised for the same reason. He distributed land grants [*iqṭā'*s] to the soldiers and made them a source of income and revenue for them. They therefore had an incentive to make [the lands] prosper, and in the shortest time they returned to the best state of adornment. The sultan had relatives by marriage who prided themselves on their relationship to him, on account of which they continually claimed that they were his kinsmen. [Nizam al-Mulk] clipped their wings and prevented them from causing harm. He ruled the masses with prudence and arranged their affairs with his policy . . . With his pen he apportioned the kingdom which had been won by the sword in the best way, and carried out the most just assessment of the land. He investigated endowments and public works and established trustworthy men in their charge . . .'[238]

Isfahani exaggerates. Nizam al-Mulk was not the first to introduce the system of *iqṭā'* (land grants, see further pp. 79–80), which had been widely used during the Buyid period.[239] Indeed, rather than administrative reform, Nizam al-Mulk's ambition was to cement his own position and that of his relatives through a vast network of patronage and clientalism that reached across the empire.[240] There is evidence that all was not well, both economically and politically. In Khuzistan, the revenue from tax farms actually seems to have fallen precipitously in Malikshah's reign compared with Tughrıl's, although it is unclear whether the cause was reduced productivity, an inability to collect revenues – or simply unreliable figures.[241] Matthew of Edessa, despite his praise for Malikshah personally, describes the years around 1079–80 as marred by famine, depopulation, insecurity and migration.[242] A passage in the *Siyasatnama* suggests that by the end of

[238] Bundari, *Zubda*, 57. Cf. Bosworth, 'Towards a Biography of Niẓām al-Mulk', 302–4; Ibn al-'Adim, *Bughya*, 89–91.

[239] Durand-Guédy, *Iranian Elites*, 117–18.

[240] *Ibid.*, 126–9.

[241] Nanette Pyne, 'The Impact of the Seljuq Invasion on Khuzestan: An Inquiry into the Historical, Geographical, Numismatic and Archaeological Evidence', PhD dissertation, University of Washington, 1982, 130; cf. Peter Christensen, *The Decline of Iranshahr: Irrigation and Environments in the History of the Middle East 500 B.C. to A.D. 1500* (Copenhagen, 1993), 112–13. Concerns about excessive taxation during Malikshah's reign seem to be reflected by Mafarrukhi: see Paul, 'Histories of Isfahan', 128–9. For another indication of financial difficulties in the period see Stefan Heidemann, 'Unislamic Taxes and the Unislamic Monetary System in Seljuq Baghdad', in İsmail Safa Üstün (ed.), *Islam Medeniyetinde Bağdat (Medinetü's-Selām) Uluslararası Sempozyumu (International Symposium on Baghdad (Madinat al-Salam) in the Islamic Civilization)* (Istanbul, 2011), 503.

[242] Matthew of Edessa, *Armenia and the Crusades*, 143–4.

Malikshah's reign the cost of sustaining the military was becoming unacceptably high.[243] Politically, the vast power of Nizam al-Mulk suggests sultanic weakness.

As early as around 472/1080, Malikshah seems to have begun to turn against Nizam al-Mulk.[244] The vizier's growing alienation was signalled by the execution of his grandson 'Uthman b. Jamal al-Mulk.[245] Nonetheless, Malikshah felt insufficiently strong to actually remove him, fearful, perhaps, of the Charybdis of the alienated Türkmen. It was not until the end of his reign that the sultan dared to move directly against Nizam al-Mulk, promoting his rival, the Jibali bureaucrat Taj al-Mulk. Terken Khatun, Malikshah's wife, seems to have been particularly anxious to undermine the vizier, apparently to secure the succession for her own son.[246] Some sources even accuse Malikshah of having a hand in the assassination of Nizam al-Mulk in Ramadan 485/October 1092.[247] Malikshah started to spend more time in Baghdad, and was evidently plotting the removal of the caliph. Yet Malikshah's own death, barely a month after Nizam al-Mulk's, put paid to these schemes. He may have been murdered on the caliph's instructions.[248] The underlying tensions in the Seljuk political system would ensure that Malikshah's vision of a powerful sultanate was never realised.

243 Nizam al-Mulk, *Siyar al-Muluk*, 223–4, trans. 165.

244 Cf. Ibn al-Jawzi, *al-Muntazam*, XVI, 205–6, s.a. AH 472, recounting the arrest of Nizam al-Mulk's ally Ibn 'Alan, the Jewish tax collector of Basra. See also *ibid.*, XVI, 216–17; Ibn al-Athir, *al-Kamil*, X, 116.

245 Ibn al-Athir, *al-Kamil*, X, 205; Lambton, *Continuity and Change*, 43–4; Safi, *Politics of Knowledge*, 65–7; Makdisi, *Ibn 'Aqil*, 137–8.

246 See Nishapuri, *Saljuqnama*, 32, who even claims that Nizam al-Mulk was replaced as vizier by Taj al-Mulk; but also the discussion in Durand-Guédy, *Iranian Elites*, 115, and in more detail on Taj al-Mulk, Durand-Guédy, 'Un fragment inédit'.

247 Ibn al-'Adim, *Bughya*, 91; Hamadhani, *'Unwan*, 100; Subki, *Tabaqat*, IV, 324; Safi, *Politics of Knowledge*, 74–9.

248 For an analysis of the deaths of Nizam al-Mulk and Malikshah, see Carole Hillenbrand, '1092: A Murderous Year', in A. Fodor (ed.), *Proceedings of the 14th Congress of Union européene des arabisants et islamisants* (Budapest, 1995), 281–96. See also David Cook, 'Were the Ismaili Assassins the First Recorded Suicide Attackers? An Examination of their Recorded Assassinations', in Paul M. Cobb (ed.), *The Lineaments of Islam: Studies in Honour of Fred McGraw Donner* (Leiden, 2012), 98–102.

2

Crisis, Consolidation and Collapse: The Great Seljuk Empire and the Sultanate of Iraq, 1092–1194

> Wars between [the rival sultans Berkyaruq and Muhammad] went on and on, corruption spread, possessions were plundered, blood was shed, the land was ruined, the villages were burned, the sultanate was the object of ambitions and was condemned. The [rival] princes [*maliks*] were overcome whereas previously they had been victorious, and the great amirs (*al-umarā' al-kubarā'*) preferred that. They chose it in order that their domination, happiness and freedom might endure (*li-yadūma taḥakkumuhum, wa-inbisāṭuhum wa-idlāluhum*).[1]

Ibn al-Athir's bleak picture of the Seljuk Empire after Malikshah's death is replicated in much modern scholarship. The period is characterised as one of 'decline',[2] and the main culprit for the dissipation of sultanic authority is usually considered to be the rising power of amirs.[3] Amirs had been major players in Buyid and Samanid politics too; their emergence as a political force in the Seljuk period is not well understood, but is clearly connected with the development of state structures, the recruitment of military slaves and the gradual dilution of the role of the Türkmen.[4] An amir could, in principle, be anyone, slave or free, Türkmen, Iranian or Arab, who had troops at his command, although the term is particularly associated with the *mamlūk*

[1] Ibn al-Athir, *al-Kamil*, X, 369.

[2] M. F. Sanaullah, *The Decline of the Saljūqid Empire*, with an introduction by E. D. Ross (Calcutta, 1938); cf. S. G. Agadshanow, *Der Staat der Seldschukiden und Mittelasien im 11.–12. Jahrhundert* (Berlin, 1994), 162–6, 315–16; Carole Hillenbrand, 'The Career of Najm al-Dīn İl-ghāzī', *Der Islam*, 58 (1981), 254; Eric J. Hanne, 'Death on the Tigris: A Numismatic Analysis of the Decline of the Great Saljuqs', *American Journal of Numismatics*, 16–17 (2004–5), 145–72, which deals with the period 1092–1105.

[3] See, for example, Lambton, 'Internal Structure', 225, 267–8; Lambton, *Continuity and Change*, 244–6; Bosworth, 'Political and Dynastic History', 112, 114, 119, 200.

[4] Bosworth, 'Political and Dynastic History', 80–1.

commanders who were generally (but not exclusively) Turkish (see further Chapter 6). Since the reign of Tughrıl, and especially under Malikshah, amirs had been appointed to represent the coercive force of the sultan in towns and provinces, bearing a wide variety of titles such as *shiḥna, wālī, muqṭaʿ* or *ʿamīd.*[5] Over the twelfth century, many amirs became increasingly entrenched in the territories they governed, taking advantage of succession disputes among rival contenders for the sultanate to strengthen their own positions, as Ibn al-Athir describes. This development was at first particularly marked in the west of the Seljuk domains – Khurasan under Sanjar in the early twelfth century superficially appears to have enjoyed greater stability. Some amirs were able to establish their own dynasties which outlasted the Seljuk state, such as Zangi of Mosul, founder of the Zangid state (Syria and the Jazira, 521/1127–631/1233), the Salghurids of Fars (543/1148–681/1282), or the Burids of Damascus (497/1104–549/1154). These amirs legitimised their status by claiming the title of '*atabeg*', indicating that they were guardians of a Seljuk prince, even if in practice this was sometimes a fiction and no prince existed.

Although amirs often get a bad press, in fact these strongmen had an interest in making their own patch flourish, and in promoting their own claims to legitimacy through the lavishness of the patronage of their own courts. Such rulers relied on the prosperity of their lands to raise revenues to allow them to project power and resist the encroachments of their neighbours, and some amirs seem to have been genuinely popular with the people of their *iqṭāʿs*. Indeed, in some ways growing amiral independence actually seems to have contributed to deepening Seljuk influences. Thus – to take one of the few examples that has been studied in detail – northern Syria actually seems much more integrated into the empire and 'Seljuk' in the early twelfth century, with Seljuk officials now present not just in the large cities but also smaller centres and the countryside.[6] The Seljuk sultan's court served as the amirs' model, and they brought its ideals and its practices to their *iqṭāʿs*.

The other characteristic contributing to the designation of the post-Malikshah period as one of decline was the re-appearance of the division

5 *ʿAmīd* is often said to have been a governor's title held by civilian bureaucrats or tax collectors. However, as Ibn Banna' makes clear (see p. 58 above), the title *ʿamīd* was also used by Turkish amirs in the Seljuk period. On the office, see C. E. Bosworth, 'Amīd', *EI*[3]; Lambton, *Continuity and Change*, 301; Durand-Guédy, *Iranian Elites*, 106, 130, 134 and further references as per the index.

6 Heidemann, *Die Renaissance der Städte*, 145–75, 440–2; cf. Stefan Heidemann, 'Arab Nomads and the Seljūq Military', in Stefan Leder and Bernard Streck (eds), *Shifts and Drifts in Nomad–Sedentary Relations* (Wiesbaden, 2005), 293–4.

of the Seljuk territories into eastern and western halves. Initially, the centre of gravity remained in the west, as it had been under Malikshah. Isfahan and Baghdad served as the twin capitals of Malikshah's sons Berkyaruq (r. 485/1092–498/1105) and Muhammad Tapar (498/1105–511/1118), although from the early twelfth century Hamadhan was beginning to emerge as the third Seljuk capital in the west. Khurasan throughout this period was dominated by Malikshah's third son Sanjar, first as *malik* (prince), vassal to the sultans in the west, then from 511/1118 as Great Seljuk Sultan. The earlier parts of Sanjar's reign in some respects represented a second zenith of Seljuk rule, marked by successful campaigns across Central Asia and a flourishing intellectual and cultural life at his oasis capital of Merv, but the sultan was unable to assert direct control of the west. Sanjar was obliged to recognise the Sultanate of Iraq under Muhammad Tapar's descendants as vassals holding the title of sultan.[7] From the death of Muhammad, then, we are dealing with two Seljuk sultans concurrently: the senior one, Sanjar (*al-sulṭān al-aʿẓam*), and the junior Sultan of Iraq (*al-sulṭān al-muʿaẓẓam*). These grandiloquent titles ('the greatest sultan' and 'the great sultan', respectively) could not mask the crises that increasingly enveloped both east and west from the 1130s. Sanjar faced external foes in the form of the Qarakhitay, and internally both rebel vassals and restive nomads. It was these latter that would eventually destroy him through their revolt in 1152–7. Meanwhile, the Sultanate of Iraq was beset by financial problems that sapped the power of the sultans. Factions of amirs and bureaucrats intrigued incessantly, while the Caliphs of Baghdad started to play an increasingly important role in Seljuk politics, as well as asserting their authority over most of central and southern Iraq.

Although under Sanjar Seljuk rule in Khurasan appears more robust than the politically troubled western sultanate, it was the latter that survived for nearly another half century after the collapse of the 1150s. The Sultanate of Iraq, became, however, a very different creature, run in the second half of the twelfth century by what has been described as a 'dyarchy'[8] – a system of dual rule whereby a Seljuk sultan reigned in name, while effective power was exercised by his *atabegs*, a dynasty of slave origin

[7] Sanjar's difficulty in asserting control of the Sultanate of Iraq is documented more fully below. See further Köymen, *Büyük Selçuklu İmparatorluğu Tarihi*, II, 113–17, 181–215. As will be seen, Sanjar's attempts to intervene militarily nearly ended in diasaster, forcing him to adopt a circumspect approach, and even his efforts to impose his favoured candidate, Tughrıl II, as Sultan of Iraq, eventually failed.

[8] The term is Luther's: see Kenneth Alun Luther, 'The Political Transformation of the Seljuq Sultanate of Iraq and Western Iran: 1152–1187', PhD dissertation, Princeton University, 1964, 1.

from Nakhchivan in the Caucasus known as the Ildegüzids. This dyarchy functioned until the last Seljuk sultan, Tughrıl III, tried to free himself from its shackles and assert his own authority as ruler. Tughrıl, however, was surrounded by enemies on all sides who had no desire to see a resurgent Seljuk state, and was killed in battle, finally bringing an end to the Seljuk line in Iran and Iraq.

It is often hard to see beyond the vicious world of elite infighting which is the prime interest of our sources. There is reason to think, however, that the depressing picture painted by Ibn al-Athir and others does not really do justice to the realities of life under Seljuk rule in the twelfth century. True, even Sanjar's nominal authority extended over a reduced area compared with Alp Arslan's; and at times the fighting caused hardship in individual areas – Baghdad and Isfahan, both key to a sultan's legitimacy, but also the focus of many of our sources, were probably disproportionately badly affected. Despite, or perhaps because of, the atmosphere of more or less permanent political crisis at the heart of the Sultanate of Iraq, individual towns and cities prospered, a vibrant trade was still carried out on the land and sea routes that linked the Middle East to China, and, especially from the mid-twelfth century, art flourished, developments which will all be discussed in more detail in subsequent chapters. To understand this apparent contradiction we must bear in mind that centralised authority was not necessarily to the advantage of many subjects, meaning in essence more effective collection of taxation. Moreover, despite the political fragmentation of the empire into eastern and western halves and the establishment of *de facto* independent atabegates, the Seljuk territories shared an elite political culture and to some degree an artistic culture that was promoted by the regional amiral courts. Works of art produced in Iran do not really reflect regional variation, but are closely connected in style and iconography, and eastern architectural styles are increasingly attested in Syria under the Zangids.[9] In a sense, then, precisely the political disunity of the later Seljuk Empire brought it a greater cultural cohesiveness with courts in Shiraz, Maragha, Nakhchivan, Hamadhan and Mosul (to name but a few) all seeking to emulate the Seljuk legacy.

[9] Lorenz Korn, 'Saljuqs. VI. Art and Architecture', *EIr*; Robert Hillenbrand, 'Eastern Islamic Influences in Syria: al-Raqqa and Qal'at Ja'bar in the later 12th Century', in Julian Raby (ed.), *The Art of Syria and the Jazira, 1100–1250* (Oxford, 1985), 21–48. On artistic links between Syria and Iran, see also Lorenz Korn, 'The Sultan Stopped at Ḥalab: Artistic Exchange between Syria and Iran in the 5th/11th Century', in Lorenz Korn, Eva Orthmann and Florian Schwarz (eds), *Die Grenzen der Welt. Arabica et Iranica ad honorem Heinz Gaube* (Wiesbaden, 2008), 105–121.

The Succession to Malikshah

With Malikshah's death, amirs and palace elites sought to assert power by promoting one of his youthful sons as sultan. Berkyaruq was no more than thirteen,[10] Muhammad eleven[11] and Mahmud four.[12] In contrast, the main adult claimant, Tutush, who had ruled Syria on Malikshah's behalf, attracted little support from the Turkish military elites who increasingly emerged as major power brokers.[13]

Initially, Malikshah's wife Terken Khatun took control of his troops in Baghdad, securing their loyalty by disbursing huge sums of cash in secret and persuading them to swear the oath of allegiance to her son Mahmud, while also sending the amir Qiwam al-Dawla Kirbuqa to seize control of Isfahan for her and capture Berkyaruq. She also persuaded the caliph to have the *khuṭba* said in Mahmud's name and to appoint her favoured candidates to key positions: the amir Onor to command the military, and Taj al-Mulk to the vizierate, in charge of civilian affairs and tax collection. She was, however, undone by her association with Taj al-Mulk, who was bitterly hated by the partisans of Nizam al-Mulk. The latter's private army of slave soldiers, known after him as the Nizamiyya, remained intact and held Taj al-Mulk responsible (probably, at least in part, rightly) for their master's murder. The Nizamiyya thus gave their support to the adolescent Berkyaruq, and fighting broke out between the two sides.[14]

By 488/1095, Berkyaruq seemed secure at least in Iran and Iraq. He had entered Baghdad and been recognised as sultan at the beginning of the previous year when he had also finally seized Isfahan, and in the meantime all his rivals had been killed or died: the sickly infant Mahmud in Shawwal 487/October 1094, then Terken Khatun, and finally, Tutush himself, in battle on 16 Safar 488/25 February 1095.[15] Meanwhile,

10 Ibn al-Athir, *al-Kamil*, X, 381.

11 *Ibid.*, X, 525.

12 *Ibid.*, X, 214.

13 *Ibid.*, X, 220–2, 233, 244. The most detailed accounts in English of Tutush's role in the succession struggle are El-Azhari, *Saljūqs of Syria*, 73–9 and Durand-Guédy, *Iranian Elites*, 153–7. See also Sevim, *Suriye ve Filistin Selçukluları*, 137–60. See further the discussion in Chapter 3.

14 Bundari, *Zubda*, 82–3; Husayni, *Akhbar*, 74–5; Ibn al-Athir, *al-Kamil*, X, 211, 214–16; Ibn al-Jawzi, *al-Muntazam*, XVII, 14; Nishapuri, *Saljuqnama*, 35–6.

15 Ibn al-Athir, *al-Kamil*, X, 229, 234, 240, 244; Husayni, *Akhbar*, 76; Sibt, *Mir'at*, ed. Ghamidi, 239–42. The most detailed study of these events, and indeed the whole reign of Berkyaruq, remains C. Defrémery, 'Recherches sur le règne du sultan seldjoukide Barkiarok (485–498 de l'hégire, 1092–1104 de l'ère chrétienne)', *Journal asiatique*, sér. 5, 1 (1853), 425–58; 2 (1853), 217–322.

Malikshah's brother, Arghun Arslan, sought to carve out for himself a realm in Khurasan.[16] Berkyaruq's dispatch of an army under the nominal command of his ten-year-old brother Sanjar[17] to restore his authority in the region was pre-empted by Arghun Arslan's murder by a disgruntled slave in 490/1097.[18] Sanjar was established as vassal ruler (*malik*) of Khurasan, where he was to reign for the next six decades, although Berkyaruq also came in person to the region, campaigning as far east as Tirmidh, and confirming the Qarakhanids Sulayman-tegin and Mahmud-tegin in possession of Transoxiana as Seljuk vassals.[19] No sooner had Berkyaruq returned to the west, however, than a series of revolts broke out, including one involving another Seljuk prince, Dawlatshah.[20] Berkyaruq's name started to be omitted from coins struck at Nishapur, signalling the gradual collapse of the sultan's authority in Khurasan.[21]

Preoccupation with these internal threats explains why the arrival of the First Crusade in Syria in 1097 met with little response from Berkyaruq, despite their siege of Antioch and the brutal sacking of Maʿarrat al-Nuʿman, an atrocity allegedly accompanied by acts of cannibalism.[22] Furthermore, Berkyaruq would have felt little desire to help the Syrian Seljuks, the sons of his erstwhile rival Tutush. These had themselves now split into the warring parties of Ridwan in the north and his brother Duqaq in Damascus, manipulated by their respective *atabegs* Janah al-Dawla and Tughtegin, for both Seljuk princes were still youths.[23] Almost exactly as the Crusaders finally broke into Syria in September 1097, Ridwan – who had thrown off the tutelage of Janah al-Dawla – went so far as to drop Berkyaruq's name from the *khuṭba*, instead proclaiming his loyalty to the Fatimid caliphate. Although the step was rescinded after a few weeks, the sources continue to accuse

16 Bundari, *Zubda*, 85, 256; Husayni, *Akhbar*, 85. For details, see Jürgen Paul, 'Arslan Arghun – Nomadic Revival?', in C. Lange and S. Mecit (eds), *The Seljuqs: Politics, Society and Culture* (Edinburgh, 2011), 99–113.

17 Ibn al-Athir, *al-Kamil*, XI, 222, states he was born in 479; but Bundari, *Zubda*, 255, gives his date of birth as 25 Rajab 481.

18 Ibn al-Athir, *al-Kamil*, X, 262–5; Bundari, *Zubda*, 258.

19 Bundari, *Zubda*, 258.

20 Ibn al-Athir, *al-Kamil*, X, 266–7, 279. Cf. Ibn al-Qalanisi, *Dhayl Ta'rikh Dimashq*, ed. H. F. Amedroz (Leiden, 1908), 140.

21 Hanne, 'Death on the Tigris', 169.

22 Ibn al-Athir, *al-Kamil*, X, 269–73, 279.

23 El-Azhari, *Saljuqs of Syria*, 79–87; Sevim, *Suriye ve Filistin Selçukluları*, 161–78; Jean-Michel Mouton, *Damas et sa principauté sous les Saljoukides et les Bourides 468–549/1076–1154* (Cairo, 1994), 32–3. For Ridwan, see Anne-Marie Eddé, 'Riḍwān, Prince d'Alep de 1095 à 1113', *Revue des Études Islamiques*, 54 (1986), esp. 103–8.

Ridwan of a dubious association with the Ismailis, perceived by Sunnis as arch heretics (see below, pp. 85–7, 265–6).[24]

Syria was a side show, however. The real challenge Berkyaruq faced was the rebellion of his half-brother Muhammad in 492/1098–9. The impetus for revolt apparently came from Nizam al-Mulk's son Mu'ayyid al-Mulk, who had previously served Berkyaruq and was credited with the latter's defeat of Tutush. After dismissal from Berkyaruq's service, he managed to get himself appointed as Muhammad's vizier, a position which he proceeded to use to avenge himself on his enemies, doubtless helped by Muhammad's comparative youth – he would have been around 17 years old at the time.[25] The notable families of Isfahan and the Nizamiyya decided to throw their weight behind Muhammad (known as Tapar, 'he who obtains'), barring Berkyaruq from the city.[26] The fragility of Berkyaruq's regime is striking, for Muhammad seems to have little difficulty in advancing south from his base at Ganja in the Caucasus to seize Rayy, while the defection of the long-serving *shiḥna* of Baghdad, Sa'd al-Dawla Gawhara'in, meant that city too recognised the new sultan.[27] It would be wearisome to detail every clash between the two sides over the next five years.[28] Yet despite Berkyaruq's weakness, Muhammad was unable to gain a decisive victory, with defections swinging the advantage from one side to another, and Baghdad changed hands repeatedly. Even the intervention of Sanjar – who hated Berkyaruq[29] – on Muhammad's side could not secure final victory. Nonetheless, Berkyaruq's position was weakening, as is attested by the increasing number of mints striking coins in the names of Muhammad, and in 497/1104, Berkyaruq recognised that his money was exhausted and that the prolongation of hostilities served only the interests of his amirs, and sued for peace. The ensuing agreement allotted to Muhammad southern Iraq, northern Iran from the Caspian to the Bab al-Abwab, the Diyar Bakr, Mosul and Syria, while Baghdad and the rest of Iran,

24 El-Azhari, *Saljuqs of Syria*, 88–90; Sevim, *Suriye ve Filistin Selçukluları*, 202–5; Hillenbrand, *Crusades*, 79–80, 82; Hodgson, *Secret Order*, 89–92; Eddé, 'Riḍwān', 118–22; Ibn al-Athir, *al-Kamil*, X, 499; Sibt, *Mir'at*, ed. Ghamidi, 276–8.

25 Bundari, *Zubda*, 86–8, 259; Husayni, *Akhbar*, 76–7; Ibn al-Athir, *al-Kamil*, X, 287–8; Ibn al-Jawzi, *al-Muntazam*, XVII, 48. His date of birth is given by Ibn al-Athir, *al-Kamil*, X, 525 as 18 Sha'ban 474/21 January 1082.

26 See Durand-Guédy, *Iranian Elites*, 162–6

27 Husayni, *Akhbar*, 77; Ibn al-Athir, *al-Kamil*, X, 288–9; Ibn al-Jawzi has a rather different account of Gawhara'in's fluctuating loyalties, see *al-Muntazam*, XVII, 52–3, 56–7.

28 See Sanaullah, *Decline*, 105–13, and Bosworth, 'Political and Dynastic History', 108–11 for a summary of these events, and for more detail, Defrémery, 'Recherches', *Journal asiatique*, ser. 5, 2 (1853).

29 Husayni, *Akhbar*, 77; Ibn al-Athir, *al-Kamil*, X, 347.

including Muhammad's stronghold of Isfahan, went to Berkyaruq, who recognised Muhammad as sultan over the territories he controlled.[30] Whatever was agreed on paper most likely did not reflect the reality. By the time of his death the following year, no mints in the central Islamic lands were mentioning Berkyaruq as the legitimate sovereign on their coinage issues,[31] suggesting his rule was not recognised even in theory on the ground.

The *Iqṭāʿ* System and Amirs as Local Rulers

The *iqṭāʿ* had been the Buyid answer to the problem of paying the military in a period when specie was in short supply: in lieu of salary an amir would be granted the right to collect the taxes of a given area.[32] An *iqṭāʿ* could thus vary in size from a whole province to much smaller subdivision, to a single town or village. In principle, the *iqṭāʿ* remained in the gift of the sultan, and could be withdrawn at any moment. Under the Buyids, this system was widely credited with economic disaster, as absentee amirs sought to reap the swiftest possible profits before their *iqṭāʿ* was removed them. The system was greatly expanded under the Seljuks, and *iqṭāʿs* were now used to pay senior bureaucrats as well as amirs and were also granted to members of the Seljuk dynasty. However, *iqṭāʿ* holders became much more than tax collectors, and often functioned effectively as the local ruler (particularly amirs: bureaucrats seem to have become less entrenched in their *iqṭāʿs*, perhaps because their duties required their presence at court). For Seljuk amirs, in contrast to Buyid ones, the *iqṭāʿ* was the basis of

30 Ibn al-Athir, *al-Kamil*, X, 369–371; Bundari, *Zubda*, 261; Ibn al-Jawzi, *al-Muntazam*, XVII, 85. Husayni, *Akhbar*, 78, adds that Sanjar got Khurasan and Transoxiana as part of this arrangement.

31 Hanne, 'Death on the Tigris', 169.

32 On the *iqṭāʿ* see Claude Cahen, 'L'évolution de l'*iqṭā* du IXe au XIIIe siècle', *Annales, économies-sociétés-civilisation*, 8 (1953), 25–52; Lambton, *Landlord and Peasant*, 53–75; Lambton, *Continuity and Change*, 97–115; Lambton, 'Eqṭāʿ', *EIr* with full bibliography; also Heidemann, *Renaissance der Städte*, 310–15. Lambton subdivides the *iqṭāʿ* into five different categories, which, as she states, are often overlapping: those granted to members of the royal family; administrative (i.e., the *muqṭaʿ* also functioned as a governor); military; those granted to members of the bureaucracy; and personal *iqṭāʿs*. No such distinction is drawn in the sources, which is not surprising. Clearly, *iqṭāʿs* did function in different ways. In some instances, they were purely tax-farms; in other instances, they were closer to provincial governorships, or might be used separately to fund provincial governorships in the vicinity, but not actually be identical with them. However, almost never do our sources tell us exactly which of these they mean, and it is not clear what the practical differences might have been. For examples of two different *iqṭāʿ* grants, see Juwayni, *'Atabat al-Kataba*, 83–5.

their power and usually their place of residence. Some amirs succeeded in making their *iqṭā‘s* effectively hereditary possessions.

Although we do read of oppressive *muqṭa‘s* (*iqṭā‘* holders), collaboration with the local inhabitants offered amirs a way of securing their position against attempts to remove them. Thus, Chökermish, the amir and *muqṭa‘* of Mosul appointed by Berkyaruq, was strongly supported by its people against Sultan Muhammad 'because of their love for him because he treated them well' (*li-maḥabbatihim li-Jigirmish li-ḥusn sīratihi fihim*).[33] Chökermish's decision to surrender on 10 Jumada I 498/28 January 1105, on learning of Berkyaruq's death, was taken after consulting with the people of the town, his troops [*jund*] and his amirs. Conversely, wearying of Sultan Muhammad's siege of the town when it was controlled by Chökermish's unpopular replacement, Chavli Saqqa'u, a group of the populace took the sultan's side and massacred Chavli's garrison.[34] Similarly, Boz-aba, the ruler of Fars, and 'Abbas, lord of Rayy, both amirs who were a major thorn in the side of Sultan Mas'ud, are praised as local rulers. Ibn al-Athir is predictably full of praise for Zangi as ruler of Mosul, where the amir is said to have undertaken major construction works for the public good and restored a city which was in ruins.[35]

Muhammad Tapar, 1105–18

On Berkyaruq's death aged twenty-five in 498/1105 after a reign devoted almost exclusively to fighting, Muhammad Tapar entered Baghdad with little resistance, and an attempt by some amirs to install Berkyaruq's infant son Malikshah as sultan soon faltered.[36] Isfahan too welcomed the new sultan, who is claimed to have put a stop to the excesses of the military 'so that the word of the civilian became stronger than that of the soldier and the soldier had no power over the civilian thanks to the majesty and justice of the sultan'.[37]

Muhammad Tapar gets a good write up in most sources. Isfahani, for instance, calls him 'the perfect man of the Seljuk dynasty and their strongest steed'.[38] True, he was certainly more successful than subsequent rulers in

[33] Ibn al-Athir, *al-Kamil*, X, 383, also 242.

[34] *Ibid.*, X, 383–4, 457.

[35] Zarkub-i Shirazi, *Shiraznama*, ed. Muhammad Jawwad Jiddi and Ihsanallah Shukrallahi (Tehran, 1389), 136; Ibn al-Athir, *al-Kamil*, XI, 177; Ibn al-Athir, *al-Ta'rikh al-Bahir*, 76–7. On Ibn al-Athir's pro-Zangid sentiments, see above, p. 16.

[36] Ibn al-Athir, *al-Kamil*, X, 382–7; Ibn al-Jawzi, *al-Muntazam*, XVII, 90–2; cf. Bundari, *Zubda*, 90.

[37] Ibn al-Athir, *al-Kamil*, X, 396.

[38] Bundari, *Zubda*, 118: *kāna rajul al-saljuqiyya wa-faḥlahum al-bāzil.*

the west in navigating the turbulent waters of Seljuk politics. His younger brother, Sanjar, remained loyal in Khurasan, and a revolt in the Hamadhan region in 499/1105–6 by his nephew, Alp Arslan's grandson Mengubars, was crushed without much difficulty.[39] The sultan retained command of substantial resources,[40] a luxury subsequent later sultans of Iraq did not enjoy.

However, the tendency of amirs to assert themselves at the expense of the sultan's authority could not be reversed. Muhammad's strategy was simply to grant a recalcitrant amir's *iqṭāʿ* to another one and leave them to fight it out. It was by setting amir against amir, by allotting *iqṭāʿs* to different *muqṭaʿs* simultaneously, that the sultan managed to keep his vast domains united under his nominal rule. Events in Mosul between 500/1105 and 502/1108 illustrate this phenomenon. The sultan initially left Berkyaruq's governor Chökermish in place; when this latter stopped remitting revenue in an attempt to assert independence, Muhammad assigned the *iqṭāʿ* of Mosul to the amir who governed Fars and Khuzistan, Chavli Saqqa'u. After Chavli had successfully kicked the forces loyal to Chökermish out of Mosul, he himself started down the same path of independence,[41] trying to draw on a web of alliances with regional powers, including the Frankish County of Edessa. Chavli had, moreover, obtained control of the valuable prize of a Seljuk prince, Alp Arslan's grandson Bektash b. Tekish.[42] The danger that the latter could be used as a potential rival for the sultanate meant that when Muhammad sent a third army to retake Mosul under amir Mawdud, Chavli had to be treated with care. He sought the sultan's forgiveness, yielded up the prince, and was eventually reinstated as ruler of Fars.

Chavli's career underlines the limits of sultanic power. Far from meeting with retribution, he was rewarded with a new appointment. Chavli's position was, of course, helped by his control of a potential rival for the Seljuk throne, and not every amir who crossed Muhammad was so lucky: Ayaz, for instance, a leading loyalist to Berkyaruq and the latter's son Malikshah who changed sides at the last minute, ensuring Muhammad's entry in Baghdad, was murdered on the sultan's instructions.[43] The same combination of brutality and circumspection can be seen in Muhammad's dealings with his bureaucrats. The vizier Saʿd al-Mulk, for instance, accused of Ismaili tendencies by the

[39] Ibn al-Athir, *al-Kamil*, X, 398.

[40] See, for example, Bundari, *Zubda*, 117, for the vast sums distributed by the sultan to the poor on his deathbed; cf. *ibid.*, 98. Also Durand-Guédy, *Iranian Elites*, 185

[41] This is a much simplified summary of an extremely complicated sequence of events. See further: Ibn al-Athir, *al-Kamil*, X, 422–30; Ibn al-Qalanisi, *Dhayl*, 147, 150, 156, 158; Heidemann, *Die Renaissance der Städte*, 189–211.

[42] Ibn al-Athir, *al-Kamil*, X, 458–60, 462.

[43] *Ibid.*, X, 387–9.

influential qadi of Isfahan, al-Khatibi, was crucified, but when it came to choosing his successor, Muhammad was unwilling or unable to antagonise either of the main factions in his court who backed rival candidates, Khatir al-Mulk Maybudi and Diya' al-Mulk b. Nizam al-Mulk, and so appointed them both to senior positions.[44]

Muhammad's positive image in the sources can be largely attributed to his role as a fighter for Islam who 'rooted out the castles of the heretics and raised the banners of the Muslims', as Isfahani put it.[45] Although in reality Muhammad's commitment to any sort of jihad was distinctly lacklustre, he was able to use the threats the Seljuk Empire faced to his propaganda advantage. These threats were, first, the Crusaders, and, secondly, and more seriously, the Ismailis. Neither was a new phenomenon; but it was under Muhammad Tapar that the Seljuk state made some progress against them.

The Seljuks and the Jihad against the Crusaders and Ismailis

The alarm caused by the victory at Manzikert and Atsız's capture of Jerusalem had been cleverly manipulated by the Byzantine emperor Alexios to secure western support that he hoped would shore up his own position. Thus it was that the First Crusade was born.[46] Paradoxically, the arrival of the Franks in Syria in 1097 provoked little reaction in Baghdad or Isfahan, even though Frankish principalities were established in lands that had once proclaimed the *khuṭba* in the name of Seljuk sultans: Antioch, Edessa and Jerusalem. However, the latter two had already fallen to other powers – the Byzantines and Fatimids, respectively – and only Antioch was in name a Seljuk town at the time of its conquest.

Even here, the lack of interest in the fall of Antioch by much of the Islamic historiographical tradition is noteworthy, especially given that the main, unsuccessful effort to relieve the siege was led by Berkyaruq's governor of Mosul at the time, Kirbuqa. Isfahani and Nishapuri entirely ignore the fall of Antioch; Ibn al-Jawzi does mention the city's capture very briefly, but Kirbuqa not at all.[47] It is only our local Muslim sources who provide any detailed information: Ibn al-Athir, himself a native of Mosul, Ibn al-Qalanisi of Damascus, and another Syrian chronicler, 'Azimi.[48] A similar pattern is true even of the

44 Bundari, *Zubda*, 91–2, 96–7.

45 *Ibid.*, 118.

46 Alexios' policy is described in Frankopan, *The First Crusade*, esp. 87–100.

47 Ibn al-Jawzi, *al-Muntazam*, XVI, 43.

48 In addition, of course, to copious western sources, see Ibn al-Qalanisi, *Dhayl*, 134–5; Hillenbrand, *The Crusades*, 56–9. See further Tyerman, *God's War*, 140–9, who views

fall of Jerusalem to the Crusaders in 1099, which as one of Islam's holy cities one might have expected to be an event of some significance.[49]

The silence of our eastern Islamic sources and the lack of enthusiasm for intervention on the part of the sultans reflect, of course, their own preoccupations, in which the coming of the Franks played very little role. However, the Great Seljuks were not able to ignore entirely events in Syria. As early as Rabi' II 491/March 1098, six months after the arrival of the Crusaders, Muslim complaints had forced Berkyaruq to order his amirs to accompany the vizier Ibn Jahir on campaign against the Franks, although the expedition was aborted before it had left Baghdad for reasons that are unclear, but are probably connected with the deteriorating situation in Khurasan (p. 77 above).[50] Pressure for action came, however, not from Baghdadis, but from delegations of Syrian Muslims who travelled to the sultanic and caliphal courts in Baghdad to seek support:

> Abu Sa'd al-Harawi the qadi of Damascus stood up in the [caliphal] *dīwān* and made a speech which made the assembled company weep. Someone was appointed from the *dīwān* to go to the sultan's camp [*al-'askar*] and inform them of this disaster. Then apathy reigned (*thumma waqa'a al-taqā'ud*).[51]

Muhammad Tapar is said to have sent out letters 'proclaiming his intention to seek jihad',[52] and, more concretely, ordered Mawdud, the amir of Mosul, to campaign against Crusader-held Edessa in 503/1110. Although Mawdud's armies ravaged northern Syria for the next three years, these measures did not stem the criticism from Syria. In 504/1111, Ibn al-Athir reports that a Byzantine emissary also came to Baghdad to encourage the Seljuks to make

Kirbuga's relief effort as an attempt 'to create a new overlordship in Syria, ostensibly loyal to the Seljuk sultan in Baghdad' (p. 141). Heidemann, however, sees Kirbuga as acting on Berkyaruq's instructions, with the aim of bringing not just the Crusaders, but also the line of Tutush in Syria to heel. Heidemann, *Die Renaissance der Städte*, 184–6, 189–90.

49 Hillenbrand, *The Crusades*, 63–6. The status of Jerusalem was a matter of some debate among Muslim scholars, see the discussion in M. J. Kister, '"You Shall only Set Out for Three Mosques": A Study of an Early Tradition', *Le Muséon*, 82 (1969), 173–96. In our period, Nasir-i Khusraw notes how Syrians who could not make the hajj would go on pilgrimage to Jersualem instead (*Safarnama*, 28). It may be, however, that Jerusalem's renown as a holy place among Muslims was rather local in the late eleventh century, which would explain why the Iraqi chroniclers pay it little attention. In the twelfth century, Jersualem would assume a rather greater importance in Muslim eyes: Hillenbrand, *The Crusades*, 141–61.

50 Ibn al-Jawzi, *al-Muntazam*, XVII, 43. For campaigns in Khurasan in this period, see Heidemann, *Die Renaissance der Städte*, 189.

51 Ibn al-Jawzi, *al-Muntazam*, XVII, 47. For other delegations, see, for example, Ibn al-Qalanisi, *Dhayl*, 156 (AH 500).

52 Ibn al-Qalanisi, *Dhayl*, 165; Sibt, *Mir'at*, ed. Ghamidi, 521–2.

war on the Crusaders, prompting the people of Aleppo to complain to the sultan:

> Do you not fear God, given that the Byzantine king is a better protector of Islam than you are, so that he has sent to you to wage jihad against them?[53]

One of these Syrian delegations was so frustrated that it staged a protest at the lack of action by disrupting Friday prayers in Baghdad in both the sultanic and caliphal mosques. Passionate poetry by Seljuk court poets like al-Abiwardi and Mu'izzi called for war on the infidel invaders;[54] as Mu'izzi put it to 'make polo-balls of the Franks' heads in the desert, and polo-sticks from their hands and feet'.[55]

While Ibn al-Qalanisi presents the Seljuk campaigns as motivated by a newly enthusiastic jihad spirit, operations were evidently hindered, and in some instances had to be aborted, owing to the intense distrust and suspicion of Mawdud's would-be allies like Najm al-Din Ilghazi b. Artuq of Mardin and the Seljuk Ridwan of Aleppo. By far the most effective of Mawdud's campaigns came in 507/1113, when he turned his attention to Damascus, which had been threatened by Baldwin of Jerusalem. Mawdud and his allies penetrated as far as Galilee in the Kingdom of Jerusalem, even capturing Baldwin, although he was not recognised at the time and was released. However, Seljuk supply lines were over-extended in Palestine, and Mawdud ordered a withdrawal to Syria to prepare for another campaign the following spring. Although Mawdud was murdered before this could take place,[56] his replacement as amir of Mosul, Aqsonqur al-Bursuqi, was similarly ordered to fight the Franks.[57] Another Seljuk expedition was defeated in 509/1115, with Tutush's descendants, the Seljuk rulers of Aleppo and Damascus, actually allying themselves with the Crusaders.[58] However, even under Muhammad Tapar's successor Mahmud, when Bursuqi was reappointed governor of Mosul after a hiatus in

53 Ibn al-Athir, *al-Kamil*, X, 483.

54 Hillenbrand, *The Crusades*, 69–71, 78–9; Ibn al-Jawzi, *al-Muntazam*, XVII, 47–8; Ibn al-Qalanisi, *Dhayl*, 173; Sibt, *Mir'at*, ed. Ghamidi, 536; Tetley, *The Ghaznavid and Seljuk Turks*, 132–3, 142–3.

55 Amir Mu'izzi Nishapuri, *Kulliyat-i Diwan*, ed. Muhammad Rida Qanbari (Tehran, 1385), 509–10; cf. *ibid.*, 146.

56 For the campaigns under Mawdud, see Barber, *The Crusader States*, 99–104; Heidemann, *Die Renaissance der Städte*, 214–24; Hillenbrand, *The Crusades*, 79; Hillenbrand, 'Career', 260–1; Ibn al-Qalanisi, *Dhayl*, 169–70, 174–5, 184–7; Ibn al-Athir, *al-Kamil*, X, 485–7, 492, 495–7; Ibn al-Jawzi, *al-Muntazam*, XVII, 123; Sibt, *Mir'at*, ed. Ghamidi, 560–5, 589–92.

57 Ibn al-Athir, *al-Kamil*, X, 501–2; Sibt, *Mir'at*, ed. Ghamidi, 595–9.

58 Hillenbrand, *The Crusades*, 80.

515/1121–2, he was again ordered to fight the Franks.[59] The campaigns were continued with much greater success by Zangi (amir of Mosul from 521/1127, to which he added Aleppo in 1128), but Ibn al-Athir states that while all the earlier amirs were backed by the Seljuk sultans who sent them armies, 'not one of the sultans helped [Zangi] with a single horseman'.[60] Nonetheless, Zangi successfully carved out for himself a hereditary principality in northern Syria and the Jazira, capturing Edessa in 1144. The collapse of the Crusader county of Edessa spurred on the Second Crusade (1147–9), which Zangi's son Nur al-Din (d. 569/1174) won great renown for fighting.[61]

Under Muhammad Tapar, and to a lesser extent Mahmud, the Seljuk sultan thus did coordinate some efforts to fight the Crusaders, but on none of these occasions did the sultan himself, or his deputies like the vizier, command these armies operating in Syria. Instead, jihad was delegated to the amir of Mosul. Efforts were largely concentrated in northern Syria and the Jazira, and, with the exception of Mawdud's campaign of 507/1113, left the Kingdom of Jerusalem largely unaffected. This one occasion when the Seljuk armies under Mawdud do seem to have launched a concerted effort against the Franks coincides with the presence in Syria of a dangerous Seljuk refugee, Tekish b. Alp Arslan's son, who had fled there from his uncle Muhammad Tapar, taking refuge both in Muslim Hims then Crusader Antioch. One must wonder if Mawdud's sudden efforts in this period are in fact connected with the desire to capture or kill this potential threat to Muhammad.[62]

However, the Crusaders never came close to threatening the heartlands of the Seljuk state in Khurasan, Iran and Iraq, and so they were not at the forefront of the minds of most chroniclers who praised Muhammad for his defence of Islam. The real threat was represented by the Ismailis, who were not just proponents of a rival branch of Shia Islam, initially allied to the Fatimids, but rejected the whole Seljuk political edifice of a sultanate legitimised through the 'Abbasid caliphate. They intended to build an alternative state that would prepare the way before the return of Imam Nizar, the unsuccessful claimant to the Fatmid caliphate in 1095 whom most of the Ismaili movement in Iran and Syria (*al-da'wa al-jadīda*) recognised as legitimate and elevated to a messianic status. It is the Nizari Ismaili strongholds that are meant by 'the castles of the heretics' that Muhammad is praised by Isfahani for destroying (see above p. 82). Similar sentiments are reflected in

[59] Ibn al-Athir, *al-Kamil*, X, 588, 622, 628, 634.

[60] Ibn al-Athir, *al-Ta'rikh al-Bahir*, 65.

[61] Hillenbrand, *The Crusades*, 112–41; Tyerman, *God's War*, 268 ff; Barber, *The Crusader States*, 174–99.

[62] Ibn al-Qalanisi, *Dhayl*, 183; Sibt, *Mir'at*, ed. Ghamidi, 573.

the admiring biography of the sultan by Nishapuri, which has nothing at all to say about Muhammad's campaigns against the Crusaders, but discusses at length his exploits 'strengthening religion and suppressing accursed heretics'.[63]

The Ismaili challenge to Seljuk rule had developed in the reign of Malikshah when the two leaders of the Ismaili movement, Hasan-i Sabbah and Ahmad b. 'Attash, apparently independently of each other, seized a series of fortifications in Iran. To date the *da'wa* (lit. 'call', 'propaganda', the name the Ismailis gave to their movement, as had earlier the 'Abbasids whom the Ismailis intended to supplant) had largely followed a quietist policy, not seeking to challenge Seljuk rule, but Hasan-i Sabbah aimed to establish an Ismaili state.[64] The first sign of Hassan's revolt came even before the Nizari break with Cairo, when in 483/1090 he managed to seize the remote and impregnable fortress of Alamut in northern Iran from its lord, the Zaydi 'Alid ruler of Tabaristan. From Alamut, Hassan sent *dā'īs* (missionaries) across Iran. His strategy focused on seizing castles, which could then be used both as bases for propaganda into the surrounding towns and countryside, and as strongholds in case of need. The *da'wa* met with particular success in remote areas like Rudbar in the Alburz mountains and Quhistan. Expeditions launched by Malikshah in 485/1092 against Alamut and Quhistan were abandoned on his death, and the civil war allowed Ismaili influence to expand more widely, into Fars, Arrajan, Kirman and Iraq. By around 490/1096–7, Ahmad b. 'Attash had the spectacular success of capturing the major fortress of Shahdiz just outside Isfahan, and was able to collect taxes in the surrounding area. A programme of assassinations, for which the Ismailis became notorious, targeted senior Seljuk amirs and political figures, and Ismaili influence was such that several districts of Isfahan itself came under Ismaili control.[65]

The situation was more complex than a simple Ismaili versus Seljuk conflict. Even Nizari Ismailism was not a unified force, and the movement in Isfahan, subject to Ahmad b. al-'Attash, seems not to have recognised Hasan-i Sabbah's authority, while the Syrian branch of the *da'wa* also had divided loyalties.[66] The real opposition to Ismailism, which culminated in a massacre

[63] Nishapuri, *Saljuqnama*, 43; cf. Carole Hillenbrand, 'The Power Struggle between the Saljuqs and the Isma'ilis of Alamut, 487–518/1094–1124: The Saljuq Perspective', in Farhard Daftary (ed.), *Mediaeval Isma'ili History and Thought* (Cambridge, 1996), 209.

[64] See Durand-Guédy, *Iranian Elites*, 151–2; Farhad Daftary, *The Isma'ilis: Their History and Doctrines* (Cambridge, 1990), 324–5, 336–40; and Farhad Daftary, 'Hasan-i Sabbah and the Origins of the Nizari Movement', in Farhad Daftary (ed.), *Mediaeval Isma'ili History and Thought* (Cambridge, 1996), 181–204.

[65] Durand-Guédy, *Iranian Elites*, 157–62 (for events in Shahdiz and Isfahan); Daftary, *The Isma'ilis*, 343–4, 351–5.

[66] Durand-Guédy, *Iranian Elites*, 148–52; Daftary, *The Isma'ilis*, 357.

of Ismailis in Isfahan in 494/1101, came from the local Sunni population more than the Seljuks.[67] All sides in the dynastic crisis relied on Ismaili soldiers, and Berkyaruq in particular is accused of Ismaili sympathies by several chronicles.[68] Some members of the Seljuk elite embraced Ismailism themselves, including Qavurt's descendant, the Seljuk *malik* of Kirman, Iranshah b. Turanshah. Ridwan b. Tutush in Syria also relied on Ismaili support, and was sympathetic to the movement, although whether he actually converted is not clear.[69] Yet when expediency demanded, even Berkyaruq was prepared to launch an anti-Ismaili purge of his army.

The general pattern, however, is clear enough: as sultanic authority and the Seljuk state weakened, in both Syria and Iran, Ismailis were able to move into the gap. The years of the civil war between Berkyaruq and Muhammad represent the high-water mark of Ismailism. In the event, despite Ibn 'Attash's successes in the Isfahan region, the Ismailis were never able to gain control of any major urban centres. In both Syria and Iran, their territories were largely restricted to isolated fortresses and their surrounding villages, although they did control some towns in the remote and sparsely populated province of Quhistan. Beyond Quhistan and Rudbar in Iran and the Jabal Ansariyya in Syria, the Ismailis held virtually no contiguous territory. With the end of the civil war, conditions became less propitious for Ismailism. Muhammad seems to have been persuaded that his own court was a hotbed of heresy, and, encouraged by the qadi of Isfahan, 'Ubaydallah al-Khatibi, started to purge the bureaucracy of the supposedly heretical Jibalis. This was followed up by military action, and Shahdiz fell to Muhammad's forces in 500/1107, after which Muhammad issued the elaborate *fatḥnāma* (a victory proclamation, circulated throughout the Seljuk domains), which the Syrian chronicler Ibn al-Qalanisi cites.[70]

The attack on Shahdiz was followed up by expeditions against Ismaili strongholds in Fars and Arrajan. The Ismailis, unable to withstand a concerted attack by sultanic forces, responded through a programme of assassination, resulting in their labelling by European authors as the 'Assassins'. In 502/1108–9, the leader of the anti-Ismaili reaction in Isfahan, 'Ubaydallah al-Khatibi, was killed by an Ismaili assassin, and other senior bureaucrats and amirs, including Mawdud of Mosul, also fell victim.[71] From 503/1109,

67 Durand-Guédy, *Iranian Elites*, 162–70.

68 See Hillenbrand, 'The Power Struggle', 207–8.

69 Daftary, *The Isma'ilis*, 344, 358–60; Eddé, 'Ridwan'.

70 Durand-Guédy, *Iranian Elites*, 188–92; Ibn al-Athir, *al-Kamil*, X, 430–4; Bundari, *Zubda*, 90, 98; Husayni, *Akhbar*, 79; Ibn al-Qalanisi, *Dhayl*, 151–6.

71 Ibn al-Athir, *al-Kamil*, X, 471, 478, 497. Further on these assassinations, see Cook, 'Were the Ismaili Assassins the First Recorded Suicide Attackers?' *passim*.

Seljuk armies under Anushtegin Shirgir were entrusted with the task of reducing Alamut itself. After eight long years of campaigning in the Rudbar, besieging Lamasar and other Ismaili strongholds, Shirgir was on the verge of capturing Alamut when news came of the sultan's death on 24 Dhu 'l-Hijja 511/April 1118.[72]

The Ismailis had won an unexpected reprieve. With the intra-Seljuk fighting that inevitably followed Muhammad's demise, later efforts against Ismailism were distinctly half-hearted. Some minor operations were launched, but in general for the rest of the Seljuk period the relationship is best described as a stalemate.[73] The Ismailis lacked the strength or support to repeat actions like the capture of Shahdiz; and the Seljuk rulers did not seek to pursue Ismailis into these isolated mountain hideouts given they offered little direct threat to sultanic interests. As with the Crusaders, pragmatism was always the better part of valour, and the Ismailis had their uses. With their fame for assassination they could be blamed, and perhaps sometimes directly employed, for the murder of one's opponents. Thus when Sultan Mas'ud had the *mamlūk* Aqsonqur al-Ahmadili murdered, 'he gave out that that Ismailis had killed him'.[74] The same was true of the murder of Caliph al-Mustarshid in 529/1135, which certainly suited the Seljuks. According to some sources, it was falsely blamed on the Ismailis, while others directly claim that Sanjar had sent the Ismaili assassins.[75] The convenient (for Sanjar and Mas'ud) death of Caliph al-Rashid shortly afterwards should also be noted, where there are also allegations of Ismaili involvement.[76] Indeed, Sanjar seems to have maintained positively friendly relations with the Ismailis for much of his reign, an attack in 520/1126 notwithstanding.[77] Thus, an independent Ismaili state survived in Rudbar and Quhistan, surrounded on all sides by Seljuk territory, but itself refusing to accept Seljuk suzerainty. Indeed, this state would outlast the Seljuks themselves, and was destroyed only after a concerted Mongol campaign that captured Alamut in 654/1256.

[72] Ibn al-Athir, *al-Kamil*, X, 525, 527; Husayni, *Akhbar*, 82; Bundari, *Zubda*, 117. See also the discussion of these campaigns in Hillenbrand, 'The Saljuq–Isma'ili Power Struggle', 211–14.

[73] See Marshall G.S. Hodgson, *The Secret Order of the Assassins: the Struggle of the Nizari Isma 'ilis against the Islamic World* (Philadelphia, 2005 [1955]), 99–104, 145; Daftary, *The Isma'ilis*, 364f.

[74] Ibn al-Jawzi, *al-Muntazam*, XVII, 275; Ibn al-Athir, *al-Kamil*, X, 676; D. G. Tor, 'A Tale of Two Murders: Power Relations between Caliph and Sultan in the Saljuq Era', *ZDMG*, 159 (2009), 286.

[75] Tor, 'Tale of Two Murders', 288–90.

[76] *Ibid.*, 293.

[77] Daftary, *The Isma'ilis*, 365, 371–2.

The Sultanate of Iraq under Mahmud, Tughrıl II and Mas'ud, 511/1118–547/1152

With Muhammad's death and the accession of his fourteen-year-old son Mahmud, Sanjar now became the senior member of the dynasty.[78] Husayni noted the shift in power: 'Before sultan Mahmud, the [supreme] sultanate had belonged to the kings of Iraq, but from the period of sultan Mahmud it was transferred to sultan Sanjar, the king of Khurasan.'[79] Muhammad's successors in the west, of whom the most important were his two sons Mahmud (r. 511/1118–525/1131) and Mas'ud (r. 529/1134–547/1152), were thus subject to Sanjar who frequently sought to intervene in their territories. The treacherous politics of the west were further complicated by the competing and ever-shifting factions of amirs and bureaucrats that Muhammad had only held in check with some difficulty, each faction seeking to manipulate one of the numerous potential rival candidates for the Sultanate of Iraq to strengthen its own hand. Under Seljuk succession arrangements, discussed further in Chapter 3, any one of Muhammad's sons were equally entitled to the sultanate, and in fact of his progeny Mahmud, Mas'ud, Tughrıl and Sulaymanshah were at various times and in various places recognised as sultan of Iraq. At the same time, the caliphs in Baghdad also took advantage of sultanic weakness to strengthen their own power (discussed in more detail in Chapter 3).

In essence, the cause of this shift in power away from the sultan was fiscal: both Mahmud and Muhammad were permanently short of funds, as increasing quantities of land were alienated as *iqṭā'* to amirs. As a result, the authority of the sultans of Iraq came to be reduced to the Jibal and parts of Fars. In addition, the fact that the sultans came to the throne as children, and all died comparatively young, in their twenties or thirties, meant that they were more susceptible to being manipulated by the powerful entrenched interests around them. Nonetheless, both Mahmud and Mas'ud succeeded in maintaining a degree of independence as sultans in the lands of the Jibal and Iraq, and kept the ambitions of both the caliph and their amirs in check to some extent. On occasion, the sultans were able to wrong-foot their rivals and exert their authority more widely. We should not envisage power relations under Mahmud and Mas'ud as a simple rise in amiral power at the expense of the sultans. It is precisely this constant struggle between shifting coalitions of sultans, amirs and bureaucrats that makes the politics of this period so complex.

[78] Bundari, *Zubda*, 120; Husayni, *Akhbar*, 83–4.
[79] Husayni, *Akhbar*, 98.

The Reign of Mahmud, 1118–31[80]

As senior sultan Sanjar almost immediately tried to assert his authority in the west, although the precise *casus belli* is unclear.[81] Most likely, Sanjar in fact aspired to resurrect the days of Alp Arslan and Malikshah when there had been only one sultan in the Seljuk realms.[82] Although Mahmud offered to pay a substantial annual tribute of 200,000 dinars and to cede Mazandaran to his uncle, this was not enough, and Sanjar advanced west as far as Sawa in the Jibal by Jumada I 512/September 1118. The expedition nearly ended in disaster, however, for the eastern army found itself greatly outnumbered on unfamiliar terrain where Mahmud's troops had managed to monopolise the water supply. Only the presence of eighteen elephants in Sanjar's army (a Ghaznavid tactic the eastern empire had evidently inherited) saved the day at the last minute by terrifying Mahmud's cavalry. Although victorious, Sanjar realised his position was precarious, as he lacked both soldiers and any significant support in the west. He contented himself with returning everything but Rayy to Mahmud,[83] whose name he had mentioned after his own in the *khuṭba* in the east.

The immediate threat of Sanjar gone, Mahmud's position still remained weak. Inevitably, the sultan's youth only encouraged ambitions of the amirs and bureaucrats – indeed, Sanjar had used their influence as an excuse for his invasion, saying, 'My nephew is a child dominated by his vizier and the *ḥājib* 'Ali.'[84] This latter, 'Ali b. 'Umar, who had previous served as *ḥājib* (chamberlain) to Muhammad Tapar, was finally executed at the instigation of rival amirs.[85] Meanwhile, Muhammad's other sons, Mas'ud, *malik* of Mosul, the

[80] Secondary literature: Bosworth, 'Political and Dynastic History', 120–4; Köymen, *Büyük Selçuklu İmparatorluğu Tarihi*, II, 27–120, 164–73. A brief, but contemporary, account of Mahmud's reign is given in *Mujmal al-Tawarikh wa'l-Qisas*, ed. Malik al-Shu'ara Bahar (Tehran, 1381), 411–15.

[81] The account given by Isfahani differs from that Ibn al-Athir. Isfahani claims that the vizier Abu 'l-Qasim al-Darguzini had persuaded Mahmud to write to the Qarakhanid khan of Samarqand seeking an alliance against his uncle Sanjar (Bundari, *Zubda*, 120). Given Isfahani's extreme hostility to Darguzini, the reliability of such allegations should be regarded with some caution; they were, however, probably also the source for Husayni, *Akhbar*, 88.

[82] Husayni, *Akhbar*, 88, offers the wholly unconvincing explanation that Sanjar invaded to rescue Mahmud from the clutches of his amirs and strengthen him.

[83] Husayni, *Akhbar*, 89, who seems less reliable than Ibn al-Athir, *al-Kamil*, which is generally followed here, adds that Sanjar also took Mazandaran, Qumis, Damaghan and Dunbavand. See also Bundari, *Zubda*, 125 ff.

[84] Ibn al-Athir, *al-Kamil*, X, 550.

[85] *Ibid.*, X, 556–7.

Jazira and Azerbaijan, and Tughrıl, whose *iqṭā'* was based around Zanjan and Qazwin in northwestern Iran, were both pushed forward by their ambitious *atabegs*.[86]

A further challenge to Mahmud was presented by the Arab Mayzadid dynasty of Hilla in central Iraq.[87] Sadaqa b. Mazyad, who claimed the title of 'King of the Arabs', had helped Muhammad Tapar come to power, but had subsequently fallen out with the sultan, who was provoked to march on him in person.[88] In another symptom of sultanic weakness, however, Muhammad's army was considerably smaller than Sadaqa's and he only won the battle by chance.[89] Unsurprisingly, Sadaqa's son Dubays sought to emulate his father's example of asserting autonomy. As Ibn al-Athir puts it, Dubays

> was pleased when sultans quarrelled for he saw that as long as their dispute was ongoing his own affairs would prosper, just as his father Sadaqa had benefited from the dispute between sultans.[90]

By encouraging Mahmud's rivals such as his brothers Mas'ud[91] and Tughrıl,[92] Dubays sought to strengthen his own position. Meanwhile, Caliph al-Mustarshid, too, although on the surface remaining loyal to Mahmud, started to try to extend his own authority, provoking Mahmud in 520/1126 to besiege Baghdad and sack the caliphal palace (see Chapter 3).[93] Nonetheless, Mahmud was able to rely on some amirs, like Zangi, whose support enabled him to counter al-Mustarshid and Dubays to some degree.

86 *Ibid.*, X, 539–41, 547–8; Husayni, *Akhbar*, 96–7.

87 On them, see George Makdisi, 'Notes on Hilla and the Mazyadids in Medieval Islam', *JAOS*, 74/iv (1954), 249–62; on their representation by historians, see Abbès Zouache, 'Dubays b. Ṣadaqa (m. 529/1135), aventurier de legend. Histoire et fiction dans l'historiographie arabe médiéval (VI/XIIe–VII/XIIIe siècles)', *Bulletin d'études orientales*, 58 (2008–9), 88–90. See also the biography of Sadaqa in Ibn Khallikan, *Wafayat*, II, 402–3.

88 Ibn Khallikan, *Wafayat*, II, 404; Ibn al-Athir, *al-Kamil*, X, 385; Ibn al-Jawzi, *al-Muntazam*, XVI, 257; Hanne, *Putting the Caliph in his Place*, 137–8.

89 Ibn al-Athir, *al-Kamil*, X, 440–8; cf. Husayni, *Akhbar*, 80, who stresses that the sultan's forces were numerically inferior, but blames the defeat on muddy ground through which Sadaqa's horses could not pass. For accounts in English, see Sanaullah, *Decline*, 122–7; Bosworth, 'Political and Dynastic History', 115.

90 Ibn al-Jawzi, *al-Muntazam*, IX, 225; on Dubays, see Zouache, 'Dubays b. Ṣadaqa'; also the detailed biography in Ibn al-'Adim, *Bughya*, 225–50.

91 Ibn al-Jawzi, *al-Muntazam*, IX, 217–18; Ibn al-Athir, *al-Kamil*, X, 562.

92 Ibn al-Jawzi, *al-Muntazam*, IX, 252; Ibn al-Athir, *al-Kamil*, X, 610, 626.

93 See Tor, 'A Tale of Two Murders', 281–2; Hanne, *Putting the Caliph in his Place*, 150–9; Köymen, *Büyük Selçuklu İmparatorluğu Tarihi*, II, 91–112.

The vizier Anushirwan b. Khalid left in his memoirs (as quoted by Isfahani) a detailed description of the failings of the Seljuk state in Mahmud's reign. Many of these are attributed to the machinations of the vizier Abu 'l-Qasim al-Darguzini, the rival of both Isfahani's uncle 'Aziz al-Din and Anushirwan himself for office, and thus need to be treated with some circumspection.[94] We are told, for instance, that a Seljuk assault on the Ismaili stronghold of Alamut was also thwarted through the evil offices of Darguzini, who is accused of being an Ismaili sympathiser. The province of Fars, until this date 'in an excellent state . . . sending revenue consistently', is said to have been ruined by Darguzini conspiring against its governor. The chiefs of the Shabankara and Mazandaran were also alienated by Darguzini's behaviour and left the court for their castles and started to rebel, while even the sultan's slaves became increasingly unwilling to obey orders.[95]

Unfortunately, we have few independent sources to balance out this testimony. Still, it seems clear enough that finances lay at the root of these problems. One cause was the actions of Sanjar, who was able to use his position as Great Seljuk Sultan to award *iqṭā'ṣ* in the Sultanate of Iraq.[96] This may have been part of a deliberate strategy to weaken Mahmud, as Sanjar was clearly keen to assert authority in the west. His near-disaster at Sawa in 512/1118 discouraged him from intervening directly through military means, but his position as Mahmud's overlord and *al-sulṭān al-aʿẓam* allowed him to exert an indirect political authority there, which was manifested through appointments and granting *iqṭāʿs*.

Furthermore, Mahmud had to pay the price of buying the cooperation of amirs like Zangi in *iqṭāʿ* – Zangi received first the position of *shiḥna* of Iraq (516/1122–521/1127), and then the governorate of Mosul, which became his permanent base.[97] With the growing shortage of available lands as a result of these two factors, the sultan's personal estates had to be alienated to *iqṭāʿ* as a means of paying his amirs. As Isfahani puts it, after enumerating the territories lost to the sultan which comprised most of Iran and Iraq

> over each of these an amir had seized power; and what was left to the sultan was all distributed as *iqṭāʿ*. No revenue was raised from it and its income diminished. When the sultan had no personal land left (*khāṣṣ*), he had no more tax collectors (*ʿummāl*). The *dīwān* ceased to function . . .[98]

[94] See Peacock, 'Imad al-Din al-Isfahani's *Nusrat al-Fatra*', 80–5.

[95] Bundari, *Zubda*, 122–3. See also Bosworth, 'Political and Dynastic History', 123–4.

[96] Bundari, *Zubda*, 133. On the financial pressures, see also Durand-Guédy, *Iranian Elites*, 211.

[97] See S. Heidemann, 'Zangi', *EI²*.

[98] Bundari, *Zubda*, 122, 135 155; Husayni, *Akhbar*, 98–9; Durand-Guédy, *Iranian Elites*, 211.

The incessant competition for *iqṭā'* among the military elite was such that, as one of these amirs himself commented in some frustration, 'every day Mosul gets a new amir'.[99]

With the collapse in revenue, the bureaucrats seem to have turned on each other: the reign of Mahmud saw the growth of a ferocious factionalism, the effects of which were still being felt in bitter rivalries in the closing years of the twelfth century. Darguzini blamed the vizier Shams al-Mulk for destroying the glory of the sultanate – and, indeed, the latter was executed after a disastrous campaign into Shirwan – while Isfahani, predictably, credits his own uncle 'Aziz al-Din with reviving the kingdom during a brief period as *mustawfi*, having declined the vizierate, and savagely denounces Darguzini.[100] This instability is also suggested by the rapid turnover in viziers in the 1120s (below, pp. 101, 203–4).

Mahmud's increasingly precarious position only fuelled Sanjar's western ambitions. In the final years of Mahmud's reign, his uncle began to interfere ever more openly, marching on Rayy in 522/1128, and appointing Darguzini as vizier for his own daughter, Mahmud's wife.[101] Unable to win an outright victory militarily, Sanjar sought to use his prerogatives as Mahmud's suzerain to establish his own patronage networks in the west. Mahmud's brother, the *malik* Mas'ud, now resided at Sanjar's court, and his departure westwards in 524/1130 sparked rumours that he was going to fight Mahmud.[102]

Atabegs and *Maliks*

Seljuk princes were known as *maliks*, and at a young age, they were assigned a province as *iqṭā'* of which they were to be the nominal governor. In theory, the prince would be educated in the arts of fighting and governance he would need if he became ruler, a system which was also found in early Ottoman times. His education would be undertaken by an official known as an *atabeg*, a title which is not attested before Seljuk times although it may have antecedents in earlier Turkic empires, and it has been argued that a comparable term is found in the Orkhon inscriptions.[103] Typically,

[99] Ibn al-Athir, *al-Kamil*, X, 623. The quote is attributed to Aqsonqur al-Bursuqi.

[100] Bundari, *Zubda*, 140–1. On the rivalry, see further below p. 205.

[101] Ibn al-Athir, *al-Kamil*, X, 651–2; cf. Husayni, *Akhbar*, 99; Bundari, *Zubda*, 265, lists the following visits by Sanjar to the west: twice in the days of Mahmud; once under Tughrıl II; and twice under Mas'ud, although under Mas'ud he never went further than Rayy.

[102] Ibn al-Athir, *al-Kamil*, X, 666.

[103] On the atabegate, see Lambton, *Continuity and Change*, 229–33. The most detailed study remains M. Fuad Köprülü, 'Atabeg' s.v. 'Ata', *İslam Ansiklopedisi*, I, 711–18, where the possible Turkic antecedents are discussed.

the *atabeg* would be an amir, although the first individual attested to have held the office was the ubiquitous Nizam al-Mulk.[104]

Atabegs could acquire an immense degree of power, for possession of the person of a Seljuk prince allowed control over a potential claimant to the sultanate. Many *atabegs* remained in place when their *malik* became sultan, and there were no clear-cut rules in the mediaeval Islamic world about when a ruler had reached the age of majority.[105] Berkyaruq had been brought up by the *atabeg* Gümüshtegin, and when the former became sultan Gümüshtegin's 'orders were carried and his authority was so extensive it was as if he was his coregent' [*ka'annahu fi 'l-mulk shārikuhu*].[106]

Amirs might also set themselves up as rulers in their own right, legitimising themselves through the title of *atabeg* even when there was no *malik* to guard. In Damascus, for instance, the *atabeg* Tughtegin had been appointed as regent for the infant Tutush b. Duqaq in 496/1103; for some reason, he instead declared another prince, Ertash b. Tutush b. Alp Arslan, *malik* of Damascus. When Tutush b. Duqaq died in 298/1105, and Ertash fled, fearing for his life, Tughtegin was able to establish his own hereditary dynasty in Damascus, the Burids, which was recognised by Muhammad Tapar.[107]

The term could also be used purely as an honorific. Sa'd al-Dawla Yürünqüsh is known from Bundari and Ibn al-Athir to have been *shiḥna* of Baghdad from 518/1124 to 520/1126 and governor of Isfahan in about 536/1141. In between these two posts, numismatic evidence attests that he was governor of Nihawand from 521/1127 till at least 530/1135, and he minted his own coins, mentioning his own name alongside that of the senior sultan, Sanjar, and the junior, Mahmud.[108] He consistently describes himself on these coins as '*atabeg*', even though there is no evidence he ever had charge of a Seljuk prince.

104 Mirkhwand, *Rawdat al-Safa*, IV, 271, states that Alp Arslan made Nizam al-Mulk *atabeg*; Ibn al-Athir, *al-Kamil*, IX, 413, claims that Malikshah appointed Nizam al-Mulk as his own *atabeg* when he entrusted affairs to him shortly after acceding to the throne. Lambton is sceptical whether Nizam al-Mulk held the office of *atabeg*, but his use of the title is certain from contemporary inscriptions (see Köprülü, 'Atabeg').

105 See Konrad Hirschler, '"He is a Child and this Land is a Borderland of Islam": Under-age Rule and the Quest for Political Stability in the Ayyubid Period', *al-Masaq*, 19/i (2007), 34–7. The topic needs further investigation with regard to Seljuk practice, but superficially at any rate Hirschler's thesis seems to hold true. See further S. D. Goitein, 'Minority Self-rule and Government Control in Islam', *Studia Islamica*, 31 (1970), 101–16.

106 Bundari, *Zubda*, 83.

107 See Sevim, *Suriye ve Filistin Selçukluları*, 244–60; El-Azhari, *The Saljuqs of Syria*, 178–83, 186 on these events.

108 N. M. Lowick, 'Seljuq Coins', *Numismatic Chronicle*, 7th series, 10 (1970), 249–50.

The Succession Struggle and the Reign of Mas'ud

Mahmud died aged twenty-seven in 525/1131, and his death was immediately followed by chaos as competing parties sought to install their favoured candidates on the throne of the Sultanate of Iraq. Mas'ud and Mahmud's own son Da'ud had their backers (Qaraja, the governor of Fars, and Aqsonqur Ahmadili, governor of Azerbaijan, respectively), but eventually Tughrıl II b. Muhammad, who was supported by Sanjar, emerged victorious. Sanjar marched west as far as Hamadhan in 526/1131–2 to defeat Mas'ud and his brother Saljuqshah. However, as soon as Sanjar left for Transoxiana to quell a rebellion by the Qarakhanid Ahmad Khan, his protégé Tughrıl was challenged for the sultanate, first by Da'ud b. Mahmud, and then by Mas'ud.[109]

Tughrıl never came to Baghdad to be formally recognised as sultan.[110] On the contrary, in 527/1132–3, al-Mustarshid invested Mas'ud as sultan, and appointed Anushirwan b. Khalid as his vizier.[111] While the caliph sought to use his appointee to influence Mas'ud, he faced the powerful opposition of various Turkish elites: first, Mas'ud's *atabeg* Aqsonqur Ahmadili, then, after the latter's death, his successor, Yürünqüsh al-Bazdar. The Turkish amirs, however, did not form a unified front, and Mas'ud's wife Zubayda Khatun (Berkyaruq's daughter) also exerted a great influence on him, supported by the *atabeg* of Azerbaijan, Qarasonqur.[112] Thus, the jostling for power between rival Turkish and caliphal elites that was to characterise Mas'ud's reign was evident right from the start.

Despite his earlier acknowledgement by the caliph, the beginning of Mas'ud's reign is conventionally dated to 529/1134, when on Tughrıl's death he marched to Hamadhan to assert his right to the throne. Early on, he faced challenges from his nephew Da'ud, who was allied to Caliph al-Mustarshid, and then the latter's successor al-Rashid. These were not finally defeated

[109] Ibn al-Athir, *al-Kamil*, X, 681–2, 686–7; Husayni, *Akhbar*, 100-101, gives a much abridged account of Sanjar's advance, emphasising Tughrıl's reliance on Khurasani support. See also Bundari, *Zubda*, 158–63; Qummi, *Dhayl-i Nafthat al-Masdur*, 34–5, 58–9; Ibn Isfandiyar, *Tarikh-i Tabaristan*, II, 63–4; Hanne, *Putting the Caliph in his Place*, 159–61; Köymen, *Büyük Selçuklu İmparatorluğu Tarihi*, II, 174–203.

[110] Bundari, *Zubda*, 160, where predictably Abu 'l-Qasim al-Darguzini is blamed; Husayni, *Akhbar*, 101.

[111] Bundari, *Zubda*, 174, has end of Muharram 527/December 1132; Husayni, *Akhbar*, 102–3 has 25 Rabi' I/3 February 1133; Ibn al-Jawzi, *al-Muntazam*, XVII, 275, indicates the *khuṭba* was read for him as sultan in Safar 527/December 1132–January 1133; cf. Ibn al-Athir, *al-Kamil*, X, 686.

[112] Bundari, *Zubda*, 175–6.

until 532/1138 (see further Chapter 3).[113] Isfahan paid a heavy price for Mas'ud's victory, and the surrounding region was devastated by the constant campaigning, on top of bad harvests. 'Imad al-Din al-Isfahani, who witnessed these events in his youth, recalls how people were already fleeing the city and dying of hunger just as alien armies were billeted on them.[114] Nonetheless, the destruction may have been relatively localised. The fighting was a reflection of the importance of holding Isfahan for the credibility of any claimant to the sultanate.

In 533/1139, seeking a way out of the perennial crisis in the sultan's finances, Kamal al-Din Muhammad al-Khazin was appointed vizier. He seems to have initially had some success:

> Hearts relaxed and affairs were arranged properly. The vizier saw to it that monies were brought to the sultan's treasury along with taxes that he spared no efforts [in collecting]. He revived the customs of the kingdom which had gone into decline and arranged for the public interest ordinances which had fallen into oblivion. He started to break the oppressors and to restore those who had been downtrodden.[115]

Naturally this was not a popular programme with the 'oppressors' – by whom the amirs are meant. According to Isfahani, Kamal al-Din plotted with the sultan to break the power of the great amirs, starting with Qarasonqur. The latter, however, got wind of the plot, and advanced on the sultan at Hamadhan with an army 10,000 strong, plus two Seljuk princes he had managed to gain control of, Saljuqshah and Da'ud. He sent a letter stating the amirs' position in unambiguous terms:

> We do not trust the vizier Kamal, nor shall we endure what he is planning. Either kill or him hand him over to us, in which case we shall be obedient; but if you protect him, we will protect ourselves.[116]

This type of amiral 'obedience' was non-negotiable. Mas'ud had already fallen out with two of the other main amiral power-brokers, Boz-aba of Fars and Zangi of Mosul, and had no choice but to acquiesce immediately to Qarasonqur's demands. The presence of princes Saljuqshah and Da'ud with the enemy host was a sufficient reminder that Qarasonqur hardly lacked alternative candidates for the sultanate should he choose. Qarasonqur now appointed his own vizier, 'Izz al-Mulk al-Burujirdi, as the sultan's vizier, aiming to use him to

113 *Ibid.*, 185; Ibn al-Athir, *al-Kamil*, XI, 62, Ibn al-Jawzi, *al-Muntazam*, XVII, 332–3.
114 Bundari, *Zubda*, 180–1, 183–4.
115 *Ibid.*, 186. Further on him, see Qummi, *Dhayl-i Nafthat al-Masdur*, 134–42.
116 Bundari, *Zubda*, 187–8. See also Ibn al-Athir, *al-Kamil*, XI, 64

control Mas'ud. Henceforth, the appointment of viziers reflected less Mas'ud's choice than the preference of whichever amir was in the ascendant at a given moment.[117] Sensing where the balance of power lay, some bureaucrats actively sought out alliances with amirs to forward their own interests.[118] Just as under Mahmud, this amiral ascendancy had a financial as well as a political price in *iqṭāʿ*. As Ibn al-Athir put it: 'Affairs became difficult for Sultan Mas'ud and amirs demanded land without him having a choice [in the matter]. No land was left for him except the name of the sultanate, nothing else.'[119]

The amirs proved sufficiently entrenched that even their deaths did not profit the sultan. When Qarasonqur died in 535/1140–1, he was able to choose his own successor, another amir, Chavli Jandar, to whom he bequeathed 'all the lands of Qarasonqur in Arran and Azerbaijan, and appointed him over those fortresses, towns and cities [that he had possessed].'[120] 'Imad al-Din Zangi died in 541/1146, followed shortly by Chavli Jandar and Boz-aba of Fars, the latter falling in the course of a rebellion that aimed to install as sultan one of Mahmud's sons, Malikshah or Muhammad.[121] Zangi's son Nur al-Din succeeded him in Mosul and northern Syria, and Azerbaijan and Arran were seized by Mas'ud's *ḥājib* 'Abd al-Rahman Toghanyürek (whose name is sometimes distorted to read Tughayrak in the sources). The latter now became the major power in the state, imposing his own vizier, Abu 'l-Fath b. Darust, on the sultan.[122] In essence, the political dynamics of the Iranian world for next half century fell into place (see Map 2.1): Azerbaijan was the key to controlling the sultanate based in the Jibal; the Zangid lands in Mosul and northern Syria enjoyed a *de facto* independence, as did Fars, first under Boz-aba's wife, then under the his nephew Sonqur and his descendants, who became known as the Salghurid line of *atabegs*.[123]

The sultan's sole option was the traditional strategy of trying to manipulate the amirs' rivalries to his own advantage. Trapped by Toghanyürek and Ibn Darust, Mas'ud courted the favours of the Türkmen amir Khassbeg b. Palang-eri. Khassbeg was induced to murder Toghanyürek, and another over-powerful amir, Abbas, who in defiance of both Mas'ud and Sanjar had established himself in *de facto* independence in Rayy, refusing to remit

117 Cf. Lambton, *Continuity and Change*, 48.
118 Fairbanks, 'The Tarikh al-Vuzara', 198–204.
119 Ibn al-Athir, *al-Kamil*, XI, 64.
120 Bundari, *Zubda*, 191
121 *Ibid.*, 219; Ibn al-Athir, *al-Kamil*, XI, 116–7; Qummi, *Dhayl-i Nafthat al-Masdur*, 198–200.
122 Bundari, *Zubda*, 213; Ibn al-Athir, *al-Kamil*, XI, 104.
123 See B. Spuler, 'Atabakān-i Fārs', *EIr*; Erdoğan Merçil, *Fars Atabegleri Salgurlular* (Ankara, 1975).

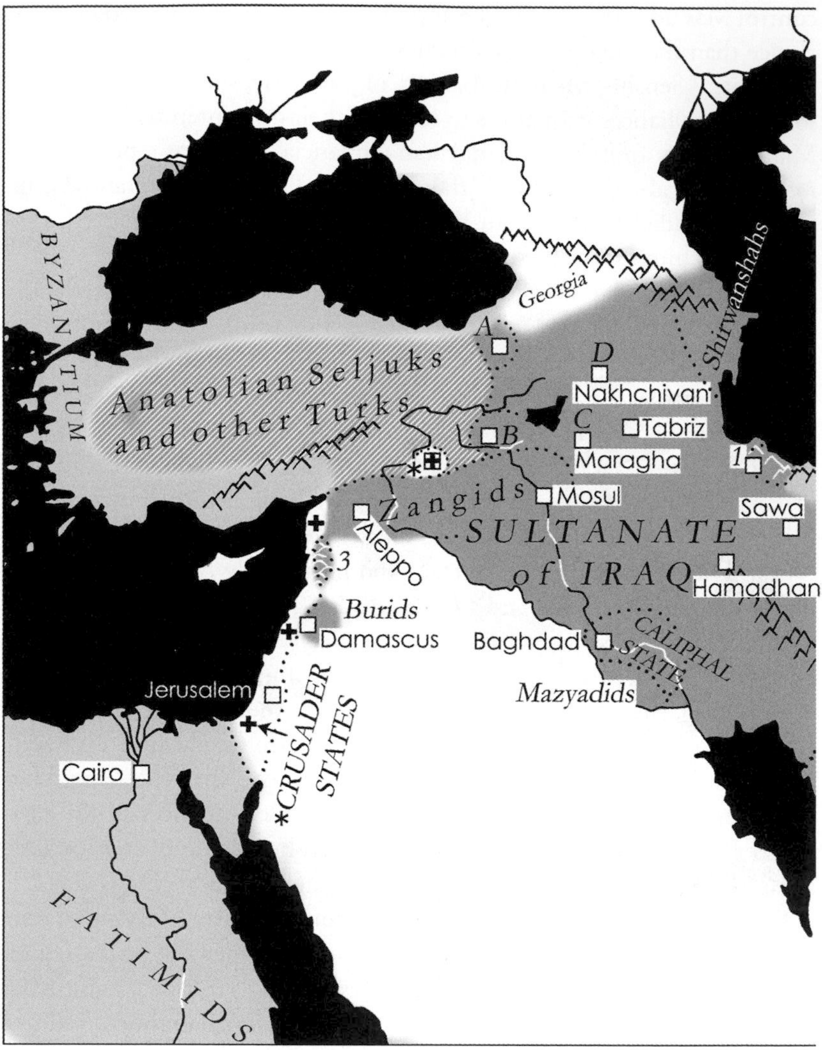

Map 2.1 The Seljuk Empire on the eve of the battle of Qatwan, 1141.
Key Ismaili territories: **1** Alamut, **2** Quhistan; **3** Jabal Ansariyya. Turkish states subject to the Sultanate of Iraq: **A** Saltuqids of Erzurum, **B** Artuqids, **C** Ahmadili *Atabegs* of Maragha, **D** Ildegüzids

revenue to the sultan, while seeking legitimacy by waging a bloody war on Ismailis in his province, such that, in Isfahani's words 'he built a minaret of their heads in Rayy from which the muezzins proclaimed the call to prayer'.[124]

[124] Bundari, *Zubda*, 191–2. See also Ibn Isfandiyar, *Tarikh-i Tabaristan*, II, 75.

The murders did the sultan little good either. His other amirs, especially a group from Azerbaijan led by Shams al-Din Ildegüz, feared they would be next. As ever, a convenient Seljuk, *malik* Muhammad b. Mahmud, the same prince whom Boz-aba had supported and whom Mas'ud had appointed as his successor and governor of Khuzistan after the failure of that revolt,[125]

[125] Bundari, *Zubda*, 222.

could be used as their figleaf for rebelling in 543/1147. Meanwhile, a second group of amirs coalesced around Malikshah. Mas'ud was summoned to Rayy by Sanjar, who attempted to resolve the crisis. Although Ibn al-Athir relates that Sanjar demanded Khassbeg's exile, Isfahani portrays the senior sultan as wholly ineffectual, readily giving in to Mas'ud's entreaties for Khassbeg.[126]

It is perhaps too easy to see only the flaws in these late Seljuk rulers. Certainly, some sources lambast Mas'ud for a dissolute lifestyle (see p. 176 below), but this may be an attempt by the chroniclers to represent impiety as leading to failure. Mas'ud's contemporary al-Fariqi judged that he was 'a just sultan, of mild disposition and so generous that he divided out all his territory amongst his associates, leaving himself only the name of sultan'.[127] Qummi also attributes the problems to Mas'ud's favouritism, claiming that he bestowed the *iqṭā's* of recently deceased amirs on Khassbeg.[128] This may well have been true, but the crisis was more deep-rooted than one personal favourite. Mas'ud did strive to curb amiral power, as his appointment of Kamal al-Din Muhammad and the murders of Toghanyürek and 'Abbas of Rayy suggest. On both occasions, other amirs had thwarted the sultan's moves to assert himself, and frustrated his attempts to build up an independent revenue stream. Mas'ud's failure may not have been a result of ineptitude, but rather the straitjacket of circumstances, or a combination of such factors.

The mere act of staying on the throne for two decades despite the constant revolts suggests considerable tenacity; and in terms of keeping caliphal ambitions in check and preserving at least a rump Seljuk Sultanate of Iraq based in the Jibal, Mas'ud had some successes. He benefited too from Sanjar's humiliation at the battle of Qatwan in 536/1141 (see below). To shore up his own position Sanjar had to write formally to Mas'ud 'permitting him to occupy Rayy in his own right according to the custom of Sultan Muhammad [Tapar], to gather armies and to reside in Rayy where he could be called on if necessary.'[129] On Mas'ud's death, Ibn al-Athir was able to write that 'the good fortune of the Seljuk dynasty died with him'.[130] However, the ultimate destruction of the empire was to come not from the west but from the east, where Sanjar had ruled supreme since the death of Muhammad Tapar.

126 Ibn al-Athir, *al-Kamil*, XI, 132–4; Bundari, *Zubda*, 222, 224; Qummi, *Dhayl-i Nafthat al-Masdur*, 201, 207–8.

127 Hillenbrand, *A Muslim Principality*, fol. 175a, p. 138.

128 Qummi, *Dhayl-i Nafthat al-Masdur*, 163.

129 Ibn al-Jawzi, *al-Muntazam*, XVIII, 26.

130 Ibn al-Athir, *al-Kamil*, XI, 160.

Crisis in the East, 1138–52

At first glance Sanjar's rule in the east as senior sultan seems to divide neatly into two phases.[131] In the first (*c.* 1118–38), an impression of invincibility was given by military feats such as the subjugation of Ghazna, whose ruler, Bahramshah, abandoned a rebellion after Sanjar marched his troops through the frozen mountains of an Afghan winter to confront him in his capital in 530/1135–6.[132] In the second phase, from *c.* 1138, the great sultan seemed increasingly beleaguered, beset by the constant rebellions of his vassal Atsız, governor of Khwarazm; a cataclysmic defeat by the invading Qarakhitay in 536/1141; the rebellion of the vassal ruler of remote Ghur, 'Ala' al-Din, which although defeated, did not prevent the emergence of the Ghurids as a major power in the Islamic east;[133] and, finally, the great Türkmen rebellion of 547/1152 in which the sultan was himself captured, dying in 552/1157 shortly after his release from three years' imprisonment by the Ghuzz.

Despite his immense resources,[134] deriving from his control of some of the most prosperous areas of the Islamic world and their connecting trade routes, Sanjar's power was even in the early phase more limited than it first appears. We have noted above his inability to impose his will on the Sultanate of Iraq, obliging him to recognise Mahmud and accept Sultan Mas'ud in place of his favoured candidate, Tughrıl. Amirs in the east frequently rebelled against Sanjar, while the eastern sultanate experienced exactly the same rapid turnover in the bureaucracy as the west in the late 1120s before the descendants of Nizam al-Mulk managed to gain more or less permanent control over the vizierate of Khurasan.[135] These factors suggest that the factionalism that plagued the bureaucracy in the Sultanate of Iraq was present in the east too, along with weak sultanic power. Isfahani – our most detailed source – portrays Sanjar as a capricious character unable to control his passions for drink and youths. He bestowed his affections on a series of slaves to whom he gave virtually unlimited power and wealth, although his love invariably turned to

131 For overviews, see Bosworth, 'Political and Dynastic History', 140–55; Tor, 'Sanjar, Aḥmad b. Malekšāh'; Köymen, *Büyük Selçuklu İmparatorluğu Tarihi*, II, *passim*; Agadshanow, *Der Staat der Seldshukiden*, 240–308.

132 Husayni, *Akhbar*, 92; Ibn al-Athir, *al-Kamil*, XI, 28–9.

133 Ibn al-Athir, *al-Kamil*, XI, 164; Minhaj-i Siraj Juzjani, *Tabaqat-i Nasiri*, ed. 'Abd al-Hayy Habibi (Tehran, 1363), I, 346–8; Nishapuri, *Saljuqnama*, 60; see further Bosworth, 'Ghurids', *EIr*; Köymen, *Büyük Selçuklu İmparatorluğu Tarihi*, II, 156–8, 353–60.

134 On Sanjar's wealth, see Bundari, *Zubda*, 275; Husayni, *Akhbar*, 124–5.

135 On amiral revolts against Sanjar, see D. G. Tor, '*Mamlūk* Loyalty: Evidence from the Late Saljūq Period', *Asiatische Studien*, 45/iii (2011), 775–80; on Sanjar's viziers, see Bundari, *Zubda*, 265–71; Klausner, *The Seljuk Vezirate*, 107; Iqbal, *Wizarat*, 191–278.

hatred, resulting in the death of the current favourite.[136] Isfahani even accuses the sultan of plotting with the Ismailis to dispose of one unwanted favourite, Jawhar.[137] As ever, it is hard to discern how much of this is simply literary fiction to explain Sanjar's ultimate humiliation and demise by portraying him as an unworthy ruler.

Problems first reared their head in Khwarazm, which was ruled by Atsız, a member of a *mamlūk* dynasty that had controlled this distant and historically always independent-minded province as Seljuk vassals since 491/1097–8.[138] Although the Khwarazmian court poet and bureaucrat Rashid al-Din Watwat wrote a triumphant qasida proclaiming,

> King Atsız ascended the throne of his kingdom: the
> Luck of Seljuk and his family came to an end,[139]

in fact, Atsız was an obedient vassal for most his first decade as ruler of Khwarazm. In 553/1138, however, Sanjar was obliged to march on Khwarazm in response to Atsız's usurpation of the sultan's privileges, in particular, it seems, his assertion of suzerain rights over the nomads of Jand and Manqishlaq.[140] Atsız was duly deposed and his son killed in battle with Sanjar's forces. Although Khwarazm was allotted in *iqṭāʿ* to Sanjar's nephew Sulaymanshah, as soon as Sanjar returned to Merv, Atsız returned to power, supported by the people of Khwarazm who had learned to hate Sanjar's soldiery.[141] As events in both halves of the empire so often underlined,

[136] Bundari, *Zubda*, 266–8, 271–3.

[137] *Ibid.*, 273–4.

[138] For the background, see İbrahim Kafesoğlu, *Harezmşahlar Devleti Tarihi (485–618/1092–1221)* (Ankara, 1956), 25–44; Ghulam Rabbani Aziz, *A Short History of the Khwarazmshahs* (Karachi, 1978), i–viii, 1–5; A. Sevim and C. E. Bosworth, 'The Seljuqs and the Khwarazm Shahs', in M. S. Asimov and C. E. Bosworth (eds), *History of Civilizations of Central Asia, vol. IV: The Age of Achievement.* A.D. *750 to the End of the Fifteenth Century, Part One: The Historical, Social and Economic Setting* (Delhi, 1999), 145–75; and Z. M. Buniyatov, *Gosudarstvo Khorezmshakhov-Anushteginidov, 1097–1231* (Moscow, 1986), 6–31. On Khwarazm, see further Barthold, *Turkestan*, 142–55, 296, 323 ff; Bosworth, 'Political and Dynastic History', 140–3.

[139] Cited by Juvaini, *History of the World Conqueror*, trans. J. A. Boyle (Manchester, 1997), 281.

[140] This is the convincing interpretation of Jürgen Paul, 'Sanjar and Atsız: Independence, Lordship and Literature', in Jürgen Paul (ed.), *Nomad Aristocrats in a World of Empires* (Wiesbaden, 2013), esp. 87–9, 93, 109–11, 115, although this is nowhere directly stated in the sources.

[141] Ibn al-Athir, *al-Kamil*, XI, 67; Bundari, *Zubda*, 278–9; Juvaini, *History*, trans. Boyle, 278–84, for an account of Seljuq–Khwarazmian relations. In general, see the discussion in Paul, 'Sanjar and Atsız'; also Kafesoğlu, *Harezmşahlar Devleti Tarihi*, 44–65; Aziz, *Short History*

without being physically present it was extremely hard for the sultan to exert his will, and gains would often be reversed as soon as his back was turned.

Broader political and demographic changes turned Sanjar's Khwarazmian problem into a full-scale disaster for the Seljuks. The twelfth century witnessed an increase in nomadism in Central Asia.[142] Turkish groups like the Ghuzz and the Qarluqs, who were at least nominally Muslim, seem to have been growing in strength, but were rapidly becoming difficult for established powers such as the Qarakhanids and the Seljuks to manage. At the same time, the Qarakhitay were starting to encroach on Islamic Central Asia,[143] their prestige undiminished by the initial defeat of their leader (the Gurkhan), Yelü Dashi, at Kashghar by the Seljuks' Qarakhanid vassals in 1131.[144] Indeed, they were soon enmeshed in Qarakhanid politics, while Atsız sought to profit from the presence of this new power to strengthen his own hand.

Both the growing nomad problem in the region and Atsız's personal ambitions have been cited as reasons for the Qarakhitay intervention. As early as 1130 the western Qarakhanid ruler Arslan Khan was finding it impossible to control the Qarluq nomads, who also comprised a good part of his army, and was obliged to call on Sanjar for help. A few years later, around 1134, the Qarakhanid ruler of Balasaghun asked Yelü Dashi for help against his own Qarluq and Qangli nomads. He got rather more than he bargained for: the Qarakhitay occupied Balasaghun itself, where they pitched their tents and henceforth made their capital. A further confrontation with the Qarakhanids in 531/1137 gave them control of the Farghana valley and the road into Transoxiana, the heart of Islamic Central Asia.[145]

Sanjar, for all his bellicosity against less powerful neighbours such as the Ghurids and Ghaznavids, does not seem to have been anxious to move to protect his Qarakhanid vassals and initially underestimated the Qarakhitay threat. A letter written from Sanjar's chancery dated 527/1133 refers to the Qarakhitay defeat at Kashghar,[146] while the Delhi historian Juzjani tells us that Sanjar even granted the Qarakhitay permission to move into pastures in Balasaghun, Qayalıq and Almalıq[147] – all Qarakhanid territories.

of the Khwarazmshahs, 4–11; and Buniyatov, *Gosudarstvo Khorezmshakhov-Anushteginidov*, 6–28.

142 See Michal Biran, *The Empire of the Qara Khitai in Eurasian History: Between China and the Islamic World* (Cambridge, 2005), 33–5, 46, 140.

143 See *ibid., passim*.

144 *Ibid.*, 37.

145 *Ibid.*, 41–2; Juzjani, *Tabaqat*, I, 261–2.

146 Bartol'd, *Turkestan v Epokhu Mongolskogo Nashestviya. Chast' 1: Teksty*, 37.

147 Juzjani, *Tabaqat*, I, 261, II, 94; Biran, *Empire of the Qara Khitai*, 39–40.

Khwarazm remained Sanjar's main concern, starting with his punitive campaign of 553/1138, the year after the Qarakhitay advance into Farghana. In 534/1139–40, Atsız sacked Bukhara; a show of force by Sanjar the following year bought him to submission again. A mere four months later, Sanjar was obliged to march to Samarqand to confront the Qarakhitay in Safar 536/ October 1141. Battle was met at Qatwan on the steppe outside the city: the Muslim and Chinese sources differ as to the details, the former claiming Sanjar was massively outnumbered. The result, however, is not in dispute: the Seljuk army suffered appalling losses, Sanjar's wife was captured, and Sanjar himself barely escaped with his life, fleeing ignominiously to Tirmidh and then Balkh. The Qarakhitay were able to establish themselves permanently in Transoxiana,[148] while to the west Atsız plundered his way through Khurasan.[149] In Merv he sat on the Seljuk throne before making off with the Sanjar's treasure chests; for several weeks in 536–7/spring 1142 Sanjar's name was dropped from the *khuṭba* in Nishapur and replaced with the Khwarazmshah's. Out of fear of the Qarakhitay Sanjar was unable to intervene.[150]

The Qarakhitay invasion thus worked out very nicely for Atsız, and several mediaeval sources suggest he incited Yelü Dashi's attack on Sanjar, both in order to free himself from his Seljuk overlord and to gain revenge for the death of his son during one of Sanjar's campaigns against Khwarazm; certainly, he does seem to have had a formal alliance with Yelü Dashi which was sealed with a dynastic marriage.[151] However, the Qarluqs seem to have been an equally important factor in prompting Qarakhitay intervention. In response to Qarakhanid requests, Sanjar had expelled the Qarluqs from his domains. The nomads took refuge with the Qarakhitay ruler – himself a tent-dwelling nomad – and encouraged his attack. Yelü Dashi had written to Sanjar asking him to forgive the Qarluqs, to which Sanjar responded by arrogantly demanding the Gurkhan's conversion to Islam and threatening him with his military might.[152]

The greatest consequence of Qatwan was less the vast number of dead than the damage to Sanjar's reputation. He lost the confidence of his amirs,[153] and with the conquest of Nishapur, Atsız seems to have openly proclaimed

[148] Bundari, *Zubda*, 278; Husayni, *Akhbar*, 94; Ibn al-Athir, *al-Kamil*, XI, 86; Juzjani, *Tabaqat*, I, 262.

[149] Bundari, *Zubda*, 280–1; Husayni, *Akhbar*, 93, 95; Ibn al-Athir, *al-Kamil*, XI, 81, 85–6.

[150] Ibn al-Athir, *al-Kamil*, XI, 87–88; Paul, 'Sanjar and Atsız', 99–101.

[151] Ibn al-Jawzi, *al-Muntazam*, XVIII, 19.

[152] Bundari, *Zubda*, 277; Husayni, *Akhbar*, 93; Ibn al-Athir, *al-Kamil*, XI, 85; Paul, 'Sanjar and Atsız', 97–8; Biran, *Empire of the Qara Khitai*, 42.

[153] Bundari, *Zubda*, 276.

his intention to supplant the Seljuk state,[154] the first time a vassal had seriously challenged the legitimacy of Seljuk rule. Indeed, the news even spread to Europe, for the Crusades chronicler Otto of Freising (d. 1158) recorded a confused account of Qatwan which identified the Buddhist Yelü Dashi with the legendary Christian king of the east, Prester John, who would save Christianity from the Muslim menace.[155]

None of these factors constituted a fatal blow to Sanjar. Yelü Dashi never followed up his conquests with an invasion further west,[156] and the establishment of a nominal Qarakhitay suzerainty over Transoxiana and Khwarazm did not affect the core lands of Seljuk Khurasan. The decade after Qatwan actually witnessed a distinct revival in Sanjar's fortunes, and Atsız proved unable to hold his gains in Khurasan. In 1143, Yelü Dashi died and Sanjar recovered sufficiently to besiege Atsız in his capital of Khwarazm in 438/1144.[157] The success of this expedition is unclear: while some sources indicate that he extracted oaths of allegiance from the Khwarazmshah, this may just have been a face-saving device. Atsız seems to have been caught in the rather awkward position of being both a Seljuk and a Qarakhitay vassal; however, a series of coins he struck between 538 and 540/1143–4 and 1145–6 mentioned not Sanjar, but the western sultan Mas'ud as his suzerain,[158] suggesting the limitations of Sanjar's authority. Yet Sanjar appears on later coins, possibly as a result of a third expedition the sultan may have sent against Khwarazm in 542–3/1147–8.[159] Even Transoxiana may have reverted to Seljuk sovereignty in some form, albeit briefly, for a coin struck in Bukhara in 541/1146–7, shows the Qarakhanid Ibrahim as vassal of both Sanjar and the Qarakhitay.[160] To the south, Sanjar launched a successful campaign against Ghur in 547/1152.[161] Thus, despite Qatwan,

154 For Atsız's victory proclamation in Nishapur, see Bartol'd, *Turkestan v Epokhu Mongolskogo Nashestviya. Chast' 1: Teksty*, 43–4; also Paul, 'Sanjar and Atsız', 99.

155 Otto, Bishop of Freising, *The Two Cities: A Chronicle of Universal History to the Year 1146 AD*, trans. Charles Christopher Mierow (New York, 1966), VII.33, p. 443. See also Biran, *Empire of the Qara Khitai*, 45.

156 Biran, *Empire of the Qara Khitai*, 45.

157 For a full discussion, see Paul, 'Sanjar and Atsız', 101–3, who proposes the expedition might be dated to the previous year; Ibn al-Athir, *al-Kamil*, XI, 95–6; Bundari, *Zubda*, 280; Husayni, *Akhbar*, 94–5; Juvaini, *History*, 282; Biran, *Empire of the Qara Khitai*, 49.

158 Paul, 'Sanjar and Atsız', 104.

159 Juvaini, *History*, 282; Paul, 'Sanjar and Atsız', 105.

160 Biran, *Empire of the Qara Khitai*, 49; cf. Paul, 'Sanjar and Atsız', 105, n. 109; Kochnev, *Numizmaticheskaya Istoriya Karakhanidskogo Kaganata*, 225.

161 Juzjani, *Tabaqat*, I, 346–7; Nishapuri, *Saljuqnama*, 60; Köymen, *Büyük Selçuklu İmparatorluğu Tarihi*, II, 374–82.

Sanjar retained the capability to assert a degree of suzerainty, at least at times, in this fractious region.

While the collapse of the Seljuk Empire in the east was not a direct result of Qatwan, the Qarakhitay infiltration had profound consequences in displacing the nomads from their traditional pasturelands. As a result, large numbers started to settle around Balkh, to the consternation of Qumaj, the local governor (and Sanjar's former *atabeg*).[162] An offer by the Ghuzz to pay 200 silver dirhams per household to be allowed to stay on their pastures was rejected for reasons that are not entirely clear.[163] Other causes of tension that the sources point to are personal animosity between the Ghuzz and Qumaj,[164] and resentment at excessive demands for taxes from the nomads (in the form of livestock) by Sanjar's court.[165] In addition, the Ghuzz leaders seem to have been in cahoots with Atsız.[166] The cause was certainly not, as later traditions alleged, that the sedentarised Seljuks had become inimical to Türkmen *per se*.[167] On the contrary, Sanjar's *dīwān* issued instructions to the official in charge of the Türkmen of Dihistan, for instance, to establish good relations with the Türkmen, to assist in securing them necessities like pasture. Chancery documents referred specifically to the kinship (*ṣilat al-arḥām*) of the sultans and the nomads.[168] It was thus not any broader anti-nomad policy, but rather local conditions in Balkh, resentment at taxation, the disruption on the steppe caused by the Qarakhitay, and the unwillingness or inability of Seljuk authorities to accommodate the displaced nomads, which combined to foment the great

162 Biran, *Empire of the Qara Khitai*, 51, 140; Husayni, *Akhbar*, 93; Ibn al-Athir, *al-Kamil*, XI, 177; cf. *ibid.*, XI, 179–80, which gives a variant of the first account.

163 Ibn al-Athir, *al-Kamil*, XI, 176; cf. Nishapuri, *Saljuqnama*, 62–3.

164 Bundari, *Zubda*, 281–3, has Qumaj apparently as the *shiḥna* of the Türkmen (although this precise word is not used: *wa-kānat [al-Turkmān] fi ihtimām al-amīr Qumaj*), who were initially loyal to the Seljuks: poor relations between them and Qumaj resulted in their murder of Qumaj's son and then a full-scale rebellion. Nonetheless, as soon as they realised the sultanic forces were mustered against them they offered to come to terms, surrender the murderers and pay tribute, but this was rejected by the sultan. Ibn al-Athir, *al-Kamil*, XI, 179, also indicates that Qumaj had initially been associated with the Ghuzz.

165 Nishapuri, *Saljuqnama*, 61.

166 See the letter from the Khwarazmian court to the Ghuzz leader Tuti (which must be dated to *c.* 551/1156), referring to their earlier relationship: Rashid al-Din Watwat, *Namaha-yi Rashid al-Din Watwat*, ed. Qasim Tuisirkani (Tehran, 1372), 29.

167 See A. C. S. Peacock, 'Seljuq Legitimacy in Islamic History', in C. Lange and S. Mecit (eds), *The Seljuqs: Politics, Society and Culture* (Edinburgh, 2011), 80–1.

168 Juwayni, *'Atabat al-Kataba*, 80–1, 85; Durand-Gúedy, 'The Türkmen–Saljuq Relationship', 46, 47–51.

Figure 2.1 The walls of Sultankala, the Seljuk city of Merv

Ghuzz revolt that broke out in Balkh in 547/1152, bringing down the Great Seljuk Empire.[169]

Five Disastrous Years: The Disintegration of the Seljuk Empire, 1152–7

Over the years 547–52/1152–7, the Seljuk state in both the east and the west unravelled. The west, as we have seen, had been beset by political problems at least since the death of Muhammad Tapar. Yet it was the Sultanate of Iraq that was to prove more resilient than Khurasan, where the Ghuzz uprising permanently destroyed Seljuk rule.

Seljuk armies sent against Balkh were rebuffed, and in the course of fighting Sanjar himself was captured along with his wife Terken Khatun. In 548/1153, the Ghuzz advanced on Merv. The city seems to have been barely defended; its walls (Figure. 2.1), perhaps, were built for show rather than protection,[170] and little effort was made to oppose the Ghuzz bands that seemingly came from nowhere in scenes reminiscent of the Seljuks' own emergence just over a century previously. Sanjar's captors made every protestation of loyalty, but these could not mask the brutal reality. Merv with its palaces, mosques, libraries and pleasure gardens was sacked and its inhabitants taken captive. The Ghuzz leader Bakhtiyar demanded to be granted Merv itself as *iqṭāʿ*, and when Sanjar protested that 'this is the abode of kingship (*dār al-mulk*) and should not be given as *iqṭāʿ* to anyone', he was greeted with derisive laughter.[171] For the next three years, Sanjar remained a captive

[169] For a more detailed study of the Ghuzz revolt, see Köymen, *Büyük Selçuklu İmparatorluğu Tarihi*, II, 398–445.

[170] See Chapter 6, p. 241 below.

[171] Ibn al-Athir, *al-Kamil*, XI, 177.

of the Ghuzz, frequently confined to a cage as a symbol of his humiliation. His court poet, Anwari, wrote a desperate plea for aid to the Qarakhanids, the famous qasida known as 'The Tears of Khurasan':

> O morning breeze if you pass by Samarqand,
> Bring the letter of the people of Khurasan to the [Qarakhanid] Khaqan;
> A letter whose beginning is bodily grief and affliction of soul,
> A letter whose end is heartache and sorrow . . .
> At the doors of the lowborn the noble stand sorrowful and bewildered,
> The virtuous are captive and restrained in the hands of pleasure seekers.
> You do not see any man happy but at death's door,
> You do not find a virgin girl save in her mother's womb.
> The congregational mosque of each city has become the stables
> For [the Ghuzz's] beasts; neither roof nor door is visible.
> They do not [even] read the *khuṭba* in the name of the Ghuzz because
> In Khurasan now there is neither preacher [*khaṭīb*] nor pulpit [*minbar*]'.[172]

While the Ghuzz marauded at will over Khurasan, the Seljuk amirs of the east began the search for an alternative representative of legitimate authority. On 19 Jumada II 548/11 September 1153 Sanjar's nephew Sulaymanshah b. Muhammad reached Nishapur and was installed as sultan.[173] Sulaymanshah proved to be wholly ineffective at putting an end to Ghuzz depredations, and he fled Khurasan in Safar 549/April-May 1154.[174] A group of amirs then called on Sanjar's nephew Mahmud Khan, who was of mixed Seljuk and Qarakhanid descent.[175] He faced opposition not just from the Ghuzz, but also from Sanjar's powerful *mamlūk* al-Mu'ayyad Ay Aba, who expelled the Ghuzz from much of western Khurasan and established himself in Nishapur as an effective and popular ruler.[176] Rayy, too, fell to another Sanjari *mamlūk*, Inanj,[177] while Herat was controlled by the *mamlūk* Sonqur al-'Azizi.[178]

172 *Diwan-i Anwari*, Introduction by Sa'id Nafisi (Tehran, 1376), 196, 197.

173 Ibn al-Athir, *al-Kamil*, XI, 180; on Sulaymanshah, see also Paul, 'Sanjar and Atsız', 94.

174 Ibn al-Athir, *al-Kamil*, XI, 181–2; Qummi, *Dhayl-i Nafthat al-Masdur*, 304–7; Ibn Isfandiyar, *Tarikh-i Tabaristan*, II, 90.

175 He was the son of Sanjar's sister who had married the Qarakhanid Muhammad b. Bughrakhan. Ibn al-Athir, *al-Kamil*, XI, 183; Bundari, *Zubda*, 284. See also Ibn Isfandiyar, *Tarikh-i Tabaristan*, I, 108–9, 113, II, 90.

176 On him, see further Ibn al-Athir, *al-Kamil*, XI, 225–6, 231–3, 236, 259–60; Qummi, *Dhayl-i Nafthat al-Masdur*, 228, 300–1.

177 Ibn al-Athir, *al-Kamil*, XI, 183–4; Husayni, *Akhbar*, 134; Qummi, *Dhayl-i Nafthat al-Masdur*, 317.

178 Ibn al-Athir, *al-Kamil*, XI, 227.

For once in Seljuk history, *mamlūk* loyalty did actually prove to be worth something. In 551/1156, al-Mu'ayyad Ay Aba managed to rescue his master Sanjar from captivity in Balkh, smuggling him in a boat to safety on the opposite side of the Oxus.[179] From the town of Tirmidh, Sanjar proclaimed the restoration of his sultanate. Surprisingly, perhaps, given his double humiliation of Qatwan and the Ghuzz rebellion, this does seem to have been taken seriously. The Khwarazmian bureaucrat Rashid al-Din Watwat wrote a letter on behalf of his master Atsız congratulating Sanjar on 'the arrival of your victorious standards to the abode of kingship, Tirmidh', crawlingly expressing his 'everlong desire to serve' and his apologies for 'previous shortcomings'.[180] That there was some substance to these sentiments is suggested by a separate letter Rashid al-Din sent to Tuti, one of the main Ghuzz leaders and a Khwarazmian ally, advising him bluntly to apologise now that Sanjar has been restored to 'the abode of kingship Tirmidh, great and honoured among his servants'.[181] Ibn al-Athir too states that Sanjar's 'kingdom was nearly restored to him'.[182]

In reality Sanjar's position was distinctly weak. Khurasan had now been ravaged by the Ghuzz for three years, and initially the sultan did not even dare leave Tirmidh to return to Merv. When he did, Nishapuri tells us, he found, 'his treasury empty, his kingdom ruined, his people dispersed and his army lost'.[183] He died in Rabi I 552/April 1157 aged seventy-two, about a year after his release from captivity, and two or three months after entering Merv,[184] and was buried in the great mausoleum he had built in the heart of the city (Figure. 2.2). The Great Seljuk Empire could not be reconstituted. In many areas, Ghuzz depredations continued,[185] alongside inter-communal blood-letting between members of rival madhhabs and between Turks and Ismailis.[186] Mahmud Khan was recognised by al-Mu'ayyad Ay Aba as suzerain, and indeed was even proclaimed by Watwat on behalf of the Khwarazmians as 'a king with imperial lineage from both

179 Nishapuri, *Saljuqnama*, 67; and see also the discussion in Köymen, *Büyük Selçuklu İmparatorluğu Tarihi*, II, 454–9.

180 Rashid al-Din Watwat, *Namaha*, 6, 10–11.

181 *Ibid.*, 30–1.

182 Ibn al-Athir, *al-Kamil*, XI, 210, 222.

183 Nishapuri, *Saljuqnama*, 68.

184 Bundari, *Zubda*, 255; Ibn al-Athir, *al-Kamil*, XI, 210, 222. For the date of Sanjar's release from captivity, wrongly given by Ibn al-Athir as Ramadan 551/October 1156, see Köymen, *Büyük Selçuklu İmparatorluğu Tarihi*, II, 454; Barthold, *Turkestan Down to the Mongol Invasion*, 330, who establish that he must have been released in Safar 551/April 1156.

185 Ibn al-Athir, *al-Kamil*, XI, 222–3, 230–3.

186 *Ibid.*, XI, 234–6, 238, 250.

Figure 2.2 The mausoleum of Sanjar, Sultankala, Merv

ancestors, on one side the noble house of Seljuk – may it last until eternity – and on the other, the noble house of Afrasiyab [the Qarakhanids]'.[187] This august lineage was not enough to secure Mahmud Khan's position, and al-Mu'ayyad seized the opportunity to kill him and his son at Nishapur in 557/1062, definitively ending any attempts by a Seljuk claimant to exercise effective rule in the east.[188] Khurasan remained convulsed by disorder as Khwarazmians, Ghurids, Qarakhitay and Ghuzz all fought over it, until at last in the late twelfth century a fragile political unity was restored to the region under the descendants of Atsız. Individual cities and regions were affected to varying degrees, depending on the strength of their fortifications and the competence of their leadership. The occasional rhetorical assertion of suzerainty aside, no material help was forthcoming from the remnants of the Seljuk sultanate in the west.[189]

In the Sultanate of Iraq, meanwhile, competing groups sought to install their favoured candidate as sultan on the death of Masʿud in 547/1152,

[187] Rashid al-Din Watwat, *Namaha*, 14.

[188] Ibn al-Athir, *al-Kamil*, XI, 273.

[189] On the situation in Khurasan in the aftermath of Sanjar's death, see Köymen, *Büyük Selçuklu İmparatorluğu Tarihi*, II, 467–75; Bosworth, 'Political and Dynastic History', 157–66; K. A. Luther, 'The End of Saljuq Domination in Khurasan', in Louis L. Orlin (ed.), *Michigan Oriental Studies in Honor of George G. Cameron* (Ann Arbor, 1976), 219–25.

the same year as the Ghuzz revolt began.[190] Over the next five years, the main contenders for power were: Muhammad b. Mahmud, the last Seljuk to aspire to assert himself as ruler until Tughrıl III; the Caliph al-Muqtafi (r. 530/1136–555/1160), who sought to turn the tables on the Seljuks by manipulating their succession disputes to ensure a pliant sultan who would maximise his own freedom for manoeuvre; and rival groups of Seljuk amirs, who may be divided into two main groups, one made up largely of amirs from the Jibal, who backed Muhammad, and their rivals, the amirs of northwestern Iran, led by the *atabeg* Nusrat al-Din Arslan Aba b. Aqsonqur Ahmadili, ruler of Maragha, and Ildegüz, the governor of the south Caucasian province of Arran, who has been described as 'the very personification of the problem of amiral disloyalty'.[191] There were also two other contenders for the sultanate: Muhammad's brother Malikshah and Sulaymanshah, both described as drink-besotted pleasure-addicts, but still useful enough for any amir who sought to challenge Muhammad.[192]

Immediately after Masʿud's death, Malikshah III was placed on the throne by the late sultan's old favourite, the great amir Khassbeg b. Palangeri who, naturally enough, sought to amass *iqṭāʿs* and wealth at Malikshah's expense, while, we are told, the new sultan devoted his days to pleasure and drinking. For reasons which are not entirely obvious if Malikshah was as pliant a candidate as the sources claim, Khassbeg resolved to replace him with Muhammad. The other amirs, anxious to cut both sultan and amir down to size, assented to Khassbeg's plan, but at the same time secretly resolved to set Muhammad against him. Muhammad's accession in Safar 548/April–May 1153 was thus accompanied by the killing of Khassbeg.[193] Muhammad seems to have aspired to assert his authority as ruler, and sent Khassbeg's head to his two most powerful amirs, Ildegüz of Arran and Nusrat al-Din Khassbeg b. Aqsonqur of Maragha in the hope that it would inspire them with fear and bring them to obedience. In fact, they drew the opposite lesson: that the new ruler presented a danger and must be opposed.[194] Just as Sultan Masʿud had found, bringing the amirs to heel was truly the Gordian knot of Seljuk politics. Unsurprisingly, the ill-fated Muhammad II b. Mahmud was unable to solve the perennial problem of

[190] Luther, 'Political Transformation', is the most detailed guide to the convoluted politics of the period in Iraq.

[191] *Ibid.*, 94.

[192] *Ibid.*, 35–6, 40.

[193] Ibn al-Athir, *al-Kamil*, XI, 161–2; Bundari, *Zubda*, 227–30; Qummi, *Dhayl-i Nafthat al-Masdur*, 212–14.

[194] Bundari, *Zubda*, 231.

the sultans of Iraq, amiral usurpation of sultanic *iqṭā's*. Moreover, in the chaotic conditions of the year 548/1152–3, when the Seljuk throne in Hamadhan was held by no fewer than three rival contenders, the amirs were able to usurp even more land for themselves.[195]

Meanwhile, Caliph al-Muqtafi li-Amr Allah sought to exploit the power vacuum by asserting his authority outside Baghdad, the first caliph to exercise effective power in Iraq since the early tenth century.[196] The caliphal vizier, Ibn Hubayra, received all the territories in *iqṭā'* that had previously belonged to the sultan's vizier, a clear demonstration of where power now lay.[197] He was even granted by the caliph the title *'Sulṭān al-'Irāq'*, previously a Seljuk prerogative, and suggestive of the caliph's ultimate ambition to destroy the dynasty that had been a millstone round the 'Abbasids' neck for a century.[198] A caliphal army captured al-Hilla and Wasit and besieged Tikrit, which the last Seljuk *shiḥna* of Baghdad, Mas'ud al-Bilali, had made his base.[199] In Tikrit two other Seljuks were imprisoned, the deposed Malikshah III and *malik* Arslan b. Tughrıl b. Muhammad. The latter was used by Mas'ud al-Bilali to legitimise his fight against the caliph to the army, especially the Türkmen, suggesting the enduring power of the Seljuk name as a token for legitimacy among a nomadic audience.[200]

A Seljuk prince in the wrong hands represented a potential challenger for Muhammad's throne. With the caliph's defeat of Mas'ud Bilal and his supporters at Bakimza in Rajab 459/September 1155, Arslan b. Tughrıl was spirited away to the amir Ildegüz, who had married his mother and proceeded to use the *malik* as the justification for the rapid expansion of his power. It was in the wake of this disaster, whereby he had been dragged into conflict with the caliph at the behest of his amirs only to lose, and furthermore producing a potential hostage to fortune in the form of Arslan, that Muhammad seems to have decided on a more proactive policy to save the sultanate.

Muhammad's efforts to assert his rule took three principal forms: he tried to clip the wings of the most powerful of his amirs; he sought to address the financial problems which beset the sultanate; and he aspired to install himself in Baghdad, the possession of which was traditionally one of the symbols of legitimate Seljuk rule. The latter would require force, and thus cash. To this end he appointed Shams al-Din Abu Najib al-Darguzini (a

[195] Luther, 'Political Transformation', 65; Fragner, *Geschichte der Stadt Hamadān*, 149–56.

[196] Ibn al-Athir, *al-Kamil*, XI, 256; Bundari, *Zubda*, 235.

[197] Bundari, *Zubda*, 235; see also Hillenbrand, *A Muslim Principality*, fol. 175b, p. 137.

[198] Luther, 'Political Transformation', 78.

[199] Ibn al-Athir, *al-Kamil*, XI, 162, 189, 194–5; Bundari, *Zubda*, 234–5; Husayni, *Akhbar*, 129–30.

[200] Bundari, *Zubda*, 236; Husayni, *Akhbar*, 131.

nephew of the notorious Abu 'l-Qasim al-Darguzini whom we met during the reign of Mahmud), whom even 'Imad al-Din al-Isfahani, usually fiercely hostile to his arch rivals in the Darguzini clan, admits was a competent administrator (although he cannot resist making some snide comments about his alleged lack of refinement).[201] Shams al-Din asked amirs who had usurped *iqṭāʿs* during the chaos of 1152–3 to return some of what they held to the sultan, and although we do not know how successful this was, rather surprisingly the financial situation did improve. Muhammad, at his vizier's urging, then resolved to march on Baghdad. The seizure of the city would solve not just the problem of legitimacy, but also aid the sultanic finances, if the *iqṭāʿs* of Iraq could be returned to Seljuk control. Shams al-Din, it should be remembered, would have had a very personal interest in a Seljuk reoccupation of Iraq, for it was there that the vizieral *iqṭāʿs*, now appropriated by Ibn Hubayra, lay.

However, Muhammad did not immediately heed his vizier's pleas, for the appearance of his uncle Sulaymanshah, backed by Ildegüz, Nusrat al-Din of Maragha and al-Muqtafi,[202] threw a spanner in the works.[203] The caliph's support for Sulaymanshah may in fact have been a double-edged sword: no amir hopeful of regaining Iraqi *iqṭāʿs* was likely to do well out of a sultan so closely allied with the caliph. This included many of the Jibali group who now gravitated towards Muhammad as their best hope of recovering them.[204] While Khuzistan and Nishapur were temporarily overrun by the Ghuzz,[205] Sulaymanshah joined forces with Malikshah III in northwestern Iran.[206] Supported by the Jibali faction of amirs, as well as by Qutb al-Din Mawdud of Mosul (Zangi's son), Muhammad marched north, defeating the caliphal northwestern amiral forces at the battle of Nakhchivan – Ildegüz's heartland – in Jumada I/June–July 551/1156.[207] Sulaymanshah was captured by Qutb al-Din's forces in the wake of the battle and imprisoned in Mosul.[208]

201 Bundari, *Zubda*, 245. See also Qummi, *Dhayl-i Nafthat al-Masdur*, 196, 205, 223, 233, who also comments on his humble origins.

202 Bundari, *Zubda*, 232.

203 Ibn al-Athir, *al-Kamil*, XI, 206–7; cf. Bundari, *Zubda*, 236, 240; Qummi, *Dhayl-i Nafthat al-Masdur*, 181–2, 215–17, 228, 229–30. For the complicated chronology, see Luther, 'Political Transformation', 282–5.

204 Bundari, *Zubda*, 236; Qummi, *Dhayl-i Nafthat al-Masdur*, 228. Bundari, *Zubda*, portrays Muhammad as reluctant to oppose the caliph at first, but drawn towards it by his amirs.

205 Ibn al-Athir, *al-Kamil*, XI, 201–2.

206 *Ibid.*, XI, 206–7.

207 For the battle and its aftermath, see Luther, 'Political Transformation', 78–82.

208 Ibn al-Athir, *al-Kamil*, XI, 206–7; Husayni, *Akhbar*, 142.

The victory gave Muhammad the opportunity to try to clip Ildegüz's wings, for the defeated amir was now obliged to beg forgiveness. However, action against such a powerful amir was out of the question, given the unpromising precedents set by Mas'ud. Instead, Muhammad promoted Nusrat al-Din of Maragha to rule over Azerbaijan, thus placing an obstacle in Ildegüz's way should he attempt to march south. Finally, the sultan was ready to advance on Baghdad.

The siege of Baghdad, lasting from Muharram 552/February–March 1157 until June of the same year, has been described as 'the last really free act of any Seljuk sultan of Iraq'.[209] His amirs were lukewarm, and some were subverted by bribes arranged by Ibn Hubayra, while the populace of Baghdad was roused to jihad against the Turks.[210] However, ultimately, it was the succession problem that scuppered Muhammad's plans: while Sulaymanshah was safely in prison, Malikshah was in the hands of Ildegüz, who now installed him on the Seljuk throne in Hamadhan and occupied the central Iranian cities of Qumm and Qashan. Isfahan remained loyal to Muhammad, but faced with the prospect of the loss of Jibal, now the core of what was left of the Seljuk Empire, he retreated eastwards.

Ildegüz then abandoned Hamadhan for reasons that are unclear, but at the same time, Muhammad fell ill, becoming wholly incapacitated just as he inherited from Sanjar the title of *al-sulṭān al-aʿẓam* (see below p. 130) which he proudly proclaimed on his coins. He died aged thirty-four in Dhu 'l-Hijja 554/November 1159, never having achieved his dream of entering Baghdad to secure recognition as sultan.[211] Henceforth, Arab Iraq was definitively lost to the Seljuks, and by the late twelfth century the resurgent caliphal state had become a significant regional power.

The 'Salvage Operation': Amiral Rule and the Dyarchy

Thus, by 1157, with Sanjar dead and Muhammad incapacitated, the Great Seljuk Empire may be said to have collapsed. The polity that survived in the Jibal was a very different creature, which we cannot investigate in detail here, but the forty-year 'salvage operation',[212] as it has been called, to rescue

[209] Luther, 'Political Transformation', 83.

[210] *Ibid.*, 89.

[211] Ibn al-Athir, *al-Kamil*, XI, 250; Husayni, *Akhbar*, 140; Qummi, *Dhayl-i Nafthat al-Masdur*, 236–8; see also Chapter 3 below.

[212] Luther, 'Political Transformation', 4. For studies of the period, see Luther, 'Political Transformation'; Fragner, *Geschichte der Stadt Hamadān*, 157–92; Durand-Guédy, *Iranian Elites*, 269–80; and in general on the Ildegüzids, K. A. Luther, 'Atabakān-e Ādarbāyjān', *EIr*; Ziya Bünyadov, *Azərbaycan Atabəyləri Dövləti, 1136–1125* (Baku, [1984] 2007).

something from the wreckage of the empire after the crises of the mid-twelfth century was surprisingly successful. The enduring prestige of the Seljuk name was such that the amirs, who were the key political force in the later twelfth century, preferred to shelter behind the legitimacy of a nominal Seljuk sultan rather than to seize power in their own names.

Initially, it seemed as if the remnants of the Seljuk sultanate might disintegrate into warring factions of amirs.[213] The amirs were themselves split between those who supported the claim of Malikshah, the partisans of Sulaymanshah and the supporters of Arslan, who was under the control of Ildegüz. Malikshah secured Isfahan, but the Hamadhan-based amirs inclined towards Sulaymanshah.[214] The latter was released by Qutb al-Din Mawdud according to instructions left by Muhammad before his death; the Mosuli amir's power was to be secured by becoming Sulaymanshah's *atabeg*, while other senior positions were assured for Mawdud's henchmen.[215] The problem of Malikshah was soon solved, for the caliphal vizier 'Awn al-Din b. Hubayra had him poisoned by a slave girl in 555/1160,[216] while Sulaymanshah himself – allegedly a total drunk whose affairs were completely managed by the amir Sharaf al-Din Girdbazu – was imprisoned by Girdbazu and other amirs who had tired of his antics in Shawwal 555/October 1160, and was then murdered.[217] This left Arslan, still in the hands of his *atabeg* Ildegüz, as the principal surviving claimant.

Ildegüz's achievement of his aim of seating his candidate on the Seljuk throne in Hamadhan marks a further diminution of the status of the sultan. As Husayni described it in a telling phrase, the sultan Arslan

> was outwardly the ruler (*kāna ṣūratan fī 'l-mulk*) and the atabeg Ildegüz was the substance (*ma'nā*), having orders executed, granting *iqṭā's*, havingcharge of the treasuries and transferring them to wherever he wanted in the country, while the sultan could not even discuss anything with him.[218]

Indeed, one of the contemporary documents that has come down to us, a confirmation of the *iqṭā's* of the amir Ildoghdi b. Qishtoghan, only

[213] Cf. Luther, 'The End of Saljuq Domination in Khurasan', 220

[214] Ibn al-Athir, *al-Kamil*, XI, 251; Qummi, *Dhayl-i Nafthat al-Masdur*, 240.

[215] Ibn al-Athir, *al-Kamil*, XI, 254.

[216] *Ibid.*, XI, 263.

[217] *Ibid.*, XI, 267; Husayni, *Akhbar*, 144; Qummi, *Dhayl-i Nafthat al-Masdur*, 240–3. Sulaymanshah's excessive drinking and general incompetence had earlier cost him the support of Ildegüz and other amirs, see Bundari, *Zubda*, 232.

[218] Husayni, *Akhbar*, 167; cf. *ibid.*, 194.

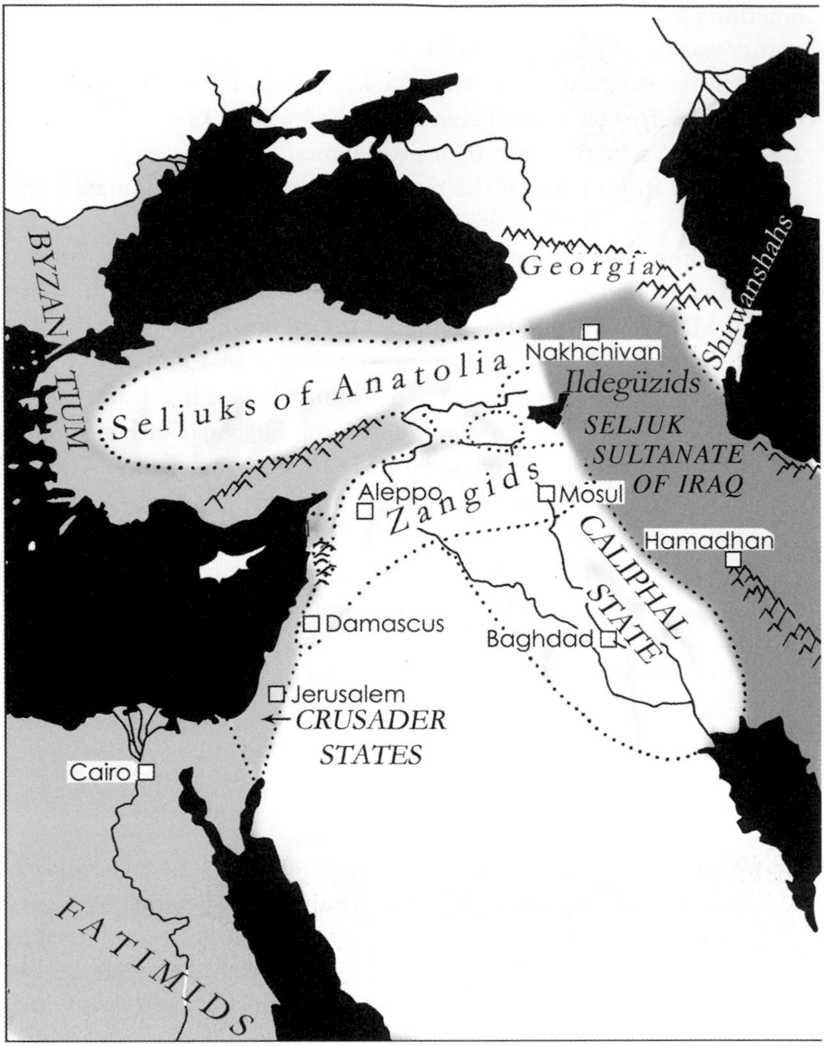

Map 2.2 The Seljuk Sultanate of Iraq and its neighbours, *c.* 1170

makes a passing reference to the sultan.[219] The document (dated 26 Muharram 553/27 February 1158) is issued in the name of Ildegüz's son Muhammad Jahan Pahlawan alone; evidently, it had not taken the Ildegüzids long to decide to dispense with the Seljuks for all practical purposes.

[219] *Al-Mukhtarat min al-Rasa'il*, 206–11.

Although Qummi alludes to a plot to restore Arslan to real power, drawing on the support of amirs disaffected with Ildegüz, nothing came of it.[220] This 'dyarchy' survived until 583/1187, with the sultan providing legitimacy for the Ildegüzid *atabegs*. More profoundly, however, the dyarchy represented basically a Caucasian takeover of the sultanate, with the Jibal effectively annexed to Arran, although Hamadhan remained politically important.

[220] Qummi, *Dhayl-i Nafthat al-Masdur*, 261.

War with Georgia features prominently in accounts of the period, reflecting this Caucasian orientation, although Ildegüzid rule saw the restoration of a modicum of stability in Jibal. Tellingly, it was in Nakhchivan, not any of the cities of the Jibal traditionally associated with legitimate rule, that Ildegüz built a tomb of exceptionally artistry and skill for his Seljuk wife, Mu'mina Khatun (see Figure 2.3). It was at the Ildegüzid court, rather than with the Seljuk sultans, that ambitious bureaucrats sought to make their careers. Control of revenue-producing lands, and thus finances, now rested with the *atabegs*.[221]

The problem of amiral destabilisation, however, was never overcome: Ildegüz's ill-documented successor, Jahan Pahlawan, attempted to circumvent it by stripping the amirs of their *iqṭā's* and granting them to his personal slaves instead, but this proved fruitless.[222] Essentially, Jahan Pahlawan's arrangement relied on his slaves being paid through booty, which required raiding. Thus, Isfahan and Fars were among the prime targets during his reign, but on his death the slave governors turned on each other and on Iraq. Yet the struggles between Pahlawan's former slaves provided a window through which the last Seljuk sultan, Tughrıl, attempted to assert his independence.

The Last Seljuk: The Reign of Tughrıl III, 571/1175–590/1194

Tughrıl was seven years old at his accession in 571/1175, and for the first ten years of his reign Jahan Pahlawan continued to exercise effective rule.[223] When, for instance, Saladin invaded northern Mesopotamia in 578/1182, besieging Mosul which still recognised Ildegüzid and ultimately Seljuk suzerainty, Jahan Pahlawan was in full control of both the diplomatic and military response: the youthful sultan is scarcely mentioned in contemporary sources.[224] On Jahan Pahlawan's death in 582/1186, wrangling broke out among his relatives – to such an extent, Rawandi tells us, that the *atabeg's* body remained unburied for two or three months.[225] His obvious successor

[221] Fairbanks, 'The Tarikh al-Vuzara', 187.

[222] Kenneth A. Luther, 'Ravandi's Report on the Administrative Changes of Muhammad Jahan Pahlavan', in C. E. Bosworth (ed.), *Iran and Islam: A Volume in Memory of the late Vladimir Minorsky* (Edinburgh, 1971), 393–406.

[223] The most detailed source on the reign of Tughrıl III is Rawandi, *Rahat al-Sudur wa-Ayat al-Surur*, ed. Muhammad Iqbal (London, 1921), 331–74. The author was a member of Tughrıl's court, and had originally planned to dedicate his work to the sultan. For an English summary of Rawandi's account, see Julie Scott Meisami, 'The Collapse of the Great Saljuqs', in Chase F. Robinson (ed.), *Texts Documents and Artefacts: Islamic Studies in Honour of D. S. Richards* (Leiden, 2003), 265–300. See also Husayni, *Akhbar*, 171–94.

[224] See the documents and discussion in Durand-Guédy, 'Diplomatic Practice in Saljuq Iran', 271–96.

[225] Rawandi, *Rahat al-Sudur*, 337.

Figure 2.3 Mausoleum of Mu'mina Khatun, Seljuk wife of Ildegüz, Nakhchivan

was his brother Qızıl Arslan, but a substantial party of amirs did not welcome the prospect of his domination and rallied around Tughrıl, who became an increasing force to be reckoned with. Tughrıl also seems to have been able to call on significant Türkmen support.[226] Caliph al-Nasir backed Qızıl Arslan, and reacted with violent fury to the sultan's request in 583/1187 that he be allowed to reoccupy the sultanic palace in Baghdad, razing the buildings to the ground. Evidently al-Nasir, understandably enough, had no wish to allow even a relatively weak Seljuk anywhere near Baghdad, but the army al-Nasir sent against Tughrıl was humiliatingly defeated at Day Marg in 584/1188.[227]

Tughrıl secured several victories over the Ildegüzids and the caliph, and attempted to solve the fundamental problems of the sultanate by appointing men with financial experience as vizier,[228] to ensure a greater coordination

226 Husayni, *Akhbar*, 178–9, 182. See further the discussion in Durand-Guédy, 'Goodbye to the Türkmen?'.

227 Ibn al-Athir, *al-Kamil*, XII, 24–6; Husayni, *Akhbar*, 177–9; Rawandi, *Rahat al-Sudur*, 245–6; Mason, *Two Statesmen*, 96–7.

228 Fairbanks, 'The Tarikh al-Vuzara', 157.

between the general strategy and its technical implementation. However, his authority was limited to the now relatively impoverished territories of Jibal. Iraq was securely under al-Nasir's control, and Tughrıl's campaigns in Azerbaijan made little headway against Qızıl Arslan. In 586/1190, Qızıl succeeded in capturing Tughrıl and deposing him, replacing him with the *malik* Sanjar b. Sulayman b. Malikshah.[229] Egged on by the caliph, Qızıl Arslan decided to do away with the Seljuk dynasty altogether and proclaim himself sultan. Yet his death shortly afterwards in 587/1191 gave Tughrıl one more chance, and in 589/1192 the sultan regained his throne.[230]

Despite the depiction of Tughrıl propagated by Husayni and Rawandi as a romantic hero charged with the noble, but ultimate hopeless, mission to revive the glories of the Seljuk dynasty, an image mirrored in Mongol era sources,[231] not everyone was sympathetic. Isfahani accuses him of alienating those amirs who had supported him,[232] while the chronicler of Tabaristan, Ibn Isfandiyar, contrasts the 'rash, wilful, proud and bloodthirsty' Tughrıl with the noble and heroic Qızıl Arslan.[233] Even more devastating is the verdict of a contemporary Jibali bureaucrat, Jurbadhqani, who regarded the death of Jahan Pahlawan as the great disaster of his age, looked on Qızıl Arslan's assumption of the sultanate sympathetically, and accused Tughrıl of conspiring with the Khwarazmians.[234] In truth, the latter were the real threat. In 593/1183, Atsız's descendant 'Ala' al-Din Tekish had been proclaimed sultan at Radkan, near Tus in Khurasan. The Khwarazmians, who since Sanjar's fall had been jousting with the Ghurids for control of Khurasan, were set on a course of expansion that would make them briefly the greatest imperial power in the Muslim world, controlling territories stretching from India to Anatolia, before they too were overwhelmed by the Mongol invasions of Central Asia and Middle East in the 1220s.[235]

Apart from his Türkmen and his amirs, Tughrıl had no significant allies; nonetheless, he may be said to have played a poor hand badly. The regional powers, Caliph al-Nasir and Qızıl Arslan's successor Qutlugh Inanj, formed common cause against him, and managed to persuade the Khwarazmians

229 Ibn al-Athir, *al-Kamil*, XII, 76; Rawandi, *Rahat al-Sudur*, 362–3; Qummi, *Dhayl-i Nafthat al-Masdur*, 338–9. For another perspective, see Ibn Isfandiyar, *Tarikh-i Tabaristan*, I, 115, 153.

230 Ibn al-Athir, *al-Kamil*, XII, 75–6, 94; Rawandi, *Rahat al-Sudur*, 363–5; Jurfadhqani, *Tarjuma-yi Tarikh-i Yamini*, 326–7; Juvaini, *History*, 299.

231 See, for instance, Hamdallah Mustawfi, *Tarikh-i Guzida*, 463–71.

232 Bundari, *Zubda*, 301–2.

233 Ibn Isfandiyar, *Tarikh-i Tabaristan*, II, 152.

234 Jurfadhqani, *Tarjuma-yi Tarikh-i Yamini*, 326–7.

235 See Kafesoğlu, *Harezmşahlar Devleti Tarihi*, *passim*.

to join their coalition. Tekish needed little encouragement, and Tughrıl's ill-advised breach of the conditions of their earlier alliance proved the perfect excuse. In Rabi' I 590/March 1194, Tughrıl reached Rayy, where Qutlugh Inanj seems to have tricked him into thinking that he was penitent and sought to join his forces. In the battle between the Khwarazmian and Seljuk forces, Tughrıl fell from his horse and was hacked to death by Qutlugh Inanj. The Khwarazamshah sent Tughrıl's head to Baghdad where it was hung on the main city gate, the Bab al-Nawba.[236] Al-Nasir's Khwarazmian alliance had finally freed the 'Abbasids from the Seljuk tutelage they had laboured under for a century and a half. The political of map of Central Asia and the Middle East was reconfigured, with the vast, but fragile, Khwarazmian state occupying most of the Seljuk lands in Iran and Central Asia, while al-Nasir reigned supreme in Iraq. The last Seljuk sultan of Kirman had fled before the Ghuzz advance in 582/1186,[237] and henceforth, the only Seljuks to bear the title of sultan were the descendants of Qutlumush b. Arslan Isra'il ruling in Anatolia (*c.* 1081–1308). In Rajab 590/June 1194, 'Ala' al-Din Tekish entered Hamadhan, where he ascended the throne in symbolic proclamation of his success in finally achieving his ancestor Atsız's aim of destroying the Seljuk dynasty.[238]

The Rise and Fall of the Seljuk Empire in Retrospect

Although the authors of our sources struggled to understand the emergence of the Seljuk Empire, they were at no loss for words to explain its demise. The chronicles persistently depict the personal faults of later Seljuk rulers in lurid terms, highlighting their drunkenness and impiety.[239] Clearly, however, there were broader structural problems in the empire. Some of the most intractable can ultimately be traced back to Seljuk succession arrangements and the question of supremacy within the Seljuk family (discussed further in Chapter 3). In the Sultanate of Iraq, the amirs were able to use the openness of the succession and their position as *atabegs* to gain control of potential candidates with whom they could threaten the incumbent sultan. At the same time, Sanjar's

[236] Ibn al-Athir, *al-Kamil*, XII, 106–18; Bundari, *Zubda*, 269–70; Husayni, *Akhbar*, 192–3; Rawandi, *Rahat al-Sudur*, 370–4; Jurfadhqani, *Tarjuma-yi Tarikh-i Yamini*, 323–4; Ibn Isfandiyar, *Tarikh-i Tabaristan*, II, 158–61; Juvaini, *History*, 302–3.

[237] On his end, see David Durand-Guédy, 'Help Me if You Can! An Analysis of a Letter Sent by the Last Seljuq Sultan of Kirman', in Robert Hillenbrand, A. C. S. Peacock and Firuza Abdullaeva (eds), *Ferdowsi, the Mongols and the History of Iran: Studies on Art, Literature and Culture from Early Islam to the Qajars* (London, 2013), 70–7.

[238] Rawandi, *Rahat al-Sudur*, 375; Ibn al-Athir, *al-Kamil*, XII, 108; Juvaini, *History*, 304; Kafesoğlu, *Harezmşahlar Devleti Tarihi*, 126.

[239] See further p. 251 below.

own sense of entitlement to suzerainty over the entirety of the Seljuk Empire was not matched by an ability to enforce this on the ground militarily, leading him to seek indirect means of asserting suzerainty and undermining the sultans of Iraq by distributing their lands as *iqṭāʿ*, exacerbating the sultanate's financial crisis caused by the rise of amirs and their financial demands.

If, despite the bewildering complexity of politics in the Sultanate of Iraq, the fundamental causes of its political and fiscal crisis seem clear enough, Khurasan is a more intractable problem. The dislocations provoked by the Qarakhitay invasion doubtless led to the Ghuzz revolt, but, as we have seen, neither of these factors was enough to demolish Sanjar's empire definitively. Rashid al-Din Watwat's correspondence reveals that Sanjar's contemporaries took his restoration to power in 1156 seriously, and, unlike after Qatwan, there was no Khwarazmian attempt to replace the Seljuk Empire. Indeed, the thirst for the legitimacy that only a Seljuk ruler could provide is indicated by the fact that some groups of Ghuzz allied themselves with Mahmud Khan, the last Seljuk claimant in the east.[240] Even after he had murdered Mahmud Khan, al-Mu'ayyad Ay Aba recognised the nominal suzerainty of the Seljuk sultans of Iraq.[241] It was not till nearly thirty years after Sanjar's demise that the Khwarazmian ruler felt able to claim the title of sultan. It was thus not so much the Ghuzz revolt itself, but the failure of Sulaymanshah and Mahmud to establish their authority in the east that led to the demise of the empire in Khurasan.

Rawandi noted the striking parallels between the Ghuzz revolt and the Seljuks' own emergence, and attributed the Ghuzz's failure to form a lasting state of their own to their lack of justice and righteousness.[242] A similar view is often taken by modern historians. However, this is to put too much emphasis on stereotypes of nomadic barbarism. The Ghuzz leaders, especially Tuti, engaged in diplomacy with other powers such as the Khwarazmians and local Iranian rulers such as the Bawandids of the Caspian to seek to further their ambitions of domination in Khurasan.[243] Another Ghuzz leader, Malik Dinar, advanced on Kirman; the desperate plea for help to the Ildegüzid Qızıl Arslan sent by the last Seljuk ruler of Kirman, Muhammad b. Bahramshah, which has survived, implies that the Ghuzz would make the Jibal their next target. Malik Dinar's activities, recorded in unusual detail in a local Kirmani chronicle, show that there was far more to the Ghuzz than random pillaging.[244]

240 Ibn al-Athir, *al-Kamil*, XI, 272.

241 Köymen, *Büyük Selçuklu İmparatorluğu Tarihi*, II, 457. Cf. Ibn al-Athir, *al-Kamil*, XI, 273.

242 Rawandi, *Rahat al-Sudur*, 186.

243 Köymen, *Büyük Selçuklu İmparatorluğu Tarihi*, II, 424–8; Bosworth, 'Political and Dynastic History', 156.

244 Durand-Guédy, 'Help Me if You Can!', 71. For the Persian text of the letter, see

Malik Dinar built alliances with both Turkish amirs and the Iranian nobility in Kirman, and as David Durand-Guédy has put it, 'Malik Dinar presented a credible political alternative to the discredited Seljuqs . . . Except for the handful of Turkish and Daylamite amirs besieged and starving in Bardasir [the last Seljuk stronghold], everyone longed for an end to the fighting and supported (or at least did not oppose) the political project of Malik Dinar'.[245] Malik Dinar employed bureaucrats to assist him, and to legitimise his rule, he married a Seljuk princess.[246]

Despite these state-building efforts, Ghuzz rule in Kirman lasted a mere two decades, collapsing shortly after Malik Dinar's death. The threat that they would emulate the Seljuks and storm westwards was never realised, nor even in Khurasan did they establish any lasting political entity. Despite their depiction in the sources as barbarians, like the Seljuks, complaints as to the devastation the Ghuzz caused are often greatly exaggerated.[247] Some communities welcomed them, and they were accepted as valued allies by the last Seljuk claimant, Mahmud. The failure of the Ghuzz and the success of the Seljuks was ultimately largely down to the difference in historical circumstances in which they found themselves. The states which the Seljuks encountered in the eleventh century all had for one reason or another weaknesses that made them unable to resist the Turkish incursions. Logistical problems had prevented the Ghaznavids from effectively countering the Seljuks in Khurasan, where much of the population was anyway content to see new political masters. Buyid and Kakuyid contenders had often actually welcomed the Seljuks as a means of defeating internal enemies. Byzantine Anatolia collapsed less under the pressure of the Turkish advance than as a result of the civil war that followed Manzikert. In Syria, the Fatimids anyway struggled to assert control. The mid-twelfth-century Ghuzz enjoyed no such advantages against their contemporaries, who were all dynasties either of nomadic origin or else employed substantial nomadic military contingents. The Qarakhitay continued to dominate Transoxiana, even on occasion making incursions into Khurasan, while the emergent Khwarazmians were able to contain, and ultimately subordinate, the Ghuzz, wiping out their polity in Khurasan. Moreover, the Ghuzz lacked one crucial component in the Seljuks' success: a royal clan that could serve as a focus for the nomads' loyalties, the prestige of which persisted beyond the dynasty's demise and which the Ghuzz themselves continued to acknowledge.

al-Mukhtarat min al-Rasa'il, 182–3. For the local chronicle, see Kirmani, *Saljuqiyan wa Ghuzz*, 514 ff.

245 Durand-Guédy, 'Help Me if You Can!', 71, 75.

246 Kirmani, *Saljuqiyan wa Ghuzz*, 569–73.

247 Cf. Bosworth, 'Political and Dynastic History', 154.

3

Sovereignty, Legitimacy and the Contest with the Caliphate

Writing for Caliph al-Muqtadi, the Turkish lexicographer Mahmud al-Kashghari commented that:

> I saw that God Most High had caused the Sun of Fortune to rise in the Zodiac of the Turks, and set their Kingdom among the spheres of Heaven; that He called them 'Turk', and gave them Rule; making them kings of the Age, and placing in their hands the reins of temporal authority; appointing them over all mankind . . .[1]

Similar sentiments were expressed in Seljuk official documents. For instance, a decree issued by Sanjar's chancery starts, 'Since God . . . has bestowed upon us lordship of the world and placed in our control the affairs of the kingdoms of the world and the ordering of the affairs of the people of the world . . .'[2] They were echoed by historians too. Alp Arslan's conquests were such that Ibn al-Athir comments, 'rightly was he called sultan of the world' (*sulṭān al-ʿālam*).[3]

Such audacious universal claims were common to rulers from the Iranian, Islamic and Turkic political traditions.[4] Yet Kashghari is strikingly silent on any role for his dedicatee, the caliph – exactly the individual who, according to traditional Islamic political theory, should himself be the universal ruler, indeed *was* the sole legitimate ruler. The caliph's position could not be so easily dismissed by religious scholars, and jurists struggled to reconcile it with the reality of Seljuk claims to supremacy. Ghazali (d. 505/1111), the greatest religious scholar of his day, argued that the Seljuk possession of

[1] Maḥmūd al-Kāšγarī, *Compendium of the Turkic Dialects*, ed. and trans. by Robert Dankoff (Cambridge, MA, 1982), 70.

[2] Juwayni, *ʿAtabat al-Kataba*, 69; trans. from Lambton, 'Internal Structure', 209.

[3] Ibn al-Athir, *al-Kamil*, X, 74.

[4] In general, see Osman Turan, 'The Ideal of World Domination among the Medieval Turks', *Studia Iranica*, 4 (1955), 77–90; on the Khazars' imperial ideology, see Golden, 'Imperial Ideology', 44–5; for Islamic rulers' universal pretensions, see Patricia Crone, *Medieval Islamic Political Thought* (Edinburgh, 2005), 162, 385; for the Perso-Islamic tradition, see Busse, 'The Revival of Persian Kingship', 47–69.

shawka (force) meant that they were legitimate rulers to whom the caliph had delegated authority, but the existence of the caliphate was the prerequisite for the legitimacy of the sultanate.[5] A rather later treatise, the *Nasihat al-Muluk*, uncertainly attributed to Ghazali and dedicated to an unnamed Seljuk ruler (probably Muhammad Tapar), dispensed even with this pretence, accepting the sultan as a divinely ordained ruler. Such a view had already been propounded by Nizam al-Mulk, from whose *Siyasatnama* the caliphate is conspicuously absent.[6] Another body of opinion, most forcefully propounded by the great scholar Imam al-Haramayn al-Juwayni (d. 478/1085), was willing to countenance the removal of the 'Abbasids entirely.[7]

Despite the competition between their claims, Seljuks could not do without the caliph. As a new dynasty, they required – to varying extents depending on the strength of the sultan – legitimation from the head of the Muslim community. While the abolition of the caliphate may have been considered by Malikshah, as we shall see, no ruler ultimately dared to take this step. Older scholarship saw the Seljuks as the saviours of the caliphate from the Shi'ite Buyids, but more recent work has pointed out that the Seljuks often displayed a fairly open hostility to the 'Abbasids.[8] Two caliphs, al-Mustarshid and al-Rashid, seem to have been murdered on the instructions of Seljuk rulers, while of the four times Baghdad, home of the caliphate, was besieged between its foundation and the Mongol conquest in 1258, two were by Seljuk sultans.[9] Nor were the 'Abbasids merely passive victims, for two sultans, Malikshah I and Malikshah III, seem to have been killed through the machinations of the caliphs, and we have noted above al-Nasir's virulent hatred for Tughrıl III and his role in his demise (pp. 119–21 above).

5 Carole Hillenbrand, 'Islamic Orthodoxy or Realpolitik?: al-Ghazali's Views on Government', *Iran*, 26 (1988), 81–94; Ann K. S. Lambton, 'Al-Juwayni and Al-Ghazali: The Sultanate' in her *State and Government in Medieval Islam: An Introduction to the Study of Islamic Political Theory, The Jurists* (Oxford, 1981), 103–30.

6 A. K. S. Lambton, 'The Theory of Kingship in the *Nasihat-ul-Muluk* of Ghazali', *The Islamic Quarterly*, 1 (1954), 47–55; cf. A. K. S. Lambton, 'The Dilemma of Government in Islamic Persia: The *Siyāsat-nāmah* of Nizam al-Mulk', *Iran*, 22 (1984), 57; Safi, *Politics of Knowledge*, 105–24.

7 Wael B. Hallaq, 'Caliphs, Jurists and Saljuqs in the Political Thought of al-Juwayni', *Muslim World*, 74/i (1984), 26–41; cf. Peacock, *Early Seljūq History*, 107, esp. n. 60 with further references.

8 The mutual antipathy between the Seljuks and 'Abbasids was noted by George Makdisi, 'Les rapports entre Calife et Sultan à l'époque saljuqide', *IJMES*, 6/ii (1975), 228–36; see also Safi, *Politics of Knowledge*, 1–42. For the older view, see, for instance, Klausner, *The Seljuk Vezirate*, 6, 27–30.

9 Tor, 'A Tale of Two Murders', 294.

Seljuk authority could not rest purely on caliphal legitimation. However useful it might be in affirming their right to rule among the conquered Muslim population, it is doubtful whether it could speak to the recently converted Türkmen, nor could it settle the question of which member of the Seljuk family was entitled to the sultanate. In this chapter, therefore, we shall investigate the various means by which Seljuk sultans sought to assert their sovereign rights. First, we will consider the steppe political heritage, elements of which can be traced back to the Gök Türks. This validated Seljuk claims to rulership in visual imagery, and influenced the Seljuk concepts of sovereignty, state and legitimate succession to the sultanate. Secondly, we will look at the Islamic titles and concepts employed by Seljuk sultans, and we will suggest that even here the Seljuks introduced innovations, despite the ostensible continuity represented by the use of caliphal legitimation. Finally, we will examine how the Seljuks' relationship with the 'Abbasids developed in practice, beyond the realms of rhetoric.

The Steppe Political Tradition in the Seljuk Empire

The Symbols of Rule and the Royal Clan

The public symbolism of the Seljuk Empire drew heavily on steppe traditions, especially the bow and arrow motif which among the steppe peoples signified sovereignty. Originally, the bow and arrow seem to have indicated the number of men a nomadic chief had at his command, and symbolised his ability to mobilise forces, but they later acquired by extension a more abstract meaning of sovereignty.[10] Bayhaqi tells us that Tughrıl wore a bow over his arm and two arrows at his waist when he entered Nishapur in 429/1038.[11] Bar Hebraeus, drawing on a version of the *Maliknama*, describes Tughrıl as sitting 'on the high throne, and before him were shields and spears and before him a very magnificent bow and in his hands were two arrows with which he used to play'.[12] Such symbols would have been meaningful first and foremost – if not initially exclusively – to the Seljuks' Türkmen subjects. The motif first appears on a Qarakhanid coin minted in Bukhara under 'Ali Tegin in 423/1032, which has no antecedents in Islamic numismatics. The Seljuks

[10] Shimizu, 'The Bow and Arrow', 91; cf. Nishapuri, *Saljuqnama*, 7. In later times the bow and arrow device was used as a tribal sign or 'tamgha'. However, it does not appear in the list of *tamghas* or brands for cattle of the Oghuz tribes given by Mahmud Kashghari. See Shimizu, 'The Bow and Arrow', 93; Faruk Sümer, *Oğuzlar (Türkmenler)* (Istanbul, 1999), 229–31.

[11] Bayhaqi, *Tarikh*, 884. For further examples, see Shimizu, 'The Bow and Arrow', 91–2.

[12] Bar Hebraeus, *Chronography*, I, 201.

Figure 3.1 Dinar of Tughrıl, showing the bow and arrow device above the central inscription on both sides of the coin. CM BMC OR 3 No. 58; CM 1906 12-4 39. © Trustees of the British Museum

followed the Qarakhanid example, and included stylised representations of bows and arrows on their coins from the first known issues (Figure 3.1) [13]

From the reign of Malikshah, the significance of the bow and arrow motif on the coinage seems to diminish, often being crudely drawn or omitted, before disappearing entirely by the reign of Muhammad Tapar.[14] However, it remained important in other contexts in the twelfth century and beyond. Bar Hebraeus records that as early as 1042, Ibrahim Yınal had had the figures of a bow and arrow drawn on a letter to the caliph, and Tughrıl is recorded to have done the same:[15]

> [Tughrıl] began to inscribe the figure of a bow at the top of his seal and alongside it were [his] titles. And that sign was called 'ṬÛGHRÂ' and he who wrote [it] being commanded, [was called] 'ṬÛGHRÂÎ.[16]

This stylised bow and arrow motif representing the sultan's name or titles came to be affixed to state documents, and the *ṭughrā'ī* was one of the most

[13] Shimizu, 'The Bow and Arrow', 87, 89, 92–3, 96. The exception was Nishapur, where, in view of its sensitive position as apparently claimed by both Chaghrı and Tughrıl, no sign of sovereignty was struck.

[14] The latest example listed by Alptekin was struck in Zanjan in 494/1100–1101. Alptekin, 'Selçuklu paraları', 518, 565.

[15] Bar Hebraeus, *Chronography*, I, 200.

[16] *Ibid.*, I, 206.

senior offices in the Seljuk bureaucracy. Such was the prestige of the *ṭughrā* – the origins of which have been traced to the Khazars – that it continued to be used by later Turkish dynasties, including the fourteenth-century sultans of Delhi, the Seljuks of Anatolia, and, most famously, the Ottomans, whose official documents and buildings it adorned until the end of the dynasty in 1923.[17]

The most important influence of steppe traditions, however, was on the concept of the ruling dynasty itself. While sultans' authority was repeatedly challenged by their relatives, the principle that sovereignty rested with members of the Seljuk family alone remained largely intact until the late twelfth century. For most rebels, the question was generally not who should replace the Seljuk dynasty, but which Seljuk should replace the current Seljuk ruler. Even those Türkmen groups which rejected the authority of Tughrıl and Chaghrı often coalesced around other descendants of Seljuk, such as the progeny of Arslan Isra'il or Ibrahim Yınal. The two eleventh-century attempts to put a non-Seljuk on throne, Tughrıl's Khwarazmian step-son Anushirwan, collapsed for almost total lack of support, and a hundred years later the Khwarazmshah Atsız was soon forced to abandon his attempts to repudiate Seljuk suzerainty. Even when Qızıl Arslan claimed the sultanate for himself at the end of the twelfth century, he was at pains to use Seljuk as well as caliphal symbolism to legitimise himself, the court poet Akhsikathi specifically calling him 'Sultan Qızıl Arslan the Seljuk' to stress this continuity.[18]

The special prestige of the Seljuk dynasty, stretching back to Khazar times, is stressed by both Mirkhwand and Ibn Hassul,[19] and is illustrated by an incident mentioned by Sibt b. al-Jawzi. When Türkmen of Syria called upon the Seljuk Qutlumush b. Arslan Isra'il b. Seljuk to lead them in place of their former chief Atsız b. Awaq, they appealed to him saying:

17 Shimizu, 'The Bow and Arrow', 91. On the *ṭughrā*, see Claude Cahen, 'La tughra seljukide', *Journal asiatique*, 234 (1943–5) 167–72, and on the possible Khazar connection, see Claude Cahen, 'Les Ḫazars et la tughra seljukide: supplement à un vieil article', *Journal asiatique*, 273(1–2) (1985), 161–2. In general, see also S. M. Stern, *Fatimid Decrees: Original Documents from the Fatimid Chancery* (London, 1964), 143–7; A. D. H. Bivar, 'The Saljuq Sign Manual Represented on a *Sgraffiato* Potsherd', *JRAS*, 2nd series, 1 (1979), 9–15; Abolala Soudavar, 'The Mongol Legacy of Persian *farmāns*', in Linda Komaroff (ed.), *Beyond the Legacy of Genghis Khan* (Leiden, 2006), 419–21.

18 Athir al-Din Akhsikathi, *Diwan*, ed. Rukn al-Din Humayun Farrukh (Tehran, 1389), 16, 44, 112, 198, 308. Qızıl Arslan did have some claim to kinship in fact, for he was Tughrıl III's uncle and half-brother of Arslan (Husayni, *Akhbar*, 174).

19 Ibn Hassul, *Tafdil al-Atrak*, 49; Mirkhwand, *Rawdat al-Safa*, 235–6.

> You are of the Seljuk dynasty and the royal house (*anta min al-saljuqiyya wa-bayt al-mulk*). If we obey you and serve you we will be honoured by you and we will be proud. Atsız was not from the royal house so we did not like to follow and obey him.[20]

Indeed, the Seljuk name itself continued to serve as a source of political legitimacy long after the demise of the dynasty, especially in Anatolia.[21]

The idea that sovereignty inhered in a certain royal clan had a long steppe pedigree. Among the Gök Türks and their successor empires like the Khazars, sovereignty was held to be the possession of the clan of Ashina, who were believed in Turkic legend to be descended from a wolf.[22] With the fall of the Khazars, the name of Ashina seems to have finally been consigned to oblivion, but aspects of the wolf legend survived. Michael the Syrian, a twelfth-century Syriac chronicler, explicitly links the Seljuks with the Gök Türks, recounting the legend that both were led westwards by the same wolf.[23] This evidently represents a Turkish oral tradition not recorded by the Islamic sources, and suggests that the idea of the lupine connections of the royal clan survived into the Seljuk period. In this sense, the Seljuk dynasty may be seen as having inherited the legitimatory legends and to an extent the prestige of the royal clan of Ashina.

Like other steppe empires such as the Gök Türks and the Qarakhanids,[24] the Seljuk state was split into eastern and western sections, an arrangement which, as we have seen, can be traced back to the *partitio imperii* after Dandanqan. The periods under Alp Arslan, Malikshah and Muhammad Tapar when there was a single sultan (1063–92, 1105–18) were exceptional, and under Muhammad, Sanjar effectively had a free hand in the east. Even these periods of unification were largely a matter of chance rather than design. If Tughrıl's bequest that the infant Sulayman b. Chaghrı should succeed him had been realised, this would inevitably have led to a continuation of the east–west split given Alp Arslan's powerful position in Chaghrı's lands. While Alp Arslan managed to add Tughrıl's lands to the patrimony of Chaghrı he had inherited and to hold them together by dint of constant campaigning

20 Sibt, *Mir'at*, 174.
21 Peacock, 'Seljuq Legitimacy'; and pp. 315–16 below.
22 Golden, 'Imperial Ideology', 40, 42, 45–6, 49, 58–9.
23 Michel le Syrien, *Chronique de Michel le Syrien, Patriarche Jacobite d'Antioche (1166–1199). Éditée pour la première fois et traduite en francais*, ed. and trans. Jean-Baptiste Chabot (Paris, 1899–1910), III, 153, 155; cf. Mark Dickens, 'The Sons of Magog: The Turks in Michael's Chronicle', *Parole de l'Orient*, 30 (2005), 441–2. Although the text refers to this creature as a 'dog', clearly a wolf is meant. See also Bar Hebraeus, *Chronography*, I, 196.
24 Golden, 'Imperial Ideology', 52–3.

(pp. 52–4 above), he does not seem to have regarded this unity as permanent or even desirable. On his death, the lands in the Jibal and the Jazira 'and what had been in the possession of Tughrıl Beg' were to go to Malikshah, while Fars and Shiraz were bequeathed to his brother Qavurt, along with the latter's traditional appange of Kirman. He appointed his son Ayaz to 'what his [own] father Chaghrı had held' (i.e., Khurasan), although he was also enjoined to aid Malikshah when necessary. Ayaz nonetheless seems to have been plotting against Malikshah when he was killed in battle with the Ghaznavids.[25] In other words, Alp Arslan aimed not to bequeath a unified, centralised empire, but to uphold the division between eastern and western territories that had prevailed in his father's day. A similar idea was voiced by Arslan Arghun (who is referred to by Husayni with the title 'sultan'), who wrote to Berkyaruq: 'I have taken control of the kingdom of my grandfather Da'ud [Chaghrı], with which I am content, and I shall not go beyond it.'[26]

It is often said that with the Seljuks 'leadership was vested in the family as a whole',[27] but this idea needs to be qualified. Even when there was a multiplicity of sultans, a single one was – in theory – senior. Thus, Sanjar was the acknowledged lord of the western sultans Mahmud and Masʿud, who were bound to him in a client–patronage (*khidma*) relationship just as their own vassals were to them (see further p. 158 below). Sanjar's seniority was reflected in the coinage struck in the west, which acknowledged him as *al-sulṭān al-aʿẓam* ('the greatest sultan'), while the junior sultan retained the traditional title of *al-sulṭan al-muʿaẓẓam*.[28] Occasions when sovereignty was actually shared (rather than delegated, as in this case) were rare. The most obvious example was the peace treaty between Berkyaruq and Muhammad, which was an unhappy compromise brought about by the inability of one member of the dynasty to deliver a decisive blow against the other. Muhammad agreed to peace on condition that:

> the sultan Berkyaruq was not to oppose his brother Muḥammad in the matter of the drums [signifying sultanic authority], and was not to be mentioned alongside him [in the *khuṭba*] in the rest of the lands he had acquired.[29]

[25] Bundari, *Zubda*, 47; Sibt, *Mir'at*, 167; Ibn al-Athir, *al-Kamil*, X, 76, 92.
[26] Husayni, *Akhbar*, 85; Bundari, *Zubda*, 256.
[27] For example, Lambton, 'Internal Structure', 218.
[28] Alptekin, 'Selçuklu paraları', 531, 536–51. For a further example of the distinction of *al-sulṭān al-aʿẓam* for Sanjar and *al-sulṭān al-muʿaẓẓam* for the western sultan, see *Mujmal al-Tawarikh*, 411–15; also Köymen, *Büyük Selçuklu İmparatorluğu Tarihi*, II, 24–7.
[29] Ibn al-Athir, *al-Kamil*, X, 370.

Insofar as it acknowledged the equality of both sultans, it can be regarded as an example of shared sovereignty, but in his own territories each sultan was absolute.

Tanistry and Succession to the Sultanate

Steppe influences can also be discerned in the sultanic succession arrangements, which, in some respects, resembled the classic steppe system of 'bloody tanistry' whereby, in the absence of a system of primogeniture or seniority, succession to the sultanate was open to any member of the family who was able to assert his right. Tanistry was designed precisely to ensure that the death of a ruler was followed by fighting, for it was through fighting and proving his martial abilities that a leader gained legitimacy in the steppe world; the candidate who won was by definition the best candidate.[30]

The function of succession struggles as conferring legitimacy on the winner helps to explain why rival Seljuks were usually treated with great leniency, and often reinstated or even showered with greater honours by the victor. Ibrahim Yınal, for instance, was forgiven twice by Tughrıl for launching major rebellions, and it was only after the third occasion that he ordered him to be executed. The killing of Qavurt on Nizam al-Mulk's orders was evidently profoundly shocking to many (see pp. 68–9 above). Likewise, after the *malik* Mas'ud's rebellion against Mahmud in 514/1120–1, the latter granted him a safe-conduct and when they met 'they embraced one another and wept'.[31] When Sanjar defeated Mas'ud in the fighting after Mahmud's death and temporarily installed his favoured candidate Tughrıl as sultan of Iraq, he nonetheless honoured Mas'ud and reinstated him in his *iqṭā'* of Ganja, although he had the *atabeg* Qaraja who had supported the losing side executed.[32] Another reason for leniency was doubtless the steppe tradition which regarded as taboo the physical shedding of the blood of members of the sacred royal clan. When, in extremis, members of the Seljuk house had to be disposed of, they were strangled with a bow strings to avoid spilling their blood: such was the fate that Ibrahim Yınal, Qavurt and Sulaymanshah all met.[33]

Despite appearances, the Seljuk succession system was not a complete

[30] The classic description of this system is Fletcher, 'The Turco-Mongolian Monarchic Tradition', *passim*.

[31] Ibn al-Athir, *al-Kamil*, X, 564.

[32] *Ibid.*, X, 678.

[33] Bundari, *Zubda*, 47; Husayni, *Akhbar*, 56–7, 144; Ibn al-Athir, *al-Kamil*, X, 78–9; Sibt, *Mir'at*, 49–50, 60, 163–4. For other examples of royal executions by strangulation, see, for example, Bundari, *Zubda*, 257 (Buri Bars b. Alp Arslan), 259 (Zubayda Khatun); also Ibn al-Athir, *al-Kamil*, X, 488.

free for all. The conflicts of the eleventh century have a markedly different character from those of later periods. Up to the end of the eleventh century, candidates came from across all branches of the Seljuk family, but even then principles of seniority influenced their expectations of their right to succeed. The descendants of Seljuk's elder son Arslan Isra'il, Qutlumush and his sons, were regarded by many Türkmen as having a strong claim to leadership, perhaps on the basis of Arslan Isra'il's seniority to Tughrıl and Chaghrı.[34] Alp Arslan's accession was challenged by his uncle Musa Yabghu b. Mika'il,[35] his cousin Qutlumush b. Arslan Isra'il,[36] and his brothers Sulayman and Qavurt of Kirman.[37] On Alp Arslan's death Qavurt openly claimed the sultanate.[38] He is said to have written to Malikshah that 'I am the elder brother while you are but a young son, and I am more worthy of the inheritance of my brother sultan Alp Arslan than you.' This was a clear assertion of a traditional Turkish concept that rule was passed from brother to brother, the same idea which may have motivated the supporters of Arslan Isra'il. Malikshah replied that 'there is no [entitlement for the brother] to inherit when a son exists'.[39]

The significant support Qavurt gained from the Türkmen – he was only defeated by Malikshah's Kurdish and Arab troops – suggests the potency the older ideas of succession retained and, until Muhammad Tapar's reign, princes not directly of sultanic descent were seen as credible claimants to the throne. After Malikshah's death, Terken Khatun had married Isma'il b. Yaquti b. Chaghrı, who was briefly recognised as sultan in the *khuṭba* and *sikka* at Isfahan before his murder by partisans of Berkyaruq.[40] Mengubars, a nephew of Muhammad and descendant of Alp Arslan, rebelled in 499/1105–6,[41] while in 502/1108–9 Chavli Saqqa'u tried to use Bektash b. Tekish b. Alp Arslan to legitimise his revolt.[42] However, a distinct narrowing in the field of candidates can be observed: whereas previously men like Ibrahim Yınal and Qutlumush, who were not descendants of Mika'il b. Seljuk but

34 Peacock, *Early Seljūq History*, 60–71; Peacock, 'From the Balkhān-Kūhīyān to the Nāwakīya', 63; on Arslan Isra'il's seniority, see also Rawandi, *Rahat al-Sudur*, 460.

35 Ibn al-Athir, *al-Kamil*, X, 34.

36 Sibt, *Mir'at*, 110–11; Ibn al-Athir, *al-Kamil*, X, 36–7.

37 Ibn al-Athir, *al-Kamil*, X, 53; Bundari, *Zubda*, 30–1. The most detailed account of Qavurt's rebellion is Sibt, *Mir'at*, 118–21, 134, 137, 141–2. See Christian Lange, *Justice, Punishment and the Medieval Muslim Imagination* (Cambridge, 2008), 27, n. 10, for variant accounts of his end.

38 Ibn al-Athir, *al-Kamil*, X, 78–9.

39 Husayni, *Akhbar*, 56. For this concept, see Peacock, *Early Seljūq History*, 63–4.

40 Ibn al-Athir, *al-Kamil*, X, 224; Nishapuri, *Saljuqnama*, 37.

41 Ibn al-Athir, *al-Kamil*, X, 398.

42 *Ibid.*, X, 462, 466.

were members of other branches of the Seljuk family, could credibly challenge for the sultanate, by the end of the twelfth century all candidates were descended from Chaghrı b. Mika'il.

Subsequently, the range of candidates was restricted still further, to Seljuk princes who were themselves sons of sultans. The numerous candidates in whose name power was contested after Mahmud's death were all either sons of Mahmud himself (Da'ud, Malikshah III, Muhammad) or Muhammad Tapar (Tughrıl II, Mas'ud, Sulaymanshah). It was probably to emphasise their sultanic descent that claimants started to use the *laqabs* (honorific titles) of their sultanic ancestors. Thus, Malikshah II b. Berkyaruq, briefly proclaimed sultan by the amirs of Baghdad on his father's death, was given the *laqab* Jalal al-Dawla like his better known namesake, his grandfather,[43] and Sanjar himself adopted another of his father's *laqabs*, Mu'izz al-Din.[44] Sulaymanshah, Sanjar's heir and would-be sultan, 'took on his father [Muhammad's] *laqab* Ghiyath al-Din and the rest of his *laqabs*' when the *khuṭba* was proclaimed in his name in Baghdad in 551/1156.[45] This tendency seems to confirm the importance of sultanic descent for legitimacy in the twelfth century. No amir contending for power in Iran and Iraq in the twelfth century seems to have considered raising the standard of revolt behind an Anatolian or Kirmani Seljuk.

No source explains exactly why this narrowing occurred, but it may be related to more general changes in the structures of power in the Seljuk state resulting from Nizam al-Mulk's campaign against the Türkmen aristocracy (see pp. 68–70 above). Qavurt and Tutush both gained widespread Türkmen support for their candidacy,[46] but by the late eleventh century it was increasingly the great amirs who were calling the shots. When Malikshah died, his brother Tutush had great difficulty in recruiting them to his cause. The *mamlūk* governor of Aleppo Aqsonqur withdrew his support from Tutush, remarking, 'We obeyed this man [Tutush] so we could wait and see what would happen with the sons of our master [Malikshah]; now his son has

43 Ibn al-Athir, *al-Kamil*, X, 382. On Seljuk *laqabs*, see also Muhammad Baqir al-Husayni, 'Dirasa tahliliyya wa ihsa'iyya lil-alqab al-islamiyya', *Sumer*, 27/i (1971), 185–231 and 27/ii (1971), 154–85.

44 Ibn al-Athir, *al-Kamil*, X, 549.

45 *Ibid.*, X, 206; Ibn al-Jawzi, *al-Muntazam*, XVIII, 106. It is noteworthy that Sanjar's successor in Khurasan, his nephew Mahmud Khan, seems to have struggled to establish his legitimacy as a Seljuk ruler. He is not included in Nishapuri's list of Seljuk sultans in the *Saljuqnama*, the twelfth-century history designed to inclucate Tughrıl III with the values of his ancestors, and he is usually referred to not by the Seljuk title of sultan, but by the distinctly Qarakhanid title of khan, alluding to his paternal ancestry.

46 Bundari, *Zubda*, 84, states that Tutush initially gained Türkmen support (*wa-qad ḥashada jumū' al-turkmān*). See also n. 38.

emerged and we want to be with him.'[47] The power of these amirs was based on their ability to manipulate youthful Seljuk sultans, and the succession of brothers, men like Tutush, who were battle-hardened and experienced, held no attractions for them, as such candidates would only be likely to clip their wings – better by far to have a weak youth. Thus, when Tutush asked amirs in Isfahan for allegiance, they prevaricated, waiting to see whether Berkyaruq would recover from his illness – and when he did, they sided with him.[48] Some sultans did seek to regulate the succession by appointing an heir apparent (*walī al-ʿahd*) from among their progeny. Although this position was confirmed by oaths of allegiance sworn by leading amirs, it seems usually to have been ineffective at securing the succession for the designated candidate.[49]

The Perso-Islamic Political Tradition

Steppe traditions explain aspects of the internal functioning of the Seljuk state: the status of the Seljuk family; the bipartite division of the empire; the nature of the succession arrangements. However, with the exception of *ṭughrā*, much of the public symbolism that the Seljuk rulers drew on was not Turkic, but rather derived from the Perso-Islamic tradition of rule – the synthesis that had been developed since the early ʿAbbasid period, bringing ancient Iranian, pre-Islamic ideas of kingship into an Islamic context.[50] The

47 Ibn al-Athir, *al-Kamil*, X, 222.

48 *Ibid.*, X, 245.

49 For the appointment of Malikshah as *walī al-ʿahd* in the presence of the leading amirs, see Ibn al-Athir, *al-Kamil*, X, 50. It has been argued that this was the first time the system of *walī al-ʿahd* had been used, and was designed by Alp Arslan and Nizam al-Mulk to prevent the succession struggles which had followed the death of Tughrıl (Bosworth, 'Political and Dynastic History', 57; Bowen and Bosworth, 'Niẓām al-Mulk'). However, shortly before his death, Tughrıl had in fact appointed a *walī al-ʿahd*, Sulayman b. Chaghrı, 'because he [Tughrıl] was married to his mother' (Sibt, *Mir'at*, 97, 100 and see further p. 183 below). Muhammad Tapar appointed his fourteen-year-old son Mahmud as his successor on his deathbed in 511/1118, which was perhaps the most successful use of this designation, despite the ensuring war with Sanjar (Ibn al-Athir, *al-Ta'rikh al-Bahir*, 20). Da'ud is mentioned by Isfahani as having been the *walī al-ʿahd* of Mahmud – although it availed him little (see Bundari, *Zubda*, 160). Sanjar made Sulaymanshah b. Muhammad his *walī al-ʿahd* (Ibn al-Athir, *al-Kamil*, XI, 205; Ibn Isfandiyar, *Tarikh-i Tabaristan*, I, 108). Ibn Balkhi also mentions that the revenues of Jahrum were designated for the heir apparent (*Farsnama*, 131); while Malikshah is said to have received Isfahan as his *iqṭāʿ* on appointment as *walī al-ʿahd* (Durand-Guédy, 'Malekšāh'; al-Mafarrukhi, *Kitab Mahasin Isfahan*, 154). However, the position of *walī al-ʿahd* is surprisingly rarely mentioned in the chronicles, testimony to its virtual irrelevance when it came to asserting a right to the sultanate.

50 For a discussion of the political legacy of ancient Iran, see D. G. Tor, 'The Long Shadow of pre-Islamic Iranian Kingship: Antagonism or Assimilation?', in Adam Silverstein and Teresa Bernheimer (eds), *Late Antiquity: Eastern Perspectives* (Oxford, 2012), 145–63.

tenth century had witnessed the heyday of this synthesis, as under ethnically Iranian dynasties like the Buyids ancient titles like *shāhanshāh* (king of kings) were revived. Turkish dynasties participated in the same phenomenon, and the Ghaznavids used similar legitimatory strategies to those of their Iranian predecessors. Praised by their Persian poets as rulers in the Iranian tradition, they also sought recognition by the caliph and to promote themselves as defenders of Islam. For most of the Seljuks' subjects, this Perso-Islamic tradition would have been a more meaningful sign of their rulers' legitimacy than any steppe tradition. Nonetheless, it was not adopted wholesale, but was substantially modified by the Seljuks, above all in the matter of the rulers' titles.

The Sultanate and Caliphal Legitimation

Literally, *sulṭān* means 'power' or 'authority',[51] but by the eleventh century the word implied 'legitimate authority', in contrast to lesser titles like *malik*, 'king' or 'prince'.[52] In 423/1032, the idea that a Buyid could have the title '*al-sulṭān al-mu'aẓẓam*' was rejected on the basis that this title was a prerogative of the caliph.[53] Such objections notwithstanding, *sulṭān* was used informally by both the Ghaznavids and Buyids.[54] Initially, Tughrıl's pretensions were strictly limited, and he used the title *amīr* favoured by previous Khurasani rulers. The Seljuk coins minted in Nishapur in the years before Dandanqan were struck in the name of *al-amīr al-ajall Ṭughril-beg* and Caliph al-Qa'im.[55] However, by 434/1042–3 Tughrıl was calling himself *al-sulṭān al-mu'aẓẓam*, 'the great sultan',[56] although he continued to signify his loyalty to the idea of the caliphate by adopting the title of *mawlā amīr al-mu'minīn* ('client of the

[51] J. H. Kraemers and C. E Bosworth, 'Sulṭān', *EI²*; C. E. Bosworth, 'The Titulature of the Early Ghaznavids', *Oriens*, 15 (1962), 210–33.

[52] See the evidence cited in Makdisi, 'Les rapports entre Calife et Sultan', 230 for the use of the term *sulṭān* for the caliph by the latter's Baghdadi partisans in the late eleventh century, while the same group would refer to the Seljuq sultan as *malik*. Nizam al-Mulk claims that Sultan Mahmud of Ghazna was the first ruler to call himself sultan: see *Siyar al-Muluk*, 63, trans. 49.

[53] Ibn al-Jawzi, *al-Muntazam*, XV, 225–6.

[54] Kraemers and Bosworth, 'Sulṭān'; Bosworth, 'Titulature', 222–3.

[55] Kucur, 'A Study on the Coins of Tughrıl Beg', 1602; Mahmoud Arafa, 'A Rare Saljuki Dinar Struck in Nisabur in 431 A.H. in the Name of Tugril Beg', *Annales Islamologiques*, 38 (2004), 307–9; cf. p. 130, n. 28 above.

[56] The earliest appearance known to me is on a Kakuyid coin of this date: see George C. Miles, 'The Coinage of the Kākwaihid Dynasty', *Iraq*, 5 (1938), 94. For slightly later examples, see Alptekin, 'Selçuklu paraları', 447. See also Kucur, 'A Study on the Coins of Tughrıl', 1602. Cf. Bosworth, 'Titulature', 227. Ibn al-Athir, *al-Kamil*, IX, 481, remarks that Tughrıl adopted the title *al-sulṭān al-mu'aẓẓam* immediately after the conquest of Nishapur in 431/1040. This should be considered unreliable given the numismatic evidence.

commander of the faithful)'.[57] Nonetheless, the term sultan was sufficiently controversial that in *khuṭbas* read in Baghdad, it was not applied to the Seljuk sultan till the reign of Alp Arslan.[58]

Turkish Titles in the Seljuk Empire

The court poet Mu'izzi described one of his patrons (probably Malikshah) as:

> The Chosroe of victorious fortune, the God-worshipping ruler, the shah with the essence of a *khāqān*, the sultan of Seljuk descent (*shāh-i khāqān-gawhar, sulṭān-i Saljūqī-nizhād*).[59]

In fact, this union of Islamic, Iranian and Turkish elements was surprisingly absent from official Seljuk titulature, although not from personal names – as Ibn al-'Adim comments, 'each of the Seljuk kings had two names, one Arabic, and one Turkish'.[60] The old Turkish sacral title of *qaghan* (Persian *khāqān, khān*), which was used by the Qarakhanids, was never formally employed by the Seljuks on their coins or correspondence. This may have been because the Qarakhanids were seen by many Turks as having a better claim to the legacy of Ashina and its title than the Seljuks: there are hints that a Qarakhanid lineage was more prestigious than a Seljuk one. Isfahani, for instance, tells us that Terken Khatun gained support for her son Mahmud because of her Qarakhanid descent, which seems to have outranked Berkyaruq's mother's Seljuk ancestry.[61] Official Seljuk titulature on their coins and documents emphasised their credentials as Perso-Islamic rulers, as sultans and *shāhanshāhs*. Ancient Turkish

57 Ibn al-Jawzi, *al-Muntazam*, XV, 289 (AH 435); cf. Bayhaqi, *Tarikh*, 693; Bosworth, 'Titulature', 226–7.

58 Ibn al-'Adim, *Bughya*, 17, 36.

59 Mu'izzi, *Diwan*, 131, No. 99, l. 10. The reference to having the 'essence of a *khaqan*' may indicate that the dedicatee of the poem was of Qarakhanid descent, which would suggest Malikshah (see n. 61 below), rather than Mu'izzi's other two royal *mamdūḥs*, Sanjar and Berkyaruq, neither of whom had a Qarakhanid mother.

60 Ibn al-'Adim, *Bughya*, 70.

61 Bundari, *Zubda*, 92; Rashid al-Din Watwat, in a letter to Mahmud Khan, Sanjar's successor, congratulates him on the prestige of both his Seljuk and Qarakhanid ancestry, but remarks specifically of the Al-i Afrasiyab (the Qarakhanid house), that 'there is no family more deep-rooted in kingship' (*az ān 'arīqtar dar mulk dūdmān nīst*) (Rashid al-Din Watwat, *Namaha*, 14). Note also how Nizam al-Mulk, congratulating Malikshah on his noble heritage from both parents, emphasises his descent from Afrasiyab (*Siyar al-Muluk*, 13, trans. 10). Cf. Peacock, 'Seljuq Legitimacy', 80; Hamdallah Mustawfi, *Tarikh-i Guzida*, 426. For Alp Arslan's Qarakhanid wife, see p. 179, n. 110 below).

titles do appear in the early years of the dynasty coupled with Semitic names: thus, Ibrahim Yınal and Musa Yabghu, who also called himself Inanj,[62] another Turkish title which was also used as a name in the Seljuk period – it can be hard to distinguish which function is intended. The twelfth century witnessed something of a vogue for Turkic titles among certain Seljuk successor states, such as the Artuqids of the Jazira, various *atabeg* dynasties such as the Ahmadilis and Zangids, and among several Anatolian Turkish dynasties.[63]

Continuity with pre-Islamic Iranian and Buyid kingship was emphasised by Tughrıl's adoption of the title *shāhanshāh*, which appeared alongside *al-sulṭān al-mu'aẓẓam* on Seljuk coins and inscriptions.[64] Tughrıl's formal recognition by Caliph al-Qa'im included a ceremony – modelled on Buyid practice – in which he was invested with regalia representing that of ancient Persian kings, such as the 'crown of Khusraw' (*al-tāj al-khusrawī*) and seven robes of honour representing the seven climes that comprised the earth in ancient Iranian cosmology. Along with the title of 'king of east and west' (*malik al-mashriq wa'l-maghrib*) that the caliph now bestowed on him, this implied claims to universal rule.[65]

At the conclusion of the coronation ceremony, the caliph enjoined Tughrıl to fear God, spread justice and prevent oppression.[66] The notion that piety and justice are the twin attributes of rulership is deeply rooted in the Perso-Islamic tradition. As Nizam al-Mulk puts it:

[62] See p. 32, n. 52.

[63] See Oya Pancaroğlu, 'The House of Mengücek in Divriği: Constructions of Dynastic Identity in the late Twelfth Century', in A. C. S. Peacock and Sara Nur Yıldız (eds), *The Seljuks of Anatolia: Court and Society in the Medieval Middle East* (London, 2013), 44–53. Some examples of such titles are also found in the Seljuk Sultanate of Iraq, but not among sultans. See *al-Mukhtarat min al-Rasa'il*, 430–1, referring to Inanj Bilge Qutlugh Ulugh Khwaja-yi Atabaki, document dated 551/1156. The reasons for this vogue in Turkish titulature need to be investigated.

[64] Alptekin, 'Selçuklu paraları', 447; Kucur, 'A Study on the Coins of Tughrıl', 1602.

[65] Bundari, *Zubda*, 14; Sibt, *Mir'at*, 24–6; Bar Hebraeus, *Chronography*, I, 212. For discussion, see Dimitri Korobeinikov, 'The King of the East and the West: The Seljuk Dynastic Concept and Titles in Muslim and Christian Sources', in A. C. S. Peacock and Sara Nur Yıldız (eds), *The Seljuks of Anatolia: Court and Society in the Medieval Middle East* (London, 2013), 67–71. For Buyid coronation ceremonies, see Busse, 'The Revival of Persian Kingship', 63–4; Wilferd Madelung, 'The Assumption of the Title Shāhanshāh by the Buyids and "the reign of the Daylam"', *Journal of Near Eastern Studies*, 28/ii (1969), esp. 85–7. See also Tor, 'The Long Shadow', 158–60.

[66] Sibt, *Mir'at*, 25.

> The person most worthy for kingship is he whose heart is a repository of justice, whose home is a haven for wise and religious men, and whose boon-companions and agents are discreet and God-fearing.[67]

Legal scholars and authors of mirrors for princes were at one in urging that the prime duty of a ruler was to protect the law (*sharīʿa*) that was the bedrock of the Islamic community.[68] Justice should be administered by the ruler through regular *maẓālim*, sessions where grievances could be presented. Even before his coronation, Tughrıl is claimed to have adopted this rhetoric of justice and piety. With the conquest of Nishapur, he made a point of sitting on the Ghaznavid sultan Masʿud's throne 'and started to sit for the *maẓālim* two days a week according to the custom of governors of Khurasan'.[69] This may be little more than propaganda, and Seljuk interest in the *maẓālim* certainly soon lapsed. Nizam al-Mulk himself provides a get-out clause, allowing the rulers who did not know Arabic to delegate their functions to a deputy.[70] It is often thought that viziers acted as the ruler's deputy at the *maẓālim*, but in fact there is little evidence of this from Seljuk times.[71] The image of the sultans dispensing justice to the masses remained the ideal, but rarely reflected the reality.

The sultans also displayed their claims to piety through the pious mottos they had inscribed on documents alongside the *ṭughrā* (e.g., *iʿtaṣamtu bi'llāh*, 'I have held fast to God'),[72] and by the *laqabs* (honorific titles) awarded by the caliphs. Ghaznavid and Buyid rulers had used *laqabs* based on 'al-Dawla' (*ʿAdud al-Dawla*, 'support of the ['Abbasid] state/dynasty', for instance), but Tughrıl is the first ruler known to have used the component 'al-Din' (of the faith) in his *laqab, Rukn al-Dīn* ('Pillar of the [Muslim] Faith').[73] Despite the ostensible piety of such a title, it also marked something of a usurpation of caliphal prerogatives: whereas previous rulers had defined themselves as supporters of the 'Abbasid *dawla*, now Tughrıl arrogated to himself the caliphal duty of upholding Islam.

67 Nizam al-Mulk, *Siyar al-Muluk*, 66, trans. 49.

68 Lambton, 'The Dilemma of Government', 56–7. Cf. Crone, *Medieval Islamic Political Thought*, 286 ff.

69 Ibn al-Athir, *al-Kamil*, IX, 459. Cf also his behaviour in Isfahan, Durand-Guédy, *Iranian Elites*, 86–7.

70 Nizam al-Mulk, *Siyar al-Muluk*, 18, 59; trans. 13–14, 44.

71 Lange, *Justice*, 41; Lambton, *Continuity and and Change*, 28, 71–2, 79. One example from a late source is Subki, *Tabaqat*, IV, 310, who states that Nizam al-Mulk sat for the *maẓālim*; but Subki is always anxious to exaggerate the role of his fellow Shafiʿi.

72 See Bivar, 'Saljuq Sign Manual'.

73 Bosworth, 'Titulature', 216; Tor, '"Sovereign and pious"', 55.

Caliphal recognition was also expressed through mentioning the sultan's name in the *khuṭba*, the Friday prayers, in Baghdad. This meant that possession of Baghdad, the surest way to enforce the mention in the *khuṭba*, became, alongside control of Isfahan (at least until the reign of Mahmud), a key element in being able to claim to be a legitimate sultan.[74]

Welcome though caliphal recognition was for securing the new dynasty's legitimacy in the broader Muslim world, it did have the distinct disadvantage of potentially subordinating the Seljuk ruler to the caliph, at least in principle. Theoretically, the sultan was bound to the caliph by a *khidma* relationship: the caliph was his patron, he was the caliph's vassal. Entering into this *khidma* relationship formed, alongside the symbolism of the *khuṭba*, a crucial part of the legitimacy of Seljuk sultans. Ibn al-Jawzi's account of the reception of Sultan Mahmud and his brother Mas'ud by Caliph al-Mustarshid in his Baghdad palace of al-Muthammina in Sha'ban 515/November 1121 emphasises this aspect of the relationship:

> When [Mahmud and Mas'ud] came close, the veil was lifted and the sultan stood in the place where his vizier was standing, with his brother behind him. They made obeisance [*khadamā*] three times, and they stood while the [caliphal vizier] Ibn Sa'id told the sultan on behalf of the caliph of the latter's affection, closeness and good faith in him. Then the Caliph ordered the robes of honour to be bestowed on him, and [the sultan] was borne to a side-chamber of the hall, with his brother and [his amirs] Yürünqüsh and Rayhan. The treasurer [*ṣāḥib al-makhzan*], Iqbal and Nazar took charge of cloaking him [in the robes], while the two [caliphal] viziers standing before the Caliph presented the amirs one by one. [Each amir] made obeisance [*khadama*], recognised his obligation of service [*ya'rifu khidmatahu*] and kissed the earth and departed. Then the sultan and his brother returned and did likewise before the Caliph. Mahmud was wearing the seven robes, the neckband, the crown and the armbands. Both did obeisance [*khadamā*], and the Caliph ordered a chair for the sultan to sit on. The Caliph admonished him and recited to him [the Qur'anic injunction] 'He who does an atom's weight of good will see it, and he who does an atom's weight of evil will see it'.[75] He ordered [the sultan] to treat his subjects well. He then gave

[74] Durand-Guédy, *Iranian Elites*, 82–3, 172. Note Tutush's difficulties as a result of his failure to secure Baghdad and his mention in the *khuṭba* there, which the caliph refused to grant him: Ibn al-Athir, *al-Kamil*, X, 233; Ibn al-Jawzi, *al-Muntazam*, XVII, 5, 15; Sibt, *Mir'at*, ed. Ghamidi, I, 199–203.

[75] Qur'an, Surat al-Zalzala, 7–8.

> permission to his vizier Abu Talib to explain that. Afterwards, it is related that [the sultan] said, 'God has entrusted me with accepting the commands of our lord the Commander of the Faithful and putting them into practice. By them is good fortune facilitated and they give tidings of boons.' The Caliph gave the two viziers two swords and ordered them to invest the sultan with them. When this was done he said, 'With them suppress the unbelievers and the heretics'.[76]

The whole ceremony was calculated to emphasise the remoteness and prestige of the caliph, with many of his commands conveyed indirectly by his officials to the sultan. The robes of honour played a particularly important role in symbolising the *khidma* relationship, showing that the sultan had been duly invested and recognised as a vassal by the caliph. This point is underlined elsewhere by Ibn al-Jawzi, when he relates a plot to make off with some of these robes of honour during the succession struggle following Mahmud's death. He relates that:

> Tughrıl [II] returned to Hamadhan. Gaining the support of the army, he secured his rule while his brother Mas'ud's situation became hopeless. The reason was that the Caliph had sent robes of honour to the Khwarazmshah, and [the Mazyadid] Dubays suggested to Tughrıl that, 'You should take these robes and make it appear that the Caliph has sent them to us. Then no one will stay with Mas'ud.'[77]

Such ceremonies and symbols were particularly important for sultans, whose legitimacy and power was otherwise weak, as was the case with Mahmud and Mas'ud. Some sultans, like Alp Arslan and Sanjar, never felt the need to meet a caliph in the flesh. Caliphal power, then, was only as potent as the sultan was weak.

The Seljuks attempted both to enhance their legitimacy and to exert control over the caliph by binding themselves to the 'Abbasids through dynastic marriages.[78] Virtually every caliph from the mid-eleventh to the mid-twelfth century had a Seljuk wife. Shortly after the Seljuk entry into Baghdad, al-Qa'im married Chaghrı's daughter Arslan Khatun;[79] his son 'Uddat al-Din, the future Caliph al-Muqtadi, wedded Alp Arslan's

[76] Ibn al-Jawzi, *al-Muntazam*, XVII, 195–6.

[77] *Ibid.*, XVII, 284.

[78] The most detailed study on this topic is Zekeriya Kitapçı, *Abbâsî Hilafetinde Selçuklu Hatunları ve Türk Sultanları* (Konya, 1994). See also Eric Hanne, 'Women, Power, and the Eleventh and Twelfth Century Abbasid Court', *Hawwa*, 3/i (2005), 80–110.

[79] Bundari, *Zubda*, 11; Ibn al-Athir, *al-Kamil*, IX, 617; Ibn al-Jawzi, *al-Muntazam*, XVI, 4–5; Sibt, *Mir'at*, 2–3.

daughter.[80] A decade later, in 474/1081–2, al-Muqtadi married a daughter of Malikshah.[81] Similar unions were celebrated in the twelfth century: in 502/1108, Muhammad Tapar arranged the marriage of another daughter of Malikshah, his own sister ʿIsmat Khatun, to Caliph al-Mustazhir,[82] while the latter's son al-Mustarshid married a daughter of Sanjar in 518/1124.[83] Al-Muqtafi too married Sultan Masʿud's sister Fatima bt. Muhammad.[84]

Seljuks also sought for themselves ʿAbbasid princesses, although such unions were rather rarer. When Tughrıl desired to marry al-Qa'im's daughter, the caliph sought to make as many difficulties as possible before reluctantly agreeing.[85] His attitude may have been born of wariness of 'the possibility of a Saljûq descendant assuming the ʿAbbasid caliphate', as George Makdisi suggested;[86] but such marriages had precedents in Buyid times. Moreover, as we have seen, caliphs usually did acquiesce in marrying Seljuk princesses, which would have carried a rather greater danger of such a consequence. Masʿud seems to have had no difficulty in arranging his own marriage to Caliph Muqtafi's daughter.[87] In all likelihood, al-Qa'im's reluctance was another manifestation of this caliph's efforts to assert a degree of independence.[88]

These marriages were designed above all as tokens of a successful deal, and marked a break with the ʿAbbasid tradition of the classical period (ninth and tenth centuries) whereby the caliphs were unmarried.[89] Al-Qa'im's own marriage to Chaghrı's daughter signified the caliph's recognition of Seljuk ascendancy after the occupation of Baghdad. Nor were they always imposed on unwilling caliphs: al-Muqtadi, for instance, actively sought the marriage,

80 Ibn al-Athir, *al-Kamil*, X, 71; Ibn al-Jawzi, *al-Muntazam*, XVI, 140; Sibt, *Mir'at*, 141, 156–7.

81 Ibn al-Athir, *al-Kamil*, X, 120; Ibn al-Jawzi, *al-Muntazam*, XVI, 222–3; Sibt, *Mir'at*, 213–14.

82 Ibn al-Athir, *al-Kamil*, X, 471; Ibn al-Jawzi, *al-Muntazam*, XVII, 112; Sibt, *Mir'at*, ed. Ghamidi, II, 501–2.

83 Ibn al-Jawzi, *al-Muntazam*, XVI, 224, 225.

84 Ibn al-Athir, *al-Kamil*, XI, 77; Ibn al-Jawzi, *al-Muntazam*, XVII, 321, XVIII, 3 (AH 531, 534); Bundari, *Zubda*, 194; Hillenbrand, *A Muslim Principality*, fol. 169a, pp. 98–9.

85 For a detailed discussion, see George Makdisi, 'The Marriage of Tughrıl Beg', *IJMES*, 1/iii (1970), 259–75.

86 *Ibid.*, 261.

87 Ibn al-Athir, *al-Kamil*, XII, 77; Ibn al-Jawzi, *al-Muntazam*, XVIII, 3–4; Hillenbrand, *A Muslim Principality*, fol. 169a, pp. 97–8.

88 Hanne, *Putting the Caliph in his Place*, 96–7.

89 Hugh Kennedy, *The Court of the Caliphs: When Baghdad Ruled the Muslim World* (London, 2004), 167–8.

for which he had to bargain hard (see p. 179 below). However, they could suffer as a result of the vicissitudes of the Seljuk–'Abbasid political relationship. Mistreating their Seljuk wives, as al-Muqtadi later did (see p. 144), represented a means by which caliphs could express dissatisfaction with the sultans. Moreover, even if the fear of the birth of a candidate for the caliphate of Seljuk descent was not the overriding motive as Makdisi has suggested, it is noteworthy that despite the frequency of these marriages, the 'Abbasids managed to exclude all children of Seljuk parentage from the succession.[90] While plenty of caliphs were of Turkish descent – as they had been in earlier periods too – this was invariably through Turkish concubines, not through these Seljuk wives.

The Seljuks and the Caliphate

Recognition by the caliph thus served to legitimise the Seljuks through public ceremonies and titulature. Although the Seljuks had deposed the Shi'ite Buyids, who had often treated the 'Abbasids with contempt, the Turks were not from the caliph's point of view much of an improvement in practice – indeed quite the opposite. Since the late tenth century, caliphs had been seeking to assert a greater measure of authority both in the religious and political sphere, in close alliance with the Hanbali religious movement that was popular among the Baghdadi masses. Already al-Qadir (r. 381/991–422/1031) had been able to take advantage of the weakness of the Buyids to assert prerogatives such as appointing qadis in Iraq, taking responsibility for the administration of Baghdad itself, and intervening in the political arena by mediating between the Buyids and their troops.[91] This new assertiveness was also proclaimed in documents issued by al-Qadir and his successor al-Qa'im, which became known as the 'Qadiri-Qa'imi creed', that sought to define the caliph's position as the defender of Sunnism. Thus, the caliphs whom the Seljuks encountered in the mid-eleventh century were 'in a position to speak and act for themselves'.[92] Nonetheless, they had access to few significant revenue sources and no military support to speak of.

The Seljuks threatened to undo the efforts of al-Qadir and al-Qa'im by imposing their own authority, personified by the *shiḥna*, a senior Seljuk amir who was the sultan's representative in Baghdad.[93] It was the *shiḥna* who in

[90] I can find no basis for Kitapçı's assertion (*Abbâsî Hilafetinde Selçuklu Hatunları*, 262, 265) that al-Rashid was the son of Mustarshid by Sanjar's daughter: according to Carole Hillenbrand, 'Al-Rās͟hid', *EI²*, his mother was a slave girl named Khushf.

[91] See Busse, *Chalif und Grosskönigen*; Hanne, *Putting the Caliph in his Place*, 65 ff.

[92] Hanne, *Putting the Caliph in his Place*, 101.

[93] On *shiḥnas* in Baghdad, see Vanessa van Renterghem, 'Controlling and Developing

practice determined in whose name the *khuṭba* would be said, underlining the impotence of the caliphs to use their legitimatory role to make political capital, even in times of internal crisis within the Seljuk Empire. Thus, during the civil war after Malikshah's death, although the *khuṭba* changed at least eight times between Berkyaruq and Muhammad, the caliph had very little influence in this. Despite the chaos, only on one brief occasion in Rabi' I 496/ January 1103 was the *khuṭba* said in the caliph's name alone. Even this was not a result of caliphal strength, but because control of Baghdad was disputed by the two rival *shiḥnas* who been appointed, one by Berkyaruq and one by Muhammad. Rather than a declaration of 'Abbasid independence, this may have been simply an attempt to avoid choosing sides.[94]

Caliphs were also frequently obliged to tolerate Seljuk interference even in prerogatives such as choosing the caliphal vizier.[95] However, they did not willingly acquiesce in surrendering the progress they had made since the late Buyid period, but continued to struggle to find a way to assert a degree of authority at least in Baghdad. Eventually, these efforts would bear fruit in the re-emergence of a caliphal state in Iraq in the later twelfth century, which would under Caliph al-Nasir li-Din Allah play a crucial role in the Seljuks' own downfall. Here, we shall examine the development of the Seljuk–'Abbasid relationship.

The Collapse of the Seljuk–'Abbasid Relationship from Tughrıl to Malikshah

Initially Tughrıl may have planned to make Baghdad one of his bases. Immediately after the occupation of the city in 447/1055, he had extensive work done to the old Buyid palace in Baghdad, adding walls and towers, and destroying a good number of neighbouring houses and markets.[96] However, he was evidently fairly swiftly forced to abandon the idea owing to the demands of his largely nomad armies (see pp. 49–50, 224). Similar exigencies must have influenced his successors, for between Tughrıl's last visit to Baghdad in 455/1063,[97] shortly before his death, and Malikshah's first sojourn in the city in 479/1086–7 for the marriage of his daughter to al-Muqtadi,[98] no Seljuk sultan set foot in Baghdad.

Baghdad: Caliphs, Sultans and the Balance of Power in the Abbasid Capital (mid-5th/11th to late 6th/12th Centuries)', in C. Lange and S. Mecit (eds), *The Seljuqs: Politics, Society and Culture* (Edinburgh, 2011), 125–6.

94 Ibn al-Jawzi, *al-Muntazam*, XVII, 80; Ibn al-Athir, *al-Kamil*, X, 355–8.
95 See Hanne, *Putting the Caliph in his Place*, 108–18.
96 Sibt, *Mir'at*, 3; Ibn al-Jawzi, *al-Muntazam*, XVI, 4; Ibn al-Athir, *al-Kamil*, IX, 614.
97 Ibn al-Athir, *al-Kamil*, X, 25; Ibn al-Jawzi, *al-Muntazam*, XVI, 82; Sibt, *Mir'at*, 97–8.
98 Ibn al-Athir, *al-Kamil*, X, 155; Ibn al-Jawzi, *al-Muntazam*, XVI, 259; Sibt, *Mir'at*, 239.

Despite the presence of the *shiḥna*, the caliphs al-Qa'im and al-Muqtadi were able to assert, cautiously at first, their authority within Baghdad. Al-Qa'im's agents seized control of the mint in 462/1069–70,[99] and he successfully insisted on the dismissal of the Seljuk *shiḥna* Aytegin al-Sulaymani in 464/1071–2.[100] The growing caliphal activism started to provoke a Seljuk reaction. Nizam al-Mulk attempted to restrict growing caliphal power by allocating some of al-Qa'im's estates to the Türkmen in 466/1073,[101] and, as discussed elsewhere (pp. 271–2), the vizier appears to have deliberately incited religious tension in Baghdad as a means of weakening the caliph's hand there.[102] Relations deteriorated further with the accession of al-Muqtadi as caliph in 467/1074. Sa'd al-Dawla Gawhara'in, Malikshah's *shiḥna*, frequently clashed with the new caliph, threatening to burn down the caliphal harem in 471/1078–9.[103] Al-Muqtadi claimed the right to implement the precepts of *sharīʿa*, traditionally a task carried out by officials appointed by temporal rulers. In 479/1086, the caliph made a show of enforcing *sharīʿa* in the market place by having wine publicly poured away,[104] and in 484/1091 he imposed the sumptuary laws on non-Muslims, a requirement which was usually more honoured in the breach than the observance.[105] Al-Muqtadi also expelled the Turkish soldiers accompanying his Seljuk wife, Malikshah's daughter, and mistreated her to such an extent that the sultan demanded she be sent back to Isfahan.[106]

In Ramadan 484/November 1091, Malikshah and Nizam al-Mulk responded to these various provocations by demanding the sacking of the caliphal vizier Abu Shujaʿ, who had been openly critical of the Seljuks.[107] Malikshah also began to spend extended periods in Baghdad towards the end of his reign.[108] On his third visit in Ramadan 485/November 1092, the

[99] Ibn al-Athir, *al-Kamil*, X, 60–61.

[100] *Ibid.*, X, 70.

[101] Ibn al-Jawzi, *al-Muntazam*, XVI, 154; Sibt, *Mir'at*, 167.

[102] Cf. Ibn al-Jawzi, *al-Muntazam*, XVI, 182; Makdisi, *Ibn ʿAqil*, 350–66, esp. 351–2, 361–2; Hanne, *Putting the Caliph in his Place*, 113.

[103] Bundari, *Zubda*, 44; Ibn al-Athir, *al-Kamil*, X, 100, 110; Ibn al-Jawzi, *al-Muntazam*, XVI, 198–9, XVII, 56–7; Sibt, *Mir'at*, 177, 195–6; Hanne, *Putting the Caliph in his Place*, 107, 113, 119.

[104] Ibn al-Jawzi, *al-Muntazam*, XVI, 255.

[105] *Ibid.*, XVI, 292; Ibn al-Athir, *al-Kamil*, X, 186.

[106] Ibn al-Athir, *al-Kamil*, X, 165, 175.

[107] *Ibid.*, X, 186–7; Ibn al-Jawzi, *al-Muntazam*, XVI, 292–3.

[108] Malikshah visited came in 479/1086–7 (n. 99 above), and stayed between Ramadan 484/October 1091 and Rabiʿ I 485/April 1092 (Ibn al-Athir, *al-Kamil*, X, 199; Ibn al-Jawzi, *al-Muntazam*, XVI, 294), in addition to his third visit (n. 110 below).

sultan came 'with an ill intent, wanting to destroy al-Muqtadi', as Ibn al-Jawzi puts it (*arāda tash'īth amr al-Muqtadī*).[109] These increasingly frequent visits were accompanied by a resumption of building work by the sultan and his officials, which had been largely abandoned since Tughrıl's efforts. A 'mosque of the sultan' (*jāmi' al-sulṭān*) was started, and Nizam al-Mulk, Taj al-Mulk and the leading amirs had houses built for their visits to the city, while Malikshah also sponsored the construction of a market near his palace.[110]

Given the sudden construction activity and the sultan's personal presence in the city, Malikshah seems to have aimed to make Baghdad the empire's capital, or at least its winter capital, as is suggested by the dates of his visits. Probably the cooler Isfahan and its environs were to remain the main base at other times, and that city's symbolic importance is suggested by the fact that it was chosen as Malikshah's burial place, rather than Baghdad where he died.[111] At any rate, it is clear that there was no place for al-Muqtadi in Malikshah's grand design, as Ibn al-Jawzi recounts:

> The sultan sent to the Caliph saying, 'You must leave Baghdad to me and depart for whatever country you wish.' The Caliph was extremely alarmed at this and replied, 'Give me a month's delay.' The reply came: 'It is not possible for you to delay even an hour.'[112]

Eventually, a respite of ten days was granted, in which time Malikshah suddenly died, quite probably killed on al-Muqtadi's instructions (see p. 71 above). Although it is not clear whether Malikshah's intention was merely to remove al-Muqtadi and replace him with a more pliant member of the dynasty – most likely Ja'far, his own grandson by al-Muqtadi's Seljuk wife[113] – or to remove the 'Abbasids altogether, it is a measure of Malikshah's self-confidence that he could contemplate such a move. Later sultans would have few scruples about removing inconvenient individual caliphs, but none attempted such an audacious step as Malikshah did.

109 Ibn al-Athir, *al-Kamil*, X, 210; Ibn al-Jawzi, *al-Muntazam*, XVI, 300.

110 Ibn al-Athir, *al-Kamil*, X, 200; Ibn al-Jawzi, *al-Muntazam*, XVI, 298. See further Vanessa van Renterghem, 'Social and Urban Dynamics in Baghdad during the Saldjūq Period (mid Vth/XIth mid VIth/XIIth c.)', in İsmail Safa Üstün (ed.), *İslam Medeniyetinde Bağdat (Medinetü's-Selām) Uluslararası Sempozyumu (International Symposium on Baghdad (Madinat al-Salam) in the Islamic Civilization)* (Istanbul, 2011), 185–7.

111 See Durand-Guédy, *Iranian Elites*, 81–2.

112 Ibn al-Jawzi, *al-Muntazam*, XVI, 299.

113 See Hanne, 'Women, Power', 95–7.

The 'Abbasid Struggle for Independence

Al-Muqtadi died shortly after Malikshah, and his successor, al-Mustazhir, played a very limited role in the Seljuk succession wars, lacking significant military forces of his own.[114] Attempts to turn the situation to his advantage by picking sides did not bear fruit. Muhammad even rejected the caliph's offer to campaign on his side in 495/1101.[115] Without any military clout of his own, al-Mustazhir could do little to influence the outcome of events, and he was not a party to the peace deal that ended the conflict. The caliph was also limited by two other major forces: the continued presence of Seljuk *shiḥnas* in Baghdad; and the growing power of the Shi'ite Mazyadid dynasty of Hilla, who were hostile to the caliph and were emerging during the succession war as the major force in central and southern Iraq.[116] Nonetheless, the caliph continued to make some progress at asserting his authority locally. The mint, evidently in 'Abbasid hands, omitted the titles (but not the name, except briefly in 486/1093) of the Seljuk sultan – in contrast to mints outside Baghdad – suggesting an effort to demote the importance of the sultan, and an increase in caliphal power. Increasing numbers of officials were appointed by the caliph, and the caliphal bureaucracy seems to have expanded, with new departments and offices.[117]

When Muhammad Tapar ascended the throne, he started to take a much greater interest in Baghdad than his predecessors, regularly wintering there.[118] His *shiḥna*, Bihruz al-Mujahid, undertook major building works, including the restoration of the sultan's mosque and official residence, the *dār al-mamlaka*.[119] It seems that Muhammad Tapar was intent on reviving Malikshah's plans to make Baghdad his winter capital, but friendly relations with al-Mustazhir were signified by exchanges of presents and the customary dynastic marriage.[120] Al-Mustazhir's only major political intervention was to seek to broker a peace between the sultan and the Mazyadid Sadaqa b.

114 In general, see Hanne, *Putting the Caliph in his Place*, 135–40.

115 Ibn al-Athir, *al-Kamil*, X, 329; Ibn al-Jawzi, *al-Muntazam*, XVII, 75.

116 Makdisi, 'Notes on Hilla and the Mazyadids', 293; C. E. Bosworth, 'Mazyad, Banū', *EI²*.

117 Hanne, 'Death on the Tigris', 158–60, 167; van Renterghem, 'Controlling and Developing Baghdad', 119; van Renterghem, 'Social and Urban Dynamics', 187, for 'Abbasid building activity.

118 The sultan is recorded as present in Baghdad in Jumada I 498/January 1105, Rabi' II 501/November 1107, Rabi' II 503/November 1109, Rajab 504/January 1111, and he spent the whole of 510/May 1116–May 1117 there. Ibn al-Jawzi, *al-Muntazam*, IX, 142, 155, 163, 166, 187; Durand-Guédy, *Iranian Elites*, 322.

119 Ibn al-Jawzi, *al-Muntazam*, IX, 159, 163, 186; cf. Sibt, *Mir'at*, ed. Ghamidi, 723; Ibn al-Athir, *al-Kamil*, X, 471.

120 Ibn al-Jawzi, *al-Muntazam*, IX, 155, 166; Ibn al-Athir, *al-Kamil*, X, 471, 483.

Mazyad of Hilla, and was apparently not even tempted by Sadaqa's offer to help the caliph throw off Seljuk tutelage by providing arms and men.[121] Al-Mustazhir was probably rightly suspicious of his fate under the Shi'ite Mazyazdids, should the gamble succeed.

Al-Mustazhir's successor, al-Mustarshid (r. 512/1118–529/1135), broke with this policy of peaceful coexistence with the Seljuks.[122] However, a much greater worry to the caliph, at least initially, were the Shi'ite Mazyadids who proved adept at using the succession dispute that followed Muhammad Tapar's death (and, coincidentally, al-Mustarshid's accession) to expand their own power in Iraq. Al-Mustarshid relied on the Seljuk sultan of Iraq, Mahmud, to protect him from Sadaqa's son and successor Dubays, who saw Baghdad as little more than a trophy to be plundered by his troops and who had plotted to install Mustarshid's brother on the throne as caliph in his place.[123] On one occasion al-Mustarshid is recorded as begging the sultan not to leave Baghdad out of fear of being left at Dubays' mercy.[124]

Like his predecessors, al-Mustarshid also sought to assert his independence. He had already in 514/1120 ordered the wine sold in the sultan's market to be poured away in an attempt to assert temporal authority reminiscent of al-Muqtadi.[125] Al-Mustarshid turned to addressing the 'Abbasids' great weakness, their lack of any military support. Kurdish and Bedouin tribes were recruited to serve in the caliphal army,[126] the caliph ordered the fortifications of Baghdad to be restored,[127] and al-Mustarshid even led these armies in person against Dubays in 517/1123[128] – the first caliph to lead armies into battle since al-Ta'i' in the tenth century.

Mahmud initially saw the caliph's growing military might as a positive advantage, regarding him as an ally against Sanjar who might help him become sole sultan. Al-Mustarshid also started to exercise a decisive influence

121 Ibn al-Athir, *al-Kamil*, X, 440–447.

122 For overviews of his reign and relations with the Seljuks, see Carole Hillenbrand, 'al-Mustarshid', *EI²*; Hanne, *Putting the Caliph in his Place*, 144–65; Tor, 'A Tale of Two Murders,' 281–91; Köymen, *Büyük Selçuklu İmparatorluğu Tarihi*, II, 91–112, 120–9, 255–84.

123 Ibn al-Athir, *al-Kamil*, X, 608; Ibn al-Jawzi, *al-Muntazam*, XVII, 207–10; Ibn al-'Adim, *Bughya*, 235–7, 239; Hanne, *Putting the Caliph in his Place*, 144–7, 151.

124 Ibn al-Jawzi, *al-Muntazam*, XVII, 197, 204–5, 207–10; cf. Hanne, *Putting the Caliph in his Place*, 150–1.

125 Ibn al-Jawzi, *al-Muntazam*, XVII, 187.

126 Ibn al-Athir, *al-Kamil*, X, 607–10, 626–8.

127 Ibn al-Jawzi, *al-Muntazam*, XVII, 217–19.

128 *Ibid.*, XVII, 216–17, 228–9; Ibn al-Athir, *al-Kamil*, X, 608, 626–8.

over appointments in the gift of the sultan. When in 515/1121–2 Abu Saʿd al-Harawi was appointed by Masʿud as chief qadi 'over all the realm', Iraq was excepted from this because of Mustarshid's preference for Abu 'l-Qasim al-Zaynabi.[129] Indeed, in 518/1124, Aqsonqur al-Bursuqi was even removed as *shiḥna* as a result of the caliph's complaints against him.[130] The caliph was able to intervene in the economic arena too, adjusting the exchange rate between dirhams and dinars to try to mitigate the effects of inflation resulting from the shortage of goods caused by the severe weather at the beginning of his reign (see also p. 288 below).[131]

Mahmud ignored warnings from his *shiḥna*, Yürünqüsh (Bursuqi's replacement), that the caliph was trying to establish his independence (*yaṭlubu al-mulk*).[132] Sanjar got wind of Mahmud's planned alliance and protested:

> You are my right arm, and the Caliph has decided to trick both you and me . . . You know I have no male child, you have waged war against me and I overcame you but did not mistreat you, I killed those who were the cause of our fighting, I reinstated you as sultan, I made you my heir and I married you to my daughter . . . I see you as my son, God forbid that you should pay attention to what [the Caliph] has said to you. You should go to Baghdad with your army, arrest the Caliph's vizier Ibn Sadaqa, kill the Kurds he has registered [in the army], take the provisions he has made and all the travel equipment and say, 'I am your sword and your servant, return to your palace according the habit of your forefathers and I will protect you from overburdening yourself.'[133]

The letter seems to have been effective in persuading Mahmud to one of those innumerable shifts of alliance that make the politics of the period so confusing.

Al-Mustarshid's intelligence network was clearly equally effective, for he then tried to prevent Mahmud from coming to Iraq.[134] Appealing directly to the leading citizens of Baghdad, on 10 Dhu 'l-Hijja 520/27 December 1126 the caliph mounted the pulpit and delivered a sermon declaring his

129 Ibn al-Jawzi, *al-Muntazam*, XVII, 193.

130 Ibn al-Athir, *al-Kamil*, X, 622–3.

131 Ibn al-Jawzi, *al-Muntazam*, XVII, 207; for inflation, see also *ibid.*, XVII, 221; Ibn al-Athir, *al-Kamil*, X, 544

132 Ibn al-Jawzi, *al-Muntazam*, XVII, 229, 231; cf. Qummi, *Dhayl-i Nafthat al-Masdur*, 86. Other sources suggest the cause of tension was in fact the behaviour of Masʿud's deputies in Iraq, but the lack of detail of these accounts suggests Ibn al-Jawzi's version is more convincing. See Hillenbrand, *A Muslim Principality*, fol. 165a, p. 67.

133 Ibn al-Jawzi, *al-Muntazam*, XVII, 231.

134 *Ibid.*, XVII, 231–2.

determination to fight, his son al-Rashid standing by the minbar with sword drawn throughout. Mahmud led his army to the outskirts of Baghdad, but the caliph still resisted his entreaties to come to terms.[135] A portion of the Seljuk army sacked the caliphal palace in Muharram 521/January 1127. The populace showed their sympathies by, apparently at al-Mustarshid's instigation, sacking the palaces of Seljuk officials, while trenches were built around the city to deter a Seljuk attack.[136] The sultan and Turkish soldiery were abused by the populace, especially in the west bank, who shouted, 'O Batini [Ismaili heretic]! You couldn't attack the Byzantines so you came to attack the Caliph and the Muslims'.[137] However, with food running out and defections by senior amirs to the sultan's camp, Mustarshid was forced to sue for peace and the sultan entered Baghdad.

Al-Mustarshid's first gamble for power thus collapsed. However, he soon resumed recruitment to his army, as before using the excuse of the threat presented by Dubays.[138] On Mahmud's death, he intervened in support of Mas'ud against Sanjar's preferred candidate, Tughrıl (see Chapter 2). The caliph then moved against other regional enemies, starting with the amir Zangi of Mosul who had earlier attempted to take control of Baghdad in the name of Sanjar and Tughrıl. Supported by a contingent of Seljuk amirs (*jamāʿa min al-umarāʾ al-saljuqiyya*) who had gone over to his side, in 527/1133 al-Mustarshid advanced on Mosul and besieged it, although fear of renewed activity by Dubays, who had now switched to Mas'ud's side, forced him to retreat.[139] Despite this failure, further Turkish amirs joined al-Mustarshid, and when the caliph reviewed his forces on 'Id al-Fitr 527/1133, they comprised 15,000 horsemen – a significant military force.[140]

Meddling in the murky world of Turkish politics was a dangerous business, and Tughrıl started to correspond with al-Mustarshid's new Turkish amirs. When the caliph found out and arrested some, the others fled to throw themselves on the mercy of Mas'ud, who refused to hand them over to his supposed ally, al-Mustarshid.[141] Within a year, the caliphal forces were reduced to a mere 5,000, and even these could not be relied on. When al-Mustarshid attempted to do battle against Mas'ud

[135] Ibn al-Jawzi, *al-Muntazam*, XVII, 232–6. See also the account of these events in Qummi, *Dhayl-i Nafthat al-Masdur*, 87–9.

[136] Ibn al-Athir, *al-Kamil*, X, 637; Ibn al-Jawzi, *al-Muntazam*, XVII, 241.

[137] Ibn al-Athir, *al-Kamil*, X, 637; Ibn al-Jawzi, *al-Muntazam*, XVII, 242; cf. XVII, 236.

[138] Ibn al-Athir, *al-Kamil*, X, 655; Husayni, *Akhbar*, 98–9.

[139] Ibn al-Athir, *al-Kamil*, XI, 5; Ibn al-Athir, *al-Ta'rikh al-Bahir*, 47–8; Ibn al-Jawzi, *al-Muntazam*, XVII, 276.

[140] Ibn al-Jawzi, *al-Muntazam*, XVII, 283.

[141] *Ibid.*, XVII, 284.

in Ramadan 529/October 1135, his Turkish commanders immediately defected and the caliph was taken prisoner.[142] The Seljuks demolished the walls of Baghdad, and al-Mustarshid was suddenly murdered by Ismaili assassins – a deed widely thought to have been instigated by Sanjar and Mas'ud.[143] Soon after, Dubays was executed by Mas'ud, for, as Ibn al-Athir tells us, 'he did not realise that the sultans kept him in order to use him as an instrument to oppose al-Mustarshid; when this reason was removed, so was he'.[144]

The willingness of al-Mustarshid to resort to force and to dabble in Seljuk succession disputes removed whatever scruples Mas'ud had. Al-Mustarshid's fate was shared by his successor: al-Rashid was also deposed and killed after a brief and bloody reign in which he had joined a group of amirs led by Zangi of Mosul in rebelling against Mas'ud.[145] Mas'ud took care to justify his removal of the caliph by producing a document allegedly signed by al-Rashid stating, 'If I recruit soldiers and rebel, then I will have deposed myself' (*khal'atu nafsī min al-amr*).[146]

While actions such as the destruction of wine at the beginning of his reign were in line with those of previous caliphs, al-Mustarshid's military recruitment and fortification programme went much further than any of his predecessors. Nonetheless, rather than a long-term strategy, one is left with the impression of something of an opportunistic power grab on the caliph's part, engendered above all by the threat posed by Dubays.[147] Indeed, Ibn al-Athir attributes the whole confrontation between Mahmud and al-Mustarshid to hostility between the *shiḥna* Yürünqüsh and caliphal officials;[148] this is probably to underestimate its significance, but there is no evidence to suggest that al-Mustarshid ever imagined a world without the Seljuks, whose support he required to fend off the more imminent threat of the Shi'ite Mazyadids.

Despite the longevity of the 'Abbasid dynasty and the lustre of its name, neither al-Mustarshid nor his successor al-Rashid could appeal to any major political constituency. The only group on whose loyalty the caliph could

142 Bundari, *Zubda*, 177; Ibn al-Jawzi, *al-Muntazam*, XVII, 295; Ibn al-Athir, *al-Kamil*, XI, 24–6. See also Chapter 6 below.

143 Ibn al-Jawzi, *al-Muntazam*, XVII, 298–9, 304; Ibn al-Athir, *al-Kamil*, XI, 27; Bundari, *Zubda*, 175–7; Hillenbrand, *A Muslim Principalty*, fol. 165b, 166a, pp. 69–70, 72–3.

144 Ibn al-Athir, *al-Kamil*, XI, 30; cf. Ibn al-Jawzi, *al-Muntazam*, XVII, 305.

145 Ibn al-Athir, *al-Ta'rikh al-Bahir*, 51–3; Ibn al-Jawzi, *al-Muntazam*, XVII, 307–12; he too was rumoured to have been killed by Ismaili assassins in 532, attempting to regain his throne: see Ibn al-Jawzi, *al-Muntazam*, XVII, 332.

146 Ibn al-Jawzi, *al-Muntazam*, XVII, 312.

147 Cf. Hanne, *Putting the Caliph in his Place*, 154–5.

148 Ibn al-Athir, *al-Kamil*, X, 635.

reasonably firmly rely was the populace of Baghdad, or at least its Sunni portions. Al-Mustarshid's defeat and capture by Mas'ud was met with widespread lamentation in Baghdad, whose people had also so enthusiastically participated in ransacking Seljuk property in the city in Mahmud's time. Even so, the Baghdadi popular support for the caliph had its limits. When al-Mustarshid had attempted to raise funds to pay for the building of the walls, the measure was so unpopular that it had to be abandoned and the funds raised returned.[149] Mas'ud's attempt to impose a punitive tax on the people of Baghdad, as well as the new Caliph al-Rashid,[150] was doubtless motivated by a desire to sap support for the caliph and his ambitions by hitting the populace where it hurt.

The End of Seljuk Tutelage

Given the lesson of the previous two caliphs' actions, Mas'ud naturally sought to hobble al-Muqtafi, who replaced al-Rashid in 530/1136, obliging him to surrender most of his wealth to the sultan in order to prevent him from raising an army. The militia he was allowed was made as weak as possible.[151] The sultan was himself frequently in Baghdad, partly no doubt to keep an eye on the caliph in person, and ostensibly friendly relations were sealed by marriages between the Seljuk and 'Abbasid dynasties (p. 141 above). Nonetheless, the Seljuk *shiḥna*, the Ethiopian eunuch Mas'ud al-Bilali, treated the caliph with astonishing rudeness, and 'Abbasid requests that he be replaced were ignored.[152]

Towards the end of his reign, Mas'ud's grip on Baghdad faltered in the face of the rebellion of his leading amirs in 543/1149 in the wake of his murder of Toghanyürek (see p. 97 above). Mas'ud al-Bilali fled Baghdad and, unable to protect the city himself, the sultan was obliged to release al-Muqtafi from the terms of his truce to allow him to defend Baghdad from the rebellious amirs led by Ildegüz and Alpqash.[153] At this stage the caliphal forces seem to have been largely composed of the Baghdad populace who stood little chance against the amirs, although when the latter returned in Rajab 544/November 1149 to demand the *khuṭba* for their candidate for the sultanate, Malikshah III b. Mahmud, the two sides' forces were more equally

[149] Ibn al-Jawzi, *al-Muntazam*, XVII, 217.

[150] *Ibid.*, XVII, 305.

[151] Ibn al-Athir, *al-Kamil*, XI, 43–4; Ibn al-Jawzi, *al-Muntazam*, XVII, 320–1, 322; Bundari, *Zubda*, 235; Hanne, *Putting the Caliph in his Place*, 169–70, 173. On the militia, see p. 236 below.

[152] Ibn Khallikan, *Wafayat*, V, 192.

[153] Ibn al-Athir, *al-Kamil*, XI, 132–4; Ibn al-Jawzi, *al-Muntazam*, XVII, 64–5.

matched and a stand-off ensued.[154] Despite his difficult financial position, al-Muqtafi had been able to recruit a militia of Armenian and Greek soldiers. Although the sultan objected, the caliph was able to persuade him that the army would help to protect him from his enemies, and Masʿud was not in a position to argue.

The architect of the newly aggressive caliphal strategy was the vizier Ibn Hubayra, who replaced the long-serving Ibn Sadaqa after the amiral attack of 543/1149.[155] He served for sixteen years both al-Muqtafi and his successor al-Mustanjid, apparently playing a crucial role in the revival of a caliphal state.[156] However, it should be noted that several sources have a reason for being biased in favour of the vizier: he was a lavish patron, and the chroniclers Ibn al-Jawzi and ʿImad al-Din al-Isfahani had both started their careers under his tutelage.[157]

With the death of Masʿud and the capture of Sanjar by the Ghuzz in 547/1152, as we have seen in Chapter 2, al-Muqtafi asserted his claims to a meaningful sovereignty more openly, with armies under Ibn Hubayra capturing Wasit and Kufa and attacking Tikrit. The Seljuk Sulaymanshah b. Muhammad took refuge with the caliph and was forced to kiss the threshold at the city gates of Baghdad in a sign of humility, which, as Isfahani commented, was an indignity to which 'no Seljuk or Daylamite [Buyid] sultan before' had been subjected.[158] The siege of Baghdad by Sulaymanshah's rival, Muhammad b. Mahmud, in 552/1157 did not deter Ibn Hubayra's machinations. When Malikshah III demanded recognition in the *khuṭba* in Baghdad in 555/1160, intent on 'restoring the system in Iraq to what it had been before, or else he would attack', Ibn Hubayra orchestrated his murder.[159] The following year, Ibn Hubayra incited an amiral rebellion against Ildegüz

154 Ibn al-Athir, *al-Kamil*, X, 143; Ibn al-Jawzi, *al-Muntazam*, XVII, 71–2; Bundari, *Zubda*, 223. Ibn Hubayra advised the caliph to pretend it was for confronting the sultan's enemies when Masʿud protested.

155 Ibn Khallikan, *Wafayat*, V, 193–5; Ibn al-Athir, *al-Taʾrikh al-Bahir*, 113; but see also Ibn al-Jawzi, *al-Muntazam*, XVIII, 71.

156 On Ibn Hubayra, see Herbert Mason, *Two Statesmen of Mediaeval Islam: Vizir Ibn Hubayra (499–560AH/1105–1165AD) and Caliph an-Nâṣir li Dîn Allâh (553–622AH–1158–1225AD)* (The Hague, 1972); also his biography in Ibn Khallikan, *Wafayat*, V, 191–203; Ibn al-Jawzi, *al-Muntazam*, XVIII, 166–70; and Qummi, *Dhayl-i Nafthat al-Masdur*, 218–19.

157 Mason, *Two Statesmen*, 34–5, and see below p. 205 for Isfahani.

158 Bundari, *Zubda*, 241. On Sulaymanshah in Baghdad, see also Ibn al-Athir, *al-Kamil*, XI, 206–7; Ibn al-Jawzi, *al-Muntazam*, XVIII, 102, 106–7.

159 Ibn al-Athir, *al-Kamil*, XI, 263; Hanne, *Putting the Caliph in his Place*, 189. See also Qummi's suspicions, based on the fact that Muhammad's two viziers were killed in the same month as him: Qummi, *Dhayl-i Nafthat al-Masdur*, 236–7.

to put Malikshah III's son Mahmud on the Seljuk throne in place of Ildegüz's favoured candidate, Arslan b. Tughrıl.[160]

For the most part, however, Ibn Hubayra concentrated his efforts on carving out territories in Iraq, and al-Mustanjid even conquered Hilla and put an end to the Mazyazdids in 558/1162. With the increasing orientation of the successor states to the Seljuk Empire towards Azerbaijan and the Jibal (in the form of the Ildegüzids) or Syria (in the case of the Zangids), al-Muqtafi's successors succeeded in keeping control of this central Iraqi territory. Al-Mustanjid formally declared his independence of the Seljuks by dropping their names from the coinage from 561/1165.[161]

This later caliphal state is little understood; it is not even clear how the caliphs managed to pay for the armies on which they relied. Moreover, the caliphs themselves played a curiously back-seat role for much of the time, with viziers such as Ibn Hubayra and Ibn al-Baladi and the leading Baghdad amir Qutb al-Din Qaymaz dominating politics. The threat to the 'Abbasids now came above all from the manoeuvrings of palace factions, which led to the murder of al-Mustanjid in 566/1170. His successor, al-Mustadi', was kept a virtual prisoner in his palace as rival factions fought with each other for influence.[162] A poem by Sibt ibn al-Ta'widhi on al-Mustanjid's vizier Ibn al-Baladi suggests that 'Abbasid independence had brought few benefits to the people of Baghdad:

> Oh journeyer to Baghdad, pass by a city
> That is dashed and overflowed by the waves of tyranny . . .
> The place is far from being what it was
> In the days when scholars filled its quarters
> And the heads of its noble families resided here
> Along with illustrious leaders and scribes . . .
> The city with its people passed away; their houses
> By the presence of our lord vizier are in a state of ruin.
> The graves imperil those who are alive,
> The stones above them and the earth are menaces.[163]

The ultimate destruction of the Seljuk house in Iran and Iraq can be laid at the door of the most effective of these later caliphs, al-Nasir li-Din allah.[164]

160 Ibn al-Athir, *al-Kamil*, XI, 269–71.
161 Hanne, *Putting the Caliph in his Place*, 196–7.
162 See Mason, *Two Statesmen*, 69–83; Hanne, *Putting the Caliph in his Place*, 181–203.
163 Sibt b. Ta'widhi, *Diwan*, ed. D. S. Margoliouth (Beirut, [1903] 1967), 47–8, trans. from Mason, *Two Statesmen*, 82–3.
164 See Mason, *Two Statesmen*, 85–132; Angelika Hartmann, *an-Nāṣir li-Dīn Allāh*

Al-Nasir tirelessly sought to exert his influence beyond the territories he controlled – limited as these were initially to Baghdad, Hilla and Wasit. Al-Nasir adopted a new legitimatory strategy for the caliphate, seeking to build a broad tent of allies by abandoning the 'Abbasids' traditional exclusive reliance on Baghdad's Hanbali masses, seeking a rapprochement with Shi'ism, and using the new tool of *futuwwa*, chivalric brotherhoods, to bind other Muslim rulers in ties of loyalty to the caliphate. Al-Nasir demanded the allegiance of the Ildegüzids and the Ayyubids, but he identified the resurgent Seljuks as the real threat to his ambitions. Without al-Nasir, Qızıl Arslan probably would never have dared to depose Sanjar b. Sulaymanshah and proclaim himself sultan, although, admittedly, the Khwarazmshahs would doubtless still have invaded at some point, for they had no more desire to see a resurgent Seljuk state under Tughrıl III than al-Nasir did. At the same time, al-Nasir provided a crucial link in the transfer of the legitimacy of the Great Seljuk sultanate to Anatolia, through investing the Anatolian sultan 'Ala' al-Din Kayqubad with the symbols of power. In this, al-Nasir was – ironically – following the example of loyalists to Tughrıl III like Rawandi who argued that the Anatolian house were now the legitimate Great Seljuk sultans.[165] In Anatolia, genealogies even circulated erasing Arslan Isra'il from the sultans' lineage and purporting to show them as descendants of Chaghrı through the bizarre expedient of conflating Sulaymanshah b. Muhammad with the Anatolian Rukn al-Din Sulaymanshah (d. 600/1204).[166]

Although the 'Abbasid–Seljuk struggle ended with the emergence of the most powerful caliph for 300 years in the person of al-Nasir and the demise of Tughrıl III, it would be mistaken to see a clear linear trajectory of rising caliphal power at the expense of declining sultanic authority. Rather, there were peaks and troughs, setbacks and triumphs for each side until the end. For much of the second half of the eleventh century, al-Qa'im was able to reign in Baghdad with only limited interference from the Seljuk sultans. Conversely, late twelfth century caliphs like al-Mustanjid and al-Mustadi',

(1180–1225): Politik, Religion, Kultur in der späten 'Abbasidenzeit (Berlin, 1975); Angelika Hartmann, 'al-Nāṣir li-Dīn Allāh', *EI²*.

165 For Rawandi, see further below, pp. 315–16 below; and Rachel Goshgarian, 'Futuwwa in Thirteenth-century Rum and Armenia: Reform Movements and the Managing of Multiple Identities on the Seljuk Periphery', in A. C. S. Peacock and Sara nur Yıldız (eds), *The Seljuks of Anatolia: Court and Society in the Medieval Middle East* (London, 2013), 230–1; Sara Nur Yıldız, 'A *Nadīm* for the Sultan: Rāwandī and the Anatolian Seljuks', in A. C. S. Peacock and Sara Nur Yıldız (eds), *The Seljuks of Anatolia: Court and Society in the Medieval Middle East* (London, 2013), 91–111.

166 A. C. S. Peacock, 'Ahmad of Nigde's *al-Walad al-Shafiq* and the Seljuk Past', *Anatolian Studies*, 54 (2004), 100–1.

captives of palace cliques, were scarcely much better off than their predecessors under Buyid rule – indeed, their position was, if anything, reminiscent of the caliphs of the 'Anarchy at Samarra' period (861–70), previously the lowest point in the 'Abbasids' fortunes, when military factions murdered caliphs at will to impose their favoured candidates. Even al-Nasir suffered some severe setbacks, such as his forces' comprehensive defeat by Tughrıl at Day Marg in 584/1188. It should be emphasised, though, that even under this most virulently anti-Seljuk caliph, ethnic differences played no part in the tensions. Al-Nasir's court poet Sibt b. Taʿwidhi praised the magnificence of the caliph's Turkish guards (*ghilmān*),[167] and wrote an elegy for al-Nasir's Seljuk wife, the daughter of the Anatolian sultan, Saljuqa Khatun bt. Qılıj Arslan b. Masʿud.[168] Until the end of the twelfth century, in spite of their rival political ambitions, marriage alliances continued to join the fortunes of the 'Abbasid and Seljuk houses.

[167] Sibt b. Taʿwidhi, *Diwan*, 159.
[168] *Ibid.*, 222–5; cf. Ibn al-Athir, *al-Kamil*, XII, 26.

4

The *Dargāh*: Courts and Court Life

> The sultan's court (*dargāh al-sulṭān*) was a real town and resounded with a thousand noises: the neighing of the Arab horses, the jingling of the gilded trappings, the call of the servants and the African *mamlūks* (*al-khashabiyya*), the cry of the haughty gate keepers, the repeated drumming of the fanfare (*nawba*), the gallop of horses brought for the race.[1]

Mafarrukhi's description of the Seljuk court (*dargāh*)[2] in eleventh-century Isfahan well evokes the noise and activity which characterised it. It was not a place of secluded magnificence, but a semi-public space, outside the walls of the main city, resounding with the sounds (and doubtless smells) of animals and men. The court was also a vast military camp (*mu'askar*) – we know of one two *farsangs* long by two wide (around 1,000 hectares[2])[3] – comprising not just the tents of the soldiers, but also bazaars to supply provisions and a *maydān*, an open space for ceremonial and games of polo. At the heart of the *mu'askar* was pitched the great red royal tent enclosure (*sarāparda* or *surādiq*) of the sultan.[4]

As with the English term court, *dargāh* can also simply evoke the body of people who accompanied the sultan wherever he went. At times the court was housed not in an extramural military camp, but in a palace complex in the heart of the city. With the political fragmentation in the Seljuk realms, there was never a single Seljuk court, but rather a whole variety of different

[1] Mafarrukhi, *Kitab Mahasin Isfahan*, 132, trans. from Durand-Guédy, *Iranian Elites*, 122.

[2] There is no exact Arabic equivalent to this Persian term, *majlis* is perhaps the closest, but *dargāh* also was used in Arabic.

[3] Nishapuri, *Saljuqnama*, 92. See also David Durand-Guédy, 'Ruling from the Outside. A New Perspective on Early Turkish Kingship in Iran', in L. Mitchell and C. Melville (eds), *Every Inch a King. Comparative Studies on Kings and Kingship in the Ancient and Medieval Worlds* (Leiden: Brill 2012), 333.

[4] Durand-Guédy, *Iranian Elites*, 94–7; David Durand-Guédy, 'The Tents of the Saljuqs', in David Durand-Guédy (ed.), *Turko-Mongol Rulers, Cities and City Life* (Leiden, 2013), 159–66, 170–1.

ones, for the senior and junior sultans, for the branches of the dynasty in Kirman, Syria and Anatolia, and for all the numerous Seljuk *maliks*. Through the court, the ruler's authority was affirmed in public rituals, and through jostling for positions at court amirs and *kātibs* sought to assert their superiority over rivals. The court was home to the ruler's household, to his slaves, his *nadīms* (boon companions) and his women, the royal harem, who also played an active part in politics. It was through the court that the ruler's entertainment and relaxation was provided – the hunting, polo games and drinking parties around which much of his life revolved. It was to the court that those desirous of the ruler's patronage or favour – petitioners, poets, artists, scholars – addressed themselves. The court thus served both a very public role, as a place where audiences were held and rituals were performed, as well as a private one, as the home to the ruler, his household and his family.

In function and organisation the Seljuk courts thus superficially resembled not just earlier and contemporary Islamic courts, but those in medieval Europe too.[5] As ever, the limitations of the sources may skew our view, with their tendency to emphasise elements familiar to the authors, and to disregard alien, Turkish elements. The *dargāh* was the backdrop against which the political history of the chronicles was written, but only occasionally does court life come directly to the foreground in our sources. Poetry, much, indeed most, of which was composed for consumption at court, can also offer descriptions of court rituals and ceremonials, albeit in idealised forms.[6] Mirrors for princes like the *Siyasatnama* and the *Qabusnama* also promote an ideal of Perso-Islamic court life that has no room for Turkish customs. However, some contemporaries certainly felt that the Seljuk court marked a break with the past. The Khurasani littérateur Nizami Arudi, who was in the service of the Ghurids, writes that because the Seljuk sultans were

> nomads [*mardumān-i bīābān-nishīn*], ignorant of the conduct of affairs and the high achievements of kings, most of these royal customs became obsolete in their time, and many essentials of dominion fell into disuse.[7]

[5] For an overview, see C. E. Bosworth, 'Courts and Courtiers. III. In the Islamic Period to the Mongol Conquest' *EIr*; A. K. S. Lambton, 'Marāsim. II. Iran', *EI*². For Seljuk courts, see Carole Hillenbrand, 'Aspects of the Court of the Great Seljuqs', in C. Lange and S. Mecit (eds), *The Seljuqs: Politics, Society and Culture* (Edinburgh, 2011), 22–38. Two works in Turkish provide overviews of the main court offices and institutions: Köymen, *Alp Arslan ve Zamanı*, II, 1–99; and Erdoğan Merçil, *Selçuklular'da Saraylar ve Saray Teşkilatı* (Istanbul, 2011). For a description of the Seljuk court in Damascus, see Mouton, *Damas et sa principauté*, 149–78.

[6] For a discussion see Tetley, *The Ghaznavid and Seljuk Turks*.

[7] Nizami Arudi, *Chahar Maqala*, ed. Muhammad Mu'in (Tehran, 1377), 40; trans.

To generalise from such normative sources and the occasional fragments of information we are given by the chronicles about 'Seljuk courts' or 'Seljuk court life' over what must have been a wide variety of actual practice is thus fraught with dangers. Bearing these caveats in mind, in this chapter we shall examine the functioning of the court, concentrating on the evidence from the politically key territories of Merv, Isfahan, Hamadhan and Baghdad. First, we look at the people of the court – the *khāṣṣ* – and court protocol and ceremonial, and then move on to consider evidence for the location and physical structures of the court. Finally, we will discuss the lifestyles of the sultans, the role of Turkish culture in their courts, and their activities as cultural patrons.

The *Khāṣṣ* and Court Protocol

The English term courtier has no exact medieval Arabic or Persian equivalent, but the word that comes closest is *khāṣṣ*, which is used for men who were bound to the sultan by personal ties of loyalty and obligation to service (*khidma*) – the sultan was their patron, they were his clients and vassals.[8] Oaths of *khidma* served to distinguish them from other elite groups, such as the *'ulamā'*, who were not tied to the sultan by the same personal ties of allegiance. The *khāṣṣ* included not just amirs, but also vassal rulers. Isfahani refers to several different groups of vassals resident at court (*muqīmīn fī 'l-khidma*) until Mahmud's reign: members of ancient Iranian families, like the amirs of Mazandaran; the chiefs of the Shabankara nomadic confederation; and the Mazyadid heir Dubays b. Sadaqa.[9]

The court was rigidly hierarchical. Rank was expressed not just through titles, but through proximity to the sultan's person. 'The order in which nobles, commoners and slaves stand must be laid. Each one must have a definite place, for standing and sitting in the presence of kings are both alike [in having different degrees]', recommended Nizam al-Mulk.[10] Positions which

E. G. Browne as *Revised Translation of the* Chahár Maqála *('Four Discourses') of Niẓámí-i-'Arúḍí of Samarqand* (Cambridge, 1921), 26; cf. Durand-Guédy, 'Ruling from the Outside', 330.

[8] Jürgen Paul, *Herrscher, Gemeinwesen, Vermittler: Ostiran und Transoxanien in vormongolischer Zeit* (Beirut, 1996), 274, 276; Paul, 'Sanjar and Atsız', 89–90, 93, 102–3, 114–16. The most detailed study of *khidma* is Antonio Jurado Aceituno, 'La "ẖidma" selyuqí: la red de relaciones de dependencia mutua, la dinámica del poder y las formas de obtención de los beneficios', PhD thesis, Universidad Autónoma de Madrid, 1995 (*non vidi*). See also Jürgen Paul, 'Khidma in the Social History of Pre-Mongol Iran', *Journal of the Economic and Social History of the Orient* 57/iii (2014), 392–422.

[9] Bundari, *Zubda*, 121–2; cf. Nizam al-Mulk, *Siyar al-Muluk*, 138, trans. 101.

[10] Nizam al-Mulk, *Siyar al-Muluk*, 163, trans. 121.

controlled access to the sultan, such as the *ḥājib* (chamberlain) and *wakīldār* (who brought messages between the sultan and the vizier) were thus of especial importance.[11] Nizam al-Mulk recommends that the *wakīl* (household steward) who was generally responsible for the running of the sultanic household, including 'the kitchen, the winehouse (*sharābkhāna*), the stables and the palaces of the elite (*khāṣṣ*), the [sultan's] sons and retinue' should have daily access to the sultan on account of his responsibilities, although he indicates that the position had fallen out of use in his day.[12] Such intimate access was a closely guarded privilege. The vizier Anushirwan b. Khalid describes in his memoirs (as quoted by 'Imad al-Din al-Isfahani) how he had served as treasurer to Sultan Muhammad Tapar. His access to the sultan inspired the bitter jealousy of his political enemies:

> The sultan appointed me over his treasury, and invited me to [attend him] in private. He singled me out with his generosity and handed over to me the treasuries of his kingdoms. Those great [men of state] only had access to the sultan in the public audience chamber (*bārgāh*)[13] when he sat [to give an audience] to the common people, but I was privileged with [attending him] in private and enjoyed [the right to] speak with him. My status grew through meeting him, and the great men of state hated me for my position and waited for me to make a mistake and be disgraced.[14]

The private and public parts of court were thus easily blurred. Nizam al-Mulk had warned against this. No official, in his view, should have access to the sultan in his private moments. Rather, *nadīms* (boon companions) should be appointed to consort with the sultan in 'everything connected with pleasure and entertainment, parties of drinking and companionship, hunting, polo and gambling'.[15] In turn, *nadīms* should not be consulted on matters of high politics – a stricture which suggests that in fact they frequently were. Isfahani relates an example of how the *nadīm* might impinge on the political sphere by giving voice to unpalatable truths that others were unable to express. When in 521/1127, Sanjar advanced to Rayy to intervene in the succession in the Sultanate of Iraq, at one point all the contenders – Mahmud, Mas'ud, Tughrıl and Sulayman – were gathered in his tent, along with the vizier Abu

[11] On the *ḥājib*, see A. K. S. Lambton, 'ḥājib', *EI*[2]; on the office of *wakīldār*, see Bundari, *Zubda*, 93–4, who indicates that it outranks the *ḥājib* (*akhaṣṣ min manzilat al-ḥijāba*); also Fairbanks, 'The Tarikh al-Vuzara', 128–32.

[12] Nizam al-Mulk, *Siyar al-Muluk*, 119; trans. 88.

[13] On this term, see Durand-Guédy, 'The Tents of the Saljuqs', 164–6.

[14] Bundari, *Zubda*, 97.

[15] Nizam al-Mulk, *Siyar al-Muluk*, 121, trans. 90.

'l-Qasim al-Darguzini. Suddenly, the *nadīm* Falak started prostrating himself in prayer, raising his hands to the heavens in supplication. When Sanjar asked him why, Falak replied,

> I was confiding in God, saying, 'This group that has gathered in this tent is the root and branches of civil strife and affliction. Make this patch of earth swallow them up, remove this plot [they stand on from beneath them] so that both Your people and what is due to You can be saved from them!'[16]

The *nadīm* might be anyone from a professional buffoon like Falak, to a man of letters or a vassal prince: Kayka'us b. Iskandar includes a section on how to act as a sultan's *nadīm*, but stresses to his son – the intended recipient of his advice – that he should not accept the position unless he is qualified.[17] Indeed, Kayka'us warns against excessive intimacy with the sultan:

> If you become a member of the sultan's retinue, serving the sultan, however much the sultan makes you close to him do not be proud of this; avoid being close to him, but do not avoid serving him; for a distance arises out of proximity to sultans, and out of service of the sultan a proximity.[18]

In practice, bureaucrats and amirs were often the sultan's companions and drinking partners, and the activities Nizam al-Mulk lists as 'connected with pleasure and entertainment' sometimes had a much broader political and social importance, as we shall investigate below.

With access to the sultan key to power, influence and prestige, court life naturally revolved around jostling for precedence among the *khāṣṣ*. Isfahani's account of the ceremonies surrounding the accession of Mahmud b. Muhammad well illustrates how this jostling could very often take on a physical form:

> [The sultan] sat on the throne in the place of his father . . . and people came to his presence according to their classes in order to congratulate him; they appeared to him before the dais of rank and prestige and kissed the earth and fulfilled their obligations in terms of performing the [requisite] ceremony. The great men [*al-'uẓamā' wa-l-kubarā'*] stood in ranks according to the order of their rank and the value of their seniority, set in order according to their stage on the ladder of precedence. [Anushirwan said], 'The vizier Rabib [al-Dawla] came forward and went up to the throne to offer congratulations and to kiss hands, and then descended. Next Khatir [al-Mulk] went forward to do as he had by virtue of the fact he was vizier.

16 Bundari, *Zubda*, 154–5.

17 Kayka'us b. Iskandar, *Qabusnama*, ed. Ghulamhusayn Yusufi (Tehran, 1345), 203.

18 *Ibid.*, 198.

> In any event, on account of his age and precedence he rightly should have had the honour of going first, but Kamal al-Sumayrami thrust himself before him and made [Khatir al-Mulk] go after him, recognising neither his precedence nor his service to the dynasty. Then Khatir al-Mulk performed the ceremony of congratulation after him.'[19]

Details of who could sit and who could stand, and where they were allowed to do so, were thus thoroughly contentious, with the honour of standing on the right side of the sultan's throne, the highest position of precedence, especially prized.[20] Already shortly after the Seljuk conquest of Baghdad the custom of arranging 'amirs and princes around the throne according to their rank' is attested.[21] It fell to the *ḥājib* to resolve these matters, as Nizam al-Mulk outlines:

> Established members of the *khāṣṣ* stand near the throne, such as the sword-bearer (*silāḥdār*), the wine-bearers (*sāqīān*) and the like; if someone [else] wants to stand among them, the *ḥājib* keeps him away and likewise if a stranger or unsuitable person stands among the group, he [the *ḥājib*] will cry out and not allow it.[22]

Rank was also signified by the *nawba*, which could mean either the beating of a drum or the playing of a musical band at set times before the presence of the honorand. The number of *nawbas* to which one was entitled signified status. The prerogative of five *nawbas* traditionally belonged to the caliph, but the Seljuk sultans (in contrast to the Buyids) adopted this right for themselves,[23] and five *nawbas* became seen as a symbol of supreme sultanic authority. One of the conditions of the peace agreement between Berkyaruq and Muhammad Tapar was that Berkyaruq 'would not stand in the way of his brother Muhammad with regard to the drums [for the *nawba*]'.[24] The privilege of having a *nawba* was not, however, restricted to the Seljuk sultans. Fadluya, chief of the nomadic Shabankara'i confederation in Fars, was granted the right 'that drums should be beaten outside his door at prayer times'.[25] On the other hand, Sanjar's settlement with Mahmud stated that

19 Bundari, *Zubda*, 119.
20 Ibn al-Athir, *al-Ta'rikh al-Bahir*, 4: Aqsonqur is said to have stood on the right-hand side of the Malikshah's throne, the position of highest precedence.
21 Sibt, *Mir'at*, 93.
22 Nizam al-Mulk, *Siyar al-Muluk*, 163, trans. 120; cf. *ibid.*, 122, trans. 91.
23 See Hillenbrand, 'Aspects', 28–31.
24 Ibn al-Athir, *al-Kamil*, X, 370.
25 Sibt, *Mir'at*, 121. Presumably, this was not done every prayer time as the five *nawbas* do seem to have been the prerogative of the caliph and the Seljuks, but rather was perhaps just

Mahmud should not be entitled to a *nawba* at all while in Sanjar's presence.[26] Having a *nawba* was thus not just a matter of how many drum rolls one had, but in whose presence and in which circumstances one was allowed them. In addition to the *nawba* on the drums the sounding of the 'Turkish horn' (*būq-i Turkī*) was an attribute of the sultanate.[27]

Clothes, armaments and titles also expressed rank. Nizam al-Mulk specifies that twenty special sets of armour, bejewelled and golden, should be kept in readiness in case it was necessary to impress ambassadors, in which case 'twenty pages finely attired can take these weapons and stand around the throne'. Nizam al-Mulk adds that:

> although our sovereign . . . has attained such a lofty state that he can do without such ceremonies, nevertheless the pomp and circumstance of the kingdom and kingship must be maintained, for every king's elegance and finery must accord with his exalted position and lofty ambition.[28]

Clothes, and robes of honour (*khil'a*) in particular, were commonly exchanged by suzerains and vassals, and like all gifts were carefully graded in quantity and quality according to the rank of the recipient (see, e.g., the description below of the gifts Tughrıl sent to the caliph and his vizier after his coronation).[29] Nishapuri notes approvingly of Mas'ud b. Muhammad that his treasury was usually empty because he gave away the revenues that reached him from distant provinces. (In reality, of course, Mas'ud's treasuries were empty for very different reasons, see pp. 95–100 above, but Nishapuri's explanation is intended to explain the financial disasters that beset the sultan in a way that enhanced his image in the prevailing culture which viewed generosity as a duty of a good ruler.[30])

Sibt b. al-Jawzi recounts how Alp Arslan tried to consolidate an alliance with Fadluya the Shabankara'i, who was in danger of supporting the sultan's

early morning and the two evening prayers, as in the case of the Buyids. Cf. Hillenbrand, 'Aspects', 29–30. Hillenbrand has also drawn attention to the fact that *nawba* bands seem to have been distinguished by wearing certain colours (*ibid.*, 30–1), and has speculated that there might be some ancient Turkic colour symbolism at work here. In particular, for red as the royal colour, see Durand-Guédy, 'The Tents of the Saljuqs', 170–2. The royal significance of colours is attested in pre-Seljuk times too, among the 'Abbasids and Fatimids. See Hillenbrand, 'Aspects', 31; and Lambton, 'Marāsim'.

26 Bundari, *Zubda*, 129.

27 Rawandi, *Rahat al-Sudur*, 170.

28 Nizam al-Mulk, *Siyar al-Muluk*, 126, trans. 94.

29 Cf. Rawandi, *Rahat al-Sudur*, 170, describing the peace agreement between Sanjar and Mahmud: Sanjar gave Mahmud's amirs honours 'in accordance with their rank' (*umarā-yi ūrā hamchunīn bar qadr-i marātib tashrīfhā bidād*).

30 Nishapuri, *Saljuqnama*, 74.

rival Qavurt (as indeed he eventually did). At a meeting in Hamadhan in 456/1064, to win him over Alp Arslan 'honoured him, bestowed upon him and everyone who had accompanied him magnificent robes of honour (*khil'a*), and gave him tents [*khiyam wa-kharkawāt*] and horses with golden saddles and jewels'.[31] Gifts of clothes constituted far more than merely signs of honour: their giving and receipt might establish a *khidma* bond of patronage and clientage (see also p. 139 above). For instance, on one occasion the vizier Ibn Jahir appeared in the caliphal *dīwān* wearing a *khil'a* bestowed on him by Alp Arslan. In this instance the *khil'a* consisted of a whole outfit – a robe, a gold-set turban, and a golden saddle. Ibn Jahir's attempt to wear this sultanic gift in the caliphal palace was considered tantamount to treason and he was summarily dismissed.[32]

Titles (*laqab*, pl. *alqāb*) were another form of rewarding service; thus, after Kunduri successfully negotiated Tughrıl's marriage to the caliph's daughter, the sultan 'increased his titles' (*zāda fī alqābihi*).[33] A newly appointed vizier, an amir or a favoured poet, might also be awarded new titles by the sultan.[34] Theoretically, there was a distinction between civilian and military titles, the former usually ending 'al-Mulk' or 'al-Din' (e.g., 'Fakhr al-Din', 'Glory of the Faith') and the latter 'al-Dawla' ('Rukn al-Dawla', 'Glory of the State/Dynasty'). Nizam al-Mulk complains bitterly, however, that this distinction was not being observed in his time, and Turks were using titles that should be reserved for civilians and vice versa.[35] Titles were awarded by both the caliph (e.g., to members of his own *dīwān*, and to the sultan) and by the Seljuk sultans.

Ceremonial

The court calendar was marked with frequent ceremonies, varying from accession rituals designed to underline vassals' allegiance to their sovereign, such as the one described by Isfahani cited above, or the appointment of a new heir apparent.[36] Some ceremonies were explicitly modelled on 'Abbasid precedents, such as the daily audience ceremony for those in favour with the ruler, which we know was emulated by the Seljuks of Damascus,[37] and prob-

[31] Sibt, *Mir'at*, 121. Fadulya's lands had been occupied by Qavurt. See Sibt, *Mir'at*, 137. For the background, see Claude Cahen, 'Fadluwayh le Shavankareh', *Studia Iranica*, 7/i (1978), 111–15.

[32] Sibt, *Mir'at*, 250–1.

[33] *Ibid.*, 99.

[34] For example, Iqbal, *Wizarat*, 251.

[35] Nizam al-Mulk, *Siyar al-Muluk*, 210–12, trans. 156–7.

[36] Nishapuri, *Saljuqnama*, 75.

[37] Mouton, *Damas et sa principauté*, 154

ably more generally. Sometimes ancient Iranian ceremonies were performed: in 484/1091, Malikshah ordered Baghdad to be lit with candles in the middle of the night, reminiscent of the Zoroastrian ritual of *sadhak*.[38] Yet we comparatively rarely read of celebrations of the great feasts of the Iranian calendar, Sada and Mihrigan, which formed an important part of Ghaznavid court life.[39] There were presumably also Turkish festivals, but again we suffer from a lack of evidence.

Some court ceremonies also were intended for public consumption, especially prestigious weddings. When Caliph al-Mustazhir married the Seljuk princess 'Ismat Khatun in 504/1111, 'Baghdad was decorated and hung [with decorations], and there was a great celebration the like of which people had never seen.'[40] An impression of what these festivities may have been like is given in the account of an earlier 'Abbasid–Seljuk marriage, between Malikshah's daughter and al-Muqtadi in 480/1087. The Seljuk princess's trousseau was transported to the caliphal palace on a caravan of 130 camels, 74 mules and 33 horses. The animals themselves were all decked in rich varieties of brocade, while the procession was led by senior Seljuk amirs, such Sa'd al-Dawla Gawhara'in, *shiḥna* of Baghdad, and Bursuq. People of districts through which the procession passed scattered coins and clothes on them, and in al-Harim, the area of Baghdad surrounding the palace, candles were lit in every shop. The bride was brought to caliphal palace in another great candle lit-procession, borne on a bejewelled golden litter surrounded by 200 Turkish slave girls, and preceded by leading men of the Seljuk state such as Nizam al-Mulk and their wives.[41]

A Seljuk Coronation: Tughrıl becomes 'King of East and West'

Our best evidence for Seljuk coronation ceremonies comes from the account preserved by Sibt b. al-Jawzi of Caliph al-Qa'im's coronation of Tughrıl in Dhu'l-Qi'da 449/January 1058. The sultan was greeted outside Baghdad where he was encamped by the caliphal vizier Ibn Muslima and other dignitaries sent by the 'Abbasid caliph, bearing al-Qa'im's gifts to Tughrıl of a gold-embroidered robe, a turban made with gold thread, and a horse with a gold saddle. When the day came for the coronation, Tughrıl

[38] Ibn al-Jawzi, *al-Muntazam*, XVII, 294; Daphna Ephrat, 'The Seljuqs and the Public Sphere in the Period of Sunni Revivalism: The View from Baghdad', in C. Lange and S. Mecit (eds), *The Seljuqs: Politics, Society and Culture* (Edinburgh, 2011), 151.

[39] For a rare example of Mihrigan, see Tetley, *The Ghaznavid and Seljuk Turks*, 99.

[40] Ibn al-Athir, *al-Kamil*, X, 483–4.

[41] *Ibid.*, X, 160–1.

entered the caliphal palace on horseback, preceded by high-ranking vassals such as the Buyid prince Abu Kalijar, Qutlumush, leading commanders and 500 Turkish *ghulāms*. He waited in the great courtyard (*ṣaḥn al-salām*) where all the dignitaries of Baghdad were in attendance, the *naqībs* (leaders of the descendants of the Prophet's family), the qadis, notables and witnesses; and eventually the gate to the inner palace (*bāb al-dihliz*) opened, the sultan dismounted and was greeted by Ibn Muslima, who brought him to the innermost part of the great hall.

The curtains were lifted to reveal the caliph seated on a great throne raised seven feet (*dhirā'*) above the ground, wearing the mantle (*burda*) of the Prophet Muhammad, and holding the mace (*qaḍīb*), all signifying his authority and his lineage. The sultan was seated on a chair below the throne, with Kunduri at his side to translate. The sultan proclaimed himself to be the caliph's 'servant' and kissed the ground before him, in formal recognition of his vassalage to the caliph. Then al-Qa'im gave permission for him to be given the garments of honour (*khil'a*), and he was taken to a side chamber and dressed in 'the accustomed *khil'a*' – which must have included the crown which, when Tughrıl returned to the caliph's presence, was so heavy he was unable to kiss the ground. Then the caliph in person girded him with a sword, addressed him as 'king of east and west', and granted him three more banners. After kissing hands, the sultan, preceded by the men of state, emerged again into the great courtyard where he sat to receive congratulations, as the banners were flown from the rooftop and balconies. Ceremonies concluded after three days with Tughrıl sending the caliph gifts of fifty Turkish slaves mounted on horseback, 50,000 dinars, and 500 robes of various kinds, while smaller gifts were dispatched to the caliphal vizier.[42]

A very different kind of court ceremonial was the tribunal, presided over by the sultan in person, to judge members of the elite accused of an offence. The tribunal might (but did not have to) include *fuqahā'* (sing. *faqīh*, jurists).[43] Such tribunals were conducted in an environment that was meant to reinforce the sultan's divinely bestowed powers, beneath banners that in Turkic and Iranian tradition symbolised royal power and justice, with the sultan himself seated on a throne the decoration of which symbolised eternity. Before the throne, the wrongdoer would receive his punishment, including summary

42 Sibt, *Mir'at*, 25–6. See also p. 137 above for more details on the content of this ceremony,

43 For this description, I am reliant on Lange, *Justice*, 32–7, although Lange does not draw the parallel with the *yarghu* that I do.

execution by the *sayyāf* (swordbearer and executioner) who was often present on such occasions. Such tribunals were held in private: a premium seems to have been put on avoiding the leaking of details of offences committed at the court into the public domain out of respect to the status of the wrongdoer, although particularly egregious offenders might be humiliated by a public punishment. This culture of secrecy is one reason why the chronicles often vary about details of the end of a particular individual. Few might actually know for sure how a high-ranking member of the elite had met his end, and rumours would swiftly circulate. These tribunals, to which our sources only occasionally allude, are reminiscent of the *yarghu* of Mongol and Timurid times, the courts which administered the traditional law of the steppe (*yasa*).[44]

Palaces, Tents, Pavilions and Caravanserais: The Location of Seljuk Rule

Rule in the mediaeval Islamic world was generally city based. The Samanids, Buyids and Ghaznavids based their rule in towns, Bukhara, Shiraz and Baghdad, and Ghazna, respectively. In Khurasan and Transoxiana, the royal palace and ancillary buildings would usually be located in a citadel.[45] Cities frequently possessed a building called the *dār al-imāra*, or in the case of capitals, *dār al-mamlaka*, which served as the governor's residence and as a physical manifestation of a ruler's authority. Sometimes in the west too, as in Damascus, these were located in the citadel, but it is not clear if this was always the case. The *dār al-imāra* might contain a throne room to be used for audiences by the ruler.[46] The Seljuks, however, ruled from a wide variety of different locations, which we will review here.

The palace attributed to Sanjar in Merv, our sole surviving Seljuk palace, must have been a vast and impressive structure despite its forlorn and desolate state today. One can just make out the four vast iwans that surrounded its central courtyard where the ruler would have held audiences. Traces of stucco from other rooms attest the palace's elaborate decoration, but little other

44 On the *yarghu* and *yasa*, see Maria E. Subtelny, *Timurids in Transition: Turko-Persian Politics and Acculturation in Medieval Iran* (Leiden, 2007), 24–8, 95–7; Lambton, *Continuity and Change*, 82–90.

45 Jere L. Bacharach, 'Administrative Complexes, Palaces, and Citadels: Changes in the Loci of Medieval Muslim Rule', in Irene Bierman, Rifaʿat Abou-el-Haj, Donald Preziosi (eds), *The Ottoman City and its Parts: Urban Change and Social Order* (New Rochelle, 1991), 111–28. In the Samanid case, the citadel appears to have fallen out of use during the later tenth century, see Yuri Karev, 'From Tents to Cities. The Royal Court of the Western Qarakhanids between Bukhara and Samarqand', in David Durand-Guédy (ed.), *Turko-Mongol Rulers, Cities and City Life* (Leiden, 2013), pp. 99–147.

46 Mouton, *Damas et sa principauté*, 154.

Figure 4.1 Sanjar's palace complex in the Shahriyar Arg at Merv: the archive or treasury (?)

evidence survives. A nearby windowless building of massive construction (Figure 4.1) has variously been interpreted as the court archive or treasury, but this is speculation. The palace was located in the heart of the citadel of Merv (the Shahriyar Arg), and would have been surrounded by administrative buildings such as a mint, a mosque, residences, bathhouses and barracks for the royal guard. Despite the modern encroachment of desert, originally the citadel grounds would have contained gardens, pools, fountains and lakes.[47] Indeed, all Seljuk residences would have been surrounded by gardens (the *bāgh*), which may have extended over several hundred hectares.[48]

What the remains cannot tell us, of course, is how much time Sanjar actually spent there. Juzjani, relying on a report from a descendant of one of Sanjar's retinue, tells us that the sultan spent the summer around Bukhara, and winter in Merv.[49] Clearly, the situation was more complicated, for Nizami 'Arudi states that he encountered Sanjar's camp one spring on the steppe near Tus, where the sultan spent two months.[50] If the situation in Khurasan can be compared

[47] This description derives from recent archaeological work undertaken at Merv. See Georgina Hermann, *Monuments of Merv: Traditional Buildings of the Karakum* (London, 1999), 97–8.

[48] Durand-Guédy, *Iranian Elites*, 97–8.

[49] Juzjani, *Tabaqat*, I, 260.

[50] Nizami 'Arudi, *Chahar Maqala*, 65.

with Baghdad at the other end of the Seljuk domains – and that is a big if – one might suggest that in fact the complex in the Shahriyar Arg may have had more an occasional ceremonial function rather than serving as a permanent residence.

Muhammad Tapar had a palace built for him in Baghdad by Mujahid al-Din Bihruz, but it was only completed shortly before his death, and burned down about three years later, in 515/1121–2. Muhammad's successor Mahmud abandoned the palace and never attempted to rebuild it 'for my father had never enjoyed [living] there'.[51] It may also have been regarded as fated as the *mamlūk* in charge of its construction, Bihruz al-Khadim, had used dubious methods of expropriation:

> it was built from the rubble of aristocrats' palaces [*min anqāḍ dūr al-nās*], and the people of Baghdad, even the qadis, noble-blooded and notables were employed on it, bringing the debris in their shawls; and when it was completed Bihruz ordered them to bring carpets, vessels and the like, which the people also bought him . . . any house which is built through expropriation will risk destruction.[52]

There was also the old Buyid palace complex on the banks of the Tigris in east Baghdad which the Seljuks inherited, and which was expanded by Tughrıl.[53] However, analysis of the use of the Seljuks' Baghdad palace during the reign of Mas'ud b. Muhammad shows that in fact the sultan seems only to have gone there for very specific purposes: to preside over the *maẓālim*, to hear a famous preacher deliver a sermon, or to receive politically important figures such as amirs or the caliphal vizier. Thus, the palace served as the backdrop to ceremonies that publicly affirmed the sultan's legitimacy as a just, Islamic ruler: it was itself a symbol of the sultan's power. It was not necessarily the sultan's primary place of residence.[54]

Even when the court was to be found in the vicinity of a settlement, frequently it preferred to stay in the *mu'askar*, the military camp, set up outside towns. Thus, when Sanjar came to the Bayhaq region on campaign, he stayed not in the town, but rather based himself in the camp in the plain in between Bayhaq and nearby settlement of Khusrawjird.[55] In Isfahan,

[51] Ibn al-Athir, *al-Kamil*, X, 595; Ibn al-Jawzi, *al-Muntazam*, XVII, 194; Sibt, *Mir'at*, ed. Ghamidi, 23.

[52] Sibt, *Mir'at*, ed. Ghamidi, 723.

[53] Sibt, *Mir'at*, 3; Ibn al-Jawzi, *al-Muntazam*, XVI, 4; Ibn al-Athir, *al-Kamil*, IX, 614.

[54] David Durand-Guédy, 'Where did the Saljuqs Live? A Case Study based on the Reign of Mas'ud b. Muhammad (1134–1152)', *Studia Iranica*, 40 (2011), 238–40; Durand-Guédy, 'Ruling from the Outside', 334–6.

[55] Ibn Funduq, *Tarikh-i Bayhaq*, 270.

where Malikshah resided more or less permanently till the last years of his reign, the *mu'askar* seems to have been the sultan's preferred residence.[56] The treasury or parts of it might also be stored in strong citadels, like Shahdiz, and we should perhaps envisage cities as having had a comparable function – secure bases, rather than places of residence.[57] Even when the sultan is described as being 'in' a given city, this may mean no more than he was in its surroundings.[58] The ambiguity is well illustrated by references to Sanjar in Merv, for that name may refer both to the city of Marw al-Shahijan and to the whole vast oasis. Within the Merv oasis Sanjar may well have held court in an array of different locations, in the great palace of the citadel, tents and *kūshks* (pavilions).

The sultans and their retinues sometimes chose to live in tents even when they were in Baghdad.[59] These might have been erected in or around the palace complex in east Baghdad, for the area had abundant gardens.[60] Evidence from the Sultanate of Iraq in the late twelfth century suggests these tent complexes could be very elaborate, replicating the buildings one might expect to find in a more permanent palace, ranging from a *sharābkhāna*, where wine and bejewelled drinking vessels were kept, to a travelling treasury.[61] The great red tent made out of material woven in Jahrum in Fars (*sarāparda-yi surkh-i jahrumī*) was considered one of the attributes of the sultanate,[62] while we have one description of Tughrıl ensconced in state in his tent (*khārkāh*) outside Baghdad, sitting on a throne and wearing royal clothes (more traditionally associated with the prerogatives of the 'Abbasids themselves) such as a tall hat (*qalansuwwa*) and black cloak (*qabā'*).[63]

Another favoured sultanic residence was the *kūshk* or pavilion. *Kūshks*

[56] Durand-Guédy, *Iranian Elites*, 93–6; cf. Durand-Guédy, 'Where did the Saljuqs Live?', 228–30; Durand-Guédy, 'Ruling from the Outside', 335–8.

[57] Tughrıl, himself so frequently on campaign, had used Hamadhan as a base to store his treasury and weapons (Sibt, *Mir'at*, 31).

[58] See Durand-Guédy, 'Ruling from the Outside', 330–2; Durand-Guédy, 'The Tents of the Saljuqs', 173, 182.

[59] Durand-Guédy, 'Where did the Saljuqs Live?', 240.

[60] *Ibid.*, 233.

[61] On the *sharābkhāna*, see Merçil, *Selçuklular'da Saraylar*, 137–9. For evidence of the *sharābkhāna* in Iran, including a mobile one, see Rawandi, *Rahat al-Sudur*, 261, 300; also Durand-Guédy, 'The Tents of the Saljuqs', 153, 186. For the mobile treasury in the Iraq sultanate, see Merçil, *Selçuklular'da Saraylar*, 157; cf. Durand-Guédy, *Iranian Elites*, 80–1. See also Ibn Isfandiyar, *Tarikh-i Tabaristan*, I, 108, 115.

[62] Rawandi, *Rahat al-Sudur*, 170; cf. Durand-Guédy, *Iranian Elites*, 95–6.

[63] Sibt, *Mir'at*, 24; cf. Bosworth, 'Courts and Courtiers'.

Figure 4.2 Ruined *Kūshk* by the mausoleum of Muhammad b. Ziyad, Merv

are mentioned several times in the sources for Isfahan, and were usually built outside the town itself in the suburban *bāgh*s.[64] Several *kūshks* were built in the region of Hamadhan by Mas'ud b. Muhammad, sometimes explicitly located in the meadows.[65] Quite a number of *kūshks* survive in Merv, which serve to give a clearer impression of their structure: they were two-storied, with the upper storey serving as the main level of use, while the lower floors were probably used as a cellar. The *kūshks* of Merv were of fortress-like appearance (Figure 4.2) even if in reality they were not strongly fortified and would have withstood only a small raid, not a concentrated assault.[66] Nothing remains of the *kūshks* of Hamadhan or Isfahan, and the extremely sparse references to them in the sources prevent us from drawing a detailed picture of them. Although not all *kūshks* necessarily resembled one another, like the *kūshks* of Merv those in the Jibal were probably two-storey buildings,[67] and

64 Durand-Guédy, *Iranian Elites*, 99. In general on *kūshks*, see Durand-Guédy, 'The Tents of the Saljuqs', 175–9.

65 Durand-Guédy, 'Where did the Saljuqs Live?', 232–3; Durand-Guédy, 'Ruling from the Outside', 334; Husayni, *Akhbar*, 174; Nishapuri, *Saljuqnama*, 110–11.

66 Hermann, *Monuments of Merv*, 81–2.

67 Durand-Guédy, 'Where did the Saljuqs Live?', 239; Durand-Guédy, 'The Tents of the Saljuqs', 175.

they presumably would similarly have 'formed the focal point of an enclosed range of buildings and gardens'.[68]

Finally, although there is no supporting literary evidence, it seems reasonable to assume that caravanserais (*ribāṭs*) were used not merely for trade, but as sultanic residences when on progress. The series of caravanserais built in Khurasan have been described as 'palaces in the desert', offering palatial comfort to high-ranking travellers making their way between Merv and Nishapur and offered facilities far beyond those a merchant would require including luxury accommodation, and even an audience chamber (see further pp. 300–1 below and Figure 8.2).[69]

Like many pre-modern courts in the Middle East and Europe, the Seljuk court is often described as being peripatetic.[70] Rawandi's description of the movements of Sultan Arslan b. Tughrıl underlines the regular seasonal nature of these movements even towards the end of the dynasty:

> In the season of spring the sultan went from Isfahan to Ganduman and the meadow of Balasan. In the summer he came to the region of Hamadhan,[71] and completed government business (*kār-i mulk nasq ū niẓām-i tamām yāft*). The sultan spent the winter in Sawa, and sometimes in Hamadhan, while in spring he was sometimes at the meadow of Na'l-bandan and the meadow of Charkh.[72]

However, the extent and nature of this itinerancy clearly varied greatly with different sultans. Alp Arslan was almost constantly on the move (although not, it seems, in any discernable pattern, unlike the rulers cited above), while Mas'ud b. Muhammad divided his time largely between Hamadhan and Baghdad, with some trips to Azerbaijan.[73] Malikshah and Muhammad Tapar, on the other hand, spent the majority of their time (around 60–65 per cent according to rough estimates) in Isfahan.[74]

[68] Hermann, *Monuments of Merv*, 81.

[69] Robert Hillenbrand, *Islamic Architecture: Form, Function and Meaning* (New York, 1994), 343–5.

[70] Lambton, 'Internal Structure', 223; David Morgan, *Medieval Persia, 1040–1797* (Longman, 1988), 35; see also Durand-Guédy, 'Ruling from the Outside', 329–30.

[71] For this translation of *bi-dār-i Hamadhān*, see Durand-Guédy, 'Where did the Saljuqs Live?' 231–2; Durand-Guédy, 'Ruling from the Outside,' 332, 340 (fig. 1).

[72] Rawandi, *Rahat al-Sudur*, 298; for the locations, see Durand-Guédy, 'Ruling from the Outside', 332.

[73] Durand-Guédy, 'Where did the Saljuqs Live?'; Qummi, *Dhayl-i Nafthat al-Masdur*, 208.

[74] Durand-Guédy, *Iranian Elites*, 75–6, 208, 321–3. For these movements, see also Ibn al-Jawzi, *al-Muntazam*, XVII, 145; and see Qummi, *Dhayl-i Nafthat al-Masdur*, 208, 221 for Baghdad as a wintering spot (*mashattā*) under Mas'ud.

The temptation to assume that this itinerant lifestyle represents a remnant of the Seljuks' nomadic heritage should thus be resisted. Numerous rulers of Iran with impeccably settled credentials, starting with Cyrus the Great, followed an itinerant lifestyle. There were sound reasons for a king to move regularly around his kingdom: with the all-encompassing importance of personal ties in the mediaeval Islamic east, it was essential for the ruler to be physically present in as many places as possible. It was less in the fact that they moved around, but rather in their preference for a life that so often avoided towns that the Seljuks differed from their predecessors. Their motives must have been varied. Simple logistics may have dictated that it was easier to accommodate a large military retinue, with all its attendant beasts of burden and camp followers, in uncluttered pastures, and the desire to avoid clashes or misunderstandings with the townsfolk such as those that had marred Tughrıl's arrival in Baghdad may have played a part.[75] On a political level, pasturelands would have provided a convenient location for audiences with nomadic subjects, a place where rituals of allegiance could be performed. Above all, such a lifestyle well suited the Seljuks' own predilections.

The Sultans' Lifestyle

When not on campaign, the sultans' lives revolved around hunting (Figure 4.3), equestrian games such polo, drinking and feasting. The *Qabusnama* offers advice on how a ruler could best divide up his time:

> Riding horses, going hunting, and playing polo are suitable occupations for powerful men, especially in youth; but everything should have a limit, measure and method. Do not go hunting every day for this is not methodical. The week has seven days. Go hunting two days, two or three days occupy yourself with drinking, and one day deal with affairs of state.[76]

It is likely that many Seljuk rulers had a similarly well-balanced week. Nishapuri, for instance, gives quite a positive assessment of Mas'ud b. Muhammad, writing that among his other praiseworthy characteristics 'he did not have his fill of the hunt'.[77] Mahmud b. Muhammad is lauded as 'the most intelligent and perceptive of the Seljuk dynasty, and no sultan was as aware as he of the details of affairs', but Nishapuri also gives prominence to his love for pigeons, falcons and hunting birds, telling us that the sultan kept 400 hunting dogs with gold collars.[78] Perhaps the most impressive hunts-

[75] Ibn al-Athir, *al-Kamil*, IX, 611–12.

[76] Kayka'us b. Iskandar, *Qabusnama*, 94.

[77] Nishapuri, *Saljuqnama*, 74.

[78] *Ibid.*, 70.

Figure 4.3 A prince on horseback, depicted on a bowl of the twelfth or thirteenth century (Iran), Metropolitan Museum of Art, Accession No. 51.53. © Metropolitan Museum of Art

man was Malikshah, who was also a keen polo player.[79] A written record of his hunting exploits was kept (a *shikārnāma*), according to which – as Nishapuri, who claims to have seen it, tells us – in a single day the sultan had hit seventy gazelles with his arrow. He built towers of the hooves of slaughtered gazelles and onagers throughout Iraq and Khurasan, and his hunting activities left their traces throughout his realms.[80] Sibt b. al-Jawzi tells us

[79] Ibn al-Athir, *al-Kamil*, X, 156.
[80] Nishapuri, *Saljuqnama*, 30.

that on one expedition in Iraq in 479/1086 he killed 4,000 or even 10,000 gazelles.[81] Whatever the exact figures, a sultanic hunt was clearly something of a holocaust for wildlife in the region.

Banquets and drinking parties in particular were also an opportunity to display kingly virtues. Nizam al-Mulk praises Tughrıl for his lavish banquets, for

> a man's magnanimity and generosity can be measured by his household management. The sultan is the paterfamilias of the world; all kings are in his power. Therefore it is necessary that his housekeeping, his magnanimity and generosity, his table and his largesse should accord with his state and be greater and better than that of other kings.[82]

The quantities of food consumed by the court were vast: the Türkmen of Balkh were obliged to send 24,000 sheep each year to Sanjar's kitchens.[83] Managing the sultanic kitchen and its supplies was a major task, and was the responsibility of an official known as the *khwānsālār*.[84] Supplying the court might be a burden, but it was also a business opportunity for some. Yaqut reminisces about having seen the fabulous library of a certain 'Aziz al-Din Abu Bakr 'Atiq al-Zanjani (or 'Atiq b. Abi Bakr) in Merv:

> He was a drink-supplier (*fuqqā'ī*) to sultan Sanjar. At the beginning of his career he used to sell fruit and flowers in the market of Merv. He then became wine supplier (*sharrābī*) and was held in [Sanjar's] esteem. [His library] contained about 12,000 volumes.[85]

To build up a collection of such magnitude suggests considerable opportunities for enrichment.

The two or three days a week Kayka'us suggests should be devoted to drinking may hardly seem moderate by the standards of any society, let alone a Muslim one, but such behaviour was expected of the elite (Figure 4.4). Rawandi, who wrote his *Rahat al-Sudur* to acculturate the Anatolian Seljuk Ghiyath al-Din Kaykhusraw to the norms of the court practice of his Great Seljuk relatives, gives prominence to a chapter on drinking, in which he gives advice on licit ways of consuming wine. He states that:

[81] Sibt, *Mir'at*, 243.

[82] Nizam al-Mulk, *Siyar al-Muluk*, 171, trans. 124–6. For examples of some normative texts dealing with the importance of generosity and feasting in Turko-Persian culture from Gök Türk to Ottoman times, see Rhoads Murphey, *Exploring Ottoman Sovereignty: Tradition, Image and Practice in the Ottoman Imperial Household, 1400–1800* (London, 2008), 28–32.

[83] Nishapuri, *Saljuqnama*, 61.

[84] See *ibid.*, 61; Merçil, *Selçuklular'da Saray*, 111–12, 114.

[85] Yaqut, *Mu'jam al-Buldan* (Beirut, 1996), V, 114 (s.v. Marw).

Figure 4.4 Statue of a figure holding a drinking bowl, probably twelfth-century Iran. Metropolitan Museum of Art, New York. Accession No. 68.67. © Metropolitan Museum of Art

> as it is necessary for the king [*pādshāh*] to imitate the praiseworthy morals of the sultans of Iraq and Khurasan, and feasting and fighting [*bazm u razm*] are essential, I have arranged it so that his wine-house [*sharābkhāna*] should not be illicit.[86]

Nizam al-Mulk devotes a short chapter of the *Siyasatnama* to warning of the danger of sultanic orders issued in drunkenness (as well as, to be fair, warning of confusion over ones issued in sobriety), advising bureaucrats to refer back to the sultan for confirmation.[87] The Ziyarid heir who was the intended audience of the *Qabusnama* was clearly expected to be drunk on a regular basis, and Kayka'us is full of sage advice on what behaviour he should avoid in such instances. Historical sources confirm this picture: there are stories of

[86] Rawandi, *Rahat al-Sudur*, 417.
[87] Nizam al-Mulk, *Siyar al-Muluk*, 118, trans. 88.

Alp Arslan's drunkenness,[88] while Malikshah b. Mahmud, Nishapuri tells us, 'adored drinking, hunting and sexual intercourse'.[89] Isfahani tells of a three-day drinking session in which Sanjar indulged as a guest of his vizier Sadr al-Din Muhammad b. Fakhr al-Mulk.[90]

This behaviour did not meet universal approbation. Some sultans were accused of indulging in their pleasure at the expense of affairs of state. Ibn Khallikan is hardly paying Malikshah a compliment when he remarks that Nizam al-Mulk was so powerful that there was nothing left for the sultan but 'the throne and hunting'.[91] We have noted elsewhere Anushirwan's comment that Malikshah was more interest in the quality of his hunting dogs than his ministers (p. 206 below), and he also remarks that Sultan Mas'ud b. Muhammad was so distracted by his amusements that he did not even ask about what his vizier, Shams al-Din Abu 'l-Najib al-Asamm al-Darguzini, was doing.[92] Isfahani describes one sybaritic winter Mas'ud spent in Baghdad, and reference by Ibn al-Jawzi to the scandalous sight of the sultan drinking in public suggest that, at least in this instance, there was more than just malice underlying Isfahani's portrayal:[93]

> The sultan [Mas'ud] resided in Baghdad that winter, enthusiastically partaking of pleasure and satisfying his desires, impassioned by the bringing near of [wine] jars, acquiring singing girls, having clowns brought into his presence and sending men of virtue away, dependent on good fortune to fend off enemies.[94]

For the broader public, however, the most notable feature of Mas'ud's debauched winter in Baghdad seems to have been his menagerie of an elephant, parrot and monkey, which the eyewitness Ibn Azraq al-Fariqi singles out for attention.[95]

Drinking, banqueting and hunting could actually form part of the business of ruling. The poet Mu'izzi's description of his patron Malikshah's winter in Baghdad (probably that of 479/1086–7), suggests how to a court audience this sort of behaviour was not just acceptable, but praiseworthy:

[88] Sibt, *Mir'at*, 130; Ibn al-'Adim, *Bughya*, 37–8. See, however, the comments on pp. 251–2 below.
[89] Nishapuri, *Saljuqnama*, 87.
[90] Bundari, *Zubda*, 366.
[91] Ibn Khallikan, *Wafayat*, II, 109.
[92] Bundari, *Zubda*, 218.
[93] Ibn al-Jawzi, *al-Muntazam*, IX, 72, 89.
[94] Bundari, *Zubda*, 193.
[95] Hillenbrand, *A Muslim Principality*, fol. 175b, pp. 135–6.

With auspicious fortune, on a blessed day, the king of kings has set out from Baghdad for the Abode of Kingship [Isfahan].
On account of his judgement and high ambition for six months has he done a thousand good works in Baghdad
With the blessing of his fortune, he has made ancient ruins beautiful and flourishing like the garden of Iram.[96]
He has hunted on the plains of Kufa, Hit, Mada'in and Tikrit, and administered justice to brave men.
He sat on the banks of the Tigris with a cup in hand; wailing out of fear of him reached the banks of the Nile.
The leaders of his army came from Byzantium and Syria, each one covered with a cloak appropriate to his rank like Qubad.[97]
Each one did homage [*khidmat*] and took the shah's robe of honour, increased in rank, and went away happy.
A king whose lifestyle and customs [*sīrat ū āyīn*] are such is happy indeed in kingship. Long may he live!'[98]

As David Durand-Guédy has put it: 'The *majlis* (for the festivities, and in particular drinking parties) and the *maydān* (for the polo games) were the two places of the sultan's social but also political life.'[99] Rawandi – himself an aspirant *nadīm* to the Anatolian Seljuk sultan Ghiyath al-Din Kaykhusraw I – recommends archery and horse racing as 'they are permissible [*ḥalāl*] because they are the cause of fighting unbelievers and [undertaking] jihad',[100] as is hunting for sport. We have several illustrations of the political utility of hunting trips, which could perform functions similar to the itinerancy of the court, allowing the sultan to project his power throughout his domains, to bring errant subjects to heel, to practise for war, and to cement bonds with the amirs and men of state who accompanied him.[101] For instance, Malikshah used a hunt in southern Iraq in 472/1080 to chastise an errant tax collector, Ibn 'Alan, a Jew who tax-farmed Basra and Ahwaz.[102] Hunts might also serve as a preliminary to warfare. The Qarakhanid Qadir Khan used a hunting party to assess Seljuk defences around Tirmidh; Sanjar sent his own hunt to

[96] The gardens of Iram (referred to in passing the Qur'an, Surah 89, verse 6–7), were often mentioned by Persian poets as a simile for an earthly paradise.
[97] A Sasanian ruler.
[98] Mu'izzi, *Diwan*, 122, No. 89, ll. 16–23.
[99] Durand-Guédy, 'Where did the Saljuqs Live?', 235
[100] Rawandi, *Rahat al-Sudur*, 429.
[101] Cf. Thomas Allsen, *The Royal Hunt in Eurasian History* (Philadelphia, 2006), 217–18; Murphey, *Exploring Ottoman Sovereignty*, 26–8.
[102] Sibt, *Mir'at*, 201; Ibn al-Jawzi, *al-Muntazam*, VIII, 323.

intercept the Qarakhanids, and Qadir Khan was captured, brought to the Seljuk court, and beheaded.[103]

Women at the Seljuk Court

Women in Islamic courts are traditionally described as confined to the harem – itself imagined as a mysterious den of pleasure and vice, cut off from the outside world. There is enough in Seljuk chronicles to give a degree of credence to such stereotypes. Mahmud, Nishapuri tells us, spent much of his time in the women's quarters or harem (*sarā-yi zanān*) and eventually became ill from an excess of sexual activity.[104] Kayka'us b. Iskandar also warns against the dangers of devoting too much time to sexual intercourse – especially in the bathhouse – but he did not envisage that the objects of affection would necessarily be female.[105] His chapter on the conduct of love affairs rather assumes that the prince's beloved would be a male *ghulām*, or slave boy. Such affairs were common in mediaeval Islamic court culture, and Mahmud of Ghazna's love for his *ghulām* Ayaz passed into literature as an example of devoted affection.[106] In Seljuk times, Sanjar was famed for his love of his *ghulām* Qaymaz to such an extent that, Isfahani tells us, he paid no attention to anything else. Isfahani depicts the sultan at a drinking party with 'his eye on the slave's eye, his hand in his hand' – although Qaymaz took a liberty too far in taking the opportunity of Sanjar's drunkenness to go and kill his vizier Sadr al-Din b. Fakhr al-Mulk, stealing the sultanic ring to authorise his actions. This was regarded as a scandal that must be hidden, and Qaymaz was duly executed. Even the most indulgent sultan had his limits.[107]

However, such stereotypes of lascivious sultans whiling away their days in the harem distracts from the prominence of women of the Seljuk house in political, social and economic life. Far from being restricted to the domain of the harem, Seljuk women played a much more public role than many of their counterparts in other contemporary Muslim dynasties.[108] Many of the Seljuk royal women were in fact descended from other dynasties, as unions were formed to cement political alliances. Tughrıl's enthusiasm for marrying an 'Abbasid princess has been discussed above (p. 141), but he also married the

103 Allsen, *Royal Hunt*, 230; Bundari, *Zubda*, 262.

104 Nishapuri, *Saljuqnama*, 70–1.

105 Kayka'us b. Iskandar, *Qabusnama*, 86–7, 88.

106 See, for example, Nizami 'Arudi, *Chahar Maqala*, 55.

107 See Bundari, *Zubda*, 366–7. As ever, Isfahani doubtless is grinding axes.

108 For a comparison of 'Abbasid and Seljuk royal women, see Hanne, 'Women, Power', 80–110. A useful overview of royal women in Seljuk and Mongol times is given in Lambton, *Continuity and Change*, 258–96; also Hillenbrand, 'Women in the Seljuq Period'.

daughter of the Buyid Abu Kalijar, whose son was married to a daughter of Chaghrı.[109] Both Alp Arslan and Malikshah married Qarakhanid princesses.[110] Seljuk princesses, meanwhile, were married off to vassal rulers as far afield as Mecca – indeed, virtually every Muslim vassal dynasty and neighbour was bound to the Seljuks by a complex network of marriage alliances.[111]

One of the most influential figures of the Seljuk court was Malikshah's wife, the Qarakhanid princess Terken Khatun.[112] When arrangements for the marriage of Malikshah's daughter to Caliph al-Muqtadi were being made, the latter's vizier Fakhr al-Dawla b. Jahir had to negotiate directly with Terken Khatun over the terms.[113] When the marriage took place, al-Muqtadi sent robes of honour to Terken Khatun 'and all the ladies of the court (*khawātīn*)'.[114] She is the target of vigorous complaints by Nizam al-Mulk in the *Siyasatnama* concerning the unhealthy influence of women on politics, confirming that her power represented a serious threat to the vizier.[115] Terken Khatun played an important role in the succession struggle on the sultan's death (see pp. 71, 76 above). After her failure to establish her son Mahmud b. Malikshah on the throne, she sought to enhance her position through marriage, seeking nuptial alliances with Ismail b. Yaquti (Berkyaruq's maternal uncle) and Tutush.[116] Although neither marriage came off, she managed to remain a leading political actor on her own terms. Ibn al-Jawzi tells us that at the time of her death she still commanded a contingent of 10,000 men – a very substantial army indeed – and describes her as having been 'the mistress of Isfahan, dealing with the wars while organising and guiding the armies'.[117]

In the extent of her power, Terken Khatun can scarcely be considered

[109] Lambton, *Continuity and Change*, 261; Ibn al-Athir, *al-Kamil*, IX, 536.

[110] For Alp Arslan's marriage to a Qarakhanid princess, see Ibn al-Athir, *al-Kamil*, X, 301; Sibt, *Mir'at*, 123. She had previously been the wife of Mahmud b. Mas'ud b. Sebüktegin of Ghazna.

[111] Malikshah's sister was betrothed to the sharif of Mecca, Abu'l-Hashim (Sibt, *Mir'at*, 156–7), while the 'Uqaylid amir only got the sultan's own foster-sister (Sibt, *Mir'at*, 238), perhaps suggesting a careful gradation of rank in arranging these marriage alliances. Seljuk women were only very rarely married to amirs, perhaps to preserve the special status of the dynasty (Lambton, *Continuity and Change*, 268–9).

[112] For her marriage to Malikshah, see Ibn al-Athir, *al-Kamil*, IX, 301.

[113] Bundari, *Zubda*, 72; Ibn al-Athir, *al-Kamil*, X, 160–1.

[114] Ibn al-Athir, *al-Kamil*, X, 161.

[115] Nizam al-Mulk, *Siyar al-Muluk*, 242–53, trans. 179–87. As will be recalled, Nizam al-Mulk's hostility to Terken Khatun doubtless derives from her anxiety to secure the succession for her infant son Mahmud, in which she was supported by Nizam al-Mulk's arch-rival, Taj al-Mulk.

[116] Hanne, *Putting the Caliph in his Place*, 127–9; Ibn al-Athir, *al-Kamil*, X, 224.

[117] Ibn al-Jawzi, *al-Muntazam*, XVII, 14; Hanne, *Putting the Caliph in his Place*, 127.

typical of Seljuk women, but her political and military role was not unparalleled. Gawhar Khatun, for instance, Malikshah's aunt who was executed on Nizam al-Mulk's advice precisely because of the political threat she posed (see p. 68 above), had devastated the region of Nishapur around 467/1074–5, suggesting that she too commanded a significant military force.[118] On occasion, women did manage to rule certain limited areas outright. The prime example is Zahida Khatun, wife of the *atabeg* Boz-Aba, who controlled Fars for twenty-one years after his death in 541/1146–7, and, the local historian tells us 'in terms of ruling, had complete control' (*az rāh-i ḥukm u farmāndahī mulk-i tamām biyandākht*).[119] Even without the backing of their own military forces, women could wield great political influence. Altunjan, wife of Tughrıl, who had previously been married to the Khwarazmshah, is said to have been 'wise, prudent and decisive: the sultan used to listen to her, obeyed her and referred affairs back to her for consideration'. It was Altunjan who recommended to Tughrıl that he should marry the caliph's daughter after her own death.[120] Peace between Sanjar and Mahmud in 513/1119 was negotiated by Sanjar's mother, Safariyya Khatun.[121] Sanjar's daughter was married to Mahmud, at whose court she exercised great influence, supporting the Mazyadid Dubays b. Sadaqa. After her death Dubays was ruined.[122] Sanjar's wife Terken Khatun (not to be confused with Malikshah's wife of the same name, but likewise a Qarakhanid princess)[123] also played an active public role, attending banquets with local notables in Khurasan,[124] and commissioning building works such as the restoration of the great caravanserai at Ribat-i Sharaf.[125]

Royal women's power derived in part from the vast sums of wealth they personally controlled. Mahmud's wife (the daughter of Sanjar) is said to have possessed 'endless precious stones, jewels, carpets and clothes'.[126]

118 Sibt, *Mir'at*, 172, 176.

119 Lambton, *Continuity and Change*, 150; Ibn Zarkub, *Shiraznama*, 136–7.

120 Sibt, *Mir'at*, 75.

121 Ibn al-Athir, *al-Kamil*, X, 552–3.

122 *Ibid.*, X, 655. According to Nishapuri, *Saljuqnama*, 70–1, Mahmud married first Mahmalak Khatun, and when she died, her sister Amirsitti Khatun was sent to him by Sanjar. Amirsitti Khatun was presumably the great supporter of Dubays.

123 Bundari, *Zubda*, 264; Husayni, *Akhbar*, 92, 94

124 Ibn Funduq, *Tarikh-i Bayhaq*, 270; Jean Aubin, 'L'aristocratie urbaine dans l'Iran seldjukide: l'exemple de Sabzavar', in P. Gallais and Y. J. Rion (eds), *Mélanges offerts à René Crozet* (Poitiers, 1966), 330.

125 R. Hillenbrand, *Islamic Architecture*, 334–6; C. Hillenbrand, 'Women in the Seljuq Period', 112.

126 Ibn al-Athir, *al-Kamil*, X, 594

Malikshah's sister, 'Ismat Khatun, was rich enough in her own right to build a madrasa in Isfahan which was among the largest in the Islamic world.[127] Some of this wealth may have derived from the exercise of patronage: Fakhr al-Mulk b. Nizam al-Mulk, for instance, managed to purchase the vizierate in 488/1095 (replacing his own brother, Majd al-Mulk) because he learned of the queen mother Zubayda Khatun's hatred of Majd al-Mulk 'and sent much wealth [to obtain] the vizierate'.[128] Royal women might possess large estates: Gawhar Khatun (the wife of Muhammad b. Mahmud, not Malikshah's aunt of the same name) derived income from the town of Sumayram, and these estates were run by her *dīwān* (*al-dīwān al-khātūnī*).[129] A document from *al-Mukhtarat min al-Rasa'il* records Mahmud's daughter Zaynab Khatun's sale to an amir of her extensive estates in the Isfahan region, comprising a village, orchards, farms and a watermill, suggesting her wide-ranging economic interests.[130] These elite women often engaged in founding charitable endowments, buildings and improving agriculture.[131]

Turkish Culture at the Seljuk Court

Turkish royal women played a much more prominent role in the historical sources than the Buyid or 'Abbasid ones who had married into the Seljuk dynasty, suggesting that their importance was specifically related to the superior status of women in steppe societies. Other fragments of evidence reinforce this impression that the court maintained more elements of steppe culture than is often credited.[132] Turkish remained the every-day language of court,[133] and was probably much more widely used than the scanty surviving evidence suggests. Tughrıl relied on his vizier Kunduri to translate from

[127] Durand-Guedy, *Iranian Elites*, 200.

[128] Ibn al-Athir, *al-Kamil*, X, 253. Although it is not directly stated she was the beneficiary, this seems the most likely interpretation. For an alternative account, see Bundari, *Zubda*, 86, which confirms Zubayda Khatun's patronage. Her political role cam at the cost of her life in the end (Ibn al-Athir, *al-Kamil*, X, 488; Bundari, *Zubda*, 87). This Zubayda Khatun, the mother of Berkayaruq, should be distinguished from Malikshah's daughter, Zubayda Khatun, who was married to Mas'ud, then Mengubars of Fars.

[129] Bundari, *Zubda*, 110.

[130] *Al-Mukhtarat min al-Rasa'il*, 458–50.

[131] Cf. Lambton, 'Aspects of Saljuq–Ghuzz Settlement', 115, for Seljuk women's activities in Yazd; Lambton, *Continuity and Change*, 150–1.

[132] The most comprehensive discussion to date of this issue is Tetley, *The Ghaznavid and Seljuk Turks*, 17–42.

[133] The evidence is collected in Erdoğan Merçil, 'Selçuklular ve Türkçe', *Belleten*, 67(248) (2003), 111–17.

Arabic and Persian into Turkish for him, and Turkish songs were sung at the wedding of Tughrıl to the caliph's daughter.[134] Later sultans, like Mahmud, are said to have known Arabic language and literature well,[135] but even so, they still spoke Turkish among themselves. When Mas'ud encountered his brother Mahmud in the battle to which he had been ill-advisedly incited, he cried out to him in Turkish.[136] The most telling evidence, however, of the importance of Turkish is the great Turkish–Arabic dictionary, the *Diwan Lughat al-Turk*, compiled in Baghdad for Caliph al-Muqtadi by the émigré Qarakhanid prince Mahmud al-Kashghari. Kashghari's introduction sets out the case for learning Turkish to his patron. God had endowed the Turks with rule and so

> every man of reason must attach himself to them, or expose himself to their falling arrows. And there is no better way to approach them than by speaking their own tongue, thereby bending their ear, and inclining their heart.[137]

Kashghari goes on to relate a hadith enjoining people to 'learn the language of the Turks for their reign will be long'. Turkish, then, was essential for getting on at court, and Kashghari's project is motivated in part by the desire to show that Turkish was fully the equal of Arabic. Yet apart from the *Diwan Lughat al-Turk*, no works written in Turkish survive from the Seljuk Empire, in contrast to the Qarakhanid domains, from which a number of examples of contemporary early Turkish literature have been preserved.[138] While the *Maliknama* was assembled from Turkish oral accounts, it was put into writing in Persian and Arabic,[139] and there is no evidence to suggest a written Turkish version was ever composed. As is suggested by Nishapuri's *Saljuqnama*, a work almost certainly written for the youthful Tughrıl III, Persian became the medium through which even the royal family were taught about the deeds of their ancestors.

Turkish was, however, on occasion committed to writing. Malikshah is said to have written a letter in Turkish to his head of chancery (*dīwān al-inshā'*),

134 Sibt, *Mir'at*, 98–9 and see p. 195, n. 37 below.

135 Husayni, *Akhbar*, 99.

136 *Ibid.*, 96–7; Bundari, *Zubda*, 132–3. For comments on Sanjar's alleged preference for a Turkish-speaking coterie, see Tetley, *The Ghaznavid and Seljuk Turks*, 159.

137 Kāšɣarī, *Compendium*, trans. Dankoff, I, 70.

138 See Tetley, *The Ghaznavid and Seljuk Turks*, 36–8; Robert Dankoff, 'Qarakhanid Literature and the Beginnings of Turco-Islamic Culture', in Hasan B. Paksoy (ed.), *Central Asian Monuments* (Istanbul, 1992), 73–80. Further on the prestige of Turkish, see Tourkhan Gandjeï, 'Turkish in pre-Mongol Persian Poetry', *BSOAS*, 49/i (1996), esp. 69–70.

139 Peacock, *Early Seljūq History*, 28.

Kamal al-Din Abu 'l-Rida Fadlallah b. Muhammad (*fa-kataba ilayhi bi'l-Turkiyya*), even though the sultan could also write Persian.[140] Kashghari's *Diwan* contains many examples of Turkish poetry, which reveal – as do the Qarakhanid Turkish works – that their authors were well acquainted with the conventions of Persian poetry.[141] The *Diwan*'s poetry also, however, suggests the existence of a literary culture in Turkish with epics on Turkish themes, independent of Perso-Islamic influences.[142]

Steppe influences are also evident in marriage. Tughrıl, in accordance with Turkish custom, married his late brother Chaghrı's widow,[143] a practice abhorred by Islam. Alp Arslan also had a Levirate marriage to Tughrıl's widow 'Akka,[144] and it seems he intended his own wife to marry Qavurt on his death.[145] Even marriage contracts between the 'Abbasids and the Seljuks might be based on Turkish norms: Ibn al-Jawzi informs us that in the negotiations over the marriage of Malikshah's daughter to the caliph, 50,000 dinars had to be handed over as compensation for a future wet nurse, which, he remarks, is 'the custom of the Turks in arranging marriages' (*hādhihi 'ādat al-atrāk 'inda al-tazwīj*).[146]

Some Seljuk sultans emphasised their distinctive heritage through their appearance. Alp Arslan was famous for his Turkish-style moustaches, which were so long that he had to tie them back when shooting arrows; Sanjar too had long and wide moustaches in addition to a beard that reached down to his chest.[147] We know very little of what the sultans wore except on major state occasions like coronations (see pp. 164–5 above). However, when in 528/1133–4 Sultan Mas'ud's support collapsed and his enemies Tughrıl II and Dubays got the upper hand through claiming that the caliph had lost confidence in him, Mas'ud sought to re-establish his position by entering Isfahan 'in Türkmen dress' (*fī zayy al-Turkmān*).[148]

140 Husayni, *Akhbar*, 68. For Malikshah's ability to write Persian, see Bundari, *Zubda*, 59.

141 Tetley, *The Ghaznavid and Seljuk Turks*, 37.

142 Robert Dankoff, 'Three Turkic Verse Cycles relating to Inner Asian Warfare', *Harvard Ukrainian Studies*, 3/4 (1979–80), 151–65; Dankoff, 'Qarakhanid Literature'; cf. Gandjeï, 'Turkish in pre-Mongol Persian Poetry', 68.

143 Ibn al-Athir, *al-Kamil*, X, 6, 29; Sibt, *Mir'at*, 97, 102, 108. On the practice, see Jean-Paul Roux, 'La veuve dans les sociétés turques et mongoles de l'Asie centrale', *L'Homme*, 9/iv (1969), 51–78, esp. 66–9; Musa Şamil Yüksel, 'Turk kültüründe "Levirat" ve Timurlularda uygalanışı', *Turkish Studies*, 5/iii (2010), 2028–58.

144 Sibt, *Mir'at*, 124.

145 *Ibid*., 165–6.

146 Ibn al-Jawzi, *al-Muntazam*, XVI, 222.

147 Nishapuri, *Saljuqnama*, 21, 69.

148 Ibn al-Jawzi, *al-Muntazam*, XVII, 284. On these events see p. 95 above.

Did the influence of Turkish culture at court remain constant – despite, say, Nizam al-Mulk's attempts to destroy parts of the Turkish aristocracy? This is a difficult question to answer, especially in view of the lack of sources comparable to Sibt for the twelfth century. I am not aware of any examples of Levirate marriage after Alp Arslan, although this might reflect the growing power of *atabegs*, who usually married the mother of their ward on her husband's death. Arabic works vaunting the virtues of the Turks and celebrating the origins of the Seljuk family in the Khazar empire were composed for the courts of Tughrıl and Alp Arslan – the *Kitab Tafdil al-Atrak* of Ibn Hassul, and the *Maliknama*, based on Turkish oral traditions. The latter work certainly continued to circulate widely, for it is cited by a large number of thirteenth-century sources.[149] A further lost work on the glories of the Turks was composed for Sanjar, indicating a continuing interest in the theme,[150] but Nishapuri's *Saljuqnama* is completely silent on the dynasty's Khazar connection, and gives Seljuk himself a lineage connecting him to Luqman, the sage of Islamic legend.[151] Furthermore, as noted above (p. 127), the bow and arrow motif on coins from the reign of Malikshah became increasingly stylised and was eventually dispensed with entirely. A shift in tastes and priorities is perhaps suggested by Nizami 'Arudi's account of Alp Arslan's son Tughanshah. He played no major political role, but was a major patron of Persian poetry who chose poets as his *nadīms*.[152] Henceforth, Perso-Islamic traditions would increasingly influence court culture, but the pace of such changes must have often been slow and uneven. On the one hand, a contemporary source attests the magnificence of Sanjar's court library;[153] on the other, according to a document issued by that sultan's own chancery, Sanjar was illiterate.[154] Further, Mas'ud's ceremonial donning of Türkmen dress to garner support, the institutions of the *ṭughrā'ī* and the *atabeg*, and the continuing use of the Turkish language and Turkish names among the dynasty to its end suggests the endurance of at least certain aspects of Turkish culture and identity, our understanding of which, in our ignorance of the oral Turkic culture of the court, will always remain partial and fragmentary.

149 Peacock, *Early Seljūq History*, 27–31.

150 Gandjeï, 'Turkish in pre-Mongol Persian Poetry', 69; Ibn Funduq, *Tarikh-i Bayhaq*, 141, 163.

151 Nishapuri, *Saljuqnama*, 5.

152 Nizami Arudi, *Chahar Maqala*, 69.

153 'Umar b. Sahlan al-Sawi, *Risala-yi Sanjariyya fi 'l-Ka'inat al-'unsuriyya*, ed. Mehmet Altay Köymen as 'Selçuklu Devri Kaynaklarına Dair Araştırmalar, II: Risale-i Senceriyye', *Doğu Dilleri*, 1/iii (1969), 23.

154 Bartol'd, *Turkestan v Epokhu Mongolskogo Nashestviya. Chast' 1: Teksty*, 38: *ma'lūm ast kih mā khāndan u nibishtan nadānīm.*

The Court and Cultural Patronage

Nizami 'Arudi remarked that all the Seljuk sultans were fond of poetry,[155] and the vast corpus of Persian verses composed for the court is the most lasting monument to their cultural patronage.[156] As early as the reign of Tughrıl, Persian and Arabic poets such as Fakhr al-Din Gurgani and Bakharzi were praising the sultan in verses that he could not understand.[157] Tughrıl III himself had a reputation as a fine Persian poet.[158] The empire provided rich opportunities for a poet trying to make his career, for there were potential patrons not just in the form of the sultan and the bureaucrats (amirs seem comparatively rarely to have patronised poetry), but in the multiplicity of different regional courts belonging to Seljuk vassals and *maliks*. Poets circulated freely from court to court, not just within the Seljuk domains but even beyond. 'A'maq, for instance, wrote poems for both the Qarakhanids and Sanjar, while Sanjar's court poet Anwari received both Seljuk and Ghurid patronage.[159] Indeed, the personal enmities of the patrons seem to have been no impediment to a poet's career: Mu'izzi, one of the greatest of the Seljuk panegyrists, worked for Malikshah, Berkyaruq and Sanjar, despite the deep-rooted antipathy between the latter two rulers (see p. 78 above).

Although a few Arabic panegyrics were written in praise of the sultans, the main market for Arabic poetry was elsewhere. The *Diwan* of al-Arrajani, for instance, an Arabic language poet of the early twelfth century, is composed almost entirely of poems addressed to caliphal and Seljuk *kuttāb* such as Anushirwan b. Khalid and various caliphs, but with only a couple of works dedicated to a Seljuk sultan. Although Arabic remained important in the eleventh-century Jibal for official and literary purposes,[160] it was gradually displaced by Persian, the language of Khurasan, which served as the main literary language of the court. Thus, a scholar like Ghazali, who usually wrote in Arabic, used Persian for composing works destined for a court audience, such as correspondence to his patrons, and his treatises

155 Nizami 'Arudi, *Chahar Maqala*, 69.

156 For Seljuk literature, see Daniela Meneghini, 'Saljuqs v. Saljuqid Literature', *EIr*; Tetley, *The Ghaznavid and Seljuk Turks, passim*.

157 See Bakharzi's qasida, *Diwan*, 143–7. For Kunduri as interpreter in Tughrıl's meetings with the Caliph, see p. 195, n. 37 below.

158 Hamdallah Mustawfi, *Tarikh-i Guzida*, 463; Hamdallah quotes some of Tughrıl's verses.

159 J. Mattini, 'A'maq-i Bok̲āri', *EIr*; J. T. P. de Bruijn, 'Anvari', *EIr*.

160 See Safi, *Politics of Knowledge*, 50; under Malikshah, Mafarrukhi's *Mahasin Isfahan* was composed in Arabic. Some Arabic documents appear in the twelfth-century Jibali *inshā'* collection, *al-Mukhtarat min al-Rasa'il*. The rise of Persian in the Jibal needs further investigation.

the *Nasihat al-Muluk* (a mirror for princes) and the *Kimiya-yi Saʿadat* (see pp. 125, 257).

Unlike later dynasties, the Seljuk dynasty seems to have evinced relatively little interest in secular prose literature like history. Apart from the various mirrors for princes we have already mentioned, most other genres of prose were produced by and for religious or bureaucratic circles. The other main area of the dynasty's intellectual patronage was science, of whom the most notable representative was ʿUmar Khayyam (*c.* 439/1048–517/1123), made famous to Anglophone audiences by Edward Fitzgerald's translation of his quatrains (*rubāʿiyyāt*).[161] In his own day, however, ʿUmar Khayyam was better known as a scholar, a philosopher, astronomer and mathematician, and he was part of the team of scholars employed by Malikshah to set up an astronomical observatory at Isfahan.[162] The purpose was doubtless, at least in part, practical, to facilitate the collection of taxes at a given date, but it may also have been connected to the general interest on the part of members of the Seljuk dynasty in matters connected with the science of the stars.

Nizami ʿArudi remarks that a properly constituted court consists of secretaries, poets, astrologers and physicians, and this does seem to have represented the practice.[163] We are told that that Tughrıl's personal astrologer and doctor never left his side,[164] and several members of the dynasty showed a fascination with the stars. Bayhaqi records how, when the Seljuks conquered Khurasan, the triumvirate of Tughrıl, Chaghrı and Yabghu prostrated themselves before the astrologer who had predicted it. Qutlumush himself had a reputation for his knowledge of the stars – which perhaps is our sources' way of telling us that he claimed the ability of the shaman to channel the forces of the sky, part of the occult knowledge that steppe rulers often claimed.[165] An interest in astrology and astronomy persisted among the dynasty into later times. A new calendar, the Jalali, taking its name from Malikshah's *laqab* Jalal al-Dawla, was inaugurated in 467/1075, which fixed the date of the vernal equinox

[161] On him, see B. A. Rosenfeld, ʿUmar Khayyām', *EI²*; for his mathematical activities, see E. S. Kennedy, 'The Exact Sciences in Iran under the Saljuqs and Mongols', in J. A. Boyle (ed.), *The Cambridge History of Iran, vol. V: The Saljuq and Mongol Periods* (Cambridge, 1968), 663–6.

[162] Ibn al-Athir, *al-Kamil*, X, 98. See further Aydın Sayılı, *The Observatory in Islam* (Ankara, 1960), 160–6.

[163] Nizami Arudi, *Chahar Maqala*, 18. The predominance of astrological imagery among artefacts connected with later Türkmen dynasties like the Artuqids, who themselves emerged from the Seljuk milieu, also suggests the Turkish enthusiasm for astrology.

[164] Sibt, *Mir'at*, 31.

[165] Bayhaqi, *Tarikh*, 958; Ibn al-Athir, *al-Kamil*, X, 37; Peacock, *Early Seljūq History*, 125.

and continued in use over much of Iran until modern times.[166] Although Ibn al-Athir tells us that the Isfahan observatory closed after Malikshah's death, the astronomer al-Khazini wrote a work on astronomy in the name of Sanjar, the *Zij-i Sanjari*, probably in Merv in 530/1135–6, which was eventually translated into Greek in the 1290s and found its way westwards.[167] A certain Abu'l-Qasim Asturulabi, who received the patronage of both Sultan Mahmud and Anushirwan b. Khalid, used the Seljuk palace in Baghdad as a basis for astronomic observations in 524/1129–30.[168] Other forms of science evidently did receive some interest, as is suggested by al-Sawi's treatise on meteorology written in Persian, rather than the more usual Arabic for scientific purposes, designed to attract the attention of Sanjar and his court.[169] However, that the bulk of Seljuk court patronage focused on astronomy and medicine, practical sciences, may be deduced from 'Umar Khayyam's complaint that 'other rational sciences are not valued in our time'.[170]

The Seljuk courts also patronised art and architecture, but relatively little art can be securely dated and attributed to a Great Seljuk context. Much of the material labelled Seljuk in museums in fact comes from the period *c.* 1150–1250, after the collapse of the Great Seljuks, when there seems to have been a sudden explosion in artistic production, apparently largely unrelated to court patronage.[171] As one scholar has put it, the Great Seljuk period is virtually a 'terra incognita' when it comes to artistic production.[172] For instance, courts throughout the Seljuk Empire must have been massive consumers of finely embroidered textiles, but the authenticity of most of the medieval pieces that have come to light (above all from Rayy) is suspect in the extreme. Authentic Seljuk metalware is equally virtually non-existent, although it is inconceivable it did not exist. Few Seljuk manuscripts survive, and none of the extant ones are illustrated.[173] Although many more examples of Great

166 S. H. Taqizadeh, 'Dj̲alālī', *EI*[2]; Kennedy, 'Exact Sciences', 670–2.

167 Sayılı, *Observatory in Islam*, 177–8. See also Joseph Leichter, 'The Zij-i Sanjari of Gregory Chioniades: Text, Translation and Greek to Arabic Vocabulary', PhD dissertation, Brown University, 2004, esp. 2–11.

168 Sayılı, *Observatory in Islam*, 175–6.

169 Al-Sawi, *Risala-yi Sanjariyya*, esp. 23–4.

170 Vaqar Ahmed Rizvi, 'Umar Khayyam as a Geometrician – A Survey', *Islamic Studies*, 24 (1985), 193.

171 The later period now studied by Oya Pancaroğlu, '"A World unto Himself": The Rise of a New Human Image in the Late Seljuk Period', PhD dissertation, Harvard University, 2000. See further Chapter 8 below.

172 Oleg Grabar, 'The Visual Arts, 1050–1350', in J. A. Boyle (ed.), *The Cambridge History of Iran, vol. V: The Saljuq and Mongol Periods* (Cambridge, 1968), 627.

173 Pancaroğlu, 'A World unto Himself', 28.

Seljuk architecture have come down to us, relatively few can be directly associated with sultanic patronage, although it may be that other members of the royal family played an important role – the royal halting place of Ribat-i Sharaf, for instance, was restored by Sanjar's wife Terken Khatun (see further pp. 180, 300–1). Only the mausoleum of Sanjar in Merv (Figure 2.2, p. 110 above), whose great blue dome (now tileless) rose from the heart of the metropolis, and was visible from a day's journey's distance to travellers across the desert,[174] gives an impression of the vast scale and ambition of some sultanic building projects.[175] Yet there is nothing to suggest that it was typical, and the resting place of most other sultans is today unknown.

[174] Yaqut, *Mu'jam al-Buldan*, V, 114.

[175] For a discussion of the mausoleum in the context of other Seljuk architecture in the region, see Robert Hillenbrand, 'The Seljuq Monuments of Turkmenistan', in C. Lange and S. Mecit (eds), *The Seljuqs: Politics, Society and Culture* (Edinburgh, 2011), 277–308.

5

The *Kuttāb*: Bureaucrats and Administration

'The good or ill of the king and kingdom depend on the vazir [vizier]', wrote Nizam al-Mulk:

> When the vazir is of good character and sound judgement, the kingdom is prosperous, the army and peasantry are contented, peaceful and well supplied, and the king is free from anxiety. But when the vazir is bad, irreparable harm is done to the kingdom; the king is constantly perplexed and distressed and the provinces are in a state of disorder.[1]

In the view of some modern scholars as much as Nizam al-Mulk, it was the bureaucracy – or rather the vizier – that actually ran the Seljuk Empire.[2] However, the example of Nizam al-Mulk is not representative; for most of Seljuk history there was no one central bureaucracy. Multiple Seljuk courts required multiple bureaucracies, and multiple viziers. Indeed, the whole system of administration was characterised by its extreme fluidity and decentralisation.

Quite apart from the vassal dynasties that continued to function in their own way, in the provinces an incredible variety of individuals were vested with authority in the name of the sultan(s). Alongside his representatives such as the *shiḥna* or qadi, the head of the community known as the *ra'īs* might be charged with functions ranging from the collection of taxes to cooperating with the *shiḥna* in the maintenance of security.[3] Some provinces, like Ganja, were assigned to *maliks* and their *atabegs*, while others, towns like Mosul, were allotted as *iqṭā'* to an ever-changing succession of amirs. Some cities, such as Bayhaq, Nishapur and Bukhara, were controlled by religious

1 Nizam al-Mulk, *Siyar al-Muluk*, 31, trans. 23.

2 See the comments of Barthold, *Turkestan*, 308; cf. Lambton, 'Internal Structure', 247–8.

3 Lambton, 'The Administration of Sanjar's Empire', 384–7; Jürgen Paul, 'Local Lords or Rural Notables? Some Remarks on the *ra'īs* in 12th Century Eastern Iran', in A. C. S. Peacock and Deborah Tor (eds), *Medieval Central Asia and the Persianate World: Iranian Tradition and Islamic Civilisation* (London, forthcoming).

elites – Bukhara, for instance, was subject to a dynasty of Hanafi *'ulamā'*, who bore the title of *ṣadr* (themselves, of course, subject to the Seljuks' Qarakhanid vassals).[4] Baghdad had several types of overlapping administration: most prominent were the sultan's *shiḥna*, and the caliphal *dīwān*; but other groups also controlled aspects of urban life, such as the *'ayyārs* (below pp. 236–7). Each area had its own distinctive arrangements, and the degree of penetration of Seljuk officials beyond the major cities ebbed and flowed according to local circumstances.[5]

Adherence to existing tradition was prized, and chancery documents enjoin appointees over provinces to govern by *istimālat*, persuasion and consent. As a decree from Sanjar's chancery to the people of Jurjan puts it, the *malik* Mas'ud b. Muhammad who had just been appointed governor,

> should act only after consulting experienced, trustworthy men so that whatever he does be in accordance with right and sound customs [*sunan-i ṣawāb wa saddād*] and he be protected from errors and shortcomings. He should know that the cornerstone of governing a province and ordering satisfactorily [all] the interests is to appease the hearts of men [*ta'līf wa istimālat-i dilhā*], and he should not allow any type of dispute between his retinue and servants on the one hand and the common people on the other . . .[6]

Adherence to established tradition was also a powerful rhetorical tool. To justify the proclamation of the *khuṭba* in his own name in Nishapur, Atsız had in 1142 issued a *fatḥnāma* proclaiming that Sanjar had 'destroyed the ancient rights of our ancestors' (*ḥuqūq-i qadīm-i aslāf-i mā bi-bād bar dād*).[7]

Traditionally, the administration of the Seljuk Empire is seen as being divided into two: a military establishment, staffed by the Turkish amirs, the 'men of the sword'; and a civilian bureaucracy, 'men of the pen', the Persian-speaking bureaucrats or *kuttāb*.[8] Nizam al-Mulk himself had emphasised the importance of maintaining the division between these two spheres.[9] In places, it is true, there does seem to have been a distinction between the military administration, represented by figures like the *shiḥna* or amir-*muqṭa's* who

[4] Paul, *Herrscher, Gemeinwesen, Vermittler*, 207–15; C. E. Bosworth, 'Āl-e Borhān', *EIr*; O. Pritsak, 'Āl-i Burhān', *Der Islam*, 30 (1952), 81–96. For Bayhaq, see Aubin, 'L'aristocratie urbaine'; for Nishapur, Bulliet, *Patricians of Nishapur*.

[5] Cf. A. H. Morton, 'Dinars of Western Mazandaran of some Vassals of the Saljuq Sultan Muḥammad b. Malik-shāh', *Iran*, 25 (1987), esp. 85–6.

[6] Juwayni, *'Atabat al-Kataba*, 20.

[7] Bartol'd, *Turkestan v Epokhu Mongolskogo Nashestviya. Chast'1: Teksty*, 43–4.

[8] Klausner, *The Seljuk Vezirate*, 14–15; Lambton, *Continuity and Change*, 28.

[9] Nizam al-Mulk, *Siyar al-Muluk*, 189–90, trans. 139.

were vested with coercive powers in the name of the sultans, and a civilian one, which was principally concerned with the collection of revenues. Indeed, it has been argued that this 'divided' or 'dual' system was deliberately devised to enable the sultans to retain control by something like a system of 'checks and balances'.[10]

Such a clean definition is too simplistic. The division of responsibilities between the various groups and individuals vested with power was never clearly defined. Quite what difference there was in practice between a region held as *iqṭā'* and one ruled by a *wālī* (governor) is often hard to say. Even if in origins the *muqṭa''s* duties were those of a tax collector, in practice both often acted as the ruler's deputy.[11] For instance, in 448/1056, Kunduri granted the Kurd Abu Kalijar Hazarasp b. Bankir the right to tax-farm Basra and Ahwaz in exchange for payment of 360,000 dinars. Hazarasp was not only granted a free hand in all the *iqṭā's* and tax-collection districts, but was even allowed to have his own name mentioned in *khuṭba*, one of the attributes of rulership.[12] Governors, whether or not members of the Seljuk family, also added their own name to the coinage, the other attribute of rulership. Some examples, such as those from mid-twelfth-century Isfahan, do coincide with periods of weakness in sultanic government,[13] but there are also plenty of early instances, such as Arslan Shah in Shiraz in the reign of Alp Arslan, or Tekish in eastern Khurasan under Malikshah.[14]

Nor is the distinction between a Turkish military and a Persian bureaucracy satisfactory. For instance, the *muḥtasib*, charged with the supervision of public morals in towns and the provision of justice, acting as a sort of 'state-appointed police force', providing basic security, might be a Turk or a member of the *'ulamā'*.[15] Indeed, the *'ulamā'* were a third pillar of Seljuk administration, providing qadis, whose appointments were ratified by the sultans.[16] While it is true that Turks seldom became bureaucrats,[17] on the

10 Klausner, *The Seljuk Vezirate*, 14, 35–6; Lambton, 'The Administration of Sanjar's Empire', 388. It should be noted that Lambton's later works do not stress this aspect and in fact in *Continuity and Change*, 28, she rejects the rigidity of the division between the civilian and military spheres.

11 Cf. Horst, *Staatsverwaltung*, 45.

12 Sibt, *Mir'at*, 1.

13 Durand-Guédy, *Iranian Elites*, 221, 325

14 Stephen Album, *Checklist of Islamic Coins* (n.p. 1998), 85.

15 See Lange, 'Changes in the Office of *Ḥisba*', 161–3.

16 Lambton, 'The Administration of Sanjar's Empire', 368.

17 One exception was Sulayman b. Muhammad Kashghari, vizier to Sanjar between 1122 and 1124, who was a Turk. Horst, *Staatsverwaltung*, 28–9; Lambton, 'The Internal Structure', 264; Iqbal, *Wizarat*, 252–3; Qummi, *Dhayl-i Nafthat al-Masdur*, 114–16.

other hand, bureaucrats frequently exercised military functions, as we will see below.

To add to the confusion, individuals bearing the same title might have widely varying responsibilities.[18] Thus, in twelfth-century Isfahan, the term *wālī* (governor) seems to be used as a synonym for *shiḥna*, that is, a senior amir vested with coercive power in the name of the sultan;[19] but in the Caspian province of Mazandaran in roughly the same period, the two positions were completely different, and *wālī* is used to mean a civilian bureaucrat, in contrast to a military *shiḥna*.[20] A *ra'īs* could mean anything from the personal representative of the ruler in a large city to a local landowner who functioned as the head of a village or rural community, who might or might not hold a diploma of appointment for his position.[21] The meaning of such titles was subject to local circumstances, and, perhaps above all, the connections of the man who held them. In the highly personalised Seljuk political system, what counted were personal contacts, *khidma*-ties, not the titles.

The purpose of this chapter is thus not to paint a general picture of Seljuk administration throughout the empire, for any attempts at such generalisation will be meaningless. Only a detailed study of local circumstances can give an impression of the impact and nature of Seljuk rule on the ground. Rather, we will examine the bureaucracy and the bureaucrats (*kātib*, pl. *kuttāb*) attached to the sultanic courts. The *kuttāb*, however, were much more important than mere administrators. They were the great opinion-formers of the day, and wrote many of our historical and literary sources. Their rivalries, their values, and their writings have helped shape our own view of the Seljuks.

The Bureaucracy, its Functions and its Structure

The aims of government in the mediaeval Islamic world tended to be strictly limited. While rulers who ameliorated their subjects' lot through good works are highly praised in the sources, in practice the most they generally provided was basic security on the roads and protection from external attack. Even functions such as the maintenance of irrigation works, the repair of city walls and the maintenance of security tended to fall to communities and their

18 Lambton, 'The Administration of Sanjar's Empire', 370.

19 Durand-Guédy, *Iranian Elites*, 210. See also Lambton, 'The Administration of Sanjar's Empire', 380.

20 Morton, 'Dinars of Western Mazandaran', 85–6.

21 Paul, 'Local Lords'.

leaders rather than the central government.[22] The prime aim of government in practice was to raise revenue.

The functions of the *dīwāns* reflect these limited aims. Conventionally, the administration attached to the sultan's court is described as being divided into five *dīwāns*, of which the chief was the vizier's *dīwān-i aʿlā*. As well as overseeing the functioning of other departments, the vizier and the *dīwān-i aʿlā* were tasked with making appointments in the name of the sultan to offices which were in his gift, such as the positions of qadi, *muḥtasib* and *shiḥna*. Other departments were the *dīwān-i istīfāʾ* (presided over by a *mustawfī*), which was responsible for raising revenue; the *dīwān-i ishrāf* (headed by a *mushrif*), charged with budgets and accountancy; the *dīwān-i ṭughra wa inshāʾ* (whose head was known variously as the *tughrāʾī* or *munshī*) or chancery; and the *dīwān–i ʿarḍ*, which was in charge of military pay.[23] In addition, the sources occasionally mention other *dīwāns*, also mainly concerned with aspects of finance and revenue: a *dīwān-i awqāf* was responsible for religious endowments,[24] while in the provinces taxation (or aspects of it) might be dealt with by the provincial administration, variously known as the *dīwān-i iyālat, dīwān-i wilāyat* and *dīwān-i riyāsat*.[25] The *dīwān-i riyāsat* was also at least sometimes concerned with the administration of customary law (*ʿurf*).[26]

Not all of these *dīwāns* necessarily existed at the same time, but we cannot be sure which existed and when owing to the unevenness of our information (see pp. 12–15 above). Even the evidence for the existence of some *dīwāns* is ambiguous: one scholar, for instance, has, on the basis of a single reference in a document, detected the existence of a *dīwān-i naẓar* which he presumes had some financial function; yet this may well just be an alternative name for the *dīwān-i ishrāf* (the words *ishrāf* and *naẓar* have similar meanings).[27]

22 Crone, *Medieval Islamic Political Thought*, 314; Paul, *Herrscher, Gemeinwesen, Vermittler*, 140–6, 260–78. On the limitations of Islamic government, see also Goitein, 'Minority Self-rule'.

23 Iqbal, *Wizārat*, 22–32, which is followed by Lambton, *Continuity and Change*, 29–30. See also Horst, *Staatsverwaltung*, 30–9; Klausner, *Seljuk Vezirate*, 155–9. The best description of the *dīwān-i ishrāf* is in Lambton, 'Internal Structure', 258–9.

24 Further on this, see A. K. S. Lambton, '*Awqāf* in Persia, 6th—18th/12th—14th Centuries', *Islamic Law and Society*, 4/iii (1997), esp. 380.

25 Lambton, 'The Administration of Sanjar's Empire', 376; Lambton, *Continuity and Change*, 30, 39–40; Horst, *Staatsverwaltung*, 50–1; Durand-Guédy, *Iranian Elites*, 211–12.

26 As *sharīʿa* only covered a limited number of eventualities, especially personal law, and certainly did not consitute anything like a coherent criminal code, jurists accepted the validity of *ʿurf*. Hiding behind the same designation may also lie the legal system of the steppe (which even in the better attested Mongol times when it is known as *yasa* probably resembled more an amorphous body of custom than a codified system). See Lambton, *Continuity and Change*, 29, 69–70, 79–81, 348.

27 Hort, *Staatsverwaltung*, 39, 135; Juwaynī, *ʿAtabat al-Kataba*, 67: *dīwān-i istīfāʿ wa ishrāf*

However, the *dīwān-i a'lā*, the *dīwān-i istīfā'* and the *dīwān-i ṭughrā wa inshā'* do appear fairly consistently, although the latter was sometimes divided into two separate departments.[28] The *dīwāns*' functions and status probably depended on the individual office holder, which is why, on occasion, the post of *mustawfi* seems to have been more powerful than that of vizier.[29]

Matters were complicated further by the pluralism in office-holding, of which Nizam al-Mulk bitterly complains:

> Whenever one officer is given two posts – or three or five or seven – by the divan it is a sign of the incompetence of the vazir and the negligence of the king. Today there are men, utterly incapable, who hold ten posts, and if another appointment were to turn up they would apply for it, giving bribes if necessary, and get it.[30]

Very likely this particular passage is directed against Nizam al-Mulk's arch-rival, Taj al-Mulk, who was treasurer to Malikshah, vizier to the sultan's offspring (*awlāduhu al-mulūk*), in charge of the *dīwān-i ṭughrā wa inshā'*, and also had some military responsibilities.[31] However, the practice to which it refers was certainly widespread, and is attested in the later Seljuk period too.[32] Thus, just because an individual occupied a given post, this does not necessarily imply that he effectively discharged any of its duties; deputies were commonly appointed to carry these out.[33]

The bureaucracy of each court was probably quite small. We have no precise figures, but some indication is given by Qummi's work which deals with the *kuttāb* in the Jibal from the 1130s to the 1180s. Over this period, Qummi mentions a total of ninety-seven individuals working in the various *dīwāns*. Most probably, each department probably consisted of little more than its

wa naẓar. Indeed, one could equally well argue from this passage that it seems here as if the *dīwāns* of *istīfā'* and *ishrāf* had been united into a single *dīwān* at this point.

28 See, for instance, the notices of appointments accompanying the appointment of a new vizier in Isfahani, in which the names of the *mustawfi* and *ṭughrā'ī* are usually recorded but not other offices: Bundari, *Zubda*, 129, 189. For the division of the two offices, see n. 61 below.

29 Bundari, *Zubda*, 141–2.

30 Nizam al-Mulk, *Siyar al-Muluk*, 214, trans. 158–9; cf. Klausner, *Seljuk Vizierate*, 61.

31 Bundari, *Zubda*, 61; Safi, *Politics of Knowledge*, 69–70.

32 Lambton, 'The Administration of Sanjar's Empire', 370.

33 For instance, when al-Amir al-'Amid was vizier to Gawhar Khatun, he seems to have relied heavily on Kamal al-Mulk al-Sumayrami to carry out the post's functions. However, when he became *'amid* of Iraq, he did not relinquish the post of vizier, but instead formally appointed Kamal al-Mulk as his deputy (*nā'ib fi wizāra*), 'who would attend the court and by his presence there would maintain his name and prestige for him' (Bundari, *Zubda*, 111). Further on these deputies, see Fairbanks, 'The Tarikh al-Vuzara', 160–4.

head – the vizier, *mustawfi*, *ṭughrāʾī* and so on – and a handful of clerks. This was a small world, many of whose members were related to one another.[34] We have little information about the emergence and growth of this bureaucracy, although (as argued in Chapter 1) clearly by the 1040s some bureaucratic structures were already in place in both Tughrıl's and Chaghrı's domains. It is reasonable to assume that these expanded in size and sophistication with the enlargement of the empire and the dominance of Nizam al-Mulk.

The senior figure in the bureaucracy was generally the vizier. Although the title could be used for the head of any bureaucratic establishment,[35] in western scholarship it commonly refers to the head of the *dīwān-i aʿlā* and thus the whole bureaucracy, or as Nizam al-Mulk puts it, 'the head of all the tax collectors and civil servants (*ʿāmilān wa mutaṣṣarifān*)'.[36] The early viziers probably functioned largely as intermediaries between the Turkish-speaking sultan and the wider world. Kunduri, for instance, served as interpreter for occasions such as Tughrıl's audiences with the caliph.[37] Isfahani writes of him that 'the sultan sees through his eyes and hears through his ears, and he raises [men] up and humbles them with his permission and as a result of his opinion'.[38] The responsibilities of the vizier were never clearly defined and there was no clear distinction between where the bureaucracy ended and the sultan's household started. Kamal al-Din Muhammad al-Khazin, for instance, briefly vizier to Masʿud, in addition to supervising taxation and tax collectors, was responsible for administering expenditure on the sultanic household's provisions.[39] Likewise, Malikshah's treasurer, Taj al-Mulk, was also given the task of 'overseeing the affairs of the [sultan's] palaces and his harem [*al-naẓar fī umūr dūrihi wa-ḥuramihi*]'.[40] Although Nizam al-Mulk

[34] See Fairbanks, 'The Tarikh al-Vuzara', 89. To take a rather distant comparative example from one of the few Middle Eastern states where the archives have in large part survived, the entire Ottoman central bureaucracy at the beginning of the seventeenth century has been estimated at some 218-strong (Murphey, *Exploring Ottoman Sovereignty*, 256). The Seljuk case, with its multiple courts and lack of a single imperial centre, was more complex, but the Ottoman figure stands as a warning against assuming that a large empire necessarily equalled a large bureaucracy.

[35] A wazir might be a sultan's personal adviser, or the head of a *dīwān* only able to communicate with the sultan indirectly: see Bundari, *Zubda*, 86; Lambton, 'Internal Structure', 226, 247. Alternatively, we find the term wazir used to refer to the official charged with administering the household of the Seljuk sultan's wife, or the minister to an *atabeg*. See, for example, Bundari, *Zubda*, 89, 100–1, 111.

[36] Nizam al-Mulk, *Siyar al-Muluk*, 230, trans. 170.

[37] Bundari, *Zubda*, 13, 17; Sibt, *Mir'at*, 25, 60; Ibn Hassul, *Tafdil al-atrak*, 45.

[38] Bundari, *Zubda*, 10.

[39] Ibn al-Athir, *al-Kamil*, XI, 64: *kāna yuqīmu maʾūnat al-sulṭān wa-waẓāʾifahu*.

[40] Bundari, *Zubda*, 61.

recommended that there should be separate treasuries for the state capital and expenses, this is probably another instance where his comments represent the ideal rather than the practice.[41]

All power and authority derived, at least in theory, from the sultan's person, which meant that administration had to be closely associated with – indeed, indivisible from – the sultan's court, the *mu'askar* or military camp, which it accompanied on campaigns. Tughrıl's vizier Kunduri described himself as someone who had 'served this dynasty by both the sword and the pen' (*wa-qad jama'a fi hādhihi al-dawla khidmat al-sayf wa'l-qalam*),[42] and led the army to suppress the revolt of Qutlumush b. Arslan Isra'il.[43] Nizam al-Mulk himself participated in Alp Arslan's Caucasian campaign of 456/1064, where he was assigned to accompany the men under the nominal command of the infant Malikshah, and took an active role in making tactical decisions.[44] He later joined Malikshah in his advance on Kashghar,[45] and was also put in charge of an expedition to crush the Shabankara'i leader Fadluya in Fars. Taj al-Mulk also had some military responsibilities in addition to all his other posts.[46] Fakhr al-Dawla b. Jahir, who had been 'Abbasid vizier, was in 476/1083–4 relieved of this office and appointed by Malikshah to lead campaigns in the Diyar Bakr against its Marwanid rulers,[47] and Ibn Hubayra also played a leading role in 'Abbasid campaigns in the mid-twelfth century.[48] Kamal al-Din Muhammad al-Khazin, Mas'ud's ill-fated vizier, had in fact been appointed to the office because of his military rather than his bureaucratic prowess, having impressed Mas'ud with his vigorous resistance to the sultan's attempts to take over Rayy.[49]

The Bureaucracy: Continuity or Change?

The system of the vizierate and the *dīwāns* originated in the 'Abbasid caliphate, and was emulated by the Buyids, Samanids and Ghanavids.[50] Throughout the *Siyasatnama*, Nizam al-Mulk repeatedly exhorts Malikshah to revive the

41 Nizam al-Mulk, *Siyar al-Muluk*, 322, trans. 239; cf. Horst, *Staatsverwaltung*, 22.
42 Bundari, *Zubda*, 17.
43 Sibt, *Mir'at*, 108.
44 Lambton, *Continuity and Change*, 30; Ibn al-Athir, *al-Kamil*, X, 38.
45 Ibn al-Athir, *al-Kamil*, X, 171.
46 Bundari, *Zubda*, 61: *fawwaḍa ilayhi amr ba'ḍ al-'askar*, 'the sultan entrusted him with some of the army's affairs'.
47 Ibn al-Athir, *al-Kamil*, X, 129, 134–5, 143–4.
48 Hanne, *Putting the Caliph in his Place*, 173–6.
49 Qummi, *Dhayl-i Nafthat al-Masdur*, 134–5; Fairbanks, 'The Tarikh al-Vuzara', 158–9.
50 Lambton, *Continuity and Change*, 28; A. A. Duri, 'Dīwān', *EI*².

administrative practice of the dynasty's predecessors.[51] Modern scholars, while admitting some of the distinctive features of the Seljuk system, have tended to emphasise these apparent continuities. Lambton, for instance, describes the *dīwāns* as 'staffed by men who were not Turks and who had inherited the administrative tradition of the preceding dynasties',[52] and remarks that 'new dynasties, having established themselves by the sword, usually left the details of administration in the hands of local officials'.[53]

The Seljuk bureaucracy, however, differed fundamentally from the classical 'Abbasid system in the way in which it was funded. Whereas 'Abbasid bureaucrats were paid set rates,[54] Seljuk office holders do not seem to have earned a salary per se. Ibn Khallikan states that the Seljuk viziers were paid 'in the form of a grant of one tenth of the produce of the soil'.[55] There were plenty of opportunities for profiting beyond the set *iqṭā'*. Despite the grim end of Muhammad Tapar's vizier Sa'd al-Mulk, publicly crucified on suspicion of Ismailism, there was plenty of competition for his job. As 'Imad al-Din al-Isfahani puts it in his characteristically caustic manner 'every Tom, Dick and Harry sought to become vizier' (*ṭamaḥa fī 'l-wizāra 'Amr wa-Zayd*).[56] Imad al-Din al-Isfahani singles out the Zangid vizier Jamal al-Din al-Isfahani – a family friend – for praise by noting that he remitted all the state's revenue to Zangi's treasury, evidently a rare characteristic indeed.[57] The wealth commanded by the top *kuttāb* is suggested by the building works undertaken by Taj al-Mulk and Nizam al-Mulk at the great Friday mosque in Isfahan, vying with one another to erect domes over each end of the courtyard (Figures 5.1 and 5.2). (Posterity has generally judged that Taj al-Mulk won this particular competition, his dome being more architecturally and mathematically perfect).

Offices were commonly sold. Shams al-Mulk b. Nizam al-Mulk, for instance, was made *'āriḍ al-jaysh* after paying 2,000 dinars.[58] Ibn Darust,

[51] For examples of Nizam al-Mulk's admiration for these earlier dynasties, see *Siyar al-Muluk*, chs 10, 11, 23, 24, 27, 36, 39, 40, 41, trans. pp.71, 72 100, 103, 117, 127–8, 131, 156, 173.

[52] Lambton, 'Internal Structure', 247; cf. Lambton, *Continuity and Change*, 297–8.

[53] Lambton, *Continuity and Change*, 297.

[54] Cf. Duri, 'Dīwān'.

[55] Ibn Khallikan, *Wafayat*, IV, 380: *'kāna iqṭā'uhu 'ushr mughall al-bilād 'alā jārī 'ādat wuzarā' al-dawla al-saljuqīya'*; Lambton, *Landlord and Peasant*, 62. Ibn Khallikan is in fact discussing the Mosuli vizier Jamal al-Din al-Isfahani. See Ibn al-Athir, *al-Kamil*, X, 437, for Maybudi's *iqṭā'*; also Safi, *Politics of Knowledge*, 88.

[56] Bundari, *Zubda*, 96.

[57] *Ibid.*, 212; cf. Qummi, *Dhayl-i Nafthat al-Masdur*, 254–5.

[58] *Ibid.*, 100.

Figure 5.1 The dome over the northeast end of the Friday mosque in Isfahan by Taj al-Mulk, a testimony to the wealth and ambition of bureaucratic classes

Figure 5.2 General view of the Friday mosque at Isfahan, largely rebuilt in the late eleventh century through the patronage of Nizam al-Mulk and Taj al-Mulk

a wealthy merchant, was so anxious to become caliphal vizier that he was willing to forgo the normal *iqṭā'* in lieu of salary and even pay for the privilege, a post at which he proved to be singularly inept.[59] More junior members of the bureaucracy, however, seem to have done less well. They were paid not in *iqṭā'*, but in cash (*rusūm* or *marsūmāt*). These were paid irregularly and, if the practice of the Sultanate of Iraq is anything to go by, at the discretion of more senior office holders: Najm al-Din Qummi complains of the stinginess of some viziers.[60]

The Seljuks also added some new offices of their own. The office of the *ṭughrā'ī* (which generally was part of the *dīwān-i inshā'*, but sometimes separate)[61] was a Seljuk innovation, and Isfahani tells us that it was the third most important position in the administration, after the vizier and the *mustawfī*.[62] The *ṭughrā'ī*'s task was to affix to sultanic correspondence the sultan's signature in the form of a *ṭughrā*. Isfahani refers to the post rather disparagingly, commenting that it was given to the incompetent 'Abd al-Rahim b. Niẓam al-Mulk on the basis that 'it is a position that needs no skill and consists of nothing other than [copying] that bow-shaped script [*al-khaṭṭ al-qawsī*]'.[63] However, in practice, the *ṭughrā'īs* generally seem to have been career bureaucrats, and other sources suggest that the ability to draw the *ṭughrā* was highly esteemed; in addition, *ṭughrā'īs* were responsible for checking the work of chancery scribes.[64]

Even when the Seljuks copied the names of 'Abbasid structures, they did not necessarily copy their contents. When Sadid al-Mulk, vizier to Caliph al-Mustazhir, was dismissed in 496/1102–3, Ibn al-Athir relates that 'the reason for his dismissal was his ignorance of the rules [*qawā'id*] of the Caliphal *dīwān*, for he had spent his life working for the sultans, and they do not have these rules'.[65] The exact nature of these 'rules' is unclear. A more concrete example of these changes is the post of *muḥtasib*, which had existed since the ninth century, functioning mainly as a market inspector, checking the accuracy of weights and measures, and the quality of foodstuff on sale. The office seems to have largely disappeared in Buyid times, but was revitalised by the Seljuks with many new powers to inflict corporal punishment and

59 *Ibid.*, 22–3; Ibn al-Athir, *al-Kamil*, X, 14, 23.

60 Qummi, *Dhayl-i Nafthat al-Masdur*, 191; Fairbanks, 'The Tarikh al-Vuzara', 76–7; Lambton, 'Internal Structure', 254.

61 Bundari, *Zubda*, 186; Ibn al-'Adim indicates that Husayn b. 'Ali the *ṭughrā'ī* was simultaneously the head of two separate *dīwāns* of *ṭughrā* and *inshā* under Muhammad Tapar (*Bughya*, 162). Also Qummi, *Dhayl-i Nafthat al-Masdur*, 66, 71.

62 Bundari, *Zubda*, 100.

63 *Ibid.*, 83; Iqbal, *Wizarat*, 23; see further pp. 126–8 above on the *ṭughrā*.

64 Fairbanks, 'The Tarikh al-Vuzara', 100–6.

65 Ibn al-Athir, *al-Kamil*, X, 362.

imprisonment on a wide range of wrongdoers. The institution of *tashhīr*, or the *muḥtasib*'s public parading of wrongdoers, seems to have become increasingly widespread.[66] Twelfth-century *muḥtasibs* acquired ever more intrusive powers, both to prevent wrong-doing and, increasingly, to act as an inquisitor, censoring heretical teachings such as Ismailism. The *muḥtasib* became a much more powerful and feared individual than the market inspector of classical ʿAbbasid times, and there seems to have been a growing sense in which, at least in the main cities like Baghdad, the state was interfering increasingly in the private activities and beliefs of its subjects.[67] *Muḥtasibs* were also employed by the later ʿAbbasids, and much of this evidence comes from Baghdad, so a more detailed study is needed to consider to what extent these increased powers, especially in the twelfth century, represent caliphal rather than Seljuk attempts to shape society.

On occasion the Seljuks consciously rejected ʿAbbasid and Ghaznavid models. Particularly telling is the case of the *barīd*, the post and intelligence service that had been established by the early ʿAbbasids, and which allowed the caliphal government to keep tabs on its most far-flung provinces. The system was used by both the Buyids and the Ghaznavids, and the latter had run a particularly effective (and unpopular) intelligence service. Despite Nizam al-Mulk's urging, Alp Arslan was steadfast in rejecting the introduction of the *barīd*.[68] Isfahani explains the sultan's hostility to the institution on the basis that intelligence agents could not be relied on to provide reliable reports.[69] Although he describes Alp Arslan's decision as a 'whimsy', no other sultan reinstituted the system. One reason may have been that Ghaznavid *barīd* reports were encrypted (*muʿammā*),[70] meaning that only a trained bureaucrat could interpret them. The Seljuks may not have wished to place such confidence in their *kuttāb*.

66 For a discussion, see Christian Lange, 'Legal and Cultural Aspects of Ignominious Parading (*tashhīr*) in Islam', *Islamic Law and Society*, 14/i (2007), 81–108.

67 See Lange, 'Changes in the Office of *Ḥisba*', esp. 160–9; but see, too, Ephrat, 'Sunni Revivalism', 149–50.

68 See Adam Silverstein, *Postal Systems in the Pre-Modern Islamic World* (Cambridge, 2007), 125–37. It has been argued that such a system existed in Kirman under the rule of Muhammad b. Malik Arlanshah (537/1142–3 to 551/1156) (see Safi, *Politics of Knowledge*, 87). However, the passage (Kirmani, *Saljuqiyan wa Ghuzz*, 394) is clearly an idealised description of the ruler, so it must be treated with a degree of scepticism as a representation of actual practice.

69 Bundari, *Zubda*, 66–7; cf. Nizami Arudi, *Chahar Maqala*, 40, trans. Browne, 46.

70 Bayhaqi, *Tarikh*, 976 (*mulaṭṭafahā rasīd muʿammā az ṣāḥib-barīd-i Balkh . . . tarjuma kardam*: 'encrypted letters arrived from the head of the *barīd* in Balkh . . . I translated them').

Thus, while the Seljuk bureaucracy is sometimes seen as a less sophisticated version of its ʿAbbasid and Ghaznavid antecedents, this is scarcely to do it justice.[71] The superficial similarity in terminology masks larger changes. Moreover, the extent of continuity varied greatly in different areas of the empire. In Khurasan, where the Ghazavid and Samanid structures of governance and personnel continued in place, Lambton's vision of continuity with the past probably broadly holds,[72] but in the west of the empire, the Seljuk conquest represented a massive administrative upheaval. Although as local knowledge was essential for administering – and above all taxing – newly annexed territories, the Seljuks were still reliant on locals for more junior positions, but the upper echelons of the bureaucracy were transformed as senior bureaucrats were replaced by Khurasanis[73] – men like Kunduri and Nizam al-Mulk himself. The Baghdadi contemporary to the Seljuk invasion, Ghars al-Niʿma, puts into the vizier Kunduri's mouth the following description of the consequences of Seljuk rule, which actually gives voice to the loathing of the displaced elites of Iraq for the new regime and its Khurasani henchmen:

> These are low people, scoundrels and wretches, who came with us [to the west] and were promoted to high offices in our noble service, for the chiefs of the land and its elites were not happy with this dynasty when it emerged. They despised it, and disassociated themselves from it. As a result they were destroyed, ruined and perished. The rabble, low life and scum followed [the Seljuk dynasty], and were promoted and raised high.[74]

The bureaucrats and their factions

The bitter resentment by the westerners of the Khurasani domination contributed to a political culture riven by factionalism. Nizam al-Mulk bitterly attacked the Jibali 'heretics and Ismailis' he claimed had penetrated the bureaucracy – a code, no doubt, for his arch-rival, Taj al-Mulk (who was

[71] Cf. Lambton, *Continuity and Change*, 28, 29.

[72] For instance, as we have seen (p. 35 above), when the Seljuks demanded Masʿud of Ghazna hand over Sarakhs, Abiward and Merv in 428/1036, they explicitly envisaged keeping in place the existing Ghaznavid administrative structures of *ṣāḥib-barīds*; qadis and the *ṣāḥib-dīwān* would remain in place to gather taxes which would be given, however, to them rather than the sultan (Bayhaqi, *Tarikh*, 727).

[73] Durand-Guédy, *Iranian Elites*, 114, 129; Mouton, *Damas et sa principauté*, 378.

[74] Ghars al-Niʿma, *al-Hafawat al-Nadira*, ed. Salih al-Ashir (Beirut, 1987), 295; on this work and its author and his family, see C. E. Bosworth, 'Ghars al-Niʿma Hilāl al-Ṣābi''s *Kitāb al-Hafawāt al-nādira* and Būyid History', in Alan Jones (ed.), *Arabicus Felix: Luminosus Britannicus. Essays in Honour of A. F. L. Beeston on his Eightieth Birthday* (Reading, 1991), 129–41.

in fact from Fars).[75] Indeed, bureaucratic appointments sometimes had to be made with a view to balancing these factional interests. When appointing Sa'd al-Mulk's successor, Muhammad Tapar appointed Diya' al-Mulk b. Nizam al-Mulk as vizier, but the westerner Khatir al-Mulk Maybudi as *mustawfī* 'to bring harmony to the hearts of his *khāṣṣ*'.[76] The Khurasani–Jibali rivalry seems to have diminished after the eleventh century, even if it did not disappear. 'Imad al-Din al-Isfahani (himself a westerner), writing in the late twelfth century, remarks of Muhammad al-Juzqani that he was appointed *tughrā'ī* 'because he was a Khurasani, not because of any human characteristics' (*li-khurasāniyyatihi lā li-insāniyyatihi*).[77] Although from the early twelfth century most bureaucrats in the Jibal were of Jibali origin,[78] regional rivalry was supplemented and to a degree supplanted by other factional conflicts, such as that between the rival law schools of Shafi'is and Hanafis (discussed in detail in Chapters 7 and 8).[79] Isfahani also relates that Muhammad al-Juzqani was such a Hanafi fanatic that he would not return a greeting without asking his interlocutor's *madhhab*.[80] Rawandi's *Rahat al-Sudur* is also permeated by a pro-Hanafi factionalism, and he repeatedly blames Ash'arites (i.e., Shafi'is) for the Seljuk dynasty's demise.[81] Factionalism was a constant, it merely changed its name.

The patronage relationships that characterised social and political life in the mediaeval Islamic east in general influenced the shape of the bureaucracy.[82] Viziers tried to appoint their own relatives or fellow townsmen to lower positions. Five viziers in fifty years came from the small town of Darguzin,[83] and 'Imad al-Din al-Isfahani – vehemently hostile to the Darguzini clan – caustically remarks of one them, Shams al-Din Abu Najib, that his origin was his sole qualification for the vizierate.[84] Qummi describes how Shams al-Din's uncle, Abu 'l-Qasim al-Darguzini, 'singled out men of

[75] See Durand-Guédy, *Iranian Elites*, 114–15 and above, p. 67. On Taj al-Mulk's origins, see Bundari, *Zubda*, 61; Ibn al-'Adim, *Bughya*, 95.

[76] Bundari, *Zubda*, 96.

[77] *Ibid.*, 101.

[78] Durand-Guédy, *Iranian Elites*, 196–7; Fairbanks, 'The Tarikh al-Vuzara', 79–80.

[79] Durand-Guédy, *Iranian Elites*, 202–3; Bundari, *Zubda*, 220.

[80] Bundari, *Zubda*, 101.

[81] Rawandi, *Rahat al-Sudur*, 30, 33, 41. See further Wilferd Madelung, 'The Spread of Maturidism and the Turks', *Actas do Congresso de Estudos Arabes e Islâmicos* (Coimbra-Lisbon, 1968), 140, n. 74 (reprinted in Wilferd Madelung, *Religious Schools and Sects in Medieval Islam* (London, 1985)).

[82] See Mottahedeh, *Loyalty and Leadership, passim*; also p. 158 above.

[83] Qummi, *Dhayl-i Nafthat al-Masdur*, 283.

[84] Bundari, *Zubda*, 218.

his province for patronage and favour (*iṣṭināʿ wa inʿām*). He was an ocean [of generosity] whose water is collected by the cloud and scattered on the world. The morn of his good fortune heralded the light of day for their circumstances.'[85]

The machinations of the rival bureaucrats, seeking positions either for themselves or their allies, was a key factor in the end of many *kātibs*' careers. Kunduri's fall from grace was doubtless precipitated by his support for Sulayman b. Chaghrı; but his exile and killing, the sources agree, was the work of Nizam al-Mulk, anxious to rid himself of a potential rival lest Kunduri one day be restored to favour. Kunduri is said to have prophetically declared to Nizam al-Mulk before his execution:

> What evil you have done, accustoming the Turks to killing viziers and the heads of *dīwāns*; whoever digs a hole falls into it![86]

The fall and subsequent execution of Mahmud's *mustawfi* ʿAziz al-Din was, according to his nephew ʿImad al-Din al-Isfahani who sought to rehabilitate his reputation, the result of the intrigues of the evil vizier Abu 'l-Qasim al-Darguzini; but other sources suggest ʿAziz al-Din was far from blameless, having arranged the killing of the vizier Shams al-Mulk b. Nizam al-Mulk in 517/1123.[87] Muhammad Tapar's execution of his vizier, Saʿd al-Mulk, who was hanged by the gate of Isfahan in 500/1106–7, seems been brought about by the plotting of the qadi of Isfahan, ʿUbaydallah al-Khatibi, and its *raʾīs*, Masʿud b. Muhammad al-Khujandi. Anushirwan b. Khalid himself was another victim of Khatibi's plotting, although he lived to tell the tale.[88]

Death or expropriation of wealth (*muṣādara*) frequently awaited fallen bureaucrats, who enjoyed no security of tenure, especially not viziers. Although some viziers remained in office for years or even decades, like Kunduri, Nizam al-Mulk and Nasir al-Din Tahir b. Fakhr al-Mulk (a descendant of Nizam al-Mulk who served Sanjar as vizier for twenty years between 528/1133–4 and 547/1152–3), these were the exceptions. In the west under Mahmud and Masʿud, viziers rarely lasted more than a couple of years, but even Muhammad Tapar got through no fewer than eight viziers

85 Qummi, *Dhayl-i Nafthat al-Masdur*, 45.

86 Ibn al-Athir, *al-Kamil*, X, 33–4; Ibn al-ʿAdim, *Bughya*, 88; Ibn Khallikan, *Wafayat*, IV, 378; Husayni, *Akhbar*, 25; Nishapuri, *Saljuqnama*, 22; Rawandi, *Rahat al-Sudur*, 118.

87 For a detailed discussion, see Peacock, "Imad al-Din al-Isfahani's *Nusrat al-fatra*', 80–5.

88 See Durand-Guédy, *Iranian Elites*, 178–9, 188–9; Bundari, *Zubda*, 94–6; Husayni, *Akhbar*, 83; Ibn al-Athir, *al-Kamil*, X, 437.

in his thirteen-year rule.[89] However, dismissal was not necessarily disastrous for a career, and bureaucrats were often reinstated: Anushirwan b. Khalid, for instance, served three times as vizier (as deputy vizier, under Muhammad, in 511/1117–18; for Mahmud, in 521–2/1127–8; for Mas'ud, in 529–30/1135–6, in addition to serving as vizier for Caliph al-Mustarshid, 526–8/1132–4).[90] The plethora of contenders for power and rival courts in much of the period meant it was easy for a *kātib* to slip from the service of one ruler to another. Thus, Muhammad Tapar's vizier Khatir al-Mulk al-Maybudi, entrusted with guarding one of the gates of Isfahan during Berkyaruq's siege of the city in 495/1101–2, slipped away during the night and later joined Berkyaruq's service,[91] while Fakhr al-Mulk b. Nizam al-Mulk passed from the employment of Berkyaruq to Sanjar.[92] Despite Maybudi's treachery to Muhammad Tapar, he was not just employed by Berkyaruq, but after the latter's demise he even re-entered his erstwhile master's service as vizier between 504/1110–11 and 511/1117–18.[93]

There seems to have been somewhat greater security in the other two great offices, *ṭughrā'ī* and especially *mustawfī*. Al-Shihab As'ad, for instance, remained as *ṭughrā'ī* for virtually all of Mahmud's fourteen-year reign, serving under six different viziers. Throughout most of the same period, Isfahani's uncle 'Aziz al-Din was *mustawfī*. Similarly, in the period between the reigns of Mas'ud and Tughrıl III (1131–75), when amirs usually succeeded in having their own candidates installed as viziers, the latter's very short tenures of office reflect the constant struggle between amirs for influence.[94] Conversely, *mustawfīs* remained in office for long periods, and in general their appointments do not seem to have been affected by amiral politics (we know little about *ṭughrā'īs* in this period).[95] This may reflect the fact that *mustawfīs* required special skills and technical knowledge of finances and revenues to do their job effectively. A vizier, on the other hand, was primarily a political appointment, even though he might have a general strategic oversight of the finances, and could therefore be much more easily removed and replaced.

[89] See Klausner, *Seljuk Vezirate*, 106–8.

[90] *Ibid.*; Bosworth, 'Anushirvān b. Ḵāled', *EIr*.

[91] Ibn al-Athir, *al-Kamil*, X, 336–7.

[92] *Ibid.*, X, 252, 418; Bundari, *Zubda*, 365.

[93] Ibn al-Athir, *al-Kamil*, X, 483; Bundari, *Zubda*, 103.

[94] Klausner, *Seljuk Vezirate*, 106–8.

[95] Fairbanks, 'The Tarikh al-Vuzara', 149.

The Bureaucrat-Littérateur: 'Imad al-Din al-Isfahani and the *Nusrat al-Fatra*

'Imad al-Din al-Isfahani (519/1125–597/1201), the author of our earliest Arabic chronicle of the Seljuks to survive intact, the *Nusrat al-Fatra*, was famous as a man of letters, poet and secretary to Saladin, the Ayyubid ruler of Syria and Egypt. Isfahani was born in the Seljuk lands, where his family had a distinguished pedigree as bureaucrats. His father and uncle had served the Seljuks and 'Abbasids, while both his paternal and maternal grandfathers had worked in the Seljuk bureaucracy – his maternal grandfather Amin al-Din 'Ali had been *mustawfi* to Muhammad Tapar. Isfahani had started in his own career in the bureaucracy under Ibn Hubayra in Baghdad.[96]

The *Nusrat al-Fatra*, written in a highly ornate rhetorical style, is replete with the bitterness of the factional conflicts among the Seljuk bureaucrats, some of which spilled over into the Ayyubid lands where many bureaucrats from Iran and Iraq were employed after the collapse of the Great Seljuk Empire. The events of the reigns of Mahmud and Mas'ud seem to have been especially traumatic for the bureaucrats. Anushirwan b. Khalid (459/1066–7–532 or 533/1137–9), who served both sultans, wrote his memoirs, the lost Persian *Nafthat al-Masdur*, as a partisan attempt to justify his own behaviour and to do down his enemies among the *kuttāb*. The *Nusrat al-Fatra* represents Isfahani's response, his attempt to promote his family's reputation, above that of his late uncle, 'Aziz al-Din. Particularly vicious are the denunciations of the vizier Abu'l-Qasim Darguzini, whom Isfahani held responsible for his uncle's death, but numerous other bureaucrats fall victim to the author's merciless lampooning. Allies of the Isfahani family, meanwhile, are extravagantly praised. Debates about the legacy of Anushirwan, Darguzini and other *kātibs* also continued in the late twelfth-century Jibal, where a third *kātib*, Najm al-Din Qummi, who served under Tughrıl III, wrote a *dhayl* or continuation of Anushirwan's lost work. In similar vein, it concentrated on the factional quarrels of these bureaucrats in sententious prose.[97]

[96] Lutz Richter-Bernburg, *Der Syrische Blitz: Saladins Sekretär zwischen Selbstdarstellung und Geschichtsschreibung* (Wiesbaden, 1998), 25–34; see also Houtsma's introduction to Bundari, *Zubda*, xxx–xxxvii.

[97] See Peacock, "Imad al-Din's *Nusrat al-fatra*'; and Peacock, 'Court Historiography of the Seljuq Empire'. For another perspective, see David Durand-Guédy, 'Mémoires d'exilés: lecture de la chronique des Saljūqides de 'Imād al-Dīn al-Isfahānī', *Studia Iranica*, 35 (2006), 181–202.

The Background of the Bureaucrats

There were no formal requirements for appointment to bureaucratic office. Such descriptions as we do have of the bureaucrat's qualifications and duties are extremely vague. The document appointing Abu'l-Barakat Majd al-Din as vizier to Sanjar in 549/1149–50 is a good example. The vizierate is described as an office responsible for 'the interests of the masses and the good order of the affairs of the people' (*maṣāliḥ-i jumhūr wa manāẓim-i umūr-i khalq*). The vizier, therefore, should be 'pious, learned, competent, of good behaviour and good heart, knowledgeable of the king's laws and about the customs of the dynasty; [he should have] read biographies of kings and learned the lessons of the experiences of time.' He should be chosen to 'encourage [the ruler to do] that which is pleasing to God, that which is praiseworthy in this world and that which will win the rewards of the hereafter', as well as being someone who would always 'remember the interests of Muslims'. The same document declares that 'the vizier should help the sultan [*pādshāh*] to remember the Creator, blessed and exalted is He, to express gratitude for his bounty and to mete justice'.[98]

The ideal was perhaps rarely met. 'Imad al-Din al-Isfahani lampoons Maybudi as a man 'so fat his body burst out of his coffin, with a brain more feeble than a spider's web' (*kāna rajulan jasīman mala'a al-tābūt wa-'aqluhu awhan min bayt al-'ankabūt*). He was, we are told, exceptional in his ignorance, which reached such an extent that he did not even realise that Muhammad was the last Prophet, the most elementary Muslim doctrine.[99] (It must be said that a much more attractive picture of Maybudi is given by Ibn al-Athir.[100]) 'Izz al-Mulk al-Burujirdi is condemned by Qummi as 'foolish and ignorant' (*safīh wa jāhil*).[101] Commenting on the low quality of bureaucrats under Muhammad Tapar, Anushirwan is said to have remarked:

> I wondered greatly at the sultan; he is meticulous in his choice of hunting dogs and his cheetahs, and chooses from them the one which he sees fit for his purpose, and asks about his offspring, descent, and origins; therefore why does he not choose for his *dīwān* and positions of authority men who are competent, virtuous and exemplary ministers?[102]

[98] Cited in Iqbal, *Wizarat*, 25 (text otherwise unpublished, from the St Petersburg *inshā'* collection; see Horst, *Staatsverwaltung*, 10, 104).

[99] Bundari, *Zubda*, 103–4.

[100] Ibn al-Athir, *al-Kamil*, X, 594. See further on him, Iqbal, *Wizarat*, 150–4.

[101] Qummi, *Dhayl-i Nafthat al-Masdur*, 160; cf. *ibid.*, 180.

[102] Bundari, *Zubda*, 102.

Although the sale of offices meant that some outsiders like Ibn Darust got the vizierate, the *kātibs* themselves had a fairly clear conception of who was a member of their class and they monopolized lower-ranking positions. Rarely did members of the great *'ulamā'* or merchant families become *kātibs*.[103] One exception was Shihab al-Islam 'Abd al-Razzaq, whom Sanjar 'brought from the madrasa' to serve as vizier: but perhaps more importantly, he was also related by marriage to the Nizam al-Mulk clan.[104] With some exceptions, most bureaucrats came from relatively modest backgrounds.[105] Although Nizam al-Mulk himself is said to have been descended from a family of local gentry (*dihqāns*), this class had begun to decline by the eleventh century, and his father had lost his money.[106] A certain pedigree as well as learning was considered a desirable attribute for a *kātib*. 'Imad al-Din mocks his family's great enemy, the vizier Abu'l-Qasim al-Darguzini, for his peasant origins,[107] while Qummi extravagantly praises Mas'ud's vizier 'Imad al-Din Abu 'l-Barakat as the most aristocratic of the Seljuk viziers because his family claimed to be members of the Arab tribe of Banu Salma.[108]

This emphasis on pedigree encouraged the formation of dynasties of bureaucrats, such as the Ibn Jahir family which was prominent in the eleventh and early twelfth century, serving both the 'Abbasid and Seljuk courts.[109] The sons and descendants of Nizam al-Mulk held prominent positions during his lifetime and after, and controlled the vizierate in Khurasan for much of Sanjar's reign.[110] It seems to have been felt that their descent alone spoke in their favour. When affairs were going badly for Berkyaruq in the absence of the dead Nizam al-Mulk, 'they thought that [the kingdom] would return to order [*niẓāmihi*] through one of his [Nizam al-Mulk's] sons', and thus the incompetent drunk 'Izz al-Mulk b. Nizam al-Mulk was appointed vizier.[111] Berkyaruq's rival and brother Muhammad Tapar also felt that a descendant

103 Bulliet, *Patricians of Nishapur*, 64–5; Fairbanks, 'The Tarikh al-Vuzara', 83–90.

104 Ibn Funduq, *Tarikh-i Bayhaq*, 78; Qummi, *Dhayl-i Nafthat al-Masdur*, 324, specifically states that apart from him no man of religion became a vizier under the Seljuks (*hīch imām wazīr nabūd*). Also Iqbal, *Wizarat*, 243; and Tor, 'Sovereign and Pious', 52.

105 Mason, *Two Statesmen of Mediaeval Islam*, 16, 39.

106 On the decline of *dihqāns*, see p. 293 below; on Nizam al-Mulk's background, Safi, *Politics of Knowledge*, 47–8; Ibn Khallikan, *Wafayat*, II, 108–9; Ibn al-Athir, *al-Kamil*, X, 207; Ibn al-'Adim, *Bughya*, 65–70; Ibn Funduq, *Tarikh-i Bayhaq*, 73.

107 Bundari, *Zubda*, 124.

108 Qummi, *Dhayl-i Nafthat al-Masdur*, 121.

109 Eric Hanne, 'The Banu Jahir and their Role in the 'Abbasid and Saljuq Administration', *al-Masaq* 20/i, (2008), 29–45.

110 Peacock, 'Court Historiography of the Seljuq Empire'; Klausner, *Seljuk Vezirate*, 107.

111 Bundari, *Zubda*, 83.

of Nizam al-Mulk was just the solution to his problems. When he had to appoint a replacement for his vizier Saʿd al-Mulk, who had just been executed on suspicion of Ismailism, Muhammad Tapar is said to have declared:

> 'My ancestors bestowed favour on Nizam al-Mulk and were well served by him. His sons too are the beneficiaries of our generosity, and there is no equal to them.' He ordered [Diya' al-Mulk b. Nizam al-Mulk] Abu Nasr Ahmad to be appointed vizier, who adopted his father's titles (*alqāb*): Qiwam al-Din, Nizam al-Mulk, Sadr al-Islam.[112]

The descendants of Nizam al-Mulk retained an important place in the bureaucracy in both east and west until the middle of the twelfth century.[113]

The same principle of the value of heredity is found in chancery documents of appointment to positions of governance. For example, a document issued by Sanjar's chancery to the people of Jurjan relates how:

> One invested with our authority was Amir Muhammad Yul Aba who, when we entrusted him with the province of Jurjan, followed the path of righteousness in serving us, protecting the subjects, exhibiting a sound judgement and in his good life and heart. Consequently, the beginning and the end of his life were sealed with goodness, and he passed a life of good repute and blessings, and acquired a better portion in life and a more satisfactory fortune than the days [he lived in]. Because it is one of our praiseworthy customs that we protect the rights of the dead with regard to the living and we do not consider it right that an heir should be deprived of the privileges of his ancestors, we gave his position to his son Hasan.[114]

The formation of dynasties of not just of bureaucrats, but also of provincial officials such as the *ra'īs*, and of *'ulamā'* was the natural consequence of this mentality.[115]

The Education of the Bureaucrats

Despite the lack of requirement for formal qualifications for appointment to senior office, the *kātibs* themselves were proud of their rigorous education and their skill at the composition of the complex rhymed prose (*inshā'*) in which official documents – and their own private literary efforts – were

112 Ibn al-Athir, *al-Kamil*, X, 437.

113 See Safi, *Politics of Knowledge*, 209–11; Klausner, *Seljuk Vezirate*, 126, n. 45; Ibn Funduq, *Tarikh-i Bayhaq*, 74–8; Iqbal, *Wizarat*, 10–68, 124–47, 163–70, 202–21, 275–8.

114 Juwayni, *'Atabat al-Kataba*, 17.

115 For the *ra'īs*, see Paul, 'Local Lords'; for the *'ulamā'*, see Bulliet, *Patricians of Nishapur, passim*.

composed. Much literature was written by bureaucrats for other bureaucrats to show how clever they were, resulting in the spread of this style. The bureaucrats provided a principal market for Arabic literature in an age when Persian dominated the court literary scene (p. 185 above). The masterpiece of Arabic literature in the period, the *Maqamat* of al-Hariri (d. 516/1122), which rejoices in its obscure verbal tricks, is said to have been composed at the behest of Anushirwan b. Khalid.[116] Judging by the efforts of Mas'ud b. Namdar, the *mustawfi* of Baylaqan in the south Caucasus, a skill at composing Arabic *inshā'* that was so dense, allusive and recondite as to verge on the incomprehensible was to be found among provincial administrators too, not just those attached to the sultanic courts.[117] Bureaucrats, of course, also used Persian (such as Anushirwan's own lost memoirs, and Qummi's continuation of them), but it was a Persian heavily laced with Arabic, and in which – in contrast to the straightforward prose of the tenth and eleventh centuries – the *inshā'* style also became popular.

An idea of the kind of training an aspiring bureaucrat might obtain is given by the Jewish convert to Islam, Samaw'al al-Maghribi (*c.* 520/1126–570/1175), who seems to have been groomed for court employment by his father, and has left us a brief autobiography. Samaw'al relates his education up to the age of eighteen in late Seljuk Baghdad which is worth quoting at some length:

> My father had me learn Hebrew writing, and then study the Torah and the commentaries until, by the age of thirteen, I had mastered this knowledge. Then he introduced me to the study of Indian reckoning and the solution of equations under Shaykh Abi-l-Hasan Ibn ad-Daskari, and the study of medicine under the philosopher Abu 'l-Barakat Hibat-Allah Ibn 'Ali, and the observation of current surgical operations and the treatment of diseases as practiced by my maternal uncle Abu-l-Fath Ibn al-Basri. As to Indian reckoning and astronomical tables, I mastered them in less than a year, by the age of fourteen, and at the same time continued to study medicine and to observe the treatment of diseases. Then I studied administrative accounting and the science of surveying under Shaykh Abu-l-Muzaffar ash-Shahrazuri, as well as algebra and equations also under him and the katib Ibn Abi Turab as well. I then frequented Master Daskari and Abu-l-Hasan Ibn an-Naqqash for the study of geometry, until I had solved the problems

116 Ibn al-Athir, *al-Kamil*, XI, 71; cf. Bundari, *Zubda*, 89, which confirms Anushirwan's friendship with Hariri. See also Ibn Khallikan, *Wafayat*, III, 492–3; Ibn al-Jawzi, *al-Muntazam*, XVII, 223–4.

117 It is thus unsurprising that Mas'ud b. Namdar's efforts have yet to find an editor. For a facsimile, see Mas'ud b. Namdar, *Sbornik Rasskazov*.

> from Euclid that they used to solve. At the same time, I was so devoted to medicine that I absorbed whatever I could from the above-mentioned two teachers of this science . . .
>
> Before I took up these sciences, that is, in my twelfth and thirteenth years, I was fascinated by records of the past and by stories, and was eager to learn what had happened in ancient times, and to know what had occurred in ages past. I therefore perused the various compilations of stories and anecdotes. Then I passed on from that stage to an infatuation with books of entertainment and long tales; later still to the larger compilations such as the tales on 'Antar, Dhu-l-Himma, al-Battal, Iskandar Dhu-l-Qarnayn, the stories of 'Anqa', Taraf b. Ludhan, etc. Upon reading these I recognized that most of [the material was derived] from the works of the historians. Therefore I sought the real historical accounts, and my interest shifted to the histories, of which I read the book of Abu 'Ali b. Miskawayh entitled Experiences of the Nations, the History of at-Tabari and other historical works . . .
>
> At the same time, engrossed in the accounts of ministers and secretaries, I acquired from this wide reading of the stories and reports about them, and from their own words, a mastery of eloquence, and a knowledge of rhetoric to an extent that evoked the praise of stylists and the admiration of rhetoricians, and that will be recognized by those who read any of the books I wrote on some scientific discipline.[118]

Samaw'al's education was evidently intended to leave his exact career path open, furnishing him both with the practical skills a *kātib* would need, such as administrative accounting (*al-ḥisāb al-dīwānī*), as well as a more specialised training in medicine, which he tells us, was his true passion. Despite his ultimate specialisation in medicine and the sciences, he was proud of his proficiency at the elaborate bureaucratic literary style. His early education was dominated by Muslim classics of heroic prose literature, before he graduated to Islamic history, only then moving on to mathematics and the sciences after the age of thirteen. Although some of his teachers were Jews (Abu'l-Barakat was also to convert to Islam), most were Muslims, and with the exception of the early study of Hebrew and the Torah, Samaw'al's education was solidly Islamic in inspiration, as indeed it needed to be if he was to succeed at court. His account gives us an idea of what the ideal curriculum for an administrator

[118] Samau'al al-Maghribī, *Ifḥām Al-Yahūd: Silencing the Jews*, ed. and trans. Moshe Perlmann, *Proceedings of the American Academy for Jewish Research*, 32 (1964), 76–7, 77–8, 79; cf. Adnan A. Husain, 'Conversion to History: Negating Exile and Messianism in Samaw'al al-Maghribi's Polemic against Judaism', *Medieval Encounters*, 8/i (2002), 5–6.

or a bureaucrat was thought to be: wide-ranging, encompassing literature, history, practical skills such as accountancy, and advanced mathematics.

For Muslim students there would have more emphasis on the religious aspect, especially the study of the Qur'an and hadith – indeed, Samaw'al also indicates that he read the Qur'an in his youth, doubtless because a thorough knowledge of the text was essential to participate in Arabic literary culture (Figure 5.3).[119] Many Muslim bureaucrats studied in the *madrasa*, the new institution of learning which had just begun to spread on the eve of the Seljuk period.[120] The essential subject of study in all of them was *fiqh* (Muslim jurisprudence); teaching *fiqh* is what made a madrasa a madrasa, but it was by no means the sole subject, and Qur'an, hadith, Arabic grammar and even *adab* (literature) might also be studied, while Shafi'i madrasas often taught Sufi texts[121] – indeed, any subject seems to have been fair game except *falsafa*, philosophical speculation.[122] Thus, madrasas were far from being the exclusive preserve of *'ulamā'* and *fuqahā'*.

The most famous madrasa of all, the Baghdad Nizamiyya, was founded by the greatest bureaucrat of all, Nizam al-Mulk, in 459/1066, and the spread of the madrasa system has been widely associated with his name. Although there were earlier madrasas, and other patrons, Nizam al-Mulk's programme was without parallel in its extent. There were also madrasas bearing his name, Nizamiyyas, in Nishapur, Isfahan and several other Iranian cities, and the institution gradually spread westwards to Syria and Egypt.[123] By the late twelfth century there were no fewer than thirty madrasas in Baghdad.[124] Unsurprisingly, scholars have frequently attempted to explain the rise of the madrasa with reference to Nizam al-Mulk's political aims. Lambton, for instance, argued that they were designed by Nizam al-Mulk to produce

[119] For Ibn Hubayra's education, see Mason, *Two Statesmen*, 25–8; for 'Imad al-Din al-Isfahani's, see Richter-Bernberg, *Der Syrische Blitz*, 34–59. On *kuttāb* with interest in hadith, see also Daphna Ephrat, *A Learned Society in a Period of Transition: The Sunni 'ulama' of Eleventh-century Baghdad* (Albany, NY, 2000), 100. For Nizam al-Mulk's study of *fiqh* and hadith, see Ibn al-Jawzi, *al-Muntazam*, XVI, 302; Ibn al-Athir, *al-Kamil*, X, 207; Ibn al-'Adim, *Bughya*, 90–1; Bosworth, 'Towards a Biography of Niẓām al-Mulk', 303.

[120] In general, see Makdisi, 'Muslim Institutions of Learning', to be read in conjunction with A. L. Tibawi, 'Origin and Character of "al-madrasa"', *BSOAS*, 25/i (1962), 225–38; G. Makdisi, 'Madrasa', *EI*².

[121] Margaret Malamud, 'Sufi Organizations and Structures of Authority in Medieval Nishapur', *IJMES*, 26/iii (1994), 431.

[122] Tibawi, 'Origin and Character', 231.

[123] Subki, *Tabaqat*, IV, 313–4.

[124] Ephrat, *A Learned Society*, 30; see below, Chapter 7, p. 252

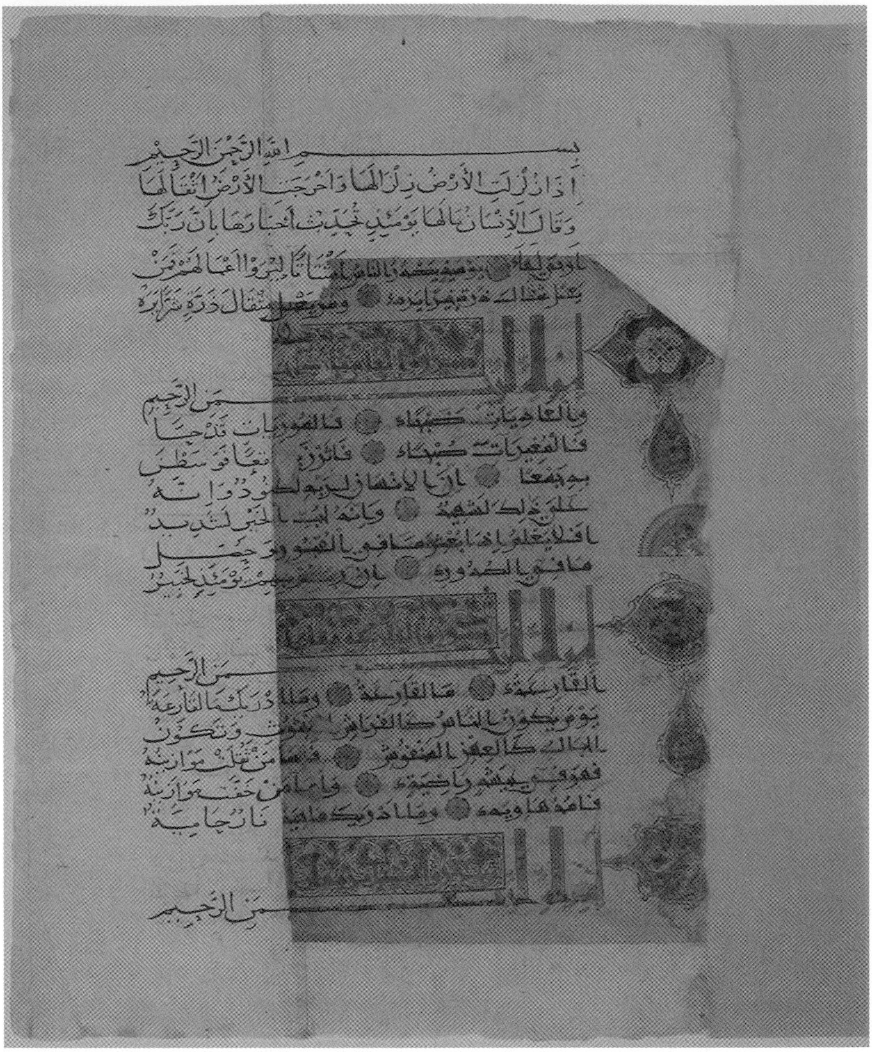

Figure 5.3 A rare folio from a surviving Seljuk Qur'an, copied by Muhammad al-Zanjani in 531/1137. The main body of the text shows the *naskh* style of script that was popularised by the Seljuk chancery. Metropolitan Museum of Art, New York, Accession No. 1996.294.2. © Metropolitan Museum of Art

'government officials trained in the tenets of orthodoxy who would replace the former secretarial class and implement his political policies; and secondly, by using the 'ulamā educated in the madrasas he hoped to control the masses and combat the spread of the Ismā'īlī sect, which had begun to threaten the existence of the state'.[125] A similar view has been propounded recently by Safi, who has seen madrasas as contributing to what he calls Seljuk 'state ideology' by promoting social order, training bureaucrats and contributing to a sense of Muslim unity.[126] A slightly different political purpose has been argued for by Richard Bulliet, who states that madrasas were 'designed to exert imperial influence on local religious politicians', to combat factionalism and to 'bring the entire patrician class under some degree of central control'.[127]

None of these theses are particularly convincing on closer examination. As the case of Samaw'al indicates, it was perfectly possible to aspire to a bureaucratic career without a madrasa education, and while the courses offered at madrasas could be very diverse, there is no evidence that they ever comprised any of the practical skills a *kātib* might need, such as the administrative accounting noted by Samaw'al. Moreover, all Nizam al-Mulk's Nizamiyyas were avowedly Shafi'i in affiliation, whereas the dynasty and most Turks were Hanafis and founded their own madrasas.[128] As we shall see in Chapter 7, the differences between these law schools were bitterly contentious, and far from contributing to social stability and cohesion, madrasas and their preachers exacerbated civil unrest and disorder. This is particularly clearly demonstrated by the controversial Baghdad Nizamiyya, a Shafi'i implant into a city whose Sunni masses were overwhelmingly Hanbali.[129] It is far from clear how offering a curriculum of Shafi'i *fiqh* would have assisted the supposed aim of central control.

Rather than being an instrument of state policy, the madrasa served as a means of extending patronage.[130] As Subki noted, Nizam al-Mulk's real innovation was not the madrasa itself, for which there are clear antecedents, but that his endowments offered stipends to their students.[131] In this way,

125 Lambton, 'Internal Structure', 214.

126 Safi, *Politics of Knowledge*, 93, 96–7; cf. Bulliet, *Patricians of Nishapur*, 73; Ephrat, *A Learned Society*, 130. For criticisms of the idea of the importance of the madrasa see Ephrat, *A Learned Society*, 68–79, 87–8. See, however, the review by Shahab Ahmed, *JAOS*, 123/i (2003), 179–82. Further on Nizam al-Mulk and the foundation of madrasas, see Makdisi, 'Muslim Institutions of Learning'.

127 Bulliet, 'Local Politics', 52; cf. Bulliet, *Patricians of Nishapur*, 73–5.

128 Madelung, 'The Spread of Maturidism', 138–47, and Chapter 7 below.

129 See, for example, Sibt, *Mir'at*, 186, who comments that because of their few numbers (*li-qillat 'adadihim*) the Shafi'is of Baghdad sought Nizam al-Mulk's support.

130 Cf. Ahmed, review of Ephrat, 180: 'the madrasa was a means by which different groups and individuals in authority in the Saljuq state sought to create for themselves networks of patronage and structures of influence among a logistically and ideologically valuable sector of the population: the 'ulama''. However, Ahmad is wrong to restrict the target audience of madrasas to the *'ulamā'*.

131 Subki, *Tabaqat*, IV, 314; Makdisi, 'Muslim Institutions of Learning', 50–1; Safi, *Politics of Knowledge*, 92–3.

Nizam al-Mulk could hope to win prestige by, essentially, offering a subsidised education to fellow Shafiʿis. Naturally, with their relatively modest backgrounds yet need for learning, prospective *kātibs* became some of the madrasas' most avid consumers – thereby, Nizam al-Mulk doubtless hoped, consolidating his own influence and status as patron throughout the Shafiʿis of the bureaucracy. It may further have offered a means of reconciling the displaced Jibali bureaucrats to the regime, for many of these would have been Shafiʿi.

The madrasa system might offer much more than just an education, as we can see from the career of ʿImad al-Din al-Isfahani himself. When he was thirteen he spent a year in the madrasa at Qashan studying the Qur'an and literature (*al-kutub al-adabiyya*). A couple of years later, after his father's move to Baghdad in 434/1139, he was enrolled in the Nizamiyya there.[132] ʿImad al-Din followed in the family footsteps in the bureaucracy, and in 552/1157–8 became deputy to the caliphal vizier Ibn Hubayra in Wasit and Basra. After his master's death, he went to Damascus, where the qadi Kamal al-Din al-Shahrazuri, father of one of his contemporaries and friends from the Nizamiyya, lodged him in the Nuriyya madrasa and helped him to secure an appointment as secretary to Nur al-Din Zangi. In Rajab 567/March 1172, he was appointed by Nur al-Din to teach in the Nuriyya, which became known after him as the ʿImadiyya, but the following year was appointed head of the chancery.[133]

ʿImad al-Din's career illustrates the function of the madrasa both in providing an education and employment for the *kātibs*, as well as even temporary accommodation. It also suggests that even if the great dynasties of *ʿulamāʾ* did not usually become bureaucrats, there was not an entirely rigid distinction between their career paths. It was possible to switch between, or even combine, serving the sultan and teaching in a madrasa.[134] In this sense, Lambton was right to argue that the madrasa was to 'bring about the integration of the members of the bureaucracy with the religious classes'.[135] Even if this was not the intention, it was the result.

However, we need a much more careful periodisation of madrasas and their functions. We cannot assume that what was true of the twelfth century

[132] Bundari, *Zubda*, 181; Ibn Khallikan, *Wafayat*, IV, 382–6; Richter-Bernburg, *Der Syrische Blitz*, 37, 39.

[133] Richter-Bernburg, *Der Syrische Blitz*, 87–8; Ephrat, *A Learned Society*, 113–14.

[134] Cf. Ephrat, *A Learned Society*, 117; David Durand-Guédy, 'An Emblematic Family of Seljuq Iran: The Khujandis of Isfahan', in C. Lange and S. Mecit (eds), *The Seljuqs: Politics, Society and Culture* (Edinburgh, 2011), 186, 199, n. 14.

[135] Lambton, 'Internal Structure', 214.

was also true of the eleventh. For instance, the *'Atabat al-Kataba* includes documents appointing professors at the Nishapur Nizamiyya and at madrasas in Balkh.[136] If in twelfth-century Khurasan, the *dīwān-i inshā'* was issuing such documents, this suggests that there was at that time and in that place a connection between the madrasa and the state, but there is no indication this was the case in earlier times. Evidence from Isfahan suggests a shift around the beginning of the twelfth century, when Muhammad Tapar – in whose rise to power the support of the Isfahani elite had played a crucial role – sought to encourage the development of a 'loyal Hanafi community' by endowing madrasas.[137] In due course, in some times and places such as Zangid Syria, the madrasa would come to fulfil the role sometimes attributed to it in earlier times, of acting as a means of propagating an official version of Sunni Islam;[138] but this does not hold for all madrasas.

[136] Juwayni, *'Atabat al-Kataba*, 6–9, 33–7.

[137] Durand-Guédy, 'An Emblematic Family', 192.

[138] See, for example, Yasser Tabbaa, *Constructions of Power and Piety in Medieval Aleppo* (University Park, 1997), 126–8.

6

The ‘*Askar*: The Seljuk Military

> God said, ‘I have a host whom I have called the Turks and whom I have set in the East; when I am wrath with any people I will make them sovereign over them.’[1]

This hadith, related by Kashghari, well expresses the fearsome reputation of the Turks as not just an invincible military force, but an instrument of God’s wrath, sentiments which are emulated by Christian writers. Already by the ninth century the Turks were frequently compared in both Muslim and Christian literature to the unclean peoples whom legend stated that Alexander the Great had enclosed behind a great wall to keep them from the civilised world, but who would finally break forth at the end of time.[2] Seljuk propaganda also vaunted these martial values. Ibn Hassul’s work ‘On the superiority of the Turks’ (*Kitab Tafdil al-Atrak*), written at Tughrıl’s court, is full of praise for the Turks’ warlike qualities and their courage.

> Let us start by mentioning their courage . . . God created them in the likeness of lions with broad faces, snub noses, well rounded limbs and irascible disposition . . . They are accustomed to deserts and steppes, are patient in the face of want and difficulty, and they consider a carefree life to consist of raiding.[3]

The arrival of the Seljuks in the Middle East is widely associated in modern scholarship with a militarisation of the state and the society. The Seljuks and their Turkish amirs are often seen as violently imposing their will on cowering subject populations, from whom they were separated by language, culture

1 Kāšɣarī, *Compendium*, trans. Dankoff, I, 274, with minor modifications.

2 On Turks as an instrument of divine wrath, see Emeri van Donzel and Andrea Schmidt, *Gog and Magog in Early Eastern Christian and Islamic Sources: Sallam’s Quest for Alexander’s Wall* (Leiden, 2010), 32–3, 39, 73–6. See also Michel Balivet, ‘Un people de l’An Mil: les Turcs vus par leurs voisins’, in Claude Carozzi (ed.), *An 1000–An 2000: Mille ans d’Histoire médiévale* (Aix-en-Provence, 2002), 25–50

3 Ibn Hassul, *Tafdil al-Atrak*, 41.

and military status. What has been called their 'fortress mentality'[4] towards their subjects is said to have been reflected in radical innovations in urban design. The Turkish military caste now built walls round the towns of the Middle East that previously had often been unfortified; and at their centre, they erected the citadels from which they ruled, a visible sign both of their own separation from the populace and of the newly militarised society they created.[5]

Although, as we shall see, there certainly is evidence for increased fortification work in some areas in the eleventh century, the arguments outlined above rest largely on assumptions about the nature of Seljuk rule and analogies with later regimes such as the Ayyubids and Mamluks. Given the prominence most authorities accord to the role of the military in the Seljuk Empire, which has been characterised as 'a military regime geared for war and expansion',[6] it has been surprisingly neglected by researchers, especially in contrast to the comparative attention that the bureaucracy has received.[7] The task of this chapter is therefore to provide an overview of the nature of the principal military groups that were associated with the Seljuk sultans and their administration; space precludes much consideration of the numerous armed groups attached to the Seljuks' vassals and enemies, such as the Qarakhanids or the Ismailis. We will look at the composition of the military, and then examine in turn the three major, overlapping military groups our sources discuss: the Türkmen, the *mamlūks* and the amirs. Finally, we will turn to assess the relationship of the military with society and the question of the spread of fortifications under the Seljuks.

The Development and Composition of the Seljuk Military: An Overview

The armies of the first Seljuks bore little relation to the famed Turkish military of the classical ʻAbbasid era. The early conquests were also great nomadic

4 Nasser Rabbat, 'The Militarization of Taste in Medieval Bilad al-Sham', in Hugh Kennedy (ed.), *Muslim Military Architecture in Greater Syria* (Leiden, 2006), 85.

5 In general, see *ibid.*; Hugh Kennedy, 'The City and the Nomad', in Robert Irwin (ed.), *New Cambridge History of Islam, vol. IV: Islamic Cultures and Societies to the End of the Eighteenth Century* (Cambridge, 2010), esp. 280; Bacharach, 'Administrative Complexes, Palaces, and Citadels', 111–28; and see also below, nn. 132–3 for further references.

6 Klausner, *The Seljuk Vezirate*, 14.

7 Kafesoğlu, *Sultan Melikşah Devrinde Büyük Selçuklu Imparatorluğu*, 155–66, and Köymen, *Alp Arslan ve Zamanı*, II, 217–89, provide general overviews of the Seljuk military. The remarks by Paul, *Herrscher, Gemeinwesen, Vermittler*, 93–146, are also useful, although not devoted specifically to the Seljuks; also Lambton, 'Internal Structure', 224–30; Lambton, *Continuity and Change*, 240–7; and for the early period, Peacock, *Early Seljūq History*, 72–98. For specific aspects of the Seljuk military, see references below.

migrations of Türkmen accompanied by their families and beasts. They were not 'professional' armies in the sense of the 'Abbasid or Samanid *mamlūk* corps, but warfare was a way of life for most adult male Türkmen; only women and children were exempted from fighting.[8] At least from the mid-eleventh century onwards (probably in the wake of the conquest of Baghdad), the Türkmen began to be supplemented, but never wholly supplanted, as a military force by *mamlūks*.[9] According to Nizam al-Mulk, by the reign of Malikshah the sultan had a great variety of forces at his disposal. There were Türkmen, *mamlūks*, a standing army paid both in cash and by *iqṭā's*, infantry and the sultan's personal guard.[10] Nizam al-Mulk claims that all Malikshah's forces amounted to the vast figure of some 400,000 men, and vigorously opposes cost-cutting plans (instituted presumably by Taj al-Mulk) to reduce these to a mere 70,000.[11] As so often, the picture presented by Nizam al-Mulk is somewhat misleading. Reflecting the diffusion of power, the sources refer to regional Seljuk armies rather than a single central one: the 'army (or: soldiers) of Diyar Bakr',[12] the 'amirs of Khurasan', the 'army of Mosul',[13] the 'army of Iraq'.[14] There was a whole array of different military forces under different commands: amirs and viziers bought their own *mamlūks*, as did the sultan. These *mamlūks* owed their loyalty not to any abstract idea of the 'state' or even the dynasty, but to their master, at least in theory. Under Malikshah, for instance, al-Hamadhani tells us that 'the overwhelming majority' of the military (*jumhūr al-'asākir*) in the Seljuk realm belonged to Nizam al-Mulk, in the form of his personal *mamlūks*.[15] The state – insofar as it was personified by the sultan and his vizier – neither possessed nor sought a monopoly of force.[16]

Nor was the military ever a strictly Turkish preserve: as we have seen (p. 196 above), viziers might serve as commanders, and there existed a wide

[8] Peacock, *Early Seljūq History*, 83–4; Bayhaqi, *Tarikh*, 712; Sibt, *Mir'at*, 5.

[9] Peacock, *Early Seljūq History*, 94–8; Tor, '*Mamlūk* Loyalty', 768–9; pp. 50–1 above.

[10] Nizam al-Mulk, *Siyar al-Muluk*, on the Türkmen, 139, trans. 102; on the standing army and its payment: *ibid.*, 134–5, trans. 99–100; on infantry and sultanic guard, 123, trans. 93; also Lambton, 'The Administration of Sanjar's Empire', 372–6; Lambton, 'Internal Structure', 228–9, 233–5.

[11] Nizam al-Mulk, *Siyar al-Muluk*, 223–4, trans. 165.

[12] Husayni, *Akhbar*, 96: *'askar al-Shām wa-Diyar Bakr*.

[13] Ibn al-Athir, *al-Ta'rikh al-Bahir*, 19: *'asākir Mawṣil*.

[14] Bundari, *Zubda*, 100: *'asākir al-'Iraq; ibid.*, 101: *al-umarā' al-Khurāsāniyya*.

[15] Hamadhani, *'Unwan*, 100; David Ayalon, 'Aspects of the Mamluk Phenomenon,' *Der Islam*, 53 (1976), 212–14.

[16] Cf. Paul, *Herrscher, Gemeinwesen, Vermittler*, 93, 136–9.

array of militias and armed groups that were ethnically Iranian, Kurdish, Arab and so on.[17] Indeed, Nizam al-Mulk himself specifically advised that the ruler should try to balance his armed forces by using different ethnic groups, such as Daylamites, Shabankara and Georgians.[18] Nonetheless, the Turkish soldier maintained a certain prestige. In their efforts to restrict the power of the caliph, the Seljuk sultans banned both al-Muqtadi (in 1078, during Malikshah's efforts to assert sultanic superiority) and al-Muqtafi (on his accession in 1136, by Sultan Mas'ud) from purchasing Turkish slaves. While Muqtafi was still allowed to purchase Greeks and Armenians for his militia, these were considered very definitely second-best, and not a serious military threat.[19]

As many *mamlūks*, as well as nomads, hailed from the steppe, sources sometimes attribute to both groups feelings of ethnic solidarity.[20] For instance, the Fatimid Turkish governor of Jerusalem, a *mamlūk*, faced with a Türkmen siege of the city in 465/1073, declared, 'I am one of you [*anā minkum*]; I resisted only out of obedience to those I served.'[21] When Caliph al-Mustarshid's Turkish forces met those of Sultan Mas'ud at Day Marg in 529/1135, the caliph was abandoned for 'each race inclined to its like, and the Turks inclined to the Turks' [*māla al-jins ilā al-jins fa-māla al-Turk ilā al-Turk*].[22] 'Fellow-feeling' or 'solidarity' (*'aṣabiyya*) is given as the reason for *malik* Da'ud b. Mahmud's Turkish amirs deserting to Tughrıl II's side in 526/1132.[23]

However, while some *mamlūks*, like the favourite of Mas'ud, Khassbeg Arslan b. Palang-eri, were of Türkmen origin,[24] others probably came from other ethno-linguistic groups denominated by the term Turk. Theoretically, the enslaving of Türkmen was disallowed under Islamic law as they were

17 Cf. Stefan Heidmann, 'Arab Nomads and the Seljūq Military', in Stefan Leder and Bernard Streck (eds), *Shifts and Drifts in Nomad–Sedentary Relations* (Wiesbaden, 2005), 289–305, who argues that, at least in the Jazira, the Arab element in the Seljuk forces was substantially reduced from the late eleventh century as the region became increasingly integrated into Seljuk political and military structures.

18 Nizam al-Mulk, *Siyar al-Muluk*, 136, trans., 100.

19 David Ayalon, 'The Mamluks of the Seljuks: Islam's Military Might at the Crossroads', *Journal of the Royal Asiatic Society*, 3rd series, 6/iii (1996), 305–33. Cf. the remarks of Ibn Hassul on the superiority of Turks over Greeks and Armenians: *Tafdil al-atrak*, 41–2.

20 See the discussion in Ayalon, 'Aspects of the Mamluk Phenomenon', 210–11, who, however, reaches different conclusions to those proposed here.

21 Sibt, *Mir'at*, 169.

22 Bundari, *Zubda*, 177.

23 *Ibid.*, 161.

24 For his *ghulām* status, see Ibn al-Athir, *al-Kamil*, XI 116; for his Türkmen origin, see *ibid.*, XI, 163, *kāna ṣabiyyan turkmāniyyan*.

Muslims. (However, there were also Türkmen who were pagan (see p. 247 below), while it is far from clear that in practice there were scruples about making Muslim Türkmen into *mamlūks* – it is possible that Khassbeg was himself a Muslim before being enslaved). Some *mamlūks*, for instance, were Qipchaqs,[25] whose language would have differed from *ghuzzī*, as the language of the Türkmen/Ghuzz was known; others probably spoke other Turkic languages.[26] There were also smaller numbers of non-Turkish *mamlūks*, such as the Habashis (Ethiopians), who were especially influential during the reign of Mas'ud b. Muhammad,[27] as well as the less favoured Greeks, Armenians and Indians.[28] These factors would have militated against a sense of solidarity,

While it is reasonable to distinguish *mamlūk*, Türkmen and auxiliary forces provided by vassal rulers, the boundaries between groups were sometimes permeable, and the terminology used to describe them is, as so often, ambiguous. When sources refer to 'Turks and Türkmen' sometimes they mean *mamlūks* and nomads, but the two terms seem to act as synonyms for one another. The term *ghulām* often refers specifically to military slaves, being equivalent in meaning to *mamlūk*; but on other occasions it is used to refer to free Türkmen, and it can also imply simply 'page' or 'serving boy'.[29]

Isfahani refers intriguingly to 'fighting in the Türkmen style' (*rasm qitāl al-Turkmān*),[30] but it is not clear how Türkmen and *mamlūk* fighting styles differed. Both groups were mounted, and famed for their prowess at archery. Their ability to let loose an accurate volley of arrows on horseback struck fear into their opponents. Both Ghaznavid and Seljuk sources recall Mahmud of Ghazna's fatal mistake of rejecting the advice of his general Arslan Jadhib to solve his Türkmen problem definitively by cutting off their thumbs, thereby

25 For Qipchaqs in Malikshah's forces, see Sibt, *Mir'at*, 164; in the Ildegüzid period, Bundari, *Zubda*, 302. Ildegüz himself is said by a late source to have been of Qipchaq origin. See K. A. Luther, 'Atābakān-e Azarbaijan', *EIr*. See also C. E. Bosworth, 'Notes on some Personal Names in Seljūq Military History,' *Der Islam*, 89/ii (2012), 106–7, s.v. Qïfchāq. Qipchaqs were purchased on a large scale by the Khwarazmians: see Lambton, *Continuity and Change*, 13, 15, 247.

26 For Turkic languages in the period, see Gandjeï, 'Turkish in pre-Mongol Persian Poetry', 68; Kāšɣarī, *Compendium*, trans. Dankoff, *passim*.

27 Bosworth, 'Ghulām. II. Persia'; Rawandi, *Rahat al-Sudur*, 243; Bundari, *Zubda*, 193–4.

28 Greeks, Armenians and Turks are all found among Zangi's *ghulāms*, see below and Bundari, *Zubda*, 208; for an Armenian *ghulām* in the service of Malikshah, see Bundari, *Zubda*, 48.

29 Cf. Nizam al-Mulk on Türkmen *ghulāms* (*Siyar al-Muluk*, 139, trans. 102); Sibt, *Mir'at*, 153, refers to Türkmen *ghulāms* (*min al-Turkmān naḥw alf ghulām*). In general on these terminological problems, see David Ayalon, *Eunuchs, Caliphs and Sultans: A Study of Power Relationships* (Jerusalem, 1999), 145, nn. 4, 5.

30 Bundari, *Zubda*, 283.

rendering them unable to wield the bow and arrow.[31] One scholar has even suggested that archery was the key technological advantage which secured the Türkmen victory over the Byzantines and allowed their infiltration into Anatolia.[32] Sanjar boasted in a letter to the Qarakhitay ruler that his soldiers could 'split a hair with their arrows'.[33]

The Türkmen and the Military

'The Türkmen . . . have a longstanding claim upon this dynasty, because at its inception they served well and suffered much, and also they are attached by ties of kinship.'[34] Nizam al-Mulk, the greatest exponent of an Islamic and Iranian orientation for the Seljuk state, was nonetheless forced to admit the debt the dynasty owed to the nomads. As we have seen (Chapter 1), even at the time Nizam al-Mulk was writing, Türkmen continued to be the driving force behind Turkish expansion in the west.

What, however, of the role of the Türkmen military *within* the Seljuk Empire under Malikshah and subsequently? David Durand-Guédy has noted that after the reign of Malikshah there are very few references to Türkmen in the Jibali heartland of the empire, particularly in their traditional axis of Rayy, Hamadhan and Hulwan.[35] Durand-Guédy suggested that under Malikshah there had been a deliberate effort to remove the Türkmen from the Iranian plateau, who were dispatched to these 'diversionary' Caucasian, Anatolian and Syrian fronts. Such an analysis does at first glance fit well with what we have seen of Nizam al-Mulk's policy of promoting a more Perso-Islamic orientation for the Seljuk state (pp. 66–70 above), although Durand-Guédy emphasises that the links between the Türkmen and the dynasty remained strong: while Türkmen were undesirable in the heartland of Iran, they were still useful militarily.

However, as Durand-Guédy himself notes,[36] the evidence is susceptible to other interpretations: the absence of references may reflect more the nature of our sources than the reality. Our best source on the Türkmen, Ghars

31 *Ibid.*, 5; Ibn al-Athir, *al-Kamil*, IX, 475–6; cf. *ibid.*, IX, 377–8; Gardizi, *Zayn al-Akhbar*, 273; Nishapuri, *Saljuqnama*, 9.

32 Walter Kaegi, 'The Contribution of Archery to the Turkish Conquest of Anatolia', *Speculum*, 39/i (1969), 96–108; for sources dealing largely with *mamlūks*, see Ayalon, 'Aspects', 218–23.

33 Ibn al-Athir, *al-Kamil*, XI, 85.

34 Nizam al-Mulk, *Siyar al-Muluk*, 139, trans. 102.

35 See Durand-Guédy, 'Goodbye to the Türkmen?'. The idea that the Seljuks sought to remove the Türkmen from their lands by 'diversionary' expeditions is discussed in Peacock, 'Nomadic Society'.

36 Durand-Guédy, 'Goodbye to the Türkmen?', conclusion.

Figure 6.1 The Kharraqan mausoleums, northern Iran, presumed monuments to nomadic chiefs, lie in an empty plain far from any settlement (photograph: Bernard O'Kane)

al-Niʿma as transmitted by Sibt, comes to an end with Malikshah's death. It would be risky to assume a whole policy on the basis of this silence, given the chroniclers' general lack of interest in nomads at the best of times. A very different impression is left by some architectural monuments.[37] Shortly after Malikshah's death, in 486/1093–4, a certain Abu Mansur [?] b. Tegin erected a stunning tomb tower at Kharraqan in northern Iran, miles from any permanent settlement, alongside an earlier such structure dating from the reign of Alp Arslan (Figure 6.1). From the Turkish names of the men who commissioned these mausoleums and their remote location, in the middle of a plain that most likely served as nomadic pastureland on the traditional Rayy–Hamadhan axis that the Türkmen frequented, it is assumed both patrons were nomadic chiefs. The tombs represent some of the masterpieces of eleventh-century architecture in Iran, and they suggest that, in the

[37] S. M. Stern, 'The Inscriptions of the Kharraqan Mausoleums', *Iran*, 4 (1966), 21–7; Blair, *Monumental Inscriptions*, 134–6, 172–3. Durand-Guédy, 'Goodbye to the Türkmen?', n. 38, has questioned whether these men can really be Türkmen chiefs on the basis that they are not mentioned in the accounts of the succession struggle on Malikshah's death when Türkmen played an important role. However, the Turkish identity of the men is undoubted, and the location of the tombs strongly indicates their nomadic associations. Given the very partial and selective evidence of the literary sources, the absence there of individuals attested epigraphically is unsurprising, and not restricted to this case (for another example, see p. 232, n. 96 below).

absence of written sources, Türkmen chiefs remained powerful, wealthy and self-confident at the end of the eleventh century. Rather than seeing Nizam al-Mulk's policies as hostile to the Türkmen in general, it is more accurate to see them as aimed purely against the sultans' immediate relatives who threatened his position, the highest ranks of the old Türkmen aristocracy. This would explain the enduring presence of other Türkmen chiefs in the heart of the empire.[38]

Some twelfth-century evidence confirms that the Türkmen continued to live in the Jibal.[39] Qummi notes Sultan Mas'ud's inability to suppress a major Türkmen uprising near Hamadhan as one of his major failures[40] – sure indication of a substantial Türkmen presence there in the middle of the twelfth century. However, these Türkmen sometimes enjoyed good relations with the Seljuks, and the growing preference of sultans for Hamadhan as their base in the Jibal from the reign of Muhammad Tapar onwards may reflect a need to make use of nomadic troops of all kinds, Turkish, Kurdish and Arab, for which Hamadhan was the prime recruiting ground and pastureland.[41] We find references to Türkmen troops in the Jibal and elsewhere to the end of the dynasty. Arslan b. Tughrıl went to fight the jihad against the Georgians surrounded by 'innumerable' Türkmen,[42] while Tughrıl III's reliance on Türkmen support is well documented.[43]

Some senior amirs were Türkmen nomads long after Malikshah's reign. In 513/1119, under Mahmud, the *amīr al-ḥajj* was a certain 'Ali b. Sökmen, 'one of the amirs of the [Turks] of Balduq', who sound as if they must be a Türkmen grouping.[44] More famous is the son of Artuq, Najm al-Din

[38] Isfahani, indeed, specifically tells us that Nizam al-Mulk targeted the sultan's relatives, confirming the evidence of Sibt (see Chapter 1, p. 70 above). Indeed, Nizam al-Mulk had actually redistributed some of the caliphal lands to the Türkmen (p. 144, n. 101), which suggests that, however much the old Tukish elite may have been horrified by the murders of Qavurt and Gawhar Khatun, Nizam al-Mulk's policy was not hostile to Türkmens *per se*.

[39] Bundari, *Zubda*, 236 (noted by Durand-Guédy with a different interpretation); Husayni, *Akhbar*, 131, mentions Türkmen in al-Lihf; Husayni, *Akhbar*, 179: Türkmen ruin area around Hamadhan.

[40] Qummi, *Dhayl-i Nafthat al-Masdur*, 208–9.

[41] On Türkmen settlement around Hamadhan, see Sibt, *Mir'at*, 31, 32, 161; Peacock, *Early Seljūq History*, 154. The rise of Hamadhan is discussed by Durand-Guedy in *Iranian Elites*, 208–9, without adducing the reasons given here – Durand-Guédy emphasises its convenient and central location, which was also doubtless a factor. For more on the pastures around Hamadhan, see Durand-Guédy, 'Where did the Saljuqs Live?', *passim*. On the rise of Hamadhan as a political centre, see Fragner, *Geschichte der Stadt Hamadan*, 121 ff.

[42] Husayni, *Akhbar*, 159.

[43] Durand-Guédy, 'Goodbye to the Türkmen?' and above p. 119.

[44] Ibn al-Athir, *al-Kamil*, X, 559.

Ilghazi (d. 514/1122), who served Muhammad Tapar as *shiḥna* of Baghdad and eventually established himself in the city of Mardin in the Diyar Bakr, which was to remain the power base of his successors in the Artuqid dynasty until the beginning of the fifteenth century.[45] Not only was Ilghazi himself a Türkmen, but his strength derived largely from nomadic support. When *shiḥna* of Baghdad in 495/1102, his men are described as 'Türkmen', and as lord of Mardin, he depended on the Türkmen who pastured around the town.[46] Ilghazi continued to rely on Türkmen forces for his operations in north Syria, the Jazira and into the Caucasus until his death.

Türkmen were difficult to control, prone to undisciplined plundering and ever ready to shift their loyalties to another leader. The biggest problem, however, was their dependence on pasturelands for their horses and cattle, which limited their range. Many of the vast regions that made up the Seljuk Empire were ecologically unsuitable for sustaining a nomadic army, including the deserts surrounding the Isfahan oasis and, above all, the pastureless land of Iraq (see pp. 50–1 above). The Türkmen's limitations are well brought home by Sibt b. al-Jawzi's account of their reaction to Tughrıl's order that they campaign in Syria in 1055, shortly after the capture of Baghdad:

> The sultan ordered his soldiers to prepare [themselves] and to send to bring their tents, children and families to Iraq and to head to Syria with him. They said, 'This land is ruined, there is neither food nor fodder here and we have no funds left. We cannot stay [indefinitely] on the backs of horses. What if our families, horses and beasts come, but our absence becomes drawn out? We must visit our families, so we are asking for permission to return to them and to go back to the place which is assigned to us.'[47]

The sultan's attempts to bring them to obedience by imprisonment and beating were unsuccessful, and Tughrıl was forced to compromise.

Indeed, even Türkmen chiefs were affected by their troops limitations. As Hillenbrand puts it, Najm al-Din Ilghazi's relationship with the Türkmen 'moulded his career, to his advantage and detriment alike'. The Türkmen would campaign only if there was a good prospect of booty, and once a battle had been won, they would inevitably wish to return to their home pastures of Mardin with their spoils. Prolonged campaigns had to be aborted owing to Türkmen demands to return home, and expeditions anyway had to be timetabled to suite the Türkmen, departing from Mardin

[45] On him, see Carole Hillenbrand, 'The Career of Najm al-Dīn İl-ghāzī', *Der Islam*, 58 (1981), 250–92.

[46] *Ibid.*, 256–7, 271–5; Ibn al-Athir, *al-Kamil*, X, 338.

[47] Sibt, *Mir'at*, 5.

in spring, returning in autumn to allow them to enjoy their winter pastures there.[48] The short-term requirements of the Türkmen made a longer term strategy impossible.

The *mamlūks*

The alternative to nomadic forces was *mamlūks*. Although also of Turkish and often nomadic origin, the same ecological limitations did not apply as they did not live a nomadic life, and they had the other great attraction that, in theory, they would owe loyalty to their owner alone. *Mamlūks* had formed a part of the later ʻAbbasid, the Samanid and the Ghaznavid armies – indeed, the Ghaznavid dynasty was itself of *mamlūk* origin.[49]

The processes of *mamlūk* recruitment and training are well attested from other places and periods in Islamic history, but we have relatively little information directly relating to the Seljuks. The main source of *mamlūks* must have been raids into the steppe. The so-called *Pand-nama-yi Sabuktagin*, which purports to be the memoirs of the Ghaznavid ruler Sebüktegin (d. 387/997), gives a sense of how a *mamlūk* was made. Sebüktegin recounts that he grew up in ʻTurkistan', a member of the Barkhan tribe (who are said by Kashghari to have lived around Lake Issyk Kul in modern Kyrgyzstan). Aged twelve he was captured by a group of raiders from another Turkish tribe, the pagan Bakhtian, who used him as a shepherd for four years. They then sold him along with other slaves in one of the towns of Transoxiana, and Sebüktegin was bought by a merchant who took him to Nakhshab (Nasaf), where he learned archery, horsemanship, and the use of the spear and the sword. He was then sold to the Samanid commander Alptegin, in whose service he rose to prominence.[50]

The Seljuks bought *mamlūks* from such dealers, as we learn from a reference to a payment dispute between the slave merchants and Muhammad Tapar.[51] Kayka'us b. Iskandar gives detailed recommendations on the difficult art of buying a slave, and discusses the merits and demerits of the various racial groups, including the different varieties of Turk one could purchase

48 Hillenbrand, ʻCareer', 268, 271–3. Further on the problems of Türkmen armies, see Durand-Guédy, ʻGoodbye to the Türkmen?'.

49 On the Ghaznavid army, see Bosworth, *The Ghaznavids*, 98–128. It has been argued that the role of *mamlūks* in these armies has been exaggerated by modern scholarship: see D. G. Tor, ʻThe Mamluks in the Military of the pre-Seljuq Persianate Dynasties', *Iran*, 46 (2008), 213–25.

50 M. Nazim, ʻThe *Pand-namah* of Subuktigin', *JRAS*, 2nd series, 3 (1933), 610–14, 621–3.

51 Ibn al-Athir, *al-Kamil*, X, 526; Lambton, *Continuity and Change*, 240–1.

(he recommends Khotan and Khalaj Turks as being more obedient than the ill-natured Ghuzz and Qipchaqs).[52] Others were captured directly by raids and warfare. Ahmad Khan, Sanjar's Qarakhanid contemporary, apparently had an army of some 12,000 Turkish *mamlūks*, as he 'ceaselessly raided the [steppe] Turks, penetrating their country for a distance of two months' journey away'.[53] In 456/1064, Alp Arslan's campaign into Georgia captured 50,000 *mamlūks*, although this number – doubtless exaggerated anyway – must have included a good number destined for domestic servitude rather than the army.[54] Alp Arslan's attacks on Türkmen in Central Asia also probably contributed to the reservoir of *mamlūks*,[55] although the sources do not explicitly state this.

Seljuk *mamlūk* training is obscure. Nizam al-Mulk gives a detailed description of the Samanid *mamlūk* training system that is clearly intended to be prescriptive of the ideal. There was a *cursus honorum* through which the *mamlūks* rose, lasting seven years. A freshly recruited *mamlūk* would start at the rank of foot-groom, and could rise by the age of thirty-five to become a fully-fledged amir.[56] Even in Samanid times the reality was probably much less rigid than Nizam al-Mulk implies.[57] The Seljuk evidence is, however, extremely scant. Ibn al-Athir informs us that Aqsonqur al-Bursuqi grew up in the company of Malikshah, whence that ruler's friendship towards him derived.[58] As the essential skills of warfare differed little for princes, *mamlūks* or *ghulāms*, all most likely trained together to some degree. Some *mamlūks* were manumitted, such as Tughtegin, who had been Tutush's slave,[59] but some very senior *mamlūk* amirs certainly remained slaves.[60] In practice, the difference between slave and free meant little, which is probably why our sources do not dwell on it.

The size of *mamlūk* armies varied considerably, although the numbers our sources give must often be treated with considerable scepticism. Nizam al-Mulk is credited with having owned 'thousands' of *mamlūks*, according to some sources up to 20,000.[61] A figure of 2,000 is given for the *mamlūk*

52 Kayka'us b. Iskandar, *Qabusnama*, 114–15.

53 Bundari, *Zubda*, 264; Husayni, *Akhbar*, 92.

54 Sibt, *Mir'at*, 117.

55 *Ibid.*, 131.

56 Nizam al-Mulk, *Siyar al-Muluk*, 141–3, trans. 103–5; Ayalon, 'Aspects', 214–16; Bosworth, *The Ghaznavids*, 102.

57 Bosworth, *The Ghaznavids*, 102; see also Lambton, *Continuity and Change*, 242.

58 Ibn al-Athir, *al-Ta'rikh al-Bahir*, 4.

59 Ibn Khallikan, *Wafayat*, I, 284.

60 See Lambton, 'The Administration of Sanjar's Empire', 372; Lambton, *Continuity and Change*, 242; Tor, '*Mamlūk* Loyalty', 284, n. 71.

61 Hamadhani, *'Unwan*, 100, puts them at 'thousands'; cf. Ibn al-'Adim, *Bughya*, 89, 92, 96;

contingent in Tughrıl's army, while Alp Arslan's *mamlūk* army at Manzikert was some 4,000 strong.[62] Most probably, a figure somewhere in the low thousands represented a reasonably large *mamlūk* contingent.

Mamlūks were in theory at the complete disposal of their owner, like any slave. Husayni relates an anecdote concerning an amir of Malikshah's who stole a watermelon. When his crime was uncovered, Malikshah made a present of the errant *mamlūk* to the watermelon seller, who sold him for the tidy profit of 300 dinars.[63] In a culture in which the beardless Turkish youth represented an ideal of beauty, frequently celebrated in literature, masters commonly used their *mamlūks* for sexual pleasure.[64] Sanjar is said to have had a particular predilection for his *ghulāms*.[65] Zangi kept the sons of notable Turks, Armenians and Greeks at his court; he allegedly used castration to punish the sons of those who had displeased him, but also 'when he found a *ghulām* beautiful he would castrate him to prolong his beardless looks'.[66] This behaviour earned Zangi the hatred of his private guard, who slept by his side at night, and they seized the opportunity for revenge, assassinating him in a drunken slumber.[67]

Eunuch *mamlūks* occupied senior positions.[68] Bihruz, who was Sultan Mahmud's *shiḥna* in Baghdad and is described as 'the amir fighting the holy war', was a eunuch, for instance (*al-amīr al-mujāhid Bihrūz al-khādim al-khaṣī nā'ib al-sulṭān fī Baghdād*).[69] The amir Savtegin, one of Alp Arslan's commanders, is even said to have castrated himself of his own volition.[70] Eunuchs were, however, probably always a small minority, being far more expensive than other slaves because of the high mortality rates as a result of the operation.[71] There were also some eunuchs who were not *mamlūks* at all, most famously the vizier al-Kunduri who

Nishapuri, *Saljuqnama*, 36, and Husayni, *Akhbar*, 67, give the figure of 20,000. See also Durand-Guédy, *Iranian Elites*, 121; Ayalon, 'Aspects', 212–14.

62 Sibt, *Mir'at*, 64, 147–8; Ayalon, *Eunuchs*, 144–5.

63 Husayni, *Akhbar*, 73.

64 Cf. Bosworth, 'Ghulām. II. Persia' *EI*[2]; see also Ayalon, *Eunuchs*, 47–8, 54–5, 57–9. For examples of some Seljuk period poems on the beauties of Turkish *ghulāms*, see al-Arrajani, *Diwan*, ed. Qadari Mayu (Beirut, 1998), I, 34–7, 66–8.

65 Bundari, *Zubda*, 266. See further above, p. 178.

66 Bundari, *Zubda*, 208. Unsurprisingly, Ibn al-Athir, with his Zangid sympathies, has nothing to say about this proclivity.

67 Bundari, *Zubda*, 208–9; Ayalon, *Eunuchs*, 166–7.

68 See Ayalon, *Eunuchs*, 153–62, 342–4.

69 Bundari, *Zubda*, 121.

70 Husayni, *Akhbar*, 30–1; for more on him, see Ayalon, *Eunuchs*, 156–7; Sibt, *Mir'at*, 27, 161, 163, 164, 224.

71 Ayalon, *Eunuchs*, 300–3.

was castrated in adulthood as punishment for a sexual misdemeanour in Tughrıl's service.[72]

The *mamlūk*'s ownership was signified by both collective and individual names: thus the Nizamiyya were the *mamlūks* of Nizam al-Mulk; while Sökmen al-Qutubi took his name from the *laqab* of his owner Qutb al-Dawla Isma'il b. Yaquti;[73] and the *mamlūk* Aqsonqur al-Bursuqi was named after his master Bursuq, himself one of Tughrıl's *mamlūks*[74] – *mamlūk* amirs often recruited their own *mamlūk* contingents. This relationship with the master might be reinforced by marriage: thus Malikshah's *mamlūk* Aqsonqur, who became governor of Aleppo, was married to the sultan's own wet-nurse.[75] An individual's *mamlūks* would often tend to stick together after his death, out of feelings of group solidarity and shared interest; thus, the Nizamiyya operated as block against Taj al-Din and Terken Khatun, and supported Berkyaruq's claim to the sultanate (Chapter 2). The *mamlūks* of the late Sultan Mahmud gathered en masse around his son Da'ud, theoretically the *walī al-'ahd* (heir apparent).[76] Even though Zangi was only ten years old at the time of the death of his father Aqsonqur, the latter's *mamlūks* still coalesced around the son.[77] This tendency towards group solidarity explains why sometimes masters' positions were inherited by their *mamlūks*. For instance, Yürünqush, governor of Isfahan between 531/1136–7 and 540/1145 was succeeded on his death by his African *mamlūk*, Jamdar Ghul Beg.[78]

The Amirs

As with other titles in the Seljuk state, amir is an ambiguous term with multiple meanings.[79] Although it appears as Tughrıl's title on his very earliest coins,[80] amir soon came to indicate a military commander, who might be free, *mamlūk* or even a nomadic chief (Figure 6.2).[81] One individual who bore the title *amīr al-umarā'* (chief amir), 'Uthman b. Malik Da'ud, was

72 Husayni, *Akhbar*, 24–5; Ibn al-Athir, *al-Kamil*, X, 32; Ibn Khallikan, *Wafayat*, IV, 278; Qummi, *Dhayl-i Nafthat al-Masdur*, 139.
73 Ibn al-Athir, *al-Kamil*, X, 384.
74 Ibn al-'Adim, *Bughya*, 204; Ibn Khallikan, *Wafayat*, I, 242.
75 Ibn al-'Adim, *Bughya*, 97; Ibn al-Athir, *al-Kamil*, X, 162.
76 Bundari, *Zubda*, 160. On this phenomenon, see Tor, '*Mamlūk* Loyalty', 780–7.
77 Ibn al-Athir, *al-Ta'rikh al-Bahir*, 15–16.
78 Durand-Guédy, *Iranian Elites*, 325.
79 Bosworth, 'Amir', *EIr*.
80 See pp. 40, 127 above.
81 For example, Nishapuri, *Saljuqnama*, 61, where the Ghuzz leaders are referred to as *umarā*. See also Durand-Guédy, 'Good-bye to the Türkmen?'.

Figure 6.2 Model statue of an amir. Walters Art Museum, Baltimore, Accession No. 24.1. © Walters Art Museum

himself a member of the Seljuk family.[82] Given the court's emphasis on protocol and rank, it is not surprising that there seems to have been a hierarchy of amirs, of which we currently only have a fairly limited understanding.[83] Nizam al-Mulk emphasises the need for a rigid military hierarchy, but gives no details as to how this worked (or might work) in practice.[84] We do know that some amiral positions were attached to certain functions, such as the *amīr-akhur* who was responsible for the sultan's stables, and it was possible to progress through the amiral ranks. The late eleventh-century governor (*'amīd*) of Khurasan, Muhammad b. Mansur al-Nasawi (whose name suggests that he

[82] Husayni, *Akhbar*, 59.

[83] For instance, Husayni (*Akhbar*, 129) tells us that al-Muqtafi 'made [his Greek and Armenian *mamlūks*] amirs [*ja'alahum umarā'*]'. However, we have little idea as to what kind of ceremonies were involved in making someone an amir. For an example from the Mamluk period, see Estelle Whelan, 'Representations of the Khassakiyyah and the Origins of Mamluk Emblems', in Priscilla Parsons Soucek and Carol Bier (eds), *Content and Context of Visual Arts in the Islamic World* (University Park, PA, 1988), 219–43.

[84] Nizam al-Mulk, *Siyar al-Muluk*, 163, trans. 120–1.

was neither Turkish nor nomadic), had started his career as a butcher to the army camp, then graduated to work in the sultanic stables. A further promotion made him *amīr aṣḥāb al-mashāʿil*, responsible for providing torch-light for the sultan, from which he then rose to become tax collector in Khurasan, and finally governor of Khwarazm.[85] His career path may not have been so unusual, for another amir, Qarategin, was also apparently a butcher by origin, although judging by his name he was a Turk.[86] The sultan's amirs (*al-umarāʾ al-sulṭāniyya*)[87] presumably enjoyed precedence over the rest. The title *al-amīr al-isfahsālār* was bestowed on the most senior amirs, such as governors of major cities like Isfahan. By the twelfth century, the greatest amirs were arrogating to themselves the title of *malik*, previously the prerogative of Seljuk princes.[88] Amirs' ranks and positions, as in later times, were probably designated by emblems on their banners, at least in the case of members of the *khāṣṣakiyya*, the sultan's personal guard.[89] From *mamlūk* to nomad to butcher to Seljuk prince, the amiral class was extremely diverse.

Equally diverse was the extent of an individual amir's power. At one extreme, Khassbeg b. Palang-eri is said to have been effectively the ruler under Masʿud (*huwa al-āmir al-nāhī*).[90] The basis for this power was his personal relationship with Sultan Masʿud, 'who had fallen passionately in love with him above [all] his peers. When he grew up he was the greatest of the amirs.'[91] Mengubars, governor of Iraq, married Nist andar Jahan, the wife of Sultan Muhammad, after the latter's death, and had absolute control of the *iqṭāʿs* of Iraq (*kāna qad istabadda bi-iqṭāʿāt al-ʿIrāq*).[92] His vizier claimed to have raised for his master taxes worth 1,300,000 dinars in cash alone, quite apart from wealth, jewellery, cattle and so on in kind.[93] He was not the only amir to become incredibly rich: at his death Savtegin's riches comprised 1

85 Husayni, *Akhbar*, 32–3.

86 Bundari, *Zubda*, 129; Husayni, *Akhbar*, 89. Lambton states Nasawi was not an amir, on the grounds of his background, but this seems to be based on a preconception of who could be an amir rather than on the evidence. He clearly did hold the title of amir, at least at one point.

87 For example, Husayni, *Akhbar*, 13.

88 Lambton, 'The Administration of Sanjar's Empire,' 372; Whelan, 'Representations', 236, n. 19.

89 The evidence for this comes from the practice not of a Seljuk sultan, but that of the Khwarazmshah Muhammad b. Tekish; but he most likely drew on Seljuk precedents. See Whelan, 'Representations', 219–20. For the *khāṣṣakiyya* in Seljuk times, see, for instance, Ibn al-Jawzi, *al-Muntazam*, XVI, 301.

90 Bundari, *Zubda*, 198; cf. Ibn al-Athir, *al-Kamil*, X, 104, 132.

91 Bundari, *Zubda*, 192; cf. Qummi, *Dhayl-i Nafthat al-Masdur*, 163.

92 Bundari, *Zubda*, 173.

93 *Ibid.*, 172–3.

Figure 6.3 The possessions of the *hajib* Abu Shuja', including his drinking cup, uncovered at Nihawand in the 1930s. British Museum, ME OA 1938.11-12.1 (bowl); ME OA 1939.3-13.1-39. © Trustees of the British Museum

million dinars, 10,000 robes (*thawb*), 5,000 horses, 1,000 camels and 30,000 sheep.[94] At the other extreme, plenty of amirs are known to us only from a single reference, or are completely nameless.

The Culture of the Amirs

Unlike the bureaucrats and the *'ulamā'*, no members of the amiral class have left us written evidence of their culture and values. These we have to deduce from passing references in the literary sources and archaeological evidence. Even in the early period, some amirs had been born and bred within the Islamic world, like Alp Arslan's amir, Savtegin, born in the Khurasani village of Khakistar where he subsequently built a *ribāṭ* (caravanserai),[95] suggesting a continuing affinity with his birthplace and a desire to promote his memory there through pious works. Such Islamic values often coexisted alongside older Turkish ones. The personal effects of Abu Shuja' Inju Tegin, a *ḥājib* unattested in the literary sources, which were dug up in Nihawand, western Iran, in the 1930s, are suggestive (Figure 6.3). The hoard consists of thirty-nine pieces of silver, including

[94] Sibt, *Mir'at*, 228–9.
[95] Husayni, *Akhbar*, 30; on the village, see Bosworth's trans. n. 119.

belt plaques, beads and an amulet case inscribed with Qur'anic verses and pictures of a peacock and a lion. Inju Tegin's clothes would thus have been richly adorned with silver accoutrements, contrary to Islamic injunctions that banned the pious from wearing precious metals. Inju Tegin also owned a gold bowl with an Arabic inscription extolling the virtues of wine drinking,[96] suggesting the traditional steppe enthusiasm for alcohol – the motif of the drunken Turkish amir crops up regularly in the sources.[97] Even a sympathetic author describes the Ildegüzid Qızıl Arslan as 'despite his chivalry (*jawānmardī*), addicted to alcohol (*mudmin al-khamr*), constantly drinking and gambling'.[98] Qızıl Arslan, at the same time, may have been the patron of one of the masterpieces of painting in the period (Figure 6.4), the *mīnā'ī*-ware plate which shows amirs – perhaps led by Qızıl himself – going into battle against a fortress in Azerbaijan, and indulging in other amiral enthusiasms such as hunting.[99]

Occasional hints suggest the persistence of steppe traditions that Muslim chroniclers sought to gloss over. They seem to have been horrified by the grisly end of the Crusader Gervase of Basoches, lord of Tiberias, on falling into the hands of his enemy Tughtegin, amir of Damascus, in 501/1107–8. Tughtegin had Gervase scalped; he turned the skull into a drinking vessel and had the knight's long white hair mounted on the tip of his spear as a *tugh*, a totemic standard that was believed to give special powers to its bearer. The use of the enemy's skull as a drinking vessel and the *tugh* are well attested traditions among steppe warriors since antiquity.[100]

Lambton has identified three groups of amir. The first comprised those based at the sultan's court, who fulfilled tasks relating to the administration of the court and the army, such as the offices of *amīr-akhur* and *amīr aṣḥāb al-mashā'il* mentioned above, and amirs responsible for the royal wardrobe, and

[96] See Basil Gray, 'A Seljuq Hoard from Persia', *British Museum Quarterly*, 13/iii (1938–9), 73–9.

[97] See, for example, Ibn Azraq al-Fariqi, *Tarikh al-Fariqi*, 160; for another example, see Merçil, *Kirman Selçukluları*, 45; see also the comments on Alp Arslan's drunken exploits at Aleppo, Chapter 7, pp. 251–2 below.

[98] Ibn Isfandiyar, *Tarikh-i Tabaristan*, II, 153.

[99] On this, see Renata Holod, 'Event and Memory: The Freer Gallery's Siege Scene Plate', *Ars Orientalis*, 42 (2012), 195–219.

[100] For Gervase, Tughtegin and these steppe traditions, see Carole Hillenbrand, 'What's in a Name? Tughtegin: "The Minister of the Antichrist"?', in Omar Alí-de-Unzaga (ed.), *Fortresses of the Intellect: Ismaili and Other Islamic Studies in Honour of Farhad Daftary* (London, 2011), 459–71.

Figure 6.4 Detail of amirs going into battle. Freer battle plate F1943.3. © Freer Gallery of Art.

the sultan's armour and weapons. The second group she describes as 'landed' amirs, who held provincial governorships or *iqṭāʿs*. A third group were 'wandering amirs', 'who owed no personal allegiance to anyone but moved about the empire serving different leaders as opportunity arose'.[101] However, no such division into these three groups is found in our sources, and as Lambton admits, the boundaries between them were very fluid. A amir might – like Muhammad b. Mansur al-Nasawi – be employed in a court position, and then become a 'landed' amir by being granted the governorate of a province. 'Wandering' amirs might become 'landed' by virtue of seizing control of a given territory, and subsequently receiving sultanic recognition.

The multiplicity of potential masters was a key factor in the amirs' power: it was a simple matter to switch from one to another, and the sources are full of examples of the amirs' machinations.[102] When Muhammad Tapar's appointed *shiḥna* of Baghdad, Najm al-Din Ilghazi, risked losing his position under the terms of the peace treaty of 497/1103–4, he switched sides to Berkyaruq. After Berkyaruq's death, Ilghazi sought to promote his own

[101] Lambton, *Continuity and Change*, 244. For an example of a wandering amir, see Ibn al-Athir, *al-Kamil*, X, 241.

[102] Further examples are given in Tor, '*Mamlūk* Loyalty', *passim*.

interests by supporting the sultanate of the infant Malikshah b. Berkyaruq, becoming reconciled with Muhammad after this moved failed – although he lost his position as *shiḥna* of Baghdad.[103] The motives of the amirs under Alpqash al-Silahi who defected to Caliph al-Mustarshid in 529/1135 are obscure, but they were concurrently negotiating with Tughrıl II, before eventually ending up in the service of the latter's rival Mas'ud.[104] Financial interests such as *iqṭā'* doubtless played a large part in amirs' calculations, but so too did their aim of maintaining a balance of power whereby no single ruler could be strong enough to control them. This was a major reason for their hostility to Mas'ud and Muhammad II. However, the reasons behind the sudden shifts of allegiance are not always so obvious owing to the inadequacy of our sources, and at times may seem downright capricious. For instance, one source states that Sanjar's attempts to fight the Qarakhitay were frustrated precisely because his 'amirs were not of the same mind' (*ghayr muttafiqī al-niyyāt*).[105]

Despite the fluidity of the amirs' loyalties, until the end of the dynasty, a nominal master was a prerequisite for the legitimacy of even the greatest amirs. The relationship of the mighty amir Khassbeg with Sultan Mas'ud illustrates this point: Bundari relates that:

> the sultan and Khassbeg travelled together and did not leave one another's side; they kept together to support one another, and they agreed with one another. Khassbeg was delighted with his privileged position [*kāna farḥan bi-ikhtiṣāṣihi*] and his master's expression of his love and devotion.[106]

Proximity to the sultan was a source of power, for it was in the sultan's name that all decrees were issued, and the sultan who was the legitimate source of all authority. As a result, distant *iqṭā's* were sometimes assigned precisely to weaken an individual's influence by removing him from court. Ibn al-Athir tells us that Nizam al-Mulk, motivated by fear of Aqsonqur's influence over Malikshah, plotted to have him awarded the *iqṭā'* of Aleppo 'to distance him from the sultan's service'.[107] The bitter hostilities that characterised the secretaries also existed among the amirs, although they are less well documented. For instance, Tughtegin inspired the hatred of a group of court amirs (*muqadammī al-dargāh al-sulṭānī*) due to his successes against the Franks in 509/1115–16.

103 Hillenbrand, 'Career', 255–8.
104 Ibn al-Athir, *al-Kamil*, XI, 19, 24–6; Bundari, *Zubda*, 174–6. See also pp. 149–51 above.
105 Husayni, *Akhbar*, 92
106 Bundari, *Zubda*, 229.
107 Ibn al-Athir, *al-Ta'rikh al-Bahir*, 4.

The court amirs tried to turn the sultan against him and have him removed, forcing Tughtegin to come to Baghdad in person to secure his position.[108]

Military Activity and the Sultans' Subjects

In classical Perso-Islamic political theory, it was axiomatic that the sultans' subjects (the *ra'āyā*) did not fight. Military activity was the task of the *'askar*, the military.[109] The sources provide us with plenty of examples of the suffering endured by the civilian population as a result of the frequent campaigning and the demands of the troops. For instance, during the struggle between Tughrıl and al-Basasiri in 448–9/1057–8, soldiers were billeted in the houses of townspeople in Mosul and Tikrit, who were also obliged to pay for the troops' upkeep.[110] Urban populations often preferred to flee rather than deal with an influx of soldiers. Mosul was left deserted by all but the weak and the poor, for instance, and Baghdad was so empty of people that robbers could act with impunity, even the notables falling victim to them.[111] In abandoned Mosul, Tughrıl's soldiers dismantled houses to make firewood, and in Baghdad, the sultan's men forcibly opened shops in broad daylight to seize their cash.[112]

Frequently, even the sultan was unable to control his troops who counted plunder as their pay. On occupying Mosul, Tughrıl granted the city as an *iqṭā'* to his ally Hazarasp, but his troops demanded their share in the spoils, saying, 'Either give us permission to plunder it, or we'll desert'. The most Tughrıl and Hazarasp could do was secretly to send word to the populace to flee before the coming destruction.[113] Food shortages and inflation often resulted. In 488/1095–6, during the civil war between Berkyaruq and Muhammad, the devastation in Iraq combined with the plague was such that, in scenes reminiscent of the worst crises of the Buyid period, the starving populace was forced to resort to eating carrion, and there were so many corpses that the dead could not be buried in accordance with Islamic rituals.[114]

However, not all subjects were passive victims, and indeed the takeover of many towns was peaceful. In Anatolia, towns often seem to have simply

108 Ibn al-Qalanisi, *Dhayl*, 192–3.
109 See the discussion in Paul, *Herrscher, Gemeinwesen, Vermittler*, 117–18; Paul, 'The Seljuq Conquest(s) of Nishapur', *passim*; David Durand-Guédy, 'Iranians at War under Turkish Dominion: The Example of pre-Mongol Isfahan', *Iranian Studies*, 38 (2005), 587–606; Lambton, *Continuity and Change*, 224.
110 Sibt, *Mir'at*, 16, 23, 30.
111 *Ibid.*, 16, 29–30.
112 *Ibid.*, 30, 31.
113 *Ibid.*, 16; cf. Ibn al-Athir, *al-Kamil*, IX, 628.
114 Ibn al-Athir, *al-Kamil*, IX, 631.

slipped into Turkish hands without much fighting, surrendered by their lord as payment for military aid. Elsewhere, prizes such as Baghdad and Nishapur fell without fighting. Indeed, the protracted siege of Isfahan was probably the exception.[115] Much of the Seljuk takeover was thus achieved without violence, and the surrender of many towns, such as Abiward, Merv and even Nishapur itself to the Seljuks was negotiated directly with the leading townsmen in the absence of any Ghaznavid government.[116] When violence did take place, it was not necessarily one-sided. The people of Herat even managed to kick the Seljuks out shortly after the conquest, in the wake of a dispute between the townsmen and the Turkish soldiery over the latter's mistreatment of Herati women, and the city seems to have survived for several years under the rule of its notables, defeating annual Seljuk attempts to take it.[117] The devastation caused by Qutlumush's Türkmen troops prompted the people of Sinjar in the Jazira to incline towards al-Basasiri. When Tughrıl attacked the following year, the townspeople stood on the walls, displaying the skulls of the Türkmen they had previously killed, shouting abuse at the advancing enemy troops.[118] When Tughrıl marched on Tikrit in Dhu 'l-Hijja 448/February 1057, its governor 'Isa b. Khamis was willing to come to terms, but its people were not. They insulted Tughrıl's envoy, declaring, 'This land belongs to al-Basasiri'.[119] Sibt b. al-Jawzi tells us that the reason the people fled Mosul was because 'they had fought with the sultan's men who were in the citadel'.[120] Civilian populations thus actively fought and resisted, and cities continued to determine their own fate even after a hundred years of Seljuk rule. As the empire in Khurasan collapsed, individual towns defended themselves against the Khwarazmians, Ghuzz and local warlords that variously sought to conquer them.[121]

There were also various urban militias and paramilitary forces.[122] In Baghdad, for instance, one militia was headed by the representative of the descendants of the Prophet, the Hashemite *naqīb*.[123] The forces we encounter most frequently in the sources, however, are groups known as *aḥdāth* and

[115] See Chapter 1, pp. 43–4.

[116] Abiward: Gardizi, *Zayn al-Akhbar*, 293; Merv and Nishapur: Peacock, *Early Seljūq History*, 89–94; Paul, 'The Seljuq Conquest(s) of Nishapur'.

[117] Paul, 'Histories of Herat', 106–7. See now also Fami, *Tarikh-i Harat*, 125–7.

[118] Sibt, *Mir'at*, 11; Ibn al-Athir, *al-Kamil*, IX, 625, 630.

[119] Sibt, *Mir'at*, 14.

[120] Sibt, *Mir'at*, 31.

[121] Paul, *Herrscher, Gemeinwesen, Vermittler*, 119–21; Durand-Guédy, 'Iranians at War'.

[122] See Paul, *Herrscher, Gemeinwesen, Vermittler*, 123–7; Lambton, 'Internal Structure', 173–4.

[123] For the militia under the *naqīb*, see van Renterghem, 'Controlling and Developing Baghdad', 127.

ʿayyār (the former term predominated in Syria, the latter in Iraq, the Jibal and Khurasan, but their function seems to have been the same).[124] The *ʿayyārs/aḥdāth* have been seen by some scholars as representing a popular 'struggle against authority',[125] but by the eleventh century they espoused Sufi ideals of chivalry (*futuwwa/jawānmardī*), in which context they are praised in the *Qabusnama*.[126] These values were thus incorporated into courtly culture and many *ʿayyārs* were of aristocratic origin, but they also remained paramilitary groups engaged in extortion, often feared by the populace.[127] *ʿAyyār* leaders were sometimes formally confirmed in their positions by the Seljuks, and on occasion the *ʿayyārs* of Baghdad operated in cooperation with Seljuk authorities like the *shiḥna*.[128]

Indeed, collaboration between subjects and Turkish rulers was perhaps more common than has been credited. As argued above (Chapter 2), amirs sought to maintain good relations with the local populace as a way of strengthening their own positions vis-à-vis the sultan. Plenty of non-combatants were involved with, and profited from, the military. Al-Basasiri's army was encouraged into battle against Tughrıl by slave girls 'standing in front of them banging the tambourines and reciting poems which contained accounts of wars'.[129] Armies were accompanied by a travelling bazaar, like the one where Nasawi the butcher-turned-amir learned his trade; even a Türkmen army like that of Turkman al-Turki, active in Syria in the late eleventh century, was accompanied by merchants to provision it.[130] Expeditions to wage war on the frontiers of Islam could also bring economic benefits in the form of cheap slaves, the

124 The major study of the *aḥdāth* and *ʿayyār* in the Seljuk period remains Claude Cahen, 'Mouvements populaires et autonomisme urbain dans l'Asie musulmane du moyen age, I', *Arabica*, 5/iii (1958), 225–50; II, *Arabica*, 6/i (1959), 25–56; III, *Arabica*, 6/iii (1959), 233–65. A useful discussion with regard to the pre-Seljuk period is D. G. Tor, *Violent Order: Religious Warfare, Chivalry and the* ʿAyyār *Phenomenon in the Medieval Islamic World* (Istanbul and Wurzburg, 2007).

125 Simha Sabari, *Mouvements populaires à Bagdad à l'époque ʿabbasside, IXe–XIe siècles* (Paris, 1981), 97, 122. See also Paul, *Herrscher, Gemeinwesen, Vermittler*, 127–30; and for a critique of previous theories about the nature of *ʿayyārs*, Tor, *Violent Order*, 1–27, 253–63, 286–7, 296.

126 Tor, *Violent Order*, 246–50; Kayka'us b. Iskandar, *Qabusnama*, 243–64, esp. 247.

127 Tor, *Violent Order*, 253–87, for a discussion of the situation in the tenth and early eleventh centuries, which broadly seems to have continued in the Seljuk period, although this is in need of further investigation.

128 For examples, see Ibn al-Jawzi, *al-Muntazam*, XVII, 30–1; Ibn al-Qalanisi, *Dhayl*, 194; cf. Tor, *Violent Order*, 268–75.

129 Sibt, *Mir'at*, 12.

130 Ibn al-ʿAdim, *Zubda*, II, 425: merchants 'in his company' (*al-tujjār al-wāṣilīn fī ṣuḥbatihi*).

price of which might fall dramatically after a successful campaign.[131] Not all subjects were long-suffering passive victims of an alien power.

Citadels, City Walls and Castles

Society, then, was itself more militarised than is often credited, and it is in this context that we should consider the question of the militarisation of the landscape in the Seljuk period that was broached at the beginning of this chapter. Viewed through the prism of archaeology, the Seljuk occupation of Syria at first glance does seem to coincide with an unprecedented explosion in the construction of urban citadels, from which it is often assumed that the Seljuk military ruled. One authority has estimated that over a hundred citadels were built there and in surrounding areas between the eleventh and thirteenth centuries, only 'a fraction' of which can be ascribed to wars with the Crusaders.[132] Inspired by the example of the Seljuks, we are told, Bedouin amirs in northern Syria also took to building themselves fortresses and citadels.[133]

Although the plan of a citadel (*quhandiz*) at the heart of an inner city (*shahristān*) is characteristically Khurasani,[134] the evidence does not support the idea that this was a Seljuk import into Syria. In the east, over the tenth and eleventh centuries, the citadel as the centre of government seems to have frequently been abandoned. The Samanids, for example, seem to have stopped using the Bukhara citadel; and while their successors in Samarqand, the Qarakhanids, did – and over time increasingly – hold court in the citadel there, it was only one locus of power among several, alongside buildings in the town and tents outside it.[135] While, as we have seen (pp. 166–7 above), Sanjar had a palace in the Shahriyar Arg (citadel) at Merv, this too was only one of many different places he occupied. In Nishapur, the *quhandiz* (Figure 6.5) was being converted into residential accommodation during the Seljuk period and most of the city was left unwalled.[136] In Isfahan, the

131 Sibt, *Mir'at*, 227.

132 Rabbat, 'Militarization of Taste', 88.

133 Heidemann, 'The Citadel of al-Raqqa', in Kennedy (ed.), *Muslim Military Architecture in Greater Syria*, 130.

134 For more on the pre-Seljuk east, see Hugh Kennedy, 'From Shahristan to Madina', *Studia Islamica*, 102/iii (2006), 301–33. Cf. V. Fiorani Piacentini, 'La resa delle grandi città del Khorāsān ai Turchi Selgiuchidi (428 e 429 HG/1038 e 1039 AD: continuità cuturale o rottura delle tradizioni?' *Studia Turcologica Alexii Bombaci Memoriae Dicata* (Naples, 1982), 199–200.

135 See Karev, 'Tents to Cities', 109–10, 133–5, 143.

136 Bulliet, *Patricians of Nishapur*, 6–7, 9; Bayhaqi, *Tarikh*, 882, confirms the lack of walls in Nishapur at the time of its conquest; cf. Rante and Collinet, *Nishapur Revisited*, 55. After

Figure 6.5 The *quhandiz* (citadel) of Nishapur

citadel was built in the tenth century, and though it served as the principal accommodation of the garrison, it does not seem to have been the prime locus of rule for either sultans or Turkish governors.[137] In the Caucasus and eastern Anatolia, and perhaps also in Khurasan, far from building fortifications at least some Seljuks sought to destroy them, apparently seeing them as a potential threat to the nomads' control of the pastureland.[138] In Herat, a local historian writing in the reign of Sanjar describes how the populace were finally freed from the oppression of the citadel by the Seljuk sultan's command:

> They say that . . . the castle of Shamiran was the first building erected after Noah's Flood. It was constantly kept in good repair and occupied, and every governor of Herat, both those of past religions and Islam, every day improved its state of repair and strengthened it, so that it ran with blood. God on high took a sort of revenge on this castle. The amir Bozghash, at the

Sanjar's reign, Shadyakh was made the centre of the town and was fortified by al-Mu'ayyad Ay Aba (Yaqut, *Mu'jam*, V, 332).

137 Durand-Guédy, *Iranian Elites*, 19, 32, 211.

138 Peacock, 'Nomadic Society', 219–20; Peacock, *Early Seljūq History*, 149–50; see also comments by Paul, 'Arslan Arghun', 107, 111–12.

> time he was governor of Herat, was appointed by the order of the greatest sultan [*al-sulṭān al-aʿẓam*, Sanjar] to destroy it, without having any reason. That happened in 498[/1104–5], and the people were freed from its harm and the inhabitants were saved from it. This is one of the good deeds of that pure dynasty [the Seljuks].[139]

The Seljuks tended to use fortresses and citadels more as temporary bases in terms of emergency than as permanent bases, and were more likely to base their camps outside rather than at the heart of cities.[140] Furthermore, the Syrian fortifications of the period can only rarely be associated with the Seljuks. It is true that literary evidence does indicate that Tutush built a citadel in Damascus, but the citadels of Aleppo, Mayyafariqin and Harran that have all been taken to exemplify the process of militarisation had all been constructed before any Turk had made his way to northern Syria – in the case of Aleppo, the citadel existed by the tenth century, when it is praised in verse, and was turned into the main government residence by the Mirdasids, the Seljuks' Arab predecessors in the city.[141] In Harran, it had been the local people themselves who had first sought to build a citadel, in the early eleventh century, before the appearance of the Turks.[142] The architectural evidence suggests that major changes in the scale and nature of fortifications in Syria came not under the Seljuks, but in the late twelfth to early thirteenth centuries,[143] which is when the vast majority of the surviving structures of the citadels in Damascus, Aleppo and other cities were constructed.

The association between the coming of the Seljuks and the emergence of the urban citadel as the ruler's base of power, characteristic of Ayyubid and Mamluk times, is thus doubtful. Responsibility for the building and upkeep of fortifications often seems to have fallen to a town's subjects, as we have noted with the citadel of Harran. At Amid (Diyarbakır) inscriptions testify to a concerted programme of restoration and reconstruction over the years from 480/1088 to 486/1092.[144] Interestingly, these works were supervised by

139 Fami, *Tarikh-i Harat*, 134–5. Sanjar at this point would, of course, have still been *malik*, not *al-sulṭān al-aʿẓam*.

140 See p. 00 above and n. 146 below,

141 Rabbat, 'Militarization of Taste', 88–91; Heidemann, 'Citadel of al-Raqqa', 130; Tabbaa, *Constructions of Piety and Power*, 54–9.

142 Heidemann, 'Citadel of al-Raqqa', 130.

143 See the discussion in Scott Redford, '*Mamālik* and *mamālīk*: Decorative and Epigraphic Programs of Anatolian Seljuk Citadels', in Scott Redford and Nina Ergin (eds), *Cities and Citadels in Turkey: From the Iron Age to the Seljuks* (Leuven, 2013), 305–46.

144 Sheila S. Blair, 'Decoration of City Walls in the Medieval Islamic World: The Epigraphic Message', in James D. Tracy (ed.), *City Walls: The Urban Enceinte in Global Perspective*

the same individual who had been in charge of a reconstruction programme under the local Marwanid dynasty in the mid-eleventh century, the city qadi,[145] testimony to the importance of the collaboration of existing local elites and the continuities with the pre-Seljuk arrangements. At Bayhaq in Khurasan, the walls were repaired 531/1136–7 at the expense of a merchant, Abu Sa'd Jurjani. Although rulers did also sometimes intervene, different Seljuk rulers adopted very different policies towards whether the town should be fortified: so in 464/1071–3, Nizam al-Mulk commanded Bayhaq's walls to be raised in height, but in 490/1097 Arslan Arghun had it pulled down. The citadel was restored in 531/1136–7, but pulled down again twelve years later on the orders of Terken Khatun, Sanjar's wife. Finally, it was restored in 548/1153–4.[146] There was no consistent citadel-building programme.

Some Seljuk towns were strongly defended. Isfahan had an impressive enceinte built by the Kakuyids, for Nasir-i Khusraw notes the strength of its walls and their battlements.[147] An impression of what they might have looked like is given by the surviving walls of Diyarbakır (Figure 6.6). However, we should not assume that such solid stone work was the rule, for many fortifications were rather flimsy, designed only to deter casual raids and localised hostilities, not properly organised armies. Ibn Funduq records that Bayhaq possessed a wall, but only the height of two men 'so that a spear could reach up to it. Nevertheless it was strongly built and had places . . . from which fighting could be carried out.' The mud-brick walls of Merv (see Figure 2.1 above), built in the eleventh century,[148] would similarly have been of only limited military use, and the same was true of the fortified villages of Khurasan.[149] Ibn Jubayr, travelling through Syria and Iraq shortly after the end of effective Seljuk power there, noted that Kufa was unwalled, Hilla's walls were limited to a mud enceinte, Tikrit's once impressive urban defences had been allowed to decay, and Mosul's walls could be easily breached owing to their rough construction.[150]

The Seljuk domains were also dotted with numerous castles, and many more of these have survived. Unfortunately, the lack of serious

(Cambridge, 2000), 489, 504–5. For a slightly earlier description of Diyarbakır's walls, see Nasir-i Khusraw, *Safarnama*, 11. The text of the inscriptions is published in Sevket Baysanoğlu, *Anıtları ve Kitabeleri ile Diyarbakır Tarihi: Başlangıçtan Akkoyunlular'a Kadar* (Ankara, [1987] 2003), I, 252–7.

145 Blair, 'Decoration', 505, 522.

146 Ibn Funduq, *Tarikh-i Bayhaq*, 269; for a comparable example from Buyid Qazwin, see Tetley, *The Ghaznavid and Seljuk Turks*, 92.

147 Nasir-i Khusraw, *Safarnama*, 137; cf. Bosworth, 'Dailamīs in Central Iran', 79–80.

148 P. Brun and A. Annaev, 'The Fortifications of Sultan Kala', *Iran* 39, (2001), 33–42.

149 Paul, 'Local Lords'.

150 *Rihlat Ibn Jubayr*, ed. Muhammad Zaynhum (Cairo, n.d.), 176, 177, 191, 192.

Figure 6.6 Walls of Amid (modern Diyarbakır), Turkey, restored in the Seljuk period

archaeological work makes it very difficult to say very much definitive about Seljuk castle-building and design. The best studied examples are in fact the Ismaili castles, especially Alamut (Figure 6.7) and Lamasar, although the Seljuk stronghold of Shahdiz near Isfahan has also been published rather scantily.[151] As far as the existing evidence indicates, it seems that there was no distinctive Seljuk style of military architecture, which shared much in common with Muslim rivals like the Ismailis. Most Seljuk castles, including Shahdiz, were built on the sites of much earlier fortifications (Figure 6.8).

Castles tended to occupy the summits of mountains, with the citadel at the uppermost point, as is best exemplified by Ismaili castles, but can also be found in Seljuk fortifications like Shahdiz.[152] Such locations naturally created problems of water supply, which was solved through complex systems of

[151] For the Ismaili castles, see W. Ivanow, *Alamut and Lamasar: Two Ismaili Strongholds in Iran, an archaeological study* (Tehran, 1960); Peter Willey, *The Eagle's Nest: Ismaili Castles in Iran and Syria* (London, 2005). For Shahdiz, see Caro Minasian, *Shah Diz of Ismaili Fame: Its Siege and Destruction* (London, 1970).

[152] See also Ibn al-Balkhi's description of Sahara near Firuzabad, 'it is a great mountain' (*Farsnama*, 158).

Figure 6.7 The mountain-top Ismaili citadel of Alamut, Iran

canals and reservoirs.[153] The achievement of the architects lay in their very ability to build in such locations, using the contours of the mountain as part of the defensive system, and solving the perennial problem of the water supply.

Ismaili castles differed in function from other fortifications, for they also served as cultural centres.[154] Alamut was famous for its library, and was a centre for the production of Ismaili philosophical treatises. As far as we can tell, most Seljuk fortresses acted purely as strongholds: of Shahdiz, we learn that, 'When the sultan was away, the treasury, armoury, his young slaves and the palace girls were [kept] there, and a group of Daylamites were its guards.'[155] There was no cultural activity, and such fortresses were merely used for the safe-keeping the sultan's valuables. They were never places of long-term residence for the Seljuk sultan and the great amirs, again in contrast to the Ismaili case – Hasan-i Sabbah did not leave Alamut for twenty-seven years.

Most castles were in the hands not of the sultan or his amirs, but local lords. Ibn al-Balkhi, writing in the early twelfth century, lists twenty-one

153 For the water supply of Alamut, see Willey, *The Eagle's Nest*; for discussion of water supply of the castles of Fars, see Ibn al-Balkhi, *Farsnama*, 156.

154 Daftary, *The Ismā'īlīs*, 325–7, 367.

155 Rawandi, *Rahat al-Sudur*, 156.

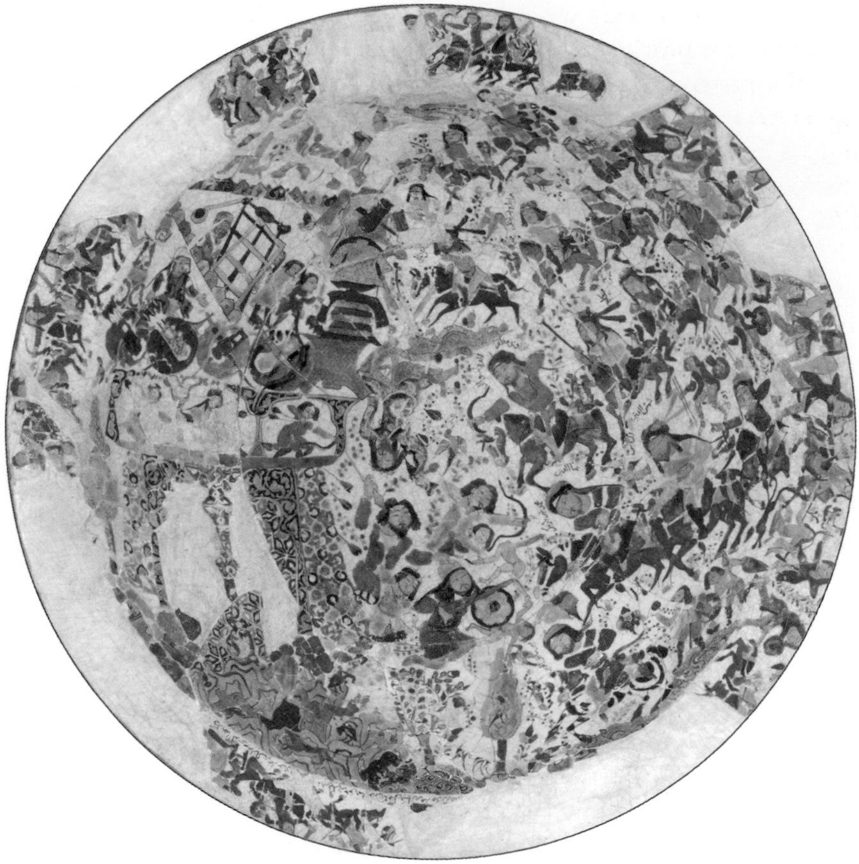

Figure 6.8 Amirs besiege a fortress, Khalkhal, Azerbaijan. Freer battle plate F1943.3. © Freer Gallery of Art

castles in Fars,[156] quite apart from the lawless region of Irahistan, of which he writes that 'there are more castles than can be counted, for in every village there is a fortress, either on a rock or the top of a hill or on the [flat] ground'.[157] We are rarely told exactly who the lords of these castles were, but two of those who are mentioned have archaic-sounding Persian names: Mil b. Bihrast of Buhskanat and Hasuyah of Istahbanan. Many castles, especially in remote and impenetrable regions like Irahistan, must have remained in the hands of the local lord, whose power might not extent much beyond his own village.

[156] Ibn al-Balkhi, *Farsnama*, 156–60.
[157] *Ibid.*, 160.

Others had been seized by the Shabankara, the possibly Kurdish nomads who devastated the province in the eleventh century.[158]

This pattern whereby castles were largely controlled by local lords whose rights were simply confirmed by their suzerains is likely to have been true of much of the Seljuk domains. The arrangements described by Ibn al-Athir for the Kurdish mountains around Mosul are probably representative: 'When [Zangi] took possession of Mosul, he confirmed the [Kurdish] lord 'Isa al-Hamidi over its surrounding regions, and did not interfere with any of his existing rights.'[159] The Khwarazmian historian al-Nasawi tells us that his ancestral castle on the steppe frontier of Khurasan had been in his family's hands since the coming of Islam.[160] Military architecture and fortifications suggest a broad continuity with regional trends in different areas of the Seljuk Empire. If society and the landscape was militarised, it was not necessarily any more so than it had been in the early eleventh or even the tenth century.

[158] *Ibid.*, 158.

[159] Ibn al-Athir, *al-Kamil,* XI, 14. On the Shabankara, see further V. F. Büchner and C. E. Bosworth, 'S͟habānkāra', *EI²*, who assert their Kurdish identity; this, however, is questioned by V. Minorsky, 'Kurds. III. History. B. The Islamic Period up to 1920', *EI²*.

[160] See Jürgen Paul, 'Where Did the Dihqāns Go?' *Eurasian Studies*, 13 (2013), 23–6.

7

Religion and the Seljuk Empire

> When [Seljuk] reached the region of Jand, God enlightened his heart with divine light. He sent a messenger to the governor of that province saying, 'The reason of my coming to this place is so that I can join the path of the people of Islam. I beseech you to send a distinguished scholar of Islam to me [*yakī az a'yān-i fuqahā wa miḥwal-i 'ulamā*] so that by teaching the Qur'an, the truths of the faith and Islam he may guide the erring pagans of the steppe to the wellsprings of true faith.' His request was accepted and Seljuk and his followers and companions became Muslim.[1]

The version of the *Maliknama* as transmitted by Mirkhwand predictably stresses the role of divine inspiration in guiding Seljuk to Islam. Duqaq and Seljuk had perhaps originally followed the Jewish faith like much of the Khazar ruling elite, although the possibility of a Christian connection has also been raised.[2] The onomastics of dynasty are suggestive of these changes: whereas Seljuk's sons and grandsons had borne names redolent of the Old Testament, such as Isra'il (Israel), Musa (Moses), Mika'il (Michael), Yusuf (Joseph) and Da'ud (David), these vanish in subsequent generations, replaced by Arabic, Turkish or, on occasion, Persian ones.

In contrast to our Muslim sources, the Christian author Bar Hebraeus (who also drew on the *Maliknama* tradition) emphasises practical motives for the conversion:

> [Seljuk] went forth from the land of TURAN, that is to say of the TURKAYE (Turks) to the land of IRAN, that is to say of the PERSIANS, under the pretence they were shepherds. And when they saw that PERSIA was flourishing with Islam, they took council together and said, 'If we do not enter the Faith of the People in the country in which we desire [to live] and make a

1 Mirkhwand, *Rawdat al-Safa*, IV, 236–7.

2 See Cahen, 'Le Maliknameh', 42, 45–6; Dunlop, *The History of the Jewish Khazars*, 259–61; Peacock, *Early Seljūq History*, 34. On Judaism in the Khazar domains, see Chapter 1, p. 24, n. 20 above.

pact with them (or, conform to their customs), no man will cleave to us, and we shall be a small and solitary people.'[3]

Whether motivated by purely practical considerations or by spiritual conviction, Seljuk's own decision to embrace Islam was one emulated over the eleventh century by numerous Turks, many of whom had adhered to shamanistic beliefs. In 435/1043, for instance, Ibn al-Athir reports that 10,000 households (lit. tents, *kharkāh*) of Turks converted in the Balasaghun region of the Qarakhanid lands, an event celebrated by their slaughter of 20,000 sheep on 'Id al-Adha.[4] Others, though, retained their old religions, and into the twelfth century documents from Sanjar's chancery occasionally allude to the 'infidel' nomads on the steppe frontier, particularly around the Seljuks' old heartland of Dihistan and the surroundings of Mount Balkhan.[5]

Although our understanding of the spread of Islam among the Turks in this period is very limited, over the eleventh and twelfth centuries the Islamic world was becoming ever more Muslim: not just pagan Turks, but also Christians and Jews were in increasing numbers embracing the faith. At the same time, Islam itself was changing, both outwardly and inwardly. The minaret, that quintessential symbol of Islam, became increasingly common throughout the Seljuk lands, spreading from Iran to Syria and witnessing a 'florescence . . . unrivalled anywhere else in the medieval Islamic world'.[6] Its classic pencil-thin form is characteristically Seljuk (Figure 7.1).[7] The same process of institutionalisation affected other aspects of Islam, with the spread of the madrasa and the emergence of its Shiʿite relative, the *ḥawza*, the seminary system based in the Iraqi

[3] Bar Hebraeus, *Chronography*, I, 195.

[4] Ibn al-Athir, *al-Kamil*, IX, 520–1.

[5] Juwayni, *'Atabat al-kataba, 19: dar jihād-i kuffār kih dar ḥudūd-i Dihistān wa biyābān-i Manqishlaq-and*. Further on pagan Turks, see Peacock, *Early Seljūq History*, 22–7.

[6] Jonathon Bloom, *Minaret: Symbol of Islam* (Oxford, 1989), 157.

[7] It has been argued that other far-reaching changes in art in this period, ranging from calligraphy to architectural ornamentation, were a direct result of a Seljuk programme (continued by the Zangids) of propagating Sunni Islam. See Yasser Tabbaa, *The Transformation of Islamic Art During the Sunni Revival* (Seattle, 2001). However, as we shall investigate further below, the extent to which the Seljuks should be identified with a 'Sunni revival' is in serious doubt; furthermore, scholars have observed parallel artistic developments in the Shiʿite Fatimid empire, which suggests that it is unlikely that an explicitly ideological agenda underlay them. See Bernard O'Kane, 'A Tale of Two Minbars: Woodwork from Syria and Egypt on the Eve of the Ayyubids', in Robert Hillenbrand, A. C. S. Peacock and Firuza Abdullaeva (eds), *Ferdowsi, the Mongols and the History of Iran: Studies on Art, Literature and Culture from Early Islam to the Qajars* (London, 2013), esp. 324–5.

Figure 7.1 The minaret of Khusrawjird, Khurasan, Iran, a typical example of the Seljuk pencil-thin minaret, dated to 505/1111–12

cities of Najaf and al-Hilla.[8] Developments in Sufism also left their imprint on the built landscape. As Sufism became ever more mainstream as it was reconciled with theology, and increasingly institutionalised, some Sufi disciples started to live temporarily or permanently in specific buildings set aside for their use, variously called *khānqāh, ribāṭ* or *zāwīya*, which would often also serve as the burial place for holy men (*awliyā'*, sing. *walī*).[9] Meanwhile, the Sevener Shi'ite Nizari Ismailis developed their own theology, ideology and state in their remote mountain hideouts within the very confines of the Seljuk Empire.

The Seljuks are traditionally characterised by their avid support for Sunnism. This formed a key part of Seljuk propaganda, and even today continues to influence scholarly and popular perceptions of the dynasty.[10] While older scholarship suggested that the Seljuks spearheaded a 'Sunni revival' after the domination of the Shi'ite Buyids, more recently this has been replaced with a view of the eleventh and twelfth centuries as witnessing a process of 'recentring' of Sunnism – which, it is argued, the *'ulamā'* sought to make increasingly homogeneous, not least through institutions like the madrasa.[11] At the same time, Sunnism was polarised by bitter disputes between adherents of the three law schools (*madhhabs*) of the Islamic east: the Hanbalis, Hanafis and Shafi'is.[12] These madhhabs lent their name not just to factional disputes among the *kātibs*, as we have seen (pp. 201–3), but to bitter rivalries that split communities in virtually every town in the Seljuk domains, frequently erupting into *fitna* (civil disorder).[13] Although Ismailism was widely

[8] For the madrasa, see references given on pp. 211–14 above; for the origins of the *ḥawza*, see Robert Gleave, 'Shii Jurisprudence during the Seljuq Period: Rebellion and Public Order in an Illegitimate State', in C. Lange and S. Mecit (eds), *The Seljuqs: Politics, Society and Culture* (Edinburgh, 2011), 205–7.

[9] On these developments, see Karamustafa, *Sufism*, 116–34; Green, *Sufism*, 51–61; van Renterghem, 'Social and Urban Dynamics', 180–2.

[10] For the image of the Seljuks as pious Sunnis, see Tor, 'Sovereign and Pious', 39–40; Safi, *Politics of Knowledge*, 1–3.

[11] For the classic demolition of the 'Sunni revival' thesis, see G. Makdisi, 'The Sunni Revival', in D. Richards (ed.), *Islamic Civilisation 950–1150* (Oxford, 1973), 155–68. See Jonathon P. Berkey, *The Formation of Islam: Religion and Society in the Near East, 600–1800* (Cambridge, 2003), 189–202, for a discussion of the Sunni 'recentring'; and Bulliet, *Islam: The View from the Edge*, 126–7, 146–8; van Renterghem, 'Controlling and Developing Baghdad',120–3; Ephrat, 'The Seljuqs and the Public Sphere', 139–40.

[12] Their names derived from those of the earlier jurists who were credited with their foundation – Ahmad b. Hanbal (d. 855), Abu Hanifa (d. 148/767) and al-Shafi'i (d. 820) – although in practice the madhhabs did not emerge in their distinctive forms till the late ninth or early tenth century. The fourth madhhab, the Malikis, did not have a significant number of adherents in the Seljuk lands.

[13] Bulliet, *Patricians of Nishapur*, 31; see further Chapter 8, pp. 312–15.

perceived by Sunnis in the Seljuk lands as a nuisance and a threat (Twelver Shiʿism rather less so), Shiʿites of either variety represented a minority in most areas of the Seljuk realm (parts of Arab Iraq, the northern Jibal between Sawa and Qumm, and Aleppo being the major exceptions with significant or majority Twelver populations).[14] The greatest challenge to public order was posed rather by these factional disputes within Sunnism.

We will discuss the social consequences of *fitna* in greater detail in Chapter 8. In this chapter, our aim is to examine the Seljuk sultans' and state's relationship with the various religious group in their domains,[15] in particular, towards Shiʿites and the various madhhabs, in order to understand the nature of the Seljuk role in the Sunni 'recentring' of the period. We also consider the fate of non-Muslim communities under Seljuk rule. First, however, we will look at the Seljuks' complex relationship with Muslim men of religion and the sultans' own personal religiosity.

Seljuk Piety and Relations with Men of Religion

The Seljuks' Sunnism is widely perceived to have been motivated as much by personal piety as it was by the demands of policy. David Durand-Guédy, for instance, writes of the sultans' patronage of madrasas that 'there is no doubt as to the sincerity of religious feelings that led them to fund these religious buildings'.[16] Deborah Tor states that 'the lives of the Great Seljuk sultans evince a significant degree of personal religiosity . . . manifested in areas ranging from personal devotional practices and expressed beliefs, through the veneration of holy men and shrines and the incorporation of religious figures into the state, to the active role of personal belief in formulating public policy'.[17]

14 A. Bausani, 'Religion in the Saljuq Period', in J. A. Boyle (ed.), *The Cambridge History of Islam, vol. V: The Saljuq and Mongol Period* (Cambridge, 1968), 294; J. Calmard, 'Le chiisme imamite à l'époque seldjoukide d'après le *kitâb al-Naqḍ*', *Le monde iranien et l'Islam*, 1 (1971), 52; Wilferd Madelung, *Religious Trends in Early Islamic Iran* (Albany, NY, 1988), 83–4. For Aleppo, see Tabbaa, *Constructions of Piety and Power*, 7, 25–6, 40–1, 105–24.

15 Earlier surveys of religion under the Seljuks concentrate largely on the eleventh century. For an overview, see Bausani, 'Religion'; also Makdisi, *Ibn ʿAqīl*; Erika Glassen, *Der mittlere Weg: Studien zur Religionspolitik und Religiosität der späteren Abbasidenzeit* (Wiesbaden, 1981); Peacock, *Early Seljūq History*, 99–127.

16 Durand-Guédy, 'Ruling from the Outside', 334. Elsewhere, however, Durand-Guédy, does distinguish between the eleventh-century sultans, whose attitude to religious affairs he describes as one of 'relative indifference', and the newly engaged policy of Muhammad Tapar as witnessed by evidence from Isfahan, see Durand-Guédy, 'An Emblematic Family', 192.

17 Tor, 'Sovereign and Pious', 41.

We cannot dismiss the possibility that some sultans were indeed (or were at least at times) genuinely pious, but making statements about the nature or degree of piety of individual rulers is fraught with difficulty. If a Seljuk ruler had left us his memoirs, like the Timurid ruler Babur in the early sixteenth century, we might be in a position to form some sort of judgement, but none did. The sources have their own reasons for extolling the piety or condemning the impiety of rulers. The sultans of the period of Seljuk greatness, Tughrıl, Alp Arslan, Malikshah and Muhammad, are regularly praised for their God-fearing nature and pious acts, while later sultans, such as Mahmud, Masʿud and their successors, are rarely if ever described as religious, and are frequently accused of debauchery.[18] Of course, it may be that the early sultans, seeking to legitimise the new dynasty to their newly conquered Muslim subjects, really did engage in ostentatious displays of piety for public consumption, a need which lapsed as the Seljuks became more firmly established. However, at times one cannot escape the suspicion that these characterisations owe something to a tendency to portray successful rulers as pious and unsuccessful ones as impious, reinforcing the moral lessons our historians often aimed to administer though their works.[19]

Indeed, the impression of personal piety even of the earlier sultans may be contradicted by other sources with their own agendas. Bar Hebraeus, for instance, perhaps ill-disposed towards the sultan because of the Turks' sacking of his home town of Melitene, highlights Tughrıl's contempt for the caliph and accuses him of burning down the congregational mosque at Sinjar; this latter outrage is confirmed by Sibt b. al-Jawzi.[20] Bar Hebraeus also records a story attributed to the chief qadi of Baghdad that reflects poorly on Tughrıl's Muslim piety, and indicates that some earlier Muslim sources had a much less favourable view of Tughrıl than that reflected by the chronicles:

> When I was sent on an embassy to him, I wrote a private letter to Baghdad, in which I described his rule, and his mercilessness, and how he prayed his prayers as a matter of form (or, routine), and not through fear of God.[21]

Ibn al-ʿAdim, the local historian of Aleppo, relates an anecdote regarding Alp Arslan's uncontrollable drunkenness at the siege of his native city.[22] Given the Turks' copious intake of alcohol (see pp. 174–6, 232), this may

[18] *Ibid.*, 41–8. See also pp. 100, 176 above for Masʿud.

[19] See Meisami, *Persian Historiography*, esp. 6–12, 282–3.

[20] Bar Hebraeus, *Chronography*, I, 204, 209, 210, 213; Sibt, *Mir'at*, 22.

[21] Bar Hebraeus, *Chronography*, I, 201.

[22] Ibn al-ʿAdim, *Bughya*, 27–8. See also Hillenbrand's discussion of this anecdote, 'Ibn al-ʿAdim's Biography of the Seljuq Sultan, Alp Arslan', 240–1.

reflect the truth at some level, but equally the anecdote may serve as a means by which Ibn al-ʿAdim could discredit this alien conqueror. Malikshah, meanwhile, is even accused by Ibn al-Jawzi of Ismaili tendencies.[23] Sanjar's image is predictably ambiguous: no doubt he was one of the greatest Seljuk sultans in terms of longevity and the magnificence of his court, but the disasters of Qatwan and the Ghuzz uprising had to be explained too. Thus, Nishapuri, for instance, praises Sanjar's piety and association with holy men; but he goes on to say, 'when the whole world had become subject to him' his amirs and retinue started to behave tyrannously and oppress the people, leading to his downfall.[24] Isfahani's account of Sanjar's love for *ghulāms* to whom 'he would give his wealth and his soul' doubtless has the same moralistic purpose.[25]

While the sultans are sometimes said in very general terms to have commissioned mosques and madrasas, there is surprisingly little evidence from either literary or epigraphic sources of precise buildings founded at their command, apart from the sultanic mosque in Baghdad commissioned by Malikshah (see p. 145 above).[26] His reign also witnessed the rebuilding of the great mosques at Damascus and Amid (Diyarbakır), and in the latter case the building inscription confirms that it was carried out at Malikshah's personal expense (*min mālihi*) (Figures 7.2(a), (b) and (c)).[27] However, other such sultanic commissions are rarely attested. Even the rebuilding of the great mosque in Isfahan was undertaken not by the sultan, but by Nizam al-Mulk and his rival Taj al-Mulk, even if Malikshah's titles are given due prominence (see Figures 5.1 and 5.2 above).[28] Tughrıl is said to have endowed a madrasa in Nishapur in 437/1045–6,[29] but of the thirty madrasas that existed in Baghdad by the late twelfth century about which information survives, only two were founded by sultans – Malikshah and Mahmud.[30] Building activity was sponsored by Seljuk bureaucrats and, on occasion, even by other

23 Ibn al-Jawzi, *al-Muntazam*, XVI, 312.
24 Nishapuri, *Saljuqnama*, 56–7.
25 Bundari, *Zubda*, 271.
26 So, for example, on Tughrıl: Bundari, *Zubda*, 27; Husayni, *Akhbar*, 23; Ibn Khallikan, *Wafayat*, III, 315. Cf. Durand-Guédy, *Iranian Elites*, 90–1; van Renterghem, 'Social and Urban Dynamics', 185–6.
27 Beysanoğlu, *Diyarbakır Tarihi*, I, 256. See also Korn, 'The Sultan stopped at Ḥalab', 112–13, for Damascus and Diyarbakır.
28 Durand-Guédy, *Iranian Elites*, 92–3; Blair, *Monumental Inscriptions*, 160–7.
29 Bulliet, *Patricians of Nishapur*, 252; Ephrat, *A Learned Society*, 25.
30 Ephrat, *A Learned Society*, 28–9; see also van Renterghem, 'Social and Urban Dynamics', 177–8, n. 11, for corrections to this list.

Figure 7.2(a) The Great Mosque (Ulu Cami) at Diyarbakır, Turkey, restored by order of Malikshah: exterior view

Figure 7.2(b) The Great Mosque (Ulu Cami) at Diyarbakır: interior view

Figure 7.2(c) The Great Mosque (Ulu Cami) at Diyarbakır: part of the inscription commemorating Malikshah's contribution of funds to the restoration of the mosque

members of the royal family, including royal women, but rarely by sultans.[31] It may be that these works were in some sense seen as redounding to the credit of the sultan, and, of course, our picture may be somewhat skewed by the bias of the sources towards interest in the activities of bureaucrats, as well as the arbitrary selection of material remains that have survived, our extant architectural and epigraphic corpus doubtless representing the tip of the iceberg of what was built. However, there is nothing to suggest any sultan ordered any construction programme to compare with the empire-wide scale of the Nizamiyyas, and the comparative lack of religious foundations that can be securely attributed to sultanic patronage is striking. The sources' praises for the sultans' construction activities may constitute a topos aimed at highlighting their devotion as much as reflecting the reality.

Links between holy men and sultans are also emphasised by the sources for their own reasons. One holy man strongly associated with the dynasty was Shaykh Abu Sa'id b. Abi 'l-Khayr (d. 440/1049) of Mayhana, a village on the northern steppes of the Kopet Dagh near Abiward (Figure 7.3). The hagiography of Abu Sa'id records his role in the emergence of the Seljuk state:

> At the time when the Seljuk family left Nur-i Bukhara and came to Khurasan and settled around Abiward and Mayhana, many people joined them. They seized most of Khurasan because of the inattention of the sultan, who at that time was Mas'ud, and his indulgence in corruption . . . Sultan Mas'ud [of Ghazna] . . . sent [the Seljuks] a threatening letter. They replied that, 'This is the work of God, what he wants will be.' Our shaykh Abu Sa'id [b. Abi 'l-Khayr] – may God sanctify his blessed soul – was, through his perspicacity, aware of this. Then Chaghrı and Tughrıl, the two brothers, came to visit the shaykh in Mayhana to pay their respects. The shaykh was sitting with a group of Sufis in the shrine. [Chaghrı and Tughrıl] came before the shaykh's dais [*takht*], greeted him and kissed his hand, then stood before his dais. The shaykh, as was his custom, immediately bowed his head. Then he

[31] See references in n. 30 for lists of patrons; also van Renterghem 'Social and Urban Dynamics', 189–90.

Figure 7.3 The shrine of Abu Sa'id at Mayhana, Turkmenistan, closely associated with the Seljuks and largely rebuilt under the Timurids.

> raised his head and said to Chaghrı, 'We have gave rule of Khurasan to you' and to Tughrıl he said, 'we have given rule of Iraq to you'.[32]

Emphasising the association between rulers and holy men suited both sides, contributing to the rulers' aura of piety and legitimacy, and enhancing the authority of holy men. The hagiography (*manāqib*) of Abu Sa'id was compiled in the late twelfth century by one of the saint's descendants for the Ghurid ruler Muhammad b. Sam,[33] and such passages were doubtless in part intended to sell the benefits of royal patronage of the shrine to the new dynasty by promising them similar legitimation. Royal patronage brought not just material advantage – Abu Sa'id himself seems to have lived much as a 'rural Khurasani aristocrat'[34] – but also helped to secure the

[32] Muhammad b. Munawwar, *Asrar al-Tawhid*, I, 156.

[33] See G. Böwering, 'Abu Sa'id b. Abi 'l-Khayr', *EIr*; Fritz Meier, *Abū Sa'īd-i Abū l-Hayr (357–440/967–1049). Wirklichkeit und Legende* (Tehran and Liege, 1976); Lambton, *Continuity and Change*, 239–40; Safi, *Politics of Knowledge*, 137–41.

[34] Green, *Sufism*, 60.

growing importance of holy men as intermediaries between their communities and the state.[35] The bargain, however, cannot be reduced to purely practical terms: there is no doubt that many rulers did genuinely believe in the *baraka* (blessings) that could be conferred by the prayers of holy men.

Thus, numerous sultans and other members of the elite patronised Sufis; especially well documented in hagiographic narratives and contemporary sources is the close relationship between Sanjar and Ahmad-i Jam, one of the few such holy men to leave an extant corpus of writings.[36] Saints were not uncritical friends of the powerful, however. ʻAyn al-Qudat al-Hamadhani (d. 525/1131), spiritual guide (*pīr*) to Sultan Mahmud's *mustawfī* ʻAziz al-Din, openly condemned the Seljuk administration, its 'wrong-doing sultans' and the very *iqṭāʻ* system of which ʻAziz al-Din was in charge.[37] Nizam al-Mulk is said to have remarked of Abu ʻAli al-Farmadhi, a Nishapuri Sufi who visited him, that: 'This shaykh tells me of the faults of my soul and the oppression I am committing; my soul is mortified as a result and I cease from much of what I am doing.'[38] Such public abasement doubtless aided the political elite's image as pious Muslims. Yet associating so closely with the ruling class had its costs too, for holy men might fall with their patrons. When Abu 'l-Qasim al-Darguzini managed to arrange the killing of his arch-rival, ʻAziz al-Din the *mustawfī*, he also had the latter's *pīr* ʻAyn al-Qudat imprisoned, tried and executed.[39]

Then there were the *ʻulamāʼ* (sing. *ʻālim*), the men with recognised expertise in the religious sciences. The question of their relationship with the Seljuks is fraught, and some scholars view them as having more or less been co-opted into legitimising the Seljuk state,[40] which controlled the juicy prizes that a careerist *ʻālim* might seek, such as appointment as qadi, *muḥtasib* or *raʼīs*.[41] Another carrot, although not strictly speaking a state-controlled one (at least until the twelfth century), was appointment to professorships in madrasas, which were privately endowed by members of the political elite, among others. *ʻUlamāʼ* who did enthusiastically collaborate with the regime were richly rewarded with appointments, such as the Khujandi family of

35 On men of religion as intermediaries, see Paul, *Herrscher, Gemeinwesen, Vermittler*, 207–10, 247–8; Green, *Sufism*, 95–8.

36 Safi, *Politics of Knowledge*, 144–56; Tor, 'Sovereign and Pious', 49–50.

37 Safi, *Politics of Knowledge*, 173–4, 182–7, 193–4.

38 Ibn al-Athir, *al-Kamil*, X, 209.

39 Safi, *Politics of Knowledge*, 191–9; Fragner, *Geschichte der Stadt Hamadān*, 131.

40 Safi, *Politics of Knowledge*, 90–7.

41 For some examples from Baghdad, see van Renterghem, 'Social and Urban Dynamics', 182–4; for Isfahan, see Durand-Guédy, *Iranian Elites*, 115–17, 201–2; for Nishapur, see Bulliet, *Patricians of Nishapur*, 64–8, 71–2.

Isfahan who dominated local city politics over the twelfth century. Skilled at delivering sermons, members of the family are also described by contemporaries as 'versed in the arts and in governance' and 'more like the viziers than the *'ulamā'*'.[42]

It was not necessary to hold worldly office to be closely associated with the Seljuk state. Abu Hamid al-Ghazali (d. 505/1111), the greatest *'ālim* of his day, was appointed to professorships at the Baghdad and Nishapur Nizamiyyas by Nizam al-Mulk and the latter's son Fakhr al-Mulk, respectively. He acted as a sort of spiritual adviser to members of the Seljuk political elite, enjoying especially close relations with Fakhr al-Mulk, and his political works increasingly explicitly supported the idea of the Seljuks' divinely bestowed sultanate.[43] Ghazali's project of promoting Sufism as the key religious science above all others, to the detriment of *fiqh* and *kalām*, was supported by Fakhr al-Mulk and Sanjar, and was articulated not just in his Arabic *Ihya' 'ulum al-Din*, but in its Persian abridgement, the *Kimya-yi Sa'adat*, which was written for the benefit of the Persophone political elite.[44] Seljuk backing also enabled Ghazali to withstand the campaign of vilification to which he was subjected by members of the *'ulamā'* whose status was threatened by his attempt to demote the importance of the sciences from the mastery of which they drew their social capital.[45]

However, there were *'ulamā'* of every madhhab who perceived secular power as intrinsically corrupt and sought to avoid any contact with it. Even some Hanafi scholars, members of the law school most closely associated with the regime, refused to have anything to do with the sultans.[46] Ghazali, too, advocated staying away from rulers, although he seems to have found it difficult to put his precepts into practice; but avoiding government appointments like qadiships and, indeed, any kind of political patronage, was widely

42 Durand-Guédy, 'An Emblematic Family', esp. 190.

43 See Chapter 3, pp. 124–5; and Kenneth Garden, *The First Islamic Reviver: Abū Ḥāmid al-Ghazālī and his* Revival of the Religious Sciences (New York, 2014), 17–29, 127–30, 138–48. For Ghazali's letters to the political elite, see Dorothea Krawulsky, *Briefe und Reden des Abu Hamid al-Ghassali* (Freiburg im Breslau, 1971).

44 Garden, *The First Islamic Reviver*, 130–3; further on the *Kimya*, see Carole Hillenbrand, 'The *Kimya-yi sa'adat* (The Elixir of Happiness) of al-Ghazali: A Misunderstood Work?', in Robert Hillenbrand, A. C. S. Peacock and Firuza Abdullaeva (eds), *Ferdowsi, the Mongols and the History of Iran: Studies on Art, Literature and Culture from Early Islam to the Qajars* (London, 2013), 59–69.

45 See Kenneth Garden, 'al-Māzarī al-Dhakī: al-Ghazālī's Maghribi opponent in Nishapur', *Journal of Islamic Studies*, 21/i (2010), 89–107; Garden, *The First Islamic Reviver*, 161–8.

46 Peacock, *Early Seljūq History*, 107–8.

regarded as praiseworthy.[47] Plenty of *'ulamā'* never received or sought an appointment, and developed their own educational networks independently of any patronage by the political elite.[48]

The Seljuks and Shi'ism

Seljuk Sunnism is often linked to a rabid prejudice against Shi'ism in both its Twelver and Sevener forms.[49] This motif runs through the primary sources as much as the secondary literature. For instance, when Alp Arslan's armies stood outside the predominantly Shi'ite city of Aleppo, the local Mirdasid ruler Mahmud b. Nasr warned the Aleppans that:

> The Egyptians' state [i.e., the Fatimids] has gone and this is a new state and a well run polity, which we fear because they consider shedding your blood licit on account of your religion [*li-ajl madhhabikum*]. The best course is to say the ['Abbasid-Seljuk] *khuṭba* . . .[50]

Nizam al-Mulk himself boasts that:

> In the days of the [Ghaznavid sultans] Mahmud and Mas'ud and Tughrıl and Alp Arslan, no Zoroastrian or Jew or Rafidi [Twelver Shi'ite] would have dared to appear in a public place or to present himself before a Turk. Those who administered the affairs of the Turks were all professional civil servants from Khurasan, who followed the orthodox Hanafi or Shafi'i sects. The heretics of Iraq were never admitted to their presence or allowed to work as secretaries and tax collectors.[51]

Further evidence of this hostility is sometimes adduced from the fact the leading Shi'ite centre of learning (*ḥawza*) at Najaf came into being because Abu

[47] See Ephrat, *A Learned Society*, 134–6; on Ghazali, see Garden, *The First Islamic Reviver*, 17–18, 27–8, 144.

[48] Ephrat, *A Learned Society*, 126–36; Ephrat, 'The Seljuqs and the Public Sphere', 140–4; Lange, 'Changes in the Office of the *Ḥisba*', 162.

[49] For example, Bausani, 'Religion', 292. Although Calmard, 'Le chiisme imamite', seriously challenged this view, it is still widely assumed. For example, Tabbaa, *The Transformation of Islamic Art*, 18: 'As staunch Sunnis the Seljuqs supported and drew legitimacy from the Abbasid state and opposed all its enemies, particularly the Fatimids and their Isma'ili sympathisers'. For another example, see Heidemann, 'Unislamic Taxes', 494: '[The Seljuks] justified their claim to rule with the renewal of Sunni Islam and the restoration of the Abbasid Caliphate, in the face of ascendant branches of Shi'ite doctrine among Muslims in the central regions and the rising power of Shi'ite dynasties, first among them being the Fatimids.'

[50] Ibn al-'Adim, *Zubdat al-Halab min Ta'rikh Halab*, ed. Sami Dahhan (Damascus, 1951–68), II, 381.

[51] Nizam al-Mulk, *Siyar al-Muluk*, 215, trans. 159.

Ja'far al-Tusi, the leading Twelver Shi'ite scholar of the period, was forced to flee there in the face of persecution in Baghdad in 449/1057–8, in the wake of the Seljuk reconquest of the city from al-Basasiri.[52]

Nonetheless, some Shi'ites had a positive view of the regime, as is suggested by a work composed *c.* 1165 entitled *Kitab al-Naqd* to refute a slightly earlier Sunni polemic against Shi'ism which is now lost. Written by one 'Abd al-Jalil Razi of Qazwin, the *Kitab al-Naqd* is a valuable source for Twelver (or Imami, as it is also known) Shi'ism in the Seljuk lands. 'Abd al-Jalil disputes the Sunni polemicist's claim that Nizam al-Mulk had obliged the Imami *'ulamā'* of Rayy to renounce their faith, alleging that the vizier had showered pensions and favours on the Imami community, especially its leaders, the sayyids or descendants of the Prophet through 'Ali.[53] Indeed, 'Abd al-Jalil is at pains throughout his work to emphasise the favour shown to the Imamis by successive Seljuk rulers and their viziers, some of whom were themselves Shi'ite.[54] 'Abd al-Jalil even claims the cult of 'Ali was very popular amongst Turkish soldiers too, recording how they would publicly chant songs in his praise.[55]

In seeking to promote the status and legitimacy of his community, 'Abd al-Jalil doubtless at times over-eggs the cake: his work is, after all, explicitly a response to a polemic. Nizam al-Mulk may well have honoured leading sayyids as they were often leading figures in local politics, and Sibt cites a poem in the vizier's praise by an 'Alid author;[56] but this need not imply any sympathy with Shi'ism. In this period, Sunnis too venerated the family of 'Ali.[57] The great shrine of the martyred eighth imam, 'Ali al-Rida, at Mashhad in Khurasan, today one of the great pilgrimage spots for Shi'ites, was patronised in the early

[52] Gleave, 'Shi'i Jurisprudence', 205–6.

[53] 'Abd al-Jalil al-Husayn b. Abi'l-Fadl al-Qazwini al-Razi, *Kitab al-Naqd ma'ruf bih ba'd mathalib al-nawasib fi naqd ba'd fada'ih al-rawafid*, ed. Jalal al-Din Urmawi (Tehran, 1331), 108 ff. (the second edition of this text (Tehran 1378), which is apparently to be preferred, was unavailable to me); Calmard, 'Le chiisme imamite', 56; see also the detailed summary in Yavari, 'Nizam al-Mulk remembered', 147–54, 174–6.

[54] Calmard, 'Le chiisme imamite', 58–9, 61–3; Bausani, 'Religion', 292; Yavari, 'Nizam al-Mulk Remembered', 150–1, 163.

[55] Razi, *Kitab al-Naqd*, 77; Madelung, 'The Spread of Maturdidism', 120–1; cf. Rawandi, *Rahat al-Sudur*, 30, on Shi'ites in the Seljuk military. No such songs have come down to us, although a taste of their content is offered by a Persian epic composed in 482/1089, which recounts 'Ali's battles: *'Ali-nama (Manzuma-yi Kuhan)*, eds Rida Bayat and Abu 'l-Fadl Ghulami (Tehran, 2010).

[56] Sibt, *Mir'at*, ed. Ghamidi, 178. The poem is attributed to Abu Talib 'Ali b. al-Hasan al-'Alawi.

[57] See Kazuo Morimoto, 'Putting the *Lubāb al-ansāb* in Context: *Sayyids* and *Naqībs* in late Saljuq Khurasan', *Studia Iranica*, 36 (2007), 179–81. Further on sayyids, see Aubin, 'L'aristocratie urbaine', 326–7.

eleventh century by that staunch anti-Shiʿite, Mahmud of Ghazna, and several senior Ghaznavid officials. With the Seljuk takeover, this elite patronage continued.[58] When heading east to fight his brother Tekish, Malikshah went in person to pray there in the company of his vizier and afterwards made presents to the local ʿAlids.[59] The shrine near Balkh in Khurasan, today known as Mazar-i Sharif and reputed to contain the tomb of ʿAli b. Abi Talib, was 'rediscovered' in 530/1135–6 and restored by the Seljuk governor of Balkh, Qumaj.[60]

The material evidence of architecture and its inscriptions does, however, allow us to confirm some elements of ʿAbd al-Jalil's evidence for the high status of at least some Shiʿites, and the public acceptance of Shiʿite practices under Seljuk rule. Especially striking is the minaret built by Tutush in Aleppo, which even bears inscriptions with a Shiʿite flavour, commemorating ʿAli and the Twelve Imams (Figure 7.4).[61] Evidently, this was an attempt to reconcile the Shiʿite populace of Aleppo to the new regime, to gainsay rumours of the Seljuks' sectarian prejudice like those propagated by Mahmud b. Nasr. Even in predominantly Sunni areas, Shiʿites were free to express their faith in the most public terms. Just outside the royal city (*dār al-mulk*) of Hamadhan, in the late twelfth century a member of the vastly wealthy Shiʿite ʿAlawiyan family – who had close connections to the Seljuk dynasty and were patrons of Rawandi – built beside his ancestors' graves a monumental cenotaph which is one of the masterpieces of Islamic architecture of the period (Figure 7.5(a) and (b)). As Raya Shani has demonstrated, the mausoleum's decorative programme and inscriptions publicly proclaims the ʿAlawiyan's Shiʿite beliefs.[62]

The ʿAlawiyan were not exceptional: members of the Shiʿite elite frequently occupied senior positions in the state. The vizier Anushirwan b.

[58] See May Farhat, 'Islamic Piety and Dynastic Legitimacy: The Case of the Shrine of ʿAli b. Musa al-Rida in Mashhad (10th—17th centuries)', PhD dissertation, Harvard University, 2002, 39–53.

[59] Ibn al-Athir, *al-Kamil*, X, 211; Sibt, *Mir'at*, ed. Ghamidi, 184.

[60] R. D. McChesney, *Waqf in Central Asia: Four Hundred Years in the History of a Muslim Shrine, 1480–1889* (Princeton, 1991), 27–8. The most detailed consideration of the Seljuk architectural and epigraphic contribution to the shrine is Lisa Golombek, 'Mazar-i Sharif: A Case of Mistaken Identity', in Myriam Rosen-Ayalon (ed.), *Studies in Memory of Gaston Wiet* (Jerusalem, 1977), 335–43.

[61] See Bloom, *Minaret*, 163–5.

[62] Raya Shani, *A Monumental Manifestation of the Shiite Faith in Late Twelfth Century Iran: The Case of the Gunbad-i 'Alawiyān, Hamadān* (Oxford, 1996), 119–30, 149–56; Rawandi, *Rahat al-Sudur*, 45. Further on the family, see Fragner, *Geschichte der Stadt Hamadān*, 114–15, 123–4, 128–30, 135–6, 175–7. Shani convincingly argues that the patron was Fakhr al-Din ʿAla al-Dawla ʿArabshah, *ra'īs* of the city (d. 584/1188).

Figure 7.4 The minaret of Tutush attached to the Great Mosque of Aleppo, Syria, destroyed in fighting in 2013. Image © Bryn Mawr College

Figure 7.5(a) The Gunbad-i 'Alawiyan, Hamadhan, Iran, twelfth century: exterior (photograph: Raya Shani, previously published in *A Monumental Manifestation of the Shi'ite Faith*, fig. 5, reproduced by kind permission of the author)

Figure 7.5(b) The Gunbad-i 'Alawiyan, Hamadhan, Iran, twelfth-century interior, mihrab (photograph: Raya Shani, previously published in *A Monumental Manifestation of the Shi'ite Faith*, fig. 95, reproduced by kind permission of the author)

Khalid, for instance, is said to have been quite open in his espousal of *tashayyu*ʿ (Shiʿism), and was buried next to ʿAli b. Abi Talib's tomb.[63] There was a dynasty of Shiʿite bureaucrats from Kashan: Mukhtass al-Mulk was one of Sanjar's viziers, and his son Fakhr al-Mulk held the same position for the short-lived Sulaymanshah (1160–1), as did his grandson for Tughrıl III.[64] The lost polemicist to whom ʿAbd al-Jalil claims to be responding is said to have written, 'now there is no palace of the Turks that has not at least ten or fifteen Imamis (Rawafid), and many of them are employed as secretaries in the *dīwāns*'.[65] A pro-Shiʿite author of the twelfth century celebrated the spread of Imami Shiʿism in exaggerated terms:

> In Iraq, praise God, it has found a ready market; in the Hijaz it is established and permitted; it has become a characteristic of the people of Syria, and its rainclouds have inundated them . . . There is no one left in Khurasan who has a hand and tongue or a sword and spear [i.e., both *kātibs* and *ʿaskar*] who does not have Shiism as his custom and his faith.[66]

The evidence of these Shiʿite sources is in fact supported by some Sunni writers. The Hanbali masses of Baghdad, who frequently rioted and fought with Shiʿites who lived predominantly in the Karkh quarter of the city, regarded the Seljuk authorities as positively pro-Shiʿite. Ibn al-Jawzi relates during one such *fitna* that:

> Whisperings against the authorities multiplied, and the masses [*ʿawāmm*] said, 'Religion is destroyed, the *sunna* is dead, heresy [*bidʿa*] has been put [in its place] and we think that God only helps the Rafidites [Shiʿites], so we apostatise from Islam.' [The Hanbali scholar] Ibn ʿAqil said, 'I went out to the mosque and said, "I heard that Muslims and Sunnis have got angry at God and abandoned his shariʿa, and have decided to apostatise . . . have you ever seen the like of what happens to Sunnis in this state? There is no religion except for the religion of the people of Karkh [i.e., Shiʿism] (*lā dīn illā dīn ahl al-Karkh*)!"'[67]

In fact, the Seljuk authorities seem to have striven to maintain a balance between the parties.[68] For instance, in 479/1086, there were two

[63] Ibn al-Jawzi, *al-Muntazam*, XVII, 334; however, Ibn al-Athir, *al-Kamil*, X, 156, has him buried next to Husayn's tomb in Karbala'.

[64] Calmard, 'Le chiisme imamite', 58–9.

[65] Razi, *Kitab al-Naqd*, 53–4; Bausani, 'Religion', 292.

[66] Ibn Isfandiyar, *Tarikh-i Tabaristan*, I, 116.

[67] Ibn al-Jawzi, *al-Muntazam*, XVI, 283.

[68] Cf. the comments of Erika Glassen on the policy of 'tolerance' she identifies with Nizam al-Mulk: *Der mittlere Weg*, 77–8, 125–6.

fitnas, in Muharram and Shawwal. In the first, the Seljuk governor [*'amīd*], Kamal al-Mulk al-Dihistani, intervened on the side of the Karkhi (i.e., Shi'ite) party, but in the second he acted against them.[69] Nonetheless, the Karkhis still seem to have seen Kamal al-Mulk as a potential ally, and when fitna erupted again in 482/1089 with a Hanbali attack on Karkh, the Karkhis sought the *'amīd'*s aid.[70] The Karkhis' pro-Seljuk sentiments were unambiguously demonstrated when Sultan Malikshah's son and heir, Ahmad, died in 481/1088. 'The women [of Baghdad] went out to lament in the markets, and many people gathered to grieve and lament, and the people of Karkh draped their entrance portals in black to show their grief for him.'[71] This is not the act of a people who feel they are living under a hostile government.

What, however, of the golden age of Tughrıl and Alp Arslan to which Nizam al-Mulk alludes and after which the Sunni polemicist too seems to have hankered? True, the highest echelons of the bureaucracy were occupied by Sunnis, Kunduri and Nizam al-Mulk. However, Tughrıl's occupation of Baghdad seems to have been welcomed by the Imami population of Karkh,[72] perhaps inspired by the long-standing Imami belief that the Turks were the soldiers of the *mahdī*, the saviour at the end of time.[73] Kunduri even intervened to stop the Hanbalis from daubing Karkh with Sunni slogans at the instigation of the fanatical Hanbali caliphal vizier, Ibn Muslima.[74] The attacks on the prominent Imami scholar Abu Ja'far al-Tusi also seem to have been orchestrated by the Hanbali masses of Baghdad, not the Seljuk officials, and the new Shi'ite centre of Najaf appears to have been allowed to flourish unmolested. Shi'ite jurisprudence continued to develop under Seljuk rule,[75] and the Seljuks were perfectly happy to allow Shi'ite dynasties like the Mazyadids of Hilla to remain in place as vassals.

The reign of Muhammad Tapar may represent something of an exception to this trend. The *Kitab al-Naqd* tells us that under this sultan Shi'ite *kātibs* had to get certificates confirming their adherence to the Hanafi faith, although such documents were evidently readily procured for cash.[76] Further testimony to these sentiments is suggested by the Friday mosque at

[69] Ibn al-Athir, *al-Kamil*, X, 157.
[70] *Ibid.*, X, 170.
[71] *Ibid.*, X, 169.
[72] *Ibid.*, IX, 611; Peacock, *Early Seljūq History*, 120.
[73] Calmard, 'Le chiisme imamite', 66 ff.
[74] Ibn al-Jawzi, *al-Muntazam*, XVI, 6; Peacock, *Early Seljūq History*, 120.
[75] Gleave, 'Shii Jurisprudence'.
[76] Qazwini Razi, *Kitab al-Naqd*, 81.

Gulpayigan in western Iran, which was built during Muhammad's reign and is decorated with inscriptions condemning Shiʿism.[77] Yet there is nothing to connect them directly with any state policy: all the evidence indicates that, as was probably usually the case, the mosque was commissioned by a private individual, likely a local dignitary. Perhaps its epigraphic programme was intended to echo what was perceived to be the attitude of Sultan Muhammad; but it may equally reflect entirely the agenda of one individual, or at least one town. Indeed, the very existence of such anti-Shiʿite slogans might be testimony to the growing popularity of Shiʿism in the period.[78]

Muhammad's reign may be an aberration, for it seems that while on a popular level there was plenty of anti-Shiʿite prejudice, it did not generally feed into Seljuk policy, despite the widely repeated allegation that 'being a Shiʿite is on the way to being a heretic' (*rāfiḍīyī dihliz-i mulḥidīst*).[79] The Seljuk attitude towards Ismailism, often designated as a heresy (*ilḥād*), was more complex. At the time of the Basasiri episode, Ismailism was linked to a foreign power, the Fatimids, but from the late eleventh century Ismailis in the Seljuk lands (both Syria and Iran) followed the new, break-away Nizari variant of the faith propagated by Hasan-i Sabbah and Ibn ʿAttash (see above pp. 85–8). The Seljuks in response seem to have changed their attitude. The chief Ismaili *dāʿī*, ʿAbd al-Malik b. ʿAttash, had been forced to repudiate the faith after being threatened by Tughrıl with execution, but under Malikshah the *daʿwa* was able to attract an ever greater number of adherents.[80] One source describes how in Malikshah's reign, Ismailism was revived in Isfahan (*madhhab-i Bāṭiniān bi-Iṣfahān tāza karda būdand*), 'and [the Ismailis] made their mission in every place, became powerful and seized strong castles'.[81] Ismailism started to spread among men of modest means working in the bazaar like carpenters, in addition to the educated elite whom Ismailism had always targeted.[82]

While the later chronicles may praise the Seljuks for their role in suppressing what Sunnis agreed was an appalling heresy, contemporaries may not have seen it that way. As noted above (pp. 86–7), most of the running in the struggle against Ismailism in the Isfahan region was made by local

[77] Lorenz Korn, 'Ein Denkmal seldschukischer Religionspolitik? Inschriften der grossen Moschee von Gulpayigan', in Hinrich Biesterfeld and Verena Klemm (eds), *Differenz und Dinamik in Islam: Festschrift fur Heinz Halm zum 70 Geburtstag* (Wurzburg, 2012), 455–71. Further on anti-Shiʿite inscriptions in mosques, see Qazwini Razi, *Kitab al-Naqd*, 110.

[78] Cf. Korn, 'Ein Denkmal', 468.

[79] Qazwini Razi, *Kitab al-Naqd*, 84, 85.

[80] Ibn al-Jawzi, *al-Muntazam*, XVII, 102.

[81] *Mujmal al-Tawarikh wa'l-Qisas*, 408.

[82] Durand-Guédy, *Iranian Elites*, 146–7.

elites, not the Seljuk sultans. It is significant, too, that despite his close links to the highest officials of the Seljuk state, al-Ghazali chose to dedicate his anti-Ismaili treatise, the *Fada'ih al-Batiniyya*, to Caliph al-Mustazhir, not to any Seljuk vizier or sultan. Indeed, contemporary praise for the Seljuks in the fight was distinctly lacking, and Sanjar, in a letter to Caliph al-Mustarshid, felt oblige specifically to deny accusations that he was lax in fighting heretics (*mulḥidān*).[83]

Nonetheless, the accusation of being a 'Batini' or Ismaili was evidently a damaging one, given the frequency with which it was used to besmirch enemies.[84] Predictably, for instance, 'Imad al-Din al-Isfahani accuses his family's enemy Abu 'l-Qasim al-Darguzini of 'Batinism'[85] – something which seems unlikely in view of Darguzini's well-attested patronage of the conservative and conventionally Sunni poet and mystic Sana'i (d. 529/1131).[86] Sometimes, however, just like hysteria over communist moles in the upper echelons of twentieth-century British public life, the rumours were entirely justified. Contemporaries, for instance, voiced doubts about the Ash'ari theologian and confidant of Sanjar, al-Shahrastani (d. 548/1153), who was accused of having converted to Ismailism.[87] Close analysis of his Qur'anic commentary, the *Mafatih al-asrar*, which is suffused with Ismaili influences, suggests that at the very least he was a fellow traveller, and more likely was indeed a fully-fledged member of the movement.[88]

The Law Schools and Factionalism

In Iran and Central Asia, the predominant madhhabs were the Shafi'is and the Hanafis, while in Iraq the contest tended to be largely between Hanbalis and Shi'ites, and to a lesser extent between Hanbalis and Shafi'is. Hanafism, traditionally pre-eminent in Transoxiana, was the madhhab of the Seljuk family.[89] It allowed a considerable latitude for the exercise of the ruler's power, although its lax definition of who might be considered a

83 Bartol'd, *Turkestan v Epokhu Mongolskogo Nashetsviya. Chast' 1: Teksty*, 37.
84 See Hodgson, *Secret Order*, 121–2, for an example.
85 Bundari, *Zubda*, 144, 145, 146.
86 Qummi, *Dhayl-i Nafthat al-Masdur*, 42–3.
87 Daftary, *The Isma'ilis*, 136–7.
88 Al-Shahrastani, Muhammad b. 'Abd al-Karim, *Mafatih al-asrar wa masabih al-abrar*, ed. and trans. Toby Mayer as *Keys to the Arcana: Shahrastānī's Esoteric Commentary on the Qur'an* (Oxford, 2009); see, in particular, the discussion of these issues in the introduction at pp. 3–19, and esp. pp. 7, 15 for his Ismailism.
89 On Hanafism and Shafiism in Iran, see Madelung, *Religious Trends*, 26–38.

Muslim – no knowledge of the Qur'an or even the religious duties of Islam was required – also had certain attractions for recently converted Turks with perhaps only shaky grasp on their new faith.[90]

Law schools were often associated with certain theological positions (and Hanbalism was in fact both a legal and a theological school). Hanafis generally tended towards Maturidi theology,[91] while Shafiʿism was closely associated with the Ashʿari theological school. The theological schools were also fierce rivals: Ashʿarism claimed to represent the theology of all right-thinking Muslims, a claim vigorously disputed by Hanbalis who felt a particular antipathy towards the Ashʿaris. The stronghold of Hanbalism was Baghdad, where it was backed by the caliphs up until al-Nasir li-Din Allah.

The differences between the madhhabs derived from disputes over the processes to be observed when reaching a legal decision (*fatwā*).[92] However, there was plenty of scope for disagreement among jurists of one school, and men might move from one madhhab to another: the famous eleventh-century Baghdadi scholar Ibn ʿAqil came from a Hanafi family and seems to have started his studies in that madhhab before becoming a Hanbali.[93] Adherence to a certain madhhab did not in principle require adherence to a given theology (except in the case of Hanbalism).

The discrepancy between the actual differences between the madhhabs and the passions aroused in their name has suggested to several scholars that there must be more to these disputes than the minutiae of legal procedures. Richard Bulliet's classic study of Nishapur argues that the denominations of Hanafi and Shafiʿi essentially stand for two different political groups competing for power and positions. Bulliet sees the Hanafis of Nishapur as the aristocratic and conservative party, while the Shafiʿis were more open to new trends in Islam, such the growing interest in Sufism. Both were patrician groups: although both probably also drew support from lower social classes, the rivalry between them aimed ultimately at political control of Nishapur.[94] A similar pattern has been identified in Isfahan.[95]

90 Madelung, 'The Spread of Maturidism', 122–3.
91 See *ibid.*, 117–19.
92 Lange, *Justice*, 203.
93 Makdisi, *Ibn ʿAqīl*, 387–8.
94 Bulliet, *Patricians of Nishapur*, 38–9; see also Bulliet, 'Political–Religious History', 73.
95 Durand-Guédy, *Iranian Elites*, 197–204.

Seljuk Hanafism and Policy Towards other the Madhhabs

The Seljuk household and the Turkish elite are often said to have been 'militant' supporters of Hanafism.[96] Some evidence does suggest that the Seljuks attempted to promote Hanafism at the expense of other madhhabs. Under Tughrıl, Isfahan, Rayy, Hamadhan and, after some delay, Nishapur, all had Hanafi qadis installed despite the Shafiʿis being much more numerous. The story was the same slightly later in Jerusalem and Damascus, despite the fact that Hanafism barely existed in Syria as a law school.[97] Sometimes, these imported Hanafis were intent on stirring up sectarian prejudice, with al-Balasaghuni, the Seljuk qadi of Damascus, declaring that Shafiʿis were infidels and should pay the jizya, the poll tax reserved for non-Muslims.[98]

On two occasions, Seljuk policies resulted in what the victims described by the emotive term *miḥna* ('trial' or 'persecution'), evoking the famous inquisition of Caliph al-Ma'mun in the early ninth century. The first of these took place in Nishapur in 445/1053, and temporarily allowed the Hanafi party to gain control of important political positions such as the office of *raʾīs*. Here the target was ostensibly the Ashʿaris, although the *miḥna* is widely regarded by mediaeval and modern sources as a pretext for excluding any but Hanafis from high office. Even the persecution's instigator, Kunduri, seems to have later given up his fanaticism, while the accession of the supposedly vehemently anti-Shafiʿi Alp Arslan in fact allowed the Shafiʿis to regain much of their earlier position in Nishapur.[99]

It was not for another ninety years that a second anti-Ashʿari *miḥna* occurred. After Sanjar ceded Rayy to Masʿud in 537/1142–3 in the wake of his defeat by the Qarakhitay, the western sultan entered the city and forced its leading Shafiʿis to disavow Ashʿarism publicly. At the instigation of Hanafi *ʿulamāʾ*, Masʿud took further measures against Ashʿaris in Baghdad and Isfahan over the next three years.[100] Isfahani notes that as a result, 'a group joined the madhhab of Abu Hanifa, seeking personal advancement and out of fear, not because of God [i.e., belief]'.[101]

[96] Madelung, 'The Spread of Maturidism', 124–9, esp. 126.

[97] *Ibid.*, 127–8. See also for Isfahan, Rayy and Hamadhan, Durand-Guédy, *Iranian Elites*, 106; for Nishapur, Bulliet, *Patricians of Nishapur*, 72; for Syria, Mouton, *Damas et sa principauté*, 126–7, 330–2, 354.

[98] Madelung, 'The Spread of Maturidism', 147; Mouton, *Damas et sa principauté*, 127.

[99] Madelung, 'The Spread of Maturdism', 131; Bulliet, *Patricians of Nishapur*, 67, 210–11; Bulliet, 'Political–Religious History'; Heinz Halm, 'Der Wesir al-Kundurī und die Fitna von Nišapur', *Die Welt des Orients*, 6/ii (1971), 205–33; Peacock, *Early Seljūq History*, 109–18.

[100] Madelung, 'The Spread of Maturidism', 131–6.

[101] Bundari, *Zubda*, 194.

Neither *miḥna* is easily explained, for they both seem to have been highly localised and short-lived. They are best understood not as a reflection of Hanafi prejudice on the part of the Seljuks, but in terms of local politics. It is perhaps significant that in both cases the *miḥna* was instituted in cities that had an ambiguous frontier status between different parts of the Seljuk realm: Nishapur, as we have seen (pp. 41, 127), was suspended awkwardly between the domains of Chaghrı and Tughrıl, while Rayy had been Sanjar's westernmost outpost, ceded only reluctantly to his nephew as a result of his deteriorating position in Khurasan. *Miḥnas* perhaps represented a convenient excuse for replacing local elites whose loyalties might lie with rival Seljuk rulers.

Plenty of evidence contradicts the description of Seljuk Hanafism as 'militant'. On the death of the famous Shafi'i jurist Abu Tahir 'Abd al-Rahman b. 'Alak in 484/1091, his funeral was attended by the leading men of the Seljuk state (*arbāb al-dawla al-saljuqiyya*) and his grave was visited by Sultan Malikshah in person.[102] Indeed, this same 'Abd al-Rahman, weary of Qarakhanid misgovernance, had been instrumental in persuading Malikshah to conquer his home town of Samarqand.[103] For this Shafi'i at any rate, the Seljuks' adherence to Hanafism did not present any obstacle to forming a close alliance. We may also question whether Hanafi prejudice lay behind the installation of a new Hanafi religious hierarchy, which seems to fit rather awkwardly with the general Seljuk principle of governance by *istimālat* (outlined on p. 190). The first Seljuk qadi of Damascus, 'Abd al-Jalil al-Marwazi, was in fact a Shafi'i.[104] As his name suggests, however, he was a native of Merv, and his appointment may reflect the desire to install a Khurasani elite in religious positions just as was done in the bureaucracy. While Hanafism and Maturidi theology were favoured by the Seljuk dynasty, there is no evidence that their officials were ever compelled to embrace them, excepting the aberrations of the two localised *miḥnas*.

Nor did Hanafism enjoy an unequivocal ascendancy. Institutionally, the greatest madrasa network was that of the Shaf'i Nizamiyyas, and patronage of Hanafi madrasas was never on the same scale, although a well-endowed Hanafi madrasa was also founded in Baghdad by a senior Seljuk official, Abu Sa'd al-Mustawfi, in the same year as the Nizamiyya, 459/1066.[105] Shafi'ism even spread among men from the staunchly Hanafi heartlands of Khurasan,

102 Ibn al-Athir, *al-Kamil*, X, 200.

103 *Ibid.*, X, 171.

104 Mouton, *Damas et sa principauté*, 353.

105 Ibn al-Athir, *al-Kamil*, X, 54. Further on this madrasa, see Makdisi, 'Muslim Institutions of Learning', 19–21.

like the *faqīh* Mansur b. Muhammad b. ʿAbd al-Jabbar, scion of a leading scholarly family of Merv, who went to seek his fortune in Baghdad where he abandoned his Hanafism for Shafiʿism. On his return to Merv, protests from the masses (*ʿawāmm*) at his conversion forced him to flee for the more congenial environment of Nishapur.[106] Nor in local politics were Hanafis uniformly dominant. Even in Isfahan, Hanafis failed to gain much advantage from the Seljuks' Hanafism. The leaders of the twelfth-century Hanafi and Shafiʿi parties in Isfahan were both immigrants from Khurasan who had established themselves in the city in the early days of Seljuk rule, but for most of the twelfth century, the Shafiʿi family of the Khujandis were the predominant local power. It was only with the final collapse of the Seljuk state after 590/1194 that, with Khwarazmian support, the Hanafi Saʿid family was able to achieve dominance. Thus, while the Seljuk period saw the gradual emergence of a Hanafi population in Isfahan, this did not immediately translate into Hanafi political ascendancy.[107]

The Seljuk attitude towards other madhhabs was thus broadly one of toleration, despite the broader atmosphere of tension. Indeed, frequently the sultans' policy seems to have aimed at achieving a balance between the various madhhabs, to avoid a feeling of excessive prejudice to one or another – just as they seem to have done with regard to Sunni–Shiʿite tensions (p. 264 above). As Nizam al-Mulk put it:

> The policy of the sultan and fairness require that we do not incline towards one madhhab more than another. It is more fitting for us to uphold the sunna than to ignite *fitna*. We proceeded with building this madrasa [the Nizamiyya] only with a view to protecting scholars and the public interest, not for disagreement and arguing. When things developed contrary to our wishes in this respect, we had no choice but to close the gate. We do not have the power to overcome Baghdad and its surroundings and to alter forcibly [its people's] established customs, for the majority here belong to the madhhab of the Imam Abu ʿAbdallah Ahmad b. Hanbal.[108]

Malikshah's visit to Baghdad of Dhu 'l-Hijja 479/February 1087, accompanied by Nizam al-Mulk, seems to have been intended to symbolise this policy of 'balance'.[109] Together the sultan and his vizier paid their respects to the shrine of the Imam Musa b. Jaʿfar (al-Kazim), the tomb of the Sufi saint Maʿruf al-Karkhi, and those of Abu Hanifa and Ahmad b. Hanbal. A

106 Ibn al-Jawzi, *al-Muntazam*, XVII, 37.
107 Durand-Guédy, *Iranian Elites*, 230–3, 281–6.
108 Ibn al-Jawzi, *al-Muntazam*, XVII, 190–1; cf. Sibt, *Mir'at*, 186–90.
109 Cf. Glassen, *Der mittlere Weg*.

visit was also made to the tombs of 'Ali b. Abi Talib at Najaf and his son Husayn at Karbala', which were especially (but not exclusively) venerated by the Shi'a.[110] These burial places represented a wide spectrum of Islamic belief in polarised Baghdad, from Shi'ism to Hanbalism, from rationalist Hanafism to mystical Sufism, but dead saints were not spared from factionalism. Even if veneration of the 'Alids was not a purely Shi'ite phenomenon, in Baghdad at any rate it could be highly contentious, and visits to tombs (*ziyāra*) had frequently been a bone of contention between Sunnis and the Shi'a, with the latter's access to the tomb of Musa al-Kazim sometimes blocked by Sunnis.[111] Nizam al-Mulk's and Malikshah's visit to shrines frequented by such bitterly opposed factions surely symbolised something more than pious pilgrimage, but rather was a public expression of the sultan's desire to stand aside from, or above, the sectarian factionalism that tore Baghdad apart.

How can this apparent desire for peace be reconciled with the vehement passions unleashed by the construction of madrasas and the activities carried out within them? The Nizamiyya became the focus of frequent disturbances between Hanbali groups hostile to the Nizamiyya's Shafi'i and Ash'ari teachers.[112] On occasion Nizam al-Mulk seems to have been quite happy to have *fitna* ignited through the Nizamiyya. In 470/1078, a riot was deliberately provoked by a student at the madrasa,[113] while, in 475/1083, another Khurasani Ash'ari, al-Sharif Abu 'l-Qasim al-Bakri, arrived in Baghdad with written permission from the vizier to preach Ash'ari theology in the Nizamiyya, which inevitably provoked further riots. On fleeing the city, al-Bakri took refuge with the sultanic camp. Enraged by this provocation, one Hanbali preacher quoted by Sibt b. al-Jawzi described the Nizamiyya in inflammatory terms: 'This madrasa which al-Tusi – meaning Nizam al-Mulk – has built is a madrasa which corrupts Muslims' religion and it should be knocked down and destroyed.'[114]

Nizam al-Mulk's precise motives for allowing the Nizamiyya to become a hotbed of unrest were doubtless complex, and are not easily understood. There may, however, have been a good dose of realpolitik about them and, as ever, we would do well to take the vizier's statements with a pinch of salt. It is striking

110 Ibn al-Athir, *al-Kamil*, X, 155–6.

111 *Ibid.*, X, 469–70. Equally the Shi'a might attempt to stop the Sunnis' paying their respects at the tomb of Mus'ab b. Zubayr.

112 In general on the Hanbali–Ash'ari clashes in eleventh-century Baghdad, see H. Laoust, 'Les agitations religieuses à Baghdad', in D. S. Richards, *Islamic Civilisation 950–1150* (Oxford, 1973), 178–85; also Sabari, *Mouvements populaires à Bagdad, passim*.

113 Ibn al-Athir, *al-Kamil*, X, 107; Makdisi, *Ibn 'Aqil*, 366–71.

114 Sibt, *Mir'at*, 217–18; Ibn al-Athir, *al-Kamil*, X, 124–5; Makdisi, *Ibn 'Aqil*, 371–5.

that the Hanbali–Ash'ari clashes seem to have been confined to Baghdad, especially given that Isfahan itself was home to substantial Shafi'i and Hanbali communities. Yet Isfahan remained free of intercommunal strife involving Hanbalis, and the director of the Isfahan Nizamiyya is never associated with Ash'arism, nor is there any evidence that Ash'ari teaching was permitted there, despite a vibrant Isfahani tradition of Ash'arism.[115] This suggests that when authorising preachers like Abu Nasr al-Qushayri and Abu 'l-Qasim al-Bakri, Nizam al-Mulk's aim was not necessarily merely to promote Ash'arism or to curry favour with Ash'aris in Khurasan, otherwise we would expect to find them preaching in Isfahan too, but rather was specific to Baghdad.

The timing of the main disturbances seems far from coincidental. The riot of 470/1078 was used as an excuse by Nizam al-Mulk to demand the dismissal of the caliphal vizier Fakhr al-Dawla b. Jahir,[116] with whom he had a history of poor relations, and for whose sacking he seems to have been angling for some time.[117] The events of 475/1083 also happened at a crucial moment, in the middle of negotiations between Nizam al-Mulk (for the Seljuks) and Fakhr al-Dawla (for the caliph) over the marriage of Malikshah's daughter to Caliph al-Muqtadi, with the Seljuk side placing onerous demands on the caliph in return for assenting to the marriage – demands to which the caliph did indeed finally agree.[118] The intercommunal riots which the Nizamiyya provoked may have played a part in allowing the Seljuks to intervene, to assert their authority in fractious Baghdad and to pressurise the caliph. In Isfahan, meanwhile, which under Malikshah had become something like a true capital for the empire, Nizam al-Mulk's interest and that of his master was in preserving stability, so Ash'aris were kept away from the Nizamiyya.

The *Ahl al-Dhimma* under Seljuk Rule

Apart from Muslims, the Seljuk domains contained Christians, Jews, some dwindling numbers of Zoroastrians and, in a few areas, small numbers of related ancient Iranian faiths, such as the neo-Mazdakite Khuramdiniyya and the followers of Muqanna'.[119] The fate of Zoroastrians in the period is

115 Durand-Guédy, *Iranian Elites*, 140–1.

116 Ibn al-Athir, *al-Kamil*, X, 109–11.

117 See Sibt, *Mir'at*, 168, 169, 170, 191: relations between Nizam al-Mulk and the caliphal household had deteriorated in 466, when Nizam al-Mulk had allocated some of Caliph al-Qa'im's estates to the Ghuzz; his relations with Fakhr al-Dawla were poor too, and Nizam al-Mulk seems to have been intent on his downfall at least from 467.

118 See Hanne, 'The Banū Jahīr', 40 and p. 179 above.

119 See Crone, *Nativist Prophets*, 178–88. However, in at least some instances these references to Mazdakism are doubtless a means of discrediting opponents, just like accusations of

almost entirely unknown, beyond the presumption that their numbers were in acute decline, especially from the eleventh century.[120] The discussion here will therefore focus on the 'protected people', or *ahl al-dhimma*, the Jews and Christians suffered by Islamic law to live under Muslim rule subject to discrimination such as the payment of the poll tax, sumptuary laws defining which clothes they should wear to distinguish them from Muslims, and restrictions on the building or restoration of their places of worship.

In plenty of individual areas within the Seljuk domains *dhimmīs* probably formed a majority. Although nowhere do we have statistics for confessional allegiances in this period, Christians were a substantial element in the populations of Syria (especially the north), the Jazira and Iraq.[121] Yet the activities of non-Muslims are only of interest to most of our Muslim sources when they come into contact with the Muslim authorities, the caliph or the sultan. We know much less about non-Muslims in the Seljuk realm than we do in the case of its great contemporary the Fatimid Empire, where Christians and Jews seem to have been more politically prominent; but in addition, the chance survival of a great Jewish archive, the Geniza from old Cairo, gives an unparalleled view of the day-to-day workings of a *dhimmī* community. We have no such source from the Muslim east, and as a result, the existence of *dhimmīs* is under-represented both in most sources and in the scholarly literature. Nonetheless, some Christian and Jewish sources help fill out the picture.

The Jews of the Seljuk Empire

Although Baghdad had been the centre of the Jewish community worldwide, by the twelfth century its position had been eclipsed by Egypt, headed by the famous scholar Maimonides. However, Jews from far-flung parts of the Muslim world such as Yemen continued to consult the Baghdadi leaders of the community on matters of doctrine.[122] We have two contemporary sources

Ismailism. 'Imad al-Din, for instance, accuses the population of Darguzin of Mazdakism (Bundari, *Zubda*, 124), which is, as so often, doubtless more an expression of his hatred for the Darguzini clan than a true reflection of the religious make-up of the area. From this source, the allegation found its way into Yaqut's *Mu'jam al-Buldan*, II, 451, s.v. 'Darkazīn'.

120 See Choksy, *Conflict and Cooperation*, 91–3, 95, 99, 107–9.

121 For Syria, see Nehemia Levtzion, 'Conversion to Islam in Syria and Palestine and the Survival of Christian Communities', in Michael Gervers and Ramzi Jibran Bikhazi, *Conversion and Continuity: Indigenous Christian Communities in Islamic Lands, Eighth to Eighteenth Centuries* (Toronto, 1990), 289–311. An overview of the situation in Seljuk Baghdad is provided by Makdisi, *Ibn 'Aqil*, 143–62.

122 On the struggle for supremacy between the Baghdad and Cairo Jewish leaders, see Sarah Stroumsa, *Maimonides in his World: A Portrait of a Mediterranean Thinker* (Princeton, 2009), 168–71.

for the Jewish community in the Seljuk realm: Rabbi Benjamin of Tudela, a Jewish traveller of the second half of the twelfth century; and Samaw'al al-Maghribi, a Jewish convert to Islam who lived in roughly the same period. Superficially, Benjamin's picture is very positive. Baghdad had 40,000 Jews who 'dwell in security, prosperity and honour under the great Caliph'. At their head was the hereditary Exilarch (known in Arabic as the Ra's al-Jalut), vested by the caliph with authority over all Jews in the east, from Yemen to China, of whom Benjamin claims that:

> every fifth day when he goes to pay a visit to the great Caliph, horsemen, Gentiles as well as Jews, escort him, and heralds proclaim in advance, 'Make way before our lord, the son of David, as is due unto him.'[123]

Like the Exilarch, the Baghdadi Jews are described as rich, respected and learned, and the community had twenty-eight synagogues. Benjamin also mentions large communities of Jews in other towns in Iran and Iraq: 10,000 in Hilla; 7,000 in Kufa; 3,000 in al-Anbar; 7,000 in Susa in Khuzistan; and 30,000 in Hamadhan, home to the tomb of Esther, a traditional Jewish place of pilgrimage.[124] The head of the Iranian Jews subject to the Exilarch was based in Isfahan, Rabbi Shar Shalom, and Isfahan and Shiraz also are alleged to have had large Jewish populations of 15,000 and 10,000, respectively. Further east, the numbers become quite incredible, with 80,000 Jews said to reside in Ghazna and another 50,000 in Samarqand.

Intriguing is Benjamin's strange account of the Jews of Khurasan, whom he claims

> are not under the rule of the gentiles, but are subject to a prince of their own, whose name is R[abbi] Joseph Amarkala the Levite. There are scholars among them . . . They are in league with the Kofar-al-Turak [Arabic *kuffār al-Turk*, Turkish infidels], who worship the wind and live in the wilderness, and who do not eat bread, nor drink wine, but live on raw, uncooked meat . . . They eat animals both clean and unclean, and they are very friendly towards the Israelites.[125]

Benjamin's account has some obviously legendary elements, such as the claim that the Turks have no noses. But it does have some historical

[123] *The Itinerary of Benjamin of Tudela*, 99–100. On the Exilarch, see further Moshe Gil, 'The Exilarch', in Daniel H. Frank (ed.), *The Jews of Medieval Islam: Community, Society and Identity* (Leiden, 1995), 33–66.

[124] *The Itinerary of Benjamin of Tudela*, 102–6, 108, 113.

[125] *Ibid.*, 115. For more details on the Jews in the Seljuk realm, see Moshe Gil, *Jews in the Islamic Countries in the Middle Ages*, trans. David Strassler (Leiden, 2004), 491–532.

foundation: these Turks are the Ghuzz, and Benjamin describes how 'fifteen years ago' they 'overran the country of Persia with a large army and took the city of Rayy'. This is evidently a reference to the great Ghuzz rebellion at the end of Sanjar's reign. Benjamin describes how the independent Jewish principality in Khurasan attempted to propitiate Sanjar while aiding their Ghuzz allies.[126] No other source that has survived refers to this alliance, nor to the existence of a Jewish principality in Khurasan. However, given the highly decentralised nature of Seljuk administration and the evidently historical nature of the remarks about the Ghuzz, it is quite possible that there is some truth to the idea of Jewish community with a strong degree of self-government. The mountainous region of Ghur, to the east of Herat, was home to a large Jewish population in the twelfth century, but there were also substantial Jewish communities in Balkh, Nishapur and Ghazna.[127]

As some of the evidently incredible and legendary elements suggest, Benjamin's account cannot thus be taken at face value. Another Jewish traveller, Rabbi Petahya of Regensburg, travelled through some of the same lands a few years after Benjamin, and he records only 1,000 Jews in Baghdad – a much more credible figure.[128] It seems likely that, as in Egypt, Iraqi and Iranian Jews made up perhaps under 1 per cent of the population, although the proportion in major cities such as Baghdad was probably much larger, perhaps say 10 per cent.[129] Nonetheless, Petahya does back up the main elements of Benjamin's account. From the perspective of a visitor from the west, the Jews under Seljuk rule formed what seemed to be a remarkably prosperous and respected community.

This positive presentation of Jews under the Seljuks is undercut by Benjamin's narrative of the rebellion of the Jewish self-proclaimed messiah, David Alroy. David had studied in Baghdad and was 'well versed in the Law of Israel, in the Halachah, as well as in the Talmud, and in all the

[126] *The Itinerary of Benjamin of Tudela*, 115–17. The dating of Benjamin's report is problematic; this date should indicate that he visited around 1170, but his references to the Seljuk sultans in Baghdad suggest that he is drawing on information ante-dating the Seljuk collapse in 1152–7, perhaps from the 1130s or 1140s.

[127] See Gil, *Jews in the Islamic Countries*, 530–1.

[128] Petahya of Regensburg, trans. in Elkan Nathan Adler (ed. and trans.), *Jewish Travellers in the Middle Ages: Nineteen First Hand Accounts* (New York, [1930] 1987), 64–91. See the discussion in Arnold E. Franklin, *This Noble House: Jewish Descendants of King David in the Medieval Islamic East* (Philadelphia, 2013), 1–7.

[129] No reliable statistical information exists for the Seljuk lands, and these figures represent guesses on analogy with the better known situation in Egypt, where the figures are still far from certain. See Franklin, *This Noble House*, 32; Gil, *Jews in the Islamic Countries*, 491.

Figure 7.6 Amadia, Iraqi Kurdistan, the base of David Alroy's Messianic revolt against the Seljuks

wisdom of the Mohammedans',[130] and from Amadia (Figure 7.6), a remote fortress-town in the mountains north of Mosul,[131] he had proclaimed himself king of the Jews, and urged his co-religionists to rebel against the Seljuk sultan, and march to liberate Jerusalem. The plot seems to have seriously alarmed the Seljuk sultan, if Benjamin is to be believed, and he threatened the Exilarch that he would 'slay all the Jews in his Empire'.[132] The Exilarch desperately pleaded with David to cease from his messianic claims for 'the time of redemption is not yet arrived'; he refused, but was betrayed and murdered by his own father-in-law who had been bribed. The Jewish community had to pay a further indemnity to dissuade the sultan from the campaign he had embarked on against the Jews of the Amadia mountains.

None of this is related by Muslim sources; indeed, it seems impossible to find the slightest allusion in the Arabic and Persian chronicles to what Benjamin portrays as a major crisis not just for the Jews, but also for the

130 *Itinerary of Benjamin of Tudela*, 111.
131 On Amadia, see Ibn al-Athir, *al-Ta'rikh al-Bahir*, 64.
132 *Itinerary of Benjamin of Tudela*, 112.

Seljuks. It would be tempting to dismiss the story as fantasy, were it not for an Arabic work by the Jewish convert to Islam, Samaw'al al-Maghribi, an anti-Jewish polemic called the *Ifham al-Yahud* ('Silencing of the Jews'). In addition to theological arguments, he denounces the Jews' tendency to 'accept the absurd and believe the impossible', of which the main example he adduces is the rebellion of 'an impostor [who] arose in the region of Mosul, a young Jew named Menahem b. Sulayman and known as Ibn ar-Rūḥī'.[133] Evidently, this is David Alroy: he made Amadia his base, and declared that he would 'free the Jews from the hands of the Muslims'. Despite the impostor's death (at the hands of the governor of Amadia in this account), Samaw'al recounts that Jewish communities of Khuy, Maragha, Tabriz and especially Amadia continued to believe in him as their messiah. Even the Jews of Baghdad, portrayed by Benjamin a few years later as so prosperous and stable, were taken in by false messages from the would-be messiah claiming that he would fly them to Jerusalem:

> The Jews of Baghdad, their claim to sagacity and pride in craftiness notwithstanding, were all led to believe it. Their women brought their moneys and jewels in order that it all might be distributed, on their behalf, as charity to those whom the two elders considered deserving. In this manner the Jews spent the bulk of their wealth. They donned green garments, and on that night gathered on the roofs expecting, they asserted, to fly to Jerusalem on the wings of angels. Women began to weep over their nursing infants. What if the mothers should fly before their children or the children before their mothers? The children might suffer hunger because of the delay in feeding. At the time, the Muslims there marvelled so greatly at what had befallen the Jews that they refrained from opposing them until the result of the Jews' vain expectations had come to light. The Jews kept crowding together for the flight until the morning disclosed their frustration and ignominy. But those two deceivers escaped with whatever they had appropriated of the Jews' wealth. Subsequently, the Jews realized the nature of the trick and how they had been fooled. Then they named that year 'the year of the flight' and began to reckon the years of their old and young as from that year: it is the era of the Jews of Baghdad at the present time. This affair should suffice to cast shame and disgrace upon them forever.[134]

It has been suggested that David Alroy died around 1160 to 1167, but his movement was not a one-off. The whole period between the 1090s and the

[133] Samau'al, *Ifham*, trans. Perlmann, 72. Cf. the analysis of this episode in Gil, *Jews in the Islamic Countries*, 425–6; Franklin, *This Noble House*, 147–8.

[134] Samau'al, *Ifham*, trans. Perlmann, 73–4.

1160s has been identified as the heyday of a messianic movement. There is some evidence to suggest that David Alroy's father may also have headed a messianic movement in the Mosul region in the late eleventh century.[135] A letter found in the Cairo Geniza shows that in 1120–1 the Jewish community in Baghdad experienced another instance of messianism. The pious daughter of a certain 'Joseph the physician' proclaimed to her co-religionists her dreams of the Prophet Elijah who told her that the redemption of Israel was at hand.[136]

These messianic movements were not merely the work of an extremist fringe, nor were they deterred by consistently unfulfilled expectation – such as the belief that a messiah would appear on the millennial anniversary of the destruction of the Second Temple in Jerusalem in 1070. Apocalyptic expectations were everywhere: the great Maimonides himself suggested that the restoration of the prophecy – itself the immediate prelude to the coming of the Messiah – was imminent in 1215/16.[137] Nor were they a uniquely Jewish phenomenon, and manifested themselves in both Christianity and Islam. The First Crusade was influenced by apocalyptic visions,[138] while Shi'ism of all strands was strongly tinged with messianic expectations, and several Muslim self-proclaimed *mahdīs* appeared in the period.[139] For instance in 483–4/1090–1, 'a man who was specialist in astrology called Tilya came to Basra and drew many people into error, claiming that he was the Imam al-Mahdi'. Tilya was far from harmless, for as part of his apocalyptic vision he burned down Basra, including its famous library.[140] These expectations started to feed into Seljuk and 'Abbasid political rhetoric. Both the ill-regarded Sultan Sulaymanshah and Caliph al-Nasir li-Din Allah were proclaimed by the court poets to be the Imam al-Mahdi.[141]

However, at least sometimes, there does seem to be a direct link between an increase in pressure on Jews and the manifestation of these messianic tendencies. Here the Muslim chronicles, which largely ignore these messianic

135 Gil, *Jews in the Islamic Countries*, 422–8, offers the most detailed analysis of these events.

136 S. D. Goitein, 'A Report on Messianic Troubles in Baghdad in 1120–21', *Jewish Quarterly Review*, 43/i (1952), 57–60 (Hebrew text at 73–6); cf. Gil, *Jews in the Islamic Countries*, 421–2; Franklin, *This Noble House*, 150–2, is more sceptical about the historicity of this event.

137 Franklin, *This Noble House*, 130–46; Joel L. Kraemer, *Maimonides: The Life and World of One of Civilization's Greatest Minds* (New York, 2008), 236–7.

138 On the role of apocalyptic thought in the First Crusade, see Jay Rubenstein, *Armies of Heaven: The First Crusade and the Quest for the Apocalypse* (New York, 2011).

139 See Gil, *Jews in the Islamic Countries*, 233–42; Franklin, *This Noble House*, 152–7.

140 Ibn al-Jawzi, *al-Muntazam*, XVI, 289, 292. See also Ibn al-Athir, *al-Kamil*, X, 183–4.

141 For Sulaymanshah, see Anwari, *Diwan*, 385; for al-Nasir, see Sibt b. Ta'widhi, *Diwan*, 158, l. 5.

elements,[142] fill in some of the background. The disturbances of the 1090s came just after Caliph al-Muqtadi had imposed stricter sumptuary laws on the *dhimmīs,* and the visions of Elijah in Baghdad in 1120–1 came just as both sultan and caliph were squeezing the Baghdadi Jews for all the cash they could. Sultan Mahmud had imposed a tax on the merchants of Baghdad, while the caliph had again imposed the sumptuary laws on Jews, which seem to have consisted of the requirement to wear yellow gowns, to distinguish themselves from Christians (who had to wear black) and Muslims. Such laws had long existed, but were irregularly enforced; when they were, it was probably largely as a way of seeking to raise funds by buying an exemption, for we are told that the Jewish community ended up paying al-Mustarshid 4,000 dinars and Mahmud 20,000.[143]

Disillusion with the false messiahs, the occasional outbreak of popular anti-Jewish violence,[144] combined with resentment at the sumptuary laws and arbitrary taxation (even if the latter was something all to which communities were subject to a degree) must have precipitated a crisis of confidence among many Jews. To be sure, there were senior Jewish bureaucrats, including the secretary to Caliph al-Mustarshid's Turkish wife, Abu 'Ali b. Fadlan, who succeeded it seems in staving off some of the worst impositions on the community.[145] But to progress in the world, a Jew had to be familiar with Muslim culture and literature, including the Qur'an: Samaw'al boasts of his education in Muslim classics (p. 210), and the great Jewish thinker Maimonides warned his co-religionists of the pernicious influence of reading Muslim historical literature, indicating its popularity.[146] Such literature naturally vaunted the superiority of Islam, and Samaw'al was not alone in converting. One of his teachers, Abu'l-Barakat, the pre-eminent philosopher of the age, had also abandoned Judaism for Islam, as had a fellow student in Baghdad, Isaac ben Abraham ben Ezra (although the latter bitterly regretted his move).[147] Various motives are imputed to Abu'l-Barakat for his embracing of Islam, ranging from fear at the consequences of the

142 An exception is the year 487/1094, when the Jews are reported to have become a laughing-stock for dreaming that they would fly [to Jerusalem, presumably], and accordingly gave away all their possessions as they waited for their flying conveyances [*al-ṭayrān*]: Ibn al-Athir, *al-Kamil,* X, 237; Ibn al-Jawzi, *al-Muntazam,* XVI, 14.

143 Goitein, 'A Report on Messianic Troubles', 61–5; Ibn al-Jawzi, *al-Muntazam,* XVII, 198; Ibn al-Athir, *al-Kamil,* X, 595.

144 Gil, *Jews in the Islamic Countries,* 416–28.

145 *Ibid.,* 417; Ibn al-Jawzi, *al-Muntazam,* XVI, 30. See also Makdisi, 'Autograph Diary, IV', 301–2, §§ 140–1.

146 These issues are discussed in Husain, 'Conversion to History', 3–34.

147 Samau'al, *Ifham,* trans. Perlmann, 16.

death of a royal patient at his hands to anger at the insults he received as a non-Muslim from his peers. The sort of casual hostility with which Jews might be confronted, à propos of nothing in particular, is well reflected by the verses composed by the Hanbali diarist, Ibn al-Banna' of Baghdad, on the occasion of the birth of a son to the future Caliph al-Muqtadi in 461/1069. Amid the celebrations, Ibn al-Banna' finds room for some anti-Jewish invective:

> Glad tidings have come with this new-born child,
> Subduing the enemy and the envious.
> O state that appears with auspiciousness,
> May you never cease to be in everlasting existence and permanence,
> Despite some abominable and ungrateful people;
> Give glad tidings of this good omen . . .
> May you ever remain in the glory of an army which is served
> From on high by the good omen, O community of Qur'anic reciters and *shuhūd*-notaries!
> And may the curse of God be on the Jews![148]

A late twelfth- or thirteenth-century Persian heresiography, the *Tabsirat al-'Awamm*, describes the Jews as 'the most hostile' people to the Muslims.[149] Even the sumptuary laws were sometimes imposed not purely as money-making exercises, but in response to the demands of the piety-minded. For instance, in Baghdad in Ramadan 450/1058:

> because of the pious masses known as the followers of 'Abd al-Samad, the sumptuary laws on *dhimmīs* were renewed. A certain Hashemite man known as Ibn Sukkara attended the *dīwān* and addressed [the caliphal vizier] Ra'is al-Ru'asa' on that subject, mentioning the liberties that that the *dhimmīs* enjoyed. He spoke to him to him roughly and made him furious [with the situation].[150]

In this sort of atmosphere, whatever the relative merits of Iran and Iraq as compared with Europe, being a Muslim was quite simply a safer, more comfortable thing to be than a Jew. Moreover, there was room for negotiation over the terms. As a condition of his conversion, Abu'l-Barakat was able to stipulate that his three daughters should be allowed to inherit in accordance

148 Makdisi, 'Autograph Diary, IV', 300, § 137.

149 Sayyid Murtada b. Da'i Hasani Razi, *Tabsirat al-'Awamm fi Ma'rifat Maqalat al-Anam*, ed. 'Abbas Iqbal (Tehran, 1364), 23.

150 Ibn al-Jawzi, *al-Muntazam*, XVI, 30. For an alternative account of Ibn Sukkara, see Makdisi, 'Autograph Diary, IV', 292–3, §§ 108, 110.

with Jewish, not Islamic, inheritance law.[151] It is unsurprising that many followed his example.

The Christian Peoples of the Seljuk Empire

Christianity was widespread in Syria, Iraq and Central Asia, even if declining in numbers.[152] Three varieties existed, distinguished from one another by their varying interpretations of Christ's divine and human nature, the Melkites, Jacobites and Nestorians. The latter, also known as the 'Church of the East', was the predominant denomination, and had made considerable headway in converting the Turkic steppe peoples.[153] In 1007 – around the time the Seljuks embraced Islam – a Turkish group converted en masse to Christianity. Traditionally, these have been described as Keraits, but it has been suggested they were actually Oghuz.[154]

Little information has yet come to light about Christianity in the core Seljuk territories of Khurasan and central and western Iran. There was apparently still a Jacobite bishop in Herat in the eleventh century, and in Sistan till the twelfth.[155] Melkites existed in Khwarazm to the eleventh century, and perhaps later.[156] Further west, Isfahan was the seat of a bishop, as were Urmiyya and Jundishapur.[157] The situation is much better attested in Iraq, which probably had a much larger Christian community, although numbers are still very uncertain. Our most valuable source for Christianity in Iraq, especially Baghdad, is the Arabic chronicle of Mari, a Nestorian patriarch, entitled the *Kitab al-Majdal*. Although mainly preoccupied with the seemingly incessant feuding among the Nestorians over who should be Catholicus, the

151 On these conversions, see Sarah Stroumsa, 'On Jewish Intellectuals who Converted in the Middle Ages', in Daniel H. Frank (ed.), *The Jews of Mediaeval Islam: Community, Society and Identity* (Leiden, 1995), 179–88; Gil, *Jews in the Islamic Countries*, 468–75.

152 For the declining income from jizya in Syria in the period, see Heidemann, 'Unislamic Taxes and an Unislamic Monetary System', 493–4; Heidemann, *Die Renaissance der Städte*, 332–4.

153 On it, see Wilhelm Baum and Dietmar W. Winkler, *The Church of the East: A Concise History* (London, 2003); in Iraq, see Jean-Maurice Fiey, *Chrétiens syriaques sous les Abbassides: surtout à Bagdad (749–1258)* (Louvain, 1980).

154 Erica C. D. Hunter, 'The Conversion of the Kerait to Christianity in 1007', *Zentralasiatische Studien*, 22 (1989–91), 158–76; Erica C. D. Hunter, 'The Church of the East in Central Asia', *Bulletin of the John Rylands Library*, 78/iii (1996), 129–42.

155 N. Sims-Williams, 'Christianity in Central Asia and Chinese Turkestan', *EIr*.

156 *Ibid.*

157 Mari b. Sulayman, *Akhbar Fatarikat Kursi al-Mashriq min Kitab al-Majdal*, ed. Henricus Gismondi as *Maris Amri et Slibae De Patriarchis Nestorianum Commentaria* (Rome, 1898), 152–3.

head of the church who was based in Baghdad,[158] it also reveals information about Christian life under Seljuk rule. Typical occupations for the Christian population of Baghdad were doctor in a *māristān* (hospital), merchant or tradesman, and *kātib*.[159] Relations between Nestorian and Jacobite Christians were poor, and intermarriage between the two groups was virtually unheard of.[160] The situation was doubtless exacerbated by the fact that the Muslim authorities recognised the Nestorian Catholicus as the representative of all Christian communities, Melkites and Jacobites included. Like the Exilarch, the Catholicus owed his office to caliphal appointment, and was responsible for gathering the jizya, the poll tax.[161]

Like Jews, Christians were subjected to discriminatory laws, and there was a constant background pressure to convert – a pressure that was doubtless much lower in those areas of Iraq where Christians formed a majority. A letter from Makkikha, bishop of Mosul, to the Christian community in Isfahan, written somewhere between 1085 and 1092, refers to the 'atrocious affairs' (*al-umūr al-shanī'a*) which had beset the Church, and had had no parallel for centuries.[162] What exactly these were is unclear: although the date of the letter does coincide with Caliph al-Muqtadi's reinstitution of sumptuary laws on *dhimmīs*, this was hardly unprecedented. The letter also refers to the recent martyrdom in Mosul of three Christians who were 'famous secretaries and viziers and known to kings and sultans', and it has been suggested these officials had converted to Islam and were martyred for apostatising – death being the usual penalty for apostasy.[163] As in the Jewish community, prominent Christian intellectuals and bureaucrats were tempted to convert – and doubtless some regretted what they had done. Others vigorously defended their new faith. Ibn Mawsilaya, for instance, secretary to Caliph al-Muqtadi, was obliged to abjure Christianity. The exact circumstances of his conversion are not entirely clear, but it came in the wake of both Tilya's messianic destruction of Basra, and a very public dispute in which the Seljuk financial agent in Baghdad, the Jew Ibn Samha, had become embroiled. After al-Muqtadi's

158 *Ibid.*, 120 ff. On Iraqi Nestorians under Seljuk rule, see also Fiey, *Chrétiens syriaques*, 198–260.

159 Mari, *Kitab al-Majdal*, 125

160 *Ibid.*, 125; Fiey, *Chrétiens syriaques*, 205–7; George Makdisi, 'Autograph Diary of an Eleventh-century Historian of Baghdad, III', *BSOAS*, 19/i (1957), 43, §§ 92, 301.

161 Mari, *Kitab al-Majdal*, 133 ff.

162 Gianmaria Gianazza, 'Lettre de Makkīḫā (†1109) sur la vérité de la religion chrétienne', *Parole d'Orient*, 25 (2000), 493–555, No. 11.

163 *Ibid.*, Nos 139–42. For further details concerning Makkikha and his letter, see the bibliography given in David Thomas and Alex Mallet (eds), *Christian–Muslim Relations: A Biobibliographical History, vol. 3: 1050–1200* (Leiden, 2011), 323–7.

imposition of sumptuary laws on the *dhimmīs*, employing a Christian in such a senior position was no longer acceptable. Ibn Mawsilaya was converted to Islam by the caliph in person, and went on to proclaim his embrace of the new faith by writing a particularly enthusiastic prayer in favour of jihad against unbelievers.[164]

Although some contemporaries expressed scepticism as to the motives of converts, it would be unfair to imagine that practical considerations were the sole impetus.[165] A Christian counterpart to Samaw'al al-Maghribi was the physician Ibn Jazla (d. Baghdad 483 or 493/1100), who converted to Islam and then penned a refutation of his former faith.[166] We are told 'he used to study with Abu 'Ali b. al-Walid the Mu'tazilite [philosopher], and kept his company; the latter did not cease from calling him to Islam and showing him the clear proofs until God Almighty guided him aright [to Islam]'.[167] Just as they had done in 'Abbasid times, public debates between Muslim and Christian intellectuals seem to have continued to be held in Baghdad, and works by Muslim authors like Imam al-Haramayn Juwayni refuting Christianity may have originated in this environment.[168] In a society permeated by Muslim thought, reinforced by Muslim political domination, inevitably some would see the claims of Islam as more convincing than their own faiths.

However, it would be mistaken to portray Christian communities as in relentless decline under Seljuk rule. Despite the use of the rhetoric of jihad by both the Ildegüzids and earlier Seljuks like Alp Arslan (pp. 56–7, 117, 284), there is little evidence this translated into attacks on the Christian population within the confines of the empire. Indeed, Turkish soldiers and dignitaries such as the *shiḥna*'s representatives would officiate at the installation of the Nestorian Catholicus.[169] In many respects Christianity remained vigorous, even ambitious to expand. The Nestorian Patriarch Elias II (d. 1133) penned a defence of the faith, aimed at explaining Christian doctrine not just to Nestorians, but also to Jacobites, Jews and Muslims.[170] Arabic works were also written to commemorate the history of the Church of the East, such as the *Mukhtasar Akhbar al-Bi'a*, copied in Iraq in 1137, and the work of

164 On Ibn Mawsilaya, see Ibn Khallikan, *Wafayat*, III, 421–2; Ibn al-Athir, *al-Kamil*, X, 186–7; Ibn al-Jawzi, *al-Muntazam*, XVI, 292; Husayni, *Akhbar*, 47–8; Hillenbrand, *Crusades*, 165.
165 See Fiey, *Chrétiens syriaques*, 203.
166 Thomas and Mallet, *Christian–Muslim Relations*, 152–4.
167 Ibn Khallikan, *Wafayat*, V, 224–5.
168 Thomas and Mallett, *Muslim–Christian Relations*, 123, 158
169 Mari, *Kitab al-Majdal*, 130, 154.
170 *Ibid.*, 418–21.

Mari himself. In Syriac too, literature and intellectual life revived, and the Seljuk period coincided with much of what has been characterised as a 'Syriac renaissance'.[171] The Christian mission to the Turks continued in the eleventh and twelfth centuries, under the auspices of the Catholicos of Baghdad. Under Tughrıl's rule, the Nestorians of Baghdad dispatched a metropolitan to Khurasan and Sistan, but he ended up going to China where he died.[172] In the 1170s, two more metropolitans were appointed to Kashghar.[173]

Christians in the Caucasus were in a rather different position from those in Iraq, as they still often lived under Christian vassal rulers to the Seljuks, despite the substantial Türkmen settlement in parts of the region.[174] Although King Akhsartan of Kakheti in Georgia was obliged to convert to keep control of his kingdom, there was no consistent attempt to impose Islam on Armenian and Georgian rulers.[175] Indeed, the Seljuk period actually saw the strengthening of the Georgian monarchy, especially from the early twelfth century, and some spectacular reverses for Islam as Tbilisi, a Muslim city for nearly 400 years, fell to the armies of the Georgian King David the Builder (1089–1125) in 1121.[176] Although Ganja in the more heavily Muslim Caucasian province of Arran was a major Seljuk centre, the *iqṭāʿ* held variously by Muhammad Tapar and Tughrıl II as *maliks*, the Georgian advance provoked little reaction from the Seljuks, preoccupied as they were by their internal disputes. However, with the rise of the Ildegüzids with their base at Nakhchivan, in the later twelfth century jihad against Georgia was used increasingly to legitimise the upstart amirs, and is commemorated by poets like Athir al-Din Akhsikhathi.[177] Nonetheless, local Christian historians often preserve a positive view of Turkish rulers, in particular Malikshah who was famous for his good treatment of Christians. The Georgian Chronicle describes him as 'both by the unequalled extent of his empire, as well as by his charming demeanour and kindness, he was the most excellent of men.

171 Herman Teule, 'La renaissance syriaque (1026–1318)', *Irenikon*, 75/ii–iii (2002), 174–94.

172 Mari, *Kitab al-Majdal*, 125; Hunter, 'Church of the East', 137.

173 Hunter, 'Church of the East', 137.

174 Robert W. Thomson (trans.), *Rewriting Caucasian History: The Medieval Armenian Adaptation of the Georgian Chronicles: The Original Georgian Texts and the Armenian Adaptation* (Oxford, 1996), 307–13; Peacock, 'Nomadic Society'; Peacock, *Early Seljūq History*, 128 ff.

175 Thomson, *Rewriting Caucasian History*, 313; cf. Husayni, *Akhbar*, 44.

176 On this period in Georgia,, see Donald Rayfield, *Edge of Empires: A History of Georgia* (London, 2012), 85–97.

177 Akhsikathi, *Diwan*, 80–4; Husayni, *Akhbar*, 156–62; for Ildegüzid engagement in Caucasia, see Bünyadov, *Azərbaycan Atabəyləri Dövləti*, 56–67, 105–10; Rayfield, *Edge of Empires*, 102–3, 112–13. Also Qummi, *Dhayl-i Nafthat al-Masdur*, 245–7.

His innumerable other virtues are known – his justice, mercy and love for the Christians.'[178]

Putting aside their use of the rhetoric of jihad, Seljuk sultans did not seek to enforce religious conformity. Instances such as Kunduri's Nishapur *miḥna* or the conversion of King Akhsartan were the exceptions rather than the rule. The Seljuk employment of senior Shiʿite and Jewish officials, the activities of al-Shahrastani in promoting the Ismaili *daʿwa* right under the nose of Sultan Sanjar, the alliance of various sultans with the Ismailis – all these factors suggest that the Seljuks viewed religious difference with a pragmatic rather than a prejudiced eye. This is not to say that the Seljuk period was characterised by interfaith peace and tolerance, and it is important to distinguish between Seljuk and ʿAbbasid policy. To bolster their own position as defenders of Islam and thus their claims to temporal authority, caliphs attempted to impose a range of measures from cracking down on un-Islamic practices like wine drinking (p. 144 above) to targeting the *dhimmī* population of Baghdad. Evidently, being a non-Muslim, and under certain circumstances a Shafiʿi or a Shiʿite, could be extremely uncomfortable. The evidence suggests, though, that this was a more a product of broader trends that had started before the arrival of the Seljuks.

[178] Thomson, *Rewriting Caucasian History*, 312. Cf. Matthew of Edessa, *Armenia and the Crusades*, 137, 153; and see above p. 00.

8

The Economic and Social Organisation of the Seljuk Lands

In his obituary notice for Chaghrı, Ibn al-Athir recounts the bitter recriminations that flew between the two sons of Mika'il b. Seljuk over the state of their lands:

> [Chaghrı] was virtuous, just and lived a praiseworthy life, recognizing Almighty God's favour to him, for which he was thankful. One indication of this is that he sent to his brother Tughrıl [a message] with 'Abd al-Samad, the qadi of Sarakhs, saying, 'I have heard that you have ruined the land which you have conquered and taken possession of, and its people have fled from it. This indubitably constitutes opposition to God with regard to His servants and his land. You know that [such behaviour] leads to a bad reputation and terrorizing the subjects [*ra'iyya*].'
>
> Tughrıl replied, saying, 'O my brother, you took possession of Khurasan which is a prosperous land, and ruined it when you should have made it prosper given you were stably established there. I came to a land which my predecessors had ruined and those who came before me had ravaged. I could not make it prosper when enemies were surrounding it and necessity forced [me] to march across it with armies, nor was it possible to prevent damage to it.'[1]

The Seljuk impact on the economies and societies they ruled is equally controversial today. Some scholars vigorously contend that Seljuk rule witnessed, or even led to, economic collapse, while others argue that the eleventh and twelfth centuries were a period of economic revival and boom.

As the quotation attributed to Tughrıl suggests, the Seljuk impact can only be understood in view of the pre-existing condition of the lands that they occupied, which varied considerably.[2] Some evidence, especially for

[1] Ibn al-Athir, *al-Kamil*, X, 6–7.

[2] For a survey of developments in urbanism in this period, see Paul Wheatley, *The Places where Men Pray Together: Cities in the Islamic Lands, Seventh to Tenth Centuries* (Chicago, 2000), esp. 95–102, 136–43, 172–90, 270–8, 305–20. See also Christensen, *Decline of Iranshahr*.

Transoxiana and the Iranian plateau, points to a massive expansion in urbanism in the ninth and tenth centuries, and the emergence of a newly prosperous city-dwelling Muslim bourgeoisie. This economic growth, it has been argued, was fed by a boom in cotton production.[3] Nonetheless, if long-term trends were to an increasingly urban economy, by the time of the Seljuk invasions, major cities in Khurasan were suffering from drought, famine and over-taxation.[4] The story in the west, however, was very different. Although Baghdad continued to grow, the evidence from the surrounding countryside suggests that Iraq's economic and demographic decline, ongoing since late antiquity, continued, exacerbated by the practice of *iqṭāʿ* so favoured by the Buyids, which left agricultural estates in the hands of the military. Khuzistan, too, was in acute economic decline even before the arrival of the Seljuks. The Jazira and northern Syria, dominated throughout the tenth century by nomadic dynasties, seem to have suffered a collapse in urban life.[5]

Some research has pointed to a severe chilling in the climate on the eve of the Seljuk invasions across the Middle East and Central Asia. Richard Bulliet, focusing above all on Khurasan, has argued that this disastrous cooling led to the contraction of agriculture and the collapse of the cotton industry, which was the mainstay of the economy of the east. Indeed, Bulliet suggests cooling even led to the coming of the Seljuks themselves, as it was especially dangerous to the camels on which the Seljuks relied, forcing them to abandon

3 For Central Asia, see G. A. Pugachenkova, 'Urban Development and Architecture. Part One: Transoxiana and Khurasan', in C. E. Bosworth and M. S. Asimov (eds), *History of Civilizations of Central Asia, vol. IV: The Age of Achievement: AD 750 to the End of the Fifteenth Century. Part Two. The Achievements* (Paris, 2000), 507–56. For the Iranian plateau, see Bulliet, *Islam: The View from the Edge*, 67–79; for the thesis of a cotton boom, see Richard Bulliet, *Cotton, Climate, and Camels in Early Islamic Iran: A Moment in World History* (New York, 2009), 8–68; for an alternative interpretation, see Andrew Watson, *Agricultural Innovation in the Early Islamic World* (Cambridge, 1983). See, however, the work of Decker cited in n. 14 below, p. 289.

4 Bosworth, *The Ghaznavids*, 258–60; Bulliet, *Cotton, Cimate and Camels*, 80–4; see p. 37 above.

5 For the archaeological evidence for the Iraqi countryside, see Robert M. Adams, *The Land Behind Baghdad: A History of Settlement on the Diyala Plains* (Chicago, 1965); and for Khuzistan, see Pyne, 'The Impact of the Seljuq invasion on Khuzestan'. A much more positive impression of the economy of Iraq in the eleventh century, drawing on literary sources, is given by Khidr Jasmin Duri, 'Society and Economy of Iraq under the Seljuqs (1055–1160 A.D.) with Special Reference to Baghdad', PhD dissertation, University of Pennsylvania, 1970. For northern Syria and the Jazira, see Heidemann, *Die Renaissance der Städte*, 1–23; for Isfahan, see Durand-Guédy, *Iranian Elites*, 226–9; for Anatolia and some general remarks, see Peacock, *Early Seljūq History*, 156–63. For Buyid *iqṭāʿ* policies, see Tsugitaka Sato, *State and Rural Society in Medieval Islam: Sultans, Muqtaʿs and Fallahun* (Leiden, 1997).

Khwarazm for the warmer territories of northern Khurasan and the Iranian plateau. The influx of nomads is said to have caused further damage to the economy, and to the Khurasani cotton industry. According to this thesis, the chill and the economic dislocation caused by the Seljuk invasions lasted into the twelfth century and triggered the flight of much of the Iranian elite to seek their fortunes in more favourable climes.[6] The idea of a precipitous chilling in this period, connected both to the Seljuk invasions and to broader economic collapse, has also been advocated by Ronnie Ellenblum, drawing on evidence largely from the Levant.[7]

This evidence, however, is not entirely clear-cut. The chroniclers do record a series of harsh climatic events in the eleventh and twelfth centuries. In 515/1121–2, for instance, Ibn al-Jawzi noted unusually heavy rains over all Iraq, which destroyed palm trees, grapes, fruit and grain. In Baghdad, the snowfall 'filled the streets and lanes and stood about a *dhirāʿ* high; the *aḥdāth* made statues out of it in the shape of wolves and elephants'.[8] Ibn al-Jawzi suggests that the events of this year were exceptional, even in a period of cooling:

> We have mentioned in this book of ours that snow fell in many years of [the reigns of the caliphs] al-Rashid, al-Muqtadir, al-Muʿtamid, al-Ta'iʿ, al-Mutiʿ, al-Qadir and al-Qa'im, but we have not heard of the like of this event. [The snow] remained for fifteen days without melting, and citrus, lemon and orange trees were destroyed. Plants and vegetables were also completely destroyed, and snowfall was never witnessed in Basra except in this year.[9]

However, severe cold in Baghdad is regularly recorded from the early third/ninth century onwards – in fact, from as soon as our sources start to take an interest in such matters, and long before the Seljuks appear in the Islamic world.[10] There does not appear to have been any sudden change of pattern around the beginning of the eleventh century that might be connected with the Seljuks. Indeed, scientific research, as opposed to the anecdotal evidence of chronicles, suggests conditions in the Middle East were actually warmer, if wetter, in this period.[11] Even if climate change was happening, it would not

6 Bulliet, *Cotton, Cimate and Camels, passim.*

7 Ronnie Ellenblum, *The Collapse of the Eastern Mediterranean: Climate and Change and the Decline of the East, 950–1072* (Cambridge, 2012), esp. 64 ff.

8 Ibn al-Jawzi, *al-Muntazam*, XVII, 196.

9 *Ibid.*, XVII, 197. Cf. Ibn al-Athir, *al-Kamil*, X, 595–6.

10 See Fernando Domínguez-Castro *et al.*, 'How Useful could Arabic Documentary Sources be for Reconstructing Past Climate?', *Weather*, 62/iii (2012), 76–82.

11 For a discussion of the Medieval Cimate Anomaly in historical context, see, for instance, Victor Lieberman, *Strange Parallels: Southeast Asia in Global Context, vol. I: Integration on the Mainland* (Cambridge, 2003), 101–12, 156–7, with references; and more recently

necessarily have triggered nomadic migrations, for most nomads will prefer to adapt to changing conditions if possible.[12] Khwarazm remained a key pasture for nomadic groups till the end of the Seljuk period, suggesting that conditions there had not changed so radically as to make the surrounding steppes uninhabitable for the Türkmen.[13]

The other arguments for collapse adduced by Ellenblum and Bulliet are also problematic. The evidence for a cotton boom in early Islamic Iran is flimsy, and it is not all clear that the textile industry in Khurasan collapsed.[14] The migrations of Iranian scholars are dated by Bulliet to the late twelfth century,[15] not to the arrival of the Seljuks and the 'Big Chill', and might be explained by the upheavals of the Khwarazmian period, and by new opportunities offered outside Iran by states in the Levant like the Zangids and then the Ayyubids, who wished to emulate the practices and prestige of the Seljuk sultanate where they themselves had their origins. Indeed, the brain-drain was not a one-way street, and it has been argued that skilled craftsmen from Egypt migrated to Iran in the late twelfth century, bringing with them new techniques.[16] Certainly, artistic production of the late twelfth and early thirteenth centuries was not undertaken solely under court patronage, but was destined for much broader sections of society.[17] The market for art, particularly the refined lustre (*mīnā'ī*) ceramics (Figure 8.1),[18] suggests widespread prosperity in Iran and Iraq, despite the political upheavals.

Henry F. Diaz *et al.*, 'Spacial and Temporal Characteristics of Climate Change in the Medieval Period Revisited', *Bulletin of the American Meteorological Society*, 92/xi (2011), 1487–99; Jessie Woodbridge and Neil Roberts, 'Late Holocene Climate of the Eastern Mediterranean Inferred from Diatom Analysis of Annually-laminated Lake Sediments', *Quarternary Science Review*, 30/xxiii–xxiv (2011), 3381–92. Neither Bulliet or Ellenblum cite much research by climate scientists in support of their theses: the sole scientific evidence Bulliet adduces comes from one set of tree rings from Mongolia. I do not necessarily dismiss their ideas, but they need to be tested against scientific research.

12 See the discussion in Peacock, *Early Seljūq History*, 44–5, with references.

13 See Paul, 'The Role of Ḫʷārazm', 1–17; also Paul, 'Sanjar and Atsız', 88.

14 For the cultivation of cotton in the Sasanian empire, which undermines Bulliet's thesis of a sudden Islamic cotton boom, see Michael Decker, 'Plants and Progress: Rethinking the Islamic Agricultural Revolution', *Journal of World History*, 20/ii (2009), 197–200, 205. For the Seljuk textile industry, see below, pp. 292, 303, 305.

15 Bulliet, *Cotton, Climate and Camels*, 117–20. See the review by Michael Morony in *Speculum*, 85/iv (2010), 944–5.

16 Oliver Watson, *Persian Lustre Ware* (London, 1985), 28.

17 Grabar, 'The Visual Arts', 648; Oleg Grabar, 'Les arts mineurs de l'Orient musulman à partir du milieu du XIIe siècle', *Cahiers de civilisation médiévale*, 11(42) (1968), 190; Pancaroğlu, 'A World unto Himself', 190–5; Lorenz Korn, 'Saljuqs, VI. Art and Architecture', *EIr* (under 'Minor Arts'); Rebecca Ward, *Islamic Metalwork* (London, 1993), 72.

18 In addition to Watson, *Persian Lustre Ware*, see also Melanie Gibson, 'The enigmatic figure:

Figure 8.1 *Mīnā'ī* ware, the luxury lustre ceramics that became popular from the second half of the twelfth century. British Museum, image AN3418000. © Trustees of the British Museum

It is beyond the scope of this chapter to resolve these debates, which need much further research. Archaeology, the main source for long-term economic trends in the absence of archival records, remains in its infancy in most of the territories of the Seljuk Empire, while the serious study of Seljuk numismatics, the other key source for economic history, has yet to begin.[19] My inten-

ceramic sculpture from Iran and Syria, 1150–1250', *Transactions of the Oriental Ceramic Society* 73 (2008–9), 39–50.

19 Heidemann's *Die Renaissance der Städte* is the sole significant contribution to understanding Seljuk economic history to make use of the numismatic data, but concentrates only

tion is purely to provide some preliminary conclusions based on a synthesis of the existing evidence dealing with three main questions that will contribute to understanding economic and social life in the empire: the Türkmen impact on agriculture and the economy; the role of trade; and urbanism in the period. First, however, it is worth stepping back to consider one of the few detailed contemporary views we have of the economic organisation of a Seljuk province.

Portrait of a Seljuk Province: Fars in the Early Twelfth Century

In the first decade of the twelfth century, a Seljuk official, Ibn al-Balkhi, wrote a description of his home province of Fars in southern Iran, which he dedicated to Sultan Muhammad Tapar.[20] Home to the ancient capitals of the Achaemenids and Sasanians, Fars had been politically important under the Buyids, and a Buyid prince held court in Shiraz, its chief city. Ibn al-Balkhi tells us that the late Buyid period saw major upheavals. It was then that there first appeared the mysterious Shabankara nomads, of whom no one had heard before.[21] Areas like Irahistan, which in the heyday of Buyid rule under ʿAdud al-Dawla in the tenth century had been a recruiting-ground for soldiers, subsequently became prone to banditry and highway robbery and were too remote and inhospitable for later rulers to attempt to garrison.[22] Dams built by ʿAdud al-Dawla had fallen into disrepair.[23] Ibn al-Balkhi blames the decline above all on the oppression of Abu Saʿd, the last Buyid ruler of Fars.[24]

Despite his royal patron, Ibn al-Balkhi's view of Seljuk rule is far from uniformly apologetic. He tells us that great damage was done to Shiraz in the fighting between the Shabankara chief Fadluya and Qavurt. Although security improved under Malikshah, the town was damaged by subsequent Shabankara raids, fighting between 'Turks and Türkmen' and expropriations (*muṣādara*). Ibn al-Balkhi expresses the hope that Shiraz will return to prosperity – indicating that the city had not yet recovered from these depredations.[25] Quite a number of places are mentioned as being currently in ruins,[26] and our author condemns the policies of the Seljuk governor Rukn

on a limited area. For a bibliography of works on Seljuk numismatics, see also Özgüdenli, *Selçuklular*, 306–8.

20 Ibn al-Balkhi, *Farsnama*, 2.

21 *Ibid.*, 164. On the Shabankara, see further references on p. 245, n. 159 above.

22 *Ibid.*, 140–1.

23 *Ibid.*, 129.

24 *Ibid.*, 142, 145, 146.

25 *Ibid.*, 133.

26 For example, Bilad-i Shapur (*ibid.*, 147).

al-Din Khumartegin, whose ineptitude he blames for the decline of the port of Siraf.[27]

Ibn al-Balkhi several times gives credit for recent improvements to the *atabeg* Chavli Saqqa'u: for instance, the revival of the formerly flourishing town of Nubanjan which had declined under Abu Sa'd.[28] The *atabeg* had once again restored order among the troublesome inhabitants of Irahistan, suppressed the Shabankara, and rebuilt 'Adud al-Dawla's dams on the River Kur.[29] The cotton and textile centre of Jahrum is mentioned with the comment that 'now it is flourishing' (*aknūn ābādān-ast*),[30] and cotton production is mentioned in several locations, with the cotton (*karbās*) of Kazarun being specially designated for the consumption of the Seljuk court – producers enjoyed an agreement with the *dīwān* insuring them fair prices and regular custom,[31] suggesting the continuing popularity of this material with the elite in the early twelfth century.[32] Silk, too, was cultivated and agriculture remained important: the town of Maybud was particularly noted for its fruits as well as silk and textiles, and wheat was widely grown in the province.[33] Ibn al-Balkhi describes the pastures of Fars at some length, confirming the economic importance of stock-breeding (an activity especially, although not exclusively, associated with the Türkmen). Occasionally, he specifies that a given pasture is divided between *mulk* (private property) and *iqṭā'*. Grazing, then, was not a free-for-all, but Ibn al-Balkhi presents no evidence that competition over these grazing rights played much part in the upheavals Fars experienced.

A picture of long-term continuity is confirmed by the statement of the Mongol period author, Hamdallah Mustawfi, that the revenues of Fars in Seljuk times were more or less what they had been under the Buyids.[34] The fourteenth-century *Shiraznama* also preserves a reasonably positive view of Seljuk rule. While admitting the failings of Rukn al-Din Khumartegin,[35] later

27 *Ibid.*, 137.

28 *Ibid.*, 145.

29 *Ibid.*, 128, 141, 146.

30 *Ibid.*, 131.

31 *Ibid.*, 145. For other examples of cotton production in Fars, see *ibid.*, 132, 134. For a discussion of the twelfth-century evidence for the textile industry, see Wheatley, *The Places Where Men Pray Together*, 148–9.

32 *Pace* Bulliet, *Cotton, Climate, and Camels*, 90–1, who argues that cotton was going out of fashion by the eleventh century.

33 Ibn al-Balkhi, *Farsnama*, 122.

34 Lambton, 'Aspects', 121; Hamdallah Mustawfi, *The Geographical Part of the* Nuzhat al-Qulūb *Composed by Ḥamd Allāh Mustawfī of Qazwīn in 740*, trans. G. Le Strange (London, 1919), 113.

35 Zarkub-i Shirazi, *Shiraznama*, 132.

governors are given credit for revitalising Shiraz through building madrasas and pious works. Such damage as had been done appears largely as the result of the oppression of Abu Saʿd or the upheavals of the Shabankara rather than Seljuk policies.

Ibn al-Balkhi himself suggests the difficulties of extrapolating about broader economic trends from the fate of individual cities in his remarks on the district of Kazarun: 'its chief town is in ruins but it has many flourishing rural estates' – although problems of security were such that the principal buildings [*sarāy*] had to be fortified.[36] Thus, there was considerable variation within the province; and, as we will investigate further below, even seemingly long-term economic trends such as the ruin of Siraf may have been less significant than they at first appear, marking a shift in trade routes rather than their abandonment. Nonetheless, evidence from other parts of the Seljuk Empire suggests changes in the nature of provincial society. The term *dihqān*, referring to the landed gentry who were so important in early Islamic Iran, from the eleventh century appears more rarely in the sources. When it does occur, it seems to indicate an increasingly diminished status, something closer to a simple farmer,[37] and there is evidence that over the tenth and eleventh centuries, in certain places, the rural gentry did move to towns.[38] Both processes were underway before the arrival of the Turks, but become more conspicuous under the Seljuks. As ever, though, one should be wary of jumping to conclusions on the basis of shifting terminology, and it is possible that the *dihqāns*' functions were taken over by *raʾīses*.[39] In other words, a rural aristocracy survived, under a different name, just as the castle lords of Irahistan mentioned by Ibn al-Balkhi evidently weathered the change from Buyid to Seljuk rule (p. 244 above).

The Türkmen Impact on Agriculture and the Economy

Proponents of the thesis of economic and especially agricultural decline during the Seljuk period point the finger at the Türkmen. The case against the nomads was made by Andrew Watson in his description of the fate of agriculture in the Islamic world in the eleventh century:

> Because the invaders had come from regions where less intensive use was made of the soil, they were on the whole unsympathetic to the kind of

[36] *Ibid.*, 145.
[37] Paul, 'Where did the Dihqāns Go?' 20, 22–3.
[38] Aubin, 'L'aristocratie urbaine', 325.
[39] Paul, 'Where Did the Dihqāns Go?' 23, 26–34; Paul, 'Local Lords'.

> agriculture which the early Islamic world had so brilliantly created . . . In many areas the balance of sedentary agriculture and nomadic life once again tipped towards the latter form of land use. Settlements were abandoned. The desert encroached on land that for some centuries – or millennia – had been tilled.[40]

A similar line of argument has been followed by Bulliet, who suggests that the Türkmen presence would have discouraged investment in irrigation and hence agriculture.[41]

Some literary evidence confirms the decline of irrigation works in places. The early thirteenth-century geographer Yaqut writes of the areas between Baghdad and Wasit that:

> They have been ruined since the days of the Seljuk kings because of the decay of the Nahrawan [canal]. The Nahrawan river silted up and the kings neglected to repair it and dig it out because of their fighting. Their troops trampled over it and the district was destroyed in its entirety.[42]

A picture of devastated countryside is also painted by the Seljuk *mustawfī* in Arran in the south Caucasus at the beginning of the twelfth century, Mas'ud b. Namdar, who complained he had charge of 'devastated rubble and provinces in turmoil (*fī yadayya tilāl khariba wa-a'māl muḍtariba*)'.[43] In Isfahan, economic decline seems to have set in with the reign of Mas'ud. The last dated building erected in the region before the Mongol invasions was put up in 529/1134–5 (although it has been suggested that undated ones derive from the later twelfth century). Starting in the 530s/1135–45, but recurring throughout the twelfth century, Isfahan suffered from severe famines, which were exacerbated by the constant campaigns of various Seljuk pretenders and Turkish amirs.[44] Regions like Arrajan in southern Iran and Sistan appear to have been in dire economic straits throughout the Seljuk period.[45]

40 Watson, *Agricultural Innovation*, 143. The secondary literature Watson cites for the Seljuk period (*ibid.*, 210, n. 13) draws almost entirely on literary sources, with exception of Adams' work on the Diyala plains.

41 Bulliet, *Islam: The View from the Edge*, 139–40.

42 Yaqut, *Mu'jam*, I, 181.

43 Minorsky and Cahen, 'Le recueil transcaucasien', 117; Mas'ud b. Namdar, *Sbornik Rasskazov*, 169, fol. 200b.

44 Durand-Guédy, *Iranian Elites*, 226–9; cf. Christensen, *Decline of Iranshahr*, 147–8.

45 Arrajan: Heinz Gaube, *Die Sudpersische Provinz Arraǧān/Kūh-Gilūyeh von der arabischen Eroberung bis zur Safawidenzeit: Analyse und Auswertung literarischer und archäologischer Quellen zur historischen Topographie* (Vienna, 1973), 74–5, 81–2. Sistan: Christensen, *Decline of Iranshahr*, 237–8; Bosworth, *Saffarids*, 393.

However, the mere occurrence of decline does not allow us to attribute its cause to the Türkmen. In fact, in none of these regions apart from Arran did many Türkmen settle, as they were ecologically unsuitable (see pp. 224–5 above). Indeed, Lambton has argued that far from being a destructive force, the Türkmen actually made a positive contribution to the economy:

> the Saljuq invasion did not create, generally speaking, dislocation, but on the contrary the introduction of a limited number of nomads with their flocks into Persia may well have contributed to the prosperity of the country, in that they helped to provision the towns with milk products, meat and wool, and may, perhaps in the field of trade, also have made some contribution in the matter of transport.[46]

As Lambton observed, there is not necessarily a contradiction between a nomadic population and prosperity.[47] Nomads might actually promote agriculture, sometimes partly to meet their own needs,[48] but also for motives of profit, as described by a near contemporary account of the actions of the Nawakiyya Türkmen in Syria in 464/1071:

> The Türkmen seized control of the entirety of Syria, and came to Ramla which was in ruins, without a single person living there; its market had no gates. They brought peasants to it, and made it prosper. They tax-farmed the sultan's portion out of the existing olive trees for 30,000 dinars, and established the town's tax obligation at half this.[49]

The economic importance of the Türkmen is reflected in a document from Sanjar's chancery preserved in the *'Atabat al-Kataba*:

> Their commercial products (*matājir*) and activities (*makāsib*) result in an increase in the wealth, tranquillity and benefits for all their contemporaries.

46 Lambton, 'Aspects', 124, cf. 115. See also Claude Cahen, 'Nomades et sedentaires dans le monde musulman du milieu du moyen age', in D. S. Richards (ed.), *Islamic Civilisation, 950–1150* (Oxford 1973), 102–3.

47 See also the critique of Watson in Jean-Luc Krawczyk, 'The Relationship between Pastoral Nomadism and Agriculture: Northern Syria and the Jazira in the Eleventh Century', *JRŪR*, 1 (1985), 15–20 (reprinted in Michael Morony (ed.), *Production and the Exploitation of Resources* (The Formation of the Classical Islamic World, 11) (Aldershot, 2002)).

48 See, for instance, on Turkish foodstuffs popular in the eleventh century which were based on agricultural produce, Buell, 'The Mongol Empire and Turkicization', 203.

49 Sibt, *Mir'at*, 153, cf. *ibid.*, 180. See also the discussion in Krawczyk, 'The Relationship between Pastoral Nomadism and Agriculture', 12–13. Note also Ibn al-Athir's comments on how Turkish rule led to a boom in fruit production in Mosul: Ibn al-Athir, *al-Ta'rikh al-Bahir*, 78. See, too, accounts of the Ghuzz leader Malik Dinar's efforts make Kirman prosper: Bosworth, 'Political History', 174.

> And these good deeds and blessings are beneficial to all, both the elite and the commoners.[50]

A similarly positive view of nomads is presented by the Qarakhanid mirror for princes, the *Qutadghu Bilig*:

> [They] provide us with food and clothing: horses for the army and pack animals for transport; koumiss [fermented mare's milk] and milk, wool and butter, yoghurt and cheese; and also carpets and felts . . . They are a useful class of men and you should treat them well.[51]

Türkmen might migrate considerable distances in order to do business with the sedentary world. In 556/1161, 'there came to Nishapur a great number of Türkmen from Fars, bringing with them numerous sheep to trade. They sold them and took their price, and went off and set up camp two stages away from Tabas Gilaki', where they were attacked by the Ismailis of Quhistan.[52] The Türkmen's route between Fars and Khurasan must thus have taken them across the vast inhospitable Dasht-i Kavir desert, where Tabas is the main oasis. It is testimony to the vibrancy of Nishapur's economy in the period that a protracted journey over such difficult conditions was worthwhile.

Other documents in the *'Atabat al-Kataba* refer to the need to restrain Kurds and Türkmen from committing acts of highway robbery against passing caravans, and more vaguely to their tendency to commit acts of 'violence or intimidation'.[53] Doubtless such events were quite common, but go largely unrecorded in our sources. Mas'ud b. Namdar complains of the ravages of the Türkmen around Baylaqan in the early twelfth century, which no chronicle mentions.[54] The ambiguous nature of the Türkmen's activities is reflected in Ibn al-Athir's report, *sub anno* 496/1102–3, of a

50 Juawyni, *Atabat al-Kataba*, 31, trans. Durand-Guédy, 'The Türkmen–Saljuq Relationship', 48–9, cf. *ibid.*, 33; Lambton, 'Aspects', 109.

51 Yusuf Khass Hajib, *Wisdom of Royal Glory (Kutadghu Bilig). A Turko-Islamic Mirror for Princes*, trans. Robert Dankoff (Chicago, 1983), 184; cf. Durand-Guédy, 'The Türkmen–Saljuq Relationship', 33–4. Further on the economic activities of the Türkmen, see Agadshanow, *Der Staat der Seldschukiden*, 233–5; for northern Syria, Krawczyk, 'The Relationship between Pastoral Nomadism and Agriculture', 17–18.

52 Ibn al-Athir, *al-Kamil*, XI, 280. On Tabas Gilaki, see G. Le Strange, *Lands of the Eastern Caliphate: Mesopotamia, Persia and Central Asia from the Moslem Conquest to the Time of Timur* (Cambridge, 1930), 259–60. Further on nomadism in Quhistan, see Lambton, 'Aspects', 121.

53 Durand-Guédy, 'The Türkmen–Saljuq Relationship', 50, 52–3.

54 Minorsky and Cahen, 'Le recueil transcaucasien', 101, 109, 123. For another example, see Sibt, *Mir'at*, 131.

group of Türkmen who were sent by Sökmen b. Artuq to Tikrit, where they sold cheese, butter and honey to the local populace. It was a trick, however, for in the night the Türkmen rose up, overwhelmed the town's guards, and let Sökmen in to seize the town for himself.[55] The story nonetheless suggests that the urban populace were accustomed to doing business with the nomads.

The Türkmen thus had a relationship of mutual dependency with the settled population, to whom they sold their animal products and from whom they would have bought grain. Even if the relationship was far from unambiguously happy, in the main the evidence bears out Lambton's contention that nomads were a positive economic force. Regions that were heavily populated by Türkmen, such as Central Asia, Jurjan and northern Syria, witnessed urban expansion and economic growth.[56] Azerbaijan, a major centre of Türkmen settlement owing to its rich pasturelands, also seems to have prospered, even if it did not witness the same degree of urban expansion as elsewhere.[57] Even the devastation of Khurasan by the Ghuzz in the mid-twelfth century was far from being a decisive blow. Nishapur, for instance, under al-Mu'ayyad Ay Aba, swiftly recovered from its sack of 548/1153. The town moved to the old residential quarter of Shadyakh, which was fortified by al-Mu'ayyad, and became, Yaqut tells us, more prosperous than it had been before 'because it was a corridor to the east and caravans could not avoid coming to it'.[58]

Trade in the Seljuk Empire

The Seljuk Empire bestraddled the collection of land caravan routes that linked China to the Mediterranean known as the Silk Road, which had been active since antiquity. Both scholars who see the period as one of economic decline and those who take the opposite view have posited a growth in trade under the Seljuks. Heidemann's findings for northern Syria indicate that from the beginning of the twelfth century the region witnessed a massive demand for Byzantine copper currency, suggesting major economic growth that existing currencies – above all gold coins imported from the Jibal and Baghdad – were unable to fill. Indeed, these Byzantine coins were worth much more in northern Syria than they were in the Byzantine lands.[59]

[55] Ibn al-Athir, *al-Kamil*, X, 355
[56] See Durand-Guédy, 'The Türkmen–Saljuq Relationship', 50; Lambton, 'Aspects', 110; Heidemann, *Die Renaissance der Städte*. See further below for urbanism in Central Asia.
[57] For Azerbaijan, see Christensen, *Decline of Iranshahr*, 209–11; Lambton, 'Aspects', 119–20.
[58] Yaqut, *Mu'jam*, V, 332.
[59] Heidemann, *Die Renaissance der Städte*, 355–435, 446–7.

Figure 8.2 Ribat-i Sharaf, Khurasan, Iran (photograph Bernard O'Kane)

Bulliet, too, has argued that instead of agriculture, the Seljuks concentrated on trade, as suggested by the prevalence of high value gold coins.[60]

Our sources only rarely discuss merchants, but it is clear enough that there were ample fortunes to be made. The Baghdadi Hanbali merchant Ibn Jarrada (d. 476/1084) by his death had wealth amounting to some 300,000 dinars. His Baghdad residence comprised some thirty buildings (*dār*), a garden, a bathhouse and two private mosques; he had been able to pay off al-Basasiri's allies when they attacked Baghdad, and had given shelter in his house to al-Qa'im's Seljuk wife Khadija, earning Tughrıl's gratitude.[61] We do not know, however, what exactly Ibn Jarrada's business interests were. We are better informed about Ramisht, a twelfth-century millionaire from Siraf on the coast of Fars, who specialised in the sea trade with the Far East. He endowed all kinds of pious works at Mecca, and even had the Ka'ba covered in priceless Chinese cloth.[62]

According to an argument advanced by Bernard Lewis which remains influential, the Fatimids adopted a policy of trying to attract the lucrative Indian Ocean trade to their own Red Sea littoral territories. With the impoverishment of Iraq under the Buyids, by the eleventh century the Fatmids had succeeded in making the Red Sea the major entrepot for Indian and Far Eastern trade.[63] However, the case of Ramisht suggests that the old Indian Ocean routes remained viable during the Seljuk period, albeit with some flux in the precise ports that were used as their western terminus. Although the decline of Siraf does seem to have set in by *c.* 1000, the Gulf route did not disappear.[64] Rather Siraf's function was displaced by Kish (or Qays), and later Hormuz itself. True, Kish was built on a considerably smaller site than Siraf, but this is no indication of the extent of the trade. In fact, a much greater proportion of Far Eastern ceramics has been identified at Kish than at Siraf,[65]

60 Bulliet, *Cotton, Climate and Camels*, 121–3.

61 Ibn al-Jawzi, *al-Muntazam*, XVI, 232–3; van Renterghem, 'Le sentiment d'appartenance', 240–1.

62 See S. M. Stern, 'Ramisht of Siraf, a Merchant Millionaire of the Twelfth Century', *JRAS*, 99/i (1967), 10–14.

63 Bernard Lewis, 'The Fatimids and the Route to India', *Revue de la faculté des sciences économiques de l'université d'Istanbul*, 14 (1953), 50–4; cf. C. E. Bosworth, 'Saldjukids.V. Administrative Social and Economic History. 1. In Persia and Iraq', *EI²*.

64 See Jean Aubin, 'La ruine de Siraf et les routes du Golfe Persique aux XIe et XIIe siècles', *Cahiers de civilisation médiévale*, 2 (1959), 295–301. On the port, see also David Whitehouse, *Sīrāf: History, Topography and Environment* (Oxford, 2009).

65 Moira Tampoe, *Maritime Trade between China and the West: An Archaeological Study of the Ceramics from Siraf (Persian Gulf), 8th–15th Centuries* AD (Oxford, 1999), 113, with a useful list of commodities traded.

indicating that, if anything, Gulf trade with China was on the increase in the Seljuk period. It is likely that the Sirafi merchants simply relocated themselves to Kish with the trade. Most of the merchandise probably consisted of perishables, in particular spices, which have not survived in the archaeological record.

There were also changes in the east–west caravan routes that linked the Middle East to China by land. Over the tenth to fourteenth centuries, routes around Merv – the most thoroughly studied area to date – saw the construction of large numbers of caravanserais, at a distance of about 10–30 km from one another, to provide shelter for travellers. The increasing aridity of the twelfth and thirteenth centuries seems to have forced a shift in some routes, as wells dried up, but this construction activity in the Seljuk period and afterwards attests the continuing economic importance of trade.[66] Less well known, but also important, were the routes that led up from Khwarazm to the Turkish principality of Bulghar on the Volga, which survived till the end of the twelfth century before collapsing in circumstances which are unclear. The furs from Russia which were Bulghar's speciality were especially prized in the Islamic world, and were exchanged for ceramics, stone beads, pepper and swords, the latter from Iran itself: Zanjan, Tabriz and Isfahan are mentioned as centres of manufacture.[67]

Taxes on long-distance trade seem to have first appeared with the Seljuks.[68] To what extent did the Seljuk rulers deliberately promote trade, beyond taxing it? There is very little evidence to suggest that they had any distinct policy towards maritime trade, but we are on firmer ground with land trade. The construction of caravanserais, in theory a pious act meant to benefit Muslims, may suggest state support for commerce, but the scale and luxurious nature of some indicates that they were also (or even mainly) intended to function as residences for the itinerant sultan (see p. 171). Ribat-i Sharaf (Figure 8.2), originally built at the beginning of the twelfth century, was restored by Sanjar's wife Terken Khatun after the Ghuzz revolt, suggesting

66 On the medieval caravan routes and caravanserais, see Buchard Brentjes, 'Caravan Routes through Central Asia', *Annales archéologiques arabes syriennes*, 43 (1999), 215–28, which represents a slightly abridged version in English of the same author's 'Karawanwege durch Mittelasien', *Archaeologische Mitteilungen aus Iran*, 25 (1992), 247–76.

67 Janet Martin, 'Trade on the Volga: The Commercial Relations of Bulghar with Central Asia and Iran in the 11th–12th Centuries', *International Journal of Turkish Studies*, 1 (1980), 85–97; see also Roman K. Kovalev, 'The Infrastructure of the Northern Part of the "Fur Road" between the Middle Volga and the East during the Middle Ages', *Archivum Eurasiae Medii Aevi*, 11 (2000–1), 25–37; Roman K. Kovalev, 'The Infrastructure of the Novgorodian Fur Trade in the pre-Mongol Era (ca. 900–1240)', unpublished PhD dissertation, University of Minnesota, 2002.

68 Heidemann, 'Unislamic Taxes'.

Figure 8.3 A caravan at rest. An illustration from the famous Arabic literary work produced in Seljuk Iraq, the *Maqamat* of al-Hariri. A copy made and illustrated by Yahya b. Mahmud al-Wasiti, AD 1237. Bibliothèque nationale de France, MS Arabe 5847, fol. 11a.

a close association of such buildings with sultanic prestige.[69] These vast sultanic caravanserais seem to have been prevalent in Khurasan, but structures on a comparable scale are not known from the rest of the Seljuk domains. Members of the dynasty sponsored other pious projects, such as shelter for

[69] See Hillenbrand, *Islamic Architecture*, 338–40.

pilgrims on the desert route to Mecca from Iraq, but these were on a much smaller scale.[70]

Seljuk Urbanism

The cities of the Seljuk period have almost entirely disappeared. Some, like Baghdad and Isfahan, were so comprehensively built over by later generations that, very rare architectural monuments aside,[71] scarcely a trace of their eleventh-twelfth century forms have survived. Others were deserted in the turmoil of the late twelfth and early thirteenth centuries, and when urban life resumed, it often did so on a different site. This is the case at Nishapur, Merv and Abiward, but the limited extent of archaeological investigations to date and the reuse of any building materials in later constructions mean that even these deserted Seljuk sites can give us only a very fragmentary picture of urban structures. With archaeology of the Seljuk period so much in its infancy, we are largely reliant on literary sources. This is a perilous path, meaning that even roughly estimating the size of cities is fraught with hazard. While Bulliet posits a population of 110,000–220,000 for Nishapur by around the year 1000, Bosworth puts it at 50,000.[72] The figures estimated by Durand-Guédy for Isfahan, the greatest city in western Iran, fall somewhere between the two, at around 65,000–130,000 in the eleventh century.[73] Sultankala (Figure 8.4), the main Seljuk urban area at Merv, has been calculated to have contained a population of 150,000.[74] A figure of between 500,000 and 1 million has been suggested for Baghdad in the late eleventh century, although the upper end of this seems excessive.[75] All these cities would have been considerably larger than average, whatever the exact figure. Nor was their size necessarily constant throughout the period. Bulliet, arguing that demographic pressure, agricultural collapse and Türkmen depredations resulted in disaster, has suggested that the population of Nishapur had decreased by 85 per cent by the end of the twelfth century.[76]

Many Seljuk cities, owing to their location on the edge of deserts or in earthquake zones, teetered on the edge of viability. Quite apart from the Türkmen, Arab nomads could cause problems, taking advantage of any

70 *Ibid.*, 342; Bundari, *Zubda*, 69–70.

71 For Isfahan, see the list in Durand-Guédy, *Iranian Elites*, 123, listing two buildings in the town itself, the Friday mosque and the minaret of Chihil Dukhtaran.

72 Bulliet, *The View from the Edge*, 73; Richard Bulliet, 'Medieval Nishapur: A Topographic and Demographic Reconstruction', *Studia Iranica*, 5 (1976), 88; Bosworth, *The Ghanazvids*, 161–2.

73 Durand-Guédy, *Iranian Elites*, 25–6.

74 Agadshanow, *Der Staat der Seldschukiden*, 211.

75 Duri, 'Society and Economy', 95–119.

76 Bulliet, *Islam: The View from the Edge*, 141; Bulliet, 'Medieval Nishapur', 88–9.

weakening in political authority to plunder the nearby cities. On Tughrıl's death in 456/1064, Bedouin tribes exploited the uncertainty over the succession to plunder the outskirts of Baghdad; after Malikshah's death, the Bedouin Banu Khafaja even entered Kufa itself before being chased away by an army from Baghdad.[77] Cities were frequently destroyed by natural disasters or devastating fires, such as that which burnt down several quarters of Baghdad in 485/1092.[78] Another conflagration, starting in a baker's shop in the city's Nahr al-Mu'alli district in 467/1075, destroyed not only houses, but also 180 shops.[79] In 515/1121, the sultan's palace in Baghdad burnt down because a slave girl had carelessly propped up a candle on a mat while applying henna one night, destroying carpets, jewels and valuables to a value of 1 million dinars. A week later, the great mosque in Isfahan caught fire, destroying 500 copies of the Qur'an, one allegedly in the handwriting of a companion of the Prophet, Ubayy b. Abi Ka'b, as well as doing 1 million dinars worth of damage to the wooden interior.[80] Earthquakes frequently struck. The people of Bayhaq in northeastern Iran were forced from their houses for forty days in 444/1052 owing to a series of earthquakes that devastated the town.[81] Plague too might strike at any time.[82]

Cities often relied on very fragile water supply and irrigation systems. Nishapur had grown very rapidly over the ninth and tenth centuries to incorporate sixty-five nearby villages.[83] Its broader agricultural hinterland comprised 2,000 villages, but even this was not sufficient to supply its needs, and foodstuffs had to be imported from nearby Sarakhs and Quchan. The agricultural basis of the region was the qanat system of irrigation through underground canals. This also allowed the widespread cultivation of cotton, and Nishapur became famous for its textile industry, as well as for ceramics and silk. Its cloths were fashionable among the Baghdadi elite, and there was a substantial export trade in them.[84] Any failure of maintenance in the qanat

77 Ibn al-Jawzi, *al-Muntazam*, XVI, 301. Further on the activities of Kurds and Arabs, see Duri, 'Society and Economy', 123–7; Lambton, 'Aspects', 121–2.

78 Ibn al-Jawzi, *al-Muntazam*, XVI, 299; for another example, see *ibid.*, XVII, 145 (510 AH).

79 Ibn al-Athir, *al-Kamil*, X, 97.

80 Ibn al-Jawzi, *al-Muntazam*, XVII, 194; Sibt, *Mir'at*, ed. Ghamidi, 722–4. For another example, see Ibn al-Jawzi, *al-Muntazam*, XVII, 156 (511 AH).

81 Ibn Funduq, *Tarikh-i Bayhaq*, 267. For more on earthquakes in the region, see N. N. Ambraseys and C. P. Melville, *A History of Persian Earthquakes* (Cambridge, 1982).

82 For example, Ibn al-Jawzi, *al-Muntazam*, XVI, 16–17 (Baghdad, 449 AH). Also Durand-Guédy, *Iranian Elites*, 216.

83 Description: Christensen, *Decline of Iranshahr*, 193–5.

84 R. B. Serjeant, *Islamic Textiles: Materials for a History up to the Mongol Conquest* (Beirut, 1972), 91–2.

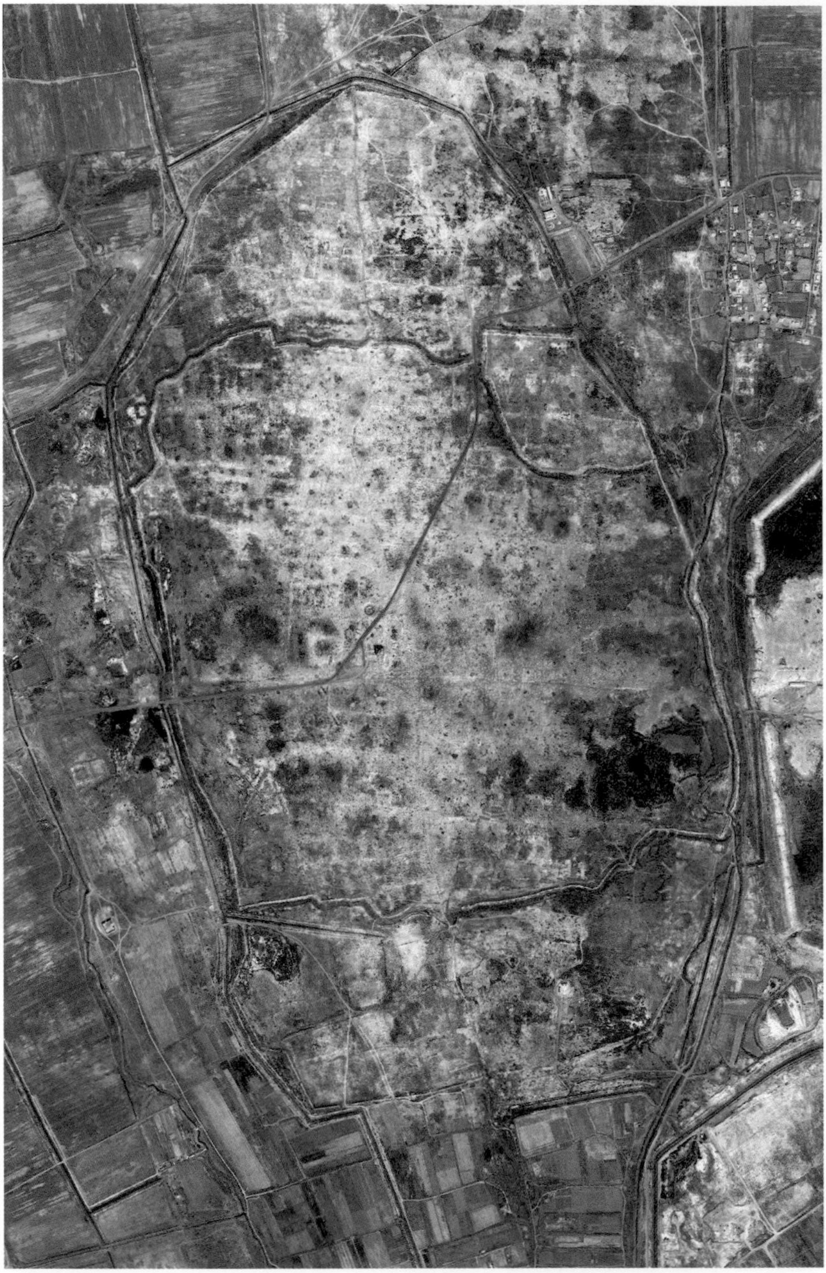

Figure 8.4 The city of Merv; the inner ring of walls marks the Seljuk city of Sultankala, with at its top right the Shahriyar Arg containing Sanjar's palace and government buildings; in the centre, Sanjar's mausoleum. Part of an IKONOS satellite image taken in April 2001. Courtesy of the UCL Ancient Merv Project

system, though, was potentially utterly ruinous, and we frequently read of the devastating impact of famine in the region. Even more acute problems beset Merv, located in a vast oasis, surrounded by inhospitable desert. The city's survival relied on a complex irrigation system, both to bring water of the Murghab River to the city and to allow cultivation of the surrounding oasis. In the tenth century, the only mediaeval period for which we have information, maintenance of the irrigation works required a workforce of 10,000 men. Yet the city was nonetheless prone to both sudden floods when the Murghab broke its banks, but equally to drought when the river and the irrigation works failed. Sands constantly threatened to choke the canals, but nonetheless the irrigation system was sufficiently robust to allow the cultivation of cotton – Merv was especially famous for the fine, almost silk-like quality of its cotton,[85] and the textile industry was essential to the town's prosperity. In reality, Merv was probably a distinctly unpleasant place to live. Quite apart from the extreme heat, its precarious location on the edge of a harsh desert, liable to Ghuzz attacks at the slightest weakening of authority, the extreme heat in summer and cold in winter, the water was notoriously brackish and bitter, and malaria was a constant hazard.[86] It is perhaps hardly surprising that Sanjar's court is said to have rapidly wearied of the place and begged the sultan to move to the more agreeable climate of Bukhara.[87]

Despite all these tribulations, there is evidence that in many areas of the Seljuk Empire cities were expanding rapidly. Perhaps surprisingly, it is exactly in places where nomads must have been present in their largest numbers that we see the most dramatic growth in urbanism over the eleventh and twelfth centuries. Archaeological research on the middle reaches of the River Syr Darya, in what is now Kazakhstan, shows that the eleventh and twelfth centuries saw the construction of several new towns. These were concentrated in the area near the confluence of the Syr Darya and the Arys rivers, in the vicinity of the great shrine of the saint Ahmad Yasavi at the town of Turkestan, and thus largely fell under the domains of the Seljuks' Qarakhanid vassals. Existing towns, moreover, expanded. Even more dramatic was the expansion of urbanism in Semirechie, especially its northeast, also part of the Qarakhanid domains; in the ninth to tenth centuries, there were about ten settlements of any size; in the eleventh to early thirteenth centuries, there

[85] *Ibid.*, 89–90.

[86] Christensen, *Decline of Iranshahr*, 189–93.

[87] Juzjani, *Tabaqat*, I, 260–1. Juzjani even attributes Rudaki's famous ode on the attractions of Bukhara, *bū-yi jū-yi Mūliyān āyad hamī*, to Mu'izzi, claiming he had been begged by the sultan's retinue to compose something to get him to leave Merv.

were something like seventy.[88] The size varied immensely: some places categorised as towns may seem to us little more than villages, with a population of say 1,500; others, like Isfijab, were much more considerable, with perhaps a population of 40,000, putting it in the same league, probably, as some of the larger settlements of Khurasan.

These towns were in many ways part of the steppe world; in some cases permanent tents seem to have been installed in the courtyards of houses, testimony to the inhabitants' continuing links with the nomadic way of life.[89] From the steppe they purchased horses, wool, leather, dairy products, meat and slaves; in return, they would have traded the products of the sedentary economy – above all, no doubt, agricultural goods, but also ceramics and metalwork produced in urban ateliers, and imported luxuries, such as jewellery and silk, trade being a mainstay of the urban economy.[90] By the end of the eleventh century, the town must have been a familiar sight to steppe dwellers. In earlier periods, too, of course, nomads had dealings with the sedentary world, but there were now far more of these towns right on the nomads' back door, and the archaeology suggests that these eleventh- and twelfth-century towns were much more classically Islamic,[91] both in terms of the presence of distinctive structures likes mosques and baths, and in the increasingly dense population within the city walls.[92]

According to Soviet archaeologists, there was also expansion in existing urban centres throughout the Seljuk and Qarakhanid realms in Khurasan and Transoxiana, ranging from Tirmidh on the Oxus to Shash (Tashkent).[93] This picture has been confirmed by more recent work at Merv, which under Sanjar witnessed rapid expansion and considerable urban prosperity.[94] Merv reached the height of its prosperity in the twelfth century, but Yaqut's account of the glories of the city where he lived for three years in the early thirteenth century suggests that despite the traumas of the Ghuzz takeover, it remained a

88 Karl M. Baypakov, 'Culture urbaine du Kazakhstan du sud et du Semiretchie à l'époque des Karakhanides', in Vincent Fourniau *et al.* (eds), *Études karakhanides* (*Cahiers d'Asie Centrale* 9) (Tashkent and Aix-en-Provence, 2001), 145.

89 *Ibid.*, 153.

90 *Ibid.*, 155–71.

91 *Ibid.*, 163.

92 *Ibid.*, 164–6.

93 See Agadshanow, *Der Staat der Seldschukiden*, 211–12.

94 Georgina Herrmann, *Monuments of Merv: Traditional Buildings of the Karakum* (London, 1999), 114; see also Tim Williams, 'The City of Sultan Kala, Merv, Turkmenistan: Communities, Neighbourhoods and Urban Planning from the Eighth to the Thirteenth Century', in Amira K. Bennison and Alison L. Gascoigne (eds), *Cities in the Pre-modern Islamic World: The Urban Impact of Religion, State and Society* (London, 2007), 42–62.

spectacularly wealthy city until the Mongol conquest.[95] The oasis countryside was, he claimed, even more splendid than the urban areas (*fa-ammā rustāq Marw fa-huwa ajall min al-mudun*).[96]

Evidence for the Iranian plateau is much harder to come by. Most Seljuk cities now lie buried under modern buildings, making archaeological investigation unfeasible. Even in those towns where some archaeological work has taken place, such as Nishapur and Rayy, investigated by American teams in the 1930s, the quality of publication sometimes leaves much to be desired. Tentatively, the limited archaeology that has been done suggests that Rayy and Jurjan grew under Seljuk rule; literary sources seem to present the same picture of growth and prosperity for Isfahan in the first quarter of the twelfth century.[97]

Even in Iraq, the pattern was not one of uniform decline despite the gloomy picture painted by Yaqut (p. 294 above). Although some areas of Baghdad were deserted, others witnessed rapid expansion.[98] A Seljuk document allegedly seen by the fourteenth-century author Hamdallah Mustawfi, indicates that the revenue collected from Arab Iraq was nearly ten times as great as it was in his day.[99] Yaqut's testimony of the decline of southern Iraq should be qualified. Yaqut himself states that the Mazyadids founded their prosperous capital of Hilla in 495/1101.[100] Indeed, despite Yaqut's accusations of Seljuk neglect in Iskaf, Ibn al-Jawzi tells us that the Seljuk *shiḥna*, Bihruz, spent considerable efforts to restore the Nahrawan canal between 522/1128 and 536/1141–2.[101]

95 Yaqut, *Muʿjam*, V, 114–15.

96 *Ibid.*, V, 115.

97 Rayy: Rocco Rante, 'The Topography of Rayy in the Early Islamic Period', *Iran*, 45 (2007), 177; see also on the medieval city the publication of an exhibition based on the findings of the unpublished excavations of 1934–6: Tanya Treptow with Donald Whitcomb, *Daily Life Ornamented: The Medieval Persian City of Rayy* (Chicago, 2007). Rocco Rante, *Rayy: from its Origins to the Mongol Invasions* (Leiden, 2014) appeared when this book was in the final stages of production. For Jurjan: M. Kiani, *The Islamic City of Gurgan* (Berlin, 1984); and for Isfahan: Durand-Guédy, *Iranian Elites*, 184–6. The main publications for Nishapur are Charles Wilkinson, *Nishapur: Some Early Islamic Buildings and Their Decoration* (New York, 1986), and, based on much more recent excavations, Rante and Collinet, *Nishapur Revisited.*

98 Van Renterghem, 'Controlling and Developing Baghdad', 123–4; van Renterghem, 'Social and Urban Dynamics,' 171–4, 190–1; Duri, 'Society and Economy', 49–95. See also Lambton, 'Aspects', 117.

99 Lambton, 'Aspects', 121–2; Mustawfi, *The Geographical Part of the* Nuzhat al-Qulūb, 47–8.

100 See Yaqut, *Muʿjam*, II, 294; Makdisi, 'Notes on Hilla and the Mazyadids', 249–62; Duri, 'Society and Economy', 22–26.

101 Duri, 'Society and Economy', 176–7; Ibn al-Jawzi, *al-Muntazam*, XVII, 250 (522 AH), XVIII, 3 (534 AH), XVIII, 17 (536).

In Syria and the Jazira the pattern was also uneven: a city like Harran seems to have remained little more than an isolated garrison town and actually declined, but elsewhere towns like Raqqa witnessed rapid construction and expansion. Indeed, Heidemann has described the Seljuk period as representing an 'urban, political and economic renaissance' that laid the foundations for urban growth under the Zangids and Ayyubids.[102] Thus, from Syria to Central Asia, Seljuk rule coincided with the growth of cities. There are occasional indications that this was the result of a deliberate policy by the sultans. Ibn al-Athir states that Tughrıl found Rayy ruined and ordered it to be restored, and we have noted elsewhere (p. 48 above) efforts to encourage the prosperity of Isfahan after the conquest.[103] Local Seljuk rulers like Ridwan and amirs like Tughtegin introduced policies designed to encourage re-population in Aleppo and Damascus.[104] Stefan Heidemann sees the proactive role of the Seljuk state as key to ensuring prosperity and laying the ground for further growth in the second half of the twelfth century.[105] Such an interpretation, however, assumes the ability of the state to project its power effectively on the ground, an ability which is not always apparent in Seljuk history. However, there is little doubt that for individual *muqṭa'*s, as argued above (pp. 73, 79–80), making their *iqṭā'*s prosper was the best way of securing both their revenue and their political autonomy. The extent of this urban revival, its consequences, and a comparison with the situation in neighbouring parts of the world, both Muslim and non-Muslim, need further research.

The Organization of Urban Life

In Khurasan and Transoxiana, cities followed a basic plan of a citadel (*quhandiz*), which was surrounded by an inner city (*shahristān*), which would also usually be walled; beyond the *shahristān* was the *rabaḍ*.[106] Although unwalled, the *rabaḍ* in fact was often the economic heart of the town, and, as we have seen, the military role of the *quhandiz* was in places declining in

[102] Stefan Heidemann, 'Charity and Piety for the Transformation of Cities: The New Direction of Taxation and Waqf and Policy in Mid-twelfth Century Northern Syria and Mesopotamia', in Miriam Frenkel and Yaacov Lev (eds), *Charity and Giving in Monotheistic Religions* (Berlin, 2009),154; cf. Heidemann, *Die Renaissance der Städte*, esp. 289 ff.

[103] Ibn al-Athir, *al-Kamil*, IX, 507–8.

[104] Heidemann, *Die Renaissance der Städte*, 315–16.

[105] *Ibid.*, 97–353, esp. 315–18; more briefly, 'Unislamic Taxes', 494: 'The Seljuqs had laid the political and economic foundations for the second blooming of the Islamic world' . . . 'The Seljuqs began to make necessary political and economic adjustments to improve the prevailing social and economic order.'

[106] Kennedy, 'From Shahristan to Madina'.

the eleventh century (pp. 238–9). As in the modern Middle Eastern city, the congregational mosque stood at the heart of the town, while certain quarters or streets were the preserve of given professions: there might be a *sūq* (market) for clothmakers, for farriers, for metalworkers and so on. A scholarly debate has raged over whether these professions were arranged into 'guilds' by analogy with Europe. There is no precise term in Arabic or Persian in this period which equates to 'guild', but circumstantial evidence suggests that each craft may have had at least some kind of loose and informal organisation, with a head and some kind of apprenticeship.[107] The absence of direct references to such organisations, or even a specific term for them, suggests their relative lack of importance, even given the comparatively limited socio-economic data at our disposal.[108]

Little more than the scantiest foundations survive of the domestic architecture of the period: the elaborate stucco work on the so-called 'rich man's house' at Merv suggests that a life of luxury could be enjoyed by some, but we know nothing of its inhabitants.[109] More revealing is a remarkable series of glazed ceramic models dating from the twelfth century which give us an impression of what a typical house looked like, at least in Iran (Figure 8.5). The function of these objects is not quite clear – they most probably served as ritual gifts on occasions such as Nawruz or weddings – but they clearly depict typical houses, probably of the middle classes. The ceramics would have been fairly cheap, generally with a monochrome glaze, and are far from being luxury items. The houses depicted are all one storey, usually rectangular in shape, based around an open courtyard with a sort of fence around the top. Human figures are often depicted too, moulded around the inside edges of the courtyard, usually about eight to ten in number. Occasionally, other objects such as wine jars and tables are depicted in the courtyard. Indeed, some of the figures seem to be drinkers or musicians, suggestive of the festivities enjoyed on the occasions for which these models may have been created. These models indicate that the typical house in Seljuk Iran was rather like

[107] See Abbas Hamdani, 'The *Rasa'il Ikhwan al-Safa* and the Controversy about the Origin of Craft Guilds in Early Medieval Islam', in Nelly Hanna (ed.), *Money, Land and Trade: An Economic History of the Muslim Mediterranean* (London, 2002), 157–73, which also offers an overview of the earlier literature. Lambton, 'Internal Structure', 276–7, uses the term guild rather freely, but appears actually to mean just groups of traders of the same products. See also Lambton, *Continuity and Change*, 343.

[108] For example, other organisations such as *aḥdāth* and *'ayyārs* which did play an important socio-economic role are discussed regularly in our sources. It is thus not simply a question of a lack of data.

[109] Hermann, *Monuments of Merv*, 114.

Figure 8.5 Model of a Seljuk house. Burrell Collection Glasgow, No. 33/235. © CSG CSC Glasgow Museums Collection.

those from a much later date that survive in Yazd in central Iran.[110] As at Yazd (Figure 8.6), the exterior of the houses was probably very plain, with few windows. Narrow, winding lanes lined with these mud-brick abodes occasionally give out into open spaces with a mosque or mausoleum, but the focus of social life was either the house courtyard or the bazaar – and we may assume the latter was a largely male preserve.

Society was highly stratified; elites were in theory themselves segregated into bureaucratic, military and religious classes, marked out by distinctive clothing, headgear and place of residence. Sources condemn the mixing of members of these different social classes, although these very condemnations suggest that these conventions were not always rigidly observed.[111] Ibn al-Jawzi, for instance, remarks with some surprise that despite his wealth the rich Baghdadi Ibn Jarrada 'never abandoned the clothing or food of merchants'.[112] Such distinctions were perhaps of greater importance in the great imperial centres such as Baghdad and Isfahan which had a substantial

[110] Margaret S. Graves, 'Ceramic House Models from Medieval Persia: Domestic Architecture and Concealed Activities', *Iran*, 46 (2008), 227–51.

[111] Van Renterghem, 'Le sentiment d'appartenance', 232–4, 235–7.

[112] *Ibid.*, 240–1; Ibn al-Jawzi, *al-Muntazam*, XVI, 232–3.

Figure 8.6 The mud streets of modern Yazd, the buildings all looking inwards, give some impression of a Seljuk townscape

bureaucratic and military presence. The constitution of these elites also changed as Khurasani families gained prominent positions in society in the wake of the Seljuks conquests.[113] In most towns, however, the dominant figures were the local 'urban aristocracy' who tended to occupy the position of *ra'īs* (on which see above, p. 192). The constitution of this urban aristocracy varied from place to place, but these families' position often rested less on the control of extensive lands or commercial interests (although they might indeed intermarry with merchants and landowners), than on social capital as descendants of the Prophet, or their status as *'ulamā'*.[114] In the few places where we have detailed local evidence, this aristocracy was in flux. In Nishapur, Hanafi then Shafi'i notables alternately came to prominence, while in Bayhaq, where the aristocracy was predominantly composed of sayyids, new sayyid families came to the fore over the eleventh and twelfth centuries.[115]

113 Van Renterghem, 'Le sentiment d'appartenance', 232; van Renterghem, 'Social and Urban Dynamics', 181–2; Durand-Guédy, 'An Emblematic Family', 183–6.

114 Bulliet, *Patricians of Nishapur*, 21–6; Aubin, 'L'aristocratie urbaine'.

115 Bulliet, *Patricians of Nishapur*, 26 ff; Aubin, 'L'aristocratie urbaine'; Morimoto, 'Putting the *Lubāb al-Albāb* in Context'.

The urban aristocracy was thus riven with rivalries which were reflected more generally in society, above all through madhhab affiliation. Tensions between members of rival madhhabs had been rising from the tenth century onwards, perhaps as an expression of broader social and economic dislocation.[116] However, there was a religious aspect too, for the belief that a rival madhhab's rituals and communal prayers were invalid meant that separate mosques for each madhhab were required. In twelfth-century Rayy Ash'ari and Hanafi *'ulamā'* issued fatwas forbidding their followers from attending each other's prayers.[117] Merv had separate Hanafi and Shafi'i mosques even before the Seljuks, and this became a common pattern.[118] In Nishapur, Nizam al-Mulk built a mosque exclusively for the Shafi'is, while use of the great mosque in Isfahan was disputed between Shafi'is and Hanafis.[119] As a result, cities across the Seljuk Empire became divided into quarters inhabited by members of rival madhhabs. In Baghdad, for instance, the Hanbalis were concentrated in the Bab al-Azaj and Bab al-Basra areas, while the Shi'ites lived in Karkh;[120] Nishapur, likewise, was divided into Hanafi and Shafi'i quarters. This spatial division must only have exacerbated the madhhabs' sense of mutual alienation and antagonism. Although the inter-madhhab tensions predated the Seljuks, they seem to have intensified under Seljuk rule. In Isfahan, for instance, both the minority Hanafis and the Shafi'is were long established in the city, but at the time of the Seljuk conquest this was not reflected in any special division of the population. By the mid-twelfth century, the polarisation was reflected in the physical layout of the city, with distinct Hanafi and Shafi'i quarters.[121]

Disputes between the parties frequently ended in violence, riots and death, or as our mediaeval sources term it, *fitna*, civil unrest. In late Buyid times, *fitna* seems to have broken out more or less every year in Baghdad, and these disturbances continued under Seljuk rule. Further east, Isfahan, Nishapur and the other major cities were ravaged by *fitna*. Yet there are also plenty of towns where we read little or nothing of any such strife. The

116 See Cl. Cahen, 'Mouvements populaires et autonomisme urbain dans l'Asie musulmane du moyen age, II', *Arabica*, 6/i (1959), 27–9; Paul, *Herrscher, Gemeinwesen, Vermittler*, 131–6.

117 Calmard, 'Le chiisme imamite', 46; cf. Rawandi, *Rahat al-Sudur*, 13, who condemns the extremes to which members of a madhhab would go in denouncing their opponents (somewhat ironically, in view of his own Hanafi partisanship).

118 Madelung, 'The Spread of Maturidism', 138, n. 72.

119 *Ibid.*, 139, n. 73; Durand-Guédy, *Iranian Elites*, 200; Husayni, *Akhbar*, 125; cf. Hamadhan: Fragner, *Geschichte der Stadt Hamadān*, 125–6.

120 Cf. Ephrat, *A Learned Society*, 25, on the location of madrasas in Baghdad according to madhhab.

121 Durand-Guédy, *Iranian Elites*, 200–4, 233.

Jazira seems to have been mainly peaceful, and in Iran, there is little evidence for *fitna* in major centres such as Tabriz and Shiraz. It is hard to be sure whether this reflects genuine regional variation or simply the unevenness of the sources, as for many cities we have no local histories.[122] The detailed chronicles of Damascus and Aleppo by Ibn al-Qalanisi and Ibn al-ʿAdim do not suggest anything like the same prevalence of strife there, although it certainly occurred from time to time.

According to the literary sources, *fitna* was the main cause of the decline of urbanism in Iran, not climate change, Seljuk maladministration or over-taxation, Ghuzz depredations or even Khwarazmian brutality. Rather, the local population had destroyed their own cities in the course of the vicious factional infighting. In Isfahan for instance, Yaqut writes:

> Its quarters have been ruined of late because of the numerous incidents of civil strife and partisanship between the Shafiis and the Hanafis and the constant wars between the two parties. Whenever one party gets the upper hand over the other, it plunders, burns and ruins the other's quarter . . . it is likewise in the rural districts and villages, each one of them is like the city.[123]

Ibn al-Athir confirms this picture for Nishapur, remarking of the Ghuzz incursions after the fall of Sanjar that:

> the *ʿayyārs* [i.e., the local urban militias] also plundered Nishapur, more severely than the Ghuzz, and behaved even worse than the latter had.[124]

The same was true of Merv, according to Nishapuri:

> When the Ghuzz left [after sacking the city in 548/1153], because of the difference in madhhab between the inhabitants there were ancient hatreds. Every evening a group from one quarter would get together and set light to the rival quarter, until the ruins that had been left by the Ghuzz were completed destroyed. Famine and plague enveloped them so that everyone who had escaped from sword and torture died in poverty.[125]

[122] However, *fitna* scarcely features in our two main city histories for the eleventh- to twelfth-century Jazira, Ibn Azraq's *Taʾrikh Mayyafariqin*, and Abu Hafs ʿUmar b. al-Khidr al-Turki's *Taʾrikh Dunaysir*, ed. Ibrahim Salih (Beirut, 1992).

[123] Yaqut, *Muʿjam*, I, 209; cf. Durand-Guédy, *Iranian Elites*, 200–4, 271, 300; for Rayy, see Yaqut, *Muʿjam*, III, 117; for Nishapur, see Bulliet, *Patricians of Nishapur*, 76–81; Bulliet, 'The Political–Religious History of Nishapur', 90–1; Rawandi, *Rahat al-Sudur*, 182; Qummi, *Dhayl-i Nafthat al-Masdur*, 318–19.

[124] Ibn al-Athir, *al-Kamil*, XI, 182.

[125] Nishapuri, *Saljuqnama*, 65–6.

Confirmation of the association between *fitna* and the relaxation of Seljuk authority comes from Ibn Funduq's chronicle of Bayhaq, which describes how civil disorder broke out in the town almost immediately after Malikshah's death, blossoming into full-scale fighting between rival groups of inhabitants during the war between Berkyaruq and Muhammad.[126]

The picture painted by our sources of the ruin of Khurasan through these 'ancient hatreds' (*ḥaqā'id-i qadīm*), as Nishapuri calls them, will doubtless need to be interpreted in the light of future archaeological work, which, in conjunction with numismatics, offers the best potential for understanding long-term economic trends. The phenomenon of urban ruin through *fitna* appears to be especially characteristic of the Jibal and Khurasan, but the underlying dynamics are more generally applicable across the Seljuk realm. Economic and social conditions were ultimately determined less by the policies of any vizier or sultan, than by the communities themselves. It was these same communities, after all, who decided whether to open the gates of their cities before the Seljuks in the conquest period, or to resist. At the same time, the fact that these rivalries resulted in fully-fledged destruction only after the empire's collapse suggests that the Seljuk officials were more efficient in, and more concerned with, maintaining public order than the sources often make apparent. The policy of balance and containment observable in Baghdad (pp. 263–4 above) seems to have obtained more generally, suggesting that even if the reach of the state was often weak, and pre-existing custom was preferred to administrative innovation, Seljuk rule was not entirely laissez-faire.

126 Aubin, 'L'aristocratie urbaine', 328–9; Ibn Funduq, *Tarikh-i Bayhaq*, 265, 275.

Conclusion
The Seljuk Legacy

The historian and littérateur Rawandi, an intimate of Tughrıl III, recounts how after the death of the last sultan, he was left in a state of utter depression, until a mysterious voice announced to him in a dream:

> Glad tidings to you! The five-fold *nawba* of the sultanate of the Seljuk dynasty is still played in this world, and a king who is refuge to the world still shines like a moon from the Seljuk constellation; he hastens in search of kingship, to take the position of his ancestors. There has arisen a Seljuk dynasty descended from [Arslan] Isra'il, the seventh generation grandfather of the sultan, who was the elder of the [Seljuk] brothers and their senior . . . From the line of Isra'il a sultan has arisen with the conduct of Solomon, the wisdom of Anushirwan, the justice of 'Umar and the virtue of Kaykhusraw, such that that both men and supernatural creatures [*ādamī wa parī*] are subject to his command.[1]

Delighted but bewildered, Rawandi remained in confusion until there appeared in Hamadhan an Anatolian merchant, Jamal al-Din Abu Bakr b. Abi 'Ala, 'a partisan of the Seljuk dynasty' (*dūstdārī wa hawākhwāhī-yi khāndān-i Āl-i Saljūq*), who told him of the virtues of the Anatolian sultan, Ghiyath al-Din Kaykhusraw. In the presence of the 'amirs of Iraq, its religious dignitaries and its notables', Jamal al-Din recounted the sultan's wondrous victories over the Byzantine infidel, 'and filled the amirs of Iraq with affection for the lord of the world [Ghiyath al-Din]'.[2] Rawandi's own enthusiasm led him to undertake the long journey from Hamadhan to Konya in central Anatolia, the principal seat of the Ghiyath al-Din's court, in the search for a new patron for his history of the Seljuk sultans, the *Rahat al-Sudur*. The book was intended to instruct Ghiyath al-Din in the practices of the Seljuk sultans of Iraq, and

[1] Rawandi, *Rahat al-Sudur*, 460–1. For the *nawba* as a symbol of rule, see above pp. 161–2. Anushirwan and Kaykhusraw are legendary Iranian kings, 'Umar is a reference to the second caliph (d. 23/644).

[2] *Ibid.*, 462.

solicit the position of *nadīm* for its author.[3] Indeed, Rawandi even seems to have envisaged Ghiyath al-Din as a world ruler whose 'banners will stretch to the extremities of the land of the Turks, the Khita [China] and Khotan, and will grant that land to his servants'.[4] By implication, then, Ghiyath al-Din was not merely the legitimate successor to the Great Seljuk sultanate, but offered the best hope of liberation from Khwarazmian oppression.

In view of the deep-rooted hostility between the descendants of Mika'il b. Seljuk – Tughrıl and Chaghrı – and those of Arslan Isra'il, the emergence of the latter's Anatolian descendants as the standard-bearers of legitimate Seljuk rule for the partisans of the Iraq sultanate is ironic. In reality, the Anatolian Seljuks showed no interest in the distant lands of Iraq – in fact, the nearest they ever came had been a century earlier in 500/1105, when Qılıj Arslan b. Sulayman briefly captured Mosul and rumours spread that he was advancing on Baghdad to claim the sultanate.[5] However, after the demise of the Iraq sultanate, the descendants of Isra'il started to promote themselves as heirs to the Great Seljuk heritage. Whereas in the twelfth century when they were rulers of a remote and undeveloped frontier polity, just one of several Turkish states in Anatolia – in essence, Nawakiyya chiefs[6] – the collapse of first the Great Seljuks and then the Iraq sultanate coincided with the emergence of the Seljuks of Rum as the leading Muslim state in Anatolia and a major power in the eastern Mediterranean. From the early thirteenth century, Anatolian Seljuk sultans started to commission vast poetic epics celebrating their dynastic history, *Saljuqnamas*.[7] Despite the dynasty's decline later in the century, victims of the Mongol invasions of the Middle East, an association with the Seljuks remained an essential attribute of legitimacy for Muslim rulers in Anatolia. Many claimed Seljuk descent, while the Ottoman court historians tried to obfuscate the question of that dynasty's obscure origins by transmitting the legend that the last Seljuk sultan had personally invested their ancestors with the right to rule. The same weapon could equally well be turned against the Ottomans, and rebellions headed by men claiming superior legitimacy on the basis of Seljuk descent occurred in Anatolia into the sixteenth century, while traces of the influence of this idea can be found as late as the eighteenth century.[8]

3 See further Yıldız, 'A *Nadīm* for the Sultan', 91–111.

4 Rawandi, *Rahat al-Sudur*, 464.

5 Ibn al-Athir, *al-Kamil*, X, 431. The rumours are said to have been spread by Ismailis in Muhammad Tapar's army to discourage a campaign against Ismaili strongholds.

6 On the Nawakiyya and the characteristic of early Seljuk rule in Anatolia, see Peacock, 'From the Balkhān-Kūhīyān to the Nāwakīya'.

7 See Peacock, 'Seljuq Legitimacy', 81–2. Unfortunately, none of these verse *Saljuqnamas* from the period has survived intact.

8 *Ibid.*, 86–91.

In the lands that had been subject to the Great Seljuks, responses to the Seljuk legacy were more varied. Most of the Seljuks' immediate successors in the west, especially in Syria and the Jazira, were connected to the dynasty in some way, and sought to stress these links as a way of justifying their rule. As parvenu military elites, they often did not feel able to adopt the title of sultan. Thus, long after Seljuk power had disappeared from Arabic-speaking Syria, Zangid rulers continued to use the Persianate titles of the Seljuk courts in the Jibal.[9] Like numerous other dynasties in the Seljuk west – the Salghurids of Fars, the Hazaraspids of Luristan, the Ildegüzids of Azerbaijan and the Ahmadilis of Maragha – they claimed the title of *atabeg*, even when there were no Seljuk princes to guard, as a means of emphasising their connection with the Seljuk Empire.[10] On their accession, Zangid rulers were seated ceremonially on the throne of Tutush, another symbol of this connection.[11] The enthusiasm for the Seljuk heritage was also expressed in architectural and artistic styles from Iran that became popular in the Zangid domains.[12] The most significant of the thirteenth-century Levantine Muslim states, the Ayyubid empire in Syria and Egypt, also had Seljuk origins. The Ayyubids' ancestors had served in the Seljuk military, and Saladin himself had been born in Tikrit where his father, Najm al-Din Ayyub, was the Seljuk military governor. It has been suggested that the decentralised structure of the Seljuk Empire influenced the Kurdish Ayyubids, whose state was run along a similar system of appanages controlled by different members of the ruling family. Seljuk influences also permeated the Ayyubid state through their employment in the bureaucracy of numerous émigrés from the Seljuk lands, exemplified by 'Imad al-Din al-Isfahani. [13]

However, this enthusiasm for all things Seljuk was not universally shared. Jurbadhqani, whose hostility to his contemporary Tughrıl III we have noted (p. 120), sniffily commented that the Seljuks had been forgotten by history because men of learning did not prosper under their rule.[14] Although Jurbadhqani is doubtless motivated by his own agenda

[9] See Nikita Elisséeff, 'La titulature de Nur ad-Din d'après ses inscriptions', *Bulletin d'études orientales*, 14 (1952–54), 155–96.

[10] On these, see Cl. Cahen, 'Atābak', *EIr.*

[11] Abu Shama, *Kitab al-Rawdatayn fi Akhbar al-Dawlatayn*, ed. Ibrahim Shams al-Din (Beirut, 2002), II, 208.

[12] Hillenbrand, 'Eastern Islamic Influences'.

[13] On Seljuq influences in Ayyubid state, see R. Stephen Humphreys, *From Saladin to the Mongols: The Ayyubids of Damascus, 1193–1260* (Albany, NY, 1977), 67–71, 190; Hirschler, 'He is a Child', 33, 37–8; Peacock, ''Imad al-Din al-Isfahani's *Nusrat al-fatra*', 85–8.

[14] Jurfadhqani, *Tarjuma-yi Tarikh-i Yamini*, 9. See further my comments in Peacock, 'Court Historiography', 336–7.

to find a suitable patron in the post-Seljuk age, the Seljuk political legacy seems at first glance rather more muted in Iran and Central Asia than in the empire's peripheral territories of the Jazira and Syria. Unlike the Zangids and most Ayyubids, the new dynasties of the Khwarazmshahs and the Ghurids did claim the title of sultan, and they did not feel the same need as the western successor states to broadcast their connection to this Seljuk heritage. Nonetheless, especially in the case of the Khwarazmians, Seljuk antecedents continued to exercise an influence in, for instance, their chancery practice.[15] The composition of Husayni's history of the Seljuks, most probably in early thirteenth-century Nishapur under Khwarazmian rule – the author himself seems to have served in the Khwarazmshahs' bureaucracy – points to a continuing interest in the dynasty. Husayni's work presents quite an idealised view of the Seljuks, perhaps with the aim of presenting them as a model to a putative Khwarazmian patron.[16] This idealisation of the Seljuks would intensify under Mongol rule. Consider the comments of the bureaucrat Hamdallah Mustawfi, writing in the early fourteenth century under the Ilkhanid Mongol dynasty that ruled in Iran, criticising the heretical tendencies or obscure origins of other dynasties, and vaunting the Seljuks even above the ʿAbbasids:

> Each of the dynasties that have existed in the epoch of Islam have been polluted by a fault: the Umayyads by heresy and secession from orthodoxy and Kharijism (*zandaqa wa iʿtizāl wa khārijīyat*), some of the ʿAbbasids by Muʿtazilism (*iʿtizāl*), the Saffarids and the Buyids by Shiʿism (*rafḍ*), and the Ghaznavids, Khwarazmshahs and Salghurids by their low origins. The Seljuks, however, were free from all these faults. They were Sunnis of pure religion and good faith, beneficent and compassionate to their subjects, so that they were not disturbed by any rebels.[17]

Hamdallah was not alone: the great Ilkhanid vizier Rashid al-Din also praised the Seljuks, and they were glorified in Yazdi's fourteenth-century *al-ʿUrada fi 'l-Hikaya al-Saljuqiyya*, which represents a repolished and elaborated version of Nishapuri's chronicle. The memory of Nizam al-Mulk as the model

[15] See Lambton, *Continuity and Change*, in general on the continuities between Seljuk and later periods in Iran; specifically on the Khwarazmshahs' administrative organisation and its Seljuk antecedents, see Horst, *Staatsverwaltung*, which should be treated with some caution. On the Ghurids, see Bosworth, 'Ghurids'. However, neither dynasty has yet been thoroughly studied and our understanding of the way they functioned is limited.

[16] See Peacock, 'Court Historiography', 332 with further references.

[17] Hamdallah Mustawfi, *Tarikh-i Guzida*, 426.

vizier was also celebrated in the Mongol period.[18] The pro-Seljuk enthusiasm among Ilkhanid bureaucrats, writing shortly after their Mongol masters had embraced Islam and themselves sought to appropriate Perso-Islamic traditions of rulership, perhaps derived from the fact that the Seljuks provided a precedent for this sort of acculturation of a steppe dynasty. This idealised view, promoting the Seljuks' legitimacy as Sunni rulers, has more basis in the imagination of these fourteenth-century bureaucrats than in reality, even if it has exerted an unwarranted influence on modern scholarship.[19] Nonetheless, the precedent was not entirely imaginary. The Mongol vizier Rashid al-Din's attempts to trace the origins of his masters in his great chronicle *Jami' al-Tawarikh*, in a sense emulate the Arabic and Persian versions of the Seljuk *Maliknama*, reflecting the dynasty's desire to preserve its memory of its steppe beginnings, translated into a language and form comprehensible to a literate Muslim audience.[20]

The Seljuks thus left a threefold political legacy. The prestige of their name continued to embody ideas of legitimate rule long after the dynasty's disappearance, above all in Anatolia; an association with the Seljuks legitimised successor states in the western territories of the empire; and the invented image of the Seljuks as the perfect Sunni dynasty made them (in theory, if not in practice) a model for later steppe dynasties. In terms of a more concrete legacy of institutions, certainty is somewhat elusive. Of the massive social and demographic changes that swept the Middle East during the eleventh and twelfth centuries, it is harder to be sure which owe a direct debt to Seljuk rule. The growth of Sufism, conversion to Islam and the increasing dominance of the Persian language in the east would all certainly have happened anyway, although possibly not all at the same pace or in the same way that they did. Would the Turks have settled the Middle East without the existence of the Seljuk Empire? Possibly they would: the 'Iraqiyya and the Nawakiyya, who introduced Seljuk settlement to Anatolia and Syria, generally operated beyond the sultans' direct control. However, these groups (especially in Syria) on occasion did receive some support and encouragement from the sultans and this was doubtless a factor in ensuring that Turkish settlement became entrenched in the region. Further, without the association with a prestigious aristocratic line – the key ingredient in earlier Turkish empires too in the form of the Ashina clan, and now embodied by the Seljuks – it is quite likely that the Turkish incursions of the eleventh century would simply have fizzled out leaving little behind but a trail of destruction, just as happened with the

18 Cf. Cook, 'Were the Ismaili Assasins the First Suicide Attackers?', 101–2.
19 Cf. Safi, *Politics of Knowledge*, 6, 36.
20 Cf. Peacock, 'Court Historiography', 345.

Ghuzz in the twelfth century, or indeed the 'Iraqiyya in the early eleventh century.

The impact of later steppe rulers makes tracing the survival of a specifically Seljuk legacy difficult, for they shared common practices. For instance, the practice of using the bow string to murder members of the royal family to avoid shedding their blood survived into Ottoman times; but the Mongols had exactly the same taboo. Similarly, although the Seljuks were first to introduce the *ṭughrā* to the Middle East, a symbol which survived in daily use until the twentieth century, it was probably common to most Turkic rulers, included those who had no connection with the Seljuks; indeed, one of the earliest surviving examples comes from the chancery of the Turkish rulers of fourteenth-century Delhi.[21] The atabegate, too, had a successor in the Ottoman post of *lala*, and till the sixteenth century the Ottomans emulated Seljuk practice in allotting territories as appanages to princes, just as the Seljuks granted their *maliks iqṭā's*.[22] While all these institutions and practices first appear in the Middle East with the Seljuks, we cannot say with any certainty that their survival is connected with the dynasty. Rather, their importance was probably reinforced by later dynasties, such as the Mongols, or the several Türkmen dynasties that ruled in the fourteenth to fifteenth centuries. Turkish dynasties in this period, both the Ottomans and Türkmen rulers like the Aqqoyunlu, showed a special enthusiasm for emphasising their steppe lineage, manifested in tales of a common ancestry (purportedly shared with the Seljuks) in Oghuz Khan, a mythical ancestor of the Turks who became conflated with Genghis Khan.[23]

Thus, it is politically, as a symbol of legitimate rule, rather than in terms of precise institutions, that the Seljuk legacy is most clearly discernable. This legacy has continued to resonate into modern times. Ironically, in view of the seventeenth-century genealogist and historian of the Türkmen Abu 'l-Ghazi's bitter recollection of the Seljuks as 'no use to their tribe or people',[24] abandoning their steppe kin for the trappings of Persianate kingship, the Seljuks have today been pressed into the service of the Republic of Turkmenistan. The Türkmen currency features Sanjar on the 5 manat note, while in the

21 Soudavar, 'Mongol Legacy'.

22 On the steppe heritage in the Ottoman empire, see Murphey, *Exploring Ottoman Sovereignty*, esp. 19–39, 77–9; Fletcher, 'Turko-Mongol Monarchical Tradition'; Leslie Pierce, *The Imperial Harem: Women and Sovereignty in the Ottoman Empire* (New York, 1993), esp. 28 ff, 273–5.

23 See İlker Evrim Binbaş, 'Oghuz Khan Narratives', *EIr*. John E. Woods, *The Aqquyunlu: Clan, Confederation, Empire* (Salt Lake City, 1999).

24 Peacock, 'Seljuq Legitimacy', 80.

Figure C.1 Statue of Seljuk, one of the Türkmen national heroes depicted at the Independence Monument, Ashgabat, Turkmenistan

heart of the capital Ashghabat, a few miles away from Tughrıl's first *iqṭāʿ* of Nasa, the independence monument made out of marble and gold (the building materials du jour in post-Soviet Central Asia) is adorned with statues of Türkmen heroes, among them in prominent positions, Seljuk, Tughrıl and Chaghrı (Figure C.1).

For historians (and indeed politicians) in the Republic of Turkey, the Seljuks also play a crucial role in state ideology, as founders of the first Turkish state in Anatolia. The Seljuk sultanate of Anatolia was seen as a direct ancestor of modern Turkey, while the Great Seljuks were thought to demonstrate the Turks' supposedly unequalled talent for state-building.[25] Such views were especially emphasised in the early years of the republic, but the Seljuk past continues to be used for political purposes today. For instance, in a speech given on the anniversary of the battle of Manzikert on 26 August 2013, Turkish Prime Minister Recep Tayyib Erdogan declared:

> The victory at Manzikert, by making the land in which our dear nation lives into our motherland, determined the fate of Anatolia. Our dear nation through the victory at Manzikert laid the foundations of a civilisation based on peace, brotherhood, tolerance and solidarity . . . With these thoughts I celebrate the 942nd anniversary of the victory at Manzikert which opened the gates of Anatolia to us and made this land into our dear nation's motherland. I remember the great commander Alp Arslan and our dear martyrs [who fell in the battle] with mercy and gratitude.[26]

[25] Strohmeier, *Seldschukische Geschichte und türkische Geschichtswissenschaft*.

[26] http://www.haberler.com/basbakan-erdogan-dan-malazgirt-mesaji-4981339-haberi, (accessed 15 October 2013): 'Malazgirt Zaferi, üzerinde yaşadığımız bu coğrafyanın aziz milletimizin anavatanı haline gelmesine vesile olarak Anadolu'nun kaderinin yeniden tayin edilmesini sağlamıştır. Aziz milletimiz, Malazgirt Zaferi sayesinde, Anadolu'da asırlar boyunca devam edecek olan barış, kardeşlik, hoşgörü ve dayanışmaya dayalı bir medeniyetin de temellerini atmıştır . . . Bu düşüncelerle bize Anadolu'nun kapılarını ardına kadar aralayan ve bu toprakları aziz milletimizin vatanı kılan Malazgirt Zaferi'nin 942. yıldönümünü kutluyor, büyük komutan Sultan Alparslan'ı ve aziz şehitlerimizi rahmetle, minnetle yad ediyorum.' Further on the reception of the battle in modern Turkey, see Hillenbrand, *Turkish Myth*.

Appendix I
Regnal Dates of Seljuk Sultans, 'Abbasid Caliphs, Khwarazmshahs and Principal *Atabegs*[1]

Great Seljuk Sultans: 428/1038–552/1157

Tughrıl, 429/1038–455/1063 (Iran and Iraq, initially using title of amir)
Chaghrı, 429/1038–451/1059 (Khurasan, *malik al-mulūk*, but does not use title of sultan)[2]
Alp Arslan b. Chaghrı, 455/1063–465/1073 (ruler in Khurasan from the death of Chaghrı, then all Seljuk territories from 455/1063)
Malikshah b. Alp Arslan, 465/1073–485/1092
Mahmud b. Malikshah, 485/1092–487/1094 (claim disputed by Berkyaruq)
Berkyaruq b. Malikshah, 485/1092–495/1105 (claim disputed by Mahmud, Tutush and Muhammad Tapar)
Tutush b. Alp Arslan, 487/1094–488/1095 (claimed disputed by Berkyaruq, recognised mainly in Syria and parts of Iran)
Muhammad Tapar b. Malikshah, 495/1105–511/1118 (asserted claim to sultanate from 492/1098–9)
Sanjar b. Muhammad Tapar, 511/1118–552/1157 (ruled Khurasan as *malik* from 490/1097)
Mahmud Khan, nephew of Sanjar, 552/1157–557/1162 (Khurasan, not universally accepted as legitimate Seljuk ruler)

Seljuk Sultans of Iraq

Mahmud II b. Muhammad Tapar, 511/1118–525/1131
Da'ud b. Mahmud, 525/1131–526/1132; d. 538/1143 (claim disputed by Tughrıl II and Mas'ud)
Tughrıl II b. Muhammad Tapar, 526/1132–529/1134 (claim disputed by Da'ud and Mas'ud)

[1] The dates given here are largely based on those provided in C. E. Bosworth, *The New Islamic Dynasties: A Chronological and Genealogical Manual* (Edinburgh, 2004), with some modifications in the case of Seljuk rulers. For *atabegs* and Khwarazshahs, only basic information about figures directly relevant to the theme of this book is given.

[2] For Chaghrı's dates, see Özgüdenli, 'Selçuklu paraların ışığında'.

Mas'ud b. Muhammad Tapar, 529/1134–547/1152 (recognised by the caliph as sultan from 527/1132–3)
Malikshah II b. Mahmud II, 457/1152–458/1153
458/1153 Sulaymanshah b. Muhammad Tapar, Muhammad II b. Mahmud II and Arslan b. Tughrıl all proclaimed sultan by different parties of amirs, with Muhammad II eventually emerging as victorious.
Muhammad II b. Mahmud II, 548/1153–555/1160
Sulaymanshah b. Muhammad Tapar, 555/1160–556/1161 (had earlier briefly been proclaimed as sultan during Sanjar's captivity in 548/1153, but was forced to flee Khurasan and abandon claim)
Arslan(shah) b. Tughrıl II, 556/1161–571/1176
Tughrıl III b. Arslan, 571/1176–590/1194 (also Sanjar b. Sulaymansah, proclaimed sultan briefly by Qızıl Arslan in 586/1190)

'Abbasid Caliphs during the Seljuk Period: 'Abbasid Dynasty in Baghdad, 750–1258

Al-Qa'im, 422/1031–467/1075
Al-Muqtadi, 467/1075–487/1094
Al-Mustazhir, 487/1094–512/1118
Al-Mustarshid, 512/1118–529/1135
Al-Rashid, 529/1135–530/1136
Al-Muqtafi, 530/1136–555/1160
Al-Mustanjid, 555/1160–566/1170
Al-Mustadi', 566/1170–575/1180
Al-Nasir li-Din Allah, 575/1180–622/1225

Khwarazmshahs: Khwarazm 490/1097–628/1231, and in the late twelfth–early thirteenth century much of Central Asia and Middle East

Anushtegin Gharcha'i (*mamlūk* of Malikshah, appointed governor of Khwarazm *c.* 470/1077)
Arslantegin Muhammad b. Anustegin, 490/1097–521/1127 (loyal vassal to Sanjar)
Atsız b. Arslantegin 521/1127–551/1156 (rebels repeatedly against Sanjar)
Ilarslan b. Atsız 551/1156–567/1172 (starts Khwarazmian expansion)
'Ala' al-Din Tekish b. Ilarslan 567–96/1172–1200 (continues expansion, proclaiming himself sultan, and destroys remnants of Seljuk Sultanate of Iraq)
'Ala' al-Din Muhammad b. Tekish 596/1200–617/1220

Ildegüzid *Atabegs* of Nakhchivan: *c.* 530/1135–622/1225

Ildegüz, 530/1135–36–571/1175 (*atabeg* to Arslan b. Tughrıl II)
Muhammad Jahan Pahlawan b. Ildegüz, 571/1175–582/1186 (*atabeg* to Tughrıl III b. Arslan)
Qızıl Arslan b. Ildegüz, 582/1186–587/1191 (proclaimed himself sultan shortly before his death)
Qutlugh Inanj, dates uncertain, active in 1090s (step-son of Muhammad Jahan Pahlawan, assigned the Jibal in the latter's division of territories)
Abu Bakr b. Muhammad Jahan Pahlawan, 587/1191–607/1210 (assumed title of sultan)
Muzaffar al-Din Uzbek, 607/1210–622/1225

Zangid *Atabegs* during the Seljuk Period: Mosul, the Jazira and Syria, 521/1127–631/1233

Aqsonqur, *mamlūk* of Malikshah, governor of Aleppo, 480/1087–487/1094
'Imad al-Din Zangi b. Aqsonqur (d. 541/1146) (governor of Iraq 516/1122–521/1127, of Mosul from 521/1127, expanding to control most of the Jazira and northern Syria. *Atabeg* to Mahmud II's son Alp Arslan)
Nur al-Din Mahmud b. 'Imad al-Din Zangi, 541/1146–569/1174

Appendix II
Genealogical Chart of the Seljuk Sultans

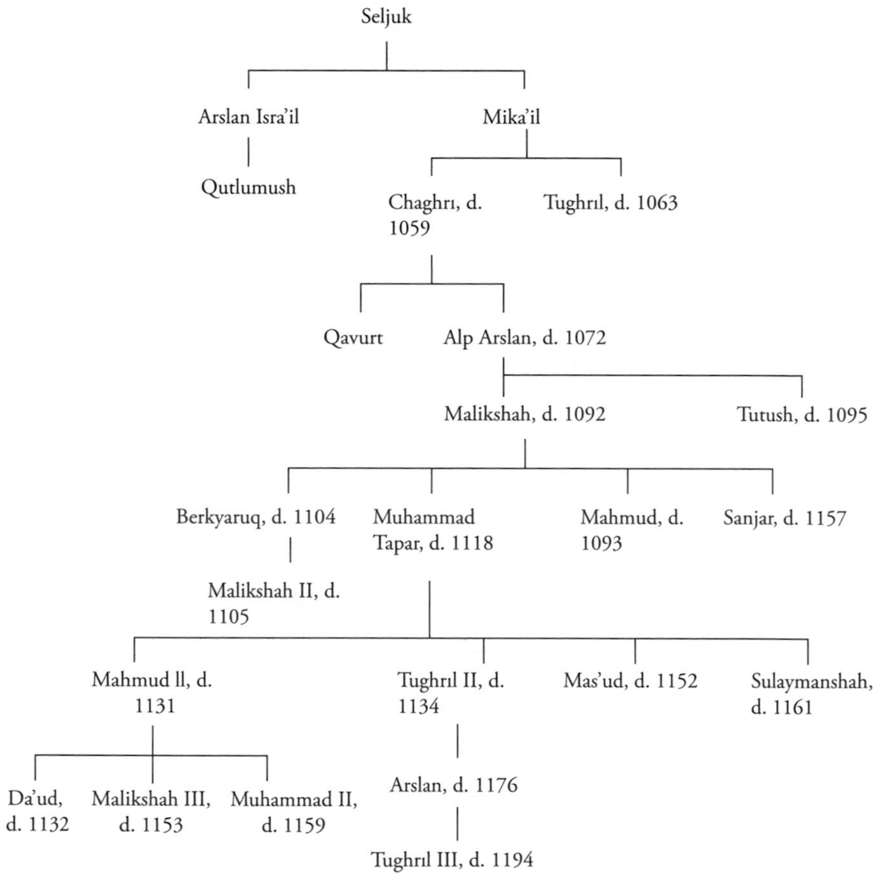

Appendix III
Chronological Outline

Date	Central Asia and Eurasian steppe	Iranian plateau and Iraq	Syria and Anatolia
Late tenth century	Collapse of Khazar empire; rise of Qarakhitay in Manchuria	Buyid rule	Fatimid rule in Syria; Byzantine expansion into eastern Anatolia and Armenia
c. 985–6	Migration of Seljuk and his followers from Khazar lands to Jand		
991		Accession of Caliph al-Qadir	
999	Collapse of Samanid state in Transoxiana; territories divided between Qarakhanids and Ghaznavids		
1009	Traditional date for death of Seljuk		
1020s	Arslan Isra'il b. Seljuk intervenes in Qarakhanid politics; subsequently imprisoned by Mahmud of Ghazna; eventually replaced by Tughrıl and Chaghrı as Seljuk leader		
1030	Death of Mahmud of Ghazna; accession of his son Mas'ud to Ghaznavid throne		
1030		First 'Iraqiyya incursions reach western Iran	Some 'Iraqiyya may reach eastern Anatolia
1031		Death of Caliph al-Qadir; accession of al-Qa'im	

Date	Central Asia and Eurasian steppe	Iranian plateau and Iraq	Syria and Anatolia
1034–5	Seljuk flight from Transoxiana to Khwarazam and then into Khurasan		
1038	Seljuk conquest of Nishapur, Merv and other major cities in Khurasan; Ghaznavid control subsequently partially reasserted		
1040	Battle of Dandanqan; definitive Seljuk takeover of Khurasan		
1040s		Seljuk conquest of Iranian plateau; establishment of Qavurt in Kirman	Byzantine annexation of Armenian kingdom of Ani in 1045; Seljuk campaigns reach eastern Anatolia
1055		Tughrıl occupies Baghdad; end of Buyid state	
1058–9	Death of Chaghrı, 1059	Baghdad occupied by Fatimid-supported Basasiri; major rebellion against Tughrıl by Ibrahim Yınal	
1063		Death of Tughrıl; Alp Arslan emerges victorious from struggle with Qutlumush and Sulayman b. Chaghrı	
1064		Defeat of Qavurt's rebellion	Alp Arslan captures Ani from Byzantines
1067		Qavurt rebels	
1071			Battle of Manzikert, defeat of Byzantines; Atsız b. Awaq temporarily captures Jerusalem

Date	Central Asia and Eurasian steppe	Iranian plateau and Iraq	Syria and Anatolia
1072	Death of Alp Arslan; succession of Malikshah		
1073		Execution of Qavurt	Atsız b. Awaq again attacks Jersualem
1076–7			Atsız's unsuccessful expedition against Cairo
1081	Seljuk prince Tekish rebels		Sulayman b. Qutlumush seizes Nicaea in western Anatolia; traditional date for foundation of Seljuk sultanate of Anatolia (Rum)
1089–90	Malikshah reduces Qarakhanids to vassal status and campaigns east as far as Kashghar	1090, Hasan-i Sabbah seizes Alamut, marking beginning of Ismaili state	
1092		Deaths of Malikshah, Nizam al-Mulk and al-Muqtadi	
1092–7	Arslan Arghun b. Alp Arslan asserts control of Khurasan	Succession wars for sultanate between Berkyaruq and Mahmud and then Tutush	Ridwan succeeds Tutush in Syria, 1096, marking effective secession of Syrian branch of Seljuk family
1097	Sanjar installed as *malik* in Khurasan		First Crusade reaches Antioch
1098–1105		Civil war between Berkyaruq and Muhammad Tapar resulting in division of Seljuk Empire; Ismailis gain control of much of Isfahan region	Crusaders seize Jersualem from Fatimids in 1099

Date	Central Asia and Eurasian steppe	Iranian plateau and Iraq	Syria and Anatolia
1104			Atabeg Tughtegin seizes control of Damascus on death of Duqaq, marking foundation of Burid dynasty
1105		Accession of Muhammad Tapar	
1107		Muhammad Tapar's forces capture Shahdiz fortress near Isfahan from Ismailis	
1118	Sanjar becomes senior sultan on Muhammad Tapar's death	Mahmud succeeds Muhammad Tapar as junior sultan in west, effective foundation of Sultanate of Iraq	
1126		Mahmud besieges Baghdad	
1128			Zangi, amir of Mosul, extends control over Aleppo, marking foundation of Zangid state in Jazira and Syria
1131–2	Qarakhanid revolt	Fighting between Mas'ud, Da'ud and Tughrıl II over succession to Mahmud	
1134–8	Qarakhitay advance into Islamic Central Asia	Fighting between Da'ud and Mas'ud over succession to Tughrıl II	
1138	Sanjar marches on Khwarazm to supress Atsız's revolt		
1141	Sanjar's defeat by Qarakhitay at Qatwan		

Date	Central Asia and Eurasian steppe	Iranian plateau and Iraq	Syria and Anatolia
1142	Atsız briefly seizes Nishapur and declares sovereignty		
1143	Sanjar's second campaign against Atsız in Khwarazm		
1144			Zangi captures Crusader County of Edessa, prompting Second Crusade
1152	Ghuzz revolt starts in Balkh	Muhammad II, Malikshah III and Sulaymanshah compete for succession to Mas'ud	
1153	Ghuzz capture of Merv and Sanjar		
1157	Death of Sanjar; collapse of Seljuk empire in Khurasan	Muhammad II's unsuccessful siege of Baghdad	
1157–82	1162, murder of Mahmud Khan, last Seljuk claimant in Khurasan; Khwarazmian, Ghurid and Qarakitay empires dominate east	Fighting between amirs results in triumph of Ilduzids and beginning of 'dyarchy'	
1183	'Ala' al-Din Tekish proclaimed Khwarazmian sultan		
1186		Disputes follow death of Ildegüzid Jahan Pahlawan; Tughrıl III succeeds in asserting himself as sultan; Seljuk Kirman surrenders to Ghuzz	
1194		Death of Tughrıl III in battle against allied Khwarazmian and Ildegüzid forces	

Glossary

A. = Arabic
P. = Persian
T. = Turkish

aḥdāth (A.)	paramilitary groups, militias, often claiming inspiration by ideals of *futuwwa*
ahl al-dhimma	see *dhimmī*
ʿālim see *ʿulamāʾ*	
ʿamīd (A.)	governor, usually responsible for tax collection
amīr (A.)	(1) a military commander; (2) a prince, a ruler's title; (3) a Türkmen chief (in this sense equivalent to *beg*)
ʿaskar (pl. *ʿasākir*) (A.)	military; soldiers; army
atabeg (T.)	guardian to a prince (*malik*), usually a senior *amir*
ʿayyār (A.)	see *aḥdāth*
bāgh (P.)	garden
bārgāh (P.)	audience hall
barīd (A.)	intelligence and postal service
beg (T.)	a Türkmen chief
dāʿī (A.)	propagandist, especially an Ismaili missionary
dār al-imāra (A.)	(lit. 'abode of commanding') a palace or government complex
dār al-mamlaka (A.)	(lit. 'abode of the realm') a palace or government complex, usually in capital city

dār al-mulk (A.)	(lit. 'abode of kingship') an epithet given to cities that regularly served as a royal residence such as Merv, Hamadhan
dargāh (P.)	the royal court
da'wa (A.)	(lit. 'the call'), propaganda, missionary activity, especially that of the Ismaili movement
dawla (A.)	dynasty; state
dhimmī (A.)	non-Muslim protected by Islamic law, such as Jews and Christians
dhirā' (A.)	a unit of measurement, approximately 30 cm
dihqān (P.)	landed gentry; farmer
dīwān (A., P.)	(1) a government department or ministry; (2) a collection of poems
dīwān-i a'lā (P.), *dīwān al-a'lā* (A)	the main government department with responsibility for all others
dīwān-i 'arḍ (P.), *dīwān al-'arḍ* (A.)	government department responsible for military pay
dīwān-i inshā' (P.), *dīwān al-inshā'* (A.)	the chancery
dīwān-i ishrāf (P.), *dīwān al-ishrāf* (A.)	government department responsible for budgets and accountancy
dīwān-i istīfā' (P.), *dīwān al-istīfā'* (A.)	government department responsible for raising revenue
dīwān-i ṭughrā (P., T.)	see *dīwān-i inshā'*
faqīh (pl. *fuqaha'*)	a jurist, one who specialises in *fiqh* (q.v.)
farsang (P.), *farsakh* (P., A.)	a measurement of distance, approx. 6 km
fatḥnāma (P.)	a victory proclamotion
fiqh (A.)	Islamic jurisprudence
fitna (A.)	civil strife, disorder
futuwwa (A.)	Sufi-influenced chivalric ideals or organisation
ghulām (A.)	(1) a military slave, equivalent to *mamlūk*; (2) any male slave; (3) a youthful male, a page
ḥājib (A)	chamberlain
inshā' (A.)	the elaborate, often rhymed prose in Arabic and Persian used in

	the chancery for official correspondence and in vogue with bureaucrats for their own personal compositions
iqṭāʿ (A.)	a land grant (of varying sizes, but sometimes constituting an entire province or region)
istimālat (A., P.)	governance by conciliation
jawānmardī (P.)	see *futuwwa*
kalām (A.)	dialectical theology
kātib (pl. *kuttāb*) (A.)	bureaucrat, government secretary
khānqāh (P.)	building for Sufi gatherings
khāqān (T., P.)	the senior Turkic royal title, derived from Turkish *qaghan*
khārkāh (P., A.)	tent, especially the felt-covered tents in use by Turkish nomads
khāṣṣ (A.)	the elite, people bound to the ruler by ties of clientage and *khidma*
khātūn (pl. *khawātīn*) (T., P.)	lady, especially one of royal descent
khidma (A.)	ties of clientage, service and patronage established by oaths and ceremonies that bound members of the elite in vassalage-type relationships
khilʿa (A.)	robes of honour, often given by a patron to a vassal as part of a *khidma* ceremony
khuṭba (A.)	the sermon given in mosques at mid-day prayers on Fridays; mention of the name of a ruler in the *khuṭba* signified recognition of his sovereignty and legitimacy
khwānsālār (P.)	majordomo, official in charge of *fiid* and dining arrangements for the court
kūshk (P.)	pavilion, usually a two-storeyed suburban or extra-urban palace

laqab (A.)	a title awarded by the sultan or caliph
madhhab (A.)	legal school, especially one of the four *fiqh* schools of Sunni Islam: Hanafi, Hanbali, Maliki and Shafiʿi
madrasa (A.)	an educational establishment specialising in teaching the *fiqh* of a given *madhhab*
mahdī (A.)	the saviour whose coming is expected at the end of time
majlis (A.)	(lit. 'a sitting session') may signify any kind of gathering (esp. at court), including a literary soiree; but in a Seljuk context especially suggests a drinking party
malik (A.)	a prince, especially the son of a Seljuk sultan
mamlūk (A.)	a slave, especially a military slave
manshūr	decree of appointment
maydān (A.)	an open space; a polo field
maẓālim (A.)	a public audience held by the sultan or his deputy for the redress of petitioners' wrongs
miḥna (A.)	(lit. 'trial'), persecution, esp. religiously motivated persecution
mīnāʾī (P.)	enamelled, polychrome ceramics
muʿaskar (A.)	military camp, often synonymous with the Seljuk court
muḥtasib (A.)	market inspector; city official responsible for upholding public morals
muqṭaʿ (A.)	holder of an *iqṭāʿ*, sometimes synonymous with governor
mustawfī (A.)	senior revenue official, head of the *dīwān-i istīfāʾ*
nadīm (A.)	boon companion
nāʾib (A.) (pl. *nuwwāb*)	deputy, especially the deputy for a vizier or other government office holder
naqīb (A.)	head of the community of *sayyids*

nawba (A.)	the musical fanfare which, played in the presence of a ruler, was a sign of his sovereignty
Nawrūz (P.)	Iranian new year, celebrated at the vernal equinox
quhandiz (P.)	citadel
ra'āyā (A.)	subjects of the sultan or ruler
rabaḍ (A.)	unwalled area of a city
Rāfiḍī (pl. *Rawāfiḍ*) (A.)	Shi'ite, heretic
ra'īs (A.)	a community head, an intermediary between the sultans officials and the populace
ribāṭ (A.)	(1) a caravanserai; (2) a *khānqāh*
sarāparda (P.)	the red-coloured great tent of the sultan, one of the symbols of rulerships
sayyid (A.)	a descendant of the Prophet Muhammad
shāhanshāh (P.)	(lit. 'king of kings') the titled used by the pre-Islamic Sasanian rulers of Iran, revived in the tenth century and used by Seljuk sultans
shahristān (P.)	the inner city, the walled area of a city
sharābkhāna (P.)	the 'wine house' of a court
sunna (A.)	the practice and customs of the Prophet Muhammad
surādiq (A.)	see *sarāparda*
shiḥna (A.)	a governor; an amir vested with coercive powers by the sultan
al-sulṭān al-a'ẓam (A.)	'the greatest sultan', title used by Sanjar
al-sulṭān al-mu'aẓẓam (A.)	'the great sultan', title used by Tughrıl and his successors, including the sultans of Iraq
tashhīr (A.)	'display', the public parading and humiliation of a convict
ṭughrā (T.)	the bow and arrow device symbolising sovereignty in the Turkish tradition, affixed to sultanic correspondence and depicted on coins

ṭughrā'ī (T.)	official responsible for affixing the *ṭughrā* to correspondence, one of the most senior Seljuk bureaucratic offices
'ulamā' (sign. 'ālim) (A.)	Muslim scholar
wakīldār (A., P.)	official responsible for bringing messages between sultan and vizier
wālī (A.)	governor
walī, pl. *awliyā'* (A.)	a Muslim saint or holy man
waqf, pl. *awqāf* (A.)	a religious endowment
yabghu (T.)	a Turkish title of a ruler, below the rank of *khāqān*; by the Seljuk period, sometimes a proper name

Bibliography

Primary Sources

Abū Shāma, *Kitāb al-Rawḍatayn fī Akhbār al-Dawlatayn*, ed. Ibrāhīm Shams al-Dīn (Beirut, 2002).

Adler, Elkan Nathan (ed. and trans.), *Jewish Travellers in the Middle Ages: Nineteen First Hand Accounts* (New York, [1930] 1987).

Aḥmad b. ʿAlī Kātib, *Tārīkh-i Jadīd-i Yazd*, ed. Īrāj Afshār (Tehran, 1386).

Akhsīkathī, Athīr al-Dīn, *Dīwān*, ed. Rukn al-Dīn Humāyūn Farrukh (Tehran, 1389).

ʿAlī-nāma (Manẓūma-yi Kuhan), ed. Riḍa Bāyat and Abū ʾl-Faḍl Ghulāmī (Tehran, 2010).

Anna Comnena, *The Alexiad*, trans. E. R. A. Sewter (Harmondsworth, 1969).

Anwarī, *Dīwān-i Anwarī*, Introduction by Saʿīd Nafīsī (Tehran, 1376).

Aristakes Lastiverttsi, *History*, trans. Robert Bedrosian (New York, 1985) (available at www.rbedrosian.com).

al-Arrajānī, *Dīwān al-Arrajānī*, ed. Qadarī Māyū (Beirut, 1998).

al-Bākharzī, ʿAlī b. al-Ḥasan, *Ḥāyatuhu wa-Shiʿruhu wa-Dīwānuhu*, ed. Muḥammad al-Tunjī (Beirut, 1994).

Bayhaqī, Abūʾl-Faḍl, *Tārīkh-i Bayhaqī*, ed. Khalīl Khaṭīb Rahbar (Tehran, 1376); trans. C. E. Bosworth and revised by Mohsen Ashtiany as *The History of Beyhaqi (The History of Sultan Masʿud of Ghazna, 1030–41) by Abu'l-Fazl Beyhaqi* (Boston, MA, 2011).

Bar Hebraeus, *The Chronography of Gregory Abu'l-Faraj . . . commonly known as Bar Hebraeus*, trans. Ernest A. Wallis Budge (London, 1932).

Bartol'd, V. V. (ed.), *Turkestan v Epokhu Mongolskogo Nashestviya. Chast' 1: Teksty* (St Petersburg, 1898).

Benjamin of Tudela, *The Itinerary of Benjamin of Tudela: Travels in the Middle Ages*, trans. A. Asher (New York, 2010).

Bundārī, *Zubdat al-Nuṣra*, ed. M. Th. Houtsma as *Histoire des Seljoucides de l'Irâq par Bondârî d'après Imâd al-dîn al-Kâtib al-Isfahânî* (Leiden 1889) (Recueil de textes relatifs à l'histoire des Seljoucides, II).

Gardīzī, Abū Saʿīd b. ʿAbd al-Ḥayy, *Zayn al-Akhbār*, ed. Raḥīm Riḍāzāda Malik (Tehran, 1384); partially trans. C. E. Bosworth, *The Ornament of Histories: A History of the Eastern Islamic Lands* AD *650–1041: The Persian Text of Abu Saʿid b. ʿAbd al-Hayy Gardizi* (London, 2011).

Ghars al-Niʿma, Muḥammad b. Hilāl al-Ṣābiʾ, *al-Hafawāt al-Nādira*, ed. Ṣāliḥ al-Ashīr (Beirut, 1987).

al-Ghazālī, *Briefe und Reden des Abu Hamid al-Ghassali*, trans. Dorothea Krawulsky (Freiburg im Breslau, 1971).

Fāmī Harawī, 'Abd al-Raḥmān, *Tārīkh-i Harāt*, facsimile edition prepared by Muḥammad Ḥusayn Mīr Ḥusaynī and Muḥammad Riḍā Abūnī Mihrīzī (Tehran, 1387).

al-Hamadhānī, Abū l-Ḥasan Muḥammad, *Qiṭ'a Ta'rīkhiyya min kitāb 'Unwān al-Siyar fī Maḥāsin Ahl al-Badw wa 'l-Ḥaḍar, aw al-Ma'ārif al-Muta'akhkhira, wa-bi-Dhaylihi Shadharāt min kitāb Umarā' al-Ḥajj*, ed. Shāyi' 'Abd al-Hādī al-Hājiri (Tunis, 2008).

Ḥamdallāh Mustawfī, *Tārīkh-i Guzīda*, ed. 'Abd al-Ḥusayn Nawā'ī (Tehran, 1339).

Ḥamdallāh Mustawfī, *The Geographical Part of the* Nuzhat al-Qulūb *composed by Ḥamd Allāh Mustawfī of Qazwīn in 740* (1340), trans. G. Le Strange (London, 1919).

Hillenbrand, Carole (ed. and trans.), *A Muslim Principality in Crusader Times: The Early Artuqid State* (Istanbul, 1990) (edition and translation of Artuqid sections of Ibn Azraq al-Fāriqī's *Ta'rīkh Mayyāfāriqīn*).

al-Ḥusaynī, Ṣadr al-Dīn 'Alī, *Akhbār al-Dawla al-Saljuqiyya*, ed. Muḥammad Iqbāl (Beirut, 1984); trans. C. E. Bosworth as *The History of the Seljuq State: A Translation with Commentary of the* Akhbār al-dawla al-saljūqiyya (London, 2011).

Ibn al-'Adīm, *Bughyat al-Ṭalab fī Ta'rīkh Ḥalab: al-tarājim al-khāṣṣa bi-ta'rīkh al-Salājiqa*, ed. Ali Sevim as *Buğyat at-Ṭalab fī Tārīḫ Ḥalab: Selçuklularla İlgili Haltercümeleri* (Ankara, 1976).

Ibn al-'Adīm, *Zubdat al-Ḥalab min Ta'rīkh Ḥalab*, ed. Sāmī Dahhān (Damascus, 1951–68).

Ibn al-Athīr, *al-Kāmil fī 'l-Ta'rīkh*, ed. C. Tornberg (Beirut, 1965–7); partial trans. D. S. Richards, *The Annals of the Saljuq Turks: Selections from* Al-Kāmil Fī'l-Ta'rīkh *of Izz Al-Dīn Ibn Al-Athīr* (London, 2002).

Ibn al-Athīr, *al-Ta'rīkh al-Bāhir fī 'l-Dawla al-Atābakiyya*, ed. 'Abd al-Qādir Ṭulaymāt (Cairo, 1963).

Ibn Azraq al-Fāriqī, *Ta'rīkh al-Fāriqī: al-Dawla al-Marwāniyya*, ed. Badawī 'Abd al-Laṭīf 'Awaḍ (Beirut, 1974) (see also Hillenbrand, *A Muslim Principality*).

Ibn al-Balkhī, *Fārsnāma*, ed. G. Le Strange and R. A. Nicolson as *The* Fársnáma *of Ibnu'l-Balkhí* (Cambridge, [1921] 1962).

Ibn al-Bannā', *Diary*, ed. and trans. by George Makdisi as 'Autograph Diary of an Eleventh-century Historian of Baghdad', I: *BSOAS*, 18/i (1956), 9–32; II: *BSOAS*, 18/ii (1956), 239–60; III: *BSOAS*, 19/i (1957), 13–48; IV: *BSOAS*, 19/ii (1957), 281–303; V: *BSOAS*, 19/iii (1957), 426–43.

Ibn Funduq, *Tārīkh-i Bayhaq*, ed. Aḥmad Bahmanyār (Tehran, n.d.); selections trans. C. E. Bosworth, 'Historical Information from Ibn Funduq's *Tarikh-i Bayhaq* (563/1167–68)', *Iran*, 48 (2010), 81–106.

Ibn Ḥaṣṣūl, *Kitāb Tafḍīl al-atrāk 'alā sā'ir al-ajnād*, ed. Abbas Azzavi as 'Ibni Hassulün Türkler hakkında bir eser', *Belleten*, 4 (1940) (Arabic text as separately paginated *ilave*).

Ibn al-Jawzī, *al-Muntaẓam fī Ta'rīkh al-Mulūk wa'l-Umam*, ed. Muḥammad 'Abd al-Qādir 'Aṭā and Muṣṭafā 'Abd al-Qādir 'Aṭā (Beirut, 1995).

Ibn Jubayr, *Riḥlat Ibn Jubayr*, ed. Muḥammad Zaynhum (Cairo, n.d.); trans. R. C. Broadhurst, *The Travels of Ibn Jubayr* (London, 1952).

Ibn Khallikān, *Wafayāt al-A'yān wa-Anbā' Abnā' al-Zamān*, eds Yūsuf 'Alī Ṭawīl and Mariyam Qāsim Ṭawīl (Beirut, 1998); trans. M. de Slane, *Ibn Khallikan's Biographical Dictionary* (London, 1843).

Ibn al-Qalānisī, *Dhayl Ta'rīkh Dimashq: History of Damascus 363–555*, ed. H. F. Amedroz (Leiden, 1908); partial trans. H. A. R. Gibb, *The Damascus Chronicle of the Crusades* (London, 1932).

Idrīs 'Imād al-Dīn, *'Uyūn al-Akhbār*, ed. Ayman Fu'ad Sayyid as *The Fatimids and Their Successors in Yaman: The History of an Islamic Community. Arabic edition and English summary of volume 7 of Idris 'Imad Al-Din's* 'Uyūn Al-Akhbār (London, 2002).

al-Iṣfahānī, 'Imād al-Dīn, *Nuṣrat al-Fatra*, Bibliothèque nationale, Paris, MS arabe 2145; for the published abridgement see sub Bundārī above.

Jurfādqānī, *Tarjuma-yi Tārīkh-i Yamīnī, bih inḍimām-i khātima-yi Yamīnī yā Ḥawādith-i Ayyām*, ed. Ja'far Shi'ār (Tehran, [1345] 1382).

Juvaini, 'Ata Malik, *History of the World Conqueror*, trans. J. A. Boyle (Manchester, [1958] 1997).

al-Juwaynī, Muntakhab al-Dīn Badī' Atābak, *'Atabat al-Kataba: majmū'a-yi murāsalāt-i dīwān-i Sulṭān Sanjar*, eds Muḥammad Qazwīnī and 'Abbas Iqbāl Ashtiyānī (Tehran, [1329] 1389).

Jūzjānī, Minhāj-i Sirāj, *Ṭabaqāt-i Nāṣiri yā Tārīkh-i Īrān wa Islām*, ed. 'Abd al-Ḥayy Ḥabībī (Tehran, 1363); trans. H. Raverty, *The Tabakat-i-Nasiri: A General History of the Muhammadan Dynasties of Asia* (London, 1881).

al-Kāšγarī, Maḥmūd, *Compendium of the Turkic Dialects*, ed. and trans. Robert Dankoff (Cambridge, MA, 1982).

Kaykā'ūs b. Iskandar, *Qābūs-nāma*, ed. Ghulāmḥusayn Yūsufi (Tehran [1345] 1378); trans. Reuven Levy as *A Mirror for Princes. The Qabus Nama by Kai Ka'us ibn Iskandar, Prince of Gurgan* (London, 1951).

Kirmānī, Afḍal al-Dīn Abū Ḥāmid, *Saljūqīyān wa Ghuzz dar Kirmān*, ed. Bāstanī Pārīzī (Tehran, 1373).

al-Māfarrukhī, Mufaḍḍal b. Sa'd, *Kitāb Maḥāsin Iṣfahān*, ed. 'Ārif Muḥammad 'Abd al-Ghanī (Damascus, 2010).

Mārī b. Sulaymān, *Akhbār Faṭārikat Kursī al-Mashriq min Kitāb al-Majdal*, ed. with a Latin translation by Henricus Gismondi as *Maris Amri et Slibae De Patriarchis Nestorianum Commentaria* (Rome, 1898).

Mas'ūd b. Nāmdār, *Sbornik Rasskazov, Pisem i Stikhov*, facsimile prepared by V. M. Beylis (Moscow, 1970).

Matthew of Edessa, *Armenia and the Crusades, Tenth to Twelfth Centuries: The Chronicle of Matthew of Edessa*, trans. Ara Dostourian (Lanham, MD, 1993).

Michel le Syrien, *Chronique de Michel le Syrien, Patriarche Jacobite d'Antioche (1166–1199). Éditée pour la première fois et traduite en francais*, ed. and trans. Jean-Baptiste Chabot (Paris, 1899–1910).

Mīrkhwand, *Rawḍat al-Ṣafā* (Tehran, 1338).

Muḥammad b. Munawwar, *Asrār al-Tawḥīd fi Maqāmāt al-Shaykh Abī Sa'īd*, ed. Muḥammad Riḍā Shafi'ī Kadkanī (Tehran, 1366)

Mu'izzī Nīshāpūrī, Amīr, *Kullīyāt-i Dīwān*, ed. Muḥammad Riḍā Qanbarī (Tehran, 1385).

Mujmal al-Tawārīkh wa'l-Qiṣaṣ, ed. Malik al-Shu'arā' Bahār (Tehran, 1381).

Al-Mukhtārāt min al-Rasā'il, eds Ghulāmriḍā Ṭāhir and Īraj Afshār (Tehran, 1378).

Nāṣir-i Khusraw, *Safarnāma*, ed. Muḥammad Ghanīzāda (Berlin, 1341); trans. W. Thackston, *Nasir-i Khusraw's Book of Travels* (Costa Mesa, 2001).

Nāṣir-i Khusraw, *Dīwān*, ed. Mujtabā Minuwī (Tehran, 1353).

Nīshāpūrī, Ẓahīr al-Dīn, *Saljūqnāma*, ed. A. H. Morton (Cambridge, 2004).

Niẓām al-Mulk, *Siyar al-Mulūk (Siyāsatnāma)*, ed. Hubert Darke (Tehran, 1340); trans. Hubert Darke, *The Book of Government or Rules for Kings: The* Siyar al-Mulūk *or* Siyāsat-nāma *of Nizam al-Mulk* (Richmond, [1978] 2002).

Niẓāmī 'Arūḍī, *Chahār Maqāla*, ed. Muḥammad Mu'īn (Tehran, 1377); trans. E. G. Browne, *Revised Translation of the* Chahár Maqála *('Four Discourses') of Niẓámí-i-'Arúḍí of Samarqand* (Cambridge, 1921).

Otto, Bishop of Freising, *The Two Cities: A Chronicle of Universal History to the Year 1146 AD*, trans. Charles Christopher Mierow (New York, 1966).

al-Qazwīnī al-Rāzī, 'Abd al-Jalīl al-Ḥusayn b. Abī'l-Faḍl, *Kitāb al-Naqḍ ma'rūf bih ba'ḍ mathālib al-nawāṣib fī naqḍ ba'ḍ faḍā'iḥ al-rawāfiḍ*, ed. Jalāl al-Dīn Urmawī (Tehran, 1331, 2nd edn 1378).

Qummī, Najm al-Dīn Abū 'l-Rajā', *Dhayl-i Nafthat al-Maṣdūr*, ed. Ḥusayn Mudarrasī Ṭabāṭabā'ī (Tehran, 1383).

Rāwandī, Muḥammad b. 'Alī, *Rāḥat al-Ṣudūr wa Āyat al-Surūr*, ed. Muḥammad Iqbāl (London, 1921).

Rāzī, Sayyid Murtaḍā b. Dā'ī Ḥasanī, *Tabṣirat al-'Awāmm fī Ma'rifat Maqālāt al-Anām*, ed. 'Abbās Iqbāl (Tehran, 1364).

Samau'al al-Maghribī, *Ifḥām Al-Yahūd: Silencing the Jews*, ed. and trans. Moshe Perlmann, *Proceedings of the American Academy for Jewish Research*, 32 (1964).

al-Sāwī, 'Umar b. Sahlān, *Risāla-yi Sanjariyya fī 'l-Kā'inat al-'unṣuriyya*, ed. Mehmet Altay Köymen as 'Selçuklu Devri Kaynaklarına Dair Araştırmalar, II: Risale-i Senceriyye', *Doğu Dilleri*, 1/iii (1969), 15–55.

al-Shahrastānī, Muḥammad b. 'Abd al-Karīm, *Mafātīḥ al-asrār wa maṣābīḥ al-abrār*, ed. and trans. Toby Mayer as *Keys to the Arcana: Shahrastānī's Esoteric Commentary on the Qur'an* (Oxford, 2009).

Sharaf al-Zaman Tahir Marvazi on China, the Turks and India, ed. and trans. Vladimir Minorsky (London, 1942).

Sibṭ b. al-Jawzī, *Mir'āt al-Zamān fī Ta'rīkh al A'yān: al-Ḥawādith al-khāṣṣa bi-ta'rīkh al-Salājiqa bayna al-sanawāt 1056–1086*, ed. Ali Sevim as *Mir'âtü'z-Zeman fî Tarihi'l-Âyan* (Ankara, 1968); rev. edn in *Belgeler: Türk Tarih Kurumu Dergisi*, 14/xviii (1989–1992), 1–260.

Sibṭ b. al-Jawzī, *Mir'āt al-Zamān fī Ta'rīkh al-A'yān (481–517/1088–1123)*, ed. Musfir b. Sālim al-Ghāmidī (Mecca, 1987).

Sibṭ b. al-Jawzī, *Mir'āt al-Zamān fī Ta'rīkh al-A'yān*, ed. Kāmil al-Jubūrī et al. (Beirut, 2013).

Sibṭ b. al-Ta'wīdhī, *Dīwān*, ed. D. S. Margoliouth (Beirut, [1903] 1967).

Solomon ben Joseph Ha-Kohen, *The Turkoman Defeat at Cairo*, ed. and trans. Julius. H. Greenstone (Chicago, 1906).

al-Subkī, *Ṭabaqāt al-Shāfi'iyya al-Kubrā*, eds Maḥmud Muḥammad Tanāḥī and 'Abd al-Fattāḥ Muḥammad Ḥulw (Cairo, 1964).

Sümer, Faruk and Ali Sevim (eds), *İslam Kaynaklarına Göre Malazgirt Savaşı (Metinler ve Çevirleri)* (Ankara, 1971).

Tārīkh-i Sīstān, ed. Muḥammad Taqī Bahār (Tehran, 1381); trans. Milton Gold, *The Tārīkh-e Sīstān* (Rome, 1976).
Thomson, Robert (trans.), *Rewriting Caucasian History: The Medieval Armenian Adaptation of the Georgian Chronicles: The Original Georgian Texts and the Armenian Adaptation* (Oxford, 1996).
Yāqūt al-Ḥamawī, *Mu'jam al-Buldān* (Beirut, 1996).
Yusuf Khass Hajib, *Wisdom of Royal Glory (Kutadghu Bilig). A Turko-Islamic Mirror for Princes*, trans. Robert Dankoff (Chicago, 1983).
Zarkūb-i Shīrāzī, *Shīrāznāma*, eds Muḥammad Jawwād Jiddī and Iḥsānallāh Shukrallāhī (Tehran, 1389).

Secondary Literature

Aceituno, Antonio Jurado, 'La "hidma" selyuqí: la red de relaciones de dependencia mutua, la dinámica del poder y las formas de obtención de los beneficios', PhD thesis, Universidad Autónoma de Madrid, 1995.
Adams, Robert M., *The Land Behind Baghdad: A History of Settlement on the Diyala Plains* (Chicago, 1965).
Ahmed, Shahab, Review of Daphna Ephrat, *A Learned Society in a Period of Transition: The Sunni* 'Ulama' *of Eleventh-century Baghdad*, *JAOS*, 123/i (2003), 179–82.
Agadshanow, S. G. *Der Staat der Seldschukiden und Mittelasien im 11.–12. Jahrhundert* (Berlin, 1994).
Agadzhanov, S. G., 'The States of the Oghuz, the Kimek and the Qipchaq', in Asimov and Bosworth (eds), *History of Civilizations of Central Asia*, V, 61–76.
Album, Stephen, *Checklist of Islamic Coins* (n.p., 1998).
Alptekin, Coşkun, 'Selçuklu paraları', *Selçuklu Araştırmaları Dergisi*, 3 (1971), 435–591.
Allsen, Thomas, *The Royal Hunt in Eurasian History* (Philadelphia, 2006).
Ambraseys, N. N. and C. P. Melville, *A History of Persian Earthquakes* (Cambridge, 1982).
Arafa, Mahmoud, 'A Rare Saljuki Dinar Struck in Nisabur in 431 A.H. in the Name of Tugril Beg', *Annales Islamologiques*, 38 (2004), 305–9.
Asimov, M. S. and C. E. Bosworth (eds), *History of Civilizations of Central Asia, vol. IV: The Age of Achievement: A.D. 750 to the End of the Fifteenth Century, Part One: The Historical, Social and Economic Setting* (Delhi, 1999).
Aubin, Jean, 'La ruine de Siraf et les routes du Golfe Persique aux XIe et XIIe siècles', *Cahiers de civilisation médiévale*, 2 (1959), 295–301.
Aubin, Jean, 'L'aristocratie urbaine dans l'Iran seldjukide: l'exemple de Sabzavar', in P. Gallais and Y. J. Rion (eds), *Mélanges offerts à René Crozet* (Poitiers, 1966), I, 323–32.
Ayalon, David, 'Aspects of the Mamluk Phenomenon', *Der Islam*, 53 (1976), 196–225.
Ayalon, David, 'The Mamluks of the Seljuks: Islam's Military Might at the Crossroads', *JRAS*, 3rd series, 6/iii (1996), 305–33.
Ayalon, David, *Eunuchs, Caliphs and Sultans: A Study of Power Relationships* (Jerusalem, 1999).
Aziz, Ghulam Rabbani, *A Short History of the Khwarazmshahs* (Karachi, 1978).

Bacharach, Jere L., 'Administrative Complexes, Palaces, and Citadels: Changes in the Loci of Medieval Muslim Rule', in Irene Bierman, Rifa'at Abou-el-Haj and Donald Preziosi (eds), *The Ottoman City and its Parts: Urban Change and Social Order* (New Rochelle, 1991), 111–28.

Balivet, Michel, 'Un people de l'An Mil: les Turcs vus par leurs voisins', in Claude Carozzi (ed.), *An 1000–An 2000: Mille ans d'histoire médiévale* (Aix-en-Provence, 2002), 25–50.

Barber, Malcolm, *The Crusader States* (New Haven, 2012).

Barthold, W., *Turkestan Down to the Mongol Invasion* (London, 1928).

Basan, Aziz, *The Great Seljuqs: A History* (London, 2010).

Bausani, A., 'Religion in the Saljuq Period', in Boyle (ed.), *The Cambridge History of Islam*, V, 283–302.

Baypakov, Karl M., 'Culture urbaine du Kazakhstan du sud et du Semiretchie à l'époque des Karakhanides', in Vincent Fourniau *et al.* (eds), *Études karakhanides* (*Cahiers d'Asie Centrale* 9) (Tashkent and Aix-en-Provence, 2001), 141–75.

Berkey, Jonathan P., *The Formation of Islam: Religion and Society in the Near East, 600–1800* (Cambridge, 2003).

Beysanoğlu, Sevket, *Anıtları ve Kitabeleri ile Diyarbakır Tarihi: Başlangıçtan Akkoyunlular'a Kadar* (Ankara, [1987] 2003), I.

Binbaş, İlker Evrim, 'Oghuz Khan Narratives', *EIr*.

Biran, Michal, *The Empire of the Qara-Khitai in Eurasian History: Between China and the Islamic World* (Cambridge, 2005).

Bivar, A. D. H., 'The Saljuq Sign Manual Represented on a *Sgraffiato* Potsherd', *JRAS*, 2nd series, 1 (1979), 9–15.

Blair, Sheila S., *The Monumental Inscriptions from Early Islamic Iran and Transoxiana* (Leiden, 1992).

Blair, Sheila S., 'Decoration of City Walls in the Medieval Islamic World: The Epigraphic Message', in James D. Tracy (ed.), *City Walls: The Urban Enceinte in Global Perspective* (Cambridge, 2000), 488–529.

Bloom, Jonathan, *Minaret: The Symbol of Islam* (Oxford, 1989).

Bosworth, C. E., 'The Titulature of the Early Ghaznavids', *Oriens*, 15 (1962), 210–33.

Bosworth, C. E., *The Ghaznavids: Their Empire in Afghanistan and Eastern Iran, 994–1040* (Edinburgh, 1963).

Bosworth, C. E., 'Dailamīs in Central Iran: the Kākūyids of Jibāl and Yazd', *Iran*, 8 (1970), 73–95

Bosworth, C. E., 'The Political and Dynastic History of the Iranian World (A.D. 1000–1217)', in Boyle (ed.), *The Cambridge History of Iran*, V, 1–202.

Bosworth, C. E., 'The Heritage of Rulership in Early Islamic Iran and the Search for Dynastic Connections with the Past', *Iran* (1973), 51–62.

Bosworth, C. E., 'Ghars al-Ni'ma Hilāl al-Ṣābi''s *Kitāb al-Hafawāt al-nādira* and Būyid History', in Alan Jones (ed.), *Arabicus Felix, Luminosus Britannicus: Essays in Honour of A. F. L. Beeston on his Eightieth Birthday* (Reading, 1991), 129–41.

Bosworth, C. E., *The History of the Saffarids of Sistan and the Maliks of Nimruz (247/861 to 949/1542–3)* (Costa Mesa, 1994).

Bosworth, C. E., 'Towards a Biography of Niẓām al-Mulk: Three Sources from Ibn al-'Adīm', in Geoffrey Khan (ed.), *Semitic Studies in Honour of Edward Ullendorf* (Leiden, 2005), 299–308.

Bosworth, C. E., 'The Origins of the Seljuqs', in Lange and Mecit (eds), *The Seljuqs*, 13–21.

Bosworth, C. E., 'Notes on Some Personal Names in Seljūq Military History', *Der Islam*, 89/ii (2012), 97–110.

Bosworth, C. E., 'Āl-e Borhān', *EIr*.

Bosworth, C. E., "Amīd', *EI*[3].

Bosworth, C. E., 'Anushirvān b. K̲āled', *EIr*.

Bosworth, C. E., 'Čaġrï Beg Dāwud', *EIr*.

Bosworth, C. E., 'Courts and Courtiers. III. In the Islamic Period to the Mongol Conquest', *EIr*.

Bosworth, C. E., 'G̲h̲ulām. II. Persia', *EI*[2].

Bosworth, C. E., 'G̲h̲ūrids', *EIr*.

Bosworth, C. E., 'Īlek-Khāns or Ḳarak̲h̲ānids', *EI*[2].

Bosworth, C. E., 'Kākuyids', *EIr*.

Bosworth, C. E., 'Khwārazmshahs', *EIr*.

Bosworth, C. E., 'Mazyād, Banū', *EI*[2].

Bosworth, C. E., 'Sald̲j̲ūḳids', *EI*[2].

Bosworth, C. E., 'Ṭog̲h̲ril (I) Beg', *EI*[2].

Bowen, Harold, 'Notes on Some Early Seljuqid Viziers', *BSOAS*, 20/i (1957), 97–110.

Bowen, Harold, 'Niẓām al-Mulk', *EI*[2].

Böwering, G., 'Abu Sa'id b. Abi 'l-Khayr', *EIr*.

Boyle, J. A. (ed.), *The Cambridge History of Islam, vol. V: The Saljuq and Mongol Period* (Cambridge, 1968).

Brentjes, Buchard, 'Karawanwege durch Mittelasien', *Archaeologische Mitteilungen aus Iran*, 25 (1992), 247–76.

Brentjes, Buchard, 'Caravan Routes through Central Asia', *Annales archéologiques arabes syriennes*, 43 (1999), 215–28.

Brun, P. and A. Annaev, 'The Fortifications of Sultan Kala', *Iran*, 39 (2001), 33–42.

Büchner, V. F. and C. E. Bosworth, 'S̲h̲abānkāra', *EI*[2].

Buell, Paul D., 'The Mongol Empire and Turkicization: The Evidence of Food and Foodways', in Reuven Amitai-Preiss and David Morgan (eds), *The Mongol Empire and its Legacy* (Leiden, 1999), 200–23.

Bulliet, Richard W., *The Patricians of Nishapur: A Study in Medieval Islamic Social History* (Cambridge, MA, 1972).

Bulliet, Richard W., 'The Political–Religious History of Nishapur in the Eleventh Century', in Richards (ed.), *Islamic Civilisation, 950–1150*, 71–91.

Bulliet, Richard W., 'Numismatic Evidence for the Relationship between Tughrıl Beg and Chaghrı Beg', in Dickran K. Kouymjian (ed.), *Near Eastern Numismatics, Iconography, Epigraphy and History: Studies in Honor of George C. Miles* (Beirut, 1974), 289–96.

Bulliet, Richard W., 'Medieval Nishapur: A Topographic and Demographic Reconstruction', *Studia Iranica*, 5 (1976), 67–89.

Bulliet, Richard W., 'Local Politics in Eastern Iran under the Ghaznavids and Seljuks', *Iranian Studies*, 11/i (1978), 35–56.

Bulliet, Richard W., *Islam: The View from the Edge* (New York, 1994).

Bulliet, Richard W., *Cotton, Climate, and Camels in Early Islamic Iran: A Moment in World History* (New York, 2009).

Buniyatov, Z. M., *Gosudarstvo Khorezmshakhov-Anushteginidov, 1097–1231* (Moscow, 1986).

[Buniyatov, Z. M.] Bünyadov, Ziya, *Azərbaycan Atabəyləri Dövləti, 1136–1225* (Baku, [1984] 2007).

Busse, Heribert, *Chalif und Grosskönigen: die Buyiden in Iraq (945–1055)* (Beirut, 1969).

Busse, Heribert, 'The Revival of Persian Kingship under the Buyids', in Richards (ed.), *Islamic Civilisation, 950–1150*, 47–69.

Cahen, Claude, 'La tughra seljukide', *Journal asiatique*, 234 (1943–5), 167–72.

Cahen, Claude, 'La première pénétration turque en Asie Mineure', *Byzantion*, 18 (1946–8), 5–67 (reprinted in Cahen, *Turcobyzantina et Oriens Christianus*, 1974).

Cahen, Claude, 'Le Maliknameh et l'histoire des origines seljukides', *Oriens*, 2/i (1949), 31–65 (English translation 'The Malik-nama and the history of Seljuqid origins', in C. Edmund Bosworth (ed), *The Formation of the Classical Islamic World, vol. 9: The Turks in the Early Islamic World* (London, 2007)).

Cahen, Claude, 'L'évolution de l'*iqṭāʿ* du IXe au XIIIe siècle', *Annales: économies, sociétés, civilisation*, 8 (1953), 25–52.

Cahen, Claude, 'Mouvements populaires et autonomisme urbain dans l'Asie musulmane du moyen age', I: *Arabica*, 5/iii (1958), 225–50; II: *Arabica*, 6/i (1959), 25–56; III: *Arabica*, 6/iii (1959), 233–65.

Cahen, Claude, 'The Historiography of the Seljuqid Period', in Bernard Lewis and P. M. Holt (eds), *Historians of the Middle East* (London, 1962), 59–78.

Cahen, Claude, *Turcobyzantina et Oriens Christianus* (London, 1974).

Cahen, Claude, 'Qutlumush et ses fils avant l'Asie mineure', *Der Islam*, 39 (1964), 14–27 (reprinted in Cahen, *Turcobyzantina et Oriens Christianus*, 1974).

Cahen, Claude, 'Nomades et sedentaires dans le monde musulman du milieu du moyen age', in Richards (ed.), *Islamic Civilisation, 950–1150*, 93–104.

Cahen, Claude, 'Fadluwayh le Shavankareh', *Studia Iranica*, 7/i (1978), 111–15.

Cahen, Claude, 'Les Hazars et la tughra seljukide: supplement à un vieil article', *Journal asiatique*, 273/i–ii (1985), 161–2.

Cahen, Claude, 'Atābak', *EIr*.

Cahen, Claude, 'Chaghrï', *EI*[2].

Cahen, Claude, 'Ibn al-Muslima', *EI*[2].

Calmard, Jean, 'Le Chiisme imamite en Iran à l'époque seldjoukide d'après le *Kitâb al-Naqḍ'*, *Le monde iranien et l'islam: sociétés et cultures*, 1 (1971), 43–66.

Canard, Marius, 'La campagne arménienne du sultan salğuqide Alp Arslan et la prise d'Ani en 1064', *Revue des études arméniennes*, 2 (1965), 239–59.

Canard, Marius, 'al-Basāsirī', *EI*[2].

Choksy, Jamsheed K., *Conflict and Cooperation: Zoroastrian Subalterns and Muslim Elites in Medieval Iranian Society* (New York, 1997).

Christensen, Peter, *The Decline of Iranshahr: Irrigation and Environments in the History of the Middle East, 500 B.C. to A.D. 1500* (Copenhagen, 1993).

Cook, David, 'Were the Ismaili Assassins the First Recorded Suicide Attackers? An Examination of their Recorded Assassinations', in Paul M. Cobb (ed.), *The Lineaments of Islam: Studies in Honour of Fred McGraw Donner* (Leiden, 2012), 97–117.

Crone, Patricia, *Medieval Islamic Political Thought* (Edinburgh, 2004).

Crone, Patricia, *The Nativist Prophets of Early Islamic Iran: Rural Revolt and Local Zoroastrianism* (Cambridge, 2012).
Daftary, Farhad, *The Ismāʿīlīs: Their History and Doctrines* (Cambridge, 1990).
Daftary, Farhad, 'Hasan-i Sabbah and the Origins of the Nizari Movement', in Farhard Daftary (ed.), *Mediaeval Isma'ili History and Thought* (Cambridge, 1996), 181–204.
Dankoff, Robert, 'Three Turkic Verse Cycles relating to Inner Asian Warfare', *Harvard Ukrainian Studies*, 3/4 (1979–80), 151–65.
Dankoff, Robert, 'Qarakhanid Literature and the Beginnings of Turco-Islamic Culture', in Hasan B. Paksoy (ed.), *Central Asian Monuments* (Istanbul, 1992), 73–80.
de Bruijn, J. T. P., 'Anvari', *EIr*.
Decker, Michael, 'Plants and Progress: Rethinking the Islamic Agricultural Revolution', *Journal of World History*, 20/ii (2009), 187–206.
Defrémery, C., 'Recherches sur le règne du sultan seldjoukide Barkiarok (485–498 de l'hégire, 1092–1104 de l'ère chrétienne)', *Journal asiatique*, sér. 5, 1 (1853), 425–58; 2 (1853), 217–322.
Diaz, Henry F. *et al.*, 'Spacial and Temporal Characteristics of Climate Change in the Medieval Period Revisited', *Bulletin of the American Meteorological Society*, 92/xi (2011), 1487–99.
Dickens, Mark, 'The Sons of Magog: The Turks in Michael's *Chronicle', Parole de l'Orient*, 30 (2005), 433–50.
Domínguez-Castro, Fernando *et al.*, 'How Useful could Arabic Documentary Sources be for Reconstructing Past Climate?', *Weather*, 62/iii (2012), 76–82
Dunlop, D. M., *The History of the Jewish Khazars* (Princeton, 1954).
Durand-Guédy, David, 'Iranians at War under Turkish Dominion: The Example of pre-Mongol Isfahan', *Iranian Studies*, 38 (2005), 587–606.
Durand-Guédy, David, 'Un fragment inédit de la chronique des Salǧūqides de 'Imād al-Dīn al-Iṣfahānī: le chapitre sur Tāǧ al-Mulk', *Annales Islamologiques*, 39 (2005), 205–22.
Durand-Guédy, David, 'Mémoires d'exilés: lecture de la chronique des Saljūqides de 'Imād al-Dīn al-Isfahānī', *Studia Iranica*, 35 (2006), 181–202.
Durand-Guédy, David, 'Diplomatic Practice in Saljuq Iran: A Preliminary Study based on Nine Letters about Saladin's Campaign in Mesopotamia', *Oriento Moderno*, 89/ii (2008), 271–96.
Durand-Guédy, David, *Iranian Elites and Turkish Rulers: A History of Iṣfahān in the Saljūq Period* (London, 2010).
Durand-Guédy, David, 'The Türkmen–Saljuq Relationship in Twelfth-century Iran: New Elements based on a Contrastive Analysis of Three *Inšā'* Documents', *Eurasian Studies*, 9 (2011) (special issue: *Nomads in the Political Field*, eds Johann Büssow, David Durand-Guédy and Jürgen Paul), 11–66.
Durand-Guédy, David, 'An Emblematic Family of Seljuq Iran: The Khujandis of Isfahan', in Lange and Mecit (eds), *The Seljuqs*, 182–202.
Durand-Guédy, David, 'Where Did the Saljuqs Live? A Case Study based on the Reign of Masʿūd b. Muḥammad (1134–1152)', *Studia Iranica*, 40 (2011), 211–58.
Durand-Guédy, David, 'Ruling from the Outside: A New Perspective on Early Turkish Kingship in Iran', in Lynette Mitchell and Charles Melville (eds),

Every Inch a King. Comparative Studies on Kings and Kingship in the Ancient and Medieval Worlds (Leiden, 2012), 325–42.

Durand-Guédy, David (ed.), *Turko-Mongol Rulers, Cities and City Life* (Leiden, 2013).

Durand-Guédy, David, 'The Tents of the Saljuqs', in Durand-Guédy (ed.), *Turko-Mongol Rulers*, 149–89.

Durand-Guédy, David, 'Help Me if You Can! An Analysis of a Letter sent by the Last Seljuq Sultan of Kirman', in Hillenbrand, Peacock and Abdullaeva (eds), *Ferdowsi, the Mongols and the History of Iran*, 70–7.

Durand-Guédy, David, 'Goodbye to the Türkmen? The Military Role of Nomads in Iran after the Saljuq Conquest', in K. Franz and W. Holzwarth (eds), *Nomadic Military Power: Iran and Adjacent Areas in the Islamic Period* (Wiesbaden, in press).

Durand-Guédy, David, 'Malekšāh', *EIr*.

Duri, A. A., 'Dīwān', *EI*².

Duri, Khidr Jasmin, 'Society and Economy of Iraq under the Seljuqs (1055–1160 A.D.) with Special Reference to Baghdad', PhD dissertation, University of Pennsylvania, 1970.

Eddé, Anne-Marie, 'Riḍwān, Prince d'Alep de 1095 à 1113', *Revue des études islamiques*, 54 (1986), 101–25.

Elisséeff, Nikita, 'La titulature de Nur ad-Din d'après ses inscriptions', *Bulletin d'études orientales*, 14 (1952–54), 155–96.

El-Azhari, Taef, *The Saljuqs of Syria During the Crusades, 463–549 A.H./1070–1154 A.D.* (Berlin, 1997).

Ellenblum, Ronnie, *The Collapse of the Eastern Mediterranean: Climate Change and the Decline of the East, 950–1072* (Cambridge, 2012).

Ephrat, Daphna, *A Learned Society in a Period of Transition: The Sunni 'Ulama' of Eleventh-century Baghdad* (Albany, NY, 2000).

Ephrat, Daphna, 'The Seljuqs and the Public Sphere in the Period of Sunni Revivalism: The View from Baghdad', in Lange and Mecit (eds), *The Seljuqs*, 139–56.

Fairbanks, S., 'The *Tārīkh al-Vuzarā'*: A History of the Saljuq Bureaucracy', PhD dissertation, University of Michigan, 1977.

Fairbanks, S., 'Atābakān-e Yazd', *EIr*.

Farhat, May, 'Islamic Piety and Dynastic Legitimacy: The Case of the Shrine of 'Ali b. Musa al-Rida in Mashhad (10th–17th centuries)', PhD dissertation, Harvard University, 2002.

Fiey, Jean Maurice, *Chrétiens syriaques sous les Abbassides surtout à Bagdad (749–1258)* (Louvain, 1980).

Finster, Barbara, 'The Saljuqs as Patrons', in Robert Hillenbrand (ed.), *The Art of the Saljuqs in Iran and Anatolia* (Costa Mesa, 1994), 17–28.

Fletcher, Joseph, 'The Turco-Mongolian Monarchic Tradition in the Ottoman Empire', *Harvard Ukrainian Studies*, 3–4 (1979–80), 236–51.

Fragner, Bert, *Geschichte der Stadt Hamadān und ihrer Umgebung in den ersten sechs Jahrhunderten nach der Hiğra von der Eroberung durch die Araber bis zum Untergang der 'Irāq-Selčuken'* (Vienna, 1972).

Franklin, Arnold E., *This Noble House: Jewish Descendants of King David in the Medieval Islamic East* (Philadelphia, 2013).

Frankopan, Peter, *The First Crusade: The Call of the East* (London, 2012).

Frenkel, Yehoshua, 'The Turks of the Eurasian Steppes in Medieval Arabic Writing', in Reuven Amitai and Michal Biran (eds), *Mongols, Turks and Others: Eurasian Nomads and the Sedentary World* (Leiden, 2005), 201–41.
Frye, Richard N. and Aydın M. Sayılı, 'The Turks in the Middle East before the Saljuqs', *JAOS*, 63/iii (1953), 194–207.
Gandjeï, Tourkhan, 'Turkish in pre-Mongol Persian Poetry', *BSOAS*, 49/i (1996), 67–75.
Garden, Kenneth, 'al-Māzarī al-Dhakī: al-Ghazālī's Maghribi opponent in Nishapur', *Journal of Islamic Studies*, 21/i (2010), 89–107.
Garden, Kenneth, *The First Islamic Reviver: Abū Ḥāmid al-Ghazālī and his* Revival of the Religious Sciences (New York, 2014).
Gaube, Heinz, *Die Sudpersische Provinz Arrağān/Kūh-Gilūyeh von der arabischen Eroberung bis zur Safawidenzeit: Analyse und Auswertung literarischer und archäologischer Quellen zur historischen Topographie* (Vienna, 1973).
Gianazza, Gianmaria, 'Lettre de Makkīḫā (†1109) sur la vérité de la religion chrétienne', *Parole de l'Orient*, 25 (2000), 493–555.
Gibson, Melanie, 'The Enigmatic Figure: Ceramic Sculpture from Iran and Syria, 1150–1250', *Transactions of the Oriental Ceramic Society*, 73 (2008–9), 39–50.
Gierlichs, Joachim, 'A Victory Monument in the Name of Sultan Malikshah in Diyarbakır: Medieval Figural Reliefs used for Political Propaganda?', *Islamic Art*, 6 (2009), 51–79.
Gil, Moshe, 'The Exilarch', in Daniel H. Frank (ed.), *The Jews of Medieval Islam: Community, Society and Identity* (Leiden, 1995), 33–66.
Gil, Moshe, *Jews in the Islamic Countries in the Middle Ages*, trans. David Strassler (Leiden, 2004).
Glassen, Erika, *Der mittlere Weg: Studien zur Religionspolitik und Religiosität der späteren Abbasidenzeit* (Wiesbaden, 1981).
Gleave, Robert, 'Shii Jurisprudence during the Seljuq Period: Rebellion and Public Order in an Illegitimate State', in Lange and Mecit (eds), *The Seljuqs*, 205–27.
Goitein, S. D., 'A Report on Messianic Troubles in Baghdad in 1120–21', *Jewish Quarterly Review*, 43/i (1952), 57–76.
Goitein, S. D., 'Minority Self-rule and Government Control in Islam,' *Studia Islamica*, 31 (1970), 101–16.
Golden, Peter B., 'The Migrations of the Oğuz', *Archivum Ottomanicum*, 4 (1972), 45–84.
Golden, Peter B., 'Imperial Ideology and the Sources of Political Unity amongst the pre-Činggisid Nomads of Western Eurasia', *Archivum Eurasiae Medii Aevi*, 2 (1982), 37–76 (reprinted in Golden, *Nomads and their Neighbours* (Study I)).
Golden, Peter B., 'The Karakhanids and Early Islam', in Denis Sinor (ed.) *The Cambridge History of Early Inner Asia* (Cambridge, 1990), 343–70.
Golden, Peter B., 'The Qipchaqs of Medieval Eurasia: An Example of Stateless Adaptation in the Steppes', in G. Seaman and D. Marks (eds), *Rulers from the Steppe: State Formation on the Eurasian Periphery* (Los Angeles 1991), 132–57 (reprinted in Golden, *Nomads and their Neighbours*, Study IX).
Golden, Peter B., *An Introduction to the History of the Turkic Peoples: Ethnogenesis and State Formation in Medieval and Early Modern Eurasia and the Middle East* (Wiesbaden, 1992).

Golden, Peter B., *Nomads and their Neighbours in the Russian Steppe* (Aldershot, 2003).
Golden, Peter B., 'The Türk Imperial Tradition in the pre-Chinggisid Era', in David Sneath (ed.), *Imperial Statecraft: Political Forms and Techniques of Governance in Inner Asia, 6th–20th Century* (Bellingham, 2006), 23–61 (reprinted in Golden, *Turks and Khazars*, Study III).
Golden, Peter B., *Turks and Khazars: Origins, Institutions and Interactions in Pre-Mongol Eurasia* (Farnham, 2010).
Golden, Peter B., 'The Turks: Origins and Expansion', in Golden, *Turks and Khazars* Study I.
Golden, Peter B., *Central Asia in World History* (Oxford, 2011).
Golden, Peter B., 'Courts and Court Culture in the Proto-urban and Urban Developments among the pre-Chinggisid Turkic Peoples', in Durand-Guédy (ed.), *Turko-Mongol Rulers*, 21–73.
Golombek, Lisa, 'Mazar-i Sharif: A Case of Mistaken Identity', in Myriam Rosen-Ayalon (ed.), *Studies in Memory of Gaston Wiet* (Jerusalem, 1977), 335–43.
Goshgarian, Rachel, 'Futuwwa in Thirteenth-century Rum and Armenia: Reform Movements and the Managing of Multiple Identities on the Seljuk Periphery', in Peacock and Yıldız (eds), *The Seljuks of Anatolia*, 227–63.
Grabar, Oleg, 'Les arts mineurs de l'Orient musulman à partir du milieu du XIIe siècle', *Cahiers de civilisation médiévale*, 11(42) (1968), 181–90.
Grabar, Oleg, 'The Visual Arts, 1150–1300', in Boyle (ed.), *The Cambridge History of Iran*, V, 626–58.
Graves, Margaret S., 'Ceramic House Models from Medieval Persia: Domestic Architecture and Concealed Activities', *Iran*, 46 (2008), 227–51.
Gray, Basil, 'A Seljuq Hoard from Persia', *British Museum Quarterly*, 13/iii (1938–9), 73–9.
Green, Nile, *Sufism: A Global History* (Oxford, 2012).
Hallaq, Wael B., 'Caliphs, Jurists and Saljuqs in the Political Thought of al-Juwayni', *Muslim World*, 74/i (1984), 26–41.
Halm, Heinz, 'Der Wesir al-Kundurī und die Fitna von Nišapur', *Die Welt des Orients*, 6/ii (1971), 205–33.
Hamdani, Abbas, 'The *Rasa'il Ikhwan al-Safa* and the Controversy about the Origin of Craft Guilds in Early Medieval Islam', in Nelly Hanna (ed.), *Money, Land and Trade: An Economic History of the Muslim Mediterranean* (London, 2002), 157–73.
Hanne, Eric, 'Death on the Tigris: A Numismatic Analysis of the Decline of the Great Saljuqs', *American Journal of Numismatics*, 16–17 (2004–5), 145–72.
Hanne, Eric, 'Women, Power, and the Eleventh and Twelfth-century Abbasid Court', *Hawwa*, 3/i (2005), 80–110.
Hanne, Eric, *Putting the Caliph in his Place: Power, Authority and the Late Abbasid Caliphate* (Madison, 2007).
Hanne, Eric, 'The Banū Jahīr and their Role in the 'Abbāsid and Saljūq Administration', *al-Masāq*, 20/i (2008), 29–45.
Hartmann, Angelika, *an-Nāṣir li-Dīn Allāh (1180–1225): Politik, Religion, Kultur in der späten 'Abbasidenzeit* (Berlin, 1975).
Hartmann, Angelika, 'al-Nāṣir li-Dīn Allāh', *EI*[2].
Heidemann, Stefan, *Die Renaissance der Städte in Nordsyrien und Nordmesopotamien:*

Städtische Entwinklung und wirtschaftliche Bedingungen in ar-Raqqa und Ḥarrān von der Zeit der beduinischer Vorherrschaft bis zu den Seldschuken (Leiden, 2002).

Heidemann, Stefan, 'Arab Nomads and the Seljūq Military', in Stefan Leder and Bernard Streck (eds), *Shifts and Drifts in Nomad–Sedentary Relations* (Wiesbaden, 2005), 289–305.

Heidemann, Stefan, 'The Citadel of al-Raqqa and Fortifications in the Middle Euphrates Area', in Kennedy (ed.), *Muslim Military Architecture in Greater Syria*, 122–50.

Heidemann, Stefan, 'Charity and Piety for the Transformation of Cities: The New Direction of Taxation and Waqf and Policy in Mid-twelfth Century Northern Syria and Mesopotamia', in Miriam Frenkel and Yaacov Lev (eds), *Charity and Giving in Monotheistic Religions* (Berlin, 2009), 153–74.

Heidemann, Stefan, 'Unislamic Taxes and an Unislamic Monetary System in Seljuq Baghdad', in İsmail Safa Üstün (ed.), *Islam Medeniyetinde Bağdat (Medinetü's-Selām) Uluslararası Sempozyumu (International Symposium on Baghdad (Madinat al-Salam) in the Islamic Civilization)* (Istanbul, 2011), 493–506.

Heidemann, Stefan, 'Zangī', *EI*².

Heidemann, Stefan, 'Zangids', *EI*².

Herrmann, Georgina, *Monuments of Merv: Traditional Buildings of the Karakum* (London, 1999).

Hillenbrand, Carole, 'The Career of Najm al-Dīn İl-ghāzī', *Der Islam*, 58 (1981), 250–92.

Hillenbrand, Carole, 'Islamic Orthodoxy or Realpolitik? al-Ghazali's Views on Government', *Iran*, 26 (1988), 81–94.

Hillenbrand, Carole, 'Ibn al-'Adīm's Biography of the Seljuq Sultan, Alp Arslan', in Concepción Vázquez de Benito and Miguel Angel Manzano Rodriguez (eds), *Actas XVI Congreso UEAI* (Salamanca, 1995), 237–42.

Hillenbrand, Carole, '1092: A Murderous Year', in A. Fodor (ed.), *Proceedings of the 14th Congress of Union européene des arabisants et islamisants* (Budapest, 1995), 281–96.

Hillenbrand, Carole, 'The Power Struggle between the Saljuqs and the Isma'ilis of Alamut, 487–518/1094–1124: The Saljuq Perspective', in Farhard Daftary (ed.), *Mediaeval Isma'ili History and Thought* (Cambridge, 1996), 205–20.

Hillenbrand, Carole, Review of S. G. Agadshanow, *Selğukiden und Turkmenien im 11–12 Jahrhundert*; S. G. Agadshanow, *Der Staat der Seldshukiden und Mittelasien im 11–12 Jahrhundert, JRAS*, 3rd series, 2 (1996), 255–7.

Hillenbrand, Carole, *The Crusades: Islamic Perspectives* (Edinburgh, 2000).

Hillenbrand, Carole, 'Some Reflections on Seljuq Historiography', in Antony Eastmond (ed.), *Eastern Approaches to Byzantium* (Aldershot, 2000), 73–88.

Hillenbrand, Carole, 'Women in the Seljuq Period', in Guity Nashat and Lois Beck (eds), *Women in Iran from the Rise of Islam to 1800* (Urbana, 2003), 103–20.

Hillenbrand, Carole, *Turkish Myth and Muslim Symbol: The Battle of Manzikert* (Edinburgh, 2007).

Hillenbrand, Carole, 'Aspects of the Court of the Great Seljuqs', in Lange and Mecit (eds), *The Seljuqs*, 22–38.

Hillenbrand, Carole, 'What's in a Name? Tughtegin: "the Minister of the

Antichrist"?', in Omar Alí-de-Unzaga (ed.), *Fortresses of the Intellect: Ismaili and Other Islamic Studies in Honour of Farhad Daftary* (London, 2011), 459–71.

Hillenbrand, Carole, 'The *Kimya-yi sa'adat* (The Elixir of Happiness) of al-Ghazali: A Misunderstood Work?' in Hillenbrand, Peacock and Abdullaeva (eds), *Ferdowsi, the Mongols and the History of Iran*, 59–69.

Hillenbrand, Carole, 'al-Mustarshid', *EI*².

Hillenbrand, Carole, 'al-Rāshid', *EI*².

Hillenbrand, Robert, 'Eastern Islamic Influences in Syria: al-Raqqa and Qal'at Ja'bar in the Later 12th Century', in Julian Raby (ed.), *The Art of Syria and the Jazira, 1100–1250* (Oxford, 1985), 21–48.

Hillenbrand, Robert (ed.), *The Art of the Saljuqs in Iran and Anatolia* (Costa Mesa, 1994).

Hillenbrand, Robert, *Islamic Architecture: Form, Function and Meaning* (New York, 1994).

Hillenbrand, Robert, 'The Seljuq Monuments of Turkmenistan', in Lange and Mecit (eds), *The Seljuqs*, 277–308.

Hillenbrand, Robert, A. C. S. Peacock and Firuza Abdullaeva (eds), *Ferdowsi, the Mongols and the History of Iran: Studies on Art, Literature and Culture from Early Islam to the Qajars* (London, 2013).

Hirschler, Konrad, '"He is a Child and this Land is a Borderland of Islam": Underage Rule and the Quest for Political Stability in the Ayyūbid Period', *al-Masāq*, 19/i (2007), 29–46.

Hodgson, Marshall G. S., *The Secret Order of the Assassins: The Struggle of the Early Nizârî Ismâ'îlîs against the Islamic World* (Philadelphia, [1955] 2005).

Holod, Renata, 'Event and Memory: The Freer Gallery's Siege Scene Plate', *Ars Orientalis*, 42 (2012), 195–219.

Horst, Heribert, *Die Staatsverwaltung der Grosselǧūqen und Ḫōrazmšāhs (1038–1231)* (Wiesbaden, 1964).

Humphreys, R. Stephen, *From Saladin to the Mongols: The Ayyubids of Damascus, 1193–1260* (Albany, NY, 1977).

Hunter, Erica C. D., 'The Conversion of the Kerait to Christianity in 1007', *Zentralasiatische Studien*, 22 (1989–91), 158–76.

Hunter, Erica C. D., 'The Church of the East in Central Asia', *Bulletin of the John Rylands Library*, 78/iii (1996), 129–42.

Husain, Adnan A., 'Conversion to History: Negating Exile and Messianism in Samaw'al al-Maghribi's Polemic against Judaism', *Medieval Encounters*, 8/i (2002), 3–34.

al-Ḥusaynī, Muḥammad Bāqir, 'Dirāsa taḥlīliyya wa iḥṣā'iyya lil-alqāb al-islāmiyya', *Sumer*, 27/i (1971), 185–231; *Sumer*, 27/ii (1971), 154–85.

Iqbāl, 'Abbās, *Wizārat dar 'ahd-i salāṭīn-i buzurg-i Saljūqī az tārīkh-i tashkīl-i silsila tā marg-i Sulṭān Sanjar 432–552* (Tehran, 1338).

Ivanow, W., *Alamut and Lamasar: Two Ismaili Strongholds in Iran, an Archaeological Study* (Tehran, 1960).

Kaegi, Walter, 'The Contribution of Archery to the Turkish Conquest of Anatolia', *Speculum*, 39/i (1969), 96–108.

Kafesoğlu, İbrahim, *Sultan Melikşah Devrinde Büyük Selçuklu İmparatorluğu* (Istanbul, 1953).

Kafesoğlu, İbrahim, *Harezmşahlar Devleti Tarihi (485–618/1092–1221)* (Ankara, 1956).

Karamustafa, Ahmet T., *Sufism: The Formative Period* (Edinburgh, 2007).

Karev, Yuri, 'From Tents to Cities. The Royal Court of the Western Qarakhanids between Bukhara and Samarqand', in Durand-Guédy (ed.), *Turko-Mongol Rulers*, 99–147.

Kennedy, Hugh, *The Court of the Caliphs: When Baghdad Ruled the Muslim World* (London, 2004).

Kennedy, Hugh (ed.), *Muslim Military Architecture in Greater Syria from the Coming of Islam to the Ottoman Period* (Leiden, 2006),

Kennedy, Hugh, 'From Shahristan to Madina', *Studia Islamica*, 102/iii (2006), 301–33.

Kennedy, Hugh, 'The City and the Nomad', in Robert Irwin (ed.), *New Cambridge History of Islam, vol. IV: Islamic Cultures and Societies to the End of the Eighteenth Century* (Cambridge, 2010), 274–89.

Kiani, M., *The Islamic City of Gurgan* (Berlin, 1984).

Kister, M. J., '"You Shall only Set out for Three Mosques": A Study of an Early Tradition', *Le Muséon*, 82 (1969), 173–96.

Kitapçı, Zekeriya, *Abbâsî Hilafetinde Selçuklu Hatunları ve Türk Sultanları* (Konya, 1994).

Klausner, Carla L., *The Seljuk Vezirate: A Study of Civil Administration 1055–1194* (Cambridge, MA, 1973).

Kochnev, Boris, *Numizmaticheskaya Istoriya Karakhanidskogo Kaganata (991–1209)* (Moscow, 2006).

Köprülü, M. Fuad, 'Atabeg' s.v. 'Ata', *İslam Ansiklopedisi* (Istanbul, 1978), I, 711–18.

Korn, Lorenz, 'The Sultan stopped at Ḥalab: Artistic Exchange between Syria and Iran in the 5th/11th Century', in Lorenz Korn, Eva Orthmann and Florian Schwarz (eds), *Die Grenzen der Welt: Arabica et Iranica ad honorem Heinz Gaube* (Wiesbaden, 2008), 105–21.

Korn, Lorenz, 'Ein Denkmal seldschukischer Religionspolitik? Inschriften der grossen Moschee von Gulpayigan', in Hinrich Biesterfeld and Verena Klemm (eds), *Differenz und Dinamik in Islam: Festschrift fur Heinz Halm zum 70 Geburtstag* (Wurzburg, 2012), 455–71.

Korn, Lorenz, 'Saljuqs. V. Art and Architecture', *EIr.*

Korobeinikov, Dimitri, '"The King of the East and the West": The Seljuk Dynastic Concept and Titles in Muslim and Christian Sources', in Peacock and Yıldız (eds), *The Seljuks of Anatolia*, 68–90.

Kovalev, Roman K., 'The Infrastructure of the Northern Part of the "Fur Road" between the Middle Volga and the East during the Middle Ages', *Archivum Eurasiae Medii Aevi*, 11 (2000–1), 25–37.

Kovalev, Roman K., 'Mint Output in Tenth-century Bukhara: A Case Study in Dirham Production and Monetary Circulation in Northern Europe', *Russian History/Histoire Russe*, 28/i–iv (2001), 245–71.

Kovalev, Roman K., 'The Infrastructure of the Novgorodian Fur Trade in the pre-Mongol Era (ca. 900–1240)', unpublished PhD dissertation, University of Minnesota, 2002.

Kovalev, Roman K., 'The Production of Dirhams in the Coastal Caspian Sea Provinces of Northern Iran in the Tenth–eleventh Centuries and their Circulation in the Northern Lands', *Archivum Eurasiae Medii Aevii*, 19 (2012), 133–83.

Köymen, Mehmed Altay, 'Selçuklu Devri Kaynaklarına Dâir Araştırmalar, I. Büyük Selçuklu İmparatorluğu devrine ait münşeat mecmuaları', unpublished offprint held in Türk Tarih Kurumu, Ankara, from *Ankara Üniversitesi Dil ve Tarih-Coğrafya Fakültesi Dergisi*, 8 (1951), 539–648.

Köymen, Mehmed Altay, *Büyük Selçuklu İmparatorluğu Tarihi, II: İkinci İmparatorluk Devri* (Ankara, 1954).

Köymen, Mehmed Altay, *Tuğrul Bey ve Zamanı* (Istanbul, 1976).

Köymen, Mehmed Altay, *Büyük Selçuklu İmparatorluğu Tarihi, I: Kuruluş Devri* (Ankara, 1979).

Köymen, Mehmed Altay, *Alp Arslan ve Zamanı* (Ankara, 1983).

Kraemer, Joel L., *Maimonides: The Life and World of One of Civilization's Greatest Minds* (New York, 2008).

Kraemers, J. H. and C. E Bosworth, 'Sulṭān', *EI*[2].

Krawczyk, Jean-Luc, 'The Relationship between Pastoral Nomadism and Agriculture: Northern Syria and the Jazira in the Eleventh Century', *JRŪR*, 1 (1985), 1–22 (reprinted in Michael Morony (ed.), *Production and the Exploitation of Resources* (The Formation of the Classical Islamic World, 11) (Aldershot, 2002)).

Kucur, Sadi S., 'A Study on the Coins of Tughrıl Beg, the Sultan of the Great Seljuqs', in Carmen Alfaro, Carmen Marcos and Paloma Otero (eds), *XII Congreso Internacional de Numismática, Madrid, 2003. Actas* (Madrid 2005), I, 1599–1608.

Lambton, A. K. S., 'The Theory of Kingship in the *Nasihat-ul-Muluk* of Ghazali', *Islamic Quarterly*, 1 (1954), 47–55.

Lambton, A. K. S., 'The Administration of Sanjar's Empire as Illustrated in the *'Atabat al-kataba'*, *BSOAS*, 20 (1957), 367–88

Lambton, A. K. S., 'The Internal Structure of the Saljuq Empire', in Boyle (ed.), *The Cambridge History of Iran*, V, 203–82.

Lambton, A. K. S., 'Saljuq–Ghuzz Settlement in Persia', in Richards (ed.), *Islamic Civilisation 950–1150*, 105–26.

Lambton, A. K. S., *State and Government in Medieval Islam: An Introduction to the Study of Islamic Political Theory. The Jurists* (Oxford, 1981).

Lambton, A. K. S., 'The Dilemma of Government in Islamic Persia: The *Siyāsat-nāmah* of Niẓām al-Mulk', *Iran*, 22 (1984), 55–66.

Lambton, A. K. S., *Continuity and Change in Medieval Persia: Aspects of Administrative, Economic and Social History* (Albany, NY, 1988).

Lambton, A. K. S., '*Awqāf* in Persia, 6th–8th/12th–14th Centuries', *Islamic Law and Society*, 4/iii (1997), 298–318.

Lambton, A. K. S.,'Eqṭā'', *EIr*.

Lambton, A. K. S., 'Ḥājib', *EI*[2].

Lambton, A. K. S., 'Marāsim. II. Iran', *EI*[2].

Lambton, A. K. S., 'Shiḥna', *EI*[2].

Lange, Christian, 'Legal and Cultural Aspects of Ignominious Parading (*tashhīr*) in Islam', *Islamic Law and Society*, 14/i (2007), 81–108.

Lange, Christian, *Justice, Punishment and the Medieval Muslim Imagination* (Cambridge, 2008).

Lange, Christian, 'Changes in the Office of *Ḥisba* under the Seljuqs', in Lange and Mecit (eds), *The Seljuqs*, 157–81.

Lange, Christian and Songül Mecit (eds), *The Seljuqs: Politics, Society and Culture* (Edinburgh, 2011).

Laoust, H., 'Les agitations religieuses à Baghdad', in Richards (ed.), *Islamic Civilisation, 950–1150*, 169–85.

Le Strange, G., *Lands of the Eastern Caliphate: Mesopotamia, Persian and Central Asia from the Moslem Conquest to the Time of Timur* (Cambridge, 1930).

Leichter, Joseph, 'The Zij-i Sanjari of Gregory Chioniades: Text, Translation and Greek to Arabic Vocabulary', PhD dissertation, Brown University, 2004.

Leiser, Gary (ed. and trans.), *A History of the Seljuks: İbrahim Kafesoğlu's Interpretation and the Resulting Controversy* (Carbondale, 1988).

Levtzion, Nehemia, 'Conversion to Islam in Syria and Palestine and the Survival of Christian Communities', in Michael Gervers and Ramzi Jibran Bikhazi (eds), *Conversion and Continuity: Indigenous Christian Communities in Islamic Lands, Eighth to Eighteenth Centuries* (Toronto, 1990), 289–311.

Lewis, Bernard, 'The Fatimids and the Route to India', *Revue de la faculté des sciences économiques de l'université d'Istanbul*, 14 (1953), 50–4.

Lieberman, Victor, *Strange Parallels: Southeast Asia in Global Context, vol. I: Integration on the Mainland* (Cambridge, 2003).

Lowick, N. M. 'Seljuq Coins', *The Numismatic Chronicle*, 7th series, 10 (1970), 241–51.

Luther, K. A., 'The Political Transformation of the Seljuq Sultanate of Iraq and Western Iran, 1152–1187', PhD dissertation, Princeton University, 1964.

Luther, K. A., 'A New Source for the History of the Iraq Seljuqs: The *Tārīkh al-Vuzarā*'', *Der Islam*, 45 (1969), 117–28.

Luther, K. A., 'Rāvandī's Report on the Administrative Changes of Muḥammad Jahān Pahlavān', in C. E. Bosworth (ed.), *Iran and Islam: In Memory of the Late Vladimir Minorsky* (Edinburgh, 1971), 393–406.

Luther, K. A., 'The End of Saljuq Domination in Khurasan', in Louis L. Orlin (ed.), *Michigan Oriental Studies in Honor of George G. Cameron* (Ann Arbor, 1976), 219–25.

Luther, K. A., 'Atābakān-e Ādarbayjān', *EIr*.

Madelung, W., 'The Spread of Maturidism and the Turks', *Actas do Congresso de Estudos Arabes e Islâmicos* (Coimbra-Lisbon, 1968), 109–68 (reprinted in W. Madelung, *Religious Schools and Sects in Medieval Islam* (London, 1985)).

Madelung, W., 'The Assumption of the Title *Shāhanshāh* by the Buyids and "the reign of the Daylam"', *Journal of Near Eastern Studies*, 28/ii (1969), 84–108; 28/iii (1969), 168–83.

Madelung, W., *Religious Trends in Early Islamic Iran* (Albany, NY, 1988).

Makdisi, George, 'Notes on Ḥilla and the Mazyadids in Medieval Islam', *JAOS*, 74/iv (1954), 249–62.

Makdisi, George, 'Muslim Institutions of Learning in Eleventh-century Baghdad', *BSOAS*, 24/i (1961), 1–56.

Makdisi, George, *Ibn 'Aqīl et la résurgence de l'Islam traditionaliste au XIe siècle* (Damascus, 1963).

Makdisi, George, 'The Marriage of Tughril Beg', *IJMES*, 1/iii (1970), 259–75.
Makdisi, George, 'The Sunni Revival', in Richards (ed.), *Islamic Civilisation, 950–1150*, 155–68.
Makdisi, George, 'Les rapports entre Calife et Sultan à l'epoque saljuqide', *IJMES*, 6/ii (1975), 228–36.
Makdisi, George, 'Madrasa', *EI²*.
Malamud, Margaret, 'Sufi Organizations and Structures of Authority in Medieval Nishapur', *IJMES*, 26/iii (1994), 427–42.
Martin, Janet, 'Trade on the Volga: The Commercial Relations of Bulghar with Central Asia and Iran in the 11th–12th Centuries', *International Journal of Turkish Studies*, 1 (1980), 85–97
Mason, Herbert, *Two Statesmen of Mediaeval Islam: Vizir Ibn Hubayra (499–560 AH/1105–1165 AD) and Caliph an-Nâṣir li Dîn Allâh (553–622 AH/1158–1225 AD)* (The Hague, 1972).
Mattini, J., 'A'maq-i Boḵāri', *EIr*.
McChesney, R. D., *Waqf in Central Asia: Four Hundred Years in the History of a Muslim Shrine, 1480–1889* (Princeton, 1991).
Meier, Fritz, *Abū Sa'īd-i Abū l-Hayr (357–440/967–1049). Wirklichkeit und Legende* (Tehran and Liege, 1976).
Meisami, Julie Scott, *Persian Historiography to the End of the Twelfth Century* (Edinburgh, 1999).
Meisami, Julie Scott, 'The Collapse of the Great Saljuqs', in Chase F. Robinson (ed.), *Texts, Documents and Artefacts: Islamic Studies in Honour of D. S. Richards* (Leiden, 2003), 265–300.
Meneghini, Daniela, 'Saljuqs. V. Saljuqid literature', *EIr*.
Merçil, Erdoğan, *Fars Atabegleri Salgurlular* (Ankara, 1975).
Merçil, Erdoğan, *Kirman Selçuklular* (Ankara, 1989).
Merçil, Erdoğan, 'Selçuklular ve Türkçe', *Belleten*, 67(248) (2003), 111–17.
Merçil, Erdoğan, *Selçuklular'da Saraylar ve Saray Teşkilatı* (Istanbul, 2011).
Miles, George C., 'The Coinage of the Kākwaihid Dynasty', *Iraq*, 5 (1938), 89–104.
Minasian, Caro, *Shah Diz of Ismaili Fame: Its Siege and Destruction* (London, 1970).
Minorsky, V., 'Kurds. III. History. B. The Islamic Period up to 1920', *EI²*.
Minorsky, Vladimir and Claude Cahen, 'Le recueil transcaucasien de Mas'ûd b. Nâmdâr (debut du VIe/XIIe siècle)', *Journal Asiatique*, 237 (1949), 93–142.
Molé, M., '"Vis u Ramin" et l'histoire seldjoukide', *Annali: Istituto Orientale di Napoli*, 9 (1960), 1–30.
Morimoto, Kazuo, 'Putting the *Lubāb al-ansāb* in Context: *Sayyids* and *Naqībs* in late Saljuq Khurasan', *Studia Iranica*, 36 (2007), 163–83.
Morton, A. H., 'Dinars from Western Mazandaran of Some Vassals of the Saljuq Sultan Muḥammad b. Malik-shāh', *Iran*, 25 (1987), 77–90.
Morton, A. H., 'Qashani and Rashid al-Din on the Seljuqs of Iran', in Yasir Suleiman (ed.), *Living Islamic History: Studies in Honour of Professor Carole Hillenbrand* (Edinburgh, 2010), 166–77.
Mottahedeh, Roy, *Loyalty and Leadership in an Early Islamic Society* (London, [1981] 2001).

Mouton, Jean-Michel, *Damas et sa principauté sous les Saljoukides et les Bourides, 468–549/1076–1154* (Cairo, 1994).
Murphey, Rhoads, *Exploring Ottoman Sovereignty: Tradition, Image and Practice in the Ottoman Imperial household, 1400–1800* (London, 2008).
Nagel, Tilman, 'Buyids', *EIr*.
Nazim, M., 'The *Pand-nāmah* of Subuktigin', *JRAS*, 2nd series, 3 (1933), 605–28.
Noonan, Thomas, 'The Onset of the Silver Crisis in Central Asia', *Archivum Eurasiae Medii Aevii*, 7 (1987–91), 228–48.
O'Kane, Bernard, 'A Tale of Two Minbars: Woodwork from Syria and Egypt on the Eve of the Ayyubids', in Hillenbrand, Peacock and Abdullaeva (eds), *Ferdowsi, the Mongols and the History of Iran*, 316–26.
Özgüdenli, Osman G., 'Yeni paraların ışığında kuruluş devri Selçuklularında hakimiyet münasabetleri hakkında bazı düşünceler', *Belleten*, 45(242–4) (2002), 547–70.
Özgüdenli, Osman G., 'Selçuklu paraların ışığında Çağrı Bey'in ölüm tarihi meselesi', *Ankara Üniversitesi Dil ve Tarih-Coğrafya Fakültesi Tarih Bölümü Tarih Araştırmaları Dergisi*, 22(35) (2004), 155–70.
Özgüdenli, Osman G., *Selçuklular, vol. I: Büyük Selçuklu Devleti Tarihi (1040–1157)* (Istanbul, 2013).
Özgüdenli, Osman G., 'Musa Yabgu', *EIr*.
Pancaroğlu, Oya, '"A World unto Himself": The Rise of a New Human Image in the Late Seljuk Period', PhD dissertation, Harvard University, 2000.
Pancaroğlu, Oya, 'The House of Mengücek in Divriği: Constructions of Dynastic Identity in the late Twelfth Century', in Peacock and Yıldız (eds), *The Seljuks of Anatolia*, 25–67.
Paul, Jürgen, *Herrscher, Gemeinwesen, Vermittler: Ostiran und Transoxanien in vormongolischer Zeit* (Beirut, 1996).
Paul, Jürgen, 'The Histories of Herat', *Iranian Studies*, 33/i–ii (2000), 93–115.
Paul, Jürgen, 'The Histories of Isfahan: Mafarrukhi's *Kitāb maḥāsin Iṣfahān*', *Iranian Studies*, 33/i–ii (2000), 117–32.
Paul, Jürgen, 'The Seljuq Conquest(s) of Nishapur: A Reappraisal', *Iranian Studies*, 38/iv (2005), 575–85.
Paul, Jürgen, 'The role of Ḫʷārazm in Seljuq Central Asian Politics, Victories and Defeats: Two Case Studies', *Eurasian Studies*, 6 (2007–8), 1–17.
Paul, Jürgen, 'Arslan Arghun: Nomadic Revival?', in Lange and Mecit (eds), *The Seljuqs*, 99–113.
Paul, Jürgen, Review of Aziz Basan, *The Great Seljuqs: A History, Eurasian Studies*, 9 (2011) (special issue: *Nomads in the Political Field*, eds Johann Büssow, David Durand-Guédy and Jürgen Paul), 268–71.
Paul, Jürgen (ed.), *Nomad Aristocrats in a World of Empires* (Wiesbaden, 2013).
Paul, Jürgen, 'Sanjar and Atsız: Independence, Lordship and Literature', in Paul (ed.), *Nomad Aristocrats in a World of Empires*, 81–130.
Paul, Jürgen, 'Where did the Dihqāns Go?' *Eurasian Studies*, 11 (2013), 1–34.
Paul, Jürgen, 'Khidma in the Social History of Pre-Mongol Iran', *Journal of the Economic and Social History of the Orient* 57/iii (2014), 392–422.
Paul, Jürgen, 'Local Lords or Rural Notables? Some Remarks on the *Ra'īs* in 12th-century Eastern Iran', in A. C. S. Peacock and D. G. Tor (eds), *Medieval Central Asia and the Persianate World: Iranian Tradition and Islamic Civilisation* (London, forthcoming).

Peacock, A. C. S., 'Aḥmad of Niğde's *al-Walad al-Shafiq* and the Seljuk Past', *Anatolian Studies*, 54 (2004), 95–107.
Peacock, A. C. S., 'Nomadic Society and the Seljuq Campaigns in Caucasia', *Iran and the Caucasus*, 9 (2005), 205–30.
Peacock, A. C. S., *Early Seljūq History: A New Interpretation* (London, 2010).
Peacock, A. C. S., 'Seljuq Legitimacy in Islamic History', in Lange and Mecit (eds), *The Seljuqs*, 79–95.
Peacock, A. C. S., 'From the Balkhān-Kūhīyān to the Nāwakīya: Nomadic Politics and the Foundations of Seljūq Rule in Anatolia', in Paul (ed.), *Nomad Aristocrats in a World of Empires*, 55–80.
Peacock, A. C. S., ''Imad al-Din al-Isfahani's *Nusrat al-fatra*, Seljuq Politics and Ayyubid Origins', in Hillenbrand, Peacock and Abdullaeva (eds), *Ferdowsi, the Mongols and the History of Iran*, 78–91.
Peacock, A. C. S., 'Court Historiography of the Seljuq Empire in Iran and Iraq: Reflections on Content, Authorship and Language', *Iranian Studies*, 47 (2014), 327–45.
Peacock, A. C. S., 'Saljuqs. III. Saljuqs of Rum', *EIr*.
Peacock, A. C. S. and Sara Nur Yıldız (eds), *The Seljuks of Anatolia: Court and Society in the Medieval Middle East* (London, 2013).
Piacentini, V. Fiorani, 'La resa delle grandi città del Khorāsān ai Turchi selgiuchidi (428 e 429 HG/1038 e 1039 AD): continuità cuturale o rottura delle tradizioni?' *Studia Turcologica Alexii Bombaci Memoriae Dicata* (Naples, 1982), 193–204.
Pierce, Leslie, *The Imperial Harem: Women and Sovereignty in the Ottoman Empire* (New York, 1993).
Pritsak, O., 'Āl-i Burhān', *Der Islam*, 30 (1952), 81–96.
Pugachenkova, G. A., 'Urban Development and Architecture. Part One: Transoxiana and Khurasan', in C. E Bosworth and M. S. Asimov (eds), *History of Civilizations of Central Asia, vol. IV: The Age of Achievement: AD 750 to the End of the Fifteenth Century. Part Two. The Achievements* (Paris, 2000), 507–56.
Pyne, Nanette, 'The Impact of the Seljuq Invasion on Khuzestan: An Inquiry into the Historical, Geographical, Numismatic and Archaeological Evidence', PhD dissertation, University of Washington, 1982.
Rabbat, Nasser, 'The Militarization of Taste in Medieval Bilad al-Sham', in Kennedy (ed.), *Muslim Military Architecture in Greater Syria*, 84–105.
Rante, Rocco, *Rayy: from its Origins to the Mongol Invasions* (Leiden, 2014).
Rante, Rocco, 'The Topography of Rayy in the Early Islamic Period', *Iran*, 45 (2007), 161–80.
Rante, Rocco and Annabelle Collinet, *Nishapur Revisited: Stratigraphy and Ceramics of the Qohandez* (Oxford, 2013).
Rayfield, Donald, *Edge of Empires: A History of Georgia* (London, 2012).
Redford, Scott, '*Mamālik* and *mamālīk*: Decorative and Epigraphic Programs of Anatolian Seljuk Citadels', in Scott Redford and Nina Ergin (eds), *Cities and Citadels in Turkey: From the Iron Age to the Seljuks* (Leuven, 2013), 305–46.
Richards, D. S. (ed.), *Islamic Civilisation, 950–1150* (Oxford, 1973).
Richards, D. S., ''Emād al-Din al-Iṣfahāni', *EIr*.
Richter-Bernburg, Lutz, *Der Syrische Blitz: Saladins Sekretär zwischen Selbstdarstellung und Geschichtsschreibung* (Wiesbaden, 1998).

Rizvi, Vaqar Ahmed, "Umar Khayyam as a Geometrician: A Survey', *Islamic Studies*, 24 (1985), 193–204.
Rosenfeld, B. A., "Umar Khayyām', *EI*².
Roux, Jean Paul, 'La veuve dans les sociétés turques et mongoles de l'Asie centrale', *L'Homme*, 9/iv (1969), 51–78
Rubenstein, Jay, *Armies of Heaven: The First Crusade and the Quest for the Apocalypse* (New York, 2011).
Sabari, Simha, *Mouvements populaires à Bagdad à l'époque 'abbasside, IXe–XIe siècles* (Paris, 1981).
Safi, Omid, *The Politics of Knowledge in Premodern Islam: Negotiating Ideology and Religious Inquiry* (Chapel Hill, 2006).
Sanaullah, M. F., *The Decline of the Saljūqid Empire*, with an introduction by E. D. Ross (Calcutta, 1938).
Sato, Tsugitaka, *State and Rural Society in Medieval Islam: Sultans, Muqṭa's and Fallāḥūn* (Leiden, 1997).
Sayılı, Aydın, *The Observatory in Islam* (Ankara, 1960).
Schnyder, Rudolf, 'Political Centres and Artistic Powers in Saljuq Iran', in Richards (ed.), *Islamic Civilisation, 950–1150*, 201–9.
Serjeant, R. B., *Islamic Textiles: Materials for a History up to the Mongol Conquest* (Beirut, 1972).
Sevim, Ali, 'Sultan Melikşah devrinde Ahsa ve Bahreyn Karmatilerine karşı Selçuklu seferi', *Belleten*, 24(94) (1961), 209–32.
Sevim, Ali, *Suriye ve Filistin Selçukluları Tarihi* (Ankara, 1983).
Sevim, A. and C. E. Bosworth, 'The Seljuqs and the Khwarazm Shahs', in Asimov and Bosworth (eds), *History of Civilizations of Central Asia*, IV, 145–75.
Shani, Raya, *A Monumental Manifestation of the Shiite Faith in Late Twelfth Century Iran: The Case of the Gunbad-i 'Alawiyān, Hamadān* (Oxford, 1996).
Shimizu, Kosuke, 'The Bow and Arrow on Saljuqid Coins', *Memoirs of the Toyo Bunko*, 56 (1998), 85–106.
Silverstein, Adam, *Postal Systems in the Pre-Modern Islamic World* (Cambridge, 2007).
Sims-Williams, Nicholas, 'Christianity in Central Asia and Chinese Turkestan', *EIr*.
Sinor, Denis, 'The Establishment and Dissolution of the Türk Empire', in Denis Sinor (ed.), *The Cambridge History of Early Inner Asia* (Cambridge, 1990), 285–316.
Soudavar, Abolala, 'The Mongol Legacy of Persian *Farmāns*', in Linda Komaroff (ed.), *Beyond the Legacy of Genghis Khan* (Leiden 2006), 407–21.
Spuler, B., 'Atābakān-i Fārs', *EIr*.
Stern, S. M., *Fatimid Decrees: Original Documents from the Fatimid Chancery* (London, 1964).
Stern, S. M., 'The Inscriptions of the Kharraqān Mausoleums', *Iran*, 4 (1966), 21–7.
Stern, S. M., 'Ramisht of Siraf, a Merchant Millionaire of the Twelfth Century', *JRAS*, 99/i (1967), 10–14.
Strohmeier, Martin, *Seldschukische Geschichte und türkische Geschichtswissenschaft: die Seldschuken im Urteil moderner türkischer Historiker* (Berlin, 1984).
Stroumsa, Sarah, 'On Jewish Intellectuals who Converted in the Middle Ages', in Daniel H. Frank (ed.), *The Jews of Medieval Islam: Community, Society and Identity* (Leiden, 1995), 179–88.

Stroumsa, Sarah, *Maimonides in his World: A Portrait of a Mediterranean Thinker* (Princeton, 2009).
Subtelny, Maria E., *Timurids in Transition: Turko-Persian Politics and Acculturation in Medieval Iran* (Leiden, 2007).
Sümer, Faruk, *Oğuzlar (Türkmenler)* (Istanbul, 1999).
Tabbaa, Yasser, *Constructions of Piety and Power in Medieval Aleppo* (University Park, PA, 1997).
Tabbaa, Yasser, *The Transformation of Islamic Art During the Sunni Revival* (Seattle, 2001).
Tampoe, Moira, *Maritime Trade between China and the West: An Archaeological Study of the Ceramics from Siraf (Persian Gulf), 8th–15th Centuries AD* (Oxford, 1999).
Taşagıl, Ahmet, *Gök Türkler I–II–III* (Ankara, 2012).
Tekin, Talat, *Orhon Yazıtları* (Ankara, 1988).
Tetley, G. E., *The Ghaznavid and Seljuk Turks: Poetry as a Source of History* (London, 2009).
Teule, Herman, 'La renaissance syriaque (1026–1318)', *Irenikon*, 75/ii–iii (2002), 174–94.
Thomas, David and Alex Mallet (eds), *Christian–Muslim Relations: A Biobibliographical History, vol. 3: 1050–1200* (Leiden, 2011).
Tibawi, A. L., 'Origin and Character of "Al-madrasa"', *BSOAS*, 25/i (1962), 225–38.
Tor, D. G., *Violent Order: Religious Warfare, Chivalry and the* 'Ayyār *Phenomenon in the Medieval Islamic World* (Istanbul and Würzburg, 2007).
Tor, D. G., 'The Mamluks in the Military of the pre-Seljuq Persianate Dynasties', *Iran*, 46 (2008), 213–25.
Tor, D. G., 'A Tale of Two Murders: Power Relations between Caliph and Sultan in the Saljuq Era', *ZDMG*, 159 (2009), 279–97.
Tor, D. G., '*Mamlūk* Loyalty: Evidence from the Late Saljūq Period', *Asiatische Studien*, 45/iii (2011), 767–96.
Tor, D. G., '"Sovereign and Pious": The Religious Life of the Great Seljuq Sultans', in Lange and Mecit (eds), *The Seljuqs*, 39–62.
Tor, D. G., 'The Long Shadow of pre-Islamic Iranian Kingship: Antagonism or Assimilation?' in Adam Silverstein and Teresa Bernheimer (eds), *Late Antiquity: Eastern Perspectives* (Oxford, 2012), 145–63.
Tor, D. G., 'Sanjar, Aḥmad b. Malekšāh', *EIr*.
Treptow, Tanya with Donald Whitcomb, *Daily Life Ornamented: The Medieval Persian City of Rayy* (Chicago, 2007).
Turan, Osman, 'The Ideal of World Domination among the Medieval Turks', *Studia Iranica*, 4 (1955), 77–90.
Tyerman, Christopher, *God's War: A New History of the Crusades* (London, 2006).
van Donzel, Emeri and Andrea Schmidt, *Gog and Magog in Early Eastern Christian and Islamic Sources: Sallam's Quest for Alexander's Wall* (Leiden, 2010).
van Renterghem, Vanessa, 'Le sentiment d'appartenance collective chez les élites baghdadiennes des Ve–VIe/XIe–XIIe siècles', *Annales Islamologiques*, 42 (2008), 231–58.
van Renterghem, Vanessa, 'Controlling and Developing Baghdad: Caliphs, Sultans

and the Balance of Power in the Abbasid Capital (mid-5th/11th to late 6th/12th Centuries)', in Lange and Mecit (eds), *The Seljuqs*, 117–38.

van Renterghem, Vanessa, 'Social and Urban Dynamics in Baghdad during the Saldjūq Period (mid. Vth/XIth mid. VIth/XIIth c.)', in İsmail Safa Üstün (ed.), *İslam Medeniyetinde Bağdat (Medinetü's-Selām) Uluslararası Sempozyumu (International Symposium on Baghdad (Madinat al-Salam) in the Islamic Civilization)* (Istanbul, 2011), 171–92.

Ward, Rebecca, *Islamic Metalwork* (London, 1993).

Watson, Andrew M., *Agricultural Innovation in the Early Islamic World* (Cambridge, 1983).

Watson, Oliver, *Persian Lustre Ware* (London, 1985).

Wheatley, Paul, *The Places Where Men Pray Together: Cities in the Islamic Lands, Seventh to Tenth Centuries* (Chicago, 2000).

Whelan, Estelle, 'Representations of the Khassakiyyah and the Origins of Mamluk Emblems', in Priscilla Parsons Soucek and Carol Bier (eds), *Content and Context of Visual Arts in the Islamic World* (University Park, PA, 1988), 219–43.

Whitehouse, David, *Sīrāf: History, Topography and Environment* (Oxford, 2009).

Wilkinson, Charles, *Nishapur: Some Early Islamic Buildings and their Decoration* (New York, 1986).

Willey, Peter, *The Eagle's Nest: Ismaili Castles in Iran and Syria* (London, 2005).

Williams, Tim, 'The City of Sultan Kala, Merv, Turkmenistan: Communities, Neighbourhoods and Urban Planning from the Eighth to the Thirteenth Century', in Amira K. Bennison and Alison L. Gascoigne (eds), *Cities in the Pre-modern Islamic World: The Urban Impact of Religion, State and Society* (London, 2007), 42–62.

Woodbridge, Jessie and Neil Roberts, 'Late Holocene Climate of the Eastern Mediterranean Inferred from Diatom Analysis of Annually-laminated Lake Sediments', *Quarternary Science Review*, 30/xxiii–xxiv (2011), 3381–92.

Woods, John, E., *The Aqquyunlu: Clan, Confederation, Empire* (Salt Lake City, 1999).

Yavari, Neguin, 'Nizam al-Mulk Remembered: A Study in Historical Representation', PhD dissertation, Columbia University, 1992.

Yavari, Neguin, 'Mirror for Princes or a Hall of Mirrors? Nizam al-Mulk's *Siyar al-Mulūk* Reconsidered', *al-Masāq*, 20/i (2008), 47–69.

Yıldız, Sara Nur, 'A *Nadīm* for the Sultan: Rāwandī and the Anatolian Seljuks', in Peacock and Yıldız, *The Seljuks of Anatolia*, 91–111.

Yüksel, Musa Şamil, 'Türk kültüründe "Levirat" ve Timurlularda uygalanışı', *Turkish Studies*, 5/iii (2010), 2028–58.

Zouache, Abbès, 'Dubays b. Ṣadaqa (m. 529/1135), aventurier de légend. Histoire et fiction dans l'historiographie arabe médiéval (VI/XIIe–VII/XIIIe siècles)', *Bulletin d'études orientales*, 58 (2008–9), 87–130.

Index

Page numbers in *italics* indicate illustrations